Witchcraft and Magic in Europe
Ancient Greece and Rome

WITCHCRAFT AND MAGIC IN EUROPE

Series Editors
Bengt Ankarloo
Stuart Clark

The roots of European witchcraft and magic lie in Hebrew and other ancient Near Eastern cultures and in the Celtic, Nordic, and Germanic traditions of the continent. For two millennia, European folklore and ritual have been imbued with the belief in the supernatural, yielding a rich trove of histories and images.

Witchcraft and Magic in Europe combines traditional approaches of political, legal, and social historians with a critical synthesis of cultural anthropology, historical psychology, and gender studies. The series provides a modern, scholarly survey of the supernatural beliefs of Europeans from ancient times to the present day. Each volume of this ambitious series contains the work of distinguished scholars chosen for their expertise in a particular era or region.

Witchcraft and Magic in Europe: Biblical and Pagan Societies
Witchcraft and Magic in Europe: Ancient Greece and Rome
Witchcraft and Magic in Europe: The Middle Ages
Witchcraft and Magic in Europe: The Period of the Witch Trials
Witchcraft and Magic in Europe: The Eighteenth and Nineteenth Centuries
Witchcraft and Magic in Europe: The Twentieth Century

Witchcraft and Magic in Europe

Ancient Greece and Rome

Edited by
BENGT ANKARLOO
and STUART CLARK

PENN

University of Pennsylvania Press
Philadelphia

First published in 1999 by
The Athlone Press
1 Park Drive, London NW11 7SG

First published 1999 in the United States of America by
University of Pennsylvania Press
Philadelphia, Pennsylvania 19104−4011

British Library Cataloguing in Publication Data
A catalogue record for this book is available
from the British Library

Library of Congress Cataloging-in-Publication Data
Witchcraft and magic in Europe : ancient Greece and Rome / edited by
Bengt Ankarloo and Stuart Clark.
    p.   cm.
    Includes bibliographical references and index.
    ISBN 0−8122−3517−7 (hardcover : alk. paper). — ISBN 0−8122−1705−5
(pbk. : alk. paper)
    1. Witchcraft — Greece — History.   2. Magic — Greek — History
3. Witchcraft — Rome — History.   4. Magic, Roman — History.
I. Ankarloo, Bengt, 1935−   II. Clark, Stuart.
BF1567.W58   1999
133.4′3′0938 — dc21   99−26082
                                                                        CIP

Typeset by Ensystems, Saffron Walden, Essex
Printed and bound in Great Britain

Contents

Note on Citations

Readers should note that we have not attempted to standardize the citations to classical authors and texts in this volume. The contributors have aimed for consistency within each essay but have been allowed to cite in their preferred manner. This applies in particular to the choice of either Latin or English titles and of either full or abbreviated names and titles.

All secondary works, identified by date, are listed in the Bibliography, which also contains a list of the abbreviations that have been adopted throughout the volume when citing modern source collections or other items common to all the essays.

Introduction

Bengt Ankarloo and Stuart Clark

The chronological scope of this volume ranges from the heroic age of Homer to the late western empire of Augustine and Theodosius, a period of well over a thousand years.[1] Passing through the centuries, our focus of interest will slowly move from the Greek East to the Latin West. In this long millennium the geo-political and cultural landscape of the Mediterranean basin underwent significant changes. Bustling urban centres such as Miletos, Alexandria and Rome developed cosmopolitan attitudes and offered markets not only for commodities and services but also for ideas and beliefs. The melting-pot religious syncretism of the Roman empire is only one aspect of a more general convergence of cultures, languages and mentalities. The political diversity of the early city-states both in Greece and Italy eventually gave way to large uniform commonwealths under military rule and centralized bureaucracies. In succession, the two great empire builders, the Macedonians and the Romans, set their stamp on the history of the ancient world.

The historiography of witchcraft and magic in the ancient world relies primarily on a multiplicity of texts. Most of these written sources have come down to us as part of a glorious cultural and scientific tradition, the 'classical heritage', created by, and for the consumption of, the social élites. Only rarely, indirectly, and probably at times in a biased form, do these narratives deal with the beliefs and practices of ordinary men and women. But some material remains unearthed by the archeologists, and, most importantly, magical papyri and curses inscribed on durable material such as metal sheets, give evidence of the everyday concerns of people all over the classical world, from Egypt to Britannia.

The major groups of sources for the study of magic beliefs and actions in classical antiquity are: (1) fictional literature from Homer and Euripides to Apuleius and Lucian; (2) historical narratives from the Bible and the *Lives* of Christian Saints to historians proper such as Plutarch, Lucan, Porphyry and Suetonius; (3) philosophical and scientific discourses from Plato and Hippocrates to Plotinus and Celsus; (4) religious texts from the Gospels to the Church Fathers; and finally (5) performative sources, i.e. texts created as part of social actions, whether legal (such as court decisions and records), religious (prayers, ritual invocations), or magical (papyri, curse tablets). The four authors in this volume each focus on different groups of sources: Daniel Ogden on magical inscriptions on curse tablets unearthed by archeologists; Georg Luck primarily on fictional and philosophical discourses; Richard Gordon on legal rulings and court cases as well as literary and philosophical texts in general; and Valerie Flint on biblical and patristic texts.

A fundamental and highly interesting problem is the way in which these various sources relate to each other. To take but one example: Flint demonstrates how dogmatic statements by Church Fathers about the nature of angels and demons can be fully understood only against the background of the ambitions of a church militant in a pagan world where miracles were expected of religious leaders and where theurgists and gnostics were powerful adversaries of Christians. The visibility of this conflict suggests that magic through the centuries and over the wide area of Greek and Roman culture was many different things. Any attempt to circumscribe the area of the occult must be open to the possibility of historical change and fundamental differentiation between regions and classes in the use of, and attitude to, magical practices. The fact that competing creeds and denominations accused each other of sorcery and deceit indicates that magic had a somewhat inferior status as compared with religion proper. Such a classification is, therefore, relative and culturally determined. When used as scientific terms, magic and religion should, perhaps, be based on more universally acceptable criteria. Following a basically Durkheimian tradition Ogden suggests an essential distinction between religion and magic applicable at least to sacrifices and rituals: When they unite the community they are religious, whereas magical operations serve to distance the operator or practitioner from his fellow men. This social/anti-social dichotomy is underlined by the fact that magical practice sometimes defined itself 'by the countercultural cloak that it took on, at least partly of its own accord.' Secrecy, inversion and perversion were important elements of such a countercultural identification. Things were done in the opposite way, objects were twisted and placed upside down, texts were jumbled and juxtaposed. Yet all these operations were made with reference to a concept of 'proper' use; magic, in spite of its rebellious, anti-social nature, was directly dependent on, and formed in accordance with, the norms and values of society itself.

To us the classical heritage is primarily made up of three dominant components – Greek philosophy, Roman law and the Christian religion. But we know history only after the fact, as a closed chapter. When it was still open, numerous other cultural options were available and all kinds of creeds and world-views vied for people's attention. Witchcraft and magic in antiquity should be of particular interest in this perspective. Firstly, they are an integral part of the understanding of Graeco-Roman civilisation.

Magic beliefs and practices held a place in the minds of the ancients and so tell us a good deal about the motives people acted on. The transmission and diffusion of various transcendent ideas was part of a general process of cultural interaction in the Mediterranean region over a period of a thousand years or more. The hegemony of Greek philosophy was never complete even in Greece itself. It developed in competition with old agrarian cults and an emerging cosmopolitan Pantheon. Tensions and oppositions between learned cosmologies and sociologies on the one hand and vulgar creeds on the other is a dominant *topos* in the classical literature studied by Luck in his contribution to this volume.

Secondly, the tradition from antiquity in both philosophy and religion was the basic foundation for medieval and modern European culture. The classical elements were transmitted in a number of ways, both as a precarious cultural, mostly monastic, continuity through the 'dark ages' and also as a result of recurrent 'renaissances' – Carolingian, Arabic and Italian – in which the study of ancient sources was revived. This process of unbroken traditions, discontinuities and rediscoveries occurred in both popular mentalities and scholarly discourses. But for obvious reasons it can be more readily discerned in written texts biased in favour of the learned tradition. Again, the popular substratum of magic beliefs poses a methodological problem to the modern observer.

The continuity of a tradition based on texts would seem to be more secure than that of practices and creeds transmitted only orally, directly from one generation to another. This may be true in principle, but applied as a general methodology it has its limitations. Given the immense geographical spread of the curse tablets within the Roman empire, the overall stylistic uniformity is striking and seems to indicate some form of literary tradition, for example in the form of handbooks. The existence of such magic manuals is well established. Nevertheless, the interpretation of similarities within a given body of archeological finds, such as the deposit of curse tablets in Roman Bath, is also open to suggestions of an established, largely oral culture of magical expertise. A central problem concerning the permanence and durability of mentalities through the centuries, even their transmission from one historical civilisation to another, such as that from antiquity to the medieval West, is that of the relative importance to be given to oral as opposed to written traditions. Scholars, strongly disposed as they are in favour of the literary, have been inclined to emphasise the radical cultural discontinuity caused by the fall of the western empire, such that classical culture had to be rediscovered centuries later in the manuscripts buried in monastic libraries. The striking similarities between ancient and modern Western magic should, according to such a methodology, be regarded as the result of later scholarly interpretations and adaptations from literary sources, not as an oral tradition of folk beliefs. This position has been challenged, of course, both by ethnologists and historians of religion.

Finally, the ancient world can supply us with material for comparison. What are the similarities and dissimilarities in the encounter with 'otherness' that the Romans experienced in Egypt and Mesopotamia and the early modern Europeans in the New World? How does the political demonisation of magic in the late Roman empire (as discussed by Flint) compare with the association of witchcraft with the Devil that accelerated in sixteenth-century Europe as the combined result of reforming zeal within the churches and the interventionist ambitions of the bureaucracies of the early modern monarchies? Why did magic catch the attention of emperors and princes at all, if not for political reasons? Was it because they were no longer satisfied with ruling over the bodies and labours of their subjects, wanting to control their passions and creeds as well? In developing such Foucauldian ambitions the political order sometimes interfered with the religious. With the differentiation in the late empire of state and church élites, conflicts about the interpretation of magical transgressions emerged. It is interesting to note that the leading churchmen, both in late antiquity and the early modern period, soon found it proper and expedient to soften the harsh commands and ruthless methods of the secular lords in persecuting the crime of magic. The privilege of interpretation was contested and this gave some members of the Christian church a chance to act protectively towards the magical operator and so perhaps to gain friends and converts. To some extent, the 'demonisation' of their practices put magicians in Christian hands, and subjected them to quite different kinds of discipline than the imperial alternatives. Through emphasising the invasiveness and power of demons in matters of magic, Christianity may have meant to bypass the punishment for magic recommended by imperial magistrates, and so to save many of the accused, magicians though a few of them may truly have been. These different interpretations have interesting similarities with those prevailing in early modern Europe, where the secular arm tended to exercise a much harsher justice in witchcraft cases than ecclesiastical legal practice was prepared to accept.

Such an emphasis on similarities may conceal important differences between ancient and early modern mentalities. How was ancient magic affected by the various influences from a multiplicity of 'pagan' gods and cults? The insistence on conformity and the fight against heresy in the Christian churches during the early modern European Reformations offered a market for popular magic which was probably more limited and at least quite different from that in late republican Rome. How deeply rooted were the official and socially approved cults among the general population of, say, Medicean Toscana as compared to Periclean Attica?

We may ask, with Paul Veyne, if the Greeks really believed in their myths – or, by extension, if the ancients were universally credulous. When phrasing the question in such an extreme form, we hesitate to affirm the underlying proposition. It seems more reasonable to assume that the levels of 'truth' and acceptability must have been as varied and as disputed in Plato's days as they are today. This is the constructivist position. Gordon demonstrates how several of the dynamic aspects of magic can be attributed to successive periods and different social settings. In archaic times magic was 'embedded', that is, an integrated part of everyday practice. Nobody thought about it as 'magic'. And it long continued to have this degree of invisibility among ordinary people. The practices of wise women remained unaffected by the processes of rationalisation and modernization of the divine world which set in with the formation of the city state. The cultural and social differentiation that took place in this process alone makes it impossible to speak of a single ancient view of magic. A whole range of representations and claims eventually competed in the marketplace. Gordon identifies five successive transformations in which legitimate knowledge was forced to adapt to new conditions: (1) the formation of the city state; (2) the passage from independent cities to the Hellenistic kingdoms; (3) the emergence of the Principate; (4) the crisis of the third century leading up to the tetrarchy; and (5) the fourth-century transition to a Christian Empire.

Again we must focus on the relationship between continuity and change. On the one hand, there was stability; the case of the stylistic uniformity of the curse tablets should be stressed again here. On the other hand, we find a multiplicity of magical practices and versatile adaptations to changing market conditions. It is noteworthy how certain curses came into vogue (such as erotic spells) only to disappear a few centuries later, superseded by other styles of invocation associated with circus and athletic games or with legal litigation. These changes are clearly linked with more general trends in society and culture. There is also a fairly clear one-directional development from simple, laconic curses to highly elaborate, even verbose, descriptions of the victim and the terrible fate intended for him, indicating stages from the purely verbal to standardised and widely diffused literate invocations, items of a professional magic trade market.

The problem of unbelief in history has been widely discussed. Sometimes it has been defined, rather narrowly, as the informed scepticism of scientifically trained minds – as a kind of positivism. According to this view only the modern West has developed the intellectual tools necessary for such a mentality. Not even the free and audacious heroes of the Renaissance, such as Rabelais, were able to take the final step into agnostic rationalism or downright atheism. Without going further into this discussion, one thing is abundantly clear: it was indeed possible for the ancients to think in critical terms of gods and mythical lore. Some philosophers were accused of being atheists (the very word is Greek). Thus, the concept of unbelief and the intellectual tools for it were available. It was within the reach of many to imagine a completely immanent world.

It is important to acknowledge this, since it has recently been argued that traditional cultures in the past were so completely embedded – so immersed in their own categories – that it was impossible for their members to step outside of the common beliefs. This is probably not true even in very small, isolated village communities, where life and culture are so tightly linked as to be the same. But it is certainly not true of the 'high' cultures of the ancient world. It was common knowledge that other people had other gods and other beliefs. And even if those others were condemned as heathens and barbarians, many must have had the relativistic insight that 'they' had the same deprecatory thoughts about 'us'. Conversion and proselytising, syncretism and aggressive orthodoxy lived side by side. It was possible to choose, and it was also possible to doubt. But it was not always easy; the pressures toward conformity were strong. Tolerance was not always the companion of multiculturalism.

Diversity, therefore, was long the rule. The repertoire of ancient magic included Persian, Egyptian and Hebrew formulas as well as Greek *grammata* and Roman *sortes*. In Flint's words, the 'daimones' of the classical world offered to humans a tremendous range of employment and exploitation, as they streamed into the world of late antiquity. Only towards the end of the classical period, in the late Roman republic, was political control of magic and religious practice forcefully exercised by magistates. There were mass executions of people accused of magic in the second century BC. The emperors and later the Christian church forcefully interfered with the freedom of magic manipulation. The persecution of witches in sixteenth- and seventeenth-century Europe was a late manifestation of the importance accorded by the powers, both secular and ecclesiastical, to the necessity of unity and control in the face of dark and dangerous enemies threatening the order of Christian republics and pious princes.

Notes

1. The editors would like to thank Richard Gordon for his help with this volume, in particular with the compiling of the Bibliography.

PART 1

Binding Spells: Curse Tablets and Voodoo Dolls in the Greek and Roman Worlds

Daniel Ogden

We do not need recourse to the problematic abstraction of 'magic' to define a catalogue for study in this essay.* The curse tablets and voodoo dolls from the Greek and Roman worlds, both of which were used to 'bind' victims in various ways, present reasonably tight syndromes of evidence, even if there are some 'penumbral' cases. The definition of curse tablets generated by Jordan for his survey of the Greek ones runs as follows:

> *Defixiones*, more commonly known as curse tablets, are inscribed pieces of lead, usually in the form of small, thin sheets, intended to influence, by supernatural means, the actions or the welfare of persons or animals against their will. (*SGD* p. 151)

Although the word 'supernatural' here could be considered almost as problematic as 'magic', the definition functions just as well for our purposes even if the 'supernatural' clause is omitted. An evidential syndrome can also be defined for voodoo dolls. Faraone includes figurines in his catalogue of them if they display two or more of the following criteria: (1) the doll's arms or legs are twisted behind its back as if bound; (2) the doll is transfixed with nails; (3) the head or feet or upper torso of the doll has been twisted back to front; (4) the doll is tightly shut in a container; (5) the doll has been inscribed with a victim's name; (6) the doll has been discovered in a grave, sanctuary or in (what was) water (*VD* p. 200).

THE CURSE TABLETS: AN OVERVIEW

More than 1,600 tablets are currently known. Most are in Greek: the *DTA* corpus contains 220, the *DT* corpus 305 in all of which around 166 are Greek (tablets written in multiple languages or vestigially inscribed are difficult to classify), and the *SGD* list 'over 650', making a subtotal of around 1,100. On the Latin side, the *DT* corpus contains around 120, the corpus of Besnier 1920 contains 61, the list of Solin 1968 contains 48, the

* Thanks to Stuart Clark and Richard Gordon for their comments on a draft of this essay. They are not responsible for the views expressed.

Tab. Sulis corpus 130, the Uley cache around 140, and there remain a few tablets not included in any of these corpora or lists, making a subtotal of over 500. Not all of these tablets are currently available for study: some are lost (e.g. the *DTA* corpus, on which see Jordan, 1988b: 274 and 1990: 441 n. 10); others are too delicate to unroll or too damaged to decipher (e.g. the Uley cache). Despite the decline in excavatory archaeology, it is likely that significant numbers of curse tablets will continue to come to light. This is partly due to the identification of likely cache-sites: thus the 130 tablets from Bath represent the fruits of the investigation of merely one sixth of the deposit of the sacred spring, which suggests that there may be 500 or more tablets remaining in it. It is also partly due to the heightened awareness of excavators about the appearance of curse tablets, which is concomitant with the general rise of scholarly interest in the documents. (See *SGD* p. 152; *Tab. Sulis* pp. 59–61 and 100; Faraone, 1985: 153, and 1991b: 22 n. 4 and 30 n. 74; Jameson et al., 1993: 125.)

The earliest batch of Greek tablets is that of 22 from the Greek colony of Selinus in Sicily, dating from the early fifth century BC, with some perhaps from the late sixth (listed at Jameson et al., 1993: 125–6). The great majority of all known curse tablets prior to the imperial period hail from Attica, where they are found in large numbers from throughout the classical, hellenistic and imperial periods. They are found chiefly in the Agora, i.e. the market place and civic centre (there are about a hundred tablets from here alone), and in the Ceramicus cemetary (*DTA*; *DT* nos. 45–79; *SGD* nos. 1–54). Other pre-imperial curses are found in small numbers scattered around various Greek states. The chief concern of classical-period curse tablets that are 'diagnostic' (i.e., that provide information about their subject matter) is litigation, but this subject is relatively rare in them after the classical period. Indeed, all extant Attic litigation examples, of which there are many, appear to be classical. Trade curses and theatrical-competition curses are also found from the fifth century BC, the former not being found much after the hellenistic period. Erotic-separation curses and prayers for justice are found from the fourth century BC. It was the imperial period above all, and especially the second century AD, that witnessed the spread of the curse tablets around the Mediterranean: they are found in every modern country around the sea, and also in Britain. Given the immense geographical spread of the tablets, the overall stylistic uniformity of their texts is striking. From the second century AD onwards many of the tablets are highly syncretistic, with heavy inputs from Egyptian and Jewish culture in particular. From the second century AD also two new curse types appear, erotic-attraction spells and athletic and circus spells, the bulk of them belonging to the third and fourth centuries AD. Circus spells are found predominantly in North Africa and Syria, and they also constitute the subject of the distinctive 'Sethian' batch of 48 tablets from Rome. This is also the period in which tablets of the prayers-for-justice type came to flourish. The Latin tablets, predictably, are found mostly in the Western half of the Roman empire. Most of them date from the third and fourth centuries AD, and most of them belong to the prayer-for-justice type, this being largely a function of the two major find-batches from the Severn estuary, Bath (*Tab. Sulis*) and Uley. It is difficult to pinpoint exactly when the tradition of cursing seen in the tablets dies out: it is apparently at some point between the sixth and eighth centuries AD. (See Faraone, 1985: 153 and 1991b: 3, 11–13, 16; Jordan, 1988b: 274; *CT* pp. 27–9, 50, 177 and 244.)

It is unclear what standard term (if any) the ancients applied to these curse tablets. The best Greek candidate is *katadesmos* 'a binding' (plural: *katadesmoi*), which expresses either the physical form of the curses in their rolled up state, or their fundamental function of restraint, or both. The word is classical, being used by Plato (*Republic* 364c), and it is sanctioned by the Greek magical papyri (e.g. *PGM* IV 2176–7). It is derived from a verb that often appears in the tablets, *katadein*, 'bind down.' A possible title given to an early tablet from Selinus is *eucha*, 'prayer.' The best Latin candidate is *defixio* (plural: *defixiones*). This word is only found in one obscure source, a bilingual gloss (See *LSJ* s.v., ii.40). However, it is a derivative of the verb *defigere*, 'fasten,' which is actually found in some British curse tablets (e.g. *RIB* nos. 6–7), and may refer either to the piercing of the curse tablets with nails, as was common, or again to the binding of the victim, or to both. Despite the obscurity of the word *defixio*, it has become the standard technical term for curse tablets in the scholarly literature, although Versnel is anxious that the term should not be applied to the prayers-for-justice category. The British evidence throws up some other candidate terms: *execratio*, 'curse', *devotio*, 'dedication/curse/ spell', *commonitorium*, 'memorandum', or *petitio*, 'petition'. Tomlin, however, considers that the likeliest term to have been applied by their users to the British texts, which almost all belong to the prayers-for-justice category, is *donatio*, 'giving/dedication' (i.e. of lost goods or of an offending thief to a god). (See Gow, 1952; ii: p. 37; Preisendanz, 1972: 1–3; Tomlin, 1988: 59; Faraone, 1991b: 21 n. 3; Versnel, 1991 especially 60–3; *CT* p. 30 n. 1; Jameson et al, 1993: 125).

Figure 1 illustrates a unrolled tablet from the Bath cache (*Tab. Sulis* no. 9a); Figure 2 illustrates some tablets from the same cache still in their rolled state.

THE DEVELOPMENT OF THE CURSE TABLETS ACROSS TIME

The texts of the curse tablets vary in their elaborateness and informative-ness. Three quarters of them either consist of no more than the name of the intended victim or provide no information diagnostic for context. The earliest name-only texts appear to have recorded names in their nomina-tive forms. Some name-only texts imply a verb of cursing by recording the name(s) in the accusative case (e.g. *DTA* no. 34), but since none of the accusative-name-only texts can be positively dated prior to the fourth century BC, they appear to represent an eliptical development of the verb-of-cursing-included texts, rather than an intermediate stage before them. Most of the earliest Attic and Sicilian curse tablets belong to the name-only types. No doubt to know and use a victim's name was itself to exercise power over him, the name probably being seen in some way as an embodiment of the victim. Their use should perhaps be seen as an instance of *pars pro toto* ('part for whole' or 'synecdochic') magic. This basic type of tablet decreases in frequency until it disappears entirely in the first century AD. Of the texts that go beyond the mere listing of (a) name(s), the earlier ones tend to be more succinct, and the later ones more prolix and elaborate. (See Preisendanz, 1972: 5; Jordan, 1980a: 231 with nn.21 and 22; Faraone, 1985: 151 and 1991b: 5 and 10). The main trends in the development of the curse tablets across time may be highlighted by the juxtaposition of an early tablet and a late one. We begin with one of the very oldest Greek tablets, one of the litigation curses from Selinus, from the early fifth or possibly even the late sixth century BC:

> The tongue of Eucles and the tongue of Aristophanis and the tongue of Angeilis and the tongue of Alciphron and the tongue of Hagestratos. The tongues of the advocates of Eucles and Aristophanis. (*SGD* no. 95 = *CT* no. 49 = Jameson et al., 1993: 126 *c* side A)

This is a simple text restraining the author's enemies (with the verb of binding suppressed). A minimal term, 'advocates', tells us that the context of the spell is litigation, and the most relevant and potentially dangerous parts of their bodies, their tongues, are singled out for special restraint. With this may be contrasted a tablet from fourth-century Rome, also written in Greek. It is one of the so-called 'Sethian' hoard (first published by Wünsch, 1898, with elaborate drawings of the texts and illustrations), and it is of the circus-competition type:

EULAMON, restrain, OUSIRI OUSIRI APHI OUSIRI MNE PHRI,
. . . and archangels, in the name of the underworld one, so that, just

as I entrust to you this impious and lawless and accursed Cardelus, whom his mother Fulgentia bore, so may you bring him to a bed of punishment, to be punished with an evil death, and to die within five days. Quickly! Quickly!

Spell: You, Phrygian goddess, nymph goddess, Eidonea [=ADO-NAI?] NEOI EKATOIKOUSE, I invoke you by your . . ., so that you may help me and restrain and hold in check Cardelus and bring him to a bed of punishment, to be punished with an evil death, to come to an evil condition, him whom his mother Fulgentia bore. And you, holy EULAMON, and holy Characters, and holy assistants, those on the right and those on the left, and holy Symphonia [?]. These things have been written on this (EULAMON, restrain, OUSIRI OUSIRI API OUSIRI MNE PHRI) tablet made from a cold-water pipe, so that, just as I entrust to you this impious and accursed and ill-fated Cardelus, whom his mother Fulgentia bore, bound, tied up and restrained, Cardelus whom his mother Fulgentia bore, so that you may so restrain him and bring him to a bed of punishment, to be punished and to die an evil death, Cardelus whom his mother Fulgentia bore, within five days, because I invoke you by the power that renews itself under the earth, the one that restrains the [sc. zodiacal] circles and [more *voces magicae* follow]. (Wünsch, 1898 no. 16 = *DT* no. 155 = *CT* no. 13 side A)

A mere transcription and translation does not do justice to the richness of this tablet (see Figure 3). Firstly, each alternate line is written upside down – in other words the text 'snakes' back and forth across the tablet. Secondly, the tablet is decorated with a number of pictures. In the centre stands an elaborate horse-headed demon holding a whip and a chariot-wheel (?), doubtless one of the powers that controlled chariot-racing. It may also have affinities with the Egyptian god Seth, who could be depicted as ass-headed, whence the 'Sethian' label, or with a 'Gnostic' demon concerned with the punishment of murderers (cf. Preisendanz, 1926: 22–41; Moraux, 1960: 15–23). Beneath him are two figures perhaps representing the 'assistant' demons (*paredroi*), or perhaps even the charioteers themselves. At the top of the tablet, a figure peeps out from his coffin: this may be Osiris, who was murdered by Seth, or it may be a wishful representation of the curse-victim. The dead figure and his coffin are transfixed by nails. At the bottom of the tablet is a horizontal mummy, around which coil two (chthonic) snakes, which attack the head. 'Osiris', the assistant-demons and the mummy are covered in criss-cross lines, which probably represent binding ropes. The tablet is further decorated with Characters and vowel-patterns. The ways in which the second tablet differs from the first may be tabulated:

1. A massive increase in the scale of the text. One result of this is that, for all its formulaicness, the Sethian tablet gives the (probably deceptive) appearance of being a more personal document, into which the 'personalities' of the author and the victim intrude. However, some fifth-century texts can be lengthier than the one quoted (e.g. 'The Great Defixio from Selinus,' *SGD* no. 107 = Dubois, 1989 no. 38 = *CT* no. 50 = Jameson et al., 1993 *f*, on which see Calder, 1963; or, from the Athenian Ceramicus, *SGD* no. 1 = *CT* no. 105).

2. A developed interest in the inherent magical power of letters and writing, evidenced by the 'snaking' of the text and by the vowel-patterns. The use of the Characters, which are broadly comparable in form and complexity with alphabetic letters, also belongs here.

3. The development of a high degree of syncretism (cf. Preisendanz, 1972: 11–13). The tablet invokes a great many powers from a wide range of cultures and types: Greek, mainline and traditional ('Phrygian goddess', i.e. Demeter); Greek, minor but traditional (Nymph-goddess), Greek, new (Symphonia: possibly a Gnostic invention, if the word is read correctly); Egyptian (Osiris, Apis, Mnevis, Ra [garbled at the beginning], Bachuch [and Seth?]); Judaeo-Christian (angels, archangels and Adonai). Other powers invoked are more specific to magical practice itself and less easy to locate in their cultural origins: the dead man in the underworld; Eulamo(n), a great favourite in syncretistic curse tablets, whose origins may be Greek, Egyptian, Semitic or Assyrian (see Youtie and Bonner, 1937: 62; *CT* p. 267); the Characters; the *voces magicae* or 'words of power', which can occupy between 80 per cent and 90 per cent of some of the imperial period tablets (*CT* p. 6).

4. The recourse to a formulary or magical recipe book, as is indicated by the phrase 'The spell:', apparently included by mistake.

5. The use of elaborate, 'persuasive' and emotive descriptions of the victim.

6. The heavy development of repetition, which is already latent in the Selinus tablet.

7. The varied developments of the basic notion of binding and restraining.

8. The identification of the curse-victim by his mother's name, instead of his father's, as was usual in antiquity. This became quite common from the second century AD.

The context of these developments will be picked up in the subsequent discussion. For now it is sufficient to note the apparent difference in mentalities underlying the two texts. The Sethian tablet at first sight appears to be a baroquely alien and bizarre production, but its magical agenda and strategies are paradoxically easier to explain than those of the

Selinus tablet. The Sethian tablet draws much of its magical power from its direct appeal to gods and demons. It finds power too in the counter-cultural: gods and demons that are monstrous, inexplicable words and symbols and maternal (as opposed to paternal) relations. Its repetitiveness is incantatory. It is richly clothed in heavily characterised magical para-phernalia. By contrast the Selinus text is remarkable for its lack of explicit magical paraphernalia. It probably drew its magical power chiefly from the site of its deposit, a tomb of the dead, and through association with the pollution (*miasma*) of a dead man. The Selinus tablet may also have drawn power from the mechanical act of inscription itself: unlike later tablets from elsewhere, it does not pretend that anyone or anything will read it at some point in the future (see Jameson et al., 1993: 128–9).

Two antecedents to curse tablets can be identified: uninscribed metal voodoo dolls and verbal curses. An example of the sort of verbal concoction that preceded written curses may be found in the 'binding song' (*hymnos desmios*) sung by the Furies in Aeschylus' *Eumenides*, which has the function of restraining Orestes' success in his trial, a function very much akin to that of litigation curse tablets (line 306; cf. Gow, 1952, ii: p. 39; Faraone, 1985 and 1991b: 4–5). The fifth-century sophist Gorgias was to elaborate notions of verbal cursing into a semi-philosophical justification of rhetoric in his *Helen* (cf. Segal, 1962; de Romilly, 1975; MacDowell, 1982). There is some debate as to how central the principal innovation of the curse tablets, writing, was to their magical identity. It is hard to believe that uninscribed voodoo dolls had been used without accompanying verbal curses: how else were they to be associated with their victim? So perhaps the earliest tablets should be seen as simplified voodoo dolls and vestigial physical accompaniments to verbal curses. Some take the fact that the majority of the earliest curse tablets consist merely of names to indicate the necessity of verbal accompaniment to accomplish the magic (e.g. Petropoulos, 1988: 215; Faraone, 1985: 153 and 1991b: 4; *CT* p. 7). But a small degree of independence from any verbal context should perhaps be conceded to the earliest, nominative-name-only tablets, since the names upon them are inscribed in their 'default' grammatical case rather than in that in which they would have appeared in an accompanying verbal curse, the accusative. At the other end of the tradition the recipes for curse tablets and their activation in the Greek magical papyri still require many 'extraneous' incantations and rituals (see Kotansky, 1991: 108–9; *CT* p. 20). That the introduction of curse tablets was not considered a great conceptual innovation is implied by the fact that the ancient terminology applied to them was not specific to their written nature. Verbal accompaniment was probably necessary in the case of an undated cache of 40 curse tablets, rolled and nailed but blank, deposited at Rom in France (*DT* no. 109).

Nonetheless, writing may have been attributed with some magical power of its own: initially the very act of writing a name, of 'freezing' it permanently in lead, could in itself have been considered a way of tying it down by comparison with the transience of uttering it (cf. Tupet, 1976: 43; Bernand, 1991: 76 and 399–408; Graf, 1994a: 152). An episode of Homer's *Iliad* is often referred to in connection with the magical power of writing in archaic Greece (6. 167–70 = *CT* no. 138). King Proteus sends off Bellerophon to Lycia with a folded tablet on which are written 'many life-destroying baleful signs' in order to kill him. When the Lycian king reads the signs, he realises that he is to contrive Bellerophon's death, and attempts to do so. As is the case with much of the Homeric poems, it is uncertain at what point in the history of the epic tradition these lines were composed. Are they a dim dark-age recollection of the lost Mycenean writing system, Linear B? Or were they composed in the early seventh century, to refer to the newly developed alphabetic writing system? Or do they refer not to writing as such at all, but merely to some dark-age pre-arranged coded picture or symbol? (See Harris, 1989: 48–9 with n. 17; Kirk, 1990 ad loc.) Whichever is the case, it is not certain that a curse tablet or a precursor of one is described: we may simply be dealing with a letter, the contents of which prosaicly ordered the Lydian king to kill Bellerophon. However, the phrase 'life-destroying signs' (*sēmata . . . thymophthora*) does recall a phrase used elsewhere by Homer, *pharmaka thymophthora*, which could be translated 'life-destroying spells', though this too could similarly be translated more prosaicly as 'life-destroying poisons' (Homer, *Odyssey* 2.329).

THE PROCESS OF MANUFACTURE

Almost all extant curse tablets are inscribed on lead or lead alloy. This appears to be due not only to the fact that lead is a more durable medium than some of the others that may have been used, but also to the fact that lead was the medium of choice, because of the specific magical associations that it developed. Lead aside, curse tablets were inscribed in other durable media: bronze (e.g. *DT* no. 196), copper (Jerome, *Life of Saint Hilarion* 23), tin (e.g. *PGM* VII 417–22), ostraca, i.e. potsherds, (e.g. *PGM* ostraca, of which nos. 1 and 2 = *CT* nos. 111 and 35), limestone (e.g. the cache of 51 from Tell Sandahannah near Jerusalem: see Wünsch, 1902 and *CT* no. 107), talc (e.g. the cache from Amathous in Cyprus: Aupert and Jordan, 1981), and gemstone (Bonner, 1950: pp. 103–22). The Greek magical papyri contain recipes for curse tablets in the durable media of other metals, such as gold or silver (e.g. *PGM* X 24–35) or iron (*PGM* IV 2145–2240). It is, however, puzzling that, although many magical texts inscribed on gold or silver survive, they wholly constitute protective amulets (Jordan, 1985c: 165; Tomlin, 1988: 81; Kotansky, 1994: pp. xv–xvi). The special conditions of the Egyptian environment have preserved some curse tablets in the relatively non-durable medium of papyrus (e.g. *PGM* VIII 1–63 and CIX). An Aramaic spell written on cloth was preserved in the Cairo Geniza (Naveh and Shaked, 1985 Geniza no. 1 = *CT* no. 32). No curse tablets survive in the similarly non-durable medium of wax (although there remain wax voodoo dolls: e.g. *VD* nos. 28–9), but a fourth-century BC Attic curse tablet apparently refers to the phenomenon (*DTA* no. 55a) and literary sources also indicate that they were made, such as Ovid's reference to 'red wax' inscribed with a needle (*Amores* 3.7.29; cf. *CT* no. 142). Ovid's reference to the redness of the wax may be mistaken or misleading, and so indicate that wooden writing-tablets coated with red 'gum lac', like a cache found near Pompeii, could also be used for cursing. A number of curse tablets are made from reused objects. This is obviously true of the ostracon tablets. One of the Bath tablets is inscribed on an old pewter plate (*Tab. Sulis* no. 30). (See Tomlin, 1988: 81; Faraone, 1991b: 7 and 25 n. 30; *CT* p. 3.)

Some of the curse tablets reported to be of lead on the basis of visual inspection may in fact be of lead alloy. This possibility is raised by the systematic metallurgical analysis of the Bath tablets, which were similarly assumed to be pure lead at first sight. The alloyed metal is tin (the tablets are consequently better considered 'pewter'), and a trace of copper is also sometimes present. But it is unsafe to extrapolate from a single cache, and tin in particular was a speciality of Britain, as was, by consequence, pewter (Tomlin, 1988: 82; *CT* pp. 3–4).

Lead was likely to have been used for curse tablets initially because it was cheap and readily available in the ancient world, and provided an easily inscribable surface for a stilus. Already in fifth-century BC Greece it was used for a number of document types: financial documents (Corinth, Nemea, Athens); civic membership tokens (Piraeus, Euboea, Camarina); private letters (Athens, Olbia and elsewhere); questions to and replies from Zeus at Dodona; sacrificial calendars (Corinth). Among these letters and civic membership tokens in particular could be close to curse tablets in form. The superficial resemblance between scrolled lead letters and curse tablets may indicate that curse tablets were initially conceptualised in part as letters to the dead or to infernal powers. At any rate some curse tablets seem to exploit this conceit in their phraseology: one calls itself a letter sent to the demons and Persephone (*DTA* no. 102, Attic, iv BC). Some scrolled tablets carry an address to chthonic powers on their external exposed side, just as if they were letters (e.g. *SGD* no. 62, Attic, iii BC). The superficial resemblance of the name-only curse tablets to various sorts of lead name-tickets that acted as membership or allotment tokens in

Athens and elsewhere should probably not be taken as significant, but it can be unclear to us to which category certain finds should be ascribed (e.g. *DT* no. 45). (See *DTA* pp. ii–iii; Preisendanz, 1972: 7 and 20; Jordan, 1980a: 226–9 with nn.6–13 and 1985b: 212; Tomlin, 1988: 81 and 84; Faraone, 1991b: 4, 22 n. 4 [for *DTA* no. 45] and 23 n. 10; Versnel 1991: 65; *CT* p. 18.)

Despite the banality of lead, in the context of cursing its properties came to be re-rationalised and regarded as providing sympathetic magical power. Some Attic curse tablets request that their victims become as cold and useless (*achrēstos*) as the lead upon which the curse is written (e.g. *DTA* nos. 105–7, iv BC). Another Attic tablet wishes that the victim's tongue should come to resemble lead (*DTA* no. 67, iv BC), and two related tablets wish that the victim's tongue should actually become lead (*DTA* nos. 96–7 [97 = *CT* no. 66], iv BC). Latin tablets sometimes wish that their victim should be rendered as heavy as their lead (e.g. *DT* no. 98, i–ii AD, Germany). A more tenuous analogy is made by an erotic tablet which wishes that Zoilos may be separated from Antheira, just as the lead is in a place separate from humans (*DT* no. 85 = *CT* no. 20, iii–ii BC, quoted below). No tablet explicitly draws the analogy between the oxidised blotchiness of lead and deathly pallor, but the elder Pliny compared the colour of lead to that of death (*Natural History* 11.114) and the body of Germanicus, who was killed with the aid of curse tablets, was said to have been blotchy (Tacitus, *Annals* 2.69 and 74 and Suetonius, *Caligula* 1). A newly inscribed text would have shone out in an alluring silver against this background. Perhaps lead was also thought appropriate for the fact that some of its chemical compounds were poisonous. (See Tupet, 1976: 43; Guarducci, 1978: 240; Jordan, 1985b: 207; Tomlin, 1988: 81–4; Bernand, 1991: 20; Faraone, 1991b: 7; *CT* p. 4; Graf, 1994a: 154–6.)

In the imperial period lead from water pipes seems to have become particularly significant. The Sethian tablet quoted above actually claims to have been made of lead from a cold-water pipe (*psychrophoros*, *DT* no. 155b = *CT* no.13). A papyrus recipe for a curse tablet accordingly instructs that the lead should be taken from a (presumably public) cold-water pipe (*PGM* VII 396–404; cf. also XXXVI 1–34 and Jordan, 1990: 440 for lead 'worked cold'). A recipe from the Jewish spell collection *Sepher ha-Razim* instructs one to take a lead pipe from an aqueduct with which to make the curse tablet (Morgan, 1983: 49 = *CT* no. 114). Since lead was cheap, this suggestion is not made, it seems, to direct the user to a convenient free source of a precious commodity. Rather, lead from a water pipe will have been valued because it was colder even than usual and because of the high importance of (especially underground) water in the activation of curse tablets (for which see below), or simply because the destruction of a public water pipe was a dangerous, antisocial and countercultural act, which in itself conferred magical power on the cursing process. It is common for ancient magical ingredients to be either extremely dangerous or difficult to obtain: thus a Greek magical papyrus spell to attract a lover through wakefulness requires the eyes of a bat (the creature that sees all night), which is then to be released alive (*PGM* IV 2943–66; cf. Luck, 1985: 101).

Despite the *PGM* reference to the working of the lead for a tablet in its cold state, and despite the fact that fire could be unhelpfully purifying (cf. Bernand, 1991: 324), analysis of the Bath cache suggests that there at any rate smelting was employed in the tablets' manufacture. Since no two of the Bath tablets have exactly the same metallurgical composition, it appears that they were made separately, with the metal perhaps smelted in a ladle over a small fire. The sheet could then be made by pouring the metal out over a flat surface. The addition of tin to lead is eutectic and productive of a smoother surface, but all proportions of lead to tin are found in the Bath tablets, and there appears to have been no concerted attempt to produce the most eutectic alloy. If the metal was simply left on the flat surface, its surface tension would cause it to set in a thick blob. Sometimes these were used directly (e.g. *Tab. Sulis* nos. 95–6, iv AD). But finer sheets were usually made. One method was to hammer the metal when set, which would transform the blob's projecting spurs into distinctive 'scallops,' (e.g. *Tab. Sulis* 54, iii AD). Tablets of this type sometimes exhibit 'cold shuts', holes which the molten material had failed to close before setting. Sometimes tablets were used as they came, with their irregular edges, but usually they were trimmed by repeated scoring with a knife, to form more or less regular shapes. Otherwise, the metal could be pressed thin between two flat surfaces whilst still molten. Some Bath tablets display the distinctive flanged edges that reveal that they have been made in a proper, shaped mould (e.g. *Tab. Sulis* 10 and 44, iii–iv AD). (See Tomlin, 1988: 83, qualified by Jordan, 1990: 440.)

The tablet made, it was inscribed with a stilus or similar sharp, pointed object, and then usually rolled or folded over on itself. At Bath the ends of the 'roll' were sometimes brought together too, to form a lump. The rolling may have been initially due to the influence of letters, but in curse tablets its main function was probably not to keep the contents secret. Rather, it was to achieve a sympathetic binding and perhaps a sympathetic confusion of the tablet's contents. It is unfortunate for us that the folding of the tablets can increase their rate of corrosion, and that the process of unfolding or unrolling can consequently be quite destructive. (See Tomlin, 1988: 84; Jameson et al., 1993: 125. A technique for the unrolling and conservation of the fragile tablets by gradually unwinding them onto glued polyester fabric is described by Rosenberg at Jordan, 1988c: 134–40.)

Curse tablets were often pierced with nails. The prime significance of this was also binding or restraint. Piercing is common among classical tablets, particularly the Attic ones, but rare in the imperial period (no Attic tablet of this period is pierced). One tablet displays no less than five nail holes, and in its text the curser refers specifically not only to 'binding' but to 'nailing down' his enemies (*DT* no. 49 = *CT* no.44, Attic, c. 300 BC). Another tablet asks that the opponent's tongue be 'stabbed' (*DTA* no. 97 = *CT* no. 66, Attic, iv–i BC). Four separate but related tablets with brief texts were found pinned together by a single nail (*DTA* nos. 47–50 [a–d] = *CT* no. 59, Attic, iv BC). A pair of Latin tablets containing a continuous text was nailed together to form a diptych (*DT* nos. 111–12 = *CT* no. 53, Gaul, ii AD). An undated tablet from Aegina was found folded around an iron nail (*SGD* p. 166). The context of nailing may have been different in the case of 'prayers for justice.' One of these has a nail-hole positioned in its middle top, which suggests that it was nailed up in a sanctuary for the thief it intended to punish to read (Dunant 1978 = *CT* no. 90, Asia Minor, i BC–i AD; cf. Versnel, 1991: 74). In the case of hammered or corroded tablets it can be difficult to distinguish a nail-hole from a 'cold shut' (e.g. *Tab. Sulis* no. 61, iii AD; cf. Tomlin, 1988: 84).

Sometimes the nails used could be special. Pamphile, one of Apuleius' fictional witches, maintained a supply of nails from crucifixions (*Golden Ass* 3.17 = *CT* no. 153; cf. Tupet, 1976: 37–9). We are also told here that Pamphile kept the remains of shipwrecks in her workshop, and no doubt ship's nails were prominent amongst these remains: a papyrus recipe requires that a tablet should be written not with a stilus but a copper nail from a shipwreck (*PGM* VII 462–6; cf. Fox, 1912b: 306). The same papyrus tells that magical wicks could be made from the hawser of a wrecked ship (*PGM* VII 593–619; cf. Winkler, 1990: 85–6). Magical power was doubtless conferred on such objects by their association with death and catastrophe as well as by the difficulty of their acquisition. The practice of nailing tablets was in some ways assimilated to the practice of inscribing them: another recipe encourages the curser to drive his stilus through the tablet (*PGM* V 304–69). One papyrus spell gives instructions for the writing of a curse tablet with a 'headless' (*akephalōi*) needle (*PGM* VII 429–58): was the breaking off of the 'head' of the needle a further means of restraint (cf. *VD* no. 7, and the 'headless' demon favoured by the syncretistic tablets, Akephalos)?

The tablet could be aided in its task if it was accompanied by some of the victim's 'stuff' (*ousia*), usually some of their hair of a fragment of their clothing. The underlying notion is that what is effected upon part of the victim may be effected upon the whole of him (*pars pro toto* magic). It was hoped that if a part of the victim was put into a grave with a corpse, it might have a 'deadening' or restraining effect upon the rest of him. This

Figure 1: An unrolled curse tablet from Bath (*Tab. Sulis* no. 9a), ii–iii AD.

Figure 2: Curse tablets from Bath in their rolled state, ii–iii AD. Figures 1 and 2 reproduced by kind permission of the Institute of Archaeology, University of Oxford; the help of Mr R. Wilkins, of the Institute, and of Ms Jane Bircher, of the Roman Baths Museum, where the tablets reside, is gratefully acknowledged.

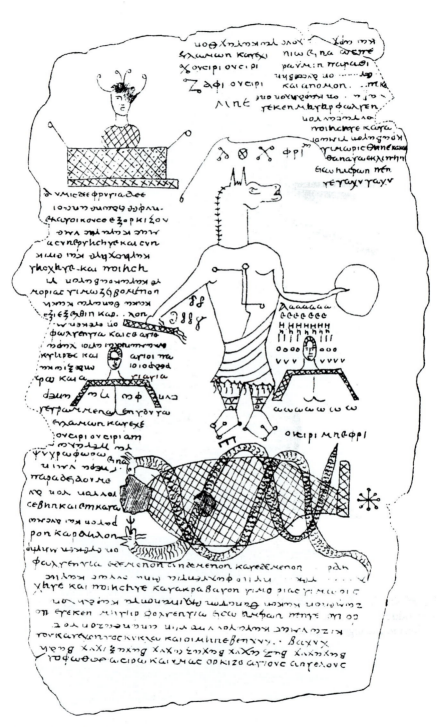

Figure 3: 'Sethian' tablet from Rome as transcribed by Wünsch, Wünsch 1898 no. 6 = *DT* no. 155 = *CT* no. 13, side A, iv AD. Reproduced from Wünsch 1898:16.

Figure 4: The Louvre voodoo doll, *VD* no. 27, Egypt ii–iii century AD. Reproduced by kind permission of the Musée du Louvre; the help of Mme Catherine Belanger is gratefully acknowledged; Louvre E27145.

*Figure 5:*Wax voodoo doll in the British Museum built around a rolled papyrus curse, *VD* no. 31, Egypt, late antique. Copyright British Museum; BM EA 37918.

technique was principally used in erotic spells, whether of attraction or separation. Lucian speaks of an attraction spell which required some of the beloved's hair, a fragment of his clothing or his boots (*Dialogues of the courtesans* 4.286 = *CT* no. 152). Euripides has Phaedra's nurse suggest that she win the love of her beloved by using a lock of his hair or a piece of his clothing (*Hippolytus* 513–15; cf. Barrett, 1964: ad loc.). The most graphic illustration of the way in which this sort of magic works is found in an episode of Apuleius' *Golden Ass*, in which the witch Pamphile's maid brings her not the hairs of her beloved as requested, but the hairs of some old goatskins; when the spell is worked, it is not the beloved but the goatskins that come knocking at Pamphile's door (2.32 and 3.16–18). Some tablets were found wrapped round wads of hair (e.g. *SGD* no. 38, Attica, iii AD), and some make explicit mention of the hair they contain (e.g. *SGD* nos. 155–6 = *Suppl. Mag.* no. 51 = *CT* no. 29, Oxyrhynchus, ii–iii AD). Some papyrus curses were also found containing hair (*PGM* XVI, ii–iii AD and XIXa, iv–v AD). (See Jordan, 1985b: 251–2; Winkler, 1990: 85–6 and 228 n. 25; *CT* pp. 16–18; Graf, 1994a: 162–3.)

DEPOSITION SITES: GRAVES AND THE DEAD

The final stage of a tablet's activation was its deposition. There were five major contexts for this: in a grave, in a chthonic sanctuary (usually one of Demeter), in a body of water, in a place of specific relevance to the curse or its victim, or in a non-chthonic sanctuary. A recipe for the manufacture of a curse tablet recommends that it be deposited in 'river, land, sea, stream, coffin or well' (*PGM* VII 451–2; cf. Fox, 1912b: 305–6; *CT* p. 18). Of approximately 625· tablets of which the provenance was known in 1985, approximately 325 came from graves and 60 from sanctuaries of Demeter; approximately 220 could be identified as deriving from underground bodies of water, mainly wells (Jordan, 1980a: 232–3 and n. 23, and 1985b: 207). Since then the discovery of the Bath cache has done much to even up the basic grave/water distribution. It is probable that graves were the first sites used, although both graves and chthonic sanctuaries are already represented in the case of the earliest curse tablets from Selinus (Versnel, 1991: 61; Jameson et al., 1993: 125–9). Deposition in non-chthonic sanctuaries is associated particularly with prayers for justice, which could be addressed to ordinary deities. It is possible that water-deposition was not used at all before the imperial period. Earlier Greek tablets found down wells or in other bodies of water may have been out of their original deposition-context, i.e., typically, thrown down the well as rubbish. Thus a fourth-century BC tablet from a well near the

Dipylon gate in the Ceramicus cemetary may have been dumped there from a nearby tomb (*SGD* no. 14 = *CT* no. 57; cf. Jordan, 1980a: especially 232 n. 24); similarly, 17 hellenistic tablets found down a well in the Agora may have been dumped from the adjacent shrine of Demeter (*SGD* p. 162; cf. Jordan, 1985b: 207–10; Faraone, 1991b: 3 and 23 n. 7; Jameson et al., 1993: 125).

The association of curse tablets with graves and the places of the dead may in part be historical, in that their antecedent voodoo dolls may originally have been placed in graves specifically to lay restless ghosts by binding. But in general the places of the dead were magically useful as imbued with pollution (*miasma*), and the physical contact of the victim's name on its curse tablet with the dead might have been considered to bring the victim himself into some restraining contact with the dead (Jameson et al., 1993: 129; cf. Parker, 1983: 198). The curse tablets were sometimes laid in the right hand of the corpse (e.g. *SGD* nos 1 and 2, Attica, v BC; cf. Jordan, 1988b: 274).

The preferred graves were those of people that had died by violence (*biaiothanatoi*) or at any rate died untimely (*aōroi*). The souls of the dead (*nekydaimones*) of these categories were supposed to remain restless until they had reached the occasion of what would have been their natural death from old age, and wander about their graves and cemetaries, particularly at night (Plato, *Phaedo* 81cd; Hippocrates, 1.38; cf. Jordan, 1980a: 234). Such souls were thought more likely to give help, through an enhanced degree either of animation or of bitterness. Their bitterness stemmed either from resentment towards their killers or regret at their deprivation of the joys of love and the prospect of progeny. (See Tertullian, *De anima* 56–7, on which text specifically see Waszink, 1947 ad loc., and Nock, 1950, and see more generally *DT* pp. cxii–xv; Wide, 1909; Rohde, 1925: 593–5; Cumont, 1945; Waszink, 1954a; Ter Vrught-Lentz, 1960; Schlörb-Vierneisel, 1964; Tupet, 1976: 82–91; Guarducci, 1978: 242; Bravo, 1987: 196; Jordan, 1988b: 273–5; Bernand, 1991: 131–55; Faraone, 1991b: 22 n. 6; *CT* pp. 19). Magicians sought to redirect the souls' bitterness towards a source of their own choosing. Thus a tablet binds Cercis and others 'with dead bachelors' (*DT* no. 52 = *CT* no. 73, Attica, iii–ii BC; cf. Bravo, 1987: 201). Whenever the age of the occupant of a grave in which a curse tablet is found can be estimated, it proves to be young (Jordan, 1988b: 273, pace Graf, 1994a: 152 and 174). A graphic literary illustration of the value of the untimely dead in this way is provided by Virgil's Dido, who, in cursing Aeneas, burns an effigy of him (perhaps a bust) alongside his possessions (*ousia*) and adds herself to the pyre so that her ghost will pursue him as an avenging demon (*Aeneid* 4.641–65; cf. Delcourt, 1939; Tupet, 1976: 232–66; Luck, 1985: 29). So too the boy killed by Horace's Canidia and her fellow witches in the course of the manufacture of a love potion exploits his own death to lay a curse upon the women (*Epode* 5; cf. Tupet, 1976: 316–17). It was believed that some magical practitioners actually went so far as the manufacture their own *nekydaimones* for their various projects by child-'sacrifice' (e.g. Cicero, *In Vatinium* 14) or even by ripping foetuses from wombs (e.g. Lucan, *Pharsalia* 6.558–9; cf. Tupet, 1976: 87–91 and 206–9).

A variation of the idea of depositing curse tablets in graves was to deposit them on a battlefield or in a place of execution. The 200 or so fragments of tablets from Amathous in Cyprus were deposited in a particularly appropriate site (some of the tablets are published at *DT* nos. 22–7, ii–iii AD; see Aupert and Jordan, 1981; *SGD* p. 193; Jordan, 1985b: 207 n. 3; Faraone, 1991b: 23 n. 11). They were found at the bottom of a shaft under a mass of human bones. These circumstances themselves suggest that the shaft was a mass grave and therefore the home of the prematurely dead, but the tablets also state as much explicitly: 'I invoke you, demons (*daimones*), many men buried together, and dead by violence, and dead before your time, and deprived of burial . . . you who lie here below, dead before your time and nameless . . .' (*DT* no. 22 = *CT* no. 45). (This text, incidentally, constitutes a problem for those who suppose that the tablets were deposited significantly prior to and separately from the dumping of the bones on top of them.) The fact that the corpses go unidentified is one of the inadequacies of their burial (see below on *ateleia*) and probably contributes to the ghosts' restlessness:

> Demons beneath . . . the earth and demons whoever you are, fathers of fathers and mothers, equals of men, male or female, demons, whoever you are and whoever lie here, having left life with all its cares, whether dead by violence, or alien, or native, or dead before your time, or denied burial, whether you are carried away from the outermost part of the stars [*or.* cities] or wander about in the air, and you [singular] who lie here below. (*DT* no. 25 = *CT* no. 46)

A third-century BC Olbian tablet actually draws its sympathetic power from the author's very ignorance of the exploited corpse's identity: 'Just as surely as we do not know you, so surely will Eupolis and Dionysius, Macareus, Aristocrates and Demopolis, Comaios, Heragores come to court for a terrible thing' (*SGD* no. 173 = Bravo, 1987: 189 and cf. 194–6).

It was no easy or pleasant task to open a grave, presumably at night, insert something into it carefully and close it again without being caught. Danger was courted on two fronts. First, one risked provoking the wrath of the ghost itself or the infernal powers. The Greek magical papyri include a hymn to accompany an erotic spell explicitly begging off the anger of the exploited dead man from the curser himself (*PGM* IV 449–56 = *CT* no. 27; cf. Gow, 1952, ii: p. 43; Graf, 1994a: 173). A prayer for justice opens and closes by begging off the wrath of the powers from the curser that is troubling them with the explanation that he is forced to do so by thieves (*SGD* no. 21 = *CT* no. 84, Attica, i AD; cf. Versnel, 1991: 72–3). Another prayer for justice asks the powers to 'preserve the one that struck the lead' (*DTA* no. 100, Attica, iv BC; cf. Jordan, 1990: 440). That the powers may have been ill-disposed towards magicians in particular may be implied by the paradoxical use of the slander in some of the Greek magical papyri that the intended victim is a witch or magician (e.g. *PGM* IV 2574–601; cf. Winkler, 1990: 91). Secondly, one – normally – risked the wrath of the corpse's relatives and the outrage of decent citizens. There seems to have been at the least strong social disapproval of the exploitation of corpses in this way throughout antiquity (Versnel, 1991: 63; Faraone, 1991b: 17). Imperial-period inscriptions from a number of places around the Greek world (Thessalonice, Thessaly, Attica, Lesbos, Attica, Asia Minor) show that those who interfered with tombs were often liable to a fine, payable either to the tomb's family or to the authorities (be it city, temple or guild) charged with protecting it. However, these interdictions appear to envisage the primary threat as being one of the eviction of the corpse and/or the insertion of another one into the grave rather than the abuse of the corpse for magical purposes (Bernand, 1991: 364–9). But in 359 AD Ammianus Marcellinus wrote that those that dug up graves for magical purposes were executed (19.12.14).

The unpleasantness and danger of opening graves doubtless enhanced the magical efficacy of tablets deposited in this way. Life was made easier for magical practitioners exploiting Greek graves in the Roman period by the development of the custom of building offering pipes leading down into them. A curse tablet could easily be dropped down one of these to the corpse: a short curse tablet was dropped down just such a pipe in Messina in Sicily (*SGD* no. 114 = *CT* no. 116, ii AD). The grave of a Roman official in Carthage contained seven separate curse tablets (*DT* nos. 233, 235, 237, 239–42 [241 = *CT* no.12], i–iii AD): perhaps access to his grave was particularly easy – or perhaps the ghost had proven to be a successful agent.

Cursers normally avoided naming themselves on their tablets, except in the cases of prayers for justice and erotic-attraction spells. This was doubtless to avoid retribution from both the living and the dead. The existence of (victim's) name-only tablets highlights the danger of depositing one's own name with a ghost in any context whatsoever. Nor would one wish to nail one's own name inadvertently (Versnel, 1991: 62–3).

Graves could themselves be protected by curses displayed at them, usually inscribed on wood or stone. These were particularly common in imperial-period Asia Minor, where more than 350 survive. The language of grave-protection curses has much in common with that of the tablets, although their aim was to bring peace rather than disturbance to the dead. Like the tablets, grave-protection curses also commonly refer to the gods of the underworld, before whom, they proclaim, violators will be impious. But, unlike the tablets, grave-protection curses were inevitably open-ended, and did not define any particular target, focusing as they did on hypothetical grievances in the future rather than actual ones in the past or the present. However, it may have been that, as with the fines for tomb violation, grave-protection curses were primarily targetted against those that were considering casting another corpse into the grave on top of the original one rather than against tablet-inserters. Thus a Cilician curse: 'We adjure you by the god in heaven [Zeus] and Helios and Selene and the underworld gods who have received us that no-one [. . .] should throw another corpse on top of our bones' (Keil and Wilhelm, 1915: 46–7, cf. Bernand, 1991: 153 and 369–79; Strubbe, 1991: esp. 35; *CT* pp. 177–8). But they did also protect against grave-robbers, and magicians could fall into this category in an unusual way: alongside the curse tablets concealed in the house of Germanicus were parts of human bodies (Tacitus, *Annals* 2.69); Apuleius' description of the contents of the witch Pamphile's workshop accordingly includes, alongside pre-inscribed curse tablets, exhumed pieces of human bodies and, magically economical alternatives, crucifixion nails with gobbets of flesh still clinging to them (*Golden Ass* 3.17 = *CT* no. 153). No doubt those inserting tablets into graves took the opportunity to avail themselves of supplies for future spells. Lucan paints a vivid picture of the horrid witch Erichtho, who is introduced to perform necromancy for the younger Pompey (*Pharsalia* 6.438–830). In a memorable paradox she puts the living into graves but takes the dead out of them (529–32). Her plundering of tombs, pyres and gallows for body-parts is lovingly dwelt upon. She is keen that battle be fought in Thessaly, so that she can avail herself of an abundance of magical supplies. As we learn from Apuleius' entertaining account of Zatchlas and the Thelyphrons, Thessalian witches snatched facial parts from corpses even before their burial (*Golden Ass* 2.28–30). Libanius accuses a magician of 'roaming around the graves and from them bringing doom upon people doing him no wrong, troubling the corpses, and refusing to let the souls remain in their own accustomed homes' (41.7; cf. Bonner, 1932a: 41). The distinctive Mnesimachos voodoo doll was found in a grave in the Athenian Ceramicus beside the pelvis of a corpse that had been mutilated and disturbed (*SGD* no. 9 = *VD* no. 5 = *CT* no. 41, c. 400 BC; see Trumpf, 1958 with plates 71–2, and below). Perhaps body-parts were particularly useful for accompanying tablets deposited in places other than in graves, as in the case of those concealed in the home of Germanicus (but see Graf, 1994a: 193 for a different interpretation). In these instances the body-parts function as the counterparts of the victim's 'stuff': in the one case a piece of the victim is brought into proximity with the corpse, in the other a piece of the corpse — the corpse's *ousia* — is brought into proximity with the victim (cf. Tupet, 1976: 85).

Cremation did not inhibit a corpse's usefulness, as can be seen from Erichtho's raiding of pyres. Curse tablets are accordingly found in urns alongside ashes: thus a group of three Latin tablets was found in three adjacent urns (Solin, 1968 nos. 26–8 = *CT* no.52, Spain, 78 AD). One of the Sethian curses was similarly found in an urn (*DT* no. 187 = *CT* no. 15).

The evidence discussed so far indicates that cursers generally preferred to exploit dead people that they did not know and that did not know them, and that the last corpse one would wish to disturb with curse tablets was that of a relative or friend. But there was also a surprising contrary trend. The text of the distinctive tablet cursing the gates of Rome implies that it was deposited in the grave of the curser's own brother (*SGD* no. 129 = *CT* no. 79, Rome, iii AD, quoted below; cf. Guarducci, 1978: 253). More generally, Libanius refers to the possibility that a magician may use the ghost of his son, who is about to be sacrificed to deliver a city from pestilence, as a familiar spirit to carry out his work (41.51; cf. Bonner, 1932a: 41–2). In such cases no doubt curse tablets were inserted into the grave with relative ease at the time of burial. We may suppose that when individual graves were used (in contrast to the mass graves of the unidentifiable dead), the dead person was often known at least vaguely to the curser, since the curser had to be sure both that the exploited corpse was fairly recently dead and that he had died before his time. This degree of acquaintance may be implied by direct addresses to the corpse, a striking example of which is found in a ii–i BC curse from Megara:

> Whenever you, O Pasianax, read these words — but neither will you ever, O Pasianax, read these words, nor will Neophanes ever bring a case against Aristander. But just as you, O Pasianax, lie here ineffectually, so may Neophanes also become ineffectual and nothing. (*DT* no. 43 = *CT* no. 43, ii–i BC; cf. Bravo, 1987: 199–200)

But some such addresses to the corpse may be based upon nothing more than the reading of the corpse's name on the tombstone: 'Whoever you are, Kames, spirit of the dead' (*SGD* no. 156 = *Suppl. Mag.* no. 50, Oxyrhynchus ii–iii AD).

Sometimes a curse promises to 'free' the spirit of the dead person from its restlessness if it does the curser's bidding (*SGD* no. 152 = *Suppl. Mag.* no. 47 = *CT* no. 28, Antinoopolis, iii–iv AD; cf. Erichtho's promise to the corpse she exploits for necromancy at Lucan, *Pharsalia* 6.762–5; see Graf, 1994a: 218). Another curse promises an excellent grave-gift to a corpse that successfully restrains (*SGD* no. 173 = *CT* no. 48, Olbia, iii–1 BC).

It is not always clear whether the restless souls are supposed to carry out the action of restraint themselves, or merely convey the curse to a greater infernal power, since they hover between the two worlds (*CT* pp. 19–20). Poor Pasianax was too helpless even to read, but the frequent placing of the curse-tablet in the right hand of a corpse implies that the dead person was indeed intended to read it (e.g. *SGD* nos. 1–2, Attica, v BC; cf. Jordan, 1988b: 273–4; Faraone, 1991b: 4 and 23 n. 14; Graf, 1994a: 151–2). More was expected of other corpses. In the Olbian tablet just cited the dead man is asked to carry out the curse directly himself. In a late circus curse actually addressed to the Characters, the spirits (*daimones*) of those that have died prematurely or violently are asked to make a very direct intervention and to materialise to frighten the horses at the starting gate (*SEG* xxxiv no. 1437 = *CT* no.6, Apamea, v–vi AD; cf. *SGD* p. 192).

The dead were also of particular use from the sympathetic angle, since a corpse presented a paradigm of lifelessness and uselessness for those attempting to restrain the actions of the living. Thus we find requests that victims be rendered as wordless as the corpses addressed (*DT* no. 25 = *CT* no. 46, Amathous, iii AD); that they be rendered as harmless as a dead puppy accompanying the tablets (*DT* nos. 111–12 = *CT* no. 53, Gaul, ii AD); that they be 'deeply buried' (*SGD* no. 48 = *CT* no. 56, Attica, iv BC); that their bodies be chilled, doubtless to resemble corpses (e.g. *SGD* nos. 22–38 [31 = *CT* no. 21], Attica, iii AD, on which see Jordan, 1985b); that they become as idle as the corpse (the curse addressed to Pasianax, quoted above); and that a circus horse should perish and fall, just as the addressed corpse lies there dead before his time (*DT* no. 295 = *CT* no. 11, Hadrumentum, late Roman). A third- or second-century BC tablet from Boeotia is particularly rich:

> Just as you, Theonnastos, are powerless in any act or exercise of (your) hands, feet, body . . . to love and see maidens (?) . . . so too may Zoilos remain powerless to screw Antheira and Antheira (remain powerless toward) Zoilos in the same way, of beloved Hermes (?) . . . the bed and the chitchat and the love of Antheira and Zoilos . . . and just as this lead is in some place separate from humans, so also may Zoilos be separated from Antheira with the body and touch and kisses of Antheira and the love-makings of Zoilos and Antheira . . . the fear of Zoilos (?). I inscribe this blocking (spell) with a seal. (*DT* no. 85 side A = *CT* no.20 (trans.); cf. Bravo, 1987: 202 and Faraone, 1991b: 13–14)

Of importance here is the concept of *ateleia* or 'unfulfilment,' as it is usually awkwardly translated (it has adjectival derivatives, *atelēs* and *atelestos*, 'unfulfilled'), a state often wished upon curse victims or their designs (*SGD* nos. 94, 97, 99, 100 and 108 = Jameson et al., 1993: 126 a, b, g, h, and i, Selinus, v BC, and *SEG* iv 93, Italian Cyme, v BC). In an Attic tablet the root is used to express a notion of uselessness and fruitlessness that sympathetically associates the corpse with the victim and her deeds:

> And as this corpse lies here 'unfulfilled' (*ateles*), so let all that comes from Theodora, both her words and her actions, towards Charias and towards other people, be 'unfulfilled'(*atelesta*). I bind Theodora before Hermes of the underworld and the 'unfulfilled' (*atelestoi*) and Tethys. (*DT* no. 68b = *CT* no. 22 = Jameson et al., 1993: 130, iv BC)

But the significance of unfulfilment here goes further than the simple conceit of restraint. The *atelestoi* are the dead that have not received the due rites (*telē*). Such spirits, like the ones of those that have died by violence or before their time, cannot achieve rest: Plato explains that those who arrive in Hades without due rites (*atelestoi*) will be left to lie in mud (*Phaedo* 69c). They are therefore bitter and troublesome: in the *Odyssey* the ghost of the unburied Elpenor warns his comrades that if he is not given a proper burial and the due rites, he will occasion the wrath of the gods against them: 'Accomplish (*telesai*) these things for me', he bids Odysseus (Homer, *Odyssey* 11.72–9). The *miasma* or pollution that arises from one that has not received the due rites is famously explained by Teiresias in Sophocles' *Antigone* (998–1032; cf. Parker, 1983: 43–8). The dead without due rites are therefore particularly desirable magical allies. (See generally *DT* on no. 68b, Jameson et al., 1993: 129–31 and Graf, 1994a: 153 and 174.) Death by shipwreck disastrously deprived one of the possibility of the due rites of burial, and this (together with the difficulty of its acquisition) no doubt accounts for the popularity of shipwreck material among the magician's paraphernalia (cf. Bernand, 1991: 140 and 154). An interesting suggestion has been made in connection with the recently discovered classical sacred law from Selinus, which attempted to free the state of *miasma*:

> While curse tablets are not mentioned in the [sacred law], their quantity at Selinous, and in particular in the *Campo di Stele* [where the law was probably discovered], suggests that the deliberate manipulation of *miasma* by means of them may have been one of the reasons why the law was written. (Jameson et al., 1993: 131)

The earlier curse tablets did not usually seek to kill their victims, even when wishfully comparing them to a corpse. But in the later tablets this aim is more frequently expressed: e.g. 'Let him perish and fall, just as you lie (here), prematurely dead' (*DT* no. 295 = *CT* no. 11 [trans., quoting

Jordan], Hadrumentum, late Roman). (See Gow, 1952, ii: p. 40; Bravo, 1987: 201 and 206; Faraone, 1991b: 8 and 26 n. 38.)

The tablets exhibit contradictory magical conceits in relation to corpses: pollution-magic requires the dead to be restless, active and effective; sympathetic magic peaceful, passive and ineffectual.

OTHER DEPOSITION SITES

The progression from grave to chthonic sanctuary as a deposition site is easy and explicable: the chthonic gods, like the dead, dwelt under the earth, but could be expected to be much more reliable and powerful. Most of the tablets that have been identified as having been deposited in sanctuaries of the chthonic gods hail from sanctuaries of Demeter: thus 10 from Demeter Malophoros at Selinus (v BC), 13 from Demeter's Cnidian sanctuary, 10 from her Morgantina sanctuary, 14 from her Corinthian sanctuary, and 12 from an Attic well, apparently dumped from an adjacent Demeter sanctuary (Jordan, 1980a: 231–1 and n. 23; cf. Faraone, 1991b: 22 n. 7; Jameson et al., 1993: 126–7).

In the imperial period if not before 'underground' bodies of water in particular came to be favoured as sites of deposition. Water, like lead, developed sympathetic significance: underground water was usually cold, and wells were normally used for refrigeration, so they were useful for 'chilling' the tablet and its victim (Guarducci, 1978: 254–5; Jordan, 1985b: 241–2 and 1990: 440). One of the Bath tablets prays that its victim should become as liquid as water (*Tab. Sulis* no. 4; cf. Tomlin, 1988: 81). Perhaps such bodies of water were initially seen as channels of communication leading to the infernal powers. Older scholars believed that water brought the tablets into contact with the ghosts of those that had died by shipwreck (*DTA* p. iv and Fox, 1912b: 301). The most important batch of curse tablets found in underground water are those from Bath, but these constitute a marginal case, since they are prayers for justice addressed to the 'respectable' goddess Sulis Minerva and deposited in her sacred spring. Perhaps more typical is the cache of twelve Latin tablets found near a spring at Gaulish Raraunum, which are addressed to obscure infernal powers (*DT* nos. 109–10 = *CT* no.16, iii AD). A Latin tablet from Spain is actually addressed to the spring in which it was deposited: 'O Mistress Spring Foyi . . .' (*AE* 1975 no. 497, ii AD; cf. Versnel, 1991: 60). A number of imperial-period tablets have been found deposited in wells in the Athenian Agora (e.g. *SGD* nos. 22–38; see inventory at Jordan, 1985b: 209).

A iv BC Attic tablet confusingly speaks of its own deposition both in water and in tombs: how could it be deposited in both? Perhaps the tablet was destined for one site, and the accompanying wax doll referred to in the text for the other (*DTA* no. 55 = *CT* no. 64). However, the shaft that contained the mass grave at Amathous in Cyprus discussed above may actually have been a well in origin, in view of its depth (Jordan, 1985b: 207 n. 3). Such a site exploited the best of both alternatives, and was particularly desirable as a deposition site for curse tablets. It is possible that another tablet addresses a ghost that inhabits a well (*SGD* no. 35, Attica, iii AD; cf. Jordan, 1985b: 231). A group of nine lead tablets from Morgantina in Sicily combine water with chthonic sanctuary as their site of deposition: they were found in a well-altar within a chthonic sanctuary (*SGD* pp. 79–80 = *CT* no. 117, i BC). A tablet which was not itself deposited in water implies that the victim's stuff was separately submerged: 'The stream in which the hair now lies awaits the head whence it came' (*DT* no. 210, Salerno, ii AD; cf. Fox, 1912b: 303–5; Fox has many interesting cross-cultural parallels for the use of water-deposition in magic).

Tablets could also be deposited at a site specific to their subject or their victim. A trade curse against bronze smiths was found in the wall (it may originally have been under the floor) of a building in Athens' industrial quarter, which exhibited traces of metal-working and which was therefore likely to have been the victims' workshop:

> I bind Aristaichmos the bronze-smith before those below, and Pyrrhias the bronze-smith, and his business and their souls and Sosias from Lamia and his business and his soul and Alegosi [an attempt to scramble 'Agesion'?] and powerfully and powerfully and Agesion, the woman from Boeotia. (*SGD* no. 20 = *CT* no. 71, iv BC; cf. Faraone, 1991b: 23 n. 9.)

The curse against the Libanius, which consisted of a chameleon voodoo doll, was concealed in his lecture room (see below).

It is quite common to find second- and third-century AD competition curses designed to bind opponents or their horses in chariot races nailed to or buried under the floor of hippodromes adjacently to the starting gates, where they would have the greatest effect, or buried in the central reserve, the *spina* (e.g. *DT* nos. 234–44 and *SGD* nos. 138–9, Carthage; *DT* no. 272–95 and *SGD* no. 144, Hadrumentum; *SGD* no. 149, Lepcis Magna; *SGD* no. 166, Damascus; *SGD* no. 167, Beirut; cf. Faraone, 1991b: 13 and 28 n. 56; *CT* pp. 18–9, with a photograph of an unpublished tablet that is folded like a handkerchief and transfixed by a large nail that formerly secured it to the floor of the Carthaginian circus, near the starting gates).

The victim's home was often used. Perhaps the most famous literary example of the use of curse tablets concerns the discoveries in the house of the imperial heir-apparent Germanicus in 19 BC:

And there were found in the floor and the walls the exhumed remains of human corpses, incantations and curses and the name of Germanicus cut into leaden tablets, ashes half-burned and smeared with putrefied flesh and other evil apparatuses, by which it is believed that souls are dedicated to the infernal powers. (Tacitus, *Annals* 2.69 = Luck, 1985 no. 13 = *CT* no. 148; cf. Goodyear, 1981: ad loc. and Dio Cassius, 58.18)

Another, rather later, literary account tells of the siting of an erotic curse:

Therefore after a year, having been taught by the priests of Asclepius, who does not cure souls but destroys them, he came in eager anticipation of illicit sex. He buried under the threshold of a girl's house certain monstrous words and monstrous figures carved into sheets of bronze from Cyprus. The virgin immediately went mad. (Jerome, *Life of St. Hilarion the Hermit* 23 [= *PL* vol. 23 col. 38] = *CT* no. 163, iv–v AD)

Similarly Sophronius tells how Theodorus of Cyprus was made lame by magic. A saint appeared to him in a dream and told him to look under the threshold of his bedroom. There he found a 'wicked instrument of a sorcerer', which perhaps included a tablet or a voodoo doll. We are further told that on the removal of the instrument the sorcerer was immediately destroyed and made to disappear (Sophronius, *Account of the miracles of Saints Cyrus and John* at *PG* vol. 87.3, col. 3625 = *CT* no. 166, vi AD; cf. Gow, 1952, ii: p. 47 for the importance of doors in magic).

The following rather ambitious third-century AD curse, apparently made by a slave anxious to escape Rome and go home, was found in a grave, but one appropriately adjacent to Rome's Adreatina gate:

Restrain Artemidoros the doctor of the Third Praetorian Cohort. The brother of the dead Demetrios is his servant, who now wants to go out to his own fatherland. Therefore do not let him [i.e. do not let Artemidoros stop me], but restrain the Italian land, knock out the gates of the Romans. (*SGD* no. 129 = *CT* no. 79)

Here we have another strategic combination of deposition sites. Similarly, some Latin tablets binding baths were found in a spring adjacent to the remains of baths: the curser was probably attempting to exploit both the water-site and the trade site (Solin, 1968: 31 = *CT* no. 82, Carthage, ii–iii AD).

THE FUNDAMENTAL NATURE OF THE IDIOM OF BINDING

The chief magical idiom employed by the texts is one of binding and restraining. We have already discussed their physical 'binding' and 'nailing'; here we turn to their use of binding language. Although the conceit of binding may initially appear to be of restricted exploitability, in practice it can be addressed to a wide range of problems in different areas of life: it is simply a matter of re-thinking the structure of the problem and representing it in the tablet as one that can be solved if the action or designs of (a) person(s) or object(s) can be restrained. The corrollary of this is that the real motivation for some of the tablets may not be immediately apparent from their text. This is particularly likely in the case of the erotic tablets, a category which ultimately deviated more than any other from the binding idiom under the pressure of their authors' real agenda.

The most basic form of tablet, and doubtless the earliest form, simply contains the name(s) of the victim(s) in the nominative. Any words of binding applied must have been verbal. Then came the addition of a simple verb of binding, with the name(s) made direct object and put into the accusative. In the Attic tablets the verb is *katadeō*, in the Boeotian *katadidēmi* (dialectal variants of the same root), which literally mean 'bind down'. Graf has interestingly argued that the *kata*-prefix, 'down', refers significantly to the desired association of the victim with the world below (1994a: 142–3 and 149, with particular attention to *DT* no. 49 = *CT* no. 44). Some of the earliest tablets, including some of those from Selinus, use a verb not of 'binding' but of 'inscribing,' such as *engraphō*, *katagraphō* or *enkatagraphō* (Jameson et al., 1993: 128, on their *f*, *h–j* and *r*). This again may imply that the act of inscription itself was seen as a kind of binding. However, these terms are usually related to a group of others found in the tablets, such as *apographō*, *katatithēmi* and *paradidōmi*, and explained as quasi-legal formulas for 'registering' the victim with a divinity or power, so that the power can do the act of binding (Faraone, 1991b: 5 and 9–10 and 24 nn. 20 and 24; cf. Bravo, 1987: 197; Tomlin, 1988: 70–1; Versnel, 1991: 71–3; Graf, 1994a: 146–7). One of the most distinctive tablets consists of a flattened voodoo doll with a curse-text written on it, the so called 'gingerbread man' (Euboea, iv BC):

> I register (*katagraphō*) Eisias, daughter of A(u)toclea, before the Hermes who restrains. Restrain her and keep her with you!
> I bind Eisias before the Hermes who restrains, her hands, the feet of Eisias, her body. (*SGD* no. 64 = Faraone, 1991b: 3 = *CT* no. 19)

The tablets soon developed more varied and indirect ways of expressing binding, going beyond the simple use of a verb such as *katadeō*, which Faraone categorises as the 'direct binding formula.' We find also 'prayer formulas' in which the gods or powers are asked to do the binding on the curser's behalf and 'wish formulas' ('*May . . .*') (Faraone, 1991b: 5). Tablets using the direct binding formula often repeat the word of binding many times, or apply it separately to different parts of the victim's body. A brief tablet includes a list of the most commonly bound parts:

> I bind Iphemythanes and Androsthenes and Simmias and Dromon. I bind their hands and feet before Hermes the restrainer; so too their soul, tongues, work and profits. (*DTA* no. 86 = *CT* no. 67, Attica, iv BC)

The parts of the body singled out are sometimes specifically relevant to the theme of the curse (Preisendanz, 1972: 10–11). Thus tongues are often singled out for binding in curses against opponents in lawsuits. We have already referred to a number of such curses (e.g. *SGD* no. 95 = Jameson et al., 1993: 126 *c* = *CT* no. 49 and *DTA* 97 = *CT* no. 66). A very early curse tablet requests that the tongue of Selinontios be twisted to the point of uselessness (*SGD* no. 99 = Dubois, 1989 no. 37 = *CT* no. 51, Selinus, early v BC). The 'binding song' sung by the Eumenides against Orestes before their suit against him in Aeschylus' *Eumenides* perhaps reflects an oral forerunner of tongue-binding curses in Attic trials (line 306; cf. Faraone, 1985). Many of the classical Attic litigation curses bind tongues, such as that against Androsthenes et al. quoted above. A noteworthy literary example of the phenomenon was that to which Thucydides son of Melesias was subject in the course of a trial which possibly took place in the early 420's (Aristophanes, *Wasps* 946–8 with scholiast; cf. Faraone, 1989). In Rome Cicero told that his opponent Curio claimed that he had been made to dry up in pleading a suit by drugs and incantations (*Brutus* 217, cf. *Orator* 129; cf. Tupet, 1976: 204–5; Graf, 1994a: 71, 139 and 189). Ovid imagines an old woman teaching girls how to bind hostile tongues using lead, thread, beans, and the head of a small fish which has been sown up and sealed with pitch and pierced with a bronze needle (Ovid, *Fasti* 2.571–82 = *CT* no. 144; cf. Tupet, 1976: 67 and 409). A Latin grave inscription records how a beloved wife, Ennia Fructuosa, was killed by curses which first rendered her mute (*CIL* viii no. 2756 = *CT* no. 136, Numidia, iii AD+). The most distinctive case of a binding spell used against a tongue was that worked against the orator Libanius, who fell ill and could not speak before his students. The cause was discovered to be a chameleon voodoo doll concealed in his lecture room: its head had been chopped off and stuffed between its hind legs; one of its forefeet closed its mouth, to symbolise silence; its other forefoot had been chopped off, to deprive Libanius of his gesticulating hand. Once the chameleon was removed, Libanius recovered (Libanius 1.245–50, iv AD; cf. Bonner, 1932a: especially 38–9; Bernand, 1991: 255–6; Faraone, 1991b: 29 n. 70). An interesting variation on this theme is provided by an inscription from Delos, which recounts how Serapis preserved his new temple by binding the tongues of litigants that threatened it (*IG* xi no. 1299 ll. 85–90, iii BC; cf. Engelmann, 1975). But the parts singled out for binding are not always of obvious relevance: why, for example, the nose of a silversmith's bellows-operator (*SGD* no. 3 = *CT* no. 72)?

Animals also can be bound, such as the horses in chariot races (e.g. *SGD* no. 167 = *CT* no. 5, Syria, ii–iii AD). So too can significant objects: another way of hindering a rival in a chariot race could be to bind his whip (*SEG* xxxiv no. 1437 = *SGD* p. 92 = *CT* no. 57, Syria, v–vi AD). Even abstractions can be bound: a Greek competition curse binds not only the legs of opponents, but also their bounding and their running (*DT* no. 241 = *CT* no. 12, Carthage, i–iii AD).

A number of techniques were available for expanding the usefulness of binding curses. The possibility of binding objects itself extended the range of problematic situations to which binding curses could be applied: the curse applied to the gates of Rome by the homesick slave, cited above, illustrates the point. A particularly useful sort of binding was the prevention from eating, sleeping and drinking. Sometimes this could be an end in itself: thus a tablet directed against athletes requests 'Keep them up all night long and keep them away from all nourishment, [so that they will have no strength] but fall behind' (*SGD* no. 157 = *CT* no.8 [trans.], Oxyrhynchus, iv AD). But more often this type of binding is conditional, and intended to torture the victim until they act in accordance with the ultimate goal of the curse. It is often used in erotic spells to force the beloved to come to the arms of his or her admirer (e.g. *SGD* no. 152 = *Suppl. Mag.* no. 47 = *CT* no. 28, Antinoopolis, ii–iii AD; cf. the closely related *PGM* IV 354–75). Similarly, prayers for justice sometimes deprive thieves of sleep until they surrender the stolen goods (e.g. *Tab. Sulis* nos. 10, 32 and 52, iii–iv AD). Another Bath tablet is quite determined: it forbids the thief to drink, eat, defecate or (probably) urinate before returning the goods (*Tab. Sulis* no. 41, iii AD). Yet another is unforgiving: on Tomlin's interpretation, the victim is to be deprived of sleep until he measures out equal quantities of cloud and smoke – an impossibility (*Tab. Sulis* no. 100, iv AD).

We perhaps get an idea of what it was supposed to feel like to be the victim of binding magic from the (unsuccessful) attempts of the sorcerer Olympius against Plotinus: though proof against the magic, he confessed that his body had felt like a purse, the strings of which had been drawn tight, and that his limbs had felt squeezed (Porphyry *Life of Plotinus* 53–5 = Luck, 1985 no. 31; cf. Merlan, 1954).

THE IMPORTANCE OF TWISTEDNESS

Closely related to the notion of binding is the notion of twistedness, which likewise operates in a sympathetic manner and restrains through confusion and 'hobbling'. The notions are associated in voodoo dolls which are often both bound and twisted (see below). But twisting and confusion have other significances too in a magical context. Twisting was seen as something inherently magical, and for that reason the Magician-god, Hephaestus, was often portrayed with twisted legs (Delcourt, 1957: esp. 110–36; Detienne and Vernant, 1978: 259–76; cf. Faraone, 1992: 119 and 133–4).

Magical texts are twisted in a number of ways. The distinctive rolling of the lead sheet gives a physical twist to the text in one dimension, but the texts themselves were often written in twisted fashion. It is quite common for texts to be written in 'boustrophedon' form, i.e., with lines written alternately from left to right and from right to left, following the pattern of the 'turns of an ox' (e.g. *DTA* nos. 33 and 34, iii BC). This had been an unremarkable form of writing in the archaic period. Its preservation in curse tablets may have been due to magic's taste for the maintenance of its arcane rituals (Faraone, 1991b: 8 and 12, with n. 35), but the inherent 'twistedness' of the style probably also played a part in securing its magical future. To this type the tablets were to add many more versions of twisted writing. A variant closely akin to boustrophedon is found in the Sethian tablet quoted above: alternate lines are written upside down and in different directions, to produce a snaking effect (*DT* no. 155 = *CT* no. 13, Rome, iv AD; see Figure 3). The tablet is appropriately illustrated with (among other things) a pair of snakes that wind back and forth around a mummy in a similar fashion. Another way to twist text was to spiral it, so that it resembled a cross-section of a rolled tablet. This is found on two early round tablets (*SGD* nos. 99 and 100 = Jameson et al., 1993: 126 *h* and *i* and cf. p. 128 [99/*h* = *CT* no. 51], Selinus, v BC); the Theonnastos text quoted above is similarly arranged (*DT* 85 = *CT* no. 20, side B, Boeotia, iii–ii BC).

The names of the individual(s) to be cursed, which in the earliest name-only tablets stood very directly and sympathetically for the victims themselves, are often singled out for distortion. The simplest and most systematic distortion of names is reverse-spelling; sometimes the victims' names are listed in reverse spelling, and followed by a line of text written normally (e.g. *DT* no. 60 = *CT* no. 42, Attica, iv BC). Or the letters of the names could be jumbled in an otherwise normal text (e.g. *DTA* no. 95 = *CT* no. 39). Sometimes the jumbled versions of the names are written in addition to undistorted versions (e.g. *SGD* no. 105 = Jameson et al., 1993: 127 *o*, Selinus, v BC, and *DTA* no. 55 = *CT* no. 64, Attica, iv BC). These last examples indicate that it was the purpose of letter-jumbling to achieve a sympathetic confusion of the bearers of the names rather than to conceal the identity of the victims. One tablet makes this explicit, requesting that just as the names have been jumbled, so may the victims' words and deeds be (*SGD* no. 40, Attica, v–iv BC). Perhaps unjumbled forms were included alongside jumbled ones out of an anxiety that the powers might not be able to decipher the jumbled ones. Another tablet perhaps attempts a different kind of sympathetic debilitating operation upon its victims' names: they have been written and then erased (*SGD* no. 22, Attica, ii–iv AD).

The entire text of a curse can also be distorted, and there are many variants available here. These techniques are particularly associated with later classical Attic tablets (Faraone, 1991b: 7). It is common for the entire text to be spelled out backwards, letter by letter (see *CT* p. 5). Sometimes with this technique the letters still face right (e.g. *DTA* no. 24 = *CT* no. 58, iv BC), sometimes they too are reversed to face left (e.g. *Tab. Sulis* no. 61, iii AD, with resulting copying-errors). A variation of this technique reverse-spells the text line by line (e.g. *Tab. Sulis* no. 44 = *CT* no. 95, iii AD). Sometimes the general flow of sentences is in the left-to-right direction, but the individual words within them are reverse-spelled, to read right-to-left (*DTA* no. 86 = *CT* no. 67, v–iv BC, and *Tab. Sulis* no. 4, iii–iv AD). The sympathetic function of retrograde writing is likewise made explicit in one tablet: 'Just as these words are cold and right-to-left (*eparistera*), so too may the words of Crates be cold and backwards' (*DTA* no. 67, Attica, iv BC; cf. Faraone, 1991b: 7).

A variation on the theme of twisted language may be found in twisted thought. In the two tablets addressed to the corpse Pasianax the thought changes direction dramatically: it begins 'Whenever you, O Pasianax, read this letter . . .', but then abruptly breaks off and begins again in contradictory fashion '. . . but neither will you, Pasianax, ever read this letter' (*DT* nos. 43–4 = *CT* no. 43, Megara, ii–i BC; the former is quoted above). That this structuring of the text does not merely reflect second thoughts during a careless writing is indicated by the fact that these phrases appear separately on both tablets.

CATEGORISATION

The curse tablets cover a moderately wide range of subjects and situations, but the vast majority of them fall into quite definable categories. The most recent scholars of the tablets employ the following sorts of categories:

1. litigation curses (including political curses)
2. competition curses
3. trade curses
4. erotic curses (separation and attraction)
5. prayers for justice

Thus divide Jordan (at Versnel, 1991: 62), Faraone (1991b: 10 and 16), Gager (1992: 42–199) and Graf (1994a: 141–2), superseding Audollent (1904: lxxxix), Kagarow (1929: 50–5), Preisendanz (1972: 9–10 and 22), Faraone's earlier division (1985: 151) and Tomlin at *Tab. Sulis*, p. 60.

Faraone has argued that the earlier Greek tablets are linked by a common theme: competitiveness or rivalry. This is particularly clear in the case of the tablets that address themselves to theatrical competitions. But the litigation curses appear to be addressed against opponents in lawsuits, the trade curses against competing traders, and the earlier erotic curses, the separation ones, against rivals in love. The competitive or 'agonistic' spirit is one of the characteristic features of classical Greek civilisation, a feature visible not only in the classical Greeks' athletic and theatrical competitions, but also in their legal, military and literary culture. The cultural context of the earliest curse tablets may therefore be characteristically Greek (Faraone, 1991b and Graf 1994a: 176). Bernand similarly sites the culture of Greek magic as a whole in the context of a related, wider Greek phenomenon, that of envy (*phthonos*) (Bernand, 1991: 85–105 and passim). However, the apparent degree of competitiveness (and envy) underlying the tablets may be deceptive, since their dependence upon the idiom of binding or restraining a rival forces the curser to structure his problem in a competitive fashion. Thus if a trader wishes to use magic to become rich, he can only do so by finding trade-rivals to restrain. The eventual development of erotic-attraction spells may suggest that some of the earlier separation spells were written by people whose chief aim was to attract, but in deference to the binding idiom went about this by restraining a 'rival'.

Litigation Curses
So far there are around 67 Greek and 46 Latin published examples of litigation curses (*CT* p. 117). The earliest extant curses, from Selinus, belong to this category, and it was a popular one in classical Athens. It is

now believed that the curses were usually prepared prior to or during the trial, and were designed to influence the effectiveness of speeches made in its course: their purpose was deliverance, not revenge (Moraux, 1960: 42–4; Calder, 1963: 171; Faraone, 1985: 151 and 1989: 156–7 n. 21 and 1991b: 29 n. 67). It is also believed, on the basis of technical legal vocabulary found in the tablets, that curses relating to criminal cases were only made by defendants (i.e. the people with something to lose), although there is no obvious reason why a prosecutor should not have used a tablet to secure a conviction, especially if the prosecution was, as so often, malicious. But in a civil case either side could feel threatened and so make a tablet (*CT* pp. 117–18). We are seldom told what the subject of the relevant legal dispute was, but one late curse informs us that its dispute concerned slaves, property and papers (*SGD* no. 179 = *CT* no. 54, provenance unknown, iii–iv AD; cf. Moraux, 1960: 12–14 and 46–8).

In the early Selinuntine curse against Eucles and others (*SGD* no. 95 quoted above) we already see the chief elements of the litigation curse: the identification of the legal opponents, and the specific request that their tongues should be bound (see above for discussion of the latter phenomenon). These elements are found in the many classical Athenian litigation tablets (e.g. *DTA* no. 95 = *CT* no. 39). Classical Athens was and knew itself to be an extraordinarily litigious city: the point was well made by Aristophanes' buffoon Strepsiades, when he refused to believe that Athens had been identified for him on a map of the world, since he could not see any jurors there (*Clouds* 208; cf. Dover, 1968: ad loc.).

The forensic speeches of the Attic orators show that Greek prosecutions often had a wider political agenda. In tablets where large numbers of prosecutors and (obviously hostile) witnesses are cursed, it may be that a political faction is involved. One Athenian tablet appears (without specific legal context) to attempt to curse an entire political party: it contains a protracted list of names, some of which are known from literary and other epigraphic sources, and some of which, interestingly, are women (*SGD* no. 48 = *CT* no. 56, 350–25 BC; cf. *CT* p. 119).

Competition Curses

The earliest trace of a curse of the competition type is found in a passage in Pindar: 'Poseidon . . . bind the bronze spear of Oenomaus!' (*Olympian* 1.75–8, composed 476 BC). Surviving pre-imperial competition curses address theatrical rather than sporting competition:

> All the choral trainers and under-trainers with Theagenes, both the trainers and the under-trainers. (*DTA* no. 34 = *CT* no.1, Attica, iv–iii BC)

A group of imperial-period curses against athletes was deposited in a well in the Athenian Agora, directed against the wrestler Eutychian and others (*SGD* nos. 24–9; cf. Jordan, 1985b on nos. 1–6 and p. 214 for a list all known curses against athletes). The majority of curses falling into this category are the distinctively Roman circus (i.e. chariot-racing) curses dating from the second century AD onwards. The most important batch of these is the 'Sethian' one from Rome itself (Wünsch, 1898 = *DT* nos. 140–87, of which no. 155 was quoted above). The circuses were taken very seriously in the Roman empire: the extremity of the passions they aroused often led to riots between the supporters of the universal Blue, Green, Red and White factions. Since charioteers were also commonly the clients of local aristocracies, support for them also often had a social or political significance. As Brown has observed, charioteers were often 'undefined mediators' in urban society. Betting money could also be at stake. Doubtless both charioteers themselves and their supporters resorted to the tablets. An imperial decree of 389 AD required that those known to be using magic in the circus be publicly exposed (*Theodosian code* 9.16.11), and charioteers were punished under it on three recorded occasions (Ammianus Marcellinus 26.3.3, 28.1.27 and 29.3.5). Cassiodorus, writing in 507–11 AD, refers to a charioteer, Thomas, who was so successful that his enemies attributed his victories to magic (*Variae Epistolae* 3.51). It is curious that even in the Latin west circus curses tend to have been written in Greek: perhaps because most charioteers came from the Greek east. (On the circuses generally see Brown, 1970: 17–46; Cameron, 1973 and 1976; Segal, 1981; Humphrey 1986. On circus curses see Wünsch, 1898; Preisendanz, 1972: 15 and 22; Humphrey et al., 1972–3: 97; Jordan, 1988c: esp. 119; Faraone, 1991b: 10–13; *CT* pp. 42–77).

Trade Curses

Trade curse tablets are almost entirely confined to the classical and hellenistic Greek worlds. The best examples tend to come from classical Athens. A distinctive antecedent to them is found in the 'Homeric' or 'Hesiodic' hexameter poem *Kiln* in which the poet calls down the wrath of a series of appropriately named demons on the work of potters, Crusher, Smasher, Shatterer, Unquenchable and Unbaked-pot-destroyer, and asks that their pots be ground to dust as if in the jaws of a horse (Homer, *Epigram* 14 at [Herodotus] *Life of Homer* 32 = Hesiod F302 MW. See Milne, 1966; Faraone, 1991b: 11 and 1992: 47 and 56; *CT* p. 153; Griffiths 1995: 87–8).

Trade curses appear to have been generally made between rival tradesmen. Hesiod again provides an insight into the sort of trade rivalries in the archaic period that would go on to generate the curses we find in the classical:

> Neighbour envies neighbour as he races for wealth. This is a good kind
> of strife for men. And potter bears grudges towards potter, and joiner
> towards joiner, and beggar envies beggar, and singer envies singer.
> (Hesiod, *Works and Days* 23–6 [trans. Evelyn-White (Loeb)])

Apart from potters (*SGD* no. 44 = *CT* no. 70), the trades recorded in
discovered Greek tablets from Attica between the fifth and the third
centuries BC include: innkeepers/shopkeepers (*DTA* no. 87 = *CT* no.
62), pipemakers, carpenters (both in *DTA* no. 55 = *CT* no. 64), bronze-
workers (*SGD* no. 20 = *CT* no. 71), netmakers (*SGD* no. 52 = *CT* no.
60), frame or rope makers, fabric sellers (both in *DTA* no. 87 = *CT* no.
62), helmet makers, goldworkers (both in *DTA* no. 69 = *CT* no. 63),
painters, flour sellers, scribes (all three in *SGD* no. 48), silversmiths'
bellows-workers (*SGD* no.3 = *CT* no. 72, v BC and possibly the oldest
extant tablet from the Greek mainland), brothelkeepers and prostitutes
(both in *DT* no. 52 = *CT* no. 73). Curses are also found against shield
makers (*DTA* no. 12, undated), doctors (*SEG* xxxiv no. 1175 = *SGD* no.
124 = *CT* no. 81, Metapontum, iv–iii BC), helmsmen (*SGD* no. 170,
from Panticapaeum in southern Russia, undated) and seamstresses (*SGD*
no. 72, unknown provenance and date). Free and slave, male and female
workers are victims alike. (Cf. *CT* pp. 151–74.).

The innkeepers' profession predominates, which is gratifying in view of
their ancient literary reputation for obstreperousness and vulgar abuse;
often the distinction between innkeeper and brothelkeeper was vague, and
often they were women (Faraone, 1991b: 27 n. 46). The following Attic
tablet gives pride of place to innkeepers:

> I bind Callias, the local shopkeeper/innkeeper, and his wife Thraitta,
> and the shop/inn of the bald man, and the shop/inn of Anthemion,
> which is adjacent to . . ., and Philon the shopkeeper/innkeeper. Of all
> these people I bind their soul, work, hands, feet and shops/inns. I bind
> Sosimenes (and?) his brother, and Carpos his slave, the linen-seller, and
> Glycanthis, whom they call Malthace, and Agathon the shopkeeper/
> innkeeper, the slave of Sosimenes, of all these people I bind their soul,
> work, life, hands and feet [etc.] (*DTA* no. 87a = *CT* no. 62, iv BC)

The following Attic curse almost certainly targets amongst other people a
pimp and his prostitutes:

> Cercis, Blastos, Nicander, Glycera. I bind Cercis and her words and the
> actions of Cercis and her tongue before the unmarried (dead); and
> whenever they read this, may utterance be denied Cercis. I bind [name
> lost] himself and his girls/prostitutes and his trade and his capital and his
> business and his speech and his actions. Underworld Hermes, restrain

these things by all means until they lose their minds. (*DT* no. 52 = *CT* no. 73, iii–ii BC)

Perhaps definitions of some individuals on curse tablets as pimps should not be taken literally, but as abuse, as ritual slander to give the powers particular reason to attack the victims (e.g. *SGD* no. 11 again; cf. Versnel, 1991: 95 n. 23).

The elder Pliny indicates that curse tablets were used still in the Roman world in connection with trade, again specifically with reference to the crushing of potters' wares (*Natural History* 28.4.19). There are two reasonable Roman-period examples of trade curses: one from Nomentum dating from the first century AD or possibly even from the late republic (*DT* no. 135 = *CT* no. 80; cf. Solin, 1989: 196–7), and one from Carthage dating from the second or third century AD (Solin, 1968: 31 = *CT* no. 62).

Erotic Curses

Erotic or amatory curse tablets are of particular importance, not only because around a quarter of classifiable extant tablets fall into the category, but because they constitute the category of tablets mostly clearly forced to evolve under the pressure of the circumstances in which they were made and because of their general relevance to the study of gender relations, which is currently the prime focus of interest in Greek social history. (On erotic curses see primarily Maltomini, 1979 [reviewing unpublished work by Moke]; Jordan, 1985b: 222–3 [for a concise survey]; Petropoulos, 1988; Winkler, 1990; *CT* pp. 78–115.)

There are literary indications that the Greeks had used magic in erotic contexts at least since the archaic period: the most famous example is the 'girdle' or 'band' of Aphrodite, which Hera borrows as a love charm with which to seduce Zeus (Homer, *Iliad* 14.198–223 and 292–351; cf. Bonner, 1949 and 1950: 115). More directly antecedent to erotic tablets is the series of temporary verbal spells through which the demi-goddess Calypso detains Odysseus on her island, making him 'forget' his homeland and wife, even though he still really longs for them (Homer, *Odyssey* 1.51–9 and 5.148–59; cf 9.94–5 and 10.236 and 12.184–5 for other magical 'forgetting'; see Petropoulos, 1988: especially 128–20; Heubeck, et al., 1989 on 10.213). However, erotic curse tablets only appear first in the fourth century BC, well after the establishment of the other major types of binding spell. Perhaps this was because the binding idiom did not seem immediately useful for situations of love, and it was indeed the rather specific erotic circumstance of the presence of a rival (real or feigned) for the beloved's affections, an 'enemy' in love, that first brought curse tablets into the erotic sphere. It was not until the second century AD, when curse tablet culture had become mature, complex and syncretised, that tablets were finally used for attraction, initially in North Africa and Syria. Although the language of binding was still used in these tablets, the binding was of a type that violated the original idiom: to 'bind' a lover to oneself is not really to restrain them. The distinction between the first and second types is usually rendered in terms of 'separation curses', known in Greek as *diakopoi* (but often now referred to under the German term 'Trennungszauber'), and 'attraction' or 'aphrodisiac curses', known in Greek as *agōgai*. Separation curses disappeared in the iii AD, attraction in the fourth. (See Gow, 1952,ii: p. 37 and Faraone, 1991b: 13–15 for this development and terminology; cf., for further subcategorisation, Petropoulos, 1988: 216; Winkler, 1990: 94; *CT* pp. 79–80.)

The majority of extant erotic tablets are written by men in pursuit of women, but examples of all four sexual permutations survive. An example of a man (we assume) in pursuit of a woman is found in the separation curse addressed to the corpse Theonnastos quoted above (*DT* no. 85 = Gager no. 20, Boeotia, iii–ii BC). Women (we assume) are seen in pursuit of men in another undated separation curse from Boeotia:

> (*Side A*) I assign Zois the Eretrian, wife of Kabeira, to Earth and to Hermes – her food, her drink, her sleep, her laughter, her intercourse [probably including sexual], her playing of the kithara and her entrance [perhaps with some sexual overtones], her pleasure, her little buttocks, her thinking, her eyes . . .
> (*Side B*) and to Hermes (I consign) her wretched walk, her words, deeds and evil talk. (*DT* no. 86 = *CT* no. 18 [trans.])

Women are seen in pursuit of women in a lead attraction curse from Egypt:

> By the means of this corpse-demon set on fire the heart, liver, the spirit of Gorgonia, whom Nilogenia, bore for desire and love for Sophia, whom Isara bore. Drive Gorgonia, whom Nilogenia bore, to the bath-house, and you (corpse-demon), become a (female) bath-attendant. (*SGD* no. 151 = *Suppl. Mag.* no. 42, Hermoupolis, iii–iv AD)

The corpse-demon is to heat up Gorgonia with love, as a bath-attendant would heat up her customers with warm water. Bath-houses were appropriately believed to be favoured haunts for ghosts (see Bonner, 1932b and *Suppl. Mag.* ad loc.). Egypt has produced other homosexual curses on papyrus: a further lesbian one (*PGM* XXXII) and three male-homosexual (*PGM* XXXIIa and LXVI and *Suppl. Mag.* no. 54).

Winkler argued that attraction spells may sometimes have had a less romantic purpose than first appears. Some tablets appear to wish not simply to make the beloved reciprocate love, but actually to turn the tables on her, and make her suffer the torments of unreciprocated love for the curser. Winkler sees this process as a therapeutic one of transference and projection, in which the primary goal is not a relationship with the beloved but deliverance from the torments of desire, and in which the process is akin to sending away a disease onto another (Winkler, 1990: 87–91; cf. *CT* pp. 81–2). The archaic Lesbian poetess Sappho's hymn to Aphrodite had arguably attempted to achieve the same (F1 Voigt, early vi BC; cf. Winkler, 1990: 166–76 and Bernand, 1991: 294–7). However, many tablets do explicitly ask for a relationship (see below).

The curse tablets' custom of binding those parts of the body specifically relevant to the matter in hand and their taste for the countercultural gave rise to the use of frank and vigorous sexual language in erotic tablets, as illustrated by the curse against Zois quoted above. An Egyptian tablet is particularly full:

> I bind you Theodotis, daughter of Eus, to the tail of the snake and to the mouth of the crocodile and the horns of the ram and the poison of the asp and the hairs of the cat and the 'appendage' of the god, so that you may not ever be able to have sex with another man or be screwed or be buggered or give oral sex or take pleasure with another man, except me alone, Ammonion the son of Hermitaris . . . so that Theodotis, the daughter of Eus may no longer make trial of another man apart from me alone, Ammonion, taken in slavery, driven hysterical, searching for Ammonion son of Hermitaris, flying through the air, and so that she may bring her thigh near to thigh and genitals near to genitals for eternal sex for all the time of her life. These are the pictures. (*SGD* no. 161 = *Suppl. Mag.* no. 38 = *CT* no. 34, ii AD)

The accompanying pictures include a crocodile and a kissing couple; it is possible that an obscure figure represents with appropriate explicitness a penis entering a vagina (see *CT* ad loc.). A papyrus formulary for an attraction spell similarly expresses its purpose: ' . . . so that you may bring me woman X and fix head to head, and fasten together lips with lips, and fix stomach to stomach and bring thigh near to thigh, and fasten black together with black, and may woman X accomplish her own love-making with me, man Y, for all the length of time' (*PGM* IV 400–5 = *CT* no. 27).

Prayers for Justice

Prayers for justice constitute the most distinctive category of curse tablets. The specific sort of justice that most of them seek is the restitution of stolen goods. The category is dominated by the large Bath cache, the importance of which for our understanding of the 'prayers for justice' genre is further increased by the exemplary nature of Tomlin's analysis of them (*Tab. Sulis*). All but one of the 130 tablets in this cache seek restitution of stolen goods, as do at least 20 of the other 30 British tablets. By contrast only 20 tablets prompted by theft are known from the rest of the ancient world: the British ever, it seems, valued private property above all else. (Theft tablets from outside Bath are listed at *Tab. Sulis* pp. 60–2.)

The prayers-for-justice category is so distinctive that some scholars now insist that they should not be classed with curse tablets at all (e.g. Versnel, 1991). But we should not lose sight of the similarities:

* Both are usually written on lead, rolled and transfixed by nails (cf. *Tab. Sulis* p. 59).

* Prayers for justice conform to the latter part of Jordan's definition of curse tablets: '. . . intended to influence, by supernatural means, the actions or welfare of persons or animals against their will' (1985a: 151).

* Prayers for justice are typically deposited in sanctuaries or sacred springs, as are many curse tablets.

* A significant number of cross-over cases, which share elements both of traditional curses and prayers for justice, prevents categorical differentiation between the two groups. Excluding the Bath tablets, which all derive from a single local practice, there are, according to Versnel's classification, 20 examples of 'pure' prayers for justice and 18 examples of 'border area' cases (1991: 61 and 64–75, esp. 68; cf. *CT* pp. 179). Since the size of the 'border area' group is of a similar order of magnitude to the 'pure' type, it cannot be argued that 'prayers for justice' belong to a radically independent group. Of particular interest in this 'border area' is a tablet with a fairly traditional curse on one side, and a prayer for justice on the other, both directed to the same end (*SGD* no. 58, Delos, i BC–i AD; cf. Versnel, 1991: 66–7).

Nonetheless, the following criteria may be employed towards the construction of a syndrome for prayers for justice:

* They do not use the distinctive binding formula of words, but rather simply pray for just treatment from the god. Nor do they contain *voces magicae* or 'words of power' (*Tab. Sulis* p. 62).

* They are normally addressed to major or respectable deities, although there can still be a preference for those with chthonic connections, such as Mercury (= Hermes, as in the Uley cache: see *Tab. Sulis* p. 61 nos. 13–16), or Demeter (as in *DT* nos. 2–3, 6, 11–12 and *SGD* no. 60 = *Tab. Sulis* p. 61 nos. 2–7). However, the Athenian prayers for justice are addressed to the demons of the underworld (*DT* nos. 74–5, *SGD* no. 21 and p. 162 = *Tab. Sulis* p. 62 nos. 9–12). The Bath cache is addressed to Sulis, identified with Minerva (= Athene). While Minerva

had no chthonic associations, Sulis' sacred spring was a body of underground water.

⋆ Concomitantly, the tone of the language of prayers for justice evinces greater humility and deference towards the powers invoked than that of binding curses. Taking these first three points together, many of the prayers for justice seem to have much more in common with ordinary pious religious practice than 'magic' (*Tab. Sulis* p. 62).

⋆ Since most of the 'prayers for justice' seek the restitution of stolen goods, the petitioner is usually unaware of the identity of the one that wrongs him, with the result that the victim is usually unnamed, in contrast to traditional curse tablets, which in their most basic form consist solely of names. Some prayers for justice do, however, name suspected thieves (e.g. *Tab. Sulis* no. 15, iii–iv AD, 'Concordia'), while others include a convenient shortlist of suspects, to expedite the god's work (e.g. *Tab. Sulis* no. 90 [cf. p. 95] = *CT* no. 96, iii AD, with 18 names appended). On the other hand, the petitioner usually names himself in prayers for justice, and this again is in contrast to traditional curse tablets (except erotic attraction spells), in which self–identification may even have courted danger from both the living and the dead. In prayers relating to theft self-naming helps identify the stolen goods for benefit of god and thief alike, but it is common also in non–theft prayers for justice (*Tab. Sulis* pp. 62 and 100, Versnel, 1991; *CT* pp. 179 and 189).

⋆ Whereas other types of curse are open-ended and supposedly permanently effective, the curses in prayers for justice tend to be conditional and of finite duration, and are to be lifted when the desired justice has been achieved (e.g. *DT* no. 212 = *CT* no. 92 [and cf. p. 189], Bruttium, iii BC, quoted below).

The basic conceit of the prayers relating to theft is a quasi-legal one. The Bath tablets have been compared in the legalising of their language to appeals for the restitution of stolen property made before Roman magistrates (*Tab. Sulis* pp. 70–1; cf. Versnel, 1991: 71–2; *CT* pp. 175, 179). Usually, the stolen goods are transferred into the ownership of the deity: thus a crime of theft against a mortal is transformed into one of sacrilege against a god (temple-robbery was one of the most heinous crimes in the ancient world). Not only did a god have the power to identify a thief, but he also had the power to inflict terrible (if indirect) punishment, via illness, accident or death, and that too for a crime now far greater than mere theft (cf. Versnel, 1991: 73–4, 80, 85). Here is an example from the Bath cache, which is on the whole typical (although the vivid detail that the thief is to return the cloak 'in his beak' is unique):

I, [. . .]eocorotis, have lost my (Italian) cloak, (Greek) cloak, (Gallic) cloak (and) my tunic. I have given [it/them to] Sulis, so that the thief may deliver it in his beak within nine days, whether free or slave man, whether free or slave woman, whether boy or girl. [Let him] deliver the horse-blanket, [whether slave or free man, whether] slave or free woman, whether boy [or girl] in his beak. (*Tab. Sulis* no. 62, iii AD)

A Latin tablet from Corsica comes right to the point. Omitting preamble about the actual theft from the petitioner and the petitioner's donation of stolen goods to the god, it begins:

. . .]ulus, avenge yourself. Whoever harmed you, avenge yourself [etc.] (Solin, 1981: 121 = Versnel, 1991: 82–3, undated)

It was quite usual to profess that one was 'giving' to a god in other contexts: one would have done this in making temple dedication, a regular sacrifice, and conditionally when making a vow. Sometimes it is not the stolen goods that are given to the deity, but the thief himself directly (cf. Versnel, 1991: 80). The Bath curses are further associated with ideas of sacrifice in that they often demand that the thief should pay for his crime with his blood (see *Tab. Sulis* p. 70; cf. Versnel, 1991: 89). In the following curse from Bath, anger or wit leads the petitioner to associate the spilling of the victim's blood with the stolen object, and in a way that is particularly reminiscent of sacrificial procedure:

The one that has stolen my bronze bowl is accursed. I give the person to the temple of Sulis, whether woman or man, whether slave or free, whether boy or girl, and may the man who did this pour his own blood into the very bowl. I give you that thief who stole the item itself, for the god to find, whether woman or man, whether slave or free, whether boy or girl. (*Tab. Sulis* no. 44 = *CT* no. 95, iii AD)

In the following Bath tablet both property and thief are given:

A message from Docca to the goddess Sulis Minerva: I give to your power the money that I lost, i.e. 5 denarii, and I give the one that stole the money, whether slave or free, whether man or woman. Let the person be forced to . . . (*Tab. Sulis* no. 34, iii AD)

People that know the identity of the thief but refuse to reveal it can be cursed too (e.g. *Tab. Sulis* no. 97, iv AD; cf. p. 62 and Versnel, 1991: 89). A Latin tablet from Pagans Hill in Britain curses a named thief-couple, but then the author takes the opportunity to attack old enemies whilst he is about it, and asks for their names to be cursed also (*Tab. Sulis*: 61 no. 9; cf. p. 95).

On the (doubtless rare) occasions on which a stolen object was found, what then became of it? A range of options was available. One was to promise to give the god a specified fraction of the (value of the) property on its return. We find this in some British curse tablets, though not at Bath. Here is a Latin example from Kelvedon:

> Whoever has stolen the property of Varenus, whether woman or male, may he pay with his own blood. Half of the money he pays is dedicated to Mercury and to Virtue. (*Tab. Sulis* p. 61 no. 17 = *CT* no. 97, iii–iv AD)

The half-back deal is also offered in Silvianus' tablet (*DT* no. 106 = *Tab. Sulis* p. 61 no. 28 = *CT* no. 99, quoted below). A tablet from Uley offers a third part of the value of the recovered goods to the successful god (*Tab. Sulis* p. 61 no. 14; cf. Versnel, 1991: 87). Another British tablet, from Redhill, offers Jupiter a tenth of 112 stolen denarii (*Tab. Sulis* p. 61 no. 24 = *CT* no. 98). Another option was for the recovered item to be deemed to belong to the god, whilst its erstwhile human owner retained the right to use it. Petronius' fictional nouveau-riche Trimalchio, who had vowed to Mercury a thousandth of his profits, may be broadly compared: this dedication did not sit idly in Mercury's temple, but constituted a ten-pound gold bracelet on the donor's arm (*Satyricon* 67; cf. *Tab. Sulis* p. 70, Versnel, 1991: 84; *CT* pp. 193–4). Are we to suppose that such objects were to be returned to the goddess when worn out or broken, or on the death of their mortal keepers? But if one had promised to donate the recovered property to a god, without further qualification, as was normal at Bath, was it not ungrateful or even sacrilegious to continue to make use of it? The possibility should not be excluded that the deity was often to get not only the ownership but also the use of any stolen property that was recovered, and that the original owner effectively despaired of recovering the goods for himself, and therefore wrote the curse primarily out of a wish for revenge upon the thief (cf. Versnel, 1991: 83–4). In all cases stolen goods were to be returned in the first instance to the temple (cf. *Tab. Sulis* p. 70 and Versnel, 1991: 75–7).

A unique Greek tablet from Bruttium may be particularly vindictive. It seeks far more than the simple restitution of the goods:

> Collyra dedicates to the attendants of the goddess the dusky coat which Melitta took and has not given back and . . . and she uses it and she knows . . . it is. May she dedicate to the goddess 12 times its value along with a half-medimnus of incense as is law in the city. Let the possessor of the cloak not release her soul until she makes dedication to the goddess. Collyra dedicates to the attendants of the goddess the three pieces of gold that Melitta took and is not giving back. May she dedicate to the goddess 12 times their value along with a medimnus of

incense, as is law in the city. Let her not release her soul until she makes dedication to the goddess. But if [Collyra] were to drink or eat with her without realising it, may she be preserved, and similarly if she were to go under the same roof. (*DT* no. 212 = *CT* no. 92, iii BC)

But perhaps part of Collyra's purpose here is to magnify the incentive for the god to pursue the crime. One of the Uley tablets similarly asks for restitution of the stolen goods to Mercury and also requests that the god choose an extra 'devotion' of his own to receive from the thief (*Tab. Sulis* p. 61 no. 13; cf. Versnel, 1991: 88).

The Bath tablets (all third- to fourth-century AD) record the theft of a wide range of things: coins (*Tab. Sulis* nos. 8, 34, 54, and 98), jewelry (*Tab. Sulis* nos. 15, 59 and 97), pots and pans (*Tab. Sulis* nos. 44, 60 and 66), a ploughshare (*Tab. Sulis* no. 31), gloves (*Tab. Sulis* no. 5), a cap (*Tab. Sulis* no. 55), cloaks and capes (particularly popular: *Tab. Sulis* 10, 32, 43, 55 and 61–4) and blankets (*Tab. Sulis* nos. 49 and 62). Two tablets curiously do not specify the goods stolen, whether through carelessness, or, as Tomlin suggests, because the goddess already knew (*Tab. Sulis* nos. 99–100). The ploughshare apart, everything could have been stolen in the baths themselves. Roman baths were notoriously subject to thieves (see, e.g., Catullus 33 and Seneca, *Letter* 56.2). It is possible that some of the lost jewelry was not in fact stolen but accidentally dropped by its owner in the actual baths: the drains from the baths at Bath and Carleon have revealed a large number of rings and gemstones (*Tab. Sulis* pp. 79–81).

The elaborate so-called 'confession inscriptions' from second- to third-century AD Asia Minor, of which there are more than eighty, are often invoked in the elucidation of the mentality behind prayers for justice, and as evidence of their effectiveness. Some of them are believed to have been motivated by the use of prayers-for-justice tablets. The following is one such:

The god [Men] was angry with the thief, and after some time made him bring the cloak to the god, and he confessed. Therefore the god commanded, via an angel, that the cloak be sold and that he should inscribe his powers on a pillar. (*TAM* v.1 no. 159 = *CMRDM* i no. 69 [cf. *CT* p. 176])

(See Lane, 1971–8, iii: pp. 17–38; *Tab. Sulis* pp. 103–5; Versnel, 1991: 75–9; *CT* p. 176; Mitchell, 1993, i: 191–5). Some tablets from the temple of Demeter at Cnidus in Asia Minor also require that the guilty party publicly confess his guilt, in a gesture typical of the religious mentality of the area (*DT* nos. 1–13, i–ii AD).

A British tablet of the second half of the later fourth century AD, from the temple of the minor Romano-British god Nodens at Lydney Park, is of particular interest:

> To the god Nodens. Silvianus has lost his ring. He has given half its value to Nodens. Among those that possess the name of Senicianus do not allow good health until he brings it right to the temple of Nodens. (*DT* no. 106 = Versnel, 1991: 84 = *CT* no. 99)

A golden ring from the same period was found in a field at Silchester, 30 miles away. It has two inscriptions: the first, on the bezel, is a simple pagan one: 'Venus'. The second is a Christian one, on the band: 'Senicianus, may you live in God!' It is hard to believe that this is not the pagan Silvianus' ring, re-customised by a Christian Senicianus. We cannot be sure that Silvianus did not get his ring back, but if he had done, it would have been natural for him to obliterate the Senicianus inscription. Taken together, these two finds perhaps constitute the earliest document of British Christian hypocrisy. (See Bathurst, 1879: 45–7 with Plate 20; Goodchild, 1953.)

Sometimes prayers for justice are unconnected with theft and merely seek vengeance upon an enemy. The following example from Sicily (i AD) is to the point:

> Lady, may you eliminate Eleutheros. If you do justice for me, I will make a silver bough, if you eliminate him from the human race. (*SGD* no. 115 = *CT* no. 93)

Here the goddess appears to be employed almost amorally as a contract killer. Another prayer for justice of a more general kind, albeit dealing with an issue akin to theft, is the following tablet from Amorgos (ii BC–ii AD). It is perhaps the most narrative of any of the surviving tablets, thus providing a valuable insight into social life in ancient Amorgos. The purpose of the detailed and petulant narration seems to be to make it clear to Demeter that the petitioning couple has been subjected to a concerted campaign of victimisation by the wicked Epaphroditus. The tablet is also of interest for itself containing accusations of magic against its victim (cf. Versnel, 1985: 252–3):

> Lady Demeter, my queen, I am your suppliant. I fall before you as your slave. One Epaphroditus has lured away my slaves. He has taught them evil ways. He has put ideas into their heads, he has given them advice, he has seduced them. He has laughed at me, he has given them wings to waste time in the marketplace. He gave them the idea of running away. He himself bewitched my slavegirl, so that he could take her to wife against my will. For this reason he bewitched her to run away

along with the others. Lady Demeter, being the victim of these things, and being on my own, I take refuge with you. May I find you propitious, and grant that I should find justice. Grant that the one that has done such things to me should find no peace in body or mind anywhere, whether still or moving. May he not be served by slaves or slavegirls, by small people or a large person. May he fail to accomplish his aims. May a binding(-curse) (*katadesmos*) seize hold of his house and hold it fast. May no child cry (?). May he not lay a happy table. May no dog bark. May no cockerel crow. May he not harvest after he has sown . . . May neither the land nor the sea bear fruit for him. May he not have blessed joy, and may he himself perish miserably, and all that is with him.

Lady Demeter, I beseech you as the victim of injustices. Help me, goddess, and make a just choice, so as to bring the most terrible things and even harsher terrible things upon those who contrived such things and laughed at us and inflicted griefs upon both myself and my wife Epictesis. Queen, heed us in our plight and punish those who are glad to see us in such a condition. (*SGD* no. 60 = *CT* no. 75)

THE POWERS ADDRESSED

In addition to the dead themselves, a wide range of powers is invoked in the tablets. In the earlier tablets the powers appealed to are, understandably, particularly chthonic gods. Hermes, the escorter of souls to the underworld (*psychopompos*), and Persephone or Kore, the bride of Hades, are popular already in the early Attic tablets. Hades himself and the underworld witch-goddess, Hecate, were also appropriate powers to appeal to, as were the Furies, the avengers of those that died by violence. Earth-mother goddesses in all their manifestations were important too, such as Demeter (mother of Persephone) and Ge/Gaia ('Earth'). The Roman equivalents of these were popular in Latin tablets, such as Pluto (Hades) and Mercury (Hermes). Prayers for justice were less strongly associated with chthonic powers, and were often given to the main local god. In the imperial period the curses, particularly those found in Egypt, tended to become extremely syncretistic: Alexandria was the chief melting pot for the various religious cultures, with large contingents of Greeks, Egyptians, Jews and others (Fraser 1972: i 192–3). In these tablets are found: Egyptian gods – e.g. Thoth (also identified with Hermes), Osiris (ruler of the Egyptian underworld) and Seth (commonly identified with the Greek Typhon; cf. Kees, 1923; Moraux, 1960: 15–19); Jewish gods and powers – e.g. Iao (= Yahweh/Jehovah), Adonai and cherubim; other Near Eastern powers – e.g. the Babylonian Ereschigal. Iao was often identified in the syncretistic tablets with Seth (possibly because *Iaō* was considered similar to *eiō*, Coptic for 'ass', the animal particularly associated with Seth: see Procopé-Walter, 1933; Moraux, 1960: 23–37; Jordan, 1985b: 245–6). The demonic *voces magicae* and Characters which were also developed in this period will be discussed below. (See the catalogue of powers at Kagarow, 1929: 59–75; cf. Preisendanz, 1972: 6–9, 11–13 and 20–1; Faraone, 1991b: 6; Versnel, 1991: 62 and 64; *CT* pp. 5–6 and 12–13, with ranking in terms of popularity.)

Interestingly, it appears that some powers could be invoked in shrines belonging to others: thus in the sacred spring of Sulis were found tablets addressed to Mercury (*Tab. Sulis* no. 53) and Mars (*Tab. Sulis* nos. 33 and 97; cf. p. 70).

It is surprising that the Greeks' magician-god, Hephaestus, his feet twisted like a voodoo doll (see above), makes very little impact in the tablets. He appears only in one late tablet from Syria (*SGD* p. 192 = *CT* no. 6, v–vi AD), and is otherwise mentioned only in one of the Greek magical papyri (*PGM* XII 177–8). On the other hand, a quite unexpected deity appears in a Latin prayer for justice from Austria: it is addressed to 'deceitful Cacus' (Versnel, 1991: 83–4 = *CT* no. 101, c. 100 AD). This is presumably the Roman thief-monster made famous by Virgil's *Aeneid* (8.193–305): a curious case of setting a thief to catch a thief, or perhaps of 'fighting fire with fire' (cf. Faraone, 1992: 36–53).

The act of invocation could itself be considered to have magical effect, as is apparent from some of the later tablets which are taken up with little else. Behind this usage again lurks the conceit that to know the name is ipso facto to exercise power over the one denoted. The special power of invocation is guaranteed by the difficulty and obscurity of some of the demonic names. Some tablets, in their anxiety to use the correct name for the demon addressed, somewhat undermine themselves by adding to their addresses 'or if you wish to be addressed by any other name' (e.g. *DT* nos. 129b [Arretium, ii AD] and 196 [Cumae, undated]; cf. *Tab. Sulis* pp. 95–6).

A wide variation of tone and attitude is adopted towards the powers addressed. We discussed above a curse that expressed extreme diffidence towards the dangerous powers it disturbs ('Have respect for me the writer and destroyer, because he does this not willingly but under the compulsion of thieves': *SGD* no. 21 = *CT* no. 84, Attica, i AD). In the Bath tablets Sulis is sometimes deferentially and indirectly addressed via her 'majesty' (e.g. *Tab. Sulis* no. 32, iii AD; cf. p. 70). In the Amorgos tablet against Epaphroditus the curser shows extreme humility towards Demeter: 'Lady Demeter, my queen, I am your suppliant. I fall before you as your slave' (*SGD* no. 60 = *CT* no. 75, ii BC–ii AD).

Apparently rather high-handed in tone is the following argument presented to encourage Cybele's co-operation in a Phrygian prayer-for-justice tablet, despite the usual humility of the category:

> I dedicate to the mother of the gods all the gold coins which I lost, so that she will seek them out and bring them all to light and punish those that have them in a way that is appropriate to her power, and so that she will not be a laughing stock (*katagelaston*). (Dunant, 1978 = *CT* 1992 no. 90, i BC–ii AD; cf. Versnel, 1991: 74)

An imperative tone towards the powers appears in the imperial period (Versnel, 1991: 94 n. 7). Some tablets from Egypt import the Egyptian practice of actually threatening them if the wishes of the curser are not carried out, e.g.: 'If you do not obey me, and do not quickly bring to pass what I say to you, the sun does not set below the earth, and neither does Hades nor the universe exist' (*PGM* CI = *Suppl. Mag.* no. 45 = *CT* no. 30, v AD; cf. *PGM* XXXIV and LVII; see Faraone, 1991b: 18 and Betz, 1992: lvii).

Sometimes the maker of the spell identifies himself with the terrible powers that he invokes in order to strengthen the expression of his will in the spell: thus in the tablet against Theodotis partly quoted above, the curser asserts, 'I bind you, Theodotis . . . For I alone am LAMPSOURE OTHIKALAK AIPHNOSABAO STESEON UELLAPHONTA SANKISTE CHPHURIS ON' (*SGD* no. 161 = *Suppl. Mag* no. 38 = *CT* no. 34).

A curious tablet from Bath, although addressed to the pagan Sulis in the usual way, curses the thief of stolen money, whether pagan (*gentilis*) or Christian (*Tab. Sulis* no. 98, iv AD). *Gentilis* would normally indicate the language of a Christian, so we may have a Christian here using a pagan cursing technique. If so, it is interesting that just as the Christian feels able to cross over and make use of pagan powers, so too he perceives that Sulis has the power to chastise her own and unbelievers alike.

VOCES MAGICAE, LETTERS, SHAPES AND IMAGES

We have seen that the notion of twistedness is fundamental to the curse tablets, and that this has many implications for the organisation of language upon them. In this section we turn to some other facets of their magical language.

Voces magicae or 'words of power' are rare before the imperial period, but common thereafter. In translations they are usually transliterated in small capitals. These are mysterious words which are not *obviously* or *immediately* meaningful in Greek or any other language. The most important group of *voces magicae* are the six so-called 'Ephesian letters' (*Ephesia grammata*). It is doubtful whether in origin they had any special association with Ephesus (the name may derive from the Babylonian *epêšu*, 'bewitch'). In their usual order they are: *askion, kataskion, lix, tetrax, damnameneus* and *aision* (or *aisia*), but they can be rearranged into a hexameter. Some of these words do closely evoke some Greek words, and Damnameneus was reputedly one of the Idaean Dactyls, dwarf helpers of the magician-god Hephaestus. Despite the fact that they are only found on curse tablets from the first century AD, they are known to have been in circulation since at least the fifth century BC, and their earliest attestation is in a curse-related context, an inscription from near Mycenae apparently giving thanks for vengeance:

> The Ephesian vengeance (*mēnysis*) was sent down. Firstly Hecate harms the belongings of Megara in all things, and then Persephone reports to the gods. All these things are already so. (Jeffery, 1955: 75; cf. *CT* p. 6)

Words reminiscent of the first *Ephesia grammata*, fully meaningful in context, are found in a hexameter on an unpublished fourth-century BC tablet from Selinus, perhaps modelled on a fifth-century original: *eske kata skie[rōn] oreōn* . . . 'when under the shadowy mountains . . .' (Jordan, 1988a: 256–8). The *Ephesia grammata* could have protective qualities that made them suitable for amulets: a fragment of Menander reveals that they were used to ward off spells from newly marrying couples (F313 Körte). (See McCown, 1923; Preisendanz, 1962; Kotansky, 1991: 111–12, 126 n. 21 and 127 n. 27; *CT* pp. 5–7.)

Contradictory attitudes were probably employed towards the intelligibility of the *voces magicae*. At one level they were considered unintelligible to mortals, and for that reason powerful: in around 300 AD Iamblichus argued that 'foreign names' (*barbara onomata*), by which he may mean, or among which he may include what we call *voces magicae*, lost their power when translated into Greek, i.e., when they were rendered intelligible (*On the mysteries of Egypt* 7.5; cf. 3.14 for a similar view on the Characters). The use of *voces magicae* in the Greek magical papyri from Egypt may evidence their unintelligibility in one respect, as the Graeco-Egyptian professionals garbled phrases from the old languages, and progressively broke up the metrical patterns in which they had originally been composed (Betz, 1992: xlvi–xlvii; cf. *CT* p. 9, with modern anthropological parallels).

On the other hand, most of them were initially corruptions of things recognised as the names of deities or demons in some or other mortal language. And the more the individual *voces magicae* were used, whatever their origin, the more familiar they became; and the more they came to be addressed as powers themselves, and correspondingly personalised into the names of demons, the less 'unintelligible' and the more genuinely meaningful they would have become (cf. Graf, 1991: 188–97). Professionals probably came to feel quite at home with them (in contrast to their clients?). Thus it is actually possible to construct sketchy descriptions of some of the demons connected with individual *voces magicae*. ABRASAX (who appears in, e.g., *SGD* no. 152 = *Suppl. Mag.* no. 47 = *CT* no. 28, Egypt, ii–iii AD) was a cock-headed, armoured demon with snakes for legs, this last quality giving rise to a Latinate title, 'the Anguipede'. He was associated with the number 365 (based upon the numerical value of his name's constituent letters) and hence with the sun, and was particularly popular as an illustration on amulets (Bonner, 1950: pp. 123–39 and D162–88, with plates viii–ix; Barb, 1957; Merkelbach and Totti, 1990 and Merkelbach, 1992; further images at *LIMC* i.2 pp. 2–7). Strings of *voces magicae* in formulas were perhaps more proof against a debilitating familiarisation, but then again it is possible that specific uses or properties came to be associated with particular formulas. And, as with the *Ephesia grammata*, parts of the later *voces magicae* formulas can seem semi-translatable: thus in the formula MASKELLI MASKELLŌ PHNOUKENTABAŌ OREOBAZAGRA RHĒXICHTHŌN HIPPOCHTHŌN PYRIPĒGANYX the last three words are evocative, in Greek terms, of 'Bursting-forth from the earth, horse-earth and fire-spring-master' (e.g. *DT* no. 38 lines 27–9, Egypt, iii AD; cf. *CT* p. 268 and Betz, 1992: 336).

The 'Characters' (*charaktēres*) are a series of magical figures which broadly resemble alphabetic letters in form, but are slightly more complex in design. They only begin to appear in curse tablets in the second century AD, but from that time on they are very common in magical texts and on magical objects of all sorts. They were sometimes addressed directly as powers in their own right in curses; sometimes indeed they are the only powers invoked, as in a curse in which they are drawn above the text (*SGD* no. 163 = *CT* no. 106, Israel, iii–v AD). A fine set of 38 of them is drawn out on a pair of tablets from Apamea in Syria (*SGD* p. 192 = *CT* no. 6, with illustration, v–vi AD). Some Characters are found also in Sethian tablets, fitted in around the other elaborate images (*DT* no. 155 = *CT* no. 13, Rome, iv AD, quoted above). No doubt their effectiveness too lay in their mysteriousness, in the fact that they signified, if not nothing, then something otherwise inexpressible. They may have had an astrological origin. Their use was not always covert and personal: seven of them are found inscribed on the wall of a theatre in Miletus, with an accompanying inscription which asks them to protect the city (Grégoire, 1922 no. 221). (See Van Rengen, 1984; *CT* pp. 10–11)

The letters of the alphabet in their own right, removed from the trammels of words, could also be magically effective. Thus on some curse tablets we find the alphabet or part of it written out. Of particular interest is one of the Bath tablets, which contains only the legend ABCDEFX, where the unexpected X may associate –DEF– with the word *def(i)x–io* (*Tab. Sulis* no.1). It was the vowels above all that were held to be powerful. In the imperial period these are often found written out in series and patterns (e.g. *DT* no. 155 = *CT* no. 13, quoted above). The Greek vowels were usefully seven, a number held to be of mystical significance; they were further associated with planets, angels and sounds (*CT* p. 34 n. 40). In a papyrus curse from Egypt, found together with wax voodoo dolls, we find a long list of *voces magicae* each beginning with a different letter of the Greek alphabet in order (*PGM* CI = *Suppl. Mag.* no. 45 = *CT* no. 30, v AD).

Another means of playing around with alphabets was to employ both Greek and Latin, or in various ways to confuse Greek and Latin in the same tablet. Some tablets from Hadrumentum employ passages of Latin text written in Greek script (e.g. *DT* nos. 267 and 269–71 [271 = *CT* no. 36], iii AD), or blend the two languages (*DT* no. 291, iii AD), or, within a Latin text, record the *voces magicae* and most of the names of the horses to be cursed in Greek, this alphabet apparently being considered more powerful (*DT* no. 295 = *CT* no. 11, late Roman). A less obvious case of alphabetic perversion is constituted by a circus tablet from Carthage, on which the text is written in Greek, but the names (which are Latin) in Latin (*DT* no. 241 = *CT* no. 12, i–iii AD).

It is common to find *voces magicae* arranged into shapes: squares, triangles (isoceles), 'wing-forms' (*pterygoeidea*, i.e. right-angled triangles), and occasionally diamonds (the equivalent of two isoceles triangles). A word-square made from the word/name Eulamo, one of the commonest *voces magicae*, is found on a number of tablets: in each of the six rows one letter is transposed from the front of the word to the end, with the result that 'Eulamo' can be read down the first column too (e.g. *SGD* no. 157 = *CT* no. 8, Egypt, iv AD). Triangles are made by repeating a word beneath or above itself in aligned rows, omitting a letter from either end each time. 'Wings' are similarly made by omitting a letter each time from one end of the word. The entire, lengthy text of a Carthaginian tablet is written out in the form of a large wing (*DT* no. 237 = *CT* no. 9, late Roman).

One sort of *vox magica* well suited to the curse tablets was the palindrome: such words remained magically proof against the retrograde writing common on the curse tablets. They appear in various lengths, but they are often very long indeed, and are favourite bases for the formation of isoceles triangles, since they retain their symmetry and palindromic nature at each stage of reduction (e.g. *SGD* no. 154, Egypt, iii AD). Sometimes the palindromes functioned at the level of sound rather than that of letter, with, for example, mirroring diphthongs appearing in the same orientation in their opposite halves of the palindrome (Bernand, 1991: 325).

In one Egyptian tablet we find all the sorts of figure discussed here: the Eulamo square, a retrograde Eulamo triangle (in which letters are lost from the beginning and end of the name for three lines, with a single A on the bottom line), and two complementary Eulamo wings, the first of which loses a letter from the end in each line, the second of which a letter from the beginning. There is also a long (imperfect) palindrome triangle, which Gager regards as representative of a grape-cluster (*SGD* no. 162 = *CT* no. 115, iv–v AD). One of the Greek magical papyri is also noteworthy for its highly elaborate palindrome-triangle, squares, wings and a vowel-series diamond (*PGM* XIXa).

The later tablets are also often decorated with pictures, and in this regard they can draw near to voodoo dolls. Many images are not securely decipherable. The purpose of those that are can usually be understood as sympathetic. Pictures of mummies or otherwise bound figures are common. Often these figures are transfixed by nails. Snakes, chthonic animals par excellence, are frequently found too, coiled around the bound figure or biting it. A Beirut curse includes a strangely rotund bound figure, whose body is criss-crossed with lines apparently representing ropes, and whose legs are oddly crossed too, perhaps representing further binding. The dots that cover the body seem to represent nail-heads, and protruberances from the head may do likewise. The figure is attacked by a creature, which may be a snake, but which looks rather vulturine, and may be intended to provide a bird's head to accompany the two adjacently inscribed Eulamo 'wings' (*SGD* no. 167 = *CT* no. 5, ii–iii AD). The Sethian batch is particularly well illustrated, an exemplary tablet of which was discussed above (*DT* no. 155 = *CT* no. 13, reproduced as Figure 3).

Images of the demons invoked were popular. These too can be seen as sympathetic in a broad sense, in that the drawing of the demon was perhaps felt to help reify his presence (cf. *CT* p. 11). A famous, albeit insecurely deciphered, image on a 'prayer for justice' tablet from a well in the Athenian agora has been variously thought to represent a 'bat with outspread wings', a 'six-armed Hecate' and 'three-winged Hecate'. Hecate is at least invoked by the tablet (among other powers). To the present author the image appears to be six armed, with the top pair brandishing torches aloft, the middle pair holding whips, and the bottom pair terminating in snakes (somewhat akin to the Angipede). The central part of the image is obscured by 'binding lines' and nails, but it is possible to see it as a large head, face-on, with large eyes, bulbous nose, and a broad smile. As often, nails project from the top (*SGD* no. 21 = *CT* no. 84, i AD; cf. Elderkin, 1937: 394; Jordan, 1980b).

AMULETS, PROTECTION AGAINST CURSING AND THE MAGICAL
'ARMS RACE'

How did one go about protecting oneself and one's property from the
effects of these secret curses? Preisendanz thought that one could not
protect oneself (1972: 6–7), but this view has not found support. The
chief means would have been by wearing a protective amulet (*periapta* or
periamma, literally denoting something 'fastened round' a person). Inscribed
versions appear in the archaeological record from the fourth century BC,
the earliest being a Cretan one inscribed with the *Ephesia grammata*
(McCown 1923); uninscribed amulets can be difficult to identify as such.
Amulets came to flourish in the imperial period. The most distinctive
type, based on Punic and Egyptian models, consisted of a roll of inscribed
papyrus or gold or silver lamella ('foil sheet') hung round the neck in a
copper tube and flourished between the first century BC and the sixth
century AD. Inscribed gemstones were also popular. (See Bonner, 1950
[for gemstones] especially 1–21; Delatte and Derchain, 1964 [also gem-
stones]; Kotansky, 1991 and 1994 – [a systematic publication of the
lamellae-amulets] esp. xv–xix; *CT* pp. 218–42.)

Most amulets were designed either to give their wearers general
protection or protection specifically from a named disease, such as stomach
trouble, cholic, fever, eye-disease and or sciatica (see Bonner, 1950:
45–94). But some amulets explicitly declare their purpose to have been
the warding off of curse tablets. A Beirut amulet protected its owner,
Alexandra, from demons, spells and curse tablets (Jordan, 1991 = *CT* no.
125 = Kotansky, 1994 no. 52, iv AD; cf. Bonner, 1950: 101–2). An
amulet from Asia Minor (i AD–i BC) begs of its demon-addressee:

> Drive away, drive away the curse from Rufina. And if anyone harms
> me in the future, turn the curse back upon him. (*CT* no. 120 =
> Kotansky, 1994 no. 36)

According to Gager's interpretation the Greek term used for 'curse' here
(*hypothesis*) refers specifically to the deposition of a tablet. This amulet
appears then to have been made both to respond to an already exisiting
curse and to be generally protective against any other curse that might be
made in the future (Kotansky, however, interprets *hypothesis* here as
'lawsuit'). Another amulet protected against magic in general:

> Free Juliana from all witchcraft (*pharmaka*) and all suffering and all
> magical influence and demonic manifestations by night and by day.
> (Kotansky, 1994 no. 46, Beroia, ii–iii AD)

The Greek magical papyri include instructions for making amulets to protect against spells, one of which itself requires inscription of and drawing on lead (*PGM* XXXVI 178–87 = *CT* no. 129); the drawing prescribed is not that which is then drawn on the papyrus, which is of a bound and nailed figure carrying a disembodied head and accompanied by a dog-like animal. Another of the papyri contains a recipe for an amulet consisting of an iron lamella inscribed with three Homeric verses (*PGM* IV 2145–240, esp. 2219–26; Homer, *Iliad* 10.564, 10.521 and 10.572). The amulet can be used for a number of purposes, including the restraint of other binding spells. In this case it is to be used in conjunction with a sea-shell buried in the grave of someone untimely dead, which is itself similarly inscribed with the same verses and some *voces magicae* besides.

The availability of protective amulets not unsurprisingly led to a magical 'arms race': a Syrian tablet, aimed at a pantomime, begins by explicitly cancelling the effects of any protective amulets that the victim might be wearing (*DT* no. 15 = *CT* no. 4, iii AD). Perhaps this was also the purpose of a much earlier tablet, which insists that it 'will bind Anticles and not let him go' (*SGD* no 16 = *CT* no. 102, Attica, iv BC).

Other curative measures could be used once one had fallen victim to a curse. The ideal way to put an end to it once and for all was to locate and remove (and presumably destroy) the tablet. In practice this must have been very difficult unless the tablet was concealed in one's own home, or one had definite information of its whereabouts (see below on the Tuder incident). Another solution was to put a binding curse of one's own on the binding curse to which one was subject: another example of the magical 'arms race.' Thus, a limestone tablet from Tell Sandahannah in Israel:

> I bind Philonidas and Xenodicus, thinking it right that I should take revenge upon them and have requital against those that had me thrown out of Demetrios' house because I have headaches and other pains. If they uttered a binding spell (*peridesmos*) to envelop me, so may obscurity take it. Philonidas . . . may they be chatterless and voiceless and have no sex. (Wünsch, 1902 no.34 = *CT* no. 107, ii AD)

A group of five Roman tablets attempts to bind every part of Plotius' anatomy, listed in systematic detail. He has deposited a curse against the author, and while this is not itself cursed, it is no doubt presumed to be rendered ineffective by the restraint of its depositor (see Fox, 1912a = *CT* no. 134 [in part], i BC). The Amorgos curse against Epaphroditus discussed above seeks a magical revenge for, amongst other things, the erotic spell Epaphroditus cast upon a slave-girl (*SGD* no. 60 = *CT* no. 75). A spell for releasing from bonds in the Greek magical papyri may also have been useful against binding magic, although it seems to focus particularly on the release from physical bonds (*PGM* XII 160–78). A single literary reference shows that herbal antidotes could be concocted to curse tablets:

> If someone should be charmed and cursed (*devotus, defixus*) this is how you can release him: cook seven pedeleonis plants, without roots, when the moon is decreasing and without using water; cleanse it as well as yourself, as you do this before the threshhold outside the house on the first night; burn and fumigate the birthwort plant; then return to the house without looking behind you and you will release him (from it). ([Apuleius] *Herbarium* 7.1 = *CT* no. 131 [trans.])

A first-century BC curse from Cnidus uses magic to protect its author not against magic, but (almost paradoxically) against the accusation of it:

> I dedicate to Demeter and Kore the one that said against me that I was making poisons/spells (*pharmaka*) for my husband. (*DT* no.4 = *CT* no. 89)

Another means of protecting oneself against an accusation of magic was, again perhaps paradoxically, to make a public conditional self-curse, with the curse to be implemented if one were foresworn. This is exemplified by a confession inscription from Asia Minor, set up by the descendants of Tatias, who doubtless wished to avert the anger of the gods from themselves. The narrative reveals that Tatias had fallen under suspicion of having cast a spell when her son-in-law Iucundus went mad. In order to vindicate herself she placed conditional self-curses in the temple, but the gods then sent punishment upon Tatias herself, and also on her son, who dropped a sickle on his foot, so that it was 'proven' that she was guilty all along. The gods are then duly praised for their powers in exacting justice. But as the commentators note, one cannot help wondering whether Tatias was indeed innocent after all (*TAM* v.1 no. 318 = *CT* no. 137 = Petzl, 1994 no. 69, ii AD; cf. *Tab. Sulis* pp. 103–4; Versnel, 1991: 75–9; Graf, 1994a: 184–5).

Another example of this sort of magical 'arms race' is found in the frequent request of curse tablets that the victim be deprived of the ability to sacrifice successfully: this was a means of ensuring that he was unable to approach the gods to avert the effects of the magic (e.g. *DT* no. 110 = *CT* no. 16, Gaul, iii AD; cf. Versnel, 1985; Strubbe, 1991: 43).

A further 'arms race' development may be found in a curse which first asks the powers to prevent the runner Alcidamos from passing the starting line at a coming festival race. But the curse goes on to ask that, should Alcidamos after all get past the starting line, he should be made to lose his direction (*SGD* no. 29, Attica, iii AD). The writer of the curse is then well aware that magic did not always work, or could be thwarted, and thought it safer to have a double try (cf. Jordan, 1985b: 221–3 and 243; Faraone, 1991b: 12–13). A recipe for a similar 'try-and-try-again' spell appears in the *Sepher ha-Razim* (Morgan, 1983: p. 28).

Akin to the magical 'arms race' is what might be termed magical 'gamesmanship'. According to Versnel's reading of one of the Bath tablets, Annianus, after cursing the thief of six silver coins, asks the goddess still to punish the thief even if he has by some deceit returned the coins to his possession without his knowledge (*Tab. Sulis* no. 98, iv AD, [cf. p. 95] and Versnel, 1991: 90). If the interpretation is correct, it implies that one might deliberately trick another into making an 'unjustified' curse against oneself, presumably so that the curser might incur the anger of the justice-bringing deity for making a false accusation. Also, such a surreptitious restoration would leave the curser indebted to the goddess in his ignorance, and liable again to her anger for cheating her of her due portion.

One means to enlist the enthusiasm of the powers against a victim was 'ritual slander' of them, as in the following tablet from Messina:

> (I bind) Valeria Arsinoe, the nymphomaniac, the worm, Arsinoe, evil-doing and idle.
> (I bind) Valeria Arsinoe, the evil-doer. Sickness and decay attack the nymphomaniac! (*SGD* no. 114 = *CT* no. 116, ii AD)

In the Amorgos spell against Epaphroditus the curser accuses his victim of having used magic against him (*SGD* no. 60 = *CT* no. 75, quoted above). Ritual slander against a curse victim as himself a magician is a feature of ancient Near Eastern cursing (see below; for further ritual slander in the Greek curses see also *SGD* no. 22, *PGM* IV 2471–92 and XXXVI 138–44; cf. Eitrem, 1924b; Preisendanz, 1972: 24; Winkler, 1990: 89–91).

PROFESSIONALISM AND SPECIALISATION

Was binding magic the province of specialists, in other words 'witches' or 'magicians', or of amateurs, non-specialists, ordinary people who performed magic for themselves as and when they needed it? No clear pattern emerges: there were apparently significant amounts of specialisation and amateurism in different places, at different times and in different contexts.

The specialisation issue is complex. While many curse tablets were probably made, activated and deposited by amateurs on an ad hoc basis, there were opportunities for the involvement of different kinds of specialists, not all of whom need be perceived as 'magicians', at four separate stages in the process (cf. *Tab. Sulis* p. 98):

1. The drawing up of the curse text, with advice on any accompanying verbal procedures
2. The manufacture of the tablet
3. The inscription of a tablet
4. The deposition of the tablet, especially if in a grave

1. The simplest and commonest form of curse text, that which consisted simply of the name(s) of the victim(s), presumably did not require professional input in drafting, although any attendant verbal incantations may theoretically have done so. The simple additional texts that are found in curse tablets until the fourth century BC vary greatly, which suggests that they are mainly home-made compositions without recourse to for-mularies (Faraone apud *CT* p. 123 n. 11). But the long, complex texts of the imperial period, with all their obscurantist *voces magicae* etc., will often have depended upon handbooks. Sometimes the tablets explicitly acknowledge that they have their origin in some authoritative pre-existing paradigm. One of the Bath texts ends with the assertion 'The written page has been fully copied out' (*Tab. Sulis* no. 8 = *CT* no. 94, iii–iv AD): we can feel it implied, 'so this must work!' A Syrian tablet opens with a line that was clearly the title of the spell in a formulary and not intended to be copied onto any actual tablet: 'For restraining horses and charioteers' (*SGD* no. 167 = *CT* no. 5, iii AD). A tablet of similar date and provenance appears to be confused in its language because of the incom-petent adaptation of a formulary (*DT* no. 15 = *CT* no. 4). Another curse is arranged in an unconventional way: the names of the cursed are written separately in a column on the left, whilst the text of the curse itself is written in a column on the right, using only pronouns to refer to the victims (*DT* no. 92 = *CT* no. 76, Crimea, iii BC). Perhaps this represents a lazy refusal to integrate the relevant names into a model text. (Cf. also the Sethian tablet *DT* no. 155 = *CT* no. 13 discussed above.)

We are fortunate to have as the bulk of the Greek magical papyri (the *PGM* corpus) a superb collection of magical handbooks and recipes from Egypt, products of a fairly homogenous Graeco-Egyptian cultural syncre-tism. They mostly date from between the first century BC and the fifth AD, and particularly from the third and fourth centuries AD, although they often reflect hellenistic material. The core of the *PGM* corpus first came to the attention of modern western scholarship after it was acquired by Jean d'Anastasi, who was the Armenian-born consular representative of Sweden at the court of the Pasha of Alexandria in the earlier nineteenth century. The uniformity in style of six of the major papyri in the Anastasi collection suggests that they may have belonged to a single ancient collection: they probably represent the discovery of a temple library or a magician's tomb near Thebes (Nock, 1929; Fowden, 1986: 72; Betz,

1991: 249 and 1992: xli–iii and xlvi). Greek magical handbooks are also refracted in the Hebrew magical handbook, the *Sepher ha-Razim*, which, though preserved in medieval manuscripts, seems to date back to the third or fourth century AD (see Margalioth, 1966 for text and Morgan, 1983 for translation).

There are numerous references to collections of such magical books in antiquity, mostly in connection with attempts to eradicate them: Augustus had 2,000 magical scrolls burned in 13 BC (Suetonius, *Augustus* 31.1); Paul's Ephesian converts burned their own magical books, altogether worth 50,000 pieces of silver (*Acts* 19:19). Such attempts at suppression guaranteed the power of the books.

The *PGM* corpus includes models for curse tablets and instructions for their manufacture and deposition, mainly from the fourth century (e.g. *PGM* IV 329–433, V 304–70, VII 394–422, 429–58, 459–61, IX, XXXVI 1–35 and 231–56 and LVIII 1–14; cf. Jordan, 1985b: 234 and Faraone, 1985: 151, 1989: 155 and 1991b: 22 n. 5). It is gratifying that there are some close correspondences between the texts of extant curse tablets and those of recipes in the corpus: thus four Egyptian tablets (*SGD* nos. 152–3 and 155–6 [of which 152 = *Suppl. Mag.* no. 47 = *CT* no. 28; 153 = *SEG* viii no. 574], ii–iii AD) are similar to one recipe (*PGM* IV 329–433), whilst a tablet probably from Rome (*DT* no. 188, iv–v AD) is similar to another (*PGM* LVIII 1–14). While it is easy to conclude in these cases that the curser probably used a handbook, it is difficult to conclude in any specific case that a curser definitely did *not* use a handbook, because one simply does not know what may have been in lost handbooks. (See Jordan, 1985b: 234 and 1988a: 246–7; Faraone, 1985: 151.)

In the imperial period especially, general similarities between curse texts and manifest formulaic style can suggest that handbooks underpinned many of them. But the Bath cache sounds a warning: the texts in this group are remarkably similar and formulaic in appearance, but none are exact formulaic duplicates. This suggests that the Bath texts are not generated directly from paradigms in handbooks, but from an established, largely oral culture of expertise, which may itself have been indirectly supported by handbooks with paradigms occasionally brought down from the magician's self (cf. *Tab. Sulis* pp. 62–74 and 99). A group of tablets by the same writer from a well in the Agora can be shown to be derived from a formulary by juxtaposition, but it is also clear that the writer, whilst not being a magical expert himself, has varied and invented his phraseology to a small degree (*SGD* nos. 24–35, iii AD; 24 = *CT* no.3). However, some extant formularies themselves record alternative readings (Jordan, 1985b: 233–47, especially 234–5; *CT* p. 50).

In the Bath tablets there are many errors of the sort that are best explained as due to copying, such as dittography, e.g. *qui iuraverunt qui iuraverunt* (*Tab. Sulis* no. 94, iv AD; cf. pp. 98–9). This is not, however, evidence that a formulary has been used, simply that a prior 'rough copy' of the tablet text has been made (perhaps in disposable form, as on a wax tablet), which then serves as a model for the fair one. A prior stage is particularly useful if one is planning to pervert the line of writing in some way (e.g. *Tab. Sulis* no. 44). Long texts are particularly likely to have been written out in advance: this was useful not only for planning the structure of the curse, but for calculating how much text one would have to fit onto one of the relatively small sheets.

Since obscurity and difficulty were important sources of 'power' for ancient magic, it may have been more satisfying to visit a professional, one of supposedly arcane knowledge and mysterious skills, for the text of a tablet, however easy it was to devise one oneself. The development of the large and complex *voces magicae* in the imperial period was no doubt gratifying to client and professional alike: the former was given access to something the magical nature of which was guaranteed by its incomprehensibility, while the latter had a means of protecting his trade from the incursions of casual amateurs, a means of 'status enhancement' (*CT* p. 10). In this connection, it is curious that, while we do find binding spells used against binding spells, we do not, with the improbable exception of the Epaphroditus curse discussed above (*SGD* no. 60 = *CT* no. 75, Amorgos, ii BC–ii AD) appear to have anything resembling a trade spell cast by one magician against another: honour among thieves?

2. As we have seen, anyone could make a tablet with the simple and readily available equipment of a bit of scrap lead, a flat surface and a hammer (and possible also a fire and a ladle). The lead/tin ratio is different in all the tablets from Bath, which indicates that the tablets tended to come from small-scale individual smeltings. This does not, however, necessarily mean that the tablets were made in DIY fashion by the individual cursers as and when they needed them: it may have been usual for metalworkers to turn any pewter scraps they had left over into writing tablets for sale (*Tab. Sulis* pp. 82–3). Professional metalworkers were perhaps responsible for the tablets from Bath with flanged edges that reveal them to have been pressed in a purpose-made mould (e.g. *Tab. Sulis* nos. 10 and 44, iii–iv AD; cf. p. 82). But a professional maker of lead tablets was not ipso facto a magician: lead tablets functioned as common notepaper. We can be confident that a Bath curse inscribed on a pewter plate was not acquired from any manufacturer of purpose-made curse tablets (*Tab. Sulis* no. 30, iii AD).

3. The variation in handwriting styles (twistedness etc. apart) even in tablets of similar provenance is enormous. The issue of the degree to

which professionals were involved at this stage is entwined with the problem of literacy (cf. Faraone, 1991b: 23 n. 10). Some tablets are barely literate (some indeed are actually illiterate: see below), and in these cases at any rate it seems likely that their inscribers were not professionals of any kind. Other tablets are produced in highly literate fashion and in beautiful script, whether it be in block capitals, plain or calligraphic, or in one of the cursive hands. One tablet is said to resemble a public monument in the fineness of its lettering (*DTA* no.55 = *CT* no. 64, Attica, iv BC). Editors describe a number of hands as 'scribal' or 'secretarial', but the implication of this may be that the inscribers were clerks instead of or at any rate as well as 'magicians'. A cache of third-century AD tablets found in the Agora adjacent to civic scribal offices appears to be written in a civic scribal script and suggests that the local scribes may have 'moon-lighted' (Jordan, 1985: 235 and 1989; *CT* p. 32 n. 24 and 123 n. 12). The group of third-century AD tablets from a well in the Agora mentioned above, which was clearly underpinned by a formulary, is written out in the same beautiful hand, but there is a series of telling copying errors in the *voces magicae* (detectable by comparison between tablets) which makes it clear that the writer was not intimately familiar with the material he was reproducing. So here too was someone that could be described as a professional scribe with access to a formulary, but not necessarily as a professional magician (*SGD* nos. 24–35, with the discussion at Jordan, 1985b: 234–5 and n. 20). The same scribe evidently pre-inscribed tablets to sell 'off the peg': another tablet in his hand has its names squeezed into the inadequate spaces that had been allowed in basic the text (*SGD* no. 38; cf. *CT* p. 14).

The cache of 200 or so fragments of tablets from the common grave at Amathous in Cyprus has only been selectively read and published, but of those that have, most seem to employ identical formulas and *voces magicae*, and to be written in the same hand (*DT* nos. 22–37, ii–iii AD; cf. *SGD* p. 193; *Tab. Sulis* p. 99; Faraone, 1991b: 23 n. 11; *CT* no. 45). Even though it is unclear from how many original complete tablets these fragments derive, their writer appears to be the most prolificly preserved inscriber of spells from antiquity (Aupert and Jordan, 1981). Multiple tablets from the same hand are also found amongst the Sethian cache (*DT* nos. 140–87). In an early Sicilian tablet the writer curses in the first person, but says he is doing it on behalf of another, Eunikos (*SGD* no. 91, c. 450 AD).

The Bath tablets sometimes give reason to suppose that they were written out by someone other than the curser. The involvement of professional scribes is revealed by the occurrence of such scribal terms as *id est* (*Tab. Sulis* no. 34, iii AD) and *infrascriptis*, 'written below' (*Tab. Sulis* no. 32, iii AD, cf. p. 71). Sometimes the name of the curser is spelt wrongly, which would be unusual if the curser were the writer (e.g. *Tab. Sulis* no. 60, iii AD, *Ocnea* for *Oconea*; cf. p. 100). Sometimes too tablets are headed by the name of the curser apparently in a different hand from that of the main text, in which case we appear to have a 'signature' (e.g. *Tab. Sulis* nos. 5 and 66, iii–iv AD). A puzzling tablet from Bath seems to contain five different scripts, which probably, but not necessarily, indicates that it was inscribed by five different people (*Tab. Sulis* no. 14, iii–iv AD). Little more can be said of this puzzling text, since, while its letters are perfectly clear, the text is undecipherable, and probably written in Celtic (the only example of written British Celtic).

However, despite the presence of many beautiful and practiced hands among the 116 inscribed Bath tablets, no hand is found on more than one tablet, save on a pair of name-only blobs that apparently belong together, and this does appear to be statistically significant within the sample (*Tab. Sulis* pp. 86, 88 and 98–100; the blobs are nos. 95 and 96, iv AD). It is therefore unlikely that there was a small number of individuals that specialised in writing out tablets for Sulis: those that did not write out their own tablets must have been able to draw upon a wide range of literate helpers, perhaps the temple priests in the first instance. Tomlin concludes that a respectable number of people could write in Roman Bath, and that most people wrote their own tablets there (*Tab. Sulis* pp. 85–6 and 100–1; cf. in general *CT* pp. 4–5 and 118.) The Bath tablets were all prayers for justice, to the making of which no shame or danger attached, so that the finding of a willing literate helper by illiterate petitioners will have constituted no great difficulty. Greater discretion may have been needed in selecting people willing to write out curse texts of a more nefarious and surreptitious nature.

The tablets exhibit the full range of degrees of literacy (for poor literacy see, e.g., on the Greek side, *DT* no. 85 = *CT* no. 20 [Boeotia, iii–ii BC, quoted above], *SGD* no. 48 = *CT* no. 56 [Attica, c. 323 BC], *SGD* no. 107 = *CT* no. 50 [Selinus, c. 450 BC] and *SGD* no. 173 = *CT* no. 48 [Olbia, iii BC]; and on the Latin side Solin 1968 nos. 26–8 = *CT* no. 52 [Emporia, 78 AD] and *Tab. Sulis* nos. 6, 16 etc., iii–iv AD, with p. 84). However, they are a difficult source for the distribution of literacy in antiquity, since one can hardly ever be sure that the curser (about whom one may be given some social information) is the actual inscriber of the tablet (about whom one is not). An interesting exception, bearing upon female literacy, is a tablet from fourth-century BC Attica by Onesime, which is basically a prayer for justice, but also uses binding language: she asks the powers to preserve 'the one that struck the lead' (*tē]n molybdoko-pon*), who is probably therefore herself, even if we cannot actually read that the gender of the article here is feminine (*DTA* no. 100; cf. Versnel, 1991: 65–6).

Some of the Bath tablets are touching: their texts consist of strings of repetitive marks, such as repeated 7's or crosses or short vertical lines (*Tab. Sulis* nos. 112–16; cf. pp. 86 and 247–8). They clearly represent the attempts of illiterate people to imitate writing (and in so doing incidentally inform us of the appearance of writing to the illiterate). This could indicate one or more of a number of things: the inscribers did not wish to impart their curse to another; they felt it important (magically preferable?) that the curse be written out by the curser in person; they could not find anyone to write for them; they were proud. The mysteries of writing perhaps added to the magic of the tablets for the illiterate. The 'religiously preferable' option may also account for the 'signatures' discussed above. An illiterate inscriber may have trusted that the goddess had the ability and grace to make sense of his marks, but such an attitude can not have been shared by the literate petitioners who fussily overdescribed their lost belongings (cf. *Tab. Sulis* pp. 100 and 247–8). Other tablets without any inscription were thrown into the sacred spring, perhaps by illiterates who placed more trust in an accompanying verbal curse than in pretend writing (e.g. *Tab. Sulis* no. 118, iii–iv AD).

4. No documentary evidence relates directly to specialisation in the deposition of curse tablets. No doubt little difficulty attended their deposition in bodies of water, or perhaps in chthonic sanctuaries. But deposition in graves was as dangerous as it was unpleasant, as we have seen, and for this reason was doubtless often left to bold professionals. Skill would also be required to conceal tablets in significant places, such as the victim's house (cf. *CT* p. 10).

It is improbable that four different specialists were normally involved in the creation and deposition of curse tablets. Many were no doubt made and deposited entirely by the amateur curser himself, and many were no doubt made and deposited entirely by professionals on behalf of others (see *Tab. Sulis* p. 100 and *CT* p. 5). Plato's reference to professionals who would make a curse tablet for a fee implies, for want of further definition, that he had in mind people that took the whole operation under their control (*Republic* 364bc; the existence of professionals is also implied by *Laws* 933a; see Faraone, 1989: 156 and *CT* nos. 140–1).

GENDER

The curse tablets raise a number of important issues for gender in the ancient world, as will already have become apparent from our treatment of erotic curses. Women's names appear frequently in the tablets, alone or with those of men (witness the frequency with which 'Women's names' are noted in *SGD*).

Women are often present even in tablets that appear to address disputes entirely between men, in that individuals in the tablets are often identified not by their father's name (patronymic), as was usual and proper in the ancient world, but by their mother's name (matronymic). The phenomenon flourished between the second and fifth centuries AD, but there are some earlier examples (*DTA* no. 102, Athens, iv BC; see catalogue at Jordan, 1976: 128–30 and n. 7). Matronymics appear in many of the examples already quoted, and are particularly noticeable in the 'Sethian' curse against Cardelus quoted above, in which the charioteer is repeatedly identified as 'Cardelus, to whom his mother Pholgentia [= Fulgentia] gave birth' (*DT* no. 155 = *CT* no. 13). There is no single convincing explanation of the phenomenon, but a few suggestions may be made. Early Egyptian and Babylonian spells employ maternal parentage and the custom may have been borrowed from them. Or matronymics may have been used because maternal parentage is much more secure than paternal (*pater incertus, mater certa*), and it was felt important to identify the individuals to be cursed as accurately as possible for the binding powers. Yet the formula was felt to be so important that it came to be included in a variant form even when the identity of the mother was not actually known. We find a number of expressions of this type, of which the abbreviated Latin version *q(uem) p(eperit) vulva*, 'whom a womb bore' is the most striking (*DT* no. 300). It is perhaps for similar reasons that a fourth-century BC Attic tablet identifies as its victim 'Pataikion whom Epainetos claims to be his daughter' (*DTA* no. 55 = *CT* no. 64). Or matronymics may simply constitute another example of magic's preference for the countercultural. The custom may specifically have been adopted from slave culture (such an adoption would certainly have been countercultural), since slaves were regularly identified by their mothers. (See Jordan, 1976; Bernand, 1991: 31; *CT* p. 14.) But the slight evidence for the use of matronymics elsewhere in the ancient world indicates that they tend to appear in the context of distinctively female discourse, be it the gossip of women in the hellenistic poets, or the inscriptions of female-dominated cults (Christophilopoulos, 1946: 130–9; Cameron, 1973: 157–8; Ogden, 1996: 94–6). This might, prima facie, suggest that by the second-century AD cursing language thrived particularly within female discourse, i.e., that it was primarily an instrument of women. Other evidence, however, obstructs such a hypothesis, but also indicates that cursing was particularly associated with women at the ideological level (see below); thus the use of matronymics in cursing may have been due to the supposition that cursing was a particularly female thing, or to an attempt to give it a countercultural veneer by representing it as such (cf.

Graf, 1994a: 149). A fifth-century BC Sicilian tablet presents an interesting compromise between traditional and curse-tablet practice: most of the men are given patronymics, most of the women matronymics (*SGD* no. 87, v BC).

It is amongst the curse tablets that some of the most important documentation of women's initiative in the ancient world is found (*CT* p. 79). The actual words of women of antiquity (women's 'voice'), unfiltered through male sources, are rarely found. Little remains beyond such things as the tantalising fragments of the archaic Greek poetess Sappho and some charming private letters between the wives of Roman soldiers at Vindolanda on Hadrian's wall, the latter only recently discovered (for these see Bowman and Thomas, 1994 nos. 291–4, 'correspondence of Lepidina'). It is possible that some of the curse tablets contain the actual words of women, but we must remember that they are largely formulaic, and we can never be sure that even an apparently personally worded tablet written in the interests of a woman was not composed with the aid of or simply by a male (professional or otherwise).

The 'mismatch' between the literary evidence and the curse-tablet evidence for witchcraft in antiquity may be revelatory of the nature of gender ideology and control in those societies (see Winkler, 1990: 71–98; *CT* pp. 80 and 244; Graf, 1994a: 200, the last of whom observes the 'autonomy' of witch-portrayals in the literary tradition from actual magical practices). Almost all the detailed and distinctive portraits of witches in mainstream classical literature are of women (cf. Tupet, 1976: 164 and Graf, 1994a: 211; pace Winkler, 1990: 90), often old ones, and their prime concern is usually the acquisition of love or vengeance for love taken away. Literary female witches concerned with love include, on the Greek side: Circe (Homer, *Odyssey* 10.203–47 = Luck, 1985 no. 1, vii BC?), Deianeira (Sophocles, *Trachiniai* especially 531–812, 420's BC), Medea (Euripides, *Medea* especially 1136–1230, 431 BC; and Apollonius of Rhodes, *Argonautica* 3–4 passim, early iii BC), Antiphon's 'Clytemnestra' (*Against a stepmother for poisoning*, a highly fictionalised if not actually fictitious speech, late v BC), Simaetha (Theocritus, *Idyll* 2, early iii BC) and Lucian's old Syrian woman (*Dialogues of the courtesans* 4.286 = *CT* no. 152, i AD [and cf. 4.281]). On the Roman side are: Virgil's Amaryllis (if that is her name, *Eclogue* 8.64–109 = Luck, 1985 no.8, mid i BC) and Dido (*Aeneid* 4.450–705 = Luck, 1985 no.9, late i BC), Horace's Canidia (*Epodes* 5 and 17 and *Satire* 1.8, late i BC), Seneca's Deianeira (*Hercules on Mount Oeta* especially 449–72 and 784–841, of which the former passage = Luck, 1985 no. 10) and Medea (*Medea* especially 6–23 and 670–843 = Luck, 1985 no. 11, mid i AD), Lucan's Erichtho (*Pharsalia* 6.438–830 mid i AD, including a 130 line digression on Thessalian witches) and Petronius' 'hag' (*Satyricon* 131 = Luck, 1985 no. 12, mid i AD). Apuleius' *Golden Ass* is particularly rich: Meroe and Panthia, the terrible Thessalians (1.5–19), Pamphile (2.32 and 3.15–8 [partly = *CT* no. 153]) and an unnamed old woman (9.29 = *CT* no. 154, mid ii AD). The association these narratives make between love potions and poisons is striking, particularly in the cases of Deianeira and Antiphon's 'Clytemnestra' (and cf. Tupet, 1976: 57 and 203; Graf, 1994a: 57–61). In around 360 AD St. Basil could make the general observation that it was typical of women to attempt to attract love to themselves through spells and tablets (*Epistles* 188.8 = *CT* no. 161). More general magical practice is rooted within female culture by Ovid's vignette showing an old woman teaching magic to a group of three young girls: they are taught to bind tongues with the aid of the demon Muta Tacita, 'She that is mute and silent' (*Fasti* 2.571–82 = *CT* no. 144, early i AD; cf. Tupet, 1976: 408–16).

It is difficult to find a comparable literary portrait of anyone resembling a male witch in mainstream classical literature, let alone one with erotic concerns. The best we can do is to point to archaic Greek 'shaman' figures, such as Aristeas of Proconessus (Herodotus 4.13–16, Pindar F271, Pliny, *Natural History* 7.174 etc., early vii BC) or Epimenides of Cnossus (Diogenes Laertius 1.109–15 etc.; sources at *DK* no.3, floruit c. 600 BC?), whose principal achievement was the transmigration of the soul (cf. Dodds, 1951: 135–78), or to the later Greek miracle-workers such as Apollonius of Tyana (Philostratus, *Life of Apollonius*; cf. Dzielska, 1986). However, the *PGM* recipes usually assume that their users are going to be male (Graf, 1994a: 211) and historically identifiable herbal specialists were almost all men (see Scarborough, 1991: 140, 161–2 and 166 n. 38). Apuleius himself was prosecuted for using erotic magic in order to persuade a rich widow to marry him in Tripoli (*Apology*, mid ii AD). (For literary portraits of magical practitioners in Greek and Latin literature in general see Lowe, 1929; Graf, 1994a: 199–230; and especially Tupet, 1976: 107–64 and 223–420, and Bernand, 1991: 159–257.)

It is only occasionally possible to discern the gender of authors of curse tablets, since they tended to avoid identifying themselves (see above). There are two broad exceptions to this rule: prayers for justice, which were less dangerous to the curser, and in which the author's name helped identify the goods stolen (cf. *Tab. Sulis* p. 95), and erotic-attraction curses, where one had to identify the person to whom one wished the beloved to cleave (Faraone, 1991b: 29 n. 65). Of those cursers whose gender can be identified, either because the author's name is supplied or because of some gender-specific reference, some are indeed women, and women are found among the authors of erotic curses. But this should not disguise the fact that the vast majority of all curse tablets, including erotic ones, are written by men. Thus, in Winkler's collation of erotic curses there are 25 extant examples of curses by men in pursuit of women (counting multiple cases involving the same curser and beloved as one example), 3 cases of men in pursuit of men, 6 cases of women in pursuit of men, and 2 cases of women in pursuit of women. Thus 28 male examples as against 8 female: almost four times as many curses by men as by women (Winkler, 1990: 90 and 229 n. 32). Winkler is undoubtedly right about the scale of male involvement in cursing in comparison to female, but his collation of the relevant evidence now needs to be revised for a number of reasons: first, a significant number of relevant curses are omitted from his list (understandably, since he apparently did not have access to *SGD*); secondly, Winkler sometimes guessed precariously at the sex of the author of a curse (thus *PGM* LXVI, which seeks to separate Philoxenos the harpist from two men, may have been written by another man in pursuit of Philoxenos, but it may equally have been written by a woman in pursuit of him); thirdly, Winkler mistakenly included *DT* no. 271 in both the categories of 'male in pursuit of female' and 'female in pursuit of male' (it belongs in the latter only). Nonetheless, an updated and more careful count would doubtless arrive at a comparable gender ratio of erotic-curse authors. Of the Bath cache of third- and fourth-century AD prayers for justice 7 are definitely male-authored (*Tab. Sulis* nos. 10, 31–2, 57, 66 and 98–9), a further 4 probably male-authored (nos. 5, 34 and 62–3), and 5 are definitely female-authored (nos. 54, 59–61, and 97): a probable female/male ratio of around 1:2.

How then are we to account for this 'mismatch' in the evidence? It is theoretically possible that women were more active than men in magic as a whole and erotic magic in particular, but less active than men in the specific area of curse tablets: note Theocritus' reference, in an erotic context, to 'old women that know *incantations*' (2.91). What factors could have influenced an under-representation of women in the tablets? If one were to take the view that curse tablets were largely home-made affairs by the individual cursers, then women could have been discouraged from making tablets by more limited access to the (admittedly low) level of technology required to make lead tablets (although as we have seen, the tablets did not have to be made of lead). Perhaps a lower level of literacy among women also discouraged them. It has been suggested that the circumscribed lives of women made access to magical professionals socially more difficult for them, but this was surely only an important consideration if most professionals were male, which may have been the case, but we should not beg the question here (cf. Winkler, 1990: 90). Perhaps women had less spare cash to spend on such things as tablets, although the indications are that they were very cheap. These suppositions may go some way towards lessening the mismatch, but they do not go all the way. It seems preferable to conclude that the general association of women in particular with witchcraft in ancient Greece was primarily an ideological act. I do not mean by this that the popular association of women in particular with witchcraft was the result of a conscious lie on anyone's part, rather that in the vacuum of reliable and incontrovertible data on the subject, a prejudice was allowed to thrive. It would have been difficult for the ancients to acquire a true picture of the gender-profile of witchcraft in their societies: in days prior to the systematic collation of statistics social 'facts' were inevitably constructed from prejudice alone (cf. Ogden, 1996: 8–10); and if individuals were unable to perceive the true profile of open and public phenomena in their society, how much less able were they to perceive the profile of a phenomenon as necessarily and as significantly secretive as magic? No-one in the ancient world had a collection of 1,600 discovered curse tablets to peruse as we do. The prejudice that witchcraft was a female phenomenon in particular would have served the function of control: it validated the exclusion of women from normal means of power. Furthermore, the accusation of magical practice provided a stick with which women could be beaten: such an accusation was conveniently difficult to refute, since magic was in any case inherently secretive and its mechanisms largely inexplicable.

For Graf the fact that men were the almost exclusive producers of ancient literature is sufficient to explain why literary portrayals of the practitioners of erotic magic should be primarily female: the concept of the female magician furnished an explanation of the mad love they could feel for women (1994a: 216). On the other side, he believes that curse tablets were particularly the preserve of men because they were concerned, in their agonistic context, with a struggle for social status that was of far greater significance to men than to women (1994a: 212, qualified at 215). For Winkler the main reason for the misrepresentation of the gender of magical practitioners in literary sources was to allow men, 'weakened by invading *eros*' to seek help 'through the construction of public images which relocated both the victimage (in young women – Theokritos' Simaitha *et aliae*) and the wickeder forms of erotic depredation (in older women – Horace's Canidia *et aliae*).' Winkler relates this 'transference' to the personal 'transferences' of erotic suffering that the individual tablets hope to achieve (1990: 87–91; see above).

From a different angle, erotic spells aimed at women make it clear that 'autonomous' sexual desire in women (which, in a paradoxical way, the tablets sought to create), was regarded as a desirable thing, at any rate for the recipient of it, much as it may have been disapproved of in public. The belief in the power of such spells could be used to explain and perhaps even excuse the illicit passionate behaviour of otherwise 'respectable' women (Winkler, 1990: 97–8).

Far-reaching, but possibly unsafe, conclusions have been drawn from the language of curse tablets and from the configuration of related voodoo dolls for the character of relationships between men and women and attitudes towards sex and love in antiquity. Winkler draws attention to the 'aggression' of the language that men use towards their beloveds in the tablets (dragging by the hair, sleep deprivation etc.) and to the symbolism of the famous Louvre voodoo doll, a female figure bound hand and foot and transfixed by 13 needles, including one in the vagina (*SGD* no. 152 = *Suppl. Mag.* no. 47 = *VD* no. 27 = *CT* no. 28, ii–iii AD; see Figure 4; pace Bernand, 1991: 293 on the last point), and raises the possibility that such things evidence a 'historical misogyny' (Winkler, 1990: 72–3 and 93–8; cf. Luck, 1985: 92). But to apply a crude and all-too-contemporary feminist semiotics to these texts and images, and to conclude that the men of antiquity 'hated' women and considered sex to be a form of violence would be to mislead. Firstly, aggressive language is resident in the tradition of curse tablets. Secondly, the piercing of ancient voodoo dolls is generally symbolic not of bodily harm, but simply of bodily restraint. In the case of erotic voodoo dolls, the piercing perhaps takes on the additional significance of expressing (sympathetically?) the desired penetration of the beloved. Most importantly of all, ancient magic often likes to clothe itself in the countercultural and the paradoxical, and it could well have been the case that violent language in attraction spells was felt to be effective in part because of its paradoxical inappropriateness (cf. *CT* p. 81).

It has similarly been argued that since many erotic tablets speak only of achieving the goal of sexual conquest, without explicit mention of a permanent union, the tablets' aim was usually an exploitative and lustful fling (thus Winkler, 1990: 72, but contrast 97; cf. *CT* p. 83; against this view see Graf, 1994a: 212). But the tablets are mostly brief documents, and such arguments from silence do not carry much weight: it is understandable that they should concentrate on the achievement of the immediate goal in the first instance. And it may be significant that while some tablets do indeed plead explicitly for marriage or a more permanent union, none of them explicitly requests a finite fling. Theon's request that Euphemia be bound to him for ten months is oddly specific, and perhaps relates to a standard fertility-testing trial-marriage period, theoretically long enough for a child to be produced (*PGM* CI = *Suppl. Mag.* no. 45 = *VD* no. 28 = *CT* no. 30, with notes ad loc., Egypt, v AD). Another tablet requests a five-month period (or possibly a seven-month one), still long enough to prove pregnancy (*SGD* no. 159 = *Suppl. Mag.* no. 37, Egypt, ii AD). The following tablet is definitely 'romantic':

Bring and yoke Urbanus, whom Urbana bore, to Domitiana, whom Candida bore, in love, tortured, sleepless because of his love and desire for her, so that he may take her away to his house to live with him . . .

yoke them in marriage and love, to live together for the whole of their lives. (*DT* no. 271 = *CT* no. 36, Hadrumentum, iii AD)

Another tablet asks for 'unceasing and imperishable love' (*SGD* no. 189 = *Suppl. Mag.* no.41, provenance unknown, iii–iv AD; cf. also *SGD* no. 160 = *Suppl. Mag.* no. 39, Egypt, iii AD). A papyrus formulary for an attraction spell designs that the relationship should last for all eternity (*PGM* IV 405 = *CT* no. 27). Another tablet from Carthage or Hadrumentum, not fully published, perhaps gives fullest play to cynicism: its male author requests the affections of no less than four women (*SGD* pp. 186–7; cf. Robert, 1981). Full publication of the text may tell us whether its author was greedily attempting to construct a harem, or was merely a harmless monogamist hedging his bets.

Occasionally the tablets give insight into the wider world of the women they are aimed at. A Greek tablet from Israel implies that a woman, Valentia, would be involved in the auditing of a business:

Lord angels, muzzle and make subject and attach to yourself and bind and enslave and restrain Sarmation whom Ursa bore and Valentia whom Eva bore and Saramanas, whom Eusebis bore, before Pancharia, whom Thecla bore, choking them, throwing into bonds their ideas, their mind, their hearts, their will, so that they should not make any further enquiries into an account or a reckoning or anything else. (*SGD* no. 164 = *CT* no. 77, iv AD)

CLASS

The different classes of antiquity all alike participated in the culture of curse tablets (cf. *CT* p. 24). Just as the curse tablets restore to us, albeit in a small and problematic way, the barely unheard voices of women of antiquity, so too they give us access to the voices of a group still more oppressed and largely silenced in other sources: slaves. While it is generally surprising to find any document from antiquity produced by a slave, it is not very surprising that slaves, in their situations of utter powerlessness, should have turned to this arcane pretence of or substitute for power (see Bernand, 1991: 30–4 and 160 for the argument that magic belonged above all to those marginal to ancient societies: women, slaves, metics etc.). This is one of the most eloquent and touching of the tablets (Rome, iv AD):

PHANOIBIKUX PETRIADE KRATARNADE, restrain, lord angels, Clodia Valeria Sophrone from getting hold of Politoria.
ARTHU LAILAM SEMISILAM BACHUCH BACHAXICHUCH

MENEBACICHUCH ABRASAX, restrain, lord gods, the boss of the workhouse, Clodia Valeria Sophrone, and let her not take Politoria to the workhouse (*ergastill[o]n*), to see lifelessness (*apsychia*). (Wünsch, 1909: 37–41 = *CT* no. 78)

Perhaps Politoria was a slave-courtesan past her prime. It is possible that the 'workhouse' referred to is a brothel (the related term *ergastērion* could be used in this way).

A litigation and trade curse attempts to restrain several cook-butchers (*mageiroi*) (*DT* no. 49 = *CT* no. 44, Athens, c.300 BC). These were usually slaves. What gives this dispute special resonance is the fact that in the New Comedy that flourished at this time cook-butchers were favourite stock characters, distinguished for their vulgarity, boastfulness and quarrelsomeness (cf. Dohm, 1964; Bethiaume, 1982). Indeed one of the cooks mentioned, Seuthes, may even have appeared in a comedy of Poseidippus (F29 K-A). This tablet therefore appears to lend some credence to the stereotype. The 'Sethian' circus tablets appear to have been written largely by slaves and freedmen (*DT* nos. 140–87; cf. *CT* p. 68, Rome, iv AD). Other stock characters from New Comedy that appear frequently in the curse tablets are prostitutes (doubtless usually slave) and their pimps, such as the one whose name is lost in the tablet binding Cercis and others (*DT* no. 52 = *CT* no. 73, Attica, iii–ii BC, quoted above). As we saw, the curser was presumably a rival in trade. Lucian portrays courtesans using binding spells to attract lovers (*Dialogues of the courtesans* 4.286).

It may be assumed that most of the petitioners responsible for the Bath tablets were from the poorer classes, since almost all of the thefts referred to in them seem to have been petty and to have occurred in the bath-complex itself, and those most subject to such thefts will have been those too poor to own or hire a slave to mind their clothes whilst they bathed (*Tab. Sulis* pp. 80–1 and 97–8; cf. *CT* p. 193). Also, the prosopography of the Bath tablets indicates that their authors were generally of non-citizen class before Caracalla's bestowal of citizenship on all inhabitants of the empire in 212, and descendants of the same group afterwards. Most of the petitioners appear to be city-dwellers; the peasant Civilis, who asks for the return of his ploughshare, appears to be an exception (*Tab. Sulis* no. 31 cf. pp. 74 and 96–7). A distinct Celtic background can sometimes be detected in the names of the appellants and in their Celtic-influenced misspelling of some Latin vowels. We have seen that one of the tablets actually appears to be written in Celtic, transcribed in Roman letters (*Tab. Sulis* no. 14, iii–iv AD; cf. p. 79).

The fact that so many of the tablets appear to have been made or commissioned by relatively poor people tells us that they could often be cheap. Plato expressly states that binding spells were very cheap even when bought from professionals (*Republic* 364c = *CT* no. 140; cf. Faraone, 1991b: 4). Certainly a home-made curse tablet would cost nothing more than the lead of which it was made, and lead was very cheap indeed in antiquity. The Bath tablets give easy proof of the overall cheapness of the tablets (whether homemade or not), since some of them complain about the theft of what seem to be quite petty sums, such as two *argentioli*, (*Tab. Sulis* no. 54; cf. pp. 80 and 100). Lucian's fictional professional, an old Syrian woman, is not said to deal in tablets, but her fee for an erotic binding spell is explicitly said to be cheap. It consists of 2 drachmas and an obol (a quite trivial sum in Lucian's day), bread and wine for her to devour, along with contributions of substances necessary for the rite itself, namely a torch, sulphur, salt and some of the victim's 'stuff' (*Dialogues of the courtesans* 4.286 = *CT* no. 152). Larger sums were doubtless taken from the rich, around whose doors, Plato tells us, the dealers in curse tablets hawked their wares (*Republic* 364c; cf. Bravo, 1987: 207–8). Augustine was asked by a magician how much he was willing to pay him to secure victory in a recitation competition (*Confessions* 4.2).

The lawcourts were usually the playgrounds of the rich and influential, so most of the litigation curse tablets may be assumed to have been made by (and against) the rich (cf. Faraone, 1989: 156; *CT* p. 119). In this context a group of inscribed dolls found together in graves a few yards apart from each other in the Ceramicus is particularly intriguing. Some of the names inscribed on them are rare, but known to have belonged to people attacked or spoken of in speeches written by Lysias. Mnesimachus is the single name found inscribed on the right leg of a voodoo doll which had been enclosed in a little oval coffin made up of two lead tablets moulded to fit each other (*VD* no. 5). A Mnesimachus was attacked by Lysias at F182 Sauppe. The upper lid of this coffin was itself inscribed with a litigation curse with a series of names which included Mnesimachus' again and also that of a Nicomachus (*SGD* no. 9 = *CT* no. 41), perhaps the great lawcode-systematiser of that name. In a nearby grave were found three voodoo dolls enclosed in oblong coffins (*VD* no. 6), inscribed with the names of Theozotides (attacked by Lysias at *P. Hibeh* 14) and Micines (perhaps less of an enemy: Lysias F170–8 Sauppe prosecute his murderer). These dolls may well then have emanated from a source very close to Lysias himself. (See Trumpf, 1958; Jordan, 1988b: 274–7; Faraone, 1985 n. 20, 1989: 156 n. 20, and 1991b: 30 n. 76.)

Curses were by no means confined within class, as is shown by a remarkable inscription from Tuder in Italy (i AD):

In return for the salvation of the town and of the order of the town senate, to Jupiter best and greatest, the guardian and the preserver, because he, by his power, brought forth the names of the town senators which had been attached (*defixa*) to tombs by the unutterable crime of a most wicked public slave, and he liberated and freed the town and the citizens from the fear of dangers. Lucius Cancrius Primigenius, the freedman of Clemens, member of the board of six, both Augustan and Flavian, the first member of the order to be honoured in this way, fulfilled his vow. (*CIL* 11.2.4639 = Luck, 1985 no. 14 = *CT* no. 135; cf. Versnel, 1991: 63)

It is interesting that an individual slave could exercise such terror over the great and the good of the town with such easy magic. Indeed the episode raises an important issue. Since binding spells could, at the cost of little effort and expense, level or even invert the power-relationships between the highest and the lowest in society, how could society as it was known, with all its established hierarchies, continue to exist? Why was it not unravelled? The fact that ancient society did continue to function with all its established hierarchies perhaps suggests that there was at some level a general acceptance that binding magic could only be effective in a very limited way.

The curse tablets cross class divides in other ways too: some of the combinations of people grouped together for cursing in the classical Attic tablets can be surprising: distinguished politicians are listed alongside

Those in the greatest positions of power gave most reason to others to hate and fear them, and so were particularly likely to attract curse tablets. Hence we find Attic tablets directed against current political figures, including such famous figures as the orators Demosthenes and Lycurgus (*DT* no. 60 = *CT* no. 42, iv BC; cf. Faraone, 1985: 159–60 and 1989: 156 n. 20) and the dynasts Cassander and Demetrius of Phalerum (*SGD* no. 14 = *CT* no. 57, late iv BC; cf. Jordan, 1980a: esp. 229–31 and 234–6, and Faraone, 1989: 156 and 1991b: 31 n. 76). Perhaps the early tablet found on the floor of the Tholos, the home of the Athenian council, which has not yet been fully deciphered, was aimed against the governing body of Athens (*SGD* p. 162, early v BC). Tacitus recounts several attempts to use curse tablets against the emperor and his family: Libo Drusus was supposedly found to have made sinister and mysterious marks (*voces magicae* and Characters?) against the names of Tiberius and his family (*Annals* 2.30 = *CT* no. 147). His account of the death of Germanicus, accomplished through curse tablets and other magical paraphernalia, is well known (*Annals* 2.69; cf. Dio Cassius 57.18). He also mentions other individuals accused of using curse tablets against Tiberius, Agrippina and Nero (*Annals* 4.52, 12.65 and 16.31 = *CT* nos. 149–51; cf. Phillips, 1991: 264). The theme of curse tablets well suits Tacitus' dark world of concealed malice and dissimulation.

The curse tablets cross class divides in other ways too: some of the combinations of people grouped together for cursing in the classical Attic tablets can be surprising: distinguished politicians are listed alongside women defined as prostitutes and with names appropriate to prostitutes (e.g. *SGD* no. 48 = *CT* no. 56 and *DTA* no. 107 = *CT* no. 40, iv BC; cf. Ober, 1989: 149). It was ever so.

VOODOO DOLLS

Faraone's survey of known 'voodoo dolls' as they are now termed, or *kolossoi* as the Greeks called them, catalogues 38 separate finds, a 'find' here including as a single unit groups of dolls found in the same site (*VD* pp. 200–5; for the appropriateness of the term 'voodoo doll', see Jordan, 1988b: 273). Although the finds of dolls are dwarfed by those of the tablets, they exhibit a roughly similar geographical and temporal spread, except that they are found already in the archaic period and therefore constitute significant antecedents to them. Nonetheless, it has been useful to review the tablets first, since they give expression to a range of meanings and purposes which can be used to contextualise the dolls' images. There are 15 finds from Greece, 9 from Sicily and Italy, 4 from North Africa, 7 from Egypt, 3 from the Near East and 1 from the Black Sea. Several examples, all twisted figures in bronze, are archaic: one each from Tegea (*VD* no. 8, early vii BC) and Cephalonia (*VD* no. 10), and a group of five from Alonistena in Arcadia (*VD* no.9). The latest dolls seem to hail from fifth-century AD Egypt (e.g. *VD* nos. 28 [= *CT* no. 30] and 28a).

As with the tablets, lead is the most commonly found material of manufacture in extant examples (*VD* nos. 1–7, 12, 15–16, 18, 21, 23–26a, 32, 34; cf. Preisendanz, 1972: 4). Bronze is also quite common (*VD* nos. 8–11, 13–14, 17, 19, 33). Wax dolls are actually found only in late antique Egypt (*VD* nos. 28–9 and 31 = [Figure 5]), but the Cyrene foundation decree gives us reason to suppose the use of wax was particularly ancient (see below); also, a lead tablet from fourth-century BC Attica refers to the curser's use of 'lead and wax,' which may imply that it was originally accompanied by a wax doll (*DTA* no. 55 = *CT* no. 64); the prayer of Theocritus' Simaetha that her lover should melt like the wax she is using also suggests the use of a wax voodoo doll (*Idyll* 2.28; cf. Gow, 1952, ii: ad loc.; Bernand, 1991: 180; *CT* 36 n. 4; pace Graf, 1994a: 202–3); the Pseudo-Callisthenic *Alexander romance*, written at some point between the second and third centuries AD, was to have Nectanebo seduce Olympias by using a wax doll with which to send her a vision (5). Clay was used in its various aspects: a number of dolls are made of terracotta (*VD* nos. 20 and 22 and pp. 201 and 204); the famous Louvre doll is made of unbaked clay (*SGD* no. 152 = *Suppl. Mag.* no. 47 = *VD* no. 27 = *CT* no. 28, ii– iii AD; Figure 4); another doll is mud (*VD* no. 30). Many unbaked clay or mud dolls will have disintegrated in their deposit-sites. Sometimes it can be speculated that loose dirt in graves derives from voodoo dolls (*VD* p. 205 and Graf, 1994a: 168). A doll made of dough is employed in a necromantic ritual recounted by Heliodorus (*Aethiopica* 6.14). Horace's Canidia uses a doll made of wool, alongside one made of wax, for erotic purposes (*Satires* 1.8.30; cf. Tupet, 1976: 44–50 and 302). One of the accusations made against Apuleius under the charge that he practiced magic was that he worshipped with extravagant rites a skeleton–statue made of rare wood, and hailed it as 'king' (*Apology* 61.2; cf. Graf, 1994a: 96–8).

The artistic quality of the voodoo dolls spans the full range from careful models (e.g. *VD* nos. 18 and 27 [= Figure 4]; cf. p. 190) to objects barely recognisable as figures (e.g. *VD* no. 11). Cast bronze or terracotta dolls required a greater degree of technical expertise to manufacture than their clay or wax counterparts. However, lack of access to casting facilities need not have deprived the curser of a metal doll: lead was malleable enough to be moulded by hand, and some of the lead dolls have clearly been made this way (e.g. *VD* nos. 5–6); a group of four figurines from Delos have been cut out of a rectangular lead slab (*VD* no. 12). The unique discovery of a cache of 16 figurines in Israel from the first century BC at the latest, alongside unused curse tablets, constitutes our sole direct evidence for professional involvement in the manufacture of the voodoo dolls (*VD* no. 32; see Mariani, 1910).

A similar range of deposition sites is found for voodoo dolls as for curse tablets. Graves are the most common sites (*VD* nos. 1, 5–6, 18, 20, 22, 34 and p. 205). A group of four were found in a hellenistic house on Delos (*VD* no. 11; see Dugas, 1915). Some are found in sanctuaries, though none can positively be said to have been chthonic (*VD* nos. 12 and 32). Some dolls are found in what were bodies of water: a riverbed (*VD* no. 2, undated) and a sewer (*VD* no. 25, imperial). These finds do not obstruct the supposition that voodoo dolls began to be deposited in water at around the same time as curse tablets, i.e., the early imperial period. Plato spoke of dolls being displayed at the points where three roads meet, on doors and on parental graves (*Laws* 933a); Sophronius spoke of a doll cast into the sea (see below).

In contrast to the curse tablets, however, it seems that voodoo dolls of the wax variety at any rate were sometimes activated by melting, as we have seen (Theocritus, *Idyll* 2.28; Horace, *Satires* 1.8.43–4; *ML* no. 5 line 44–9). But not all wax voodoo dolls met this fate: a number of them deposited in tombs like dolls of other substances survive to us (*VD* nos. 28–9 and 31 [= Figure 5]).

The voodoo dolls represent in concrete form many of the themes found in the curse tablets. They are often represented as bound. Sometimes the binding is visible, but in cruder dolls it has to be imagined from the positioning of arms or legs as if bound. Arms can be bound in front, or twisted behind the back, and legs too can be bent back for binding (thus *VD* nos. 1, 2, 3, 4, 6, 7, 9, 11, 13, 14, 18, 21, 23, 24, 27 [= Figure 4], 29, 32 and p. 204). Some female dolls from Delos wear heavy collars (*VD* no. 12). Was this particularly significant in view of the fact that Delos was a major slave-trading centre (cf. Bernand, 1991: 321)? A rope or chain appears to attach the hands to the head of the 'gingerbread man' doll from Carystus (*SGD* no. 64 = Faraone no. 15 = *CT* no. 19).

The dolls are often twisted in more violent ways too, particularly in the neck and legs, so that head and legs point in the wrong direction (thus *VD* nos. 2, 3, 8, 9, 10, 16, 19, 25, 26, 33). The purpose of this appears to have been not to maim or kill the victims, but to 'confuse' their designs and efforts (*VD* p. 194). Different kinds of distortion are also found. A few dolls have enlarged male genitals (thus *VD* nos. 5, 6, 9, 11, 21, 29). This may have been apotropaic (see Bernand, 1991: 104–5 for the apotropaic phallus in magic). The face of a classical Sicilian doll is demonic, which also may have been apotropaic, or may have represented a specific demon that the doll sought to bind (*SGD* no. 122 = *VD* no. 16 and p. 195). The male doll of an Egyptian separate male and female pair has an ass' head, perhaps representing Seth (*VD* no. 29).

A yet more extreme progression is the actual mutilation of the dolls. An Attic figurine has had its head cut off (*VD* no. 7), whereas a doll from Crete was cast without head (*VD* no. 14; cf. also no. 24). The legs of an Italian doll have been broken off (*VD* no. 9). A female doll from Morocco has no hands (*VD* no. 25). The 'gingerbread man' doll from Carystus was presumably made as a three-dimensional doll and then ritually flattened (*VD* no. 15). An Italian doll that now consists only of a torso may have been subject to mutilation (*VD* no. 21). Some dolls are transfixed by nails (thus *VD* nos. 1 [possibly], 7, 21, 27 [= Figure 4] and p. 204). A group from Delos seem to give added emphasis to the 'nailing' of the mouth by holding their right hands over the nail that penetrates the mouth (*VD* no. 12). Again, the purpose of twisting, mutilation and transfixing seems to have been the restraint rather than the killing or mutilation of the victim (*VD* p. 194; cf. Faraone, 1992: 133–4).

Personal 'stuff' (*ousia*) could also be used in conjunction with voodoo dolls: one of the Egyptian wax dolls had some human hair pushed into its navel (*VD* no. 31 = Figure 5).

Dolls could be made to resemble the dead also by being shut in mini-coffins or tight-fitting containers of their own. These containers are sometimes made of sheets of lead, and are therefore physically close to curse tablets themselves (thus *VD* nos. 4 and 6 from the Ceramicus, iv BC; cf. *CT* p. 119). Indeed the sheets that make up the coffins can themselves be inscribed as a curse tablet (*SGD* no. 9 = *VD* no. 5 = *CT* no. 41, iv BC). Sophronius speaks of a doll that was shut tight in a box which was locked and sealed with lead (see below). Some Egyptian dolls are shut tight in clay pots, in which they are accompanied by curse texts (*VD* nos. 27 [= Figure 4], 28, 28a and p. 204).

Dolls are strongly associated with curse tablets in a number of further ways. They are often inscribed with the name of the curse victim (thus *VD* nos. 5, 6, 18, 20, 21 and p. 201). Ten names are inscribed on a Sicilian doll (*SGD* no. 122 = *VD* no. 16). The lead 'gingerbread man' from Carystus is apparently a doll that has simply been flattened to be used as a tablet (*SGD* no. 64 = *VD* no. 15 = *CT* no. 19, iv BC). A broken Egyptian wax figurine (the one with hair in its navel) reveals that it has been moulded around a papyrus roll, which undoubtedly contains the name of the victim and perhaps also a curse text (*VD* no. 31; Figure 5). Sometimes bound figures can simply be drawn onto curse tablets proper, as we have seen (see also *VD* nos. 23, 24, 26a, 34; cf. Jordan, 1988c no.3, with his figures 2 and 7). The group of four lead figures from Delos that has been cut out of rectangular slabs of lead would appear to have been made out of something that could as equally well have served as a curse tablet (*VD* no. 12). Rather unique is a single terracotta bust-group of a couple and a child, each of which is inscribed with names, with a curse text on the back (*VD* no. 22).

A development of the voodoo doll specifically for erotic attraction spells is the Egyptian entwined-couple type: these represent male and female twisted together in sexual congress (*VD* nos. 28 and 28a; Wortmann, 1968: 86 figure 8 is an excellent photograph of no. 28 being unrolled from its papyrus). A recipe for such an entwined pair of dolls is preserved, from the Graeco-Roman tradition, in the Arabic magical text, the *Picatrix* (Ritter and Plesner, 1962: 267; cf. *CT* p. 101). It is an oddity here that one of the dolls presumably represents the actual curser. Individual dolls deposited in pairs in the same spot, where one is male and the other female, may also sometimes stem from an erotic context, but Faraone argues that they may rather be intended to carry a *pars pro toto* significance, and attempt to blight an entire group or family, its male and female members alike. He argues that the earliest use of couples of dolls was a Roman innovation which evinced a thinking similar to that underlying the city's ancient sacrificial rite in times of crisis, in accordance with which a Gaulish and a Greek couple, standing for all the enemies of the state, would be buried alive (*VD* nos. 18, 25, 29, with p. 192; for the rite, perhaps initially an Etruscan custom, see, e.g., Livy 22.57).

A variant of the voodoo doll is prescribed in one of the Greek magical papyri: it contains a recipe for the manufacture of a wax doll of Eros, which can be animated and serve as an assistant in attracting a beloved (*PGM* XII.14–95; cf. Winkler, 1990: 79 and 91–2, and Bernand, 1991:

305–7); this is perhaps not too far removed from the Nectanebo case discussed above. Similarly Lucian tells of a Hyperborean magician who manufactures a cupid from clay, which he animates and sends to fetch his client's beloved (*Lovers of lies* 14–18 = Luck 1985 no. 27; cf. Graf, 1994a: 213–14).

There can be various representational relationships between the dolls and the curse victims. No extant doll, even those of high artistic quality, gives the appearance of having been moulded to portrary the peculiar characteristics of any curse victim (*VD* p. 190). When a doll is inscribed with a simple name, it is an obvious assumption that the doll is intended in some way to represent the named victim (e.g. *VD* no. 5 with p. 190). This neat one–to–one relationship is lost, however, in the case of dolls inscribed with more than one name (e.g. *VD* no.16 = *SGD* no. 122, inscribed with ten names). Sometimes the gender of the doll matches that of the victim: this seems to be true of a pair of dolls found in an Etruscan tomb, one male, one female, each inscribed with a name of the corresponding gender (*VD* no. 18), and so too with the family bust-group (*VD* no. 22). Graf suggests that the Euboean 'gingerbread man', the curse text of which is addressed against a woman, should in itself be considered a male figure in default of positive female characteristics. But this is a weak argument in view of the crude state of the doll, and in view of the possibility that it was originally a three-dimensional doll, which may well have had (female) sexual characteristics before being flattened (*SGD* no. 64 = *VD* no. 15 = *CT* no. 19; Graf, 1994a: 162). It would appear, however, that Dido actually burned a portrait-bust of Aeneas, alongside his remaining clothes and belongings, on her pyre as part of her suicide-curse against him. Dido's rite here hesitates between one of erotic attraction and one of more destructive cursing (*Aeneid* 4.508 and 640; cf. Tupet, 1976: 232–66, esp. 243, 248 and 259).

Dead animals could also be used as voodoo dolls. Libanius' mutilated and twisted chameleon has already been discussed; it is clear why the chameleon should have been considered a magical creature (see Pliny, *Natural History* 38.122–7; cf. Bonner, 1932a: 39). A pair of Latin tablets with continuous text reveal that a dead puppy was sympathetically used alongside the tablet (Gaul, ii AD):

I denounce Lentinus and Tasgillus, the individuals written below, so that they may go away from here to Pluto and Proserpina. Just as this puppy did harm to no-one, so . . . nor let them be able to win this lawsuit. Just as the mother of this puppy could not defend it, so may their advocates be unable to defend them, so may these enemies be turned away from this case. Just as this puppy is turned away and cannot get up, so may they not be able to do so either. So may they be transfixed, just like this puppy. Just as animals/souls (*animalia*) have become dumb in this tomb and cannot get up, so may these men not. (*DT* nos. 111–12 = *CT* no. 53)

In a spell from the Jewish *Sepher ha-Razim* collection, the purpose of which is to prevent sleep, one is instructed to insert a duly inscribed tablet into the head of a black dog that had never been allowed to see the light (which probably implies the use of deliberately killed puppies), seal up the mouth with wax, and conceal the head behind the victim's house (Morgan, 1983: 49 = *CT* no. 114). Dogs were particularly appropriate as the special animal of Hecate: one of her heads was a dog's, and dogs were sacrificed to her (cf. Gow, 1952, ii: 38 and 43; cf. Tupet, 1976: 72). One of the Greek magical papyri bids one sow a rolled-up tablet into a dead frog (*PGM* XXXVI 231–55). Ovid speaks of binding the tongues of gossips by sewing up the mouth of a fish (*Fasti* 2.577–8; cf. Tupet, 1976: 39). A sixth-century AD literary source displays a development of this notion: St. Euthymius appears in a dream to a man dying with pains in his stomach, opens the stomach and draws out a tin tablet (Cyril of Scytho-polis, *Life of St. Euthymius* 57; cf. *Tab. Sulis* pp. 104–5). An unillustrated circus tablet refers to a cockerel: 'Just as this cockerel has been bound by its feet, hands and head, so etc.' (*DT* no. 241 = *CT* no. 12, Carthage, i–iii AD; cf. Faraone, 1989: 153). This text may refer to a real cockerel that was sacrificed in conjunction with the activation of the tablet, or to an image of a cockerel that should have been drawn on the tablet, the spell perhaps being incompletely copied from a formulary, or to the head of a cockerel (Abrasax?) found drawn on a separate but adjacent tablet. (See Jordan, 1988b; Faraone, 1991b: 21 n. 3.) Possibly the wryneck bird (*iynx*), which was spread-eagled across a wheel, itself also known as a *iynx* or *rhombos*, which was then spun on two strings to attract a beloved, as used most famously by Theocritus' Simaetha, was in some sense supposed to stand for the beloved (*Idyll* 2 passim and *Palatine anthology* 5.204 [the Niko epigram]; cf. Bonner, 1932a: 38–9; Gow, 1952, ii: 39–41; Tupet, 1976: 50–5; Pirenne-Delforge, 1993).

Voodoo dolls could also represent animals. This could be specifically to bind the animals represented: a cache of nine horse figurines from Roman Antioch, inscribed, apparently, with both horse names and human names, doubtless curses horses and their chariot-drivers in the familiar circus context (*SGD* nos. 180–8, not in *VD*; cf. Seyrig, 1935 and *CT* p. 15). But the animal could also have a magical significance exstrinsic to the subject of the spell in hand: one of the Greek magical papyri includes a recipe for an attraction spell which involves the manufacture of a wax dog into the mouth of which is to be placed a fragment of the skull of a man that died by violence (*PGM* IV 1872–926); another spell for attracting a woman through wakefulness requires the manufacture of a dough dog into which the eyes of a bat have been inserted (*PGM* IV 2943–66; cf. Winkler, 1990: 93 and 95).

The most vivdly informative narrative from antiquity about the use of voodoo dolls tells us that, like curse tablets, if found they could be deactivated. Sophronius (late vi AD) tells how Theophilus of Alexandria was rendered tetraplegic, his limbs racked by pains, by the devil, who had been summoned by his enemies. Saints appeared to Theophilus in dreams and told him to hire a fisherman to cast his net into the sea. The fisherman drew from the sea a small box locked and sealed with lead. Inside was found a bronze effigy of Theophilus with a nail driven into each limb. As they were withdrawn, he was released from pain and paralysis in the corresponding limb (Sophronius, *Account of the miracles of Saints Cyrus and John*, PG 87.3 cols. 3541–8 = *CT* no. 165; cf. *DT* pp. cxxii–iii, *VD* p. 193 and Faraone, 1991b: 9). But Graf considers this late tale unreliable evidence for ealier voodoo doll culture on the ground that the doll does not operate within any of the canonical categories of binding curse, and on the ground that the portrayed relationship between the piercing of the limbs of the doll and the restraint of the corresponding limbs of Theophilus is oversimplified and anachronistic (1994a: 165).

Horace narrates, in the character of Priapus, an elaborate magical rite which includes the use of a large woollen doll and a smaller wax one, the latter of which is made to bow down in supplication before the former, as if about to be executed as a slave. The wax doll is then melted with fire. The dolls would appear to have an erotic function, but the narrative is unfortunately difficult to exploit for the historical use of the dolls as Horace appears to have deliberately contaminated the erotic rite with a necromantic one (*Satires* 1.8.30–3 and 43–4; cf. Tupet, 1976: 299–309).

One find, that including the Louvre voodoo doll, already mentioned in a number of contexts, draws together many of the themes of this essay, despite being unique in a number of ways. It dates from the second or third century AD and comes from Egypt, perhaps Antinoopolis; it consists of:

1. The most elaborate of the voodoo dolls, a female figure carefully modelled, even though made only of unbaked clay, her hands bound behind her back and her legs bound up under her. She is transfixed by 13 nails in the top of her head, eyes, ears, mouth, chest, palms of the hands, vagina, anus, and the soles of her feet. She may be presumed to represent Ptolemais, the victim of the spell (*VD* no. 27 = Figure 4).
2. A rolled lead curse tablet, with an erotic attraction curse directed against Ptolemais by Sarapammon. The curse is written by a practised hand (*SGD* 152 = *Suppl. Mag.* no. 47 = *CT* no. 28).

3. A clay vase, which contained the two objects above, perhaps serving as
   a kind of coffin.

The find is not only of interest because of the quality and graphic nature
of the voodoo doll, and its close association with a detailed and informative
tablet: it is of also of interest because the manufacture of the doll and the
text of the curse follow quite closely the instructions given in one of the
Greek magical papyri (*PGM* IV 296–408 = *CT* no. 27; cf. Faraone,
1991b: 26 n. 33), save that no *voces magicae* are inscribed on the doll's
limbs. The group therefore consitutes our best direct evidence for the use
of magical handbooks for voodoo dolls. This, taken together with the
superb quality of the doll and the inscribed text, perhaps indicates that the
assemblage is the product of a magical professional.
    An important document bearing upon the existence and use of voodoo
dolls in the archaic period is the Cyrenean foundation decree, which,
although carved in the fourth century BC, purports to relay material from
the original foundation in c. 630 (*ML* no. 5 lines 44–9). An oath is
prescribed by the decree which is to be accompanied by the burning of
wax dolls: it includes the sympathetic wish that those who do not abide
by it should melt like the dolls. Faraone compares the notion with the
Greek myth in which Meleager is killed by the sympathetic burning of a
log (Apollodorus, *Bibliotheca* 1.8.1–3 and Ovid, *Metamorphoses* 8.445–525
etc.: a wooden voodoo doll?), and a wide range of Homeric, archaic and
classical Greek oath-taking ceremonies in which the butchery of animals
(in sacrifice) and the libation of wine are taken to have sympathetic
implications for the destruction and the spilling of the blood of the
foresworn (e.g. Homer, *Iliad* 3.292–301 and Aeschines 1.114). Such oaths
are particularly used in the context of international treaties and special
pledges of loyalty (Faraone, 1993).
    Another fourth-century BC inscription from Cyrene purports to relay
purification rituals dictated to the city in the past by Apollo at Delphi.
One of the rituals is for the laying of a ghost. Ghosts can be laid by the
proclamation of their name, but if this is not known, then male and female
dolls must be made from earth or wood, entertained to a feast, and then
deposited in uncultivated land (*SEG* ix no. 72 lines 111–21). It is possible
that this ritual is inspired by Assyrian ghost-laying rituals (i.e. mock re-
burials of the dead, for which see below), but it also appears to have
affinities with the rituals behind Mycenean, archaic and classical Greek
cenotaphs, which contain effigies in place of the missing corpse. The use
of ghosts to curse and the laying of ghosts are contradictory activities, but
both alike exploit the technique of their manipulation. An ancient
commentary on Euripides speaks of Thessalian sorcerers (*goētes*), called
'spirit-conductors' (*psychagōgoi*) whose skill lay both in being able to send

ghosts out to attack people and also to send them back to the grave (Scholiast to Euripides, *Alcestis* 1128; *VD* p. 180–5).

Traces of things akin to voodoo dolls possibly prior to the archaic are period also preserved by written sources. Pausanias speaks of an ancient bound statue of the war god Enyalius at Sparta (3.15.7). In a number of early myths we hear of Ares, the principal god of war, being bound (e.g. Homer, *Iliad* 5.385–91 and *Odyssey* 8.296–99). That there may have been corresponding bound effigies of Ares is suggested is suggested by later evidence, an oracle of Apollo at Claros to the Syedrans: it advised them to avert attacks upon them by pirates by setting up a statue of Ares, bound and kneeling (Bean and Mitford, 1965 no. 26, i BC). The *Palatine anthology* preserves the inscription from what may have been a bound statue of Ares buried in Thrace to protect it against barbarian invasions (9.805). Olympiodorus of Thebes refers to the discovery, during the reign of Constantius, of three buried silver statues of bound barbarians, which protected Thrace against the Goths; when they were removed the Goths overran the country (*FHG* iv p. 63 F27). The purpose of binding Ares was apparently both to restrain war from harming the city, and also to retain the forces of destruction on ones own side. (On all this see *VD* pp. 167–72 and Faraone, 1992: 74–93).

An intriguing find from tenth-century BC graves in Lefkandi may constitute the earliest example of a voodoo doll from Greece: it is a teracotta centaur which appears to have been deliberately broken before being inserted into graves, the head in a separate one from the body: did the centaur embody some wild and disruptive spirit which was thus subjected to restraint? (See Desborough et al., 1970; *VD* p. 195.)

THE ORIGINS OF THE CULTURE OF GREEK BINDING-CURSES

It is not possible to speak of (significant) antecedents to or influences upon Greek binding-curse culture with great certainty. All ancient mediterranean cultures probably employed 'magical' rituals of some sort and there was always cross-fertilisation between the different cultures, both before and after the beginnings of the archaeological and documentary records. The appearance in other cultures of rituals akin to binding magic prior to its recorded emergence in the Greek world does not in itself require that the Greeks 'imported' it. That said, certain ancient Egyptian and Near Eastern rites deserve consideration here: these cultures were highly developed when Greek culture remained primitive, and were therefore in a strong position to exercise influence over it. The process of magical borrowing between ancient mediterranean cultures and the development of some sort of magical *koinē* between them may have been aided by internationally intinerant professionals (Tupet, 1976: 165; Burkert, 1983; *VD* pp. 198–9).

The Greek rites in which Ares the god of war was bound seem to be prefigured in a range of oriental cultures. A forerunner of striking similarity is found in the very ancient Egyptian practice of making dolls representing the enemies of Pharaoh as kneeling bound captives. These dolls, of wax or wood, usually represented at once an enemy of a god, such as Osiris' enemy Seth (later popular in Greek curse tablets), and at the same time an enemy of Pharaoh. They would be distorted and destroyed in fire. The image of the kneeling bound captive was popular in royal Egyptian art: in reliefs they cower below the feet of Pharaoh, and could be portrayed on the soles of sandals (to be trodden on). These captive dolls bring us close also to curse tablets: clay versions of them were flattened out (cf. the Greek 'gingerbread man', *SGD* no. 64 = *VD* no. 15 = *CT* no. 19), inscribed with the names of Pharaoh's enemies, perhaps sometimes then deliberately broken, sealed in clay pots and finally deposited in graveyards or near mortuary temples. The earliest examples hail from around 2,300 BC. Earthenware bowls were similarly inscribed with 'execrations' and then deliberately shattered. Akin to the captive dolls in a different way are small figures placed in graves of the dead and inscribed with the name of an individual corpse. The purpose of these is thought to have been to lay the unquiet ghost of one that had just died, to serve, that is, as 'mortuary aids' (for a possible Greek equivalent, see *SGD* pp. 179–80 and *CT* no. 117). If this type of doll did directly influence Greek cursing practice (and NB the presence of ghost-laying dolls at Cyrene), then the dolls' purpose seems to have been inverted: designed by the Egyptians to bind the dead, and to give them (and the living) peace, they came rather to bind the living, and to exploit the restlessness of the dead in order to bring further disturbance to the living. (See Raven, 1983; Bernand, 1991: 54–62; *VD* pp. 172–6 and 199; *CT* pp. 15 and 26; Ritner, 1993: 111–90; Pinch, 1994: 90–104.)

In the Near East the Babylonians appear to have used something akin to the bound captives: as part of a pre-battle ritual effigies of the enemy were made from tallow and other materials: their arms were twisted behind them, or they were distorted with cords. The Assyrians employed both private and public 'Burning rituals' (*Maqlû*), known from records of the incantations that accompanied them, in which effigies of demons (including personifications of diseases), ghosts and human enemies were distorted and burned. The effigies of human enemies were usually themselves identified as magicians (even though their precise identity might not be known). In some Assyrian *Namburbi* texts instructions are given to counteract the magic of hostile magicians. This involves the making of a series of effigies of various materials, including tallow and wax, writing the name of the magician on the dolls' left hips, twisting their arms behind their backs, and tying their feet together. The dolls are then to be all bound together and buried with the victims' hair in a container in the ground.

Assyrian texts from Nineveh give instructions for a similar ghost-laying ritual: if a ghost appears to a living person, one is to make a clay effigy of the dead person, inscribe his name on the left hip, insert it into a container made from the horn of a gazelle, and bury it. The effigy may have its feet twisted, and its mouth plugged with the tooth of a dog. These effigies can themselves be given burial rites: it is as if it were felt that the original burial rites of the dead person had failed to work properly. (See Castellino, 1953; Caplice, 1970; Abusch, 1974 and 1987; Elat, 1982; Bottéro, 1987–90; Reiner, 1988; Bernand, 1991: 48–52; *VD* pp. 176–9; *CT* p. 26; Graf, 1994a: 195–8 and 294–5, with further bibliography.) The Cyrenean use of voodoo dolls in oath-taking may also be compared with Assyrian ceremonies in which wax dolls are sympathetically burned during oath-takings (e.g. the Aramaic 'Sefire' inscription at *ANET* pp. 659–60, viii BC; cf. Faraone, 1993).

Curses akin to those found in Greek and Roman curse tablets can also be found in ancient Jewish culture. Particularly noteworthy is:

> Jeremiah, having written down in a book a full description of the disaster which would come upon Babylon, said to Seraiah, 'When you come to Babylon, look at this, read it all and then say, 'Thou, O Lord, hast declared thy purpose to destroy this place and leave it with no one living in it, man or beast; it shall be desolate, forever waste.' When you have finished reading the book, tie a stone to it and throw it into the Euphrates, and then say, 'So shall Babylon sink, never to rise again after the disaster which I shall bring upon her.' (*Jeremiah* 51:60–4 [trans. *New English Bible*])

Ezekiel appears to give a prescription for the manufacture of something quite akin to a curse tablet, with a similarly sympathetic function (4:1–3; see Fox, 1912b: 304 and 1913–14; *CT* pp. 26–7).

There are more vague indications that the Hittites too used dolls of clay, wax and other materials in the restraint of their enemies: again the dolls could be held to represent hostile magicians. In the course of the restraining ritual the dolls were flattened or melted, and the accompanying verbal curses revealed that this was supposed to have a sympathetic effect on the enemy. (See Goetze and Sturtevant, 1938; *VD* pp. 179–80; *CT* p. 26.) The Hittites too seem to have used dolls in oath-taking (e.g. the military oath *KBo* VI 34.40–rev. 5 at *ANET* p. 353, c. 1,400 BC).

DID ANCIENT BINDING MAGIC 'WORK'?

It is now commonly argued that binding magic 'worked' with reference to shared (mistaken) belief. The notion is not new, but as old as Plato:

> Another kind of witchcraft (*pharmakeia*) with its so-called sorceries, charms and binding-spells persuades those attempting to harm their victims that they really are able to achieve such a thing, and persuades their victims that, more than anything, they are being harmed by those who are able to work magic. (Plato, *Laws* 933a)

In such a sense magic can just about be said to have worked, though hardly in the way in which it was supposed to do so. In the case of prayers for justice it may be argued that the wrongdoer's sense of guilt may have helped to induce psychosomatic illness, or led him to associate any occurring illness with his guilt. A wrongdoer might at any rate have been expecting and fretting about the prospect of a curse, but an innocent victim would not normally have had any such internal prompting. (See *Tab. Sulis* pp. 101–2; Betz, 1992: xlviii; *CT* pp. 21–3, 120 and 176–7, cf. 221; for the 'resilience' and 'self-confirming' nature of magical belief systems see Evans-Pritchard, 1937: 475–8 and Thomas, 1971: 641–2.)

There certainly was a widespread acceptance in antiquity that binding magic worked: the elder Pliny asserted that everyone feared curse tablets (*Natural History* 28.4.19 = *CT* no. 146; cf. Preisendanz, 1972: 2). But the difficulty for us in believing that it worked to any significant extent in the way outlined above relates to the problems of publicity and legality. It is probable that most magical activity was carried out in secret. This must have been true to a certain degree, since tablets and dolls could be deactivated once discovered and the desecration of graves, which was a common element of the deposition of tablets and voodoo dolls, could not have been publicly countenanced. Furthermore, magic often revelled in and drew power from its own secrecy and secretiveness: Greek magical papyri often require that their readers divulge their contents to no other (e.g. *PGM* I 40–1; cf. Graf, 1994a: 117–18). It is sometimes believed that the jumbling of letters in the tablets and the rolling of them were for reasons of secrecy, though we have seen that other explanations carry more weight. A wide range of sources indicate that magical incantations were muttered in low tones, both to maintain their secrecy and so as not to alarm the necessary demons, who could be frightened by noise (Gow, 1952, ii: pp. 38 and 43; cf. Graf, 1994a: 99). Despite this, we are asked to believe that magical practitioners, before or after the rite, effectively told their victims that a spell had been or was about to be cast upon them. The evidence usually advanced to support such a hypothesis is weak: Simaetha's reference before making her spell to her intention to go to the gymnasium and tell her errant lover Delphis off (Theocritus, *Idyll* 2.8–9; cf. *Tab. Sulis* pp. 62, 72, 84 and 100; Faraone, 1991b: 17; *CT* pp. 21, 82–3 and 176–7).

A more specific reason for keeping *harmful* magical practice secret was its illegality. There is just enough evidence to suggest that harmful magical practice was generally illegal throughout Graeco-Roman antiquity (cf. Preisendanz, 1972: 11; Aune, 1980: 1515–18 [also discussing whether illegality should be considered a universal characteristic of magic]; Phillips, 1991: esp. 261 and 269). By contrast, it is unlikely that prayers for justice were illegal (*Tab. Sulis* p. 100). Perhaps the 'lack of universally accepted definitions of unsanctioned religious activity', the diverse and polytheistic nature of ancient religion, and the largely tolerated emergence of new cults prevented the comprehensive outlawing of magic (Phillips, 1991: esp. 264 and 266). There is no definite case of an actual law from classical Greece banning the use of binding spells, but they may have been covered under the rubric of 'harmful *pharmaka*' in a lawcode from Teos of 479 BC (*Syll.*[3] no.37; cf. Faraone, 1991b: 20 and *CT* p. 23). Most forms of 'magic' appear to have been prosecutable under the catch-all crime of impiety (*asebeia*) in classical Athens (cf. Phillips, 1991: 262). Plato explicitly outlaws binding spells in his hypothetical *Laws* (933a = *CT* no. 141). In Rome harmful magic is said to have been outlawed from the time of the Twelve Tables in the fifth century BC (Apuleius, *Apology* 47; cf. Segal, 1981: 356–8; Phillips, 1991: 262; *CT* p. 258), and the extant laws of the Twelve Tables do indeed define some magical crimes, namely the incantation of a harmful spell (*malum carmen*: Pliny, *Natural history* 28.17; cf. Tupet, 1976: 166–8) and the charming of crops from one field to another by song (*excantatio cultorum*: Seneca, *Natural questions* 4.7.2 and Pliny, *Natural history* 28.17–18; cf. Graf, 1994a: 52–3). Sulla's law of 81 BC, the *Lex Cornelia de sicariis et veneficis* outlawed *veneficium*, a term which covered magical procedures for encompassing death, as well as simple poisoning (*Digest* 48.8; cf. Graf, 1994a: 57–8 and 80). The emperors seem to have agreed that harmful magic should be illegal, but to have been less consistent on non-harmful magic (Barb, 1963: 102–3; cf. *CT* p. 24). Paulus (early iii AD), writing in a context in which magic was clearly illegal, gave the opinion that professional magicians should be burned, whilst magical participants should be thrown to the wild beasts or crucified; magical books were to be confiscated or burned, and their owners exiled or, if of the lower class, decapitated (*Sententiae* 5.23.15–18 = *CT* no. 157). With the development of Christianity, with its monotheist doctrine and concept of orthodoxy, magic or 'unsanctioned religious activity' became easier to define and oppress (cf. Phillips, 1991: 264–5). Eusebius, writing in 335 AD explicitly referred to binding spells as illegal (*Laus Constantini* 13 = *CT* no. 160). Ammianus Marcellinus wrote in 359 AD that execution awaited those who dug up graves for magical purposes (19.12.14). An imperial decree of 389, repeatedly renewed, required those who knew of individuals practising magic to expose them (*Theodosian code* 9.16.11; cf. *CT* p. 48 n. 29). Later in this volume Luck illustrates the common association between the sorcerer and the criminal in antiquity. Illegality placed an officially countercultural stamp upon magic, and thus conferred greater power upon it. The illegality of magical practice meant that it was extremely dangerous for the practitioner to attempt to start the victim's powers of suggestion against himself by circulating a rumour that magic had been used, and even more dangerous to accost one's victim in a public place and there declare that one was using magic against them, as Simaetha is supposed to do.

Perhaps a partial answer lies in Plato's reference to people being frightened by wax voodoo dolls fixed at the meeting-points of three roads, on their parents' tombs or on their doors (*Laws* 933ab = *CT* no. 141; cf. Preisendanz, 1972: 4; Faraone, 1989: 159 and 1993: 64). Since other evidence indicates that a located doll could have been easily deactivated by its removal, dolls in such places could not have presented any great threat in themselves. But perhaps one could deposit a 'working' doll out of reach, whilst exhibiting all too publicly a duplicate to the victim. The displayed doll would therefore have had the function of informing the victim that a curse had been placed upon him, and of unleashing his own powers of suggestion against himself. This would have constituted an effective, graphic and anonymous way of letting one's victim know that he should begin to fret.

Some prayers for justice were probably nailed up flat for display before their deposition: this may be suspected, for example, when a tablet contains a single nail-hole at the middle-top of the text (e.g. a bronze tablet from Asia Minor of between the first century BC and the second century AD, Dunant, 1978 = *CT* no. 90; cf. Versnel, 1991: 74 and 80; Faraone, 1991b: 27 n. 43). This is not to say that the nailing in these cases was purely functional. A fourth-century BC Greek magical papyrus from Egypt, one of the oldest, contains a lengthy prayer for justice (it actually calls itself a *hiketēria*, 'supplication' or 'petition') by Artemisia against the father of her dead daughter, and the text implies that it will be posted up in a public place (*PGM* XL; cf. Versnel, 1991: 68–9). We must assume that there was nothing illegal about this sort of tablet or petition. But then there was nothing anti-social or unfair about them: rather, in so far as they worked, they served the interests of law and order. The same may be said for the publicly displayed conditional curses for the future inscribed on tombstones to protect graves (cf. Strubbe, 1991; *CT* pp. 185–7). Nonetheless, many tablets even of this category, such as the Bath cache, were definitely *not* displayed publicly (see Vernsel, 1991: 80–1; *CT* pp. 176–7).

The casting of the spells may also have served a function useful to the psychology and mental well-being of the curser, whether he felt unfairly treated, or desperately wanted the love of another person, or any of the other things sought in the tablets. In Tomlin's memorable phrase, 'something at least had been done' (*Tab. Sulis* p. 102; cf. *CT* pp. 23 and 82).

BINDING SPELLS AND THE DEFINITION OF MAGIC

It is time to return to the point at which we began. Discussions of the definition of magic itself, particularly in relation to religion, occur frequently in recent publications on ancient binding spells. Virtually all the essays in Faraone and Obbink, 1991, for example, air the matter (e.g. Faraone, 1991: 17–20; Versnel, 1991: 92–3; Kotansky, 1991: 122 and 123 n. 1; Graf, 1991: 188, 195–6 and 207 n. 1; Betz, 1991: 244–7; Phillips, 1991: 260–2 and 266. See also Barb, 1963; Tupet, 1976: vii–xv; Aune, 1980: especially 1510–15; Segal, 1981; Luck, 1985: 4–5; Phillips, 1986: 2679 and 2711–32; Versnel, 1986; *Tab. Sulis* p. 60; Winkler, 1990: 72; Bernand, 1991: 65–75; *CT* pp. 24–5, 39 n. 114 and 247; Graf, 1994a: 27–9). When attempts to define magic are not merely sterile arguments about the use of words, they often threaten to recall their roots in an agenda of religious oppression (cf. Thomas, 1971: 438 etc.; Segal, 1981: 349).

There is no easy way to separate binding spells from what can uncontroversially be termed 'religion' in an ancient context. The curse tablets merge quite fully into ordinary religious practice in the 'prayers for justice' category, in which tablets can be phrased as quite normal prayers to mainline deities. In a sense any curse tablet that appeals to a mainline deity, directly or indirectly, cannot be excluded from the sphere of 'religion.' Curse tablets of all sorts mix and interchange ostensibly 'magical' procedures, such as binding formulas and 'manipulative' or 'coercive' elements (vis-à-vis the powers), and ostensibly religious ones, such as prayer formulas and 'supplicative' elements (Faraone, 1991b: 20; cf. Versnel, 1991: 93; Faraone, 1993: 77; for the significance of these concepts, see Goode, 1949; Aune, 1980: 1512–13). Indeed Plato associated incantations and prayers alike with magicians (*Laws* 909b; cf. Graf, 1991: 188–9). Furthermore, as Gager observes, the ancient world 'teemed' with all manner of supernatural beings of different orders, which most men would not have thought to distribute into categories of 'religious' and 'magical' (*CT* p. 12, against, most recently, Versnel, 1991: 64). Betz has noted that the overlap between the culture of magic in the Greek magical papyri and the culture of mystery cults is particularly strong (1991: 249–50; cf. Graf, 1994a: 107–37). It is perhaps possible to draw a distinction between religion and magic in the ancient world in the context not of utterances, of prayers, but of rituals, in particular of sacrifice: Graf argues that in a religious context sacrifice and other rituals unite the community, whereas in a magical one they distance the magician or practitioner from the rest of the community (Graf, 1991: 195–6). But the binding magic we have discussed here only makes occasional use of actual sacrifice (dead puppies, chameleons etc.).

As Gager again observes, it is not really proper to ask a question of the sort 'What are the characteristics of Greek magic?' Rather we should confine ourselves to questions of the type 'Under what conditions, by whom and of whom does the term "magic" come to be used?' (*CT* p. 25; cf. Segal, 1981: 367). What can, however, be usefully pointed to here (and this is by no means any kind of total definition of the phenomenon) is the way in which ancient magical practice sometimes *defined itself*, that is, the countercultural cloak that it sometimes took on at least partly of its own accord. Examples of purposefully adopted countercultural forms may be found in the curse tablets' retrograde writing, their penchant for matrilineal descent and their later penchant for alien deities. Graf's observation that magic tends to distance the magician from his community is again apposite; he also argues that it was this aspect of magic that made it a useful and fruitful accusation to cast against outsiders in the community, as happened to Apuleius at Oea (Apuleius, *Apology*; Graf, 1991: 195–6 and 1994a: 75–105).

BIBLIOGRAPHICAL ESSAY

The first significant corpus of curse tablets to be published was Wünsch's *Defixionum tabellae* (Wünsch, 1897), normally referred to as *Defixionum tabellae Atticae* and abbreviated to *DTA* to distinguish it from Audollent, 1904. This was a collection of Attic curse tablets known at the time. It still constitutes the basis for the study of the Attic tablets and is likely to continue as such unless the lost originals it reproduces are rediscovered. This publication was significant not only for rendering curse tablet texts generally accessible for the first time, but also for conferring on them a degree of respectability as an object of study, since it formed part of the authoritative epigraphical series *Inscriptiones Graecae*. Wünsch's collection was soon complemented by Audollent's *Defixionum tabellae* (Audollent, 1904), usually abbreviated to *DT*, which reproduced all curse tablets known to Audollent at the time in Greek, Latin and some minor languages, categorised by provenance, excluding those already published in Wünsch's volume.

Most of the Greek tablets not found in either of these corpora are listed in Jordan's indispensible 'A survey of Greek defixiones not included in the special corpora' (Jordan, 1985a), usually abbreviated to *SGD*. Jordan here lists the tablets by provenance, following an anti-clockwise geographical progression around the Mediterranean, and indicates their place(s) of publication (if any). Some short but interesting texts are reproduced in full. I have not usually cited prior places of publication for tablets in this list.

A corpus of the Latin tablets to have emerged since Audollent by 1920 was compiled by Besnier, 1920, and a list, like *SGD* without full texts, of those to have emerged since Besnier by 1968 was compiled by Solin, 1968: 23–31 (see also García Ruiz, 1967: 55 n. 1). Since then the number of Latin documents available has been significantly increased by the discovery of the Bath cache and its publication in Tomlin's contribution to Cunliffe's *The temple of Sulis Minerva at Bath* ii (*Tab. Sulis*), which is also published separately as *Tabellae Sulis*. This is to date the most meticulous and exemplary publication of any set of curse tablets and includes, amongst other things, careful drawings of each tablet. For this reason the Bath cache takes on an importance for the study of the subject as a whole that its idiosyncratic nature would not otherwise have dictated, the cache consisting almost entirely of 'prayers for justice'.

Of these works only Tomlin provides translations. An excellent set of translations of the most interesting and important texts selected from all these corpora, together with English commentaries, is provided by Gager's *Curse tablets and binding spells from the ancient world* (1992, abbreviated here to *CT*). Where possible I have drawn the examples discussed above from among the texts available in this volume, but they are given in my own translation unless otherwise indicated.

A systematic catalogue of voodoo dolls is provided by Faraone's 'Binding and burying the forces of evil: the defensive use of "voodoo" dolls in ancient Greece' (1991a, here abbreviated to *VD*) at 200–5. This article also provides the best analysis of the use of the dolls and of oriental antecedents to them. Faraone treats the use of wax dolls and their use in oath-taking ceremonies more specifically in his 'Molten wax, spilt wine, and mutilated animals . . .' article (1993). The same scholar puts the voodoo dolls in a wider Greek religious context in his *Talismans and Trojan horses* (1992). A detailed analysis of the Mnesimachos doll is provided by Trumpf 1958, and Mariani 1910 remains useful for providing photographs of some dolls not illustrated in *VD*.

The Greek magical papyri are collected in the two volumes of Henrich's revised version of Preisendanz's *Papyri Graecae Magicae* (Preisendanz and Henrichs, 1973–4; original edition 1928–31, Leipzig and Stuttgart), usually abbreviated to *PGM*. German translations are provided. The second edition of volume ii also incorporates papyri from the 'lost' original volume iii, production of which was arrested by the Allied bombing of the Teubner press in 1941. Unfortunately this second edition does not also incorporate from the lost volume the detailed and valuable indices to the entire collection. For these we depend upon photocopies of the volume's galley-proofs which are fairly rare, although copies are held by the major British classical libraries (see Jordan, 1985b: 234 n. 71 and Betz, 1992: xliv). These papyri, together with other Greek papyri that have come to light since Preisendanz's first edition, and together with the demotic-language papyri and demotic-language sections of Greek papyri which were known to Preisendanz but omitted by him, are translated into English in Betz's *Greek magical papyri in translation* (Betz, 1992; first edition was 1986). Preisendanz's sequence is preserved, with the additional papyri continuing it: hence *PGM* references from LXXXII onwards refer only to Betz. Betz's demotic papyri are referred to under the *PDM* abbreviation. Unfortunately he omits the Christian magical spells and the magical ostraka and wooden tablets included in Preisendanz's corpus (Winkler, 1990: 226 n. 2 suggests a reason for this); for these we may now turn to Meyer and Smith, 1994: 27–57. Betz's translations are contained in a single volume; a second volume, containing indices to the papyri, is long promised but has yet to appear. If one did not know better, one might think that the indexing of the papyri lay under a curse. Annotated Greek texts, also with English translations, of magical papyri that have come to light subsequently to Preisendanz's first edition are now published by Daniel and Maltomini in the two volumes of *Supplementum Magicum* (1990–2, abbreviated to *Suppl. Mag.*). *Suppl. Mag.* also includes the closely related curse tablets from Egypt, some of which Preisendanz knew but placed outside his remit. A fairly readable survey of the material in the Greek magical papyri is provided by Nock, 1929.

Greek gemstone amulets, which largely hail from Egypt, are analysed in Bonner, 1950, which includes a full descriptive catalogue at 249–323 and photographs of the complete catalogue. See also the collection of similar material by Delatte and Derchain, 1964. The wordier Greek amulets of the lamella type, which hail largely from outside Egypt, are being published in two volumes by Kotansky, the first of which has appeared (1994). A recent introduction to the Greek amulets is provided by Kotansky, 1991. Guarducci, 1978: 271–83 provides a useful introduction in Italian.

Mention should also be made of Wortmann's fine publication, with good photographs, of thirteen magical texts of various kinds in Cologne (1968). His curse tablets, papyri, voodoo dolls and amulets are subsumed in the relevant subsequent series for these materials described above.

The accessibility of the curse tablets and ancient magical technology to study by English readers has been radically transformed over the past decade or so, largely through the work of a small number of American scholars, who have also done much to reinvigorate the subject intellectually: the names of Jordan, Faraone, Gager and Kotansky deserve particular mention. The best modern short introduction to the curse tablets is Faraone's 'The agonistic context of early Greek binding spells' (Faraone, 1991b) in the volume edited by him and Obbink, *Magika Hiera* (Faraone and Obbink, 1991); a number of the other articles in this superb collection also have a bearing on the subject, notably Versnel's on prayers for justice (Vernsel, 1991) and Winkler's on erotic magic (Winkler, 1991), which can also be found in his *Constraints of desire* (Winkler, 1990, the pagination of which is used here). A more detailed and systematic introduction is provided by Gager's *Curse tablets* (*CT*), which prefaces its translations with substantial amounts of introductory material. Tomlin's analysis of the Bath cache is extremely illuminating on the processes of tablets' manufacture, and essential to any consideration of the social context of the tablets' use (*Tab. Sulis*).

The most important introductions to the tablets among older work are Preisendanz's 'Fluchtafel (Defixion)' (Preisendanz, 1972), for twenty years the first place of reference, and Kagarow's *Griechische Fluchtafeln* (Kagarow, 1929). A readable introduction in Italian is provided by Guarducci, 1978: 240–57.

Much of the important modern work on curse tablets appears in the forms of series of articles by the American scholars named above. Thus, in addition to his *SGD*, a number of Jordan's articles may be singled out, in particular 1976, 1980a, 1985b, 1988b and 1988c. Further to Faraone's 1991b piece, there is much of value in his articles of 1985 and 1989. There is a degree of repetition between these. There have also been two recent contributions to the subject in French: Bernand, 1991 translates and discusses a number of the tablets in the course of a wide-ranging treatment of many aspects of Greek magic; a more focused discussion of the tablets themselves is provided by Graf, 1994a: 139–98; mention should also be made here of Tupet's less recent but nonetheless superb *La magie dans la poésie latine* (Tupet 1976) which, although not concentrating specifically on curse tablets, provides a wealth of information on many aspects of ancient magic far beyond the confines of its deceptively narrow title.

Further to the work of Winkler on erotic magic, reference should also be made to Maltomini's review of a thesis by Moke (1979) and to the brief but important article of Petropoulos (1988).

What should scholars turn their attention to in the future? It will be clear from the above bibliographical survey that the publication and documentation of curse tablets is currently chaotic. Also, the accumulated expertise generated by the decipherment of the more recently discovered tablets, when applied to tablets published in the older series (where the originals remain available), shows that the original decipherments are often defective (no discredit, however, to the pioneers in the field). There is then a pressing need for a single, coherent and systematic new edition of all known curse tablets, and one based, where possible, on new inspections of the texts. Happily, Jordan is engaged in such a task. The availability of such an edition will render all analytical approaches to the tablets much more easy and fruitful.

To some extent the study of curse tablets and other magical texts from classical antiquity has existed in a ghetto, and has not really been fully integrated into mainstream classical scholarship. While at the beginning of this century this isolation may have been caused by a general disdain for the 'irrational' aspects of classical antiquity, it is nowadays probably sustained by the technical difficulties and philological nature of the study of the tablets. It should then be a priority to bring such an integration about. The study of women and the study of religion are perhaps currently the two dominant areas of interest for Classical historians, yet works in these areas seldom refer to magical texts. The above discussion will, I trust, have shown how important magical texts can be for both of these subjects.

Postscript. Of great importance for the history of erotic curses is the detailed publication of a newly discovered and exciting tablet published by Voutiras, E., Διονυσοφῶντος γάμοι. *Marital life and magic in fourth-century Pella* (Amsterdam, 1998). On the representation of witches see Clauss, J.J., and Johnston, S.I., eds. *Medea* (Princeton, 1997) and, more controversially, Rabinowitz, J., *The rotting goddess: the origin of the witch in classical antiquity* (New York 1998). Another good collection of essays on ancient magic is provided by Meyer, M., and Mirecki, P., eds., *Ancient magic and ritual power* (Leiden, 1995). Graf's important general book on ancient magic, 1994a, is now available in English as *Magic in the ancient world* (Cambridge, Mass., 1997). A full and interesting account of exploitable ghosts is provided by Johnston, S.I., *Restless dead. Encounters between the living and the dead in ancient Greece* (Berkeley 1999); see also Felton, D., *Haunted Greece and Rome. Ghost stories from classical antiquity* (Austin, forthcoming). Finally, I mention two works that had not come to my attention at the time of writing. A further useful introduction to the Greek magical papyri is provided by Brashear, W., Magical papyri: magic in bookform' in Ganz, P., ed., *Das Buch als magisches und als Repräsentationsobjekt* (Wiesbaden, 1992) 25–59. A detailed and informative edition of a rich erotic attraction curse is provided by Martinez, D. G., *A Greek love charm from Egypt (P. Mich. 757)* P. Michigan xvi (Atlanta, 1991).

PART 2

Witches and Sorcerers in Classical Literature

Georg Luck

No single, no collective image of the *magos* in antiquity emerges from our sources, but we can draw a composite image from texts of the fifth and sixth centuries (Heraclitus, Euripides, Gorgias, Hippocrates and Plato). We will attempt to sum up these testimonies in modern terms. We must also consider the few clues we have concerning the training of the sorcerer. The great witches of myth – Circe, Medea – will be discussed. The Near East has furnished the concept of the *magos* who could be a priest or king or both, a concept which was later Hellenized and lives on in semi-legendary figures such as Zoroastres, Hystaspes and Otanes.

To Judaism we owe religious leaders who might also be considered as *magoi*: Moses, Solomon and Jesus of Nazareth. As a Greek parallel to the Hellenized *magoi* we then shall consider Orpheus, Pyrthagoras and Empedocles. They are followed by the Egyptian Nectanebus who is connected with the Alexander romance. Theocritus, the pastoral poet, has given a fascinating portrait of an amateur witch in action, while Horace's Canidia and Lucan's Erictho are clearly professionals, though they are presented in poetry with rhetorical colors and satirical twists. A group of more or less controversial miracle-workers exhibits common features but also striking differences: Simon Magus, Apollonius of Tyana and Alexander the False Prophet. Apuleius of Madaura is a representative of Middle Platonism who was attracted by magic but in the end became an eloquent propagandist of Isis. Neoplatonism finally gives us a new type of Greek *shaman* on a high level, the theurgist, and various occult phenomena are now closely tied up with the traditions of paganism. We return to the old sorcerer with his repertory of tricks in Hippolytus' 'Unmasking'. But some Christians were also attracted by magic, as the curious story of Bishop Sophronius shows.

We have little evidence concerning the actual attire and appearance of the *magos* during the performance of a ritual. It must have varied greatly – from the rags worn by Lucan's Erictho to the priestlike robes embroidered with symbols favoured by theurgists. There are allusions to masks or heavy make-up and strong perfumes.

It might be helpful to study those prominent figures in chronological progression, as we travel from the ancient Near East to Archaic Greece and further to the Christian Roman Empire.

Greek and Roman magic had some of its roots in the Near East, and in order to understand it, we ought to study the religious and magical beliefs and practices of the Sumerians, the Hittites, the Persians and the Jews. For the purposes of this survey, it will be sufficient to deal with some of the Hellenized *magoi* of Persia and some Old Testament figures such as Moses and Solomon. The formidable witches of Greek myth, Circe and Medea, seem to belong to a non-Greek or pre-Greek culture, but they have influenced Greek thought strongly. Orpheus, Pythagoras and Empedocles are still semi-mythical but can be placed in a historical context. Hellenistic Alexandria played the role of the great melting pot. In Rome, we find, after a historical figure like Nigidius Figulus, some composite literary figures like Vergil's Dido that reflect historical and mythical antecedents. The strong yearning for healing, salvation, and peace, called forth the miracle-workers of the first century AD. Apuleius is partly *magos*, partly philosopher, partly *homme de lettres*. Theurgy, finally, may be seen as a last attack on Christianity. The Christians, for a long time, did not abandon magic completely.

To give an idea of the universality of magical beliefs, a geographical *tour d'horizon* of the Mediterranean world from East to West will be useful. It must begin in the Near East with the countries which have always been associated with magic, astrology, divination and the other occult sciences, i.e. Babylonia and Assyria (the country of the Chaldaeans) and Persia (the country of the *magoi*).

From that part of the world, various occult techniques reached Greece and Italy in the prehistorical period, perhaps via Thessaly, a region traditionally associated with witchcraft. A special method of divination through the livers of sacrificial animals was probably brought by the Etruscans from Asia Minor to Italy and became part of Roman religion. During the Hellenistic period, new ideas and practices travelled to Greece and *Magna Graecia* via Egypt. In all these Western areas, however, there were native conglomerates which combined with the new material. We may assume that many areas preserved some ancient bits of folklore or 'superstition' which cannot be documented anywhere else. At the same time, during the first centuries of our era a kind of common idiom of witchcraft established itself throughout the Roman Empire.

Another approach to the material discussed in the following pages is possible through the range of phenomena from folk religions to the sophisticated urban diversity of Hellenistic Alexandria and Imperial Rome. At these later stages we see a colorful multitude of cults and creeds (including the Mystery religions) on the one hand and philosophical schools competing with each other on the other hand. The history of ancient magic reflects to an astonishing degree the cultures which have created and shaped it. The roots, the archetypes, may be lost in the dawn of prehistory, but they can be reconstructed to some extent. In the remotest periods, magic probably claimed to provide all the answers which were later furnished by science, technology and philosophy: it was everything to everybody. But the historic cultures of the Near East already had their distinct character. They created large cities with mixed populations besides the smaller rural settlements. There was no doubt even then a lively exchange of ideas across the subcontinents and seas. When we come to the even larger cities of the Hellenistic and Roman periods, everything, of course, happened on a larger scale, and the interaction between various cultures became more intensive.

There are certain issues that have to be addressed in a survey of this kind. Throughout antiquity, we see a general awareness of the kind of person a sorcerer must be and of the powers he is most likely to possess. But there is no single image that fits all cultures and periods. The history of the terms *magos, mageia,* suggests an old misunderstanding: What, for the Persians, was their national religion, was, in the eyes of the Greeks, ritual magic. This is a phenomenon that we can observe throughout history: From the outsider's point of view, a foreign religion may be nothing more than hocus pocus. The first practitioners of magic in Greece, as described by Heraclitus, Hippocates and Plato, were certainly no priestlike figures, but 'itinerant diviners', 'vagabonds of the night'. From these texts, vague as they are, we may establish the main characteristics of these individuals. From a later period we have clues as to the apprenticeship of a magician. The great witches of Greek myth have certain features in common yet remain distinctive personalities. The 'Hellenized Magi' form an important bridge between the Near East and Classical Greece, while Moses and Solomon represent a rather different kind of spiritual power. A specifically Greek type of shaman can be studied in such semilegendary figures as Orpheus, Pythagoras and Empedocles. Poets like Theocritus, Vergil, Horace, Seneca and Lucan have given us memorable portraits of witches, partly based on timeless myth, but also mixed with contemporary reality (Canidia is supposed to have been a perfume mixer called Grattidia). Jesus of Nazareth, Simon Magus, Apollonius of Tyana, Apuleius and Alexander of Abonuteichos represent different aspects of the type of religious leader, travelling teacher, prophet or miracle worker of the early Christian era. Theurgy, as practiced by some Neoplatonists, is not a completely new type of occult technique, but rather a higher, respectable form of very ancient practices used now to prove the reality of the old gods against the attacks of the Christians. The Christians, in retaliation, unmask fraudulent magicians.

From our modern point of view, witchcraft is not only a kind of science or technology, it also has a more general cognitive function, i.e., it is a way of perceiving the world, making sense of it, explaining it, using it for its purposes. For a very long time religion and magic were the only ways for people to come to terms with the outside world (the macrocosm) and their own personalities (the microcosm). Religion and mythology provided the answers to all the questions people kept asking. As to dealing with the higher powers on which people depend, religion mainly pre-scribed prayer and sacrifice and ritual, offered in a humble, submissive, repentant or grateful spirit, while magic normally used coercion, threats, special procedures. This is only a very rough distinction, and there are exceptions to limit its validity. Religion is based on belief and tradition, and so is magic, while science, including psychology, although never completely free from myth and prejudice, is based on logic and exper-iment. There is, of course, a kind of weird logic in witchcraft as well, and this could explain its appeal and the role it played as a pseudo-science. After Thales of Miletus and the other Ionian scientists appeared, after the work done by Hippocrates and his school, people would seem to have a choice between 'real' science, old and new religion and magic, but very few will have been able to make clear-cut decisions. For a long time, as the example of Anaxagoras shows, to be a scientist was equivalent to being an atheist. The same charge was made against magicians. On the other hand, a Neo-pythagorean miracle-worker like Apollonius of Tyana can say in his own defense that he is not a magician but a scientist. Empedocles was a great thinker as well as a miracle-worker, and E. R. Dodds has asked the intriguing question whether he started out as a *magos* who lost his nerve and took to science, or whether he was a true philosopher who also experimented with magic (like Apuleius, perhaps). The problem, insoluble of course, illustrates the dilemma we are facing. For the theurgist who communicates with the highest gods (via a medium, no doubt), the messages received from another world, no matter how confused or trivial they may seem to us, represent, for the believer, the ultimate truth.

The development of magical beliefs and practices in ancient times offers a number of examples for the tensions and interactions between an 'ignorant' general population and a 'sophisticated' urban elite. Magic has its roots in prehistoric times when these distinctions were meaningless, but as soon as science and philosophy emerge, i.e. since the sixth century BC, we have, roughly speaking, these two segments of the population: an 'enlightened' minority and a 'backward' majority. This dichotomy is clearly visible in Hippocrates' treatise *On the sacred Disease*, where he characterizes the 'diviners, purifiers and humbugs' (who had their public, to be sure) and tacitly differentiates them from the scientific physicians he himself is training on Cos. Naturally, magic was practiced among the rural population, as the Law of the Twelve Tables and the healing formulas in Cato's *On agriculture* show, but also in the cities, as the curse tablets excavated in Athens prove. Theophrastus' amusing portrait of the 'Superstitious Man' in the *Characters*, written from the point of view of Aristotelian philosophy, would indicate that protective mechanisms against evil powers were used in Athens even during an enlightened period. In Alexandria, ancient beliefs and modern theories combined with a variety of religions to form a complex and sophisticated system of occult sciences, including astrology and alchemy. Long after the victory of Christianity, these ideas and practices survived, in a simplified form, among the *pagani* who were, by definition, backward and removed from the cultural centers.

We are in a good position to study the marketing and commercialization of cults by reading, for instance, Lucian's account of Alexander of Abonuteichos, the 'False Prophet', a masterpiece of satire, based on historical reality. This man was a true genius but also an accomplished charlatan who invented the cult of Glycon, the sacred snake, and appointed himself its chief priest. The naive inhabitants of Abonuteichos were persuaded to build a sanctuary which served as the basis for an ever-expanding religious enterprise. Alexander borrowed freely from other cults and relied on his practical experience as a travelling magician. Above all, he brought to his widespread enterprise a keen business sense. The whole organization is described in detail by Lucian, and what worked so well in this particular context no doubt worked equally well for other cults, in other places. Alexander realized the deep need people felt to believe, to be saved, to be guided, to worship higher powers, and he exploited these needs to the fullest extent.

We know of other cults that were practically created, if not by a single person, at least by committees of priests and politicians. The best example is the cult of Serapis (a combination of Osiris and Apis) in Egypt. The religion of Isis had an army of skilled propagandists, among them no less an accomplished literary and philosophical figure than Apuleius of Madaura.

CONCEPTS AND SEMANTICS

The distinction between 'religion' and 'magic' on the one hand and 'philosophy' amd 'magic' on the other are bound to vary according to the historical period, the cultural context, and the personal point of view of the speaker. Our earliest Greek testimonies differentiate between 'witch-craft' as a rather suspect, if not unlawful activity, something that could not possibly be mistaken for religion, because (for example) it took place at night and was not connected with any established sanctuaries and religion.

Another distinction is no less important. Again and again, we see that the religion of one culture, e.g. that of the Persians or the Egyptians or of some 'primitive' or culturally backward people might appear as 'magic' in the eyes of another, more advanced, culture. This discrimination was more often than not based on a simple misunderstanding, as the origin of the word *mageia* illustrates; but it also could be deliberate. Someone like Apollonius of Tyana was called a magician by his enemies, while he saw himself as a philosopher or a true scientist. But there are witches like Canidia or Erictho who want to be nothing else but practitioners of the black arts; they are proud to be feared and hated; they exult in their sense of power.

The complexity of the problem is partly due to the nature of our sources. Sometimes we depend almost entirely on hostile reports (Simon Magus, Alexander the False Prophet). Sometimes, we listen to the voices of admirers or loyal followers (Philostratus' *Life of Apollonius*). Sometimes, we have a fairly well balanced account (e.g. Apuleius who reports the accusations made against him and refutes them convincingly).

It may be useful to define some terms that are more or less frequently used in this chapter. It will be noticed that almost all Greek terms have a fairly close Latin equivalent and vice versa. The following glossary represents only a small selection from the magical vocabulary of Graeco-Roman antiquity whose very size testifies to the importance of the subject. In this respect, the Greeks were not different from, e.g., the Maoris who have, in their language, about twenty synonyms for 'incantation' in general and a number of more specific terms, such as 'incantation to be used by a rejected suitor'. If read with close attention to the linguistic and cultural context, the following list is more than a simple glossary: It helps open up a new understanding of the place occupied by the magical arts in ancient thought and society.

Aegyptius: 'Egyptian', but also 'sorcerer, prophet, wise man'. Hence Engl. 'gypsy' and its connotations.

Agyrtes: Used together with *mantis* by Plato, probably in the sense of 'itinerant wizard' or 'travelling diviner'.

Atheos: Literally a person who rejects the gods of the society, community or culture to which he belongs. Philosophers like Anaxagoras or Theodorus were accused of atheism, and under the Roman Emperors, 'the philosophers' were often banished together with the sorcerers and astrologers. From a pagan view, the Christians, too, could be called 'atheists'; hence the scholarly debate stirred up by Iamblichus, *On the mysteries of Egypt* 3.31 as to whether *atheoi* refers to Christians or sorcerers. In the *Acts* of the *Disputation of St. Achatius* the Roman magistrate says to the Christians: 'You are *magoi*, because you introduce some new kind of religion.'

Chaldaeus: 'Chaldaean', originally member of the ruling caste of Babylon, a priest or scholarly astrologer. Cf. *Magos*. Later any astrologer or diviner.

Curiositas: 'curiosity', specifically, like its Greek equivalent, *periergia*, 'interest in magic'. One of the themes of Apuleius'novel, *Metamorphoses*. There is another euphemism of this kind: *ta hyper anthropon eidenai*, 'to know that which is beyond a (mere) human being'.

Dynamis: 'power', especially 'supernatural power'. Related to *arete, charis* and equivalent to *potestas, virtus*. The words have different shades of meaning, varying between 'force', 'effectiveness', 'grace' and 'spiritual gift'. Obviously all of them could have religious connotations. *Exousia* in the sense of 'spiritual power' could also be mentioned. These terms reflect the belief that some people have supernatural powers as a gift. Other terms, such as *techne, ars, scientia*, reflect the conviction that magic is an art that can be acquired. Ideally, the *magos* should not only have the special gift and be favored by the gods or by nature; he should also study his subject thoroughly.

Epoide: 'charm', 'incantation'. Magical spells were often sung or chanted, and it was thought that the music — in itself a kind of magic, *thelxis* — added to the power of the words and acts. In Latin, *carmen* means 'song' and 'spell'. The English words 'charming' and 'enchanting' still reflect these ancient beliefs.

Fascinatio: 'form of bewitching', hence the English word. Probably related with Greek *baskania*, 'envy'. A person may bewitch another because of envy. According to some modern scholars, envy is, in fact, at the root of all magic. *Fascinum* is an amulet in the shape of a phallus, used as a protection against the Evil Eye.

Goeteia: 'witchcraft', hence *goes*, 'wizard, sorcerer'. Pagans and Christians alike use these terms to denote lower forms of magic, and there almost always is a connotation of fraud and deceit. In this respect, *goeteia* is practically synonymous with *manganeia* which, originally, meant something like 'engineering'. Hence, it would imply natural explanations af seemingly supernatural phenomena and, at the same time, draw attention to fraud and deceit. Alexander, the Pseudoprophet, used *manganeumata* to orchestrate the cult of his god, Glycon.

Mageia. Hence *magos, magikos, mageuein*. Probably the most general term. A Greek word which originally designated the religious rituals performed by the chief priests of the Persians. These were obviously so different from the rites practiced by the Greeks that they were easily misunderstood and assigned to a different sphere, the realm of magic. This kind of misunderstanding occurs typically when different cultures come into contact with each other. Thus the Romans misinterpreted the religions of some nations they conquered, and the victorious Church suppressed vestiges of pagan rites because it considered them forms of witchcraft and daemon-worship.

Mystes: One who is initiated into one of the Mystery religions. Applies also to the sorcerer who has reached a certain level. *Mysterion* or *telete* could designate a high degree of magical knowledge, while *telesma* (hence 'talisman') also means 'amulet', sometimes called *alexikakon*, 'averter of evil'. It is remarkable how the language of the sorcerer (for there was such a thing, as we know from Lucian's work on Alexander) borrowed from the language of the Mystery religions, and if it borrowed words, it must also have borrowed ideas and rituals.

Necromancy: Ritual designed to conjure up ghosts and force them to reveal the future. Famous examples: Homer's *Nekyia* (Book 11 of the *Odyssey*) and Lucan's Erictho episode (Book 6 of the *Pharsalia*).

Pharmakon: 'drug', either as 'poison' or 'remedy'. Hence, *pharmakeia*, 'konwledge of remedies and poisons', but also 'magical knowledge'.

Physikos: Originally 'naturalist' or 'scientist' in the sense of 'investigator of natural phenomena', but sometimes used for 'magician'.

Planos: 'vagabond' or 'deceiver', in a certain context synonymous to *thytes*, 'sacrificer', and probably related to *agyrtes* and *mantis*.

Potio: 'potion', especially 'love potion', corresponds to Greek *philtron*. There is an analogy to *poculum* which could be any 'cup', but specifically a drink that had been drugged. Whenever the possibility of magic was involved, people were careful with their language. Again, the semantic evidence is revealing: German 'Gift' today means only 'poison', but its Germanic ancestor must have meant the same as the English word. It is easy to understand why people preferred to say: 'Something has been given to him' rather than 'someone has poisoned him'.

Shaman: Term borrowed by anthropologists from the Tungusian language to designate the 'medicine-man'. In the Greek world, this was usually a 'divine man', a 'prophet', a 'medium' or an inspired teacher, but it could also be applied to a sorcerer.

Sortiarius: A late Latin word for the professional who casts and interprets the *sortes*, i.e. lots, to predict the future. These 'lots' may be sticks or dice or cards with certain symbols. The picking up of the lots was called *sortilegium*. That particular method of divination may have given us the Tarot cards. It is interesting to note the semantic extension by which the practitioner of a special technique, the *sortilegium*, could become the 'sorcerer' pure and simple.

Superstitio: The etymology of this term is controversial, but it seems to have meant, originally, 'left-over piece of an earlier (discarded) culture'. The Greek equivalent, *deisidaimonia*, has a more obvious derivation: it means 'fear of higher powers', *daimones*. This would not necessarily exclude the deities generally worshipped in the city-state. From Theophrastus' 'Portrait of the Superstitious Person', it appears that such a fear had to be really excessive and go far beyond normal devotion and religious practices; it might include the regular worship of half-forgotten native deities and all sorts of exotic gods.

Thaumatourgos: 'Miracle-workers'. The term could be applied to an archaic *shaman*, like Pythagoras, but also to a great religious teacher like Jesus of Nazareth, worshiped as the Saviour, the Son of God, as well as a travelling Neopythagorean like Apollonius of Tyana. 'Divine man', *theios aner*, and 'deity in human shape', *anthropodaimon*, are closely related terms. Miracles were demanded by those who were ready to be converted, and if the miracles were accepted as such, 'faith', *pistis*, followed.

Theourgia: 'working on the gods' or 'making the gods work', a higher kind of magic, performed in a religious context, by philosophers and priests. They were supposed to make the statues of the ancient gods smile and talk, etc. Some mystic experiences resemble 'séances' and presuppose a medium in trance. These techniques were used by the defenders of paganism in their struggle against the ever-growing popularity of the New Faith.

Thytes: 'sacrificer', perhaps 'wizard' in our earliest witnesses. Any practitioner not attached to one of the traditional sanctuaries, working outside of the established religion of the city-state, but claiming divine revelation, purification and solutions for people's everyday problems.

THE CONVENTIONAL IMAGE OF THE SORCERER

As we look at the main testimonies, we notice only a general awareness of the powers of magic and the personality of the sorcerer (Nock, 1933/1972: passim). It becomes clear that there is not a single image, which does not surprise in such a complex culture.

We may start with a passage in Euripides' *Orestes* (408 BC). Here (line 1497) three possible explanations are given for Helen's disappearance: (1) drugs; (2) magical arts; (3) theft by one of the gods. We see that divine action is put on the same level as magical operations, but no clue is given as to what magician could be powerful enough to perform such a feat. It is, however, conceivable that magicians took credit for this kind of spectacular disappearing act, just as they took credit for an eclipse of the moon.

In his *Helen*, Gorgias (c. 480–c. 375) offers four possible explanations for Helen's going to Troy: (1) divine compulsion; (2) human force; (3) persuasion by word; (4) passionate love. He comments on (3) by introducing *epoidai*, i.e. charms that give pleasure or remove pain and explains this by *goeteia* and *mageia*, adding that these employ techniques to influence the soul and deceive the mind. In other words, a powerful sorcerer could make Helen want to go to Troy by giving her some irresistible illusions. There is no doubt a connection between the two texts.

In his treatise *On the sacred Disease* (late v BC) Hippocrates writes: 'The men who first sanctified this disease must, I think, have been of the type of our present-day ... purifiers and mendicants and humbugs. They actually pretend to be very pious and to have special knowledge.' The author seems to refer to a species of practitioners who might be called low-level *shamans* and are the opposite of the scientific healers Hippocrates wished to train. These travelling medicine men are related to the *manteis kai agyrtai* that Plato (*Republic* p. 364) exposes.

Vettius Valens (ii AD), an astrological author, says (p. 74, 17 Kr.) that a particular stellar juncture produces *magoi*, deceivers (*planoi*), sacrificers (*thytai*), healers, astrologers who lead people astray (i.e. not serious astrologers like Vettius Valens), bankers who counterfeit the currency and forge signatures – all kinds of people who conduct their business through villainy, imposture and deceit. The author does not differentiate between the various occult practitioners, although the terms he uses emphasize certain aspects of their art; he lumps them together with dishonest bankers. They all operate through deceit; they are basically criminals. It is interesting to note that the 'sacrificer' is mentioned together with the *magos* by Hippocrates, *On the sacred Disease* 3.

Plato is an important witness. In the *Symposium* 202 A, Diotima, discussing daemons, places magic close to religion and says: 'Through their care goes the whole science of divination, the arts of the priests and of all those concerned with sacrifices in initiations and spells and all divining and witchcraft (*goeteia*). God has no intercourse with men: It is through this race that all intercourse happens between gods and men.' Here we have Plato's daemonology in a nutshell. Again, the 'sacrificers' are associated with the magicians; theirs must be *magica sacra*, and the initiation rites are hardly the traditional ones, as practised at Eleusis.

Nock sums up these testimonies and the others he discusses as follows:

What then did the ancients mean by *mageia*? Broadly speaking three things: the profession by private individuals of the possession of technical ability enabling them to supply recipes or perform rites to help their clients and damage their clients' enemies; and . . . the religions belonging to aliens or on any general ground disapproved. The third use is natural.

Who are the *agyrtai* and *manteis* mentioned by Plato? Whether we translate them as 'nightwandering wizards' or as 'itinerant diviners and magicians', they remain shadowy figures, working at the margins of society (Graf, 1994a: 32–3, 271 n. 8). May we equate the terms *agyrtai, manteis*, and *magoi* or *goetes*? Only Heraclitus associates the *magoi* with the 'vagabonds of the night'. That they operate at night, not during the day, like most priests and seers, also makes them suspicious.

Graf points out another passage (Sophocles, *King Oedipus* 387–8) where *magos* is used in a negative sense (Graf, 1994a: 33). Tiresias, a respected *mantis*, is insulted as a *magos*, a schemer, a crooked begging priest whose eyes are open for gain, but closed for his art. Taking money for predicting the future seems to be a further element defining the charlatan.

Whether these specialists also fabricated curse tablets and 'voodoo dolls' for their clients — for a price, of course — we can only guess. Whatever their specialty or the variety of services they offered, we may call them lower-level *shamans* of the ancient world, the Greek equivalent of the medicine men that many civilizations have produced all over the world.

One further characteristic feature deserves to be pointed out: it is one of the claims of these 'itinerant priests' and 'diviners' or whatever they were, to 'heal the consequences of an injustice done.' This refers almost certainly to sins committed by one of the ancestors of the client. Emotional distress or mental illness is seen by this school of travelling psychiatrists as a result of crimes committed in previous generations. These crimes are most likely of a religious nature. The patient who suffers the consequences is subjected to 'purifications and rites.'

As Graf remarks, the Heraclitus fragment (see below) makes excellent sense when considered from this point of view (Graf, 1994a: 34). The philosopher threatens the shady practitioners with the same punishment in the afterlife which they promise to spare their patients in this life!

Originally, the *magoi* were Persian priests, members of a special caste or a secret society. They were responsible for the religious ceremonies, the sacrifices, the funerary rites, for divination and the interpretation of dreams. As such, they were high officials of the Empire. Xenophon calls them 'experts in matters concerning the gods.' The author of the *First Alcibiades*, talking about the teachers of the Persian elite, says that they teach the *mageia* which comes from Zoroaster, the son of Horomasdus, and it is the cult of the gods.' Another Platonist, Apuleius (*Apol.* 25), quotes this passage (*Alcibiades* 122 A) to reject the accusations directed against him, and he stresses the fact that the *magoi* were the priests closest to the kings. The religion founded by Zoroaster was, after all, the national religion of the Persians until the Arab conquest (642 AD), and the *magoi* must have fulfilled their original functions during all these centuries.

Apollonius of Tyana apparently did not have too much respect for them; according to Philostratus (*Life of Apollonius* 1.26) he said: 'They know a good many things; but there are things that they do not know.'

The word *magos*, like *goes*, had a negative connotion ever since the archaic age. Heraclitus (end of vi BC) associates the *magoi* with the 'vagabonds of the night, bacchants, maenads, mystai.' With the exception of 'vagabond', these terms also had a positive connotation which can only mean that the practitioners of occult arts usurped these terms to suit their more or less shady activities. It is as if a magician called himself the priest of some unknown deity. One only has to think of Alexander, the inventor and high priest of a new god, Glycon. But these people existed in the time of Heraclitus who threatens them with tortures in the afterlife, because what they call their 'mysteries' are, in reality, 'impious rites.'

Heraclitus must have had in mind the *agyrtai* and *manteis*, the 'begging priests'. The fact that these practitioners were 'itinerant' or 'mendicant', i.e., not attached to a sanctuary, made them suspicious. No matter how lowly his status, the Greek *goes* could see himself as a descendant of the Persian *magos*, i.e. as a kind of priest. The religion whose priest he was might be remote or long forgotten, but he might still be proud of his status. But the 'vagabonds of the night', the *magoi*, the bacchants, the maenads, and the *mystai* were threatened by Heraclitus with punishment in the next life. This composite picture is very suggestive. It seems that the *magos* had a little bit of everything – the bacchantic (i.e. ecstatic) element, the initiation rites, the migratory life, the nocturnal activities. Such, no doubt, were Plato's *agyrtai kai manteis*.

According to André Bernand's thesis, the sorcerer is motivated exclusively by envy or jealousy (*phthonos*). In my opinion, the sorcerer is also motivated by greed and by his desire to gain prestige and status. He might be an astrologer by profession, but he could probably also sell you an amulet to protect you from unfavorable constellations.

Any magical operation presupposes that some sort of energy is available in the universe which can be used by the operator. The modern anthropologists call it *mana*, the Greeks called it *dynamis*, 'power', or *charis*, 'grace', or *arete*, 'effectiveness'. In a polytheistic society, it was only natural that the one Power took on the forms and names of many powers – gods, daemons, heroes, disembodied souls, etc – who were willing, even eager, to work for the *magos*.

Sometimes, the *magos* does not quite understand what is actually working through him and for him. The sorcerer and the witch only know that something is working. The sorcerer can be a priestlike figure – a theurgist in the Neoplatonist style – or, more likely, a charlatan. But he deals with a clientele whose predominant emotions are hope and fear, as Lucian said very clearly in his attack on *Alexander, the Pseudoprophet*. People everywhere are concerned about the same things: health, wealth, good looks, favorable marriage, children, protection from dangers or disasters, and so on. In a sense, the sorcerer feels that he is above the law, above the moral code that ordinary people respect. Though he may not see it in these terms, he is a law unto himself.

The Persian *magoi* were priests, and perhaps what we call magic is the survival of a very ancient religion, the cult of the mother Earth who was worshipped in historical times under a variety of names: Ge or Gaia, Demeter, Ceres, Terra Mater, Bona Dea, Cybele and so on.

This idea of priesthood may survive in the most obscure practitioners of historical times. But the borrowing of names, concepts and rituals from religions is one of the characteristics of ancient magic.

In a sense, magic, understood as a kind of science, has always tried to locate the secret forces (*dynameis*) in nature (*physis*), especially their sympathies and antipathies and use for them for specific purposes. Apollonius of Tyana whom many considered a magician, saw himself, if we can believe his biographer and hagiographer, Philostratus, as a scientist and philosopher, and Apuleius thought of himself in the same terms. Yet the magicians were less interested in knowledge for its own sake, in pure science, than in manipulating the forces in the universe. At the same time, they explored the human soul, the hopes and fears of ordinary people in order to control them. Alexander of Abonuteichos is a good example. Like the *shamans* of so-called primitive tribes, the ancient wizards also knew about the effects of certain plants. They were able to alter states of consciousness in themselves and in others. These gifts and skills were probably not developed in all practitioners to the highest degree.

In Plato's *Laws* (10.908 C/D), the Athenian mentions certain types of 'godless criminals', especially those 'who are convinced that the universe is without any gods, are the prey of their passions – pleasures and pains – and have an excellent memory and a very sharp mind . . .' Some of these atheists are frank to the point of being cynical and make fun of the gods; others are more tactful and deceive the people. They are 'gifted' and can do a lot of mischief, and from their ranks spring forth 'many diviners and charlatans . . .'

Here we have the portrait of a very clever operator who does not believe in the gods of the city-state but does not necessarily deny them openly. He is very much on his own, a victim of his emotions, but also able to work on the emotions – the hopes and fears – of others. Plato practically anticipates a figure like Alexander of Abonuteichos, and this can only mean that such figures already existed in his own time. They are outside of society, yet able, because they are so clever and have excellent memories (but of what?) to profit from ordinary people's superstitions.

How can we sum up from the testimonies we have examined the characteristics of the professional?

1. he/she manipulates higher powers
2. he pursues specific goals
3. his rites are specific, individual, although, to us, they may seem traditional and stereotyped
4. he develops a professional-client relationship. This means, e.g., that he expects satisfied clients to recommend him to other prospective clients, emphasizing what he has done for them
5. when he fails, he modifies his techniques
6. since he cannot rely on a common faith (the gods will help you sooner or later) instant success is everything to him
7. though he may wish to appear as a benefactor to mankind, he does not feel bound by ethics

It is not surprising that the sorcerer, after all, remains a shadowy figure, wrapped in secrecy, because that is his trademark. The sorcerer as a type is, perhaps, never a real person, but always a composite figure: seer, priest, healer, philosopher for those who believe in him, and a fraud, a charlatan, a criminal for those who have no use for him. This is, perhaps, the main problem. We always move in a twilight zone. There are those who need the sorcerer, and there are those who see in him a danger to society.

By the end of the last century BC, Hellenistic magic, as we know it, was fully formed as a system, and all the occult practices that we usually distinguish – ritual magic, daemonology, astrology, alchemy – had become applied sciences that could be studied and learned to a certain extent. Much of the instruction was probably carried out orally, in secret. At the same time, magic was a sacred art, a privilege of the priests of Egypt and the Hellenized *magoi*. Many magical texts on papyrus are actually religious texts. Some of the rituals described are dramatic performances.

The priests of Egypt were supposed to be the keepers of ancient mysteries that they did not share with outsiders, but they must have admitted apprentices, even though we know very little about their methods of teaching and training which makes them difficult to approach.

We have a number of technical treatises on astrology and alchemy, but they do not seem to cover their subject thoroughly, and oral instruction was no doubt necessary to fill the gaps. The same is true for the treatises on alchemy we have today. And the substantial body of recipes and formulas for specific purposes that we have in the Magical Papyri could not take the place of a complete introduction. They were intended for the experienced professional.

One more word about the image of the professional. The practicing *magos* was probably not always an astrologer and an alchemist. As these occult sciences became more and more complex, it was increasingly difficult to master them all. No doubt some sorcerers dabbled in more than one of these arts, and as an ideal, at least, the Faustian type of the magician who is also a great astrologer, alchemist, deamonologist and physician, was recognized. In his sphere, he was not unlike the 'complete' scientist trained in the Aristotelian tradition.

THE SORCERER'S APPRENTICESHIP

In Lucian's *Lovers of Lies* (34–46), Pancrates of Memphis, a 'holy scribe and an extraordinary scholar who knew everything that Egypt could teach' tells his travelling companions how he became a sorcerer. He spent twenty-three years in secret, subterranean chambers where Isis herself instructed him in the arts of magic. Lucian must always be taken with more than a grain of salt, but the *adyta* of Egyptian temples are mentioned elsewhere, for instance in the stories rejected by Arnobius, *Against the Gentiles* 43.1, that Jesus, while living in Egypt, had learned the names of 'powerful angels' (i.e. daemons) in the secret rooms of Egyptian temples. Long before Jesus, Pythagoras was supposed to have spent some time underground in Egypt, where the 'Mother' shared her knowledge with him. This tradition may reflect an initiation rite involving a descent into the land of the dead (Jones, 1986: 48–50).

One should note, perhaps, that magic, like poetry and music, or any art, was considered a gift of the gods. Apollonius of Tyana was chosen by Asclepius to spend three years in his sanctuary at Aigai in Cilicia where higher truths were revealed to him in dreams.

The apocryphal *Confession* of Cyprian (iii AD) who started out as a magician and rhetor, speaks of a training period of ten years with the priests of Memphis. He was also initiated into a number of mystery cults.

The encounter with a deity, the revelation of arcane knowledge does not always take place underground; it may also happen on the top of a mountain. The experience itself is often described as a *mysterion* or a *telete*, i.e. an initiation (Graf, 1994a: 107–37). We learn from Pliny (*Natural History* 30.16) that the Emperor, Nero, was initiated by an authentic sorcerer, the Armenian Tiridates, 'through magical banquets', but we are not told what these banquets were. Sorcerers sometimes ate figurines that they had made with flour and smoked with incense (Graf, 1994a: 125), but in this case, the sorcerer, perhaps, conjured up tables laden with food and wine (Origen, *Against Celsus* 1.68; Philostratus, *Life of Apollonius* 3.27).

An essential part of the magician's training consisted in acquiring a *paredros*, i.e. an 'assistant' (daemon). This acquisition is a step towards complete initiation, and we find instructions in *Papyri Graecae Magicae (PGM)* 1.1–42.

A period of training, possibly a ritual of initiation, is implied in a story told by Jerome in the *Life of Saint Hilarion* 12.10. A young man fell in love with a 'Virgin of God'. Obviously she had to reject him. Thereupon he devoted himself to the study of magic at the temple of Asclepius in Memphis. After only one year he returned and buried under the threshold of the young woman, among other things, a copper sheet with 'monstrous figurines' sculpted onto it. The young woman promptly loses her mind, rips her headdress off, gets into a state of trance and calls the name of her lover (cf. Goodyear on Tacitus; Goodyear, 1981: 409–11).

In the ancient world there were at all times professional sorcerers of all types, at all levels. The *PGM* and the Neoplatonist theurgists represent, in my opinion, the most advanced, the most scholarly and sophisticated type, the product of a long tradition transmitted through several ancient civilizations, possible only in the great melting pot of Egypt. But the distant ancestor of this sophisticated Greco-Egyptian *magos* is still the humble, despised travelling *shaman* we have identified in Heraclitus and Plato.

In Athens, in Rome and elsewhere, archaeologists have unearthed caches of curse-tablets, sometimes written by the same hand. These were obviously the working materials of professionals, ready to be used. Some of these professionals probably worked for lawyers whose clients were desperate to win their case. A sorcerer also might collaborate with a politician who was eager to get elected, or with the supporters of certain athletes or charioteers who wanted their favorite to win (no doubt having bet large sums on his victory).

In his introduction to the *PGM*, H. D. Betz has sketched (1992: xlvi) two different types of magicians. One may be associated with sanctuaries of Egyptian and Greek deities. We may see him as a resident member of the temple priesthood (with easy access to the temple library and the archives, I would add). On the other hand, we see the wandering practitioner for whom the gods from various cults gradually merged, and 'as their natures became blurred, . . . often changed into completely different deities.'

Anyone who is trying to define what type of sorcerer emerges from the scrolls known as the *Papyri Graecae Magicae* could hardly improve on three succinct paragraphs in H. D. Betz' Introduction (1992: xlvii):

> Applying his craft, the magician could give people the feeling that he could make things work in a world where nothing seemed to work the way it used to. He had handbooks of magic which contained the condensed wisdom of the past, wisdom made effective to solve the problems of the present.
>
> The magician claimed to know and understand the traditions of various religions. While other people could no longer make sense of the old religions, he was able to. He knew the code words needed to communicate with the gods, the demons and the dead. He could tap, regulate and manipulate the invisible energies. He was a problem solver who had remedies for a thousand petty troubles plaguing mankind: everything from migraine to runny nose to bedbugs to horse races, and, of course, all the troubles of love and money.
>
> In short, it was this kind of world in which the magician served as power and communications expert, crisis manager, miracle healer and inflicter of damages, an all-purpose therapist and agent of worried, troubled, and troublesome souls.

This is an excellent assessment, and it explains the feeling of power that we sense in these texts. One might add that the magician must have derived some of his strength – by a kind of bio-feedback – from his clients. He was not only in close contact with gods, he was also in close contact with people. This makes him a kind of intermediary, something priestlike, and this awareness is clearly present in the texts.

The scribes of the *PGM* are quite educated. Some of them were obviously trained scholars. At least five scrolls come from the library of an Egyptian specialist who was fluent in Coptic as well as in Greek and had a deep interest in theology as well as magic. H. D. Betz points out in his Introduction to the *PGM* (1992: xlii–iii) that although the person who collected the Anastasi papyri remains shadowy, comparable figures are known from later Egyptian literature. He draws attention to Prince Khamwas, the fourth son of King Ramses II and high priest of Ptah in Memphis, and apparently also a great magician and theurgist, a legendary figure who belongs to the *Stories of the High Priests of Memphis*, published by Francis Llewellyn Griffith. What is said of him (Betz quotes from volume III of Miriam Lichtheim's *Ancient Egyptian Literature*) could apply to some scribes or editors or collectors of the *PGM*:

> Prince Kham . . . was a very learned scribe and magician who spent his time in the study of ancient . . . books. One day he was told of the existence of a book of magic written by the god Thoth himself and kept in the tomb of a prince named . . . Na-nefer-ka-ptah . . . who lived in the distant past and was buried somewhere in the vast necropolis of Memphis. After a long search, Prince Khamwas . . . found the tomb . . . and entered it. He saw the magic book, which radiated a strong light and tried to seize it. But the spirits of [the dead prince and his wife] . . . rose up to defend their cherished possession . . .

CIRCE

The first magical operation recorded in Greek is found in Book 10 of the *Odyssey*. It is one of many adventures that the hero of the epic had to endure on his way back from Troy. The epic was probably composed in the eighth century BC, but it reflects the world of the Heroic Age which coincided roughly with the second half of the second millennium BC. Homer, in other words, is writing about events that were supposed to have taken place about five hundred years before he was born. He works from oral tradition – folk tales, myths, legends and, perhaps, short folk ballads that were already in verse form. The witch-like character, Circe, is found in folk tales of many cultures. Circe's magic involves the use of a wand, and Odysseus protects himself against her by a magical herb called *moly* which has been revealed to him by the god, Hermes. Several requisites of magic are here combined: A mysterious tool that looks like a stick but is obviously endowed with special powers; an herb that is not easy to find; a god who reveals to one of his favorites a secret that will save him. Thus at the beginning of recorded Greek literature we have already three ingredients that are typical for magical operations.

Circe is a beautiful woman, a seductress and temptress like Calypso, not at all the stereotypical old hag. It is not clear why she wants to change Odysseus and his companions into swine; perhaps, because she has a very low opinion of men.

Circe is the daughter of the Sun, one of the Titans, just as Medea is the granddaughter of the Sun. The Titans represent an earlier dynasty of gods, vanquished by the Olympians. So she is no ordinary witch. Not only can she transform people into animals (and give them back their human shape), she can also predict the future. Through her predictions and instructions, Odysseus is able to proceed on his voyage and carry out the necromantic scene described in Book 11 of the epic.

Odysseus confronts a great sorceress on her own territory. She accomplishes her magic by mixing a drug into a special cheese mixture that she serves Odysseus' companions, and by touching them with her wand. Here we see the typical *modus operandi* of the witch, but no chant, no spells are mentioned, just a direct order. In mythological terms, Circe may be a minor goddess, a survivor from an earlier generation of gods and removed, after the victory of the Olympians, to a distant island, like Kronos. There she is no danger to the world at large, only to those who are bold enough to visit her little realm.

ODYSSEUS IN THE LAND OF THE DEAD

The earliest extant necromantic ceremony is described in Book 11 of Homer's *Odyssey*. It is one of the models for Aeneas' descent to the underworld in Book 6 of Vergil's *Aeneid* and the magical operations of the witch, Erictho, in Book 6 of Lucan's *Pharsalia*. Odysseus is not a 'professional', but he follows the instructions of Circe.

He has to dig a ditch – apparently not a very deep one – which serves as an access to Hades. Around it he pours libations – milk, honey, wine and the blood of a black ram. The ghosts are eager to drink in order to regain, at least for a short time, some semblance of life. Tiresias, the seer, appears and tells Odysseus what he wants to know, or at least part of it. He is still a seer, even in Hades, and the way he speaks seems to indicate that Odysseus, too, has descended to Hades. This is strange, for he has been standing, if we read the text closely, near the pit. Perhaps we must assume that, by magical substitution, the pit represents the underworld. Through magic, Odysseus descends symbolically, or, possibly, part of his being actually descends while his body remains above.

In the end, Homer's Odysseus, like Goethe's Faust, is granted visions of the beautiful heroines of Greek myth whom he could not have known on earth, because they died long before his time. Here we may detect Homer's sense of humor: his hero, who was so strongly attracted to live women, is allowed to enjoy, as a special privilege, at least a glimpse of some celebrated beauties of the past.

MEDEA

Medea is one of the main characters of the *Argonautica* by Apollonius of Rhodes, an epic poet of the third century BC. She fell in love with Jason, the leader of the Argonauts, betrayed her own people and helped the Greeks obtain the Golden Fleece. On the way back from the Black Sea, she used her magic again to save them, notably in an episode which is told in 4.1635–90. The Greek heroes wish to land on the island of Crete, but its shores are patrolled by a monster called Talos, 'a bronze giant who broke off lumps of rock to hurl at them.' This colossus is introduced by the poet as a leftover of the Bronze Age, and he naturally terrifies the Argonauts (great heroes though they are). They would have rowed away, though they were exhausted, had Medea not come to their rescue.

It is obviously time for her magic, and this quasi-magical monster is a real challenge. But she knows that she will be able to destroy Talos, unless there is immortal life in him – that is, unless he is a god. A mere product of magic can be destroyed by countermagic.

The text describes the struggle between Medea and the bronze giant. She wins, because she can control and concentrate the powers of evil in and around her and direct them towards the enemy, so that he is literally knocked over. Medea works herself into a state of trance during which her hatred becomes a deadly weapon, and the 'images of death' she conjures up in her mind assume a reality all their own. This is, perhaps, the most explicit description of the power of the evil eye and the effects of black magic in all of ancient literature. The poet professes to be shocked by the mere thought that someone can be hurt at a distance, not only by an arrow, but by an invisible magical power. Whether the poet himself believed in this power or not, most of his contemporaries did, and his whole epic is actually a mine of information for folklore and so-called superstitions.

Medea may be in the same class as Circe. Later ages labelled her as a witch, but she may be a minor goddess or the priestess of a goddess from a distant age, a foreign civilization. Ovid was fascinated by Medea. Unfortunately, we no longer have the celebrated tragedy, supposed to be his greatest work, but we have a substantial episode in his epic, the *Metamorphoses* (7.179–293) which may give us, along with Seneca's *Medea*, at least an idea of the lost play. In this episode, Ovid stresses the daemonic nature of the legendary enchantress with a wealth of brilliant details that leave the reader breathless. She invokes the powers of darkness – the Night, Hecate, the Underworld – ,asserts her godlike power over all of nature and then mounts her chariot drawn by dragons, and flies through the air in search of precious herbs. The whole passage reads like an interpretation of some enigmatic cult-image left over from a half-forgotten civilization. This Medea has cosmic powers, and even the gods are astonished and jealous. Lucan (sect. 21) has exaggerated the *thaumata* in his Erictho episode but left out the more humorous features.

In his tragedies, Seneca (c. 5 BC – 65 AD) often deals with the themes of magic, necromancy and the like. From the dialogue between Deianira and her nurse (*Hercules on Mount Oeta* 449–472) we learn that it was not unusual for jealous wives to consult witches; as it turns out, most conveniently, the nurse is a witch herself. Deianira offers to pluck herbs in remote places, but she is not sure that her own magic will work in the case of her unfaithful husband, Heracles. There is an implication here, that a hero of his greatness cannot be influenced by magical means, just as a philosopher, according to Plotinus, is immune. In the end he is overcome by a deadly poison that Deianira has given him, believing it to be a potent love charm.

When we read Seneca's *Medea*, we notice how the image of Medea has changed in the three centuries since Apollonius wrote his epic. Her invocations and incantations are no longer left to the reader's imagination: they are spelled out in detail. Her power of hating which she can switch on and off, so to speak, is still the dominant theme, but Medea now has a regular cabinet of horrors from which to select the most efficient engines of destruction. Her magic now involves the whole universe; she even claims that she can force down the constellation of the Snake.

The magical papyri illustrate the sense of power that fills the operator during the course of his ritual. Alchemistic texts describe a similar experience. In fact, such texts seem to be designed to build up this very sense of power or to reinforce it. Seneca probably knew similar documents, but he gave them a fine rhetorical structure, a literary polish of which the professional magicians were, as a rule, not capable. Like Horace in his Canidia poems, he endows the possibilities of magic with a terrifying reality. Whether these plays were actually performed on a stage or simply recited, they must have shocked a contemporary audience, and shock, *ekplexis*, was thought to have therapeutic value.

In his *Medea*, Seneca presents the heroine as a witch whose powers have no limits. Two scenes (6–23 and 670–843) are typical. In the first she invokes various deities in order to curse her enemies. Like Deianira, like Dido, she feels abandoned and betrayed by the man she loved, and she is determined to hurt him as deeply as she can. What distinguishes her from these other heroines is the fact that she is a professional witch, not just an amateur. The second passage must have been one of the models for Lucan's witchcraft scene in Book 6 of the *Pharsalia*. Here, Medea invokes the powers of the underworld while she cooks in her cauldron all kinds of magical herbs. Much of both scenes is sheer rhetoric, designed to create a mood of fear and awe. To us it is just one rather tedious detail after another, but contemporary audiences or readers probably experienced the kind of *frisson* that one gets nowadays from horror movies.

DEIANIRA'S INVOLUNTARY BLACK MAGIC

Heracles' death through a sort of love magic that went wrong was dramatized by Sophocles in *The women of Trachis* and by Seneca (if the play is genuine) in *Heracles on Mount Oeta*. The myth itself embodies the ancient belief − or the experience − that certain drugs are destructive, even if they are absorbed by the skin rather than ingested.

Deianira had been carried across a river by the Centaur, Nessus, who provided this service to travellers. When he attempted to make love to her in midstream, Heracles shot and killed him from the other side with his poisoned arrows. The dying Centaur persuaded Deianira to preserve some of his blood, telling her that it was a potent love charm, to be used when she felt that Heracles was unfaithful to her. This happens, and she impregnates a new garment with the Centaur's poisonous blood. When her husband puts it on, he dies a slow and painful death, but according to another version, he cannot die and has to burn himself on a gigantic pyre constructed on Mount Oeta. Perhaps Vergil had this scene in mind when he described Dido's suicide on top of a pyre (sect. 15).

Deianira's conversation with her nurse reveals the fact that the old woman is a witch who knows that wives often pull their marriages together by magical arts and prayers. Deianira has her doubts whether this will work in the case of her husband, a hero of superhuman stature.

THE HELLENIZED MAGI

J. Bidez and F. Cumont have collected in two volumes entitled *Les mages hellénisés* (Paris, 1938) the testimonies concerning three semi–legendary figures, Zoroastres, Hystaspes and Ostanes. They were Persians, but they seem to have played a major role in the transmission of magical doctrines and practices from the East to the West. Zoroastres was probably born shortly after 600 BC. He was called to the religious life at the age of thirty after fasting and praying in the desert (typical of the apprenticeship of the *shaman*), and became a fierce opponent of the ruling religion of Mithras with its sacrifice of the bull and its narcotic Haoma drug. He had to flee and found a refuge near Vishtaspa (Hystaspes) of Chorasmia, who listened to his message and converted with his whole court. Zoroastres was essentially the prophet of a new religion, but his doctrine and the cult of fire that he introduced were misunderstood as magic in the West.

The 'Oracles of Hystaspes' probably composed by a later 'Hellenized *magos*', are a kind of apocalypse.

Ostanes (Vishtana) was a religious adviser to King Xerxes and accompanied him on his disastrous campaign against the Greeks. He is supposed to have introduced the occult sciences of Persia into Greece. Apuleius mentions him as a great magician next to Carmendas, Damigeron and – Moses. Many writings were attributed to Ostanes: on the occult forces of animals, plants and stones; on alchemy; on medical prescriptions. He is said to have taught Democritus who, in turn, is said to have taught a more shadowy figure, Bolus of Mendes in Egypt. These Persian *magoi* live on somehow in the 'three wise men' from the Orient who come to pay their tribute to Jesus. They are priests or kings or both, and astrologers as well.

MOSES THE MAGICIAN

According to *Acts* 7:22, Moses had been 'taught the whole wisdom of the Egyptians, and he was powerful in words and in deeds.' This probably means that, among other things, Moses was in the eyes of the early Christians (and the Jews; Philo, *Life of Moses* 1.5) a great magician in the Egyptian style (Schürer, 1901–09: ii, 343ff.). Having lived in Egypt for a long time, it was assumed that he was initiated into the art of Pharaoh's magicians. The same story circulated about Jesus among Jewish opponents.

An amulet from Acrae on Sicily tells how Moses became *physikos* (i.e. a 'magician'; cf. Plotinus, *Enneades* 4.4), after having climbed the Sacred Mountain (*IG* XIV 2413, 17; Graf, 1994a: 15–16; 283, nn. 25, 26).

According to Pliny (*Natural History* 30.11) Moses founded a 'sect of magic', *magices factio*, of which 'Iannes' and 'Iotapes' were also members. Pliny probably found these names in Hermippus, the Peripatetic philosopher, who was a student of Callimachus'. The whole idea must be ultimately based on the confrontation between the Jewish leaders, Moses and Aaron on the one side and the Egyptian magicians on the other, as told in *Exodus* 7: 8; 8:15. For an ancient reader – even for a philosopher – Moses was performing magic of the same sort as the Egyptians, but his magic was better, because he was serving God.

The miracles performed by Moses in his contest with the Egyptian wizards (*Exodus* 7) have been called magical in nature, but for Josephus (*Antiquitates Judaicae* 2.284 ff.) they are proof of divine authenticity. He makes Moses say that the deeds performed by him are superior to the magical arts of the Egyptians, because things divine are superior to things human.

Moses' performance is better than that of the Egyptians, because it is not magic for effect or for profit, but a kind of miracle to demonstrate that his god is superior to their gods. This makes it legitimate.

The Eighth Book of Moses is a magical text found on the Leiden Papyrus. There is a magical formula (*PGM* V 109) in which the sorcerer claims to be Moses (as he may claim to be Adam or even God: Harrauer, 1987: 32, 44, 79n.83).

The name of God, spoken by Moses, kills an Egyptian, and, inscribed on his staff, divides the waters of the Red Sea.

SOLOMON THE SORCERER

The *Testament of Solomon* is a curious document written in Greek, but based on a Jewish text. The Greek version was probably composed in the early third century AD. It is an amazing combination of 'folktales and a magician's *vademecum*', as Chester Charlton McCown (in his edition, Leipzig, 1922, p. 1) has pointed out. In McCown's opinion, its magical formulae and recipes relate it to the execration tablets, the amulets and the Greek Magical Papyri. He has identified (pp. 43–51) the chief ideas of this document, i.e. daemonology, astrology, angelology, magic and medicine.

Solomon is depicted on medallions as a rider on horseback, piercing with his lance a half-naked woman lying on the ground. The woman may originally have represented a Lilith. These medallions were worn as phylacteries (Alexander, 1986).

The *Testament of Solomon* deserves the most careful study, because, in a sense, it adds a dimension to the *PGM*. It shows the magician who calls himself King Solomon in action and gives us a good idea of his spritual world which is rather complex. This magician was not a simple charlatan, travelling through the cities of the Near East: He was a scholar, a missionary and a kind of mystic, more like an Egyptian occultist.

The much better known *Wisdom of Solomon*, considered apocryphal by Jews and Protestants, was probably composed in the first century BC (Winston, 1979: 172–3). The author of this book was familiar with Middle Platonism and belonged, perhaps, to the circle of Philo of Alexandria.

In it Solomon says:

God . . . gave me true knowledge of things, as they are; an understanding of the structure of the world and the way in which elements work, the beginning and the end of eras and what lays in-between . . . the cycles of the years and the constellations . . . the thoughts of men . . . the powers of spirits . . . the virtues of roots . . . I learned it all, secret or manifest.

Clearly, Solomon is pictured as the greatest scientist, but also as the greatest occultist, of his time: he has studied astrology, plant magic, daemonology, divination but also *ta physika*, 'natural science'. He reminds one of Bolus of Mendes, the disciple of Democritus.

Some translators obscure these facts; they write, e.g., 'the power of the winds', when the context shows that daemons are meant. Josephus certainly understood the passage in this way. He comments (*Antiquitates Judaicae* 8.45): 'God gave him (Solomon) knowledge of the art that is used against daemons, in order to heal and benefit men.' He specifically adds that Salomon was a great exorcist and left instructions on how to perform this kind of healing. This could mean, among other things, that in Josephus' time, a magical text existed which taught how to exorcise daemons in the name of Solomon.

ORPHEUS, PYTHAGORAS AND EMPEDOCLES

During the archaic age of Greece, a number of men with supernatural abilities emerge who cannot be labeled or classified precisely, though they are often described as – among other things – sorcerers. They concern the historian of philosophy and science as well as the student of Greek religion.

In his important book *The Greeks and the Irrational* (1951), E. R. Dodds suggested for them the term *shaman* which has won approval, for they certainly look like highly sophisticated medicine-men of a specifically Greek type. Thanks to anthropological research we know a great deal about *shamans* of other cultures, but it is not clear to what extent we may apply this knowledge to the ancient Greeks. Was animism, was ancestor worship involved? Was a rigorous training period, harsh asceticism required? Probably. One hears about periods of strict isolation from the community, about fasting and praying, about monotonous exercises such as whirling that leads to trance, about the use of drugs. We do not have this kind of specific information about the early Greek *shamans*, but they probably used some of the same techniques but kept them secret or passed them on to their favorite disciples.

Perhaps the three most striking *magoi* between Homer and the Hellenistic period when magic became a kind of applied science were Orpheus, Pythagoras and Empedocles. All three have similar features, but each has an identity of his own. Orpheus is a largely mythical figure, but Orphism, the movement he founded, is attested since the sixth century BC in various parts of the Greek world.

Orpheus and Pythagoras are associated with important religious and philosophical schools, while Empedocles remains a rather solitary phenomenon, though he did have followers and the medical school which he is said to have founded in Sicily flourished for a long time. All three are known to have expressed their ideas in poetry and prose, and at some point many of their words must have been written down, but few of their original writings are extant; what we have are fragments or later substitutions and elaborations.

Nevertheless, the similarities between these three figures are impressive enough to suggest the existence, in Greek civilization, of a type of sage and miracle-worker who was also an original thinker and a great teacher, someone in touch with beings of a higher order, someone who offered a new theory to explain the universe and the human soul – macrocosm and microcosm – someone who may also have been a musician and a poet. In all three instances we face the timeless image of the *shaman*, but superimposed, as it were, on a great Greek philosopher, teacher, poet or priestlike figure.

Shaman is a useful term because it is more neutral than *magos* or *thaumaturge* or 'sorcerer', but we will use these terms as synonyms in this section. A *shaman*, as Dodds has written, is a 'psychically unstable person' who has received a call to the religious (or philosophic) life, who undergoes ascetic discipline (fasting, long periods of prayer in solitude) and acquires supernatural powers. He can heal the sick, understands the language of animals or seemingly inanimate objects, can be at different places at the the same time, and so on. Of course, these are modern terms, but they seem to fit the traditional *imago*.

They fit Orpheus, Pythagoras, Empedocles and a number of others – including Apollonius of Tyana, who appears much later, at the time of Jesus Christ, as a kind of new Pythagoras – quite well. Dodds has been able to show, in particular, that tradition has given Orpheus the main characteristics of the *shaman*: He is a poet, *magos*, oracle-giver, prophet and religious teacher. With his music – a kind of magical charm in itself – he is able to summon birds, soothe wild animals, and even make trees follow him, as he sings and plays on his instrument. Like *shamans* in other cultures, he descends alive into the realm of the dead and returns to life in this world. His magical self lives on as a singing head that continues giving oracles for many years after his death which is, therefore, no ordinary death at all.

The attribution of magical powers to Pythagoras has been discarded by many historians of Greek philosophy, but such scholars as W. Burkert are willing to accept it as part of the genuine tradition (Burkert, 1972: 162ff). Pythagoras had a golden thigh; he was greeted by rivers with a resounding 'Hail, Pythagoras!'; he had the gift of prophecy; he could be at different places at the same time. Like Orpheus, he had power over animals and in turn respected them to the degree that he preached a strict vegetarianism. All these characteristics indicate that Pythagoras was no ordinary human being: he was a 'divine man', *theios aner*, or a *shaman*, to use the more objective term.

Empedocles ascribed to himself the powers to heal the sick and rejuvenate the old (Medea did that sort of thing, according to myth); he also claimed that he could predict the weather and influence it, and he was able to summon the dead. It is evident that the people of Agrigentum – at least for a while – thought of him as a miracle worker. How could he also be a great thinker and scientist? Did he start as a magician who lost his nerve and took to natural science, or was he a philosopher who later converted to a form of Orphism? This is how Dodds, amusingly, states the problem we face, but he adds, in a more serious manner, that we should not ask such questions, for Empedocles was a *shaman*, a combination of teacher, poet, scientist and *magos*. To him and to his admirers there was clearly no contradiction between these various skills, as there is to us. After the death of Empedocles, the scale and variety of these unusual gifts in certain individuals seem to shrink, and *shamanism* becomes specialized, so to speak. One either has the gift of healing or the gift of prophecy, but no longer the universal range of supernatural powers with which these early *shamans* were blessed. Compared to the great thaumaturges of archaic Greece, the later practitioners of one occult science or another seem like *shamans* who have lost the full range of their original powers. If we look at later figures, such as Simon Magus, Apollonius of Tyana and Alexander of Abonuteichos, their lives and legends clearly reflect the great miracleworkers of the distant past, but there is something artificial, fabricated, second-hand about them.

Through his legend and his doctrine, Pythagoras had great influence on Platonism, and Plato himself refers to seers and sorcerers. In his *Laws* (933A–E) he takes healers, prophets and practitioners of magic for granted. They had to be reckoned with and controlled by law. But one does not need to be afraid of them, Plato adds: 'Their powers are real, but they themselves represent a rather low form of life.'

NECTANEBUS

An extraordinary episode figures in the Alexander Romance attributed to Callisthenes (c. 370–327 BC), but probably composed in the fourth century AD. The Egyptian Pharaoh Nectanebus who claims to be the real father of Alexander the Great is a formidable magician and astrologer. In order to seduce Olympias, the wife of Philip of Macedon, he picks certain plants which will induce dreams and extracts their juices. Then he shapes a wax figure of a woman and writes the name Olympias on it. He also lights lamps and pours out the juice he prepared, and with secret oaths he invokes the 'spirits appointed to perform this function', so that Olympias may have a vision of the god, Ammon, embracing her. This whole magical operation will enable the Pharaoh to pose as the god, Ammon, and take his place in Olympias' royal bed, thus fathering Alexander the Great.

THE AMATEUR WITCH OF THEOCRITUS

Theocritus (c. 310–c. 250 BC) is mainly known as a pastoral poet, but he composed several 'idylls', describing everyday life in Alexandria, the capital of Hellenistic Egypt. One of these, No. 2 in modern editions, has the traditional title *Pharmakeutriai*, i.e. 'The Witches': the masculine equivalent would be *pharmakeutai*, 'sorcerers'. Both nouns are derived from *pharmakon*, 'drug', 'poison', 'spell', 'remedy'. We do not know whether the poet himself or an ancient editor gave the poem this title, but it is appropriate, even though the two women participating in the magical rites are not professionals.

The text is a long monologue that furnishes all the circumstances the reader needs to know. Simaetha, a young Greek woman, is in love with a young athlete. It was love at first sight, and for a short time they were very happy together. But now, since he has not shown himself at her house for eleven days, she has decided to draw him back by magical means, threatening more powerful measures if this does not work. She has already consulted some professionals, but without success: 'Did I skip the house of any old woman who knows magical songs?' Apparently, if the matter was serious, it was necessary to see as many practitioners as possible, just as you saw more than one physician and prayed in many temples, if you were very sick.

Only then, according to the 'do-it-yourself' principle, she sets up, with a few fairly simple prerequisites, a magical operation in or near her own house. The ingredients she uses are barley groats, bay leaves, bran, wax, liquids (wine, milk, or water) for libations, furthermore coltsfoot (an herb) and pulverized lizard. Her tools are a magical wheel, a bull-roarer, and a bronze gong. She has also kept a fringe from her lover's cloak – any object belonging to a person represents that person – and she shreds it and throws it into the flames. Moreover, she addresses various spells and incantations to the full moon in the sky and to Hecate in the underworld.

NIGIDIUS FIGULUS, MYSTERY MAN

We now meet a totally different sort of person. Nigidius Figulus was a prominent figure in Rome, a scholar, a prolific author and an occultist. He was a friend of Cicero's and shared some of Varro's interests. He dealt with Roman religion and Etruscan lore. If he could be described as a 'Pythagorean and *magos*' he would appear to be a Roman version of Apollonius of Tyana and Anaxilaus of Larissa (exiled from Italy in 28 BC). Apparently, he did not start any kind of movement, but he was credited with supernatural powers (telepathy, clairvoyance) and he wrote extensively on meteorology, astrology, anthropology, zoology and other subjects. Pliny the Elder used him as a source, but we have only meager remains of his many works; therefore, he is, for us, a mystery man in many ways, a man who lived on different levels, a man who might have become a thaumaturge in the Middle East, but not in Rome.

VERGIL'S WITCH

Vergil's 8th *Eclogue* is, in part, an adaptation of Theocritus' 2nd *Idyll*. It stays close to the original in most details and does not reveal any typical Italic witchcraft, it seems. The magical wheel and the bull-roarer of Theocritus are replaced by two dolls, one made of clay, the other of wax. Vergil also introduces the werewolf theme: Moeris, a local sorcerer who has sold Simaetha, the amateur witch, certain powerful herbs, can transform himself into a wolf.

Poems like these are not meant to be factual reports of rituals. Rather, they create an atmosphere that makes the reader understand the meaning of such ceremonies. In a sense, the poetry provides a kind of magic, too.

DIDO, THE TRAGIC QUEEN

The hero of Vergil's epic has landed on the coast of North Africa, where he meets Queen Dido, who has begun to build a new city, Carthage. She is not a witch but rather resembles an oriental fairy tale queen with a tragic past. She falls in love with Aeneas and invites him to stay as her prince consort. In a sense she is modelled on Circe. One is also reminded of the encounter of Jason and Medea in Apollonius' *Argonautica*. In these legends, a travelling hero with a mission meets a beautiful exotic woman who is potentially dangerous, although kind and hospitable, as long as her love for the hero lasts.

When Aeneas leaves Dido because Fate demands that he found an empire of his own, Dido's love turns to hate (*Aeneid* 4). Detemined to destroy her faithless lover and herself, she stages a complex magical rite, although she really despises magic. She builds a gigantic pyre in the main courtyard of her palace and prepares, with the assistance of a famous priestess–witch, an elaborate sacrifice to the powers of the underworld.

When she realizes that no love-magic can bring Aeneas back to her, she kills herself in despair, giving an ultimate emphasis of doom to her curse.

It was commonly believed that suicides, murder victims, men killed in battle – in short, those who died before their time – could unleash enormous powers of destruction at the moment of their death.

Dido, however, did not destroy Aeneas who, like Odysseus, was protected by his own gods and reached the coast of Italy safely after many other adventures. Her curse lingered on through the centuries and conjured up an avenger, Hannibal, who almost crushed Rome, but once again, Rome's gods prevented the worst from happening.

In her last wish to hurt Aeneas – and Rome – Dido is more like Medea than Circe. But she also resembles Cleopatra, the Queen of Egypt, who, in Vergil's lifetime, had love affairs with two Romans: Julius Caesar and Mark Antony. Cleopatra's power over these two men could easily be explained as witchcraft, an art which she might have learned from Egyptian priests. But she also died a tragic death by suicide, when her armed forces were defeated by Rome. Thus Dido is a very complex figure, combining features of at least two heroines of Greek myth and one historical figure.

CANIDIA, THE LOVE-WITCH

Canidia appears in Horace's poem more than once. She seems to have been a real person, a pharmacist or perfume-maker by the name of Grattidia, but for the poet, she is an evil witch. His fifth *Epode* is remarkable, because a child is about to be murdered by witches for magical purposes. Led by Canidia, they have kidnapped a Roman boy of noble birth and buried him up to his chin in the ground. Close to his head they have placed a dish of food which he cannot reach, to stimulate his appetite. They intend to starve him to death and then remove his liver, which, they believe, will grow bigger because of his growing hunger. In vain does the boy plead with the hags: they need his liver, in order to brew an especially potent love potion, perhaps designed to win the poet himself. The intended victim is a man called Varus, and since he has not responded to Canidia's spells and brews, she assumes that he is protected by some counter-magic given to him by a redoubtable rival of hers. The boy, realizing that he does not have a chance, directs a terrible curse against the witches, and this curse is a form of magic too, for the spirits of those who die before their time and those who die a violent death can turn into daemons of vengeance.

Satire 1.8 deals with witchcraft in a more humorous vein. Here, a wooden statue of the god Priapus is speaking. This statue has been placed in a beautiful park on the Esquiline in Rome as a threat to thieves and birds. But this park was once a cemetery for the poor, and at night, in the light of the moon, witches, again led by Canidia, still haunt the place, digging for human bones or calling up the shades of the dead for necromantic purposes. They also perform other kinds of magic, and their rituals are so revolting that even Priapus – who is not a very refined god – loses his nerve and lets out a resounding fart. This works like a charm: the witches run away screaming; one of them loses her wig, the other her false teeth.

One might say that Horace is debunking the witchcraft scene. It was real: there were sorcerers and witches, and people were afraid of them. But Horace seems to say that they are mainly weird and grotesque and ineffectual in the end, so ordinary citizens should not be afraid of them or pay them money for their services. This was exactly what Augustus' legislation intended, though we do not understand its consequences in detail. But it seems that Horace contributed his share to the Imperial message.

WITCHES IN THE LATIN LOVE ELEGY

Propertius, Tibullus and Ovid give us glimpses of the Roman demimonde. The ladies they love consult witches, and the poets, according to their mood, take magic seriously or make it look slightly ludicrous. While the practitioners of the *PGM* seem to be mostly male, those we get to know through the elegiac poets of the Augustan age, are all female, with the exception of the astrologer, Horus, of Propertius 4.1, who may be an occultist in the style of Nigidius Figulus.

Propertius gives us, in 4.5, the satirical portrait of a witch called Acanthis who is also a bawd. These women can make a man impotent (Tibullus 1.5.49–42; Ovid, *Amores* 3.7.27–36), but they can also enhance his potency (cf. Petronius, *Satyricon* 131). A theme that appears in many variations is the contrast between 'internal' and 'external' magic. A woman who is truly beautiful and talented has the 'internal' magic that charms men, while those who are less fortunate must resort to the powers of witches. Once, Propertius' mistress is dangerously ill, and a witch is summoned to her bedside, after the gods have not responded and the physicians – presumably – did not leave much hope (2, 28). Finally the poet prays to Jupiter once more, and Cynthia recovers. Tibullus 1.2.39–64 is also a remarkable testimony (Luck, 1962: 45–7).

JESUS OF NAZARETH

Jesus has been called a 'magician', both in the past by some Jews and some gentiles and, more recently, by Morton Smith in a book that created a certain sensation (*Jesus the Magician*, 1978). From an outsider's point of view, to be sure, Jesus may have looked like the typical miracle-worker. He exorcised daemons, he healed the sick, he raised Lazarus from the dead, he predicted future events. On the other hand, apart from walking on waves, he never performed the kind of ostentatious magic that Moses and Aaron performed when they frustrated the magicians of Pharaoh. Neither did he practice necromancy.

Nevertheless, within three hundred years of his birth, he was accused of stealing the 'names of the angels of might' from Egyptian temples (Arnobius, *Against the Gentiles* 1.43). These 'angels of might' are probably mighty daemons who may be conjured up by pronouncing their names.

Jesus' life, as told in the Gospels, is coloured by certain features that have parallels elsewhere – he is of divine origin; his birth is of an unusual nature; he is in grave danger as an infant; he is initiated into his ministry by a precursor who yields before him; he has to face Satan, a great daemon representing the evil forces in this world and refuses to make a deal with him (i.e. he refuses to be just an ordinary magician), winning the upper hand in a trial of spiritual strength.

The important point seems to be this: Whenever Jesus is challenged to prove his divinity by performing the kind of magic that people seem to expect, he refuses to do so. He does perform 'magic' of a kind, but he does so out of compassion, not merely to impress the sceptics or score a point; in fact, he is sometimes rather impatient with those who require 'signs and wonders' in order to believe in him. It almost seems that magic 'flows' out of him, not as a conscious effort or the result of elaborate rituals, but simply because it is a power (*dynamis*) that he transmits. The power works when the patient and the bystander have faith in Jesus (*Luke* 8), but it also works when the patient is unaware of being healed (*Matthew* 8). Faith does matter, but it is not always a condition; faith helps create the miracle, but the miracle also generates faith.

It should also be noted that Jesus never claimed to perform miracles by himself; rather, he taught that his power came from the Father and was readily available, without complex rituals and spells. Moreover, Jesus did not accept any fees or gifts for what he did: He considered it part of his ministry to heal the sick, and he passed on his spiritual gifts to his disciples, without fee. The point of view of the early Christian Church is stated by Clement of Alexandria (*Stromateis* 6, 3). The pagans, he says, are wrong to reject the miracles recounted in the Gospels, for God is infinitely great and can easily cause miracles to be performed without any help from magical arts.

Matthew's report that Jesus was taken to Egypt as an infant was used by hostile sources to construe a sort of sorcerer's apprenticeship; according to one rabbinical version, he came back tattoed with spells. According to another rabbinical tradition, Jesus was 'mad', which probably means 'emotionally unstable', and this is one of the characteristics of the *shaman*. It could also mean that he was able to get into a state of trance, for instance, when receiving a vision. What a Christian would call the 'descent of the Spirit', an outsider might call 'possession by a daemon'. It has even been suggested that Jesus' tacit claim to status as the 'Son of God' is essentially a formula used in magical rites by the operator who identifies himself closely with the supernatural power he invokes.

A word of caution should be added here concerning these and similar theories, for that is all they are. Some of the material on which they are based comes from sources hostile to Jesus and the early Church. Superficial parallels from the magical papyri are of doubtful value, for they may already be influenced by stories circulating about Jesus.

The professional magicians were always eager to add to their repertory of formulas, rites and powerful names, especially if these seemed to work within the context of a new religious movement. To such professionals, Jesus may have appeared like a very successful fellow-magician from whom a great deal could be learned. This is more or less the attitude of Simon towards the Apostles. But the outsiders were incapable of understanding what was new and different in this religion, and they reduced it to their own level.

M. Goodman sees a difference between Greeks and Jews as far as illness and the healing process are concerned (Goodman, 1987: 100ff). The Greeks rely more on diet, drugs, baths, although they also employ magic. The Jews are inclined to attribute sickness to pollution and sin and resort more often to exorcism and magical rituals to heal patients. Jesus could be seen as a very successful, though not very typical Jewish healer. In *Acts* (8:9–13; 13:6–12; 16; 16–18; 19:13–19) we sense a certain animosity towards outside healers and magicians.

SIMON MAGUS

Simon is the name of a religious leader mentioned in *Acts* 8:9 ff and elsewhere, for example in the apocryphal *Acts of Peter*. He was active in Samaria at about the time of the Crucifixion, and his disciples called him 'the Power of God which is called the Great Power', but the Greek text is not altogether reliable, and the words 'which is called' may be an old interpolation in the manuscripts.

Simon was impressed by the Apostle Philip's cures and exorcisms and by the gift of the Spirit which came from the Apostles' laying on of hands. Consequently, he not only 'believed and was baptized', but he asked the Apostles to sell him their special gift so that he might practice it too. This is, of course, the typical attitude of the professional *magos*. To Simon, the specific charisma of this new religion is a kind of powerful magic that can be purchased, for a price, and he is prepared to pay the price, just as he must have paid for the kind of magic he had learned before. The sharp rebuke he draws from Peter shows the line that the early Church drew between itself and the old-fashioned practitioners of magic such as Simon who is flexible enough to take it in good grace.

It is difficult to label Simon, but he looks like a *magus* who, inspired by the example of Jesus and the Apostles, developed into a cult figure by borrowing from early Christianity (and from some pagan cults) whatever suited him. He may be called a practitioner of occult science (which he was supposed to have studied in Egypt) with Christlike aspirations.

Unlike Jesus, Simon uses daemons for his purposes, practices necromancy and even claims, according to the *Clementine Recognitiones* (2.15), to have created a human being. The text may be corrupt, but on the whole the meaning seems to be that Simon claimed to have invoked the soul of an innocent boy who had been murdered and ordered it to enter a new body that he had made from air. When people demand to see this *homunculus*, Simon answers that he has already made him disappear into air again.

The moment of truth comes when, according to the *Acts of Peter*, Simon and Peter challenge each other before the Emperor Nero in Rome. Like other confrontations between a mere magician and a true religious leader (cf. *Exodus* 7; *Acts* 13: 6–12), this is a contest of spiritual powers. Simon actually manages to fly through the air for a short time, but Peter breaks the spell and makes him crash to earth so badly that he breaks his leg and never recovers. His resurrection within three days, which he himself had predicted, provided he be buried alive, never takes place, 'because he was not the Christ', as Hippolytus (*Refutatio omnium haeresium* 6.20.3) notes sarcastically. According to him, Simon 'perverted many in Samaria by magical acts, but he was convicted and denounced by the Apostles.' At one point he sets up a religion of his own which borrows from Judaism, Christianity and some religions of Hellenistic paganism. His supreme deity may have been a mixture of Jahveh and Zeus (and perhaps Sabazius).

Like all *magi*, Simon is a great imitator; he wants to be like Christ, like the Apostles.

It was only natural that a provincial *magos* and thaumaturge would sooner or later appear in Rome. The *Acts of Peter* report that he performed a miracle there, in the absence of Paul. This detail is important, for as soon as Paul is present, Simon's magic does not work as well as before. He flies over a city gate in a shiny cloud, and people worship him as God or Christ. His 'tuneful voice' (cf. Alexander of Abonuteichos) makes an impression on many newly converted Christians, and some of them even turn against Paul, calling him a sorcerer and a deceiver. Very few remain steadfast and loyal. For the time being, Simon's 'incantation', his 'wickedness' triumph. These *Acts* are designed for entertainment, instruction and edification; they show what people expected a wizard to do.

In *Acts of Peter* we find an episode which is strangely reminiscent of a story told in Philostratus' *Life of Apollonius*. This could mean that Philostratus was not only familiar with the canonical Gospels and Acts but also with some *Apocrypha* (Palmer and More, 1936).

This particular episode is preceded by a miracle performed by Peter. The Apostle goes to the house of Marcellus who is Simon's host in Rome and tells the doorkeeper that he wishes to see Simon. The doorkeeper, however, has strict orders not to let Peter in – obviously, Simon is scared of him – whereupon Peter says very politely: 'You shall see a great and marvellous wonder.' Then he lets loose a large dog who had been tied with a massive chain. The dog asks Peter: 'You servant of the ineffable living God, what do you want me to do?' Peter dispatches him to summon Simon, the 'wicked man' and 'troubler of simple souls' which the dog does, lifting his forefeet. Simon and the simple souls who had listened to him were dumbfounded, and he 'lost his deceitful words.' Marcellus, Simon's host, who had, among other things, set up a statue to 'Simon, the young God' (i.e. Simon, the son of God?), now asks Peter for forgiveness and would have offered him cash (like Simon in *Acts*), had he not known that Peter strongly disapproved of such transactions. Peter gives him absolution and hugs him.

Now comes the episode reminiscent of a story in the *Life of Apollonius* (4.20). The dog finds Simon and delivers a message that goes beyond what Peter told him and involves Simon in a serious contest which is not specified. In ch. 5, the power-game, played by Peter, Simon and the dog, continues. It is the dog who denounces Simon – in the presence of his former admirer, Marcellus – as a 'cheat' and 'deceiver' and curses him as an enemy of Christ. The dog then runs away, followed by everybody, predicts another great contest between Simon and himself and a reward from God; finally, he collapses at Peter's feet and gives up his spirit. The crowd is amazed at the speaking dog but demands another 'sign' (i.e. miracle) so they can really believe him, because Simon had impressed them by his signs, too. The new signs Peter shows them are really feats of magic, but his magic is better than Simon's, just as Moses' magic was better than that of Pharaoh's sorcerers. And he does it in the name of Christ. One wonders whether Simon also invoked a sacred name as he performed his own 'magic'? Or did he do it in his own name, since he considered himself the 'true' son of God? All this is not told in so many words in this tantalizing text, but it is somehow suggested between the lines.

A smoked tuna-fish that Peter has thrown into a pond comes to life again and swims around, and people throw bread into the water for it. Clearly, this is no delusion, for the fish eats the bread. Hence, large crowds now follow Peter and listen to his words.

Marcellus berates Simon, has him thrown out of his house and beaten up by the servants. Pots full of filth are emptied over the head of the unmasked charlatan. But Simon is a tough customer. He runs to the house where Peter is staying and calls out: 'Here I am, Simon; so come down, Peter, and I will convict you of believing in a mere human being, a Jew, the son of a carpenter!'

This can only mean that, for Simon, as for other enemies or rivals of the early Church, Jesus is not the son of God, not the Messiah, but a Jew of humble origin. One is reminded of Jesus' saying that a prophet is despised in his own country (*Matthew* 13:57; *Mark* 6:4; *Luke* 4:24; *John* 4:44).

It is time for Peter to perform another miracle. He choses a baby held by his mother, and this baby, with the voice of a grown man, curses Simon, making it quite clear that God and Jesus Christ speak through him. After the dog, the babe from whose mouth comes the truth (cf. *Matthew* 21:16)! Simon is told to depart from Rome until the coming sabbath. He obeys, clearly not knowing what is happening to him. The woman, Peter and the other brethren glorify the Lord who has 'shown those things to men'.

In ch. 6, Jesus, smiling and clothed in a robe of splendor, appears to Peter in the night and tells him that through the 'signs' which he has performed in his name, many brethren have found their way back to him. But the battle is not yet won. There will be a 'trial by faith' on the coming sabbath, as predicted by the baby. Jesus will show himself to Peter when he asks for 'signs and miracles.' Then many will be converted to him in his name, for even though Simon will oppose Peter with the 'works of his father' (i.e. the Devil; cf. *John* 8:44; *Acts* 13:10), these works will be exposed as 'charms and illusions of magic'.

Peter reports how Simon did much harm by his 'incantation' in Judaea. Accompanied by 'two other like himself' (i.e. two other sorcerers) who were invisible to the household, he secretly entered the house of a rich lady by the name of Eubula, one of his followers. By means of a spell they robbed Eubula of her gold and vanished.

Peter fasts for three days and prays that this crime will come to light. In a vision, he sees two disciples and a naked boy who is bound. The boy offers him a loaf of wheat bread and tells him that he will see the 'wonderful works of God', if he holds out. The things stolen by Simon and 'the others' from the rich lady's house by 'magical arts' and by 'creating a delusion' will be sold by the crafty thieves to a goldsmith, a Christian sympathizer, whose name and address are furnished. Peter now goes to Eubula, informs her of his vision and then visits the goldsmith's workshop to give him specific instructions. Two suspicious characters trying to sell stolen objects (*inter alia*, a satyr in gold) are seized, brought before a magistrate and confess under torture that Simon had given them money (obviously, he thinks money can do everything) to commit the crime. Simon who is looking for them sees them bound with chains, realizes what has happened and runs away, while Eubula gives the property she recovered to the poor. And Marcellus, Simon's former host and patron, is anxious to purify his house, as if an evil daemon had dwelled there too long.

Peter's new contest with Simon is told in ch. 8. The Roman crowd (a fixture in all these miracle tales, the indispensable witnesses, the 'chorus') urges Peter to tell them who is (the true) God and what his (specific) greatness consists in – after they have seen what Simon has to offer. Simon starts off with denying (as he did before) that Jesus is divine. Clearly, the Christians now have to prove that Simon is not divine.

The Prefect sets a task for the two contestants. Simon is to kill a boy before everyone's eyes (and he does this by saying something into the boy's ear), and Peter is to bring him back to life again (which he does by telling the Prefect to shake the boy's hand). Next, he revives the dead son of a widow. The crowd cheers and praises Peter's God, the Savior, the Invisible. A third corpse is brought into the Forum, and Simon is challenged to revive it. He seems to be successful at first because of the devious techniques he uses, and the crowd is ready to burn Peter who keeps telling them that they are 'bewitched' – and, indeed, the dead man is unable to stand up which would be the requirement for a true miracle. (In the necromantic scene of Book 6 of Lucan's *Pharsalia*, the corpse does this most dramatically.) Now the crowd is all set to kill Simon, but Peter protects his enemy and performs the miracle for him in the name of Christ. From that same hour Peter is 'venerated as a god', and people bring him their sick so he can heal them.

As a *magos* or *thaumatourgos*, Simon boasts that he can throw himself from a high mountain and land safely on earth, 'as if he were held up' (*Clementine Recognitiones* 2.9). This is exactly the offer that the Devil makes to Jesus (*Matthew* 4:5–7), but Jesus rejects it. Clearly, the purpose of the Temptation was to induce Jesus to become a magician instead of the Savior of mankind. This was suggested by S. Eitrem, but very few scholars paid attention to him at the time (Eitrem, 1924a). Some other things that Simon claimed he could do can be paralleled from Philostratus' *Life of Apollonius*. But Simon also practiced theurgy: he made statues laugh, like Maximus, the Neoplatonist.

APOLLONIUS OF TYANA

The question whether Apollonius was a sorcerer or a true philosopher has been debated for centuries. St. Jerome (*Epistulae* 53.1) states the dilemma without giving an answer. Neither does St. John Chrysostom (*De Laudibus S. Pauli Apost.*, in *Hom.* 4.2.493 M.):

> Tell me then, whence came his great power? 'He was a sorcerer,' is the allegation. Then he must have been a unique kind of sorcerer. You have surely heard that sorcerers are and have always been common enough among Persians and the Indians; but they never count at all. 'Ah,' says he, 'but the man of Tyana, that impostor and charlatan – he also had a brilliant success.' Where and when? In a little portion of the world and for a short while; he was soon extinguished and abolished, leaving behind him no church, no people, nothing of the sort. (tr. J.S. Phillimore; see also Augustine, *Epist.* 102.32)

I shall argue that the historical Apollonius was a sorcerer as well as a philosopher and that his *Life* by Philostratus, our main source, is an attempt to defend the hero from the charge of magic posthumously but retains too much material that was simply part of the tradition to achieve its goal.

To prove my point, I shall first discuss some of Apollonius 'miracles', *thaumata*, and then some of his predictions and visions. First, we shall look at the *thaumata*, not only those he produced but some that he witnessed, for they also help create an atmosphere of the miraculous.

His birth is predicted by Proteus who appears to his mother in a dream. The birth itself is accompanied by a miracle, so that the natives of Tyana say he is the son of Zeus. As he is travelling with his companions in bright moonlight, they meet with an apparition: It is an Empusa which assumes various shapes and sometimes vanishes altogether. He knows right away what it is, curses the hag and tells his companions to do the same, whereupon the Empusa beats a hasty retreat, 'squeaking like the devil' (2.4). An Empusa is a vampire or ghoul with a donkey's hoof, not harmless at all and obviously a very real thing for the philosopher. Similarly,

Apollonius unmasks a Lamia – a related figure – in Corinth, 'the most celebrated of the stories about him'. Once he very cleverly catches an invisible Satyr, another character of Greek folklore.

The Brahmins he visits in India can levitate two cubits off the ground, and other wonderful things happen in their domain: Pythian three-legged tables move by themselves and flow with wine and water. He makes the writing disappear from the scroll his Roman prosecutor is holding. According to police reports, he can detect 'spirits and apparitions of idols'. He revives a girl who is mourned for dead; he talks with Achilles' ghost and describes him in detail. A tree talks to him which reminds one of the legend that Pythagoras was greeted by rivers (trees and rivers are divine). Animals – like the lion who is really King Amasis – recognize his superior nature. Like Pythagoras, he can be at two places at the same time, but nothing is said about the golden thigh which Alexander of Abonuteichos faked. He knows all the languages 'and all the silences of mankind'.

Naturally, he performs healings and exorcisms. As a prisoner in Rome, he extricates his leg from the fetter, to impress and comfort his companion, Damis. Simon Magus boasts of a similar feat in *Clementine Recognitiones* 2.32. Philostratus uses this episode to digress briefly on the nature of sorcery (7.38–9):

> The sillier sort of people ascribe this power to sorcerers . . . professional athletes call in their services, and so do all sorts of competitors; it contributes nothing to their victory, but the unhappy men rob themselves of the credit for their . . . successes and account them to these arts. Even the defeated do not lose faith in them: 'If only I had offered such and such a sacrifice, or burnt this and that incense, the victory would not have slipped through my fingers'. The sorcerer is a frequent visitor at the door of the merchants . . . We shall find them also crediting their lucky strokes of business to (the sorcerer) and their failures to their parsimony and the neglect of the appropriate sacrifice. But lovers more than all others are attached to this art . . . They will listen even to old women talking of magic; so it is no wonder if they resort to these professors . . . The sorcerer gives them a girdle or amulet to wear – mystical stones they got from the earth or the moon or the stars and spices of aromatic Indian plants, make them pay a handsome fee . . . and does nothing for it.

If their magic has been successful, they extol their craft as all-powerful; if not, the clients worry about having omitted something.

Philostratus is important here (*Lives of the Sophists* 5.12): Apollonius has foreknowledge of certain events, and this is due to 'supernatural prompting', but it does not make him a *magos*. Sorcerers are wretched people. They profess to alter the course of destiny (a) by torturing daemons; (b) by outlandish rites or charms or plasters. Apollonius, on the other hand, accepts destiny. His Second Sight is entirely due to divine revelation. He is impressed by the magic of the Indian Brahmins but does not really want to know how it works. He despises 'certain needy vagabonds' (i.e. the *metragyrtai* described by Lucian, *Lucius* 35 and *De dea Syria*; cf. Apul. *Met.* 8.24) who go about with an image of Demeter or Dionysus hung about their persons and profess to be supported by the deities they carry – but 'to feed on the gods with an insatiable appetite is a strange kind of madness'.

Apollonius also insists on the difference between himself and 'certain old wives who go round among shepherds and cowherds with a sieve hung over their arms and heal sick beasts by their incantations – they claim to be called 'wise women' and more scientific than the regular prophets . . .' This is a clear reference to *koskinomanteia* (see Lucian, *Alexander* 9; Theocritus *Idylls* 3.31, cf. Gow, 1952: ad loc).

Philostratus is careful to point out that his hero, although he seems to act occasionally like a sorcerer, is in fact a philosopher, a scientist in the tradition of Pythagoras, and that the suspicions of outsiders – the Roman authorities, for example – are completely unjustified. True, Apollonius does not charge fees, and the satiric image of the sorcerer – almost a caricature – drawn by his hagiographer, does not fit him at all. Nevertheless, the investigations made by the Roman police were on solid ground. But could they hold a man who miraculously disappeared from the Emperor's tribunal? No one else but Philostratus seems to refer to this truly sensational piece of magic, and he does so 'shyly, shamefacedly, . . . (without) the proper emphasis of conviction' (Phillimore, vol. 1, p. xviii). The suggestion is that he flew through the air. There are several accounts of his death, bordering on the miraculous; if he did die, no tomb is shown anywhere.

Perhaps we should distinguish his visions and predictions from the *thaumata*, because here we enter the field of parapsychology, and these are phenomena that are not utterly phantastic. Cases of Second Sight are fairly well documented (Anaxagoras, Socrates, Swedenborg). He seems to have thought about this specific gift of his. He has dreams that come true. He has knowledge and foreknowledge of what is right for him to do. How does this work? 'A sober soul, . . . discerning the prophetic significance of dreams . . . Soothsayers will never expound any vision without first asking the time at which a person saw it.'

For the sages of India it is normal to know what the future brings. They are omniscient, because they begin with self-knowledge. Second Sight is discussed at some length. Apollonius predicts his initiation into the Eleusinian Mysteries by a hierophant other than the one who rejected him once. He has a significant dream before sailing to Italy. The plague at

Ephesus is predicted and averted; catastrophic events in Smyrna, Chios, Miletus and other places are foreseen.

To predict the future and to worship the gods properly are part of his specific 'science'. How this 'science' works is discussed in his own 'apologia'. He also proposes a theory explaining how divination by the entrails works. His ambiguous prediction that Nero will narrowly escape death makes him suspicious to the secret police. But he refuses to prophesy to Tigellinus, because he is no 'prophet'. In another context, however, he correctly describes in advance the 'year of three Emperors'; he knows that Vespasian will rule after that and Nerva after him. This kind of prognosis could be very dangerous for the seer, as we know from Ammianus Marcellinus 29.1.25–32. While staying in Ephesus, he sees the assassination of Domitian, as it happens, in vivid detail, a feat that is also recorded by Dio Cassius, *Epit.* 67.17–18, even though he considers Apollonius (77.18.4) an 'errant sorcerer.'

May we consider Philostratus' *Life of Apollonius* as the portrait of a sorcerer? I do not think so, although it furnishes – against the will of the author – evidence that Apollonius was, among other things, a *magos*. This type of writing is, of course, quite different from what we have in the *PGM*. In the *Life* we read of magical feats and predictions, without any real explanations; in the *PGM* we read the recipes, the instructions, but we can only assume that they really worked.

In addition to what was said above about his *thaumata* and prophetic visions, I would like to assemble some evidence from the *Life* that would justify the suspicion of magic.

He travels to meet the Babylonian *magoi* and the Indian Brahmins, just as Pythagoras travelled before him, but he could have been motivated by purely philosophical interests. On the other hand, the miracles he observes abroad hint at other interests. Did he really travel to these countries, or are these trips symbolic fictions designed to illustrate his attachment to Brahmin philosophy and Greek Cynicism? He also travelled in the Greek world and was seen at the shrines, the religious centers and the great fairs where he would meet ordinary sorcerers and interpreters of dreams. Antioch and Ephesus attracted him especially.

The official charges brought against him are: (1) his peculiar dress and life-style; (2) the fact that people call him god; (3) his prediction of the plague at Ephesus; (4) the ritual murder of a child. On his diet and life style we are told this: He avoids meat, lives mainly on vegetables and dried fruit. Wine is a clean drink but tends to muddy the spirit. He walks barefoot, wears linen clothes, long hair and a beard and lives in temples (like Diogenes the Cynic). He imposes silence upon himself for long periods of time. At sunrise and at other times of the day he performs certain private rites. He begins the day by communicating with the gods;

next he converses with others about the gods; only after that does he deal with human affairs. He considers it his duty to repair old cemeteries and pour libations on neglected tombs. The last charge (4) which has a political context (Domitian's secret police suspects a plot to elevate Nerva to the throne) is probably the most serious. We are not told specifically why the boy had to die, but we read in Dio Cassius (69.11) that Hadrian had a favorite, Antinous, murdered, because he 'required a willing soul for his purposes' (Dölger, 1929–36, iv: 211–12).

Lucian seems to have taken him for a charlatan, for he refers in his *Alexander* 5 to the 'great' Apollonius and his whole *tragoidia*, a term which Phillimore translates as 'mummery', while Diskin Clay speaks of 'solemn farce'. Origen in *Against Celsus* 6.41 calls Apollonius a *magos*. What Apollonius calls his 'science' could easily be taken as magic science (*scientia, techne*) by an enemy. On the other hand he disapproves of those who use deadly drugs and 'violate the tombs of ancient kings', probably in order to steal their magical books (cf. the *PGM*). To the Roman authorities he says: 'If you regard me as a sorcerer, how will you chain me? And if you are going to chain me, how can you say that I am a sorcerer?' The future Emperor Vespasian discussed matters of the greatest importance with Apollonius in private (only Ephrates and Dio Chrysostomus were present). Vespasian even said to Apollonius: 'Make me an Emperor', and he knows Vespasian would want to be the ideal ruler that Plato had in mind and that he, Apollonius, prays for. But if Vespasian, a shrewd judge of people, had thought him to be a sorcerer, he would not have confided in him. He would have said: 'Force the Fates, force Zeus to make me supreme ruler of the Empire' or 'Fake some weather-prodigies for me' or 'Make the sun rise in the west'. For these were the claims usually made by sorcerers.

The argument that Apollonius speaks publicly and openly in temples, while sorcerers avoid such places and prefer the night for their operations does not really work; for the one does not exclude the other. Moreover, he hints at least once that he could do more impressive feats if he really wanted, but as he says, the Delphic Apollo reveals the truth without too much drama.

One big question remains: If his 'superhuman spiritual gifts' are entirely due to his 'scientific methods', why did he not teach his methods? Or are we to assume that there was some esoteric teaching that Philostratus does not mention?

Apollonius is not interested in astrology and 'all other supernatural dealings of that kind'. But he is interested in everything that is in the human soul, the human mind. Only men of extraordinary spiritual power understand, as he says, the depths of the soul whose 'immortal and unbegotten part is the origin of all being'. He probably saw it as his role to activate the collective soul of a group, and the phenomena that happen as a result of that might be called 'magic'.

One of his main defences is based on his behaviour during the last illness of his great friend Philiscus of Melos. Apollonius would have done anything to save him – even descend to the underworld – but he did none of the things a true sorcerer would have done (i.e. he did not use talismans, nor recited 'Orphic songs'). The attending physicians and their students are witnesses that he did none of these things. If he is not a sorcerer, what is he? Or is he a sorcerer plus something else? He seems to model himself after Pythagoras, and what tradition says about Pythagoras can be applied to him. Perhaps he wanted to be considered a reincarnation of Pythagoras. Or was he, as Phillimore (vol. I, p. xiv) suggests, a divinity of second-class rating, a daemon? 'Daemonships were easily obtained in the heyday of Syncretism,' Phillimore adds sarcastically. Unlike Jesus he was not a religious founder, though he became a cult figure long after his death. He was not an original thinker, not a great scholar, not a great orator, it would seem, but an effective speaker with a sense of humor, and a shrewd observer of human beings.

According to the *Vita Alexandri Severi* 29, he was *anima sanctior*, but even Hierocles did not call him a god. Ammianus Marcellinus 21.14.5 compared him to Hermes Trismegistus and Plotinus! This alone would show how difficult it was and is to label this man. Between Apollonius' death – or his 'disappearance from among men' – and Philostratus' work, a mass of lore accumulated and could be presented effectively, as literary propaganda, encouraged by the Imperial court. Phillimore has made it quite clear that it is Philostratus' purpose to honour Apollonius, to introduce him as the ideal philosopher. This is not so much a biography as a biographical novel, reminiscent of Xenophon's *Cyropaedia*. His admiration for Apollonius has a genuine ring. We may ask, with Phillimore (vol. I, p. lxxxii) what he saw in his hero: 'The picturesqueness of the character; the dramatic fascination of the period which includes Nero and Domitian; the splendid afternoon of a Hellenism which still understood and found its passwords in the language of the thousand-year-old poet.'

Philostratus vigorously defends his hero from the suspicion of being a *magos* by attributing his *thaumata* and predictions to 'science' and by differentiating him time and again from the vulgar *goes*. According to Roman law, both Apollonius and Apuleius could have been condemned as sorcerers. Apuleius defended himself successfully, as did Apollonius, but Apollonius was also whitewashed posthumously by his hagiographer. Why was this necessary? Because Apollonius had by now become a cult figure, with devotees in the highest circles. To worship someone who had really been a *magos* was unthinkable for someone like Julia Domna; therefore,

Philostratus had to work hard to emphasize the divine, superhuman nature of his hero.

That Apollonius himself knew of Jesus and imitated him consciously is very unlikely. But the literary tradition represented by Philostratus was very much aware of the Gospels, of *Acts* and some *Apocrypha* and thus created an image of Apollonius that pitted him against Christ. There is some anti-Jewish propaganda in the *Life* (5.33; 27; cf. Tacitus, *Historiae* 5.5). 'The Jews are inveterate rebels, not against Rome only, but against mankind.' This no doubt includes the Christians who were still considered by some an extremist Jewish sect.

There are striking parallels between the *Vita*, the canonical Gospels, *Acts* and some *Apocrypha*. Most of the parallels are found in Luke, while there is a cluster of New Testament reminiscences in Kayser, pp. 342–3 (*Mark, Luke, Acts*). There is an important parallel in the *Acts of Peter* 11 (cf. *Life* 4.20). The *Life* is not a direct attack on the Gospels, but it furnishes material for potential polemic of pagans against the Christians.

One point that I think has not been made: The Old Testament prophecies of Jesus' ministry have a parallel in the *Life*, too. Apollonius is a reincarnation of mythological figures and – in a sense – of previous philosophers, such as Pythagoras. This legitimizes him, confers a special status on him, just as the Old Testament predictions quoted in the Gospels define Jesus as the Messiah.

Incidentally, Apollonius lives on as Belinas, the great oriental sorcerer (Hempel, 1912: 6–12). Like Apuleius, he firmly denied being a magician, because, like Apuleius, he knew how dangerous such a claim could be. But in fact, he was a magician, and we can easily imagine him writing texts for amulets, though probably not for curse tablets. He practiced white magic, not black magic. Not to say what you were or what you thought you were was perhaps a necessary precaution. Jesus does refer to himself as 'Son of God', though rarely apart from the Gospel of John; on the other hand, God himself calls him his beloved son, and the daemons know this for a fact. Much more often Jesus calls himself the 'Son of Man'; but this title is never found in an address to him nor in a saying or tale about him.

The two pagan philosophers who emphasized that they were not magicians, were both in danger of being executed under Roman law. There is a certain irony in this. Of course, they both escaped: Apollonius through his very superior magic, Apuleius more through his rhetoric. Jesus was executed, but not as a magician.

The image of Apollonius that Philostratus projects is that of the 'Holy Man' or the 'Divine Man'. He is, in a sense, part of the religious establishment of paganism, for he is certified by various oracles (Colophon, Didyma) and shrines (Pergamon) as a true healer. In fact, he 'saves' people, absolves them from evil and ensures the peace of the dead by purifying them posthumously or letting them be purified by the local specialists. This connects him with Pythagoras and Empedocles who were great purifiers but also with the shady practitioners threatened by Heraclitus.

Edward Gibbon maintained that early Christianity was successful largely thanks to its appeal to miracles. This statement has been challenged recently by R. P. C. Hanson who declares that 'the market for miracles in the world of Christian antiquity was saturated. Everybody either performed miracles or claimed to do so, from the most despicable travelling charlatan to highly respectable philosophers like Apollonius of Tyana' (Hanson, 1980: 930). According to Hanson, there is another reason: Miracles were associated with magic, and a charge of operating with magic was one which all well-informed Christians were anxious to avoid. We might add that even 'well-informed' pagans like Apollonius and Apuleius were anxious – for very obvious reasons – to avoid this charge.

Hence there was a certain dilemma. On the one hand, if you wanted to make an impression, found a new movement, gain followers, you had to perform miracles or magic of some sort. On the other hand, if you made too much of an impression, you were likely to become the target of an investigation.

LUCAN'S SUPERWITCH, ERICTHO

In Book 6 of the *Pharsalia*, his epic on the Civil War between Julius Caesar and Pompey, Lucan has created a kind of superwitch, who seems like all the former witches, from Medea to Canidia, wrapped in one. She resides in Thessaly, the classical country of sorcery, and is consulted there by Pompey's son on the eve of the decisive battle of Pharsalus (48 BC). Lucan obviously wished to compete with Books 4 (Dido's magical sacrifice) and 6 (Aeneas' descent into the underworld) of the *Aeneid*, but also with the images of Medea, as given by Ovid, in the *Metamorphoses*, and by his uncle, Seneca, in his tragedy, *Medea*.

The poet first mentions the power of witches in general. Then he enumerates various methods of divination and adds that for Pompey's son, necromancy is the only reliable way of exploring the future. The rites involved are monstrous and disgusting, but the poet goes on and on, as if he enjoyed all the gruesome details. To be sure, he professes to be shocked and dismayed, but he manages to pass on the thrill he experiences to his readers.

Erictho has enormous powers. She emerges as a kind of minor daemon who has no scruples and is not responsible to any divine or human law. The central idea of the passage – the revival of a corpse – may have been discussed as a scientific problem at the time. Shelley, who admired Lucan, must have read this passage with his wife, Mary, for it almost certainly gave her the idea for her *Frankenstein*.

Was Lucan's treatment, so obviously influenced by literary sources, also based on a real person, someone like Horace's Canidia? Perhaps, but his rhetoric is so overpowering, his verbal artistry so sparkling that any connection with the world of everyday experience becomes very tenuous.

PETRONIUS' SORCERESS

Encolpius ('Bosom Pal'), the narrator and anti-hero of Petronius' novel *Satyricon*, describes an embarrassing episode. A beautiful woman named Chrysis ('Goldie') had allowed him to make love with her, but he had completely failed in her arms. Naturally, he is more than anxious to restore his sexual powers. First, he tries the conventional remedies: a spicy meal of onions and snails (considered an aphrodisiac) and just a little wine – not too much. He goes for a leisurely stroll and abstains from sex with his boyfriend, Giton. The next day, when he meets Chrysis again, he discovers that she, too, has given the problem some thought and brought her own witch, a little old woman, with her. First the witch ties a kind of amulet around his neck, for his temporary impotence might have been caused by black magic (a jealous rival, for instance). Three threads of 'different colors' (probably black, white and red) are twisted together and tied around his neck. She also takes some dirt, mixes it with her spittle and makes a mark on his forhead. Then she recites a spell and tells him to spit three times and to drop inside his garment three times in a row some pebbles over which she had said a spell and which she had wrapped in purple cloth. According to ancient belief, stones had occult powers, spittle, too, of course. Finally, the witch 'tests the power of his loins' by touching him there. The result is most satisfactory.

APULEIUS' SPIRITUAL JOURNEY

Among the works of Apuleius of Madaura, the Platonist and travelling lecturer, two deal with magic. One is a speech he delivered in his own defense around 160 AD before the Proconsul, Claudius Maximus, in Sabratha (North Africa). It is entitled *Apologia sive de Magia*; the other is an autobiographical novel entitled *Metamorphoses*.

Apuleius' defense was successful; if not, he could have been sentenced to death. His main argument is that he is a philosopher and scientist and, as such, interested in all kinds of phenomena that might appear bizarre. It is this intellectual curiosity of his that makes him suspicious. In fact, *curiositas* is practically a synonym of the pursuit of magic. There are certain things that one should leave alone.

Vague rumors have been spread in the community in which Apuleius is still a stranger. He has married a wealthy widow. There has been a mysterious death. One knows about certain experiments he has conducted.

Apuleius builds his denfense on the various connotations of the term *magos*. On the one hand, it could mean an ordinary sorcerer, a *goes*, on the other hand it could mean a priestlike figure, and that, Apuleius argues, was its original meaning. He quotes Plato's *Charmides* and his *First Alcibiades* (if it is genuine) to show how highly the Persians regarded these original 'magi'. Apuleius then tries to show that his experiments were harmless, only conducted in the interest of science and thouroughly misunderstood by his accusers who did not believe in the reality of witchcraft at all, for if he really were the great magician they made him out to be, they would have a great deal to worry about.

Apuleius defends not only himself, but the cause of philosophy – today we would say, the cause of pure research. As a philosopher, a Platonist, he feels free to investigate all sorts of problems, including occult phenomena. There is a bridge between philosophy and magic, just as there are bridges between religion and magic.

But, of course, the outsiders, the ordinary people, did not see it like this. Apuleius was, to them, a dangerous person. The specific accusations are the following: (1) his bride, the wealthy widow, whose relatives dislike Apuleius, called him a wizard, because she fell in love with him; (2) he bought three kinds of fish, in order to dissect them; (3) a young woman and a boy fell into trance in Apuleius' presence; (4) he owned *instrumenta magiae*; (5) he and some friends performed *nocturnalia sacra*; (6) someone made for him in secret from precious material a statue in the form of a skeleton which he worshiped in a costly ritual and which he called 'King', *basileus*.

Apuleius' defense was successful, but was he innocent? It depends. According to Roman Law, he could almost certainly have been sentenced to death. Fortunately, the judge was enlightened.

In his great picaresque novel, *Metamorphoses* (also known as the *Golden Ass*), a piece of fiction which must have autobiographical elements, the hero, Lucius, dabbles in magic, gets into serious trouble, is finally rescued by the goddess, Isis, and then finds true knowledge, salvation and peace in her religion.

The transformation of Lucius, the hero of the novel, into an ass is described in Book 3. The main characters of this part of the work are Lucius, eager young lover and student of magic, who is determined to learn the secrets of transformation, even though he has been warned of the risks; and Photis, the attractive young witch whose mistress, Pamphila, a more advanced sorceress, has a kind of magical workshop on the roof of her house — a wooden shelter hidden from view but open to the winds and full of her requisites: herbs, metal plates inscribed with magical characters, various ointments in little boxes, and, most gruesome of all, parts of dead bodies stolen from cemeteries or places of executions.

What makes it difficult to compare such figures as Apollonius of Tyana, Simon Magus, Apuleius af Madaura and Alexander the 'False Prophet' is the nature of our evidence. In the case of Apollonius we have mainly the testimony of an uncritical admirer who lived a few centuries later. In the case of Simon and Alexander we have practically only the hostile tradition. As far as Apuleius is concerned, we have his own story — in two versions.

But it is conceivable that a brilliant young man like Apuleius, a representative of 'Middle Platonism', wished to explore the possibilities of magic, natural or otherwise, just as some Neoplatonists were attracted, later on, by the possibilities of theurgy. The message of the novel seems to be that Apuleius found salvation in religion through a kind of spiritual pilgrimage, connected with much real hardship. This does not mean that he gave up philosophy, and we do not even know whether he renounced magic for good.

LUCIAN ON MAGICIANS

Lucian was born at about the same time as Apuleius (c. 125 AD); he died after 180 AD. Like Apuleius he travelled from city to city, giving lectures. He had studied philosophy but did not belong to any particular school, though he sympathized with the Epicureans, because they fought superstition under all its disguises.

Superstition is, indeed, one of the recurrent themes of Lucian's writings. It appears, for instance, in a devastating satire on the fraudulent founder of a new religion, Alexander of Abonuteichos, a contemporary of Lucian's whom he knew personally and detested sincerely.

Alexander, the 'Pseudoprophet', claimed to have control over a new manifestation of the god, Asclepius, in the form of a snake called Glycon. Thanks to this divine agent, he dispensed oracles and conducted mystery rites to which outsiders, especially Christians and Epicureans, were not admitted. In his essay, Lucian takes great pleasure in revealing the fraudulent magic that Alexander employed in order to capture the ignorant and credulous. The questions submitted to the oracle were sealed and came back with answers, the seals apparently unbroken, but Alexander had several techniques for opening them, adding a response and cleverly replacing the seal.

Alexander was probably just one of many accomplished impostors of later antiquity. He obviously knew how to manipulate crowds by his appearance, his delivery of the message and his use of mechanical devices (*manganeumata*) to produce sham miracles. Another type of fraud is discussed in the *Lovers of Lies*. Several philosophers, including a Stoic, a Peripatetic, and a Platonist, along with a physician, talk about miraculous cures. Some amazing instances are quoted. This leads to love-magic and other astonishing phenomena.

And here we come across the earliest version of the story of the sorcerer's apprentice, as told by the apprentice himself. His name is Eucrates, and he has studied with a great magician called Pancrates, who had spent twenty-three years underground learning magic from Isis herself. Pancrates needed no servants: he took a piece of wood − a broomstick, for instance − dressed it in some clothes and made it into a kind of robot that looked like a human being to all outsiders. One day, the apprentice overheard the master whispering a magical formula of three syllables and when the master was away tried it on the broomstick. The results are well known from Goethe's poem *The Sorcerer's Apprentice*.

At the end of this conversation, even the sceptic (Lucian himself, presumably) is confused and has lost faith in the venerable philosophers who are supposed to teach the young the truth yet perpetuate ancient superstitions instead. Still, he is not quite sure what to believe and what not to believe. As far as the story of the great Hyperborean magician is concerned (*Lovers of Lies* 14−18), Lucian seems to put his finger on the main problem. The magician charges a large fee for a feat that would take place anyway, due to purely natural causes. But his prestige, the build-up in front of his audience, and the whole hocus-pocus are all so impressive that people willingly pay and gladly give him credit.

In his dialogue *Menippus on Necromancy*, Lucian uses motifs from Book 11 of Homer's *Odyssey* but produces a picture of a more complex necromantic ritual. The satirist, Menippus, one of Lucian's heroes, wishes to visit the underworld, and he travels all the way to Babylon to consult one of the *magoi*. The preparations he has to make are formidable: Purification by ablutions and fumigations, strict diet, sleeping out of doors, taking special precautions.

After all has been said, it still remains difficult to draw the line between philosophers (or scientists) who were just that and philosophers who also did or were supposed to do magic. The archaic combination of both (Orpheus, Pythagoras, Empedocles) survives into later antiquity, but on a lower level, as it were. Neo-Pythagoreans like Apollonius of Tyana and Middle Platonists like Apuleius of Madaura may be accused of being sorcerers, and in their defence they could simply say: 'As a philosopher (or scientist) I am interested in everything and anxious to investigate every phenomenon under the sun. If there is such a thing as magic – and almost everyone seems to believe that there is – I want to find out whether it works or not. But let me assure you that this does not make me a magician, and any miracles that I seem to perform can be explained in purely scientific terms.'

Apuleius was a highly educated man, but many real magicians were not. Augustine (*Contra academicos* 1.7.19ff) was impressed by Albicerius, a sorcerer, who had helped him find a silver spoon and could 'thought-read' lines from Vergil in the mind of a proconsul. But this practitioner, acording to Augustine, lacked education; therefore, he could not be 'good'. On the other hand, it is sometimes said that an educated person, a 'philosopher', can never become the victim of magic.

In the *Lovers of Lies* (10–13) Lucian tells through one of the interlocutors the story of a Babylonian miracle-worker who instantly healed a man who had been bitten by a snake. This Babylonian could also destroy all the snakes that infested the farm on which the accident had happened; moreover, he was able to fly through the air (like Simon Magus) and walk on water. This has all the characteristics of folklore and tall tales, and the way in which it is presented suggests that the narrator himself doubts the stories he passes on. The old dragon who fails to obey the wizard's command seems like a built-in clue, and so are the heavy brogues the wizard wears as he sails through the air. By retelling such folk tales with a satiric twist Lucian manages to refute them.

LUCIAN, *ALEXANDER OR THE FALSE PROPHET*

Lucian addresses his 'unmasking' of Alexander, the 'false prophet', to an Epicurean named Celsus who had himself written a work 'Against the Magicians' (cf. 21; Origen, *Against Celsus* 1.68; 5.86; Hippolytus, *Refutatio* 4.28–42). Hippolytus in his chapters against the magicians (Ganschinietz, 1913: 1ff) seems to have used this lost work, but there are also remarkable parallels between Hippolytus and Lucian. Lucian's work has several definite themes. One of them appears right at the beginning: Alexander's operation is really a *tragoidia*, a 'solemn farce', as Diskin Clay translates who lists related terms: *drama, skeue* etc. in Lucian and his contemporaries and compares *agonizomai* in Philostratus (of the performances of sophists). He adds 'Lucian's Peregrinus Proteus and his Alexander are very much at home in . . . [the] theatrical culture [of the second sophistic]. They are always on stage and . . . histrionic; their success hung on their ability to convince their audience' (Clay, 1992: 3418).

Lucian leaves no doubt from the beginning of his treatise, our main source, that, for him, Alexander is a 'sorcerer' (*goes*) and 'an accursed villain'. At the same time, he is tall and handsome, 'truly godlike', with radiant eyes that look divinely inspired (3). He is highly intelligent, vivacious and businesslike; he has intellectual curiosity and a quick grasp of any subject. All these admirable qualities make him, in effect, a very dangerous criminal, and though he sees himself as a new Pythagoras, he is a master of lies, deceit, perjury and 'evil art' (*kakotechnia*, i.e. magic). He is unscrupulous, bold, works hard to realize his plans; he is also persuasive, inspires confidence and disguises his evil intentions under a mask of kindness (4; cf. his reception of Lucian, 55). He gives the impression of being honest, pleasant, rather simple-minded and naive. Add to this his tendency to 'think big' and execute grand schemes and his rejection of everything that is on a modest scale (4) – and you have the portrait of a real wizard of antiquity.

As a boy, he was very handsome, and one of his lovers was a professional sorcerer (*goes*), one of those who promised magical operations (*mageias*), miraculous incantations and love charms and curses against enemies, as well as the 'digging up' of hidden treasures and inheritances (perhaps by hastening the death of a wealthy relative?). Alexander proves to be a talented sorcerer's apprentice and accomplice in crime; so his lover gives him a thorough education and employs him as an assistant, servant and domestic. The teacher – incidentally a disciple of the 'great Apollonius of Tyana' – pretends to be a healer, and, in fact, he knows 'how to mix good and bad drugs'. Alexander inherits all this knowledge from him. He now takes an associate by the name of Kokkonas who 'participated in compositions' and was even more corrupt than Alexander himself. As sellers of medicine and tellers of fortunes, as wizards and sorcerers, but not yet specialized on oracles, they travel around. What they are doing, they call in their slang, 'fleecing the fatsoes'. It is interesting to note that these travelling frauds had their own slang, perhaps comparable to the *Rotwelsch* of medieval crooks in Central Europe. Alexander and his congenial accomplice are characterized as 'very wicked', as 'daredevils', as 'totally willing to commit any crime'.

One basic fact these villains – who are much more dangerous than the characters in picaresque novels, such as Petronius' *Satyricon* – understand very well is this: human beings are governed by hope and fear (cf. Vettius Valens, *Anthol.* 5.4), and if you know how to manipulate these emotions you will get rich fast. Those who hope and those who fear depend on the arts of divination; this is the reason why the famous Oracles (Delphi, Clarus, etc.) flourished for such a long time. Lucian is in agreement with Oenomaus of Gadara, the Cynic, who 'debunked the charlatans', i.e. unmasked the incompetence and fraudulence of the Oracles.

Alexander and Kokkonas are joined by a rich Macedonian lady who encourages them, and as they 'twist' and 'churn' their ideas and experiences, they hit upon the idea of establishing a new prophetic shrine. They do this and succeed beyond their own 'prognosis and their boldest hopes' – one of Lucian's typical jokes.

The two accomplices operate in a rational, businesslike manner. They are aware of the stupidity of the Paphlagonians: If any charlatan accompanied by a flute-player, predicting the future with a sieve, comes to town, these people stare at him in awe, as if he had just come down from heaven. Needless to say, Alexander is much more sophisticated.

They plot their strategy and get the population prepared for a new cult by planting bronze tablets in the old sanctuary of Apollo in Chalcedon. Kokkonas remains there and fabricates 'ambiguous, obscure, impenetrable oracles', anticipating Alexander's later techniques. Soon afterwards he departs from this life. In the meantime, the people of Abonuteichos start the construction of a temple. Alexander now creates an even more impressive image of himself: Long, flowing locks, a purple *chiton* with white stripes, a white mantle, in his hand a *harpe*, i.e. a kind of sickle, and he now calls himself the 'divine Alexander.' The Paphlagonians, hopeless fools that they are, believe in him, although they are fully aware of his humble origins.

Another oracle, skilfully concocted, announces in Pythagorean terms the arrival of a great prophet. Alexander manages to fake states of trance by chewing root of soapwort. The foam that comes out of his mouth strikes the simpletons as something 'divine' and 'awesome'. He now fashions a dragon's head that looks vaguely human and can be manipulated with horse hair, like a marionette. And, of course, there is the tame snake from Pella, nurtured in secret, destined to become one of the main actors in this show. His mystic arrival in this world is prepared by means of an egg. Then Alexander leaps into the market-place, clad only in a golden loin-cloth, carrying a sickle, shaking his flowing locks in the manner of the fanatical dervish priests of the Great Mother. Here, as elsewhere in Lucian's account, and through the stories concerning Simon Magus, it becomes clear, that a great *magos* is always a great imitator. He climbs onto a high altar and starts addressing the crowd, congratulating the city on the imminent epiphany of 'the god'. Practically the whole population is there. The people are awestruck, fall on their knees and pray. Alexander now utters a series of unintelligible words (perhaps the *onomata barbara* of the papyri; Lucian says they could have been Hebrew or Phoenician), and the names 'Apollo' and 'Asclepius' occur frequently.

The rest of this 'epiphany' is told by Lucian with superb skill. Every detail counts, but what seems particularly relevant is Alexander's declaration that he now holds Asclepius in the form of Glycon, i.e. he is the priest, the manager or impresario and (who knows?) the son of Glycon; at any rate, he is in control of him. The crowd, once more, is amazed.

(There always seems to be a crowd in ancient cities, ready to stare and listen, to admire a true or false prophet, and to embrace a new religion, if the miracles they see are good enough.)

Alexander creates a kind of mass hysteria through *ekplexis*, 'shock', and feeds the hopes, intensifies the fears of the average person. What are those hopes? Lucian tells us: wealth, health 'and the rest' (14). Now he waits for the rumors to go around; then he installs himself in a room, on a couch, 'in very goodlike fashion'. The first viewing of the divine snake is staged as a miracle by Alexander; it is also a cleverly arranged show.

His tricks, his sorcery are so accomplished that only very superior minds such as Democritus or Epicurus, would have realized that everything is deceit (*pseudos*) and cannot possibly be real.

But so far everything is only an elaborate preparation for the biggest humbug of all, i.e. the oracle that Alexander wants to establish. This is his real specialty, and as soon as the temple stands, the stage is set. Alexander's tricks are fairly obvious to Lucian and his friend, Celsus, but to the simpletons they seem a miracle, and they experience great wonderment. Some of Alexander's specific devices are revealed, although Celsus, an authority on fake magic, is probably familiar with them. The oracles that are given in response to the people's questions are sometimes obscure, sometimes downright unintelligible, but his medical advice is often based on common sense and reflects his knowledge of 'useful drugs'. He employs a large staff of paid helpers, assistants and spies, including secretaries and interpreters. This is no longer a two-man enterprise, this is a big business with international connections, for Alexander now sends his agents abroad to propagate the cult. He advertises his ability to catch runaway-slaves, thieves and robbers, to dig up hidden treasures (a specialty of certain sorcerers), to heal the sick and to restore the dead to life. The response is most heartening, but now he is attacked by a few sensible people, mostly Epicureans, but implicitly also Christians of whom, in his opinion, there are too many around. His 'magic', the secrets of his *mise-en-scène*, are by now fairly obvious to them. In his defense he uses shock-tactics against the Epicureans and the Christians. Naturally, a sorcerer type like Alexander, a friend of the marvellous must hate an 'inflexible' thinker like Epicurus who had undermined the religious establishment and denounced superstition in its various forms. With Platonists, Stoics, and Neo-Pythagoreans Alexander lives in peace.

With the help of an accomplice, he produces another *ekplexis*: The god now emits oracles *viva voce*, directly. Another very clever trick works as follows. When events prove one of his oracles wrong, he furnishes recantations *ex eventu*. He is also an expert on generating rumors, and through his knowledge of questions submitted to the oracle, he is in a position to blackmail the rich and the powerful. No ordinary crook would have hit upon this idea, Lucian says with reluctant admiration. Alexander also decides to export his oracles over the whole Roman Empire, warning the population against plagues, fires, earthquakes and other catastrophes and assuring them of his help. A hexameter attached to the city gates would act as a kind of talisman. Unfortunately, it proves to be completely ineffective, probably because people, in a false feeling of safety, neglect all the normal precautions, Lucian says. His army of spies in Rome informs him of people's thoughts even before they reach his shrine in the form of specific questions. One is impressed at the network of communications that must have been at the man's disposal. Lucian sees such activities as 'preparatory tricks'.

In Abonuteichos, Alexander now organizes initiation rites modelled after those practices at the Mystery Cults in Eleusis and elsewhere. They involve torchbearers, hierophants and dramatized myths. Christians and Epicureans are strictly excluded from these ceremonies (*orgia*), which culminate in the representation of the *hieros gamos*, the 'sacred marriage', of Alexander-Endymion and Selene; the goddess is played by a beautiful woman, the wife of a Roman official. She is lowered from the ceiling (probably by the kind of *machina* used to produce a stage-deity) and the two then hug and kiss on a couch before the eyes of her husband. Then Alexander appears dressed as a hierophant, and into the profound silence he shouts '*Ie*, Glycon!' to which the crowd responds '*Ie* Alexander!' As Alexander jumps around in 'mystic dances', his gold thigh becomes clearly visible in the light of the torches, indicating that he is a reincarnation of Pythagoras himself.

Many women are in love with him and bear him children, and their husbands are proud of this. He encourages the belief that he is really a god who spends a certain time on earth – his *epidemia*. The word, incidentally, has a similar meaning in *First Clement* 5:59, and some followers of Apollonius of Tyana think of him in this way.

Who was Alexander, after all? A charlatan? An *anthropodaimon*? Lucian's judgement is clear: Alexander was not a harmless eccentric, not an ordinary charlatan, but a master-criminal, ruthless and extremely dangerous under a mask of kindness and concern. Any critic or challenger wo dared to unmask him, including Lucian himself, would risk his life. His hatred of true philosophers who see through him takes on grotesque forms; thus, he burns the 'Main Principles' of Epicurus in public with such zeal, as if he were burning the Master himself. Epicureanism is, for Lucian, a sane, sensible philosophy, the very opposite of Alexander's obscurantism and deceit, for it provides peace of mind and happiness and real purification.

What emerges from Lucian's account, even though he does not stress it, is the fact that a sorcerer of Alexander's type is, among other things, a great imitator who borrows shamelessly what suits him from various cults, religious rituals, occult practices and ancient doctrines. He manipulates the emotions of the people who seek his help and operates with phantoms, with carefully staged miracles. Caster (1937: 47–9, in his commentary on para. 26) compares the 'speaking statues' in Egyptian and Graeco-Roman temples, and he specifically mentions a bronze statue of Diana, found in a temple of Apollo in Pompeii whose lips are half open and whose neck has a hole through which a tube could be inserted. He also makes a very interesting point: the people were not completely fooled; most of them probably knew that those statues were being manipulated by the priests. When the Emperor Julian was initiated at Ephesus, under the direction of Maximus, the theurgist, he saw a statue of Hecate smiling, moving, her torches being lit spontaneously, etc. He almost certainly knew that this was not a true miracle but had to be understood symbolically. It was a show, but a very good show, and it had a strong emotional effect on the faithful.

During Marcus Aurelius' campaign against the Marcomanni and the Quadi, Alexander issues a major oracle, involving sacrifices, aromatic essences and two hapless lions. He invents 'nocturnal oracles', just as fraudulent as the others, and once more Lucian emphasizes the element of 'shock' and 'amazement', but concedes that even Democritus might have been disturbed for a moment, but he would soon have understood the principle behind the 'miracle' and spat out in disgust. Lucian amuses himself at playing a trick an the 'prophet' in order to test him: He asks, through an agent: 'When will Alexander be unmasked as a charlatan?' It is a case of his *mechane* versus that of Alexander. But the charlatan gets bolder and bolder: he has coins with the image of Glycon minted to propagate his cult. Once more, Lucian refers to Alexander's 'magic' as *tragoidia*: 'This was the end of Alexander's show, and such was the dénouement of the drama, that one might have supposed that something like this was the work of providence, even though it happened by chance.' In the very last section Lucian briefly characterizes the purpose of his work. He wants it to be a *deigma*, an example, and he hopes that it will be useful by exposing fraud and deceit and reassure people that there is such a thing as reality and common sense.

As a work of 'unmasking' Lucian's satire is related to the 'Unmasking of the Charlatans' by Oenomaus of Gadara, a Cynic who was slightly older. It has been pointed out that Oenomaus' work, preserved in excerpts by Eusebius, has parallels in Lucian's *Iupiter Confutatus*.

In my summary of the *Alexander* I have drawn attention to the author's high opinion of Alexander's intelligence and the cleverness of his magical tricks. As a contrast we find everywhere references to the amazing stupidity of his followers. Since Alexander's operation is really a show, it has its protagonist (Alexander himself), its deuteragonist (the divine snake,

Glycon) and its chorus of dumb Paphlagonians. Lucian has a whole palette of epithets for them: They are thick-headed, naive, superstitious, brainless, witless, distinguishable from animals only by their appearance, confused, easily frightened, impressed in advance, buoyed by vain hopes, stupid and with dripping noses. The thumbnail-sketch of Rutilianus, a worthy, but exceptionally superstitious Roman, deserves to be read in its entirety; he is – sarcastically – called 'very sharp' and is one of the 'foolish wise' (*morosophoi*); he is also mindless and deranged. Lucian would not be Lucian if he did not deliver, *en passant*, a kick to the representatives of philosophical schools he dislikes: They are just as stupid as the dumbest Paphlagonians! How different was Epicurus!

PLOTINUS AND THE EGYPTIAN PRIEST

According to Porphyry's *Life of Plotinus* 56–60, the leading Neoplatonist (c. 205–270 AD) had 'some very special gifts' from the time of his birth. 'Special' means 'occult' or 'psychic'. Once, an Egyptian priest (i.e. a theurgist) came to Rome and wanted to give Plotinus a demonstration of his own 'science'. He invited him to be present at an appearance of his (Plotinus') 'familiar spirit'. The conjuring took place in the temple of the Egyptian goddess Isis, because this was, as the Egyptian priest declared, the only 'pure place' to be found in all of Rome. But when the spirit was asked to show himself, a god appeared that did not belong to 'that category of spirits'. At this point, the Egyptian cried: 'Blessed are you who have a god as a familiar and not a spirit of the lower class!' Unfortunately there was no opportunity to ask the apparition any questions or even to look at it any longer, for the friend who shared the experience strangled the chickens that he held as a safeguard, 'either because he was jealous or because he was afraid of something.' Since Plotinus had a higher divine being as a familiar, Porphyry adds, he concentrated his 'divine eye' for a while on that being. This experience prompted him to write a monograph, *On the Spirit That Alotted Us to Himself.* A monograph with this title is preserved among Plotinus' writings (Tract 15 Harder = *Enneads* 3.4), but no mention is made of this particular incident.

What the priest granted to Plotinus was a vision, *autopsia*, of his own familiar spirit, *genius*, his personal 'daemon'. The priest, who had expected an ordinary *genius*, was amazed that a deity of a higher order appeared. A theurgist was, of course, able to spot these differences.

We also learn that an attendant was needed to hold a couple of chickens. This adds a touch of simple folklore to theurgic rites of the highest order. The chickens must be strangled at once if the spirit that appears turns out to be awesome. Such a sacrifice was probably conceived as an instant peace offering, after which the spirit would leave without harming any of the participants. In this case the attendant panics, and the spirit departs prematurely, but the priest – and, of course, Plotinus – at least had a look at him.

PLOTINUS AND THE EVIL SORCERER

Plotinus had an enemy, Olympus of Alexandria, who tried to hurt him through magic. In Porphyry's *Life of Plotinus* 53–5, we are told that this sorcerer first appealed to the stars, but in vain. Second, we learn that Plotinus, being a 'wise man', was able to resist the evil forces directed against him, and in fact, redirected them against the enemy who had unleashed them in the first place. Thus, the very real anguish that Plotinus had felt at one point, rebounded on the magician. All this sounds like a personal experience that Plotinus told his disciples: His body had felt like a purse whose strings are pulled together. The message is this: A great philosopher like Plotinus can hurt hostile magicians, not by technical sorcery, but by his wisdom.

The two stories illustate Plotinus' attitude towards magic and theurgy. Ordinary 'black' magic can hurt him slightly, but he is able to defend himself. Theurgy of a higher order reveals his rank on earth.

THE THEURGIST AS *MAGOS*

Theurgy was considered a higher form of magic, designed to establish a contact between the practitioner – a more priestlike figure than the ordinary *magos* – and deities of the highest order. According to Proclus (*In theologiam Platonis*, ed. Dodds [1963]), theurgy is a 'power higher than all human wisdom, embracing the blessings of divination, the purifying powers of initiation, and in a word all the operations of divine possession.'

Theurgy, as opposed to the more vulgar *goeteia*, i.e. 'witchcraft', was supposed to be grander, more exalted, full of a deep religious feeling, but its principles and procedures were not essentialy different. Naturally, a Neoplatonist philosopher who was also a priest and practised theurgy, was quite different from the shady practitioners who sold love-charms and interpreted dreams for money at fairs and festivals all over the Greek world.

Porphyry gives us the portrait of a theurgist (*Philosophy from Oracles*, ed. Wolff [1856]: 164–5; cf. Eusebius, *Praeparatio evangelica* 4.50ff). He actually describes a statue but the reference to a living theurgist is unmistakable. We hear of the head wreathed with bandages and flowery branches, the face anointed or actually painted, the laurel twig in one hand, the magical symbols on the shoes. Fine robes, liquids, flowers, scents and certain gestures and sounds were also distinctive.

Iamblichus (c.250–c.330 AD), the Neoplatonist philosopher and theurgist, wrote among other works a treatise *On the Pythagorean Life* which is essentially a highly romanticized biography of the Master, with an outline of his doctrines.

Iamblichus himself was the subject of a hero-worshipping biography composed by Eunapius (c.345 – c.420 AD), the sophist and historian who admired the Emperor Julian and hated the Christians. He tells how Iamblichus' disciples once asked him to perform something special (i.e. a *thauma*) for them. He does not oblige them at once but puts them off until a suitable occasion arises. This reluctance stems from his own doctrine: to demand a miracle from the gods is an act of arrogance, in a sense, and could be dangerous. But he also teaches that some 'miracles' are not caused by divine intervention at all. In the end he succeeds in materializing two divine presences, Eros and Anteros, from two separate hot springs. The two divine beings look like handsome young boys; they hug Iamblichus and cling to him as if he were their father. 'After this, the crowd of his pupils demanded nothing more, but considering the proofs that had been given to them, clung to him as if by an unbreakable chain', concludes Eunapius. This is a typical pattern: Unbelief or doubt, however timid, demands a *thauma*, and the *thauma*, duly performed, produces *pistis*, 'belief'.

HECATE AND THE THEURGIST

Maximus of Ephesus, the most famous theurgist of the fourth century, had great influence on the Emperor, Julian, but was executed under Valens. Eunapius dedicated a biographical sketch to Maximus in which he tried to do justice to his charismatic teaching. At least once Maximus performed the miracle that was practically required from this type of teacher and theurgist. He takes a number of people into the temple of Hecate, reverences the statue of the goddess, burns a grain of incense and chants to himself 'some sort of hymn' from one end to other. At this the statue of the goddess begins to smile and even appears to laugh. Then flames burst out of the torches she holds in her hands. Everybody is impressed by the show. But Eunapius warns his readers not to admire any of these things: he certainly does not. Rather, one should believe that 'purification through reason is something very important.' This may be Eunapius' way of saying that miracles can be arranged and should not be over-estimated; they serve only as a symbol, a reinforcement of serious philosophical training. But when the 'divine Julian' heard this, Eunapius adds, he left the teacher whom he had at the time and departed for Ephesus at once, in order to satisfy his 'thirst for occult science' (Eunapius, *Lives of the Philosophers and Sophists*, pp. 473–5 Boissonade [1849]).

SOSIPATRA, A 'DIVINE WOMAN', AND ANTONINUS, HER SON

Thanks to Eunapius (pp. 456–60) we have an impressive portrait of Sosipatra who was roughly his contemporary (iv AD). She was a great philosophical teacher and a psychic, as we would say today. The story of her early youth sounds like a fairy-tale: One day, two old men arrive at her father's estate and offer, under certain conditions, to educate the little girl who 'is brightened by beauty and good manners.' The father does not have much choice, and the old men – whether they were actually minor gods or major daemons, is not clear – take the girl away and bring her back five years later, fully trained and initiated into 'ancient mysteries'. During her absence, her father's business flourishes beyond belief. When she returns, she is tall and 'of a different kind of beauty'. She gives an impressive demonstration of her Second Sight and the so-called Chaldaean wisdom she has achieved. Before her mentors leave, they bestow on her a whole set of robes, add certain mystic symbols and put certain scrolls into her chest. Never having had any other teachers, she is able to quote the poets, philosophers and orators.

The story can be read as a piece of pagan propaganda. Eunapius, like Julian, seems to say that the ancient gods are not dead. They still walk the earth and take care of their favourites, as they did during the Golden Age.

In the middle of a serious philosophical discussion, Sosipatra, now a respected philosopher and teacher, has a telepathic experience. This convinces everyone that she is omnipresent, and whenever anything happens, she is there, 'which is what the philosophers say about the gods' (p. 470).

In another part of his *Lives*, Eunapius records the impressive career of Sosipatra's son, Antoninus 'the anchorite', a priest, philosopher and – so it would appear – theurgist who seems to have inherited his 'psychic' gifts from his mother. Antoninus served as a priest in the temple at the Canobic mouth of the Nile and trained candidates for the priesthood. The rites of the gods worshiped there were secret, as Eunapius implies. Antoninus must have been a theurgist as well as a teacher, but not openly. When he lectured on Plato, he avoided any 'theological' (which means no doubt 'theurgical') questions. Eunapius uses a picturesque phrase worth quoting: 'Whoever proposed one of the more divine problems, encountered a statue.' That can only mean that the teacher froze and acted as if nothing had been said. One had to be careful. Theurgy had flourished under Julian, but there was a reaction under his successors, and Maximus was one of its victims.

One day Antoninus had a vision which came true. He told his disciples that soon after his death (he died in 390 AD), the temple would cease to be the great sanctuary it was, and that the magnificent shrine of Sarapis would be transformed into 'the dark and shapeless', and that 'something fabulous and formless' (i.e. fictitious and hideous) would rule over the most beautiful things on earth. This prophecy is also recorded – but not credited to Antoninus – in the Hermetic dialogue *Asclepius* (Luck, 1986: 153–6).

Eunapius describes in some detail the ways in which the prediction was fulfilled:

> The temple of Sarapis was demolished, the temple of Canobus, too. The statues of the gods and the votive offerings were removed. Only the vast floor of the temple of Sarapis was left intact for some time, because the stone slabs were too heavy to be carried off. Monks took over the ancient sacred sites, and the bones and skulls of criminals (i.e. the remains of martyrs) were buried inside the sanctuaries and worshiped there.

The Sarapeion was destroyed in 391 AD, and the temples of Canobus were ransacked between 390, the year of Antoninus' death, and 412 AD.

A NECROMANTIC SCENE IN A LOVE ROMANCE

Heliodorus, author of the novel, *Ethiopian Tales*, or *The Story of Theagenes and Charicleia*, probably lived in the third century AD. He seems to have been a Neopythagorean, at least for part of his life. Later, according to tradition, he converted to Christianity and became Bishop of Tricca in Thessaly.

In Book 6 of his novel (14–15) the beautiful heroine, Charicleia, accompanied by Calasiris, an elderly Egyptian priest, comes across a large number of bodies. It looks as though very recently Egyptians and Persians had fought a fierce battle. The only living being they see is an old Egyptian woman who mourns the loss of a son. She tells the two travellers to spend the night there and promises to escort them to the next village in the morning. As they try to rest on top of a little hill they observe in the bright moonlight, much against their will, a gruesome necromantic scene. The old woman who is a witch tries to revive the corpse of her own son who lies among the slain. The motive is similar to the scene in Book 6 of Lucan's *Pharsalia*, but the ditch she digs, the libation she pours and the sword she handles, are reminiscent of the Homeric *Nekyia* (Book 11 of the *Odyssey*). She also uses a kind of voodoo doll made of dough mixed with fennel and laurel. The operation is successful up to a point, but the witch is told by her son that she is committing a sin, because she violates the Fates. Death — actually provided by Roman law for such rituals — would be the appropriate punishment for her. Moreover — this we also know from Lucan — the dead resent being called back to life. All this is made even worse by the fact that a priest, a holy man beloved by the gods, is forced to to be a witness to this horrible scene. The dead man knows this well and reproaches his mother. We learn from Heliodorus that priests attached to certain cults were not allowed to watch magical rites, much less perform them.

THE SORCERER UNMASKED

In Hippolytus' *Refutatio* 4.28–42, we have a pamphlet 'Against the Magicians', perhaps of the type that Lucian's friend, Celsus, wrote. Text and interpretation are often doubtful, but Ganschinietz and others have cleared up a number of problems. We meet here the type of *magos* or *goes*, described so memorably in Lucian's *Alexander* and his *sympaiktai*, 'assistants', literally 'playmates' (perhaps an idiom from the sorcerers'slang). These assistants are often boys who can be easily influenced (perhaps hypnotized) by the sorcerer.

The information that Hippolytus (c.165 – c.235 AD) passes on is not always well organized. He may have used several sources and possibly misunderstood some technical details. He certainly does not want to tell people how they can become sorcerers. Thus, even though his sources may have been highly technical, he seems to stop at a certain point. To him, it is enough to show without going into details how fraud and deceit were feasible. Thus the reader gets impressions and snatches of information rather than solid instruction throughout.

There is a secret chamber (*adyton*). Messages in exotic languages are carried back and forth. Sacrifices are performed. One of the boys gets into a trance and behaves like an epileptic (cf. Apuleius, *Apologia* 42). His screams frighten the people who are waiting for an answer to the questions they have proposed to the great Egyptian god Rê (who takes the place of Alexander's Glycon). The boy appears by now to be unconscious, and the sorcerer places him on a mattress and pronounces magical formulas over him. Then the room is plunged into darkness, because divine beings of a higher rank (higher than Rê?) are expected to appear. An assistant mumbles prayers while the sorcerer beats on a gong. Then he orders silence, and at this point, apparently, the speaking tubes come into action (cf. Lucian, *Alexander* 26). A sort of lecanomancy is practiced: the sorcerer places a (papyrus?) sheet that seems to be empty into a bowl full of water mixed with vitriol. The message, written with a *pharmakon* (in this case the juice of oak-apples) now becomes visible. A wonder!

An excursus on various techniques to frighten the boys follows. The author then lists some tricks from the repertoire of *magia naturalis* based on simple chemistry. They enable the sorcerer to give the impression that a house is on fire, to produce thunder claps, to stick his hands into hot pitch without getting them burnt, to walk barefoot on a bed of glowing coals, to swallow and spit fire. Some of these tricks were probably used in stage productions over a long period of time.

Most of the effects described above apparently served as a kind of prelude to the epiphany of a 'fiery' Asclepius, not so much a theurgical operation, it would seem, as a kind of necromancy. The various techniques were not always neatly separated. After that we find out how to open a seal and substitute another one (cf. Lucian, *Alexander* 19). We are also told that sorcerers can fake ecstasy (cf. Lucian 40).

This, as G. Anderson says, represents an impressive inventory of the 'hardware' of *goeteia* (Anderson, 1994: 68). Two motifs are stressed: the quasi-miraculous distractions and atmospheric effects and the techniques of writing down something on a sheet so that it disappears but then can be reread. He also points out that the deception lies in the arbitrary association of these techniques with the invocation of a deity. It is interesting that nothing is said about the technique of the *engastrimythoi*, the ancient ventriloquists.

Eusebius of Caesarea (c.263–339 AD) wrote his *Preparation of the Gospel* to prove that even before the ministry of Jesus, pagans had at least a glimpse of the word of God. He rejects what are, to him, the errors of paganism, but he does not dismiss all the claims made for magic in general. He thinks that many 'supernatural' events are not the work of gods or daemons but the result of human fraud. He is also aware of the psychological factors that enter into this process. A mood of expectation can be created in certain ways (Alexander of Abonuteichos was very skilful at this) and there is such a thing as mass suggestion. In 4.1.6–9 Eusebius seriously considers the possibility that all 'occult' phenomena are mystifications produced by sorcerers and, therefore, fraudulent in nature. He continues as follows:

Certain perfumes go to the head and make you sleepy, while others produce visions. Moreover, the places, the locations where something is going on, also contribute a great deal, not to mention the instruments and the apparatus which sorcerers have held ready long beforehand . . . They also benefit from all sorts of outside assistance . . . The inner sanctum and the recesses inside the temple, which are not accessible to the public, also hide many secrets. The darkness certainly helps them in their fraudulent scheme.

THE BISHOP DABBLES IN MAGIC

In a chapter entitled 'Die geheimen Praktiken eines syrischen Bischofs', E. Peterson (*Frühkirche, Judentum und Gnosis*, Herder 1959, pp. 222–45) deals with a fascinating testimony which has been overlooked by many historians of witchcraft in antiquity. It is found in the records, written in Syriac, of the so-called Robber Synod of Ephesus, 449. Here, Sophronius, the Bishop of Tella is accused not only of being a heretic, but also of being a magician and an astrologer.

The Bishop had lost a sum of money while traveling. He rounded up some suspects and made them first swear on the Gospel that they were innocent. Then he forced them to undergo the 'cheese-sandwich' test (*tyromanteia*).

In a note (p. 334, n. 2) Peterson documents how often people went to consult magicians when they had lost money or had been the victims of theft. Apuleius (*Apologia* 42) had read in Varro that Nigidius Figulus, the famous occultist, thanks to his gift of clairvoyance, once apprehended a thief, and Porphyry, in his *Life of Plotinus* 11, tells a similar story of the great Neoplatonist who had a special gift of *emblepein*, 'visionary intuition'.

As the cheese-sandwiches were offered, the Bishop attached the following spell to a tripod: 'Lord Iao, Bringer of Light, deliver the thief I am looking for,' observing the suspects, because the one who was unable to eat his sandwich must be the thief. The test was inconclusive (apparently all the suspects ate their sandwiches). The Bishop next tried *phialomanteia*. He poured water and oil into a bowl. We must assume that either Sophronius himself or a medium then conjured up a daemon or a ghost (of a *biaiothanatos*, i.e. a murder victim or a suicide) and asked who the culprit was. This operation was successful.

The Bishop practiced *phialomanteia* on at least one other occasion in his mansion. The son of his personal servant and a Deacon were summoned to the Bishop's bedroom where they saw a table, a 'frankincense offering' under the table and a bowl filled with oil and water on the table. The boy was told to stand naked beside the table, and everything was covered with a linen sheet. (According to the Demotic Magical Papyri, the boy medium normally wears a linen shirt). The Bishop himself plays the role of the professional magician, and the Deacon whispers magical words which the Bishop recites into the boy's ears.

Peterson assumes that the deity or daemon or ghost summoned now establishes himself on the table and manifests his presence in the bowl. The boy first sees lightning (the prelude of an epiphany) in the magical bowl, then a man, sitting on a golden throne, clothed in a golden robe, a crown on his head. Who is this? A pagan god? Or Iao? Or Jesus Christ? Or an angel?

The following operation seems to be a separate ritual, not a continuation of the preceding one. Oil and water are poured into a hole 'behind the door', and the boy is asked to describe what he sees. Peterson (p. 341) thinks that this happens out of doors, not in the Bishop's bedroom, and that the hole is in the ground. The boy sees the Bishop's son, sitting on a black mule, accompanied by two men, returning from Constantinople. The truth of this telepathic experience is confirmed by the son himself, after his return. Peterson compares this to Sosipatra's vision, as told by Eunapius, *Lives of the Philosophers and Sophists*, pp. 469–70, and other reports.

An egg is now produced and the white of it poured out, whereupon the boy sees in the egg once more the Bishop's son, travelling. This technique is called *ooskopia*, and it seems to be very ancient. After all this the boy medium undergoes a serious emotional crisis which lasts for eight months. He is 'without his mind' during that time and has hallucinations: each time he goes for a walk, he sees seven men in white walking ahead of him. Those who care for him take him to the 'holy places' and anoint him with 'holy oil' and finally manage to cure him, but with great efforts. The disastrous effects of the Bishop's occult experiments on the boy's health were no doubt the main reason why these charges, based on eyewitness reports, were brought against him.

CONCLUSION

What has the journey from Homer to Julian the Apostate taught us about the cultural and social dynamics of religion and magic? We have seen that Circe and Medea, the great sorceresses of Greek prehistory actually had the rank of goddesses. Circe, to be sure, must obey the commands of higher deities, but Medea is a law unto herself and literally gets away with murder in a hostile society. The practitioners mentioned by Hippocrates and Plato are shady, controversial figures on the margin of society, feared rather than respected. This situation probably did not change over the centuries. Though most practitioners may have been despised and ridiculed, like Horace's Canidia, they might have been filled with self-importance, and some of them, as we know from Tacitus, were formidable poisoners with very real scientific knowledge. The 'divine men' of the early Christian era were essentially travelling teachers who also performed exorcisms and miracles but wished to be seen as true scientists or philosophers or prophets. Apuleius was a Platonist, a lecturer and story-teller whose *curiositas* transcended philosophy and got him into trouble, but in the end he found salvation in the religion of Isis and became as successful in the existing social order as anyone could be. Within the context of the pagan resistance against Christianity theurgy, as practiced by priests and philosophers in holy places, became the highest and noblest form of magic and re-established for a short time a system of values reminiscent of the age of myth when gods freely communicated with human beings.

Two further issues should be addressed: What was the impact of Empires (the kingdom of Alexander, the Roman world)? What was the impact of urbanization? The history of ancient civilizations may be understood as a succession of smaller and larger Empires: Egypt, Persia, Athens, Macedonia, the Diadochi, Rome. The Romans, the last imperialists in this series, recognized its immanent law clearly and predicted their own decline and fall. Through the territorial conquests which led to the formation of the greatest Empire ever, various cultures with their native religions and customs were brought into close contact with each other. Alexander, for example, founded new cities and settled Greeks in them. Thus, Greek culture spread throughout the East, and there was an exchange of ideas and lifestyles. The conquered nations usually adopted the religion of their conquerors, and their own religion was more often than not degraded to the level of magic, while their main gods became minor deities or evil daemons in the new hierarchy. Moreover, the capitals of these Empires were more than political centers. They propagated a new unified culture thanks to a common language (Greek in Alexander's realm, Latin in the Roman Empire). The urbanization favored intellectual centers (the Alexandrian Library, for instance), and the large cities became melting pots for a great variety of movements, cults and philosophical schools.

Magic, being to a certain extent based on imitation and adaptation, profited greatly from these conditions. For a long time, Egypt was considered a 'Holy Land', and its 'Mysteries' were propagated vigorously. Alexandria was seen as a center of pagan religions at the time when the old rituals had been abandoned elsewhere. Wherever Christianity found roots, it could claim a new universality, because its power was not of this world and did not depend on the ancient sanctuaries. Antiochia provides another example. Berossus, a Hellenized *magos*, was attached to the Seleucid court at this Eastern capital (c.280 BC) and composed substantial works on Babylonian 'wisdom' (i.e. magic) and astrology. The concept underlying these systems copies, in a sense, the hierarchy of a Hellenistic court, just as daemonology of a later period copies the hierarchy of the Roman army. Power structures observed in real life were superimposed on the ranks and orders of planetary gods and daemons, and the same laws of politics, diplomacy and etiquette which promised success in this world were applied to spiritual realms.

Another consequence of urbanization was the disintegration of many features of village life, as observed in Egypt in the third century AD. The temples were allowed to decay, and along with them the knowledge of religious and magical texts written in hieroglyphs lapsed into oblivion.

Finally we should consider the significance of the Christian attitude towards miracles both in a religious and in a magical context. Every culture tends to define magic according to its own roots, norms and specific needs. And every culture assumes that there actually are women and men endowed with unusual powers. The problem is how to define these powers, how to explain them and how to make them work for you.

During the first few centuries of our era, Christians were not expressly forbidden to practice magic. Priests provided amulets and charms for the faithful, and a fifth-century Bishop was very familiar with pagan magic.

It is imposible, sometimes, to separate religious rituals from magical rites, because they could be performed alongside throughout one and the same ceremony. This kind of synthesis or accumulation was not unususal in the Middle Ages and the Renaissance, it seems, and one only has to think of the Satanists of the late nineteenth century to realize how little had changed.

But in 391 the Roman temples were closed, and in 529 Justinian shut down the Academy of Athens which was then under the leadership of Damascius, the distinguished Neoplatonist and militant opponent of the new religion. This dealt the last blow to theurgy, but lower forms of magic no doubt lived on everywhere and survived until the Middle Ages and later. As far as miracles are concerned, we must remember that the Church for the first few centuries was the Church militant *par excellence*. It had to fight the outside enemy, paganism, as well as a host of heresies inside. Hence the intensity of the struggle, the reliance not only on sound dogma but on miracles which had to prove that the God of the new religion was more powerful than all the deities of the old one. Miraculous cures became the domain of holy men, especially monks, and even today, the Roman Catholic Church requires two attested miracles for canonization.

PART 3

Imagining Greek and Roman Magic

Richard Gordon

In memory of Martin Hollis

INTRODUCTION

The founder of the Department of Classics at the University of Malawi, Caroline Alexander, records that the local hospital had a case during her stay in the 1980s of a man who had broken both his legs due to an unusual accident (Alexander, 1991: 74). The nurses stated that he had been flying one night in a maize-basket north of Zomba and crashed on Mt Chinduzi. His legs certainly were broken, but thereafter opinions will doubtless differ. Dr Alexander's pupils found nothing surprising in the report, one observing merely that it was stupid to fly anywhere near Chinduzi, an area notoriously unsafe for flying. When, by contrast, Mr Justice Powell observed at the trial for witchcraft of Jane Wenham in 1712 that there was no law against flying, he summarized more than a century of growing scepticism in western European intellectual and legal circles of the very possibility of magical action (Thomas, 1971: 547).

Taking their cue from the heirs of that scepticism, the founding fathers Tylor and Frazer, anthropologists once took for granted that magic is a primitive mode of thinking. Even the publication of Fortune's *Sorcerers of Dobu* (1932), Malinowski's *Coral Gardens and their Magic* (1935), and Evans-Pritchard's *Witchcraft, Oracles and Magic among the Azande* two years later hardly dented the consensus. Although English social anthropologists had already shifted to the study of accusations, it was not until the 1970s, in the context of the structuralists' wider challenge to the naive essentialism of other anthropological topoi – totemism, animism, myth – that the point was widely taken and magic seen as a medium for thinking, embedded within a mass of other representations of the world, and on its own premisses unfalsifiable. Subsequently, both religion and science, the other members of the Frazerian triangle, have themselves been historicized and relativized (Tambiah, 1990; Lloyd, 1990). The cynosure of prestidigitation, Robert Houdin (1805–71), has taken his place in the history of colonialism (cf. Moore, 1997); in our own days magic has been reinvented as a living praxis (Luhrmann, 1989). The most urgent current academic debate about magic is whether the Frazerian ghost can be exorcized fully without embracing some more or less objectionable form of cultural relativism.

One promising avenue here may be Raymond Boudon's notion of good reasons for false beliefs (Boudon, 1995: 59–201).

In this context, the continuing interest of concepts of magic in the Greek and Roman worlds is that in these societies for the first time such practices ceased to be embedded, that is, simply taken for granted, and where necessary condemned, and came to be examined, contested and defended in terms other than their own. We owe to the Graeco-Roman world both the word magic and many of the semantic implications which it still has, above all the conflict between magic as specious show, as prestidigitation (in the manner of David Copperfield), and magic as a special power to achieve real effects both for good and for ill (in the manner of the Museum of Witchcraft at Boscastle in North Cornwall). In trying more precisely to locate magic in Greek and Roman society, the starting-point must be that there was no single 'ancient view of magic'. Rather, a whole gamut of representations and claims competed in the market-place, each with its own agenda. It is this variety of representations, and the ideological functions they served, that I denote by the phrase imagining magic. That is, magic in the Graeco-Roman world became good to think with. Beneath the overt representations and images deeper questions are being raised, positions staked out: Where are we to locate the boundary between the possible, the marvellous, and the sheerly impossible, the fantastic? Between belief and credulousness? How far can we trust common sense? Can people control the inhabitants of the Other World? Can gods will harm? If so, ought they to do so? What are the limits of the power of utterance? Is magical power part of nature, or is it a purely human invention or skill? Where lies the boundary between legitimate and illegitimate use of the Other World?

This variety of opinion about magic – or perhaps rather magics – was due to two factors. On the one hand, the civic compromise, the absence from the Greek and Roman state of an autonomous priestly class, meant that there was no institution with the monopoly of the means of salvation, in the Weberian sense of access to the sum of the benefits supplied by the Other World. The final decision about what belonged to, or was permissible within, civic religion lay, both in the Greek world and at Rome, with the highest political instances, and was therefore always primarily a matter of political rather than theological discussion. But there always was plenty of free space for debate below the level of such final decision-making. On the other, the development in the fifth century BC by the Sophists of a determinedly rationalistic discourse later institutionalised as the practice of philosophy made it widely impossible for the educated to accept traditional religious beliefs without some mental reservations. Immediately, quite extreme conclusions were drawn, such as the claims of the satyr-play *Sisyphus*, usually ascribed to Critias but more probably by Euripides (Dihle,

1977), that religion is a mere device ('concealing the truth with lying words') to reinforce the moral-political order (88 B25 *DK*, cf. de Romilly, 1988: 152–5); Epicureanism and Euhemerism are later and milder variants of the same tack. More usually, intellectuals – who could hardly saw off the branch their class sat on – tended to move in the direction of natural theology, inferring a rational and providential deity from the order of the cosmos (Gerson, 1990). But that too was not without its difficulties: if the Stoic Chrysippus could persuade himself that bedbugs are natural alarm-clocks and that flies have been created to make us tidier in the home (*SVF* 2: 1163), not many others shared his confidence (Dragona-Monachou, 1994).

The imbrication of these two factors produced over time a general conception of civic religion, not merely among the élite, which empha-sized the collective and beneficent aspects of traditional belief – what has been dubbed the religion of everyday – both inasmuch as it was this set of practices which defined the city in relation to the Other World and because this form of religion was the simplest to defend on rational and moral grounds. The other aspect of traditional belief, the religion of the special case, a heterogeneous collection of rituals for empowering individ-uals or groups in particular contexts for specific ends, came to be thought of as more or less at odds with the values expressed in the religion of everyday (cf. Montano, 1993). But this is simply a specifically Graeco-Roman version of the classic tendency, pointed out by Weber and refined by Pierre Bourdieu (1971), towards the monopolisation of legitimate religious capital by a particular social group or interest. Given this ideological and institutional context, it will come as no surprise that the notion of magic, at any rate in what I shall call a strong sense, was formed in the ancient world discontinuously and, as it were, with everybody talking at once.

It is said that the location of the original flowerbeds of Thomas Jefferson's garden at Monticello was rediscovered by shining car-headlights over the lawn at night. But no amount of serendipity of this archaeological kind will rediscover for us the reality of ancient magic. It might seem, for example, that the emergence of the word itself might provide a decisive insight into the nature of that reality. But that is not so. In all probability the substantive *magos*, which later came to mean magician, was coined at a specific juncture in Greek history, around the period of the Persian Wars in the early Classical period. But equally certainly it did not then connote a notion approximating to our 'magic'. It was rather a form of insult, associating Greek practitioners of the religion of the special case with the Persian or Median priestly caste made familiar by those wars and the preceding Persian occupation of the Ionian coastal cities (cf. Nock, 1933/ 1972).[1] That is certainly its force in a passage of Sophocles' *Oedipus*, where the king scornfully reproaches Teiresias the seer with being a 'scheme-hatching *magos*' (387). Diviners are typical practitioners of the religion of the special case (cf. Culianu, 1980; Brown, 1981); and the Persian magi are several times said by Herodotus to have interpreted royal dreams (1.120.1, 3; 7.19.1; cf Carastro, 1997: 26–33). Although both text and interpretation are much disputed, it seems likely that the earliest surviving use of the word, c.500 BC, occurs in a list of other practitioners of that religion of the special case, denounced by Heraclitus of Ephesus for offering an impious – because false – view of the gods and the hereafter: 'people of the night – magi, male bacchants, maenads, initiates into the mysteries' (12 B 14a D–K).[2] This list seems to have a marked internal structure: the *bakkhoi* (masc.) are opposed to the *lenaiai* (fem., here translated as 'maenads'), though both are worshippers of Dionysus, so that it is probable that *magoi* in first place are both contrasted with, but also somehow linked to, the *mystai* in fourth. Rather than suppose that official priests – why should they be Persian? – are being contrasted with private mysteries (Bollack and Wismann, 1972: 93; Conche, 1986: 167f.), it is easier to believe that the *magoi* are precisely the sort of people we shall meet in the Hippocratic *On the sacred disease*, experts in religious healing, contrasted with the *mystai*, people who receive initiation, whether at Eleusis or elsewhere.[3]

The noun *mageia* is not known to have been used until two hundred years later, and even then, coupled with the word *alexipharmaka*, antidotes, seems to mean 'magical rites' (pl.) (Theophr. *HP* 9.15.7; cf. Steier, 1933: 30). Its earliest surviving abstract use to mean 'magic' occurs in a Hellenistic fragment, from a work falsely ascribed to Aristotle,[4] in the context of the Persian Magi: 'They did not know goetic *mageia*', goetic meaning in this context, as usual, specious or fraudulent claims to magical power (Arist. frg.36 Rose).[5] *Mageia* was still an ambivalent notion; and even during the Principate we can find positive evaluation of the word's allusion to the Persian priesthood:

> You think it your duty to call philosophers who follow Pythagoras, or Orpheus, 'magicians' (*magoi*). But in my view followers of any philosophy should be called 'magi' if they aim to become holy and righteous. (*Epist. Apoll. Tyan.* 16 [tr. Conybeare, adapted])

From the very beginning, magic has been a term whose semantic implications can only be understood by close attention to context, to the values and claims that it is made to sustain.

The fragment of pseudo-Aristotle suggests at any rate a partial truth, that a strong notion of magic ('goetic magic') seems to have been a creation of the Hellenistic period. Sadly, given the massive loss of Hellenistic texts, we can hardly do more than gaze into an empty cage.

But it would be quite false to suppose that, in so far as magic also connotes the transgressive, the illicit use of religious power, there had not always, in the Dark Ages already, been rules for the exercise of such power: in that sense, magic existed far earlier than any familiar word for it. There has probably been no society, certainly no complex society, without rules concerning the use of whatever forms of religious power are deemed possible. We may conceive of these as distributed along a continuum between the wholly normal/acceptable i.e. fully legitimate uses, and the wholly abnormal/unacceptable, i.e. fully illegitimate uses. In the Greek world there is plenty of evidence – in Homer, in other Archaic literature, and in documentary evidence – of 'magic before magic', of the more or less negatively-marked deployment of religious power for socially doubtful ends.

The same is true of the Roman world. By all accounts the word *magia* begins to be used there towards the end of the civil-war period: the first surviving Latin usage, *magicis . . . sacris*, with or by magic rites, occurs in Vergil, *Eclogue* 8.66 (composed around 40 BC), an imitation of Theocritus' second *Idyll*, the so-called *Pharmakeutria*, *Witch* – although Theocritus himself does not use the Greek word, simply a periphrasis, 'an Assyrian stranger', for *magos* (162).[6] It seems to me likely however that the word had already been transposed into Latin in Varro Atacinus' *Argonautae*, a reworking of Apollonius Rhodius' *Argonautica* written c.45–44 BC (Arcellaschi, 1990: 197–230). Varro Atacinus linked Medea's name to Persia through the homonymity of Medus, her son by Aegeus, king of Athens, and the land of Media (Probus ad Verg. *Georg.* 2.126). Such an etymology would have been superfluous if he had not regarded her, in accord with the Hellenistic history of magic we shall look at later, as indeed a magician. Still earlier, probably in the early 50s, Catullus had also written an imitation of Theocritus' second *Idyll* (Pliny, *HN* 28.19), a poem which was probably one important source of much of the specific imagery of (Italian) witchcraft we find in the Augustan poets, and in which he may well have used the adjective *magicus*. But the Roman world had already developed a number of words for negatively-marked use of religious power, nouns such as *veneficus*, *saga*, local adjectives such as *Marsus*, also *Sabellus*, *Paelignus*, relating to the Sabellian people, traditional enemies, famous for being able to burst snakes open by magic, or *Thessalus*, borrowed from the Greek word commonly used for male witch; and technical terms such as *cantus*, *cantio*, *incantio*, *carmen*, probably *nenia*. Catullus' (7.12) and Vergil's (*Ecl.* 3.103) casual use of the word *fascinare* implies that another, innate or natural, aspect of such power, the evil eye, was already long familiar in Italy (Tupet, 1986: 2606–10).

Moreover, if there can be said to have been magic before magic in the ancient world, the concept never ceases to develop, in response both to ideological changes and to political ones. If we can locate the emergence of a strong view of magic in the Hellenistic period, for example, it is partly because of the appearance then of books, often ascribed to (pseudo-) Democritus and Pythagoras, which absorbed much of the traditional healing practice of 'root-cutters' and wise-folk, together with a mass of other lore, into a quite new concept of natural magic. Natural magic is a key concept, inasmuch as it draws upon the essentially rationalist notion of Nature, autonomous and enruled. So far from treating the praxeis of wise-folk and root-cutters as marginal or transgressive, the pseudo-Democritean tradition saw them as exploiting the innate powers of Nature to heal, to divine – but also to perform marvels. The rationalist position, that such beliefs are either impious or nonsense, is turned on its head by the claim that Nature herself is the source of the practitioners' powers. But this view is exclusively that of learned outsiders: the practitioners themselves have, generally speaking, no category Nature with which to work – insofar as they are concerned to account for their powers, they use a different conceptual language.

As for political changes, the transition from Republic to Principate occasioned a relatively sharp increase in the visibility of illicit religion, magic linked with private divination: such charges expressed as plainly as anything else the shift from political pluralism to autocracy. The *Calendar of 354 AD*, in the section Chronicle of the City of Rome, which often includes sensational titbits (Salzman, 1990: 52–6), reports for example that 45 men and 85 women were executed under Tiberius (*Chron. ann. 354* [*MGH* 9, Chronica minora, pt.16, p. 145.26–8, ed. Mommsen]), almost certainly after the *senatus consultum* of 16 or 17 AD condemning private divination and magic. Illicit religious practice came to be viewed typically, but not by any means exclusively, in terms which underwrote the centrality of the Princeps to the political system of the Empire.

But alongside the tendency to define illicit religion in terms of its political rather than its social danger, we find during the Principate an inclination to deploy magic, still in close alliance with private divination, as part of a wider, hesitant, attempt to give substance to the imagined community of the Roman empire – 'old' Roman religion had no symbolic purchase at this level – through its negative inversions, atheists on the one hand (that is, Christians and Epicureans), and practitioners of illicit religion, magicians and private diviners, on the other. This tendency becomes more strongly marked from the late second century, and is linked with hesitant moves to sanction the very knowledge of magic and divination, not merely the harm they did; but its full expression had to wait until the creation of a Christian empire.

My aim in this chapter is to set out a number of contexts for understanding Greek and Roman representations of magic. An approach through historical narrative is inadvisable, both because we simply do not possess enough relevant documents – what would we not give, for example, to see the protocols of the hearings before which the unfortunates mentioned by the *Calendar of 354* were executed under Tiberius? – and because narrative, despite its revived fashionability, is a discursive mode inept for cultural history and the history of ideas. Moreover, narrative constantly naturalizes the objects of its discourse, and if anything is obvious about magic, it must be that it is a matter of representations that shift more or less subtly in relation to processes of change in other dimensions. Instead, I have divided the chapter into four thematic sections, with due acknowledgement made, where appropriate, to time-scales.

The first argues that the most general context for Greek and Roman views of magic is the category of the marvellous, which we can characterize roughly as the coal-face at which any religious view of the world must continuously labour if it is to sustain its truth-claims. The marvellous can of course be sub-divided into numerous departments, but that is not here to my purpose: rather, the tinkling of exclamation marks should not deafen us to the ideological work involved in the recogition of a marvel, and especially the moral evaluation it evokes. The key questions are always: Whose marvel? To what sub-category is it properly to be assigned? What are we to do with it? Magic in a strong sense occupies simply one corner of the realm of the marvellous, which is the magical in the weakest sense.

Before moving on to survey some explicit ancient views of magic in the strong sense, we need – this is the second section – at least a schematic account (indeed none other is possible) of the emergence of the category magic in antiquity, and of four main groups of magical practitioners. The differences between these, and their conceptions of their powers, make clear that no concise definition can do justice to such diversity. The third section, ancient discussion of magic, relies heavily upon literary texts. It has attractively been argued that we should think of magic as Utopia, without substance but with a history (Daxelmüller, 1993: 23–6). In my view, it is much too easy to be distracted by the archaeological survival of curse- and vindicative-tablets, and the remains of Graeco-Egyptian magical receptaries (grimoires), from the essential point, which is that the true home of magic is a body of narrative, what Cicero calls 'old women's tales', which construct the social knowledge to which any event, real or supposed, fearful or peculiar, may be referred and in terms of which, if need be, explained. Literary texts, emanating from an élite educated within a rationalistic philosophy, supply us, by default, with elaborate and distanced, often ironic, examples of such tales as well as images of witches and magicians (cf. Phillips, 1994). But negotiation with magic also took place in a variety of other literary modes and genres. The receptaries themselves, which allude repeatedly to the marvellous effects of this or that spell, can be thought of as part of this process of negotiation.

I turn finally to consider the legal repression of magic in Greece and Rome, a history which reveals the difficulty, within the context of polytheistic practice and the sheer diversity of views about what constitutes magic and what it might really be, of defining what precisely, if anything, was criminal about magic. But, because the concept of *Rechtsstaat* in antiquity either did not exist (in the Greek world) or was very different from the modern one (Rome), the absence of laws by no means prevented the repeated condemnation, to summary execution or exile, of individuals who could convincingly be accused of magical practices. Here again, the old women's tales played their part in forming a horizon of expectation, images of the illicit, the shape of the forbidden, by means of which, in the theatre of justice, the political community defined its religious enemies and so also imagined its own ideal religious self.

THE MARVELLOUS

Magic may be a practice, but more than anything else it is a shared construction, a child of the imagination. It is that quality which makes it both interesting to the social historian and exasperatingly elusive: magic defies common sense quite as much as it resists definition. We might indeed say that magic represents the inverse of common sense, a more or less boundless world made possible by cutting the ropes that bind the imagination to the world of hard facts. Magic thus belongs to the realm of the marvellous. 'The image of the magician grows from story to story, and from teller to teller, precisely because he is a favourite hero of folk imagination . . . the image of the magician was created outside magic' (Mauss, 1902–3/1972: 33).

The marvellous is a construction of the imagination, made possible by another, equally massive, effort of the human imagination, the enrulement of the world of experience. The marvellous (which here includes the category of the strange) is in effect simply the totality of perceived infringements of culturally-stated rules for normality. Thus the big toe of King Pyrrhus' right foot, which failed to be cremated (c.272 BC) and was preserved inside a closed chest in a temple in Epirus, cured those afflicted with diseases of the spleen by mere touch (Pliny, *HN* 7.20). A point of regular intersection between the Other World and this one is constructed through a set of leading questions: fire consumes dead bodies, why did it refuse to burn the toe? parts of dead bodies belong out of sight, under the ground, why is this one kept above ground? Normality is of course neither fixed nor necessarily agreed: the marvellous is always produced within a micro-climate of evaluative assertions. The most tempting marvels rely upon tacit or implied norms — in the case of Pyrrhus' toe the empirically absurd claim that crematory fire consumes a body completely. Nor is the marvellous necessarily the inverse of a norm: denials of the normal may take any contrastive form. In the same passage in which Pliny mentions Pyrrhus' big toe, he alludes to a famous Italic people, the Hirpi Sorani, among whom were to be found a number of families whose members were gifted with the power of walking over blazing fires without injury (*HN* 7.19; cf. Vergil, *Aen.* 11. 785–8 with Servius ad loc., p. 564.14–23 Thilo). This ability was recognised officially as marvellous by the Roman Senate's grant of immunity from military service; but the Hirpi themselves expressed their difference from the norm by stressing that in their language, Samnite, the word *(h)irpus* meant wolf (Servius ibid. on 1.787, p. 564.28–31, citing Varro). Wolves belong to the wild, to the mountain; what wolves are to the tame, the Hirpi are to ordinary men (cf. Piccaluga, 1976; Buxton, 1987: 63f.).

The natural world is that part of the empirical world which provides both the model and the matrix of the marvellous: the human effort invested since the Palaeolithic in the enrulement of the natural world is repaid many times over in that world's endless, obliging, productivity of marvels. Everyone in the ancient world knew, for example, that there exists a fish, a very small fish, the *echenêis*, ship-stayer, known in Latin later as the *remora*, which by attaching itself to a ship can prevent it from moving (the earliest text is Aristotle, *HA* 2.14, 505b18–20; cf. Pliny, *HN* 9.79). 'If a horse,' writes Aelian, 'happens to step onto a wolf's track, it is struck immobile; if you throw a wolf's vertebra under a running quadriga, it will suddenly stop as though freeze-dried, when the horses tread on the bone' (*NA* 1.36). The second clause offers the empirical proof of the claim in the first: it is a second-order marvel, constructed on the back of another. But it also reveals why knowledge of the power of the wolf's vertebra, from among all the hundreds and thousands of curiosities of nature, observed or merely asserted in the Graeco-Roman world, should have become widespread, 'settled knowledge' and so relatively immune to the corrosive effects of disconfirmatory experience: it was potentially useful, it could be deployed in a claim to power over events in the world.

Here we may try to distinguish between the strange and the marvellous: the strange is the unmarked product of a discrepancy between any norm and any claimed empirical event; the marvellous is the strange appropriated into a network of claims to power. The hippopotamus, writes Pliny elsewhere,

is a real consultant in one department of medicine: when it has stuffed itself by incessant feeding, it finds a place on the bank where reeds have been newly cut and, when it espies a sharp stubble,[7] presses its body down onto it and so cuts a certain blood-vessel in its leg. By thus letting blood, it frees its body from other disorders, and covers the wound up again with mud. (*HN* 8.96)

Here the marvellous provides a natural precedent and justification for the human doctor's claim that bleeding is a necessary part of his practice: the hippopotamus's behaviour is elevated beyond the merely strange by being appropriated into a medical discourse. Much the same can be said of the most famous examples of the marvellous in ancient nature, the magnet, the 'breathing stone'; or the imputrescent meat of the peafowl. St. Augustine became convinced of this last by means of his own experiment:

One day at Carthage I was served with a roast peacock, and I gave orders that what seemed a sufficient quantity of meat should be cut from the breast and kept. After an interval of some days, long enough to have ensured the putrefaction of any other kind of cooked meat, this was brought out and presented to me; and I found it had no offensive smell. It was then put back in store, and after more than thirty days it was found to be in the same condition; and there was no change in a year's time except that the flesh was somewhat dry and shrivelled. (*Civ. Dei* 21. 4, p. 762.15–23 Dombart-Kalb [tr. Knowles])

Augustine's interest in this property of peafowl meat is that it is a natural marvel admitted as such by pagans: *a posteriori*, they should admit that God can ensure that quasi-material souls can survive the purgative fire after death (ibid. 21.7). If what is undeniably fully material can negate the general rule that flesh must rot, then there is at least a good chance that the only partly material can negate another general rule, that fire consumes.

If the natural world models the realm of the marvellous as a whole, its most interesting inhabitants are other humans. Marvellous peoples belong to the earliest reports in Greek literature – we have only to think of the one-eyed Cyclopes, the giant cannibal Laistrygones or the navel-knowledge of the Phaeacians' ships of the *Odyssey*. Neither in that poem nor in Herodotus are such reports merely fabulous: taken as a whole – despite many 'free' details – they reveal a structure of differences by which Greek social rules and institutions are shown to be both natural and normative (Buxton, 1994: 69–144). In the Hellenistic and Roman periods, after Alexander's conquest of the Persian empire and the creation by the poet Callimachus of a specific genre of *Mirabilia* (Giannini, 1964), fantastic reports multiply, such as those of the Hippodes, a people with horses' hooves, and the Panotii, whose enormous ears covered their modesty (Pliny, *HN* 4.95), the marvellous tending to decline into the (merely) bizarre. For the most part however reports of strange foreign peoples serve agenda individual to the writer. One marked tendency, to be found already in the work of Onesicritus of Astypaleia in the lifetime of Alexander the Great (d.323 BC), is the discovery of philosophical peoples, such as the land of Musikanos, whose inhabitants ate in common as in Sparta, possessed no slaves and enjoyed no law-courts other than those for murder and assault (Strabo 15.1.34, 701–2C = Jacoby, *FGrH* 134 F24).

The creation of the genre of *Mirabilia* also made it possible to fuse geographical marvels with natural ones. Philostratus' *Life of Apollonius of Tyana* provides a fine example, the detailed account of the different species of snakes (*drakontes*) to be found in India.[8] Those that live in the mountain foothills but hunt in the marshes are reddish, with serrated backs, and beards, while

> their scales glitter like silver; and the pupils of their eyes consist of a fiery stone, and they say that this has an uncanny power for many secret purposes. (3.7, p. 246.5–8 Mumprecht [tr. Conybeare])

The proper mountain snakes however are much more terrible and may be taken, if at all, only by means of a clever ruse:

> [The Indians] embroider golden letters (*grammata*) on a scarlet cloak, which they lay in front of the animal's lair, casting a spell on it by means of the letters (for this is the only way to overcome the snake's unwavering eyes); and they sing mysterious chants to it, by means of which the snake is induced to stretch his neck out of his lair and fall asleep over the letters. (3.8, p. 246.24–248.7 Mumprecht [tr. Conybeare, adapted])

An account of Indian snake charming has here been read in terms of a trope of ancient ethnography going back at least to Herodotus' description of the collection of cassia and cinnamon in Arabia (3.61, cf. Detienne, 1972/1977: 5–36), of which the burden is that the value of natural products is inversely proportional to their availability. What the Indians are after are the precious stones to be found in the dragons' heads which, like the magical ring of Gyges which made its possessor invisible (Plato, *Rep.* 2, 359d–60c), have 'an uncanny power'. In order to acquire them, the Indians use 'letters' which in themselves have the power to cast a spell upon the dragons' unblinking eyes – 'letters' which immediately recall the *charactêres*, the incomprehensible signs that can only be read in the Other World used in the learned magical practice of the Imperial period,[9] but with a history going back to one interpretation of the 'baneful signs' that were to ensure the death of Bellerophon(tes) (Homer *Iliad* 6.168f.); the enchanting figures on the *kestos himas*, the embroidered girdle of Aphrodite to which we shall return (ibid. 14.214–17); and its cousins, the feet, belt and diadem of the statue of Artemis of Ephesus that bore the most famous ancient incantatory names, the 'Ephesian letters' (*grammata Ephesiaka*) (Pausanias Grammaticus, frg. 185, p. 165.15–17 Schwabe = ε 85 Erbse; cf. Arnold, 1989: 23).

The true medium of the marvellous however is narrative. Narrative, like the medium of film, is accorded the right to refuse the opposition between objective report and downright falsehood: its realm is that middle world we call fiction (cf. Searle, 1979/1981), and the ancient world as often as not 'history'. One or two examples will enable us to explore this theme a little further. We may first pick up Aphrodite's girdle, in Homer's 'virtuoso performance' (Janko, 1992: 168). Hera is plotting to distract Zeus while her brother Poseidon helps the Achaeans, and to this end she proposes to seduce him. First, she bathes and perfumes herself, as a woman would, but then decides she needs something stronger, and pretends to Aphrodite that she wants to reconcile Okeanos and Tethys, to 'bring them back to their bed to be merged in love with each other' (*Iliad* 14.209). From her breasts, Aphrodite

> . . . unbound the elaborate, pattern-pierced
> zone, and on it are figured all beguilements (*thelktêria*), and loveliness
> is figured upon it, and passion of sex is there, and the whispered
> endearment that steals the heart away even from the thoughtful.
> She put this in Hera's hands, and called her by name and spoke to her:
> 'Take this zone, and hide it away in the fold of your bosom.
> It is elaborate, all things are figured therein. And I think
> whatever is your heart's desire shall not go unaccomplished'.
> So she spoke, and the ox-eyed lady Hera smiled on her
> and smiling hid the zone away in the fold of her bosom.
>
> (*Iliad* 14. 214–23 [tr. Lattimore])

Hera also takes the precaution of offering Hypnos a small inducement to make Zeus fall fast asleep; and Zeus falls promptly, and heavily, into the trap:

> So speaking, the son of Kronos caught his wife in his arms.
> There underneath them the divine earth broke into young, fresh
> grass, and into dewy clover, crocus and hyacinth
> so thick and soft it held the hard ground deep away from them.
> There they lay down together and drew about them a golden
> wonderful cloud, and from it the glimmering dew descended.
>
> (14. 346–51 [tr. Lattimore])

This narrative fuses different forms of the marvellous. The one that interests me here is the use of the girdle to evoke the tension between men's desire for sexual excitement and their fear that the very act of pleasure is merely another feminine wile, that the moment of male *jouissance* is actually the point of deepest subjection, the point when 'Hera smiles'.[10] The narrative voice, even-handed as ever, both confirms the suspicion – we hear the two goddesses colluding – and, in the final passage, offers the thought that the pleasure experienced may outweigh the shame at being so gulled. More important, though, to the general theme is that the subjective experience of the force of desire is represented as something created from outside, manipulable, subject to wile and skill: the narrative transposes one of the basic assumptions of love magic into the realm of the marvellous (Pirenne-Delforge, 1993: 278–80). And the fiction can admit what otherwise could hardly be admitted, that being compelled to pleasure allows many potential questions to be left quite simply unanswered.

The vagaries of passion might not only affect gods and humans. Pausanias mentions in his *Description of Greece*, one of the indispensable sources for the Greek marvellous, a bronze statue at Olympia, by Dionysius the Argive, of a mare and attendant. The mare was neither tall nor attractive, and its tail was cropped, which made it look ugly,

> but stallions go wild for it, not only in spring but every day in the year – they break their halters and escape from their grooms and come galloping into Altis [the sacred precinct of Zeus' temple] and leap upon it much more madly than they would on the finest living mare that was used to being mounted. Their hooves slip on it, but they go on and on whinnying all the more and leaping up on it more and more eagerly until you manage to drag them away with whips and main force: until you do so nothing can release them from that bronze. (5.27.3–4 [tr. Levi, adapted])

The vividness of the narrative here, the precisely observed detail of the hooves slipping ineffectually off the metal flanks, of the grooms desperate to control their concupiscent charges, is typical of the marvellous: the audience must be brought to belief by the force of rhetorical accomplishment. The story certainly resonates with many others that have to do with the ambivalent status of art-objects, those concerning human attempts to couple with divine statues for example, or the competition between Zeuxis and Parrhasius ('I have deceived the birds, but you have deceived me': Pliny, *HN* 35.65, cf. Elsner, 1995: 17); but it also alludes to one of the most famous items in the pharmacopoeia of ancient love magic, the object or substance named *hippomanes*, 'mad-horse' – the statue was indeed known by this name. According to Aristotle, there were two different things to which this name was given, one a kind of thin semen-like discharge from the vulva when mares are on heat, the other a growth on the foal:

> After parturition a mare will at once swallow the afterbirth and also eat
> off the growth on the foal's forehead known as *hippomanes*: the size of
> this is slightly smaller than a dried fig, and to look at is flat and round,
> and black in colour. If anyone gets hold of it before <the mare does>
> and she gets scent of it, the scent drives her mad and frantic. That is
> why it is in demand by sorceresses (*pharmakides*), who collect it for their
> purposes. (*Hist. Anim.* 6.22, 577a7–13 [tr. Peck])

There came in due course to be considerable disagreement about where
exactly the growth was to be found, on the forehead, the rump or the
genitals, even whether it was a growth rather than, for example, a plant
(Servius ad *Georg.* 3. 280). The mares eat the *hippomanes*, says Aelian,

> for had this continued to be attached always to the foal, both horses and
> mares would be inflamed with a passion for uncontrolled mating. This
> may, if you like, be a gift bestowed by Poseidon or Athena, the god
> and goddess of horses, upon these animals to ensure that their race is
> perpetuated and does not perish through an insane indulgence. (*NA* 14.
> 18 [tr. Scholfield]; cf.3.17)

In this context – and the issue of *hippomanes* is much more interesting and
complex than I have space here to explore – the narrative of the bronze
mare in the Altis does not merely proclaim a marvel, it provides an
example of a divinely-ordained system of restraint in disorder. Nothing
could be more absurd than stallions dashing themselves in frenzy onto an
inanimate object: the natural purpose of the sexual act is frustrated by the
uncanny power of Dionysius' creation. And the cause of that disorder?
'Anyway', says Pausanias, 'it is clear that what happens to the stallion is
due to the arts of some magician (*andros magou*)' (5.27.3). The story
concludes with a judgement about the proper location of this instance of
the marvellous: within the magical.

Although magic shares the realm of the marvellous with religion, the
creation of the city-state began an inexorable process of moralizing the
divine world, which in turn affected the way in which the marvellous was
perceived. Older reports of the marvellous tolerate ambivalences which
would later be rejected, edited out, rationalized. But even so there is often
a trace of unease in ascribing to gods powers already negatively marked in
human society. If we take for example Homer's account of how Sarpedon
managed to kill the Trojan Alkathoös:[11]

> But now Poseidon beat him down at the hands of Idomeneus,
> for he bewitched his shining eyes, made moveless his bright limbs,
> so that he could not run backward, neither evade him,

but stood like a statue or a tree with leaves towering
motionless, while fighting Idomeneus stabbed at the middle
of his chest with the spear. (*Iliad* 13.434–39 [tr. Lattimore])

What motivates recourse here to the marvellous is Alkathoös' strange behaviour. According to normal expectation, he might have done one of two things: he might have put up a proper fight or, giving way to fear, have run away. But no, he simply stood still to be butchered. The oddity of this is registered in two ways, first in the distorted appeal to the analogy between man and rooted thing – column or tree – which is normally an image of steadfastness; and then in the extraordinary behaviour of Idomeneus' spear, which

was stuck fast in Alkathoos' heart
but the heart was panting still and beating to shake the butt end
of the spear. (ibid. 442–3 [tr. Lattimore, adapted])[12]

The explanation offered for the marvel is divine intervention: the Homeric gods have such powers. But there is at the same time in the word *thelxas*, correctly translated by Lattimore 'bewitch', a suggestion that the exercise of such power is untoward, even improper – the gods may have such powers but they ought not to use them.

A similar ambivalence is to be be found in the late Archaic *Homeric Hymn to Hermes*, a bright exploration of the theme of divine cunning (whose very cleverness has suggested to some that it may have been composed only in the first half of the fifth century) (Janko, 1982: 143). Apollo and the infant Hermes have been directed by Zeus to make up their quarrel and search for Apollo's stolen cattle together. When they reach Pylos, where Hermes has hidden them, Apollo is furious to find that Hermes has already sacrificed two of them, and makes handcuffs of willow to bind Hermes:

<but the bands would not hold him>, and the withes of osier fell from him and began at once to grow from the ground there beneath their feet. And intertwining with one another, they quickly grew and covered all the wild-roving cattle by the will of thieving Hermes, so that Apollo was astonished as he looked. (*Hymn to Hermes* 410–14 Allen [tr. Evelyn-White, adapted])

This account, which recalls an earlier scene in which Hermes plaits marvellous sandals to outwit Apollo (79–81), seems to allude to a conception of Hermes also to be found in the Athenian curse-tablets, which are precisely binding-tablets, and, at least in the fourth-century BC, often invoke Hermes *katochos*, the binder (Kahn, 1978: 106–11). That is, by the fourth century BC, and doubtless considerably earlier, an aspect of Hermes' power which was still tolerable in the high Archaic period has been bracketed off, negatively marked, and associated with malign magic. Already in the *Hymn*, the tacit question of whether Hermes' binding power may properly be invoked is answered obliquely, by way of the moral judgement that emerges just before Apollo's amazement, in the epithet for Hermes, *klepsiphrôn*, 'with the heart/cunning of a thief'.

The process of moralizing the gods required not merely that their powers be curtailed in certain ways but also that boundary-lines within the realm of the divine should be more clearly drawn. One result was the gradual creation in the Archaic period of a more or less distinct category of divine beings called *daemones*, the double advantage of which was to separate the good gods of civic cult from morally ambivalent divine powers active at folk-level while at the same time opening up a new realm, of the 'dark' marvellous, based on the older view of *daemones*, as connected with the souls of the dead (cf. Detienne, 1963; Sfameni Gasparro, 1997: 70–3). The local history of Temese in Lucania, for example, includes an account, first known from Callimachus' *Aitia* (frgs. 98–9 Pfeiffer, tr. Trypanis p. 74 n. a), of how the famous athlete Euthymus wrestled with a *daemon*, a spirit, called Hero, the ghost of one of Odysseus' sailors who had raped a local girl and been stoned to death (Domínguez Monedero, 1992). This spirit for centuries persecuted the people of Temese so unforgivingly that they would have abandoned their city but for the express command of the Delphic oracle; when he was thrown, Hero vanished under the sea, and Euthymus, who had first won the Olympic crown in wrestling in 484 BC, himself became a hero and the recipient of cult (Paus. 6.6.7–11; cf. Aelian, *VH* 8.18). In the version offered by Pausanias, the malign *daemon* is provided with an identity that fits Temese into Homeric geography, but which also turns him into a *biaiothanatos*, those who have been killed by violence, part of the wider class of the restless dead, who came to be thought of as the typical instruments of malign magic (Waszink, 1949; Johnston, 1997a).[13] Once again (it is difficult to guess when this might have taken place, but presumably in the Hellenistic period) an inhabitant of the older divine world has been re-defined and given an unequivocal, morally negative, identity.

Once invented, the category of the restless dead gave rise to numerous tales, in effect ghost stories, which explored the dimensions and possibilities of the new corner of the marvellous devoted to them (cf. Plato, *Leg.* 9, 865d–e). One of the most famous, evidently widely current in the second century AD, is told us by the younger Pliny in a letter to Licinius Sura about belief in the supernatural (though he does not use that term). It concerns a house in Athens that was for long haunted by the ghost of a filthy old man rattling chains. The philosopher Athenodorus decided to rent the house and spend the night there.

> At first there was nothing but the general silence of night; then came the clanking of iron and dragging of chains . . . The noise grew louder, came nearer, was heard in the doorway, and then inside the room. He looked round, saw and recognized the ghost (*effigies*) described to him. It stood and beckoned, as if summoning him.

Athenodorus eventually follows the old man until he vanishes at a particular point in the courtyard.

> The following day he approached the magistrates, and advised them to give orders for the place to be dug up. There they found bones, twisted round with chains, which were left bare and corroded by the fetters when time and the action of the soil had rotted away the body. The bones were collected and given a public burial, and after the shades had been duly laid to rest the house saw them no more. (Pliny, *Ep.* 7.27.5–11 [tr. Radice, excerpted])

The association with Athenodorus would date this version of the story to the period of Augustus, but the story is likely in origin to be Hellenistic, since it turns on the cliché of the rational philosopher contrasted with the childish fears of the crowd. In this case, the dry tone – it has been observed that Pliny's report 'would not disgrace the annals of a psychic research bureau' (Sherwin-White, 1966: 437) – vouches for the trustworthiness of the account: it becomes a fact, whereas in the other version we possess, by Lucian (*Philops.* 31f.), it is just another tall story. Pliny's version makes the point that all such a ghost wanted was the burial to which he had a rightful claim; Lucian's proclaims the power of the magician's spells over the spirit. But both take for granted the underlying point, which was what interested practitioners of magic, namely the belief that the souls of those who died by violence, whether criminal, retributive or suicidal (Lucian, *Philops.* 27), or even by shipwreck or other misfortune (Achilles Tatius, 5.16.1f.), were somehow attached to the body they belonged to:

> and that is why many of them have been seen complaining and why souls of the dead who have not been buried remain near the corpse – these are the ones the magicians (*goêtes*) use as their servants, forcibly constraining them by retaining possession of the body or a part of it. (Porphyry, *Abst.* 2.47.2)

Here, as also in the case of *hippomanes*, we can, in reports of the marvellous, already glimpse a view of magical practitioners as delighting in the discovery of anomalous things-in-the-world, possession of which will provide the key to a door, down there at the end of the corridor, marked POWER.

THE CATEGORY OF MAGIC AND ITS PRACTITIONERS

It will be evident that the texts I have adduced – a small sample of hundreds – to illustrate aspects of the marvellous have been carefully selected in order to suggest the place of social and moral judgement in the apparently wide-eyed presentation of marvellous tales, and how intimately magic in the strong sense is linked at least from the Hellenistic period with such tales. That point made, we may now turn to the category of magic itself (which is of course not the same issue as the appearance of a word akin to our own).

The basic difficulty in making clear to oneself what one takes magic to be is that it is janus-faced, there being little point in choosing to stress exclusively (as has been the recent tendency) one side or the other. One face is that of religious power used illegitimately, the other the dream of power to effect marvellous changes in the real world. This paradox certainly runs right through Graeco-Roman views of magic.[14] Both views may be termed ideological, in the sense that they represent choices of value and significance within a particular shared conception of the world-order. We may illustrate the point by looking briefly first at the emergence in the Greek world (the Roman case is too heavily overlaid by the Greek view to be analysable here) of a view of the magician conceived as one who disposes of negatively-marked religious power; and then at some categories of practitioners who claimed power marked in varying degrees as negative in the Graeco-Roman world, ending with the Graeco-Egyptian magical papyri, which have to stand as representatives of a now lost tradition among learned or ritual magicians in the wider Graeco-Roman world.

In Archaic Greece we can find several figures of myth emblematic of 'magic before magic', all more or less divine: Circe in Book 10 of the *Odyssey* (Marinatos, 1995), Medea in the myth of the Argonauts (Graf, 1997b: 30–3), the smith-god Hephaestus (Delcourt, 1957), and the Idaean Dactyls, who resemble in several respects another group of magical smiths, the Telchines. In each case, a negative note sounds solely in the background of their marvellous stories. They are mythical representatives of what Pierre Bourdieu has called 'objective profanation' (1971: 309), the practices of dominated groups such as wise women, herbalists and smiths, which are inaccessible to, and largely unaffected by, the processes of rationalization and moralization of the divine world which set in with the formation of the city state. Medea, the daughter of the Okeanid Idyia, 'the wise one' (Hesiod, *Theog.* 352, 360; Sophocles frg.546 Radt; cf. Gantz, 1993: 340, 358) in particular represents the female herbalist, wise in the lore of plants; her beneficent double is Agamede, 'who knew of all the medicines that grow in the broad earth' (*Iliad* 11.740, tr. Lattimore);[15] an etymological double is Polymede, daughter of the Autolycus blessed by Hermes with all the arts of trickery (*Od.* 19. 395–8). All of them are in one or more ways deviant or other : Circe and Medea live at opposite ends of the earth, the one not far from the rim of Ocean, where Odysseus can create a passage to Hades, the other in Colchis, the mysterious land in the far east whose inhabitants are blackened by the proximity of the sun.[16] Hephaestus is 'deformed in both (his feet)' (Antigonus, *Hist. mir.* 45 = Giannini, 1966: 55), which was sometimes evoked as meaning that one foot pointed in one direction, the other in another, and sometimes that his head faced in a direction different from his feet (Delcourt, 1957: 91–9). The earliest surviving account of the Idaean Dactyls, in the anonymous archaic epic, *Phoronis* (7th–6th cent. BC), describes them as marvellous smiths who work in the mountains far away from human habitation:

> there Idaean Phrygians, magicians (*goêtes*), mountain-dwellers, had their homes, Kelmis and tall Damnameneus, and mighty Akmôn, skillful servants of mountain-haunting Adrasteia, who, using the arts of cunning Hephaestus, were the first to discover dark iron in mountain clefts, and bring it to the fire and work it into a splendid thing. ('Phoronis' frg. 2 Bernabé = Σ Apoll. Rhod. 1, 1126/31b)

The Telchines were supposed to have been the first inhabitants of the (floating) island of Rhodes, who came out of the sea and imparted useful arts to the human inhabitants; apart from being smiths and making the first statues of the gods, they were natural magicians (*goêtes*), who could change their shapes at will – and they were jealous of the secrets of their trade (Diod. Sic. 5.55.2–3, ultimately from ?Zeno of Rhodes). In all this, they are closely comparable to Hephaestus (Detienne 1970/1974). But, apart from the point that the Telchines could also raise at will hail-, snow- and wind-storms 'just as they say magicians can do', in general the otherness of these mythical figures is merely the condition of their extraordinary power. They are marvellous more than they are suspect, a fact noted by their common divine status.

By the fifth century, the negative marking is much clearer: the category of the marvellous has been subdivided in numerous ways, with a distinctive corner for illegitimate religious goals (Versnel, 1990: 96–205), including what are already clearly malign magical arts. Images representing Bourdieu's objective profanation begin to give way to images of intentional profanation, that is, the deliberate use of inverted religious rituals to obtain illicit power. This is evident in the shift of tone with regard to

Medea in the second half of the century, not merely in Euripides' extant tragedy *Medea*, but also in his lost *Daughters of Pelias*, and in Sophocles' lost *Women of Colchis* and *The Rootcutters* (cf. Lesky, 1931: 32, 35f., 39f.). The topic of the *Women of Colchis* was Medea's love for Jason and her betrayal of her family for his sake: here for the first time she is made to kill her brother Apsyrtus while still in Colchis (frg. 343 Radt). Of *The Rootcutters*, which like the *Daughters of Pelias* apparently dealt with her revenge on Pelias (whose daughters she tricked into boiling their father to death – a favourite subject of red-figure vase-painters), we have a fragment that describes Medea

> collecting in bronze vessels the milky juice that drips from the incision, turning her eye away from her hand. (frg. 534.1–3 Radt)

This is an obvious allusion – and also the first – to the kinds of rules we know were applied by rhizotomists (herbalists) in their collection of herbs. There also survives from the same tragedy an invocation of the goddess Hekate 'crowned with oak-leaves and twisted coils of horrid serpents' (frg.535.4f.), which is the earliest evidence for her as the goddess who attends crossroads, the gathering place for the restless dead (Johnston, 1990: 23f.; 1991: 223f.).

Whereas the figure of Medea lent itself to the exploration of malign power as the particular province of women (Moreau, 1994: 191–217, cf. 271–8), we can use the marginal smith to support the view that a strong view of magic developed only in the Hellenistic period, magical practice being until then simply one of many more or less suspect uses of symbolic power, acknowledged or merely claimed. The details of that evolution however can no longer be reconstructed. On the one hand, Hephaestus was rescued already in the fifth century for the civic pantheon, and thereafter is associated only with technical marvel positively marked. By contrast, the Dactyls and Telchines acquired a well-defined character as magicians. Pherecydes of Athens, for example, in the first half of the fifth century, distinguished, like others, between two groups of Dactyls, one, 'on the left' which specialised in casting spells, and one 'on the right', which lifted them. Predictably, those on the left were female, those on the right male (*FGrH* 3 F47; cf. Kern, 1901: 2018f.). It is the Hellenistic reports of the Telchines, especially Strabo 14.2.7, 654C and the epitome of Suetonius' *On Words of Insult* (p. 417 Erbse) which must derive from Hellenistic sources, that characterise them as particularly envious and spiteful, able to cast the evil eye: they are root-cutters who specialised in making poisons, and use their magical arts to cause natural catastrophes (this theme at least being derived from much earlier tradition) and to make the land infertile by means of water carried from the Styx, the river of the Underworld (cf. Herter, 1934: 205–9). In other words, they cease to be marvellous-divine and become representatives of a new category that fuses three distinct forms of malign magic: the evil eye (which is inborn and involuntary), root-cutting in its negative aspect, knowledge of (marvellous) poisons, and command over malign aspects of nature, i.e. natural phenomena whose unexpected or untimely incidence causes devastation to growing crops. Neither the Dactyls nor the Telchines however was suited to fulfil the role of the male counterpart of Medea; the ambiguity of the smith, interesting and topical in the Archaic period, failed thereafter to stimulate the imagination: both groups declined to the status of curiosities, stuff for local historians. By the Hellenistic period, after Alexander's conquest of the Persian Empire, the male equivalent of Medea is the (Persian) magus, student of Zoroaster, Pythagoras and Democritus, heir to the mantle of the *goês*, one of whose narrative guises is 'Thracian' Orpheus whose singing charmed the Underworld (Pausanias 6.20.18, cf. Sabbatucci, 1991).

The other face of magic, the dream of power, is in fact perceptible in these negative representations. The nature of practitioners' claims to power varied with their place on a notional scale of acknowledged competence. Distance forbids us here to be more than schematic: we simply do not know how many of the words denoting some sort of magical practitioner referred to distinguishable skills rather than acting as general designations for persons claiming negatively-marked symbolic power (cf. Riddle, 1993). It would be grand if we could provide for the ancient world the kind of graduated list that Matthew Ramsey has given us of folk-healers in France before and after the Revolution (Ramsey, 1988: 229–76). A close examination of the vocabulary with the aid of the Thesaurus Linguae Graecae on CD-ROM and *TLLatinae*, including the unpublished slips at the Bavarian Academy in Munich, is urgently needed. As it is, we can scarcely navigate even the most rudimentary distinctions. If it is certain that no one would have claimed to be a *pharmakeus* or *veneficus* in the negative sense of 'poisoner', or a *lena*, 'witch-bawd', the connotations and implications of many other terms are quite unclear. Would, for example, anyone have referred to herself as a *Thett(ss)alê*, or *pharmakis*, or even as a *saga*? Moreover, it is difficult even to guess how far people in antiquity – particularly before the Hellenistic period – relied upon practitioners for obtaining magical services rather than inventing their own rituals on the basis of rumour, common knowledge and their own imagination. Did Theocritus simply invent the figure of Simaetha for his *Idyll* 2, the logic of whose binding rituals to recover her faithless lover is far from plain (cf. Meillier, 1991)? All we can be sure of is that any lay-person who did invent his or her own ritual for a specific end after the development of a strong sense of magic in the Hellenistic period would not have laid much store by it. It was acknowledged by then in cities (though surely not, or at least not to the same degree, outside them) that such things required special competence. Magic became, more exclusively than earlier, a service.

At the lowest and least prestigious level is the wise-man or woman (for whom a Latin word may have been *plus scia*: Petronius *Sat.* 63, with Scobie, 1978: 75 n. 6) who commands only the simplest skills and knowledge, a few uncomplicated rituals, incantations, plant remedies. An example would be the 'Egyptian woman' in Achilles Tatius' novel, *Leucippe and Clitophon* (say second half of the second century AD), who taught Leucippe two charms (*rhêmata*) against wasp- and bee-stings; when her mistress Clio is stung, Leucippe pronounces them 'and almost immediately Clio said that she was much better' (2, 7 tr. Gaselee). A more specific case would be the old woman in Ovid's *Fasti* who seeks to control spiteful gossip:

> An old hag sitting among the girls performs rites to Tacita . . .: with three fingers she places three bits of incense beneath the threshold, where the house-mouse has made its hole. She utters charms over some threads, and ties them round dark lead, and mumbles seven black beans in her mouth. Then she takes a fish, the *maena*, smears its head with pitch, sews its mouth up, drops wine upon it, and roasts it before the fire: the rest of the wine she drinks with the girls. 'Now,' she says, 'we have bound the hostile tongues and spiteful mouths' (*hostiles linguas inimicaque vinximus ora*). (*Fast.* 2. 571–81 [tr. Warde Fowler, adapt.] = CT no.144)

Such men and women, who in principle lived in villages but who later had equivalents in cities and towns, such as the *peritus* who might tell you what it portended if you met a weasel (Ammianus Marcellinus 16.8.1, AD 356), were the persons routinely to consult for a variety of troubles, from bee-stings to marital difficulties. They depended largely upon popular consensus for their authority: to operate without that backing meant failure. They also routinely practised simple inductive divination, like the old Sabine woman sketched by Horace, who divined an enquirer's fate by drawing lots (*mota . . . urna*):

> He will not be carried off by horrid poison [*dira venena*, perhaps implying witchcraft] or the enemy's sword, not by pneumonia or a cough or hindering gout. (*Sat.* 1.9.30–2)

– the series of questions, each decided by the lot, is here (uniquely) intimated by a deft series of negatives. Such men and women were believed to work, like all of the practitioners we shall look at, as well for good as for ill. The example from the *Fasti* will make it obvious that an unequivocal decision about that was never possible: the person who is protected against malicious gossip thinks of the ritual as beneficent; those against whom it is directed experience it as a threat – just as the 'malign gossip' is in their own eyes 'reporting the facts'. The husband who is forced to return to his wife, or who becomes impotent when with a mistress, experiences a malign attack upon his mind or body; the wife rejoices that justice and the claims of duty have been made to prevail.

At a higher level of competence and knowledge – there is of course no sharp dividing-line – we may place root-cutters (*rhizotomoi/-ai*; *pharmako-pôlai*; *pigmentarii*, but a regular agentive noun was never formed in Latin: the verb is *succidere*; cf. *herbas dividere*), who specialized in the collection, preparation and sale of an extensive range of medicinal and other plants, as well as simples derived from animal parts. We know from Theophrastus *History of Plants* Book 9 and from Pliny's *Natural History* Books 24–7 scattered details of the varied rules that nominally protected the cutter from the power inherent in such materials, but which in fact constructed that power (Delatte, 1938; better: Martini, 1977). For example, says Theophrastus, root-cutters

> enjoin that in cutting some roots one should stand to windward – for instance in cutting *thapsia* [perhaps *Thapsia garganica*, Deadly Carrot] among others, and that one should first anoint oneself with oil, for one's body will swell up if one stands the other way . . . Also that some roots must be gathered at night, others by day, and some before the sun strikes them, for instance the plant called *klymenon* (honeysuckle) . . . They say that the peony, which some call *glykyside*, should be dug up at night, for if a man does it in the day-time and is observed by a woodpecker while he is gathering the fruit, he risks the loss of his eyesight; and if he is cutting the root at the time, he gets prolapse of the anus. (*HP* 9.8.5f. tr. Hort [adapted])

Very often the plants that were of particular interest to root-cutters were those which possessed some striking natural feature, such as the glaring red 'eyes' of the open seed of the peony, or the stately spike of Celsia (*Verbascum creticum*); or which were anomalous within the structure of rules through which these practitioners approached the natural world. Theophrastus makes a particular point (though not in the same connection) about the squill and narcissus, both well-known medicinal plants:

> whereas in most plants, whether those originally planted or those which are produced from them in season, the leaf comes up first, and then presently the stem, in these plants the stem comes up first. (ibid. 7.13.6. tr. Hort)

But in general we may say that the power of the natural world was constituted by way of the rules for collection: if it is to be used for curing pains in the ear, the semen of a boar must not be allowed to touch the ground but be caught as it drips out of the sow's vulva (Pliny *HN* 28. 175); the hind-leg of a frog caught when neither Sun nor Moon is visible will cure podagra (*Cyranid.* 2.5, p. 123.10–13 Kaimakis).

Just as in the case of the wise-man or woman, root-cutters were thought capable of acting both for good and ill: after all many of the simples they gathered and prepared – mainly plants – were recognised to be poisonous, even if they might be administered to heal. Root-cutters also covered a wide range of abilities and skills: some are known to have experimented with the properties of plants, some were certainly literate – the Graeco-Roman herborist tradition, from the drugs and plants mentioned in the Hippocratic Corpus to the massive compilation of Pedanius Dioscorides in the second century AD, which mentions 700 plants and over 1000 drugs, depends largely upon their work (Singer, 1927; Scarborough, 1991); a few were indeed of sufficient eminence to be named, as they were by Asclepiades the Younger in his *Pharmacopoeia* at the end of the first century AD (Galen, *de compos. medic.* 1, 16; 17 [13: 441f., 447f. Kühn]). The marvellous likewise played a different role in the practice of different individuals. But it must be clear that, while the image of the witch, a Medea, Canidia, or Erictho, collecting poisonous or merely powerful plants, which is dominant in Graeco-Roman literary tradition, is a selective fusion of traits taken from the wise-woman and the root-cutter, it is not in any sense an ethnological account of their practice. It is rather a wholly fantastic composite image, that turns these roles into a night-witch, a term we shall have occasion to explore later – essentially a nightmare creature who, unlike the day-witch, can never be encountered but who by her activity erodes the very foundations of human society: woman as the hideous negation of the nurturant mother.

One of the reasons for arranging these practitioners in a notional hierarchy becomes clear when we consider what kind of an account they could give of their practice. The group I classify as wise-men and women relied for their authority upon the tradition they had learned from a parent or mentor. They certainly adapted and invented, especially in their charms, but they had no wider explanatory matrix than the skills they had learned – they could not for example provide an explicit account of the individual lesions they undertook to cure. Root-cutters, by contrast, had not only the structure of differences enshrined in the particular rules for collecting and preparing plant- and animal-substances, which enabled each individual to define his or her own practice from that of others, including his teacher; but very often also particular reasons (analogical and metonymic), which they could state, for using specific remedies. Moreover, neither practice remained isolated from wider change. The Hellenistic learned scheme of sympathies and antipathies, proximately Stoic but probably ultimately derived from the intuitive ideas of *oiônistai*, diviners by the movements of birds (cf. Dillon, 1996), gradually penetrated the practice of some root-cutters.[17] But in the long run, probably even more significant was the practice of writing, which came decisively to influence both the nature of charms and of phylacteries (cf. Gordon, 1995). It was writing which encouraged the systematization of schemes of collection based on movements of the heavenly bodies, and indeed the entire project known as iatromathematics, in which astrological considerations determined both diagnosis and the choice of plant- and animal-materials (Pfister, 1938; Rothschuh, 1978). It was such schemes that enabled root-cutting to figure at all in the learned ritual magic of the Principate.

More sophisticated still, or at any rate learned in a different way, was the Greek *goês*, who is later represented as a magus (cf. Burkert, 1962a). The etymology of this term connects it with the ritual lament for the dead (actually a female responsibility). It has been argued that death came in the late Archaic and early Classical periods to seem more terrible, and that this anxiety led to an imaginative elaboration of the process of transition between this life and the world of the dead (cf. Sourvinou-Inwood, 1981; 1995: 298–361). A by-product of this shift was the democratization of an older belief about heroes, that they were potentially active and capable of direct intervention in human life as *daemones* (Snodgrass, 1982), and in particular a greater awareness of the restless dead, the *ahôroi* and *biaiothanatoi*. The *goês* seems to have emerged as a specialist 'singer' to mediate between the newly-particularized dead and the living, invoking Hekate, the goddess of passages and communications, and likewise Hermes (Johnston, 1999b). The importance of Hekate at least in later Greek representations of (malign) magic, as well as the association between Orpheus and magic almost certainly goes back to their practice (Plato *Rep.* 2, 364c-e, cf. Graf, 1974: 14–17). The *goês* seems to have been, along with begging-priests and 'prophets', the heir of 'a small portion of a divided patrimony', that of the Archaic healer-seers such as Melampus, Thaletas or Abaris (Parker, 1983/1996: 208f.; cf. Reverdin, 1945: 224–7).

The process of rationalising civic religion made such practitioners immediately suspect, and there are of course no 'objective' reports of their activity; but two fifth-century passages give us some idea of the kind of claims they then might be represented as making. The earlier is from Empedocles, and has recently been the focus of a radical – too radical – reassessment of this figure (Kingsley, 1995):

And all the remedies that exist as defence against sufferings and old age,
These you will learn, because for you alone will I make all these things
    come true.
And you'll stop the force of the tireless winds that chase over the earth

And destroy the fields with their gusts and blasts;
But then again, if you so wish, you'll stir up winds as requital.
Out of a black rainstorm you'll create a timely drought
For men, and out of a summer drought you'll create
Tree-nurturing floods that will stream through the ether.
And you will fetch back from Hades the life-force of a man who has
    died.

(31 B111 *DK* [tr. Kingsley])

I am not here concerned to discuss the place of this passage in Empedocles' thought, if indeed we accept that it is genuine (doubts inevitably remain). For my purpose, it is enough to note the positive presentation of a range of claims: the ability to heal; control over the weather, particularly untimely or excessive wind and rain (cf. Lanata, 1967: 66f.); and the ability to summon individual souls from Hades. Here Empedocles offers his reader a sketch of the powers of the *goês* – though the word is not used – to which he offers access (whether literally or not is precisely the issue) to the disciple who thoroughly masters his teaching. But it is an entirely positive list: hardly a hint of the ability to cause harm, just the suggestion of 'requital' – but as we saw earlier, one man's justice is another man's malign attack. Empedocles is determinedly looking on the bright side of things.

The second passage, though violently hostile, largely confirms what Empedocles has to say about goetic claims (cf. Lloyd, 1979: 37f.):

If these people <that is, those who heal epilepsy by ritual intervention> claim to know how to draw down the moon, cause an eclipse of the sun, make storms and fine weather, rain and drought, to make the sea too rough for sailing or the land infertile, and all the rest of their nonsense, then, whether they claim to be able to do it by ritual intervention (*teletai*) or by some other kind of knowledge or skill (*gnômês ê meletês*), they seem to be impious rogues. ([Hippocrates] *Morb. sac.* 4 = 1.29, p. 64.61–5 Grensemann [tr. Chadwick and Mann, adapt.])

The author had earlier classified these healers as 'what we nowadays call *magi*, purifiers, begging-priests, mountebanks' (cf. Graf, 1996: 25). It is evident from the subsequent account given by this author of the healing practice he so violently depreciates that they had developed a complex nosology of the disease they recognised as 'sacred':

if the sufferer acts like a goat, and if he roars, or has convulsions involving the right side, they say the Mother of the Gods is responsible. If he utters a high-pitched and louder cry, they say he is like a horse and blame Poseidon. If the sufferer should be incontinent of faeces . . . Einodia (i.e. Hekate) is the name. If the stools are more frequent and thin like those of birds, it is Apollo Nomius. (ibid. = 1.33–6, p. 64.75–66.80 Grensemann)

Their diagnostic method was simply a specialised version of many inductive systems, involving the reading of a meaning (stored in the memory of the practitioner) from a given matrix; their healing practice, intended to regain a pristine purity or integrity, included mainly sacrifices and purifications to allay the god's anger, but also incantations (*epaoidas*) and specific ritual avoidances. It has been suggested that the use of civic gods as the causative agents overlies an older representation of attack by anonymous *daemones* (Lanata, 1967: 38f.); it certainly is possible that we have here an example of the way in which such religious practitioners attempted to accommodate their beliefs and representations to those of the city-state. What is in the present context more important to note is the complexity of the diagnostic system that these practitioners had developed, which was certainly very much more detailed and elaborate than the Hippocratic author can be bothered to expound. And he also mentions what Empedocles omits: 'The man who can get rid of a disease by purifications and magic (*mageuôn*, i.e. by performing magian ceremonies) could equally well bring it on' (3 = 1.26, p. 64.53f. Grensemann).

There were besides many different representations of the causes of illness and other misfortune: other healer-seers for example evidently understood illness as a sort of 'dirt' (cf. Parker, 1983/1996: 216f.). But the *goês* seems typically to have claimed to be able to diagnose daemonic influence, understanding *daemones* precisely as souls of the dead capable of bestowing wealth but also of causing harm to individuals (e.g. Euripides, *Alc.* 1003f.), often as punishment for wrong-doing. Probably the earliest surviving such representation, much quoted in later discussions of *daemones* by Plato and others, is Hesiod's account of the Race of Gold once it had passed away, which speaks of them as 'keeping watch on judgements and wicked actions' (*Op.* 124 = 254).[18] Late Homeric passages also view the restless dead as capable of bringing harm upon the living (*Il.* 22.358–60; *Od.* 11.72f.). The recently-published sacred law from Selinus in Sicily speaks of certain *daemones* as *elastoroi*, and seems to envisage them as causing disease and, apparently, a period of crop-failure.[19] And the new fragments of the Derveni papyrus (early-mid fourth century BC) seem to represent the *magoi* – in my view not the Persian priests but the familiar *goêtes* – as capable of 'keeping off the *daemones* when they get in the way – *daemones* in the way are hostile to souls'.[20]

The basis of the *goês*' claim to power lay in his ability to affect the real world through his understanding of the world of *daemones*. This claim was in the long run, thanks to the Christian re-interpretation of *daemones* as demons, to have a determinate effect upon European views of magic:

'Without the demon magic could not have been born' (Daxelmüller, 1993: 56). Meanwhile what survived of the *goês* in the Hellenistic and Roman worlds was a double legacy. On the one hand he contributed a number of elements to the composite image of the malign witch: power over weather, crops and the land, control over the heavenly bodies, inversions of the natural order. On the other, as manipulator of spirits, he gave rise to the popular image of the necromancer, as we see him in Lucian's Mithrobarzanes, for example, the 'disciple and follower of Zoro-aster's magi' (*Menipp.* 6), who conducts veritable safaris into the Underworld.

The fourth group of practitioners in our scheme are the authors of the Graeco-Egyptian receptaries put together in the Principate, several dozen of which now known, albeit mostly in pitiful fragments.[21] These texts are grounded in the tradition of late-Egyptian temple magic, though they diverge in many respects from that earlier practice; they date from a period at which 'Egyptian magic' was a by-word in the Roman Empire. Documentary, that is activated, examples of ritual malign magic dependent on this tradition have been found both in Egypt[22] and in caches at diverse sites in the Roman Empire, though it has proved possible to read very few: the best examples are those from Amathous in Cyprus (?second cent. AD: *DT* 22–37 = Mitford, 1971: nos.127–42 with Drew-Bear, 1972); from a Roman well in the Athenian Agora (first half of third cent.: Jordan, 1985b); from Carthage and Hadrumetum in Africa (see esp. *DT* 229–62 and 264–98 resp.; many others have since been found, e.g. Jordan, 1988c); from Fiq near Lake Tiberias in Palestine (*DT* nos.15f. with Robert, 1938: 99–102); and from Porta S. Sebastiano at Rome (Wünsch, 1898). Several similar caches remain unpublished, in particular from Athens and from Rhodes.

The papyrus texts seem to assume that the practitioner will be closely attached to a temple, with access to hieratic papyrus and other sacred materials; this cannot have been the case with ritual magicians working outside Egypt. For my purpose, the receptaries are valuable because they illustrate the intimate relation between writing and sophisticated claims to magical power of a practically unlimited kind.[23] Through these texts we can glimpse not merely how a highly self-conscious and learned magical tradition used a book, the receptary, to protect its claims to power, but also how the book provides a convenient retreat from the demand to test one's claims in action.

Although one of the rules of the genre of the receptary, like that of the traditional cookery book, was that editorial comment be severely restricted, many recipes begin or end with a simple statement of their marvellous power: 'a wonderful binding philtre' (*PGM* IV 296), 'an amazing 'winner' (*nikêtikon*)' (VII 919), 'a 'goblet' (*potêrion*) – quite astonishing' (643), 'you will marvel at the unsurpassed holy power' (IV 3170f. tr. M. Smith), ''Restrainer' for every problem – even works on chariots' (VII 429), ''Bringer' within the hour' (300a), 'Prayer to Helios . . . there is none greater' (XXXVI 211f.). Often it is the 'barbaric names' (*onomata barbarika*), the unintelligible words of power, which are singled out in this way: 'protect me, oh mighty and wonderful names of (the great) God' (VII 497f.; 501f.); 'and from that moment he was called by the mighty and wonderful name *Danoup Chratôr Berbali Balbith Iaô*' (XIII 508–10; cf. 560, 738). Occasionally the astonishment is not the private emotion of the implied reader, but that of others, visitors or customers. Thus a recipe to make a place prosperous is prefaced as follows:

> Whenever you want a place to prosper greatly, so that those in the temple where the phylactery is hidden will marvel, <use this rite>. For wherever this <phylactery> be placed, if in a temple, the temple will be talked about throughout the whole world; if in some otherplace, <the place> will prosper greatly. (*PGM* IV 3125–30 [tr. M. Smith])

But the receptaries contain many other ways of reassuring the implied reader that the book he is holding really is something quite different from your ordinary papyrus roll or codex, containing as it does matter of the highest significance and moment: the injunctions to secrecy ('when you have learned the power of the book, you are to keep it secret, child, for in it there is the name of the lord, which is Ogdoas, the god who commands and directs all things': *PGM* XIII 741–3; cf. VII 805–8); the advice to equip yourself with paper and pencil when you summon an authentic vision, lest you forget what the god says (VIII 89–91); the occasional descriptions of what you or the medium will see if you perform the recipe correctly ('and a black-skinned boy [or slave] will appear to him': VII 348f.); the authentication of the recipe, whether by claiming a famous author (e.g. '"Imp" of Pnouthis, the *hierogrammateus*': I 42), or that the text has been found in a temple (VII 862–5). We might read all these, and many others, as so many devices to reassure the implied reader that the success of magic as envisaged by any collection of such spells is no dream but a very fact. The most subtle of such reassurances are those which occur not in authorial or editorial glosses but are part of the prayer itself, as in a request for the power to divine correctly in 'Hermes' Ring':

> <Make me know> what is going on in the minds of everyone, Egyptians, Greeks, Syrians, Ethiopians, of every race and kind . . . what has happened and is going to happen . . . their skills, habits, trades and livelihoods, and their names and the names of their fathers and mothers and siblings and relatives, including those who are dead . . ., those who ask me questions, coming before me, whether they speak or keep silent,

that I may announce to them what has happened to them, is presently happening and what will happen to them in the future . . . that I may tell them everything truthfully. (*PGM* V 256–303)

In the earnestness of such a prayer for true insight one catches no hint of the rough real world of the magical diviner, with its steaming open of sealed letters, its army of spies and informants, its Boy's Own Paper glues and invisible inks (Hippolytus, *Ref. haer.* 4. 28 = Totti, 1985, no 78) – no, this magic, this true magic, has no need of such stuff: only of piety and the recipe in front of you. It is telling that references to 'sacred magic' (*hiera mageia*) tend to occur at points of highest daring, of the most elaborate flights of fancy, as in a complex spell for acquiring a *paredros*, a daemonic servant:

he will serve you suitably for <whatever> you have in mind, o bl[ess]ed initiate of the sacred magic, and will accomplish it for you, this most powerful assistant, who is also the only lord of the air. (*PGM* I 126–9)

The claim that it is impossible for the Moon to 'escape the fate of my words' is bolstered by the image of the practitioner's magic as a winged arrow racing 'headlong to the target' (IV 2319f., with Smith, 1981: 651).

Another interesting device in this connection is the development of the omnium-gatherum recipe. Whereas the great majority of Graeco-Egyptian recipes are for a specific purpose, a dream-vision, a lecanomancy by medium (a vision of a god beneath oil spread over water in a bowl), a 'bringer' (of a person desired), a 'victory-bringer', some are claimed to be so powerful that they will do anything at all the practitioner wishes. A text cited earlier as working even on chariots, 'also causes enmity, and sickness, cuts down, destroys and overturns, for <whatever> you wish' (VII 429–31 tr. M. Smith); a phylactery in the same receptary is 'a bodyguard against daimons, against phantasms, against every sickness and suffering . . . when worn it works mightily for it is the name of power of the great god and his seal' (579–83 tr. Smith). The most ambitious of them is a

'Bringer' . . . it attracts people who are unmanageable, and of whom you have no 'essence' [i.e. some physical part of the person, generally hair], in a single day. It is a sovereign means of causing sickness, is a powerful means of killing, a splendid sender of dreams [i.e. to victims], a marvellous bringer of dream-visions [i.e. to the practitioner]; and in many demonstrations has caused <witnesses> to marvel having never failed in these matters. (IV 2441–6)

The omnium-gatherum recipe is an extension of the claim that the ritual magic of the receptaries, with its injunctions to purity and its assumption of learned competence, is without fail effective in gaining its ends. If that is really the case, then there is no reason to confine spells to a specific purpose – the traditional generic rule becomes an irksome restraint upon the practitioner's vaulting ambition. It is at this point, of course, that we must be reminded that these are only books, that the recipes are never at hand when the desired result cannot be obtained. Some do indeed contain 'compulsions', texts to recite when the desired result does not come about (e.g. II 45–62), but these are themselves devices to reinforce the claim that the recipes do always work, since they never envisage the possibility of final failure. The receptaries are volumes offering thought-voyages of unlimited range; and they use divination recipes, which depend heavily upon (what we would classify as) dream–induction, hallucination, medium–trance, as the experiential confirmation that all their other claims are likewise true. They are only partly directed towards action in the world: one eye is always cocked towards the mighty magicians of the glorious Egyptian past (Gordon, 1997b).

MAGIC GOOD TO THINK

We may distinguish four main strategies by which the idea of magic in antiquity is put to ideological work. Most obviously, as some form of the Other, whether religious, social or moral, it may be used to defend an asserted or implied norm. This view takes it for granted that magic is real, and a threat. An alternative strategy assumes that it is, on the contrary, vain, specious, or trifling; this view, again based on a binary inversion, asserts the superior validity of other symbolic sets. A third strategy also takes magical claims seriously, but understands them in the first place as raising a puzzle, or as it may be interesting, tricky, or unwelcome, intellectual problems; a fourth takes them at face value, as telling a guarded truth about the relation between the divine, or nature, and this world. The janus-face that we noted in the previous section re-appears clearly in these strategies. I propose to discuss here the first three only, for it is they that provided the context for ancient actors' decisions about the nature, and so the social meaning, of any action that might be represented as magical.

Magic as Other

By far the greater number of texts takes magic as the transgressive other, the inversion of any number of implied norms. Taking a Weberian standpoint, we may say that legitimate religious knowledge in antiquity can roughly be defined in terms of performance, political-social location, objectivity and ends. In relation to each, we can posit a normatively ideal form from which actual forms diverge in greater or lesser degree: the ideal form constructs the positive pole of a notional continuum of legitimacy whose opposite pole is constituted by fully illegitimate religious knowledge. In the Graeco-Roman world we can point to at least five periods in which legitimate knowledge was forced to adapt to new politico-social conditions: the formation of the city-state in the early Archaic period; the passage from independent city states to the Hellenistic kingdoms; the emergence of the Principate; the crisis of the third century leading up to the Tetrarchy; the fourth-century transition to a Christian Empire. Part of the process of establishing new understandings of legitimate religious knowledge during these periods was the creation of images of forbidden or illicit knowledge, of which magic is one; these are the periods which were particularly productive of such socio-moral imagery. Graeco-Roman representations of magic are thus both historically variable and elaborated in contrast to understandings of, or claims to, legitimate religious knowledge.

The value of conceptualizing a continuum of possible values between fully normative and wholly illicit is that, while allowing the negative pole to be wholly imaginary, it leaves plenty of room for religious activity which for one reason or another is viewed askance, as strange, outlandish, extreme. Theophrastus' Superstitious Man (Theophr. *Char.* 16 = 28 Jebb-Sandys) is an excellent example of such behaviour: nothing he does is exactly wrong, let alone illicit, but the sheer scale of his enterprise, his credulity before religious professionals, the unmanliness of his fears, all make him ridiculous to a sound understanding. Although 'descriptions' of magical rituals at the negative pole, such as Lucan's account of Erictho attempting to arouse a dead man for the purposes of necromancy (*BC* 6. 642–830), are wholly imaginary, there is no reason to doubt that others, to be located further from that point, may indeed be based on observation and, less specifically, authentic social knowledge – we may recall Ovid's account of the ritual to close up the mouths of ill-wishers, or cite his account of the ritual carried out by the nymph Cranaë to save the infant Procas from further attack by night-witches (*striges*):

> She at once brushed the door-posts in turn three times with an arbutus-twig, and with an arbutus-twig three times tapped the thresholds, sprinkled the entrances with water (water too had its healing power), and took in her hand the raw innards of a two-month-old piglet: 'Have pity: a small victim is slain in place of a small (boy). I implore you, take a heart for a heart, liver for liver: this life we give you in place of a better one'. When she had thus paid her libation, she set the offering (*prosecta*) out in the open, and forbade all those who were present at the ritual to look back. (*Fasti* 6. 155–64)

This ritual is magical only in the weak sense that in Ovid's circle such things were considered quaint, believed to be typical of the superstitious behaviour of the peasant population – for all that it is calqued on a proper ritual of the State religion – for who else would believe in *striges* either? To apply the Weberian criteria: although the performance has good credentials, and its purpose is benign, its social location, its objective validity and its meaningfulness as an act are all questionable. And precisely to that extent is it magic.

It is obvious too that some knowledge of magical healing was widespread at least among the country population: everyone would have known (of) some simple recipes, such as the Italian charm to cure podagra (?gout) recorded by the Sasennas father and son during the first century BC: 'My mind's on you – make my feet well; let the earth take the pain, and my feet not complain' (Varro, *Rust.* 1.2.27, cf. Tupet, 1976: 172–4), whose sole strangeness lies in its rhythmicality and rhyme; or the ritual for healing dislocated joints recorded by the Elder Cato in the mid-second century BC, whose strangeness lies in the unintelligible utterances prescribed (*de agric.* 165; cf. Tupet, 1976: 169f.). In such cases, only the social location makes the usage suspect – and Cato himself endorses the cure for dislocation without a hint of unease: 'Any kind of dislocation may be cured by the following charm (*cantio*)'. On the other hand, the very availability of such charms was an index of their low therapeutic value. In this realm, the market principle holds good: scarcity drives up value.

The ideal form of religious knowledge is not 'free', is not a matter of mere ideas or speculation, but encoded or inscribed in the performance of civic sacrifice, a performance which in turn is imbricated in the sets of norms governing perceptions and judgements of civilised versus savage life. Civic sacrifice is in turn embedded in the calendar of civic festivals, themselves the meeting-point of formal laws or rules of organisation and of aetiological myth, and in the sacred topography of the city and its *chora*. Both in Greece and at Rome, that aspect of legitimate religious knowledge which consists in knowing the pantheon is inseparable from active participation in the calendar of civic festivals. All claims to religious knowledge which depart from this normative centre are more or less problematic, from 'disrespectful' Homeric stories about the gods to individual claims to Teiresias-like insight, from Bacchic ecstasy to purification cults, from hero-cults to the worship of new divinities, from Xenophanes' mockery of anthropomorphism to Anaxagoras' hot-metal sun (cf. Sourvinou-Inwood, 1988). But they can be tolerated, even incorporated into 'tradition', so long as their challenge to the norms inscribed in civic sacrifice remains indistinct.

With the political location goes also a social location: legitimate religious knowledge is a collective property of men in the context of their identity as citizens. Illegitimate religious knowledge is presumptively to be found among individual non-citizens and non-men, that is, women. In each case the presumption is a consequence of the normative exclusion of these categories of persons from full membership in 'our' tradition: the notion of legitimate religious knowledge is just one of many boundary markers whose function is to define those who belong from those who in one way or another do not. For obvious reasons not all prescriptive outsiders were equally problematic: the religious knowledge of slaves was ordinarily of no concern at all. But both resident or non-resident foreigners claiming religious expertise and the outsiders who nevertheless belonged inside, namely women, were suspect: the men because they transferred Here practices that classificatorily belonged Over There, the women because of their biological openness to daemonic attack and inherent susceptibility to unreason.

Given this ground-work, the topic of magic as Other becomes unmanageably large, and I propose to limit myself here to a brief account of the social value of one kind of everyday malign magic, amatory – that is the magic relating to problems and crises in relationships viewed under their private, and particularly sexual, aspect; and of the fantastic figure of the night-witch. In each case, what interests me is magic as a means of negotiation, which the actors approach with all the self-interest, selective vision and concern for their social figure of the characters in Jane Austen, or, for that matter, the generally less familiar records of witchcraft-hearings in the English Star Chamber Court (Ewen, 1938).

The Magic of Everyday: Love Magic in Action   Lucian tells us, in his inimitably humorous way, of a prostitute named Glykera whose best customer, a soldier, has just gone off with her friend Gorgona. Now Gorgona's charms are not plentiful: she is practically bald, her lips corpsepale, her neck so scrawny you can count the veins. All becomes clear when it turns out that her mother, Chrysarion, is a witch:

> She has learned some sort of Thessalian incantations and can bring the moon down; she's even supposed to go flying at night. At any rate, she got him to drink a love-potion, and now they're picking him clean. (*Dial. meret.* 1)

The allegation of witchcraft satisfyingly explains Glykera's misfortune, but it also evokes a milieu in which the witch was at home – the brothel, the world of easy virtue and purchased pleasures. The main overt value of the witch-bawd in Roman poetry is precisely as foil to the lover, who whispers temptation into his or her ear, and thus taints pure love with the breath of decay: the most fully-imagined are Acanthis in Propertius 4. 5 and Dipsas in Ovid *Amor.* 1.8, both of whom, to enhance their own security, are made to persuade the girl that her best interests lie elsewhere than the speaker. Dipsas, true to her name, is a wrinkled lush, with emigrant hair. Acanthis is more perfectly imagined:

> Through her tight-drawn skin you could count her bones.
> I saw how her cough closed up her wrinkled throat,
> And how through the gaps of her teeth oozed blood-flecked spittle,
> On her worn-out rug she was breathing her last rank breaths;
> Her tumbledown hovel was fireless and shivering cold.
>
> (Propert. 4.5.64; 67–70 [tr. Musker])

The inversions of the image of the desirable do not need to be stressed: the malice of the bawd is figured in her appearance. But at the same time such images serve both to suggest the negative side of the speakers' passion and to provide a convenient account of its transience, an account in which the fault never lies with the speaker.

In the brothel, magic is ever-present as a cover for the institutionalized fabrication of intense emotion (cf. *Anth. Pal.* 5. 205 (204) = Gow-Page, *Hellenistic Epigr.*, 1:207, Anon. XXXV; Antiphanes of Macedonia ap. *Anth. Pal.* 6.88 = Gow-Page, *Garland*, 1: 84 no.1). But it also provides an excuse for male sexual failure – Ovid ironically evokes an occasion when the speaker's 'languid loins' (*inguen effetum*) refused to budge:

> But the other day I took Chlide twice,
> Pitho three times, Libas three,
> and as for Corinna – she inspired my record:
> in one short night I counted nine.
> Could some witch have laid me under a spell?
> Given me a magical decoction?
> Moulded my image in red wax
> and stuck pins in its guts?
> Magic can turn a wheat-field into weed,
> drain well-springs dry,
> make grapes and chestnuts drop,
> strip fruit trees bare.
> Couldn't it also emasculate muscle?
> Yes, it was probably witchcraft –
> that and humiliation too –
> aggravating the collapse.
> (*Amores* 3.7.27–38 [tr. Lee], part in *CT* no.142)

That said, we are not far removed from an insight into the insistent poetic and dramatic interest in the ancient world in the figure of Deianeira, who tried to use magic to recapture the affections of her errant husband Heracles. As we have already seen, judgements about the use of magic in conflictual situations are unavoidably ambiguous. So also here. Deianeira sees her position threatened by a new love:

> My mind fails me at the thought, a chill sweeps
> through my frame, and my hand lies nerveless in
> my lap. Me too you have possessed among your many
> loves – but me with no reproach.
> (Ovid, *Heroid.* 9.135–7 [tr. Showerman])

Freeborn men in antiquity claimed the right to sexual freedom outwith the marriage-bond. Not only did they naturally refuse to countenance such freedom in their wives – the sexual freedom of wives was a perfectly dystopian thought, an image of social disorder – they also claimed that wives had no right to sexual fidelity on their part. Most wives learned nevertheless to tolerate their husband's behaviour under normal circumstances: that is what men are like. But what they could not accept – the wife of Gorgias the sophist is a famous case (Plutarch *Praec. coniug.* 43, 144b-c) – was the endangering of their place in the house (cf. Faraone, 1994: 115–23). As the chorus in Euripides' *Andromache* sagely puts it:

> There's a touch of jealousy in the female psyche.
> It's inclined to be rather tart where concubinage enters.
> (181f. [tr. Nims, adapted])

It was in this extreme situation, that, unless independently wealthy or able to exert powerful leverage through male relatives, a wife might consider the last recourse of the weak – magical redress, a philtre (cf. 'moon water' in modern Morocco: Westermarck, 1926: 1, 126). Resort to the use of such magical means, we might say, varies inversely with the status and security of the woman in marriage, or in a marriage-like relationship (cf. Quintil. *Inst.* 7.8.2; 7.3.30bis). Philtres, which were combinations of natural substances ('drugs') and magical ritual, were supposed to influence the victim's mind. The Suda defines the *iunx* as 'something which compels the mind to desire and passion' (s.v. ἴυγξ, 2: 677f. Adler); philtres likewise were means 'whereby the mind is deranged' (Pliny, *HN* 25.25).[24] 'You'll never get your wits back, Varus, once I've 'caught' them with my spells', cackles Canidia (Horace *Epod.* 5.75f.). Fabia Numantina, the first wife of the Plautius Silvanus (*pr. urb.* 24 AD) who committed suicide after throwing his second wife out of the window, had to stand trial for 'driving her husband insane by magic (*carminibus et veneficiis*)' (Tacitus *Ann.* 4.22.4). Caligula's strange behaviour was supposed to have been partly caused by a philtre given him by his fourth wife, Milonia Caesonia, whom he arranged to be murdered in January 41 (Suet. *Caius* 50.2).

Philtres of this type were thus seen by the wronged wife as her last defence in a rightful cause, by the husband as a malign attack on his powers of decision, his freedom of sexual choice. In the public world of male rumour, the wife who tried to protect her position by means of one became at once a monster. From Heracles to Lucretius there was no lack of famous figures killed by a philtre; and the wives became poisoners, fitted into the wider stereotype of man-killing women, Clytemnestras (cf. Eurip. *Ion* 616f.) such as the Athenian girl who murdered her father with an axe and hid his body under the bath. Among the speeches of Antiphon is one that retells the pathetic story of a slave woman, in effect the sexual property (*pallakê*) of an Athenian named Philôneus, who was evidently ageing, or whose charms were at any rate becoming less desirable to her owner, who proposed to sell her into a brothel. In desperation, she attempted to change his mind by administering a philtre, which went disastrously wrong: Philoneus died more or less instantly (Antiphon 1.14–20); the *pallakê* was forthwith broken on the wheel without trial – no trial was necessary, the facts were clear, she was unfree – then strangled by the executioner on the orders of the Eleven.

But philtres might also be used with less dramatic results: they could account for any excessive or unusual or ridiculous male sexual passion, which is why there was so much talk of them in brothels; and a philtre administered by a wife or mistress with rights was a convenient explanation for male sexual failure, rather like the celebrated 'coconut water' of the Caribbean and Mexico (Lewis, 1961: 141). A man who is not a man, and not only in this sense, has been given a philtre. As Plutarch points out:

> Fishing with poison is a quick way to catch fish . . . but it makes them inedible and worthless. In the same way, wives who scheme by administering philtres to and putting spells (*goêteias*) on their husbands, and gain mastery over them through sexual pleasure, find themselves living with dull-witted, degenerate fools. (*Praec. coniug.* 5, 139a [tr. Babbitt, adapted])

This type of philtre confirmed social values in placing the man at the centre of the household: it reproduced the stereotype by making his sexual will the decisive issue. But magic might have other uses in domestic politics. If a husband now loved someone else, he might no longer be prepared even to fulfil his regulation sexual duty towards his wife. An obvious way of explaining that refusal was that he had been *made* to feel that she was repulsive, by means of a spell to divide two people who belong together, what the magical papyri call a *diakopos*, 'breach' (e.g. *PGM* VII 429, XIII 239–42, LXI 60–6; *Suppl. Mag.* no.95 with p. 222 n. 1). But it might also be that her own status in the house was ambivalent, if for example she had not, after the lapse of some years, yet had a child:

and that too might conveniently be explained as due to malice. Both accusations are made by Hermione against Andromache:

> You! You common slave! You soldier's winnings!
> You plan to usurp this house, evicting me!
> Your drugs (*pharmaka*) have made me unlovely to my husband,
> Withered my womb and left it good for nothing.
> That is the sort of thing you Asian women
> have tricky wits for (*deinê psychê*).
>   (Euripides *Andromache* 155–60 [tr. Nims, adapted])

Here the theme of the malignant outsider offers the unsuccessful wife a means of accounting for her failure without acknowledging any personal blame or defect – but also without blaming her husband, who in this perspective is merely a victim.

We can find comparable negotiations in relation to prostitutes. Prostitutes in brothels, being mainly slaves, had of course no acknowledged rights comparable to wives; but they stood to gain much if they could attract a wealthy man to give them favours, presents, on a regular basis.[25] Conflicts over such men must have been common, and magical arts always in play; but even more important than their use in fact was their use in thought, as a rationalization of the carousel of luck and loss:

> . . . and shortly afterwards, though his friends told him not to, and Phoebis, the girl he was with then, pleaded and pleaded, he came back to me; and it was mainly the spell (*epôdê*) which brought him back. (Lucian, *Dial. meret.* 4. 5 [tr. MacLeod, adapted])

For prostitutes too had their pride:

> It would be dreadful for me not only to be deprived of [Diphilus'] payments but to become a laughing-stock for Thettalê [Diphilus' current flame] into the bargain. Now you have a philtre, you say, that you often tried when you were young. Some such help as that is what I need, something that would make a clean sweep of his thinking he can do whatever he likes (*typhos*) and of his drunken bad temper too. (Alciphron, *Epist. meretr.* 4.10.3f. [tr. Benner and Fobes, adapted])

On the other hand, magic could equally be made responsible for excessive or untoward desire on the part of (free) women, that turned them from the submissive objects of male desire, or, even more important, from the dutiful role of obedient daughter or wife (or slave), into sexual agents on their own account uncontrolled by father, brother, husband (or master). There were of course many other ways of eluding such control – nocturnal festivals of the gods provided an excellent excuse – by means of which these authority figures could save face if need be. But magic was central, inasmuch as it played on the underlying model of female sexuality, which was that violent passion lay just below the surface, ready to burst out if only the right button could be found to release it. It is this model which underlies the love-spells of the Graeco-Egyptian receptaries and their activated analogues: the spell was intended to locate and depress the button. The existence of such texts to animate desire is wholly predictable; more interesting for us is the use of the idea of magic in the social negotiation of female sexuality. I take three suggestive, and well-known, examples.

A vindicative curse on lead, perhaps of the third century AD, found in a field on Amorgos (*IG* XII 7² p. 1 = Jordan, 1985a no.60, tr. in Versnel, 1985: 252f.), seeks to invoke Demeter to take revenge for the author upon a certain Epaphrodeitos, who has in some way managed to disaffect the author's slaves, presumably field-slaves, 'has led them into evil ways, given them ideas, plotted with them . . . persuaded them to run away' (ll.2f.) and so ruined him. More particularly, he has disaffected a woman we may take to have been the author's concubine, a slave kept in the house, rather than an acknowledged mistress in a brothel: 'he has induced my *paidiskê* by magic art to leave me (*sunapethelge*), so that he may have her as his wife, though I had refused' (ll.4f.). A number of possible scenarios occur; what I want to stress is that the author specifically mentions the thought of his enemies rejoicing in his misfortune, 'those who have prepared with joy sorrows for me and my wife Epiktêsis, and hate us' (verso, ll.2f.). It is the loss of the *paidiskê* that rankles more even than the escape of the (male) slaves: not only is she his legal property, but she shares his bed when he wishes, she lives in his house, he may even be fond of her – she may have privileges. That such a woman should voluntarily leave can only be due to magic, for it is this that makes him most ridiculous: he has been cuckolded of his own slave, shown to be incapable of controlling not merely his household – slaves ran away all the time – but a slave-woman who shared his bed. She must have had her mind turned for her.

Here we have a weak claim that cannot be backed up: it satisfies the complainant, at some level, but evidently not his neighbours, who are so highly entertained by his difficulties – no sizeable group was ready to bring Epaphrodeitos before the magistrates on such a charge; the complainant has to be satisfied with a weak solution, a secret message to Demeter. Quite different is the situation that faced Apuleius at Oea in winter 158/9 AD, when he had to plead to the accusation that his marriage to the rich widow Aemilia Pudentilla had only been made possible by improper, specifically magical, means, expressed by the usual hendiadys, 'incantations and poisons', *carmina et venena* (*Apol.* 90).

The background can be quickly resumed, though we are of course dependent on Apuleius' presentation of the facts (cf. Graf, 1996: 61–82; Hunink, 1997: 1, 12–20). Pudentilla, who was in her own right fairly well-off (with four times the minimum census of a Roman senator), had been married to Sicinius Amicus, of a family that originated in Zarat in western Numidia, but had later moved to Oea. By this marriage, she had two sons, Pontianus and Pudens. After her husband's death, her former father-in-law induced her against her will to betrothe herself to another of his sons, Sicinius Clarus, whom she found repellent (68). The potent threat was the exclusion of the two sons from their father's estate (he had died *in patria potestate*). She managed to delay matters until old Amicus died; her sons were then able to inherit their father's share, which divided between two was rather limited. Thinking to protect his own long-term interest in her estate, Pontianus then with some difficulty persuaded Apuleius, who happened to be delayed in the town but knew Pontianus from their student days in Athens, to marry his mother. This step appalled Sicinius Aemilianus, the third of the three brothers, now the head of the family, who considered that Pudentilla had broken her engagement to Clarus; and Pontianus' own father-in-law, Herennius Rufinus (74). Pudentilla's estate seemed now destined to be eaten up by her new husband; they feared she might transfer most of it to him – the sons' morally unquestionable interest was unsecured (71). On Pontianus' subsequent death, his younger brother, Pudens, was induced to prosecute Apuleius for having manipulated Pudentilla into marrying him by magical means. Pudens was evidently a minor; one of the actual speakers for the complainant was Herennius Rufinus: we should probably infer that Pontianus had had time before his death to produce a child, or that his wife was pregnant, and that Rufinus was acting, or claiming to act, in this child's interest.

It is clear that we have here to do with a quite different situation from that in Amorgos. The Sicinii were evidently well-known at Oea – Pudentianus, and presumably his father too, were *equites Romani*; Herennius Rufinus had inherited a considerable sum from his father, but had allegedly squandered it. They were able to gather suspicious details about Apuleius, find witnesses to give credit to their accusations, and have them taken seriously enough for Apuleius to have to stand trial at the governor's assizes at Sabratha. They were in a position to have a serious stab at having him exiled or even executed. But of course the whole issue really resolved around control of Pudentilla. The Sicinii, having allied themselves with her, were extremely reluctant for her wealth to fall outside their family; and now she had indeed outwitted them by marrying (if we believe Apuleius, *Apol.* 73) for affection, even if there were good medical reasons for renewed sexual activity – Apuleius refers to her internal pains that were so severe that they brought her to the brink of the grave. Doctors and wise women agreed that the disease had its origin in her long widowhood . . . the remedy was that she should marry before her youth finally departed from her. (*Apol.* 69)

At the crucial meeting at which he failed to persuade Pudentilla to reconsider, Rufinus lost his temper and accused her of being an *amatrix*, a wanton hussy, and Apuleius a *magus et veneficus* (78). The first hint of what became the charge was thus formulated simply in an outburst of rage, inspired no doubt by greed, but also by the claim that Pudentilla was not properly free to do what she liked with her body (nor with her property), she (and it) *belonged* to the Sicinii. Since that was the case, she can only have had her mind turned. Pudentilla's subsequent letter to Pudentianus, in which she ironised the outburst in the words 'Apuleius is a magician (*magos*) and I have been bewitched by him (*memageumai*) and love him' (82f.), simply confirmed what they desired to believe. So Rufinus took it with him to the forum, *bacchabundus*, frothing with excitement, and kept opening it to show passers-by, the chattering class of Oea (82).[26] The folklore of the philtre, with all the component beliefs about gender roles and expectations, made it possible to turn a thought into a legal case. Apuleius was young, the widow old (over 40; Rufinus claimed 60 (89)); he was a stranger, she was independent.

But again, there were considerations which spoke against Rufinus' claim. Pudentilla had remained a widow for her children's sake. She was highly respectable. Her guardian, Cassius Longinus, evidently a man of some local figure, was prepared to confirm details of financial transactions on her behalf (101). If we are to believe Apuleius, Herennius Rufinus' social credit was low: he had a bad reputation as a vexatious litigant and spend-thrift (74). Apuleius himself happened to know the then governor of Proconsularis, L. Hedius Rufus Lollianus Avitus, sufficiently well through his studies to be able independently to write to him outlining the situation and to receive a friendly reply (94). Most decisively, as the work of gathering the information for this case proceeded, Apuleius rapidly took the most concrete steps he could to avoid the suspicion that he was only interested in Pudentilla's money: he induced her to alienate a good deal of her property, including four hundred slaves, in favour of her sons, and to hold out the prospect of their eventually inheriting the whole (to which they would not necessarily be entitled, since she must have been a *filiafamilias* whose own father was dead, and perhaps also have inherited in her own right from other relatives) (93). With the legitimate interests of the sons satisfied, he had disarmed the worst suspicions of the political class of Oea: 'All Oea was aware of this. Everyone execrated Rufinus and extolled my conduct' (94). For the real bar before which he had to appear, in a sense more important than the governor's court in Sabratha, was the significant population of the city, the Calpurnii, the Caesii, the Aemilii, the leading members of a 'provincial Punic mercantile aristocracy' (Reynolds and Ward-Perkins, 1952: 65).[27] He had to prove to them that, though he was an outsider and though he was rhetorically clever, he was an honourable man, one of them. That done, he could await the outcome of the trial with composure.

One last text, again familiar, will illustrate the use of the theme of magic in relation to a girl of marriageable age. It is set in the quite different context of the *colonia* of Palestinian Gaza, during the early fourth century, just as the city was beginning to be christianized and the influence of the ascetic movement make itself felt (Millar, 1993: 385f.). One of the miracles of St. Hilarion of Thavatha concerns a young woman who was a virgin dedicated to God. A young man who lived nearby fell in love with her, and did all he could to arouse her interest in him 'with those touches, jests, nods and whispers which so commonly lead to the destruction of virginity' (Jerome, *Vit. Hilarionis* 12.2 Bastiaensen, tr. Fremantle). Rejected he decided to try stronger means, and spent a year learning magic in the temple of Amenhotep at Memphis: on his return to Gaza, he put a binding spell on the girl (cf. *CT* no.163), and she began to show signs of possession, 'tearing off her head-scarf, whirling her (loose) hair, grinding her teeth and shrieking the young man's name' (12.4). Her parents, desperate, take her to Hilarion.

Unlike an ordinary girl, a virgin of Christ could never look forward to marriage. She was scarcely allowed out of the house, except to attend religious services – and even then, only by daylight. A mid fourth-century homily on virginity doubtfully ascribed to Basil of Caesarea calls her indeed a 'prisoner' ([Basil] *peri parth.* 2.34, p. 43.1 Amand-Moons). The same text continues:

> Keep a careful eye on her bed, even at home, for the Enemy is everywhere! Keep an eye on her laughter, her spirits, her anger, her protestations, her casual utterances, and all the other passions of the flesh. (2.38, p. 43.5–7 A–M)

The stakes were high: the virgin of God was a 'surety of the Lord . . . of the heavenly King' (ibid. 2.21f., p. 41.1,3) of whom one had to take the most scrupulous care; she was an 'altar made pure for the Lord, the holy spirit made flesh, the pure limbs of Christ . . . restitution for the sin of Eve, recall from Exile, reconciliation with mankind' (2.41, p. 43.10–45.3). As an emblem of the presence of the Lord in her parents' household, she connoted its purity and devotion as a whole: 'It was the individual householder who was thought to benefit most directly from the piety of his virgin daughter. He was encouraged to act as a 'priest of the Highest

God' in fostering the vocation and maintaining the seclusion of the family's dedicated women' (Brown, 1989: 263). The lapse of such a daughter was of the utmost concern to the parents, more even than the scandalous loss of a daughter's virginity before marriage in a pagan family (the reported experience of Herennius Rufus, whose daughter, with her painted lips and fluttering eyes, had been seduced and abandoned by another before her marriage to Pontianus: *Apol.*76). Such a Christian household stood to lose all its nurtured reputation for particular piety, the prospect of the father's admission to the bridal chamber of the kingdom of heaven shrivelled by a single act of fleshly weakness (Elm, 1994: 36f.). For the risks of holy virginity were at least as familiar as its rewards. Gregory of Nazianzus dramatizes the consequence of falling in a neat chiasmus: 'Now light, then darkness; spiritual doom (instead of) heavenly food' (*Carmen* 1.2.2, l.115 = Migne *PG* 37.588). At about the same time as this incident at Gaza, we find two church councils at either end of Christendom, Elvira in southern Spain and Ancyra in the East, concerned severely to sanction the wilful abandonment of such a vocation (*Conc. Elvir.* 13; *C. Ancyr.* 19, p. 15 and 34 Lauchert).

We may take it that the girl, far from being indifferent to the young man's approaches, found herself in an intractable dilemma between incipient feelings for him and her acknowledged duty to her father.[28] I assume the young man's supposed visit to learn Egyptian magic to be mere fabrication for effect, suggested by a familiar contrast between the heavenly Jerusalem and the 'ways of Egypt' ([Basil], *peri parth.* 7.87, p. 59.7; 89, 59.9f.); but perhaps he had been away. His return precipitated a crisis, which the girl could only resolve by retreat into a locally-acknowledged syndrome of mental distress – we must be reminded of a whole gallery of young women in Puritan households in the early modern period, for example the story of Helen Fairfax (aged 21) and her sister Elizabeth (aged 7) at Fuyston or Fewston in Yorkshire in 1621 (Fairfax, 1621/1882). Hilarion himself evidently suspected that there was more here than met the eye, since, quite unmotivated by anything earlier in the narrative, he asks the girl when she recovers 'why she had acted in such a way as to give the demon the chance to enter' (12.10).

Magic here acquires a Christian flavour, with a confessing demon and an exorcizing saint, but the scenario is familiar. The girl by her behaviour – above all by calling out the young man's name – provides the hint to the parents in time to save herself from ruin; the parents have in the folklore of powerful Egyptian magicians and knowledge of defixion the means of casting blame away from their daughter – and deflecting from themselves the charge that they had failed to 'watch her bed' – into the objective reality of possession by a demon; the role of the saint, in his hut by the sea, is to confirm this interpretation as a privileged outsider. His judgement as a holy man provides them with the authority they require to counter ill-natured gossip and so safeguard, with as little damage as possible, the status of their household in the local competition in sanctity.

But it may also be that the girl's retreat into possession was not so much a defence against the attractions of the boy as a means of evading a different sort of conflict, between the incompatible demands of her parents. 'Often', says pseudo-Basil,

> when a girl devoutly wishes to lead a perfect life, her mother, longing for (grand-) children or misled by the deceptive bonniness that she can picture, perhaps too eaten up (lit. 'melted') by jealousy, does her very best to make her daughter a child of this world rather than betrothe her to God. (*peri parth.* 8.99, p. 59.22ff. A–M)

If that were the case here, the role of the accusation of magic would be to resolve the clash between the father's inclination – no dowry had to be found for a virgin of God – and the mother's hopes, a conflict the saint can mediate indirectly. It has the added advantage that the parents can in all good faith represent themselves as jointly desperate for the health of their child. The girl's putative frailty would then be the convenient cover for a tussle between wife and husband, reminding us of the first law of the ancient household: 'it is best if [its] affairs are not known to anyone else' (Lysias 32.2).

The Night-Witch   These texts relating to magic in the context of nego-tiation between the sexes suggest how the folklore of magic as the Other was deployed by actors skilled in their understanding of their own social milieu, a medium through which one might regain one's rights, cut one's losses, do an enemy or a rival down, save a reputation. Success or failure in these enterprises depended wholly on the plausibility of the case one could make, and the social weight of the opposition; one found allies where one could. Magic at this, everyday, level must be relatively clearly distinguished from the image of the night-witch, which operates in a quite different way, and is applied to quite different problems. No one is ever accused of being a night-witch; but she does have a kind of history.

We have already encountered the distinction between the every-day witch and the night-witch, the one the kind of person one might well meet, and whom many people knew (of), the other the radical enemy of all human civilisation such as the *strix*, the night-owl that is really a flesh-devouring woman, a child-killing demon (cf. Johnston, 1994a: 140–8; 1994b). But in narrative fiction the two refuse to remain distinct: the more powerful negative image constantly overwhelms the more realistic. The typical idea of the witch conveyed particularly in the Roman poets is a composite one in which ethnographic allusion, to the *goês*, the root-cutter, and the wise-man or woman, is overlaid by images of natural reversal and the violent disruption of natural order. Ovid makes Medea in Iolcus pray to Hekate, Earth (which gives powerful plants), breezes, mountains, lakes, and the gods of the forest and night:

> When you have entered me,
> As if a miracle had drained their banks and courses,
> I've driven backs rivers to springs and fountains.
> I shake the seas or calm them at my will;
> I whip the clouds or make them rise again;
> At my command winds vanish or return,
> My very spells have torn the throats of serpents,
> Live rocks and oaks are overturned and felled,
> The forests tremble and the mountains split,
> And deep Earth roars while ghosts walk from their tombs.
> Though crashing brass and bronze relieve your labours,
> Even you, O moon, I charm from angry skies.
>
> (*Met.* 7. 199–208 [tr. Gregory])

The power of these images is generated by the repetition of the denial, almost to absurdity, of the foundational opposition between words and actions: in magic, words are actions, whereas it is settled knowledge that in the 'real world' words are precisely the opposite of actions. The night-witch's fantastic world of natural inversion implies also the possibility of the cancellation of the oppositions which construct the everyday world, and legitimate its distribution of power.

We should not be tempted to under-read these scenarios of the night-witch, tedious rhodomontade though they appear at first sight to be, their inversions crude beyond all belief. For one thing, they sometimes have a particular emphasis that repays attention. When Dido, for example, is planning her malign magical attack upon Aeneas after his departure from Carthage, she takes advice from a Massylian priestess:

> Now she claims that her spells can liberate
> One's heart, or can inject love-pangs, just as she wishes;
> Can stop the flow of rivers, send the stars flying backwards,
> Conjure ghosts in the night: she can make the earth cry out
> Under one's feet, and elm trees come trooping down from the
>   mountains.
>
> (Vergil, *Aen.* 4. 487–91 [tr. Day Lewis, adapted])

Here the images of natural reversal are metaphors for the disillusioned dream of enduring love, its hopelessness imaged in the impossible feats. More generally, the poetological gain lay in the possibility of exploiting a tension between the reader's professed distance from or scepticism of 'old women's tales' and a fear that there might just be something in them — the very tension familiar in modern African societies. As Pliny observes, speaking also for himself: 'No one is unafraid of being 'caught' by curses' (*HN* 28.19). Some awareness of this tension is already present in the Hellenistic forerunners of these Latin texts, for example in Apollonius Rhodius' flashback, during his description of Medea taking her *pharmakon* from its hiding place, to the time when she gathered it near the rock in the Caucasus where the Titan Prometheus was chained so that the eagle might daily rip his liver :

> (The plant) shot up first-born when the ravening eagle on the rugged flanks of Caucasus let drip to the earth the blood-like ichor of tortured Prometheus . . .

(she cuts it)

> And beneath, the dark earth shook and bellowed when the Titanian root was cut; and the son of Iapetus (Prometheus) himself groaned, his soul distraught with pain. (*Argon.* 3. 851–3; 864–6 [tr. Seaton])

And it is certainly no less present in the manifold distances and ironies that Theocritus works into *Idyll* 2 (cf. Segal, 1973/1981; Goldhill, 1991: 261–72). But the Roman poets of the mid-first century AD, though sheer over-use of the device, found themselves on the treadmill of hyperbole.

Catalogues of nightmarish powers however are more than textual devices. We may take as illustration what at first sight looks like another routine list:

> I have myself witnessed her drawing the stars from heaven — she has reversed a river's flow with her swift-running chant, and by incantation fissured the earth, hauled the dead from their graves and summoned bones from the inextinguished pyre: at one moment she draws the pullulating dead with a magical noise, at another she sprinkles them with milk and bids them return. At will she drives clouds from overcast sky; at will she commands snow while summer reigns. (Tibullus 1.2.43–50)

The catalogue of powers focuses almost entirely on the theme of necromantic disturbance, the fear of pyres being rifled to obtain unburned parts of corpses, sarcophagi being disturbed, the dead defiled, turned into active dangers (as far as I know, the first mention of witches deliberately looking out for bits of corpses is Apoll. Rhod. *Argon.* 4. 51). Horace imagines the same scenario in his description of Canidia and Sagana stealing into the old Esquiline cemetery, now the site of a building-boom, but where slaves were once buried in mass-graves: 'I can't stop them,' says the old statue of Priapus, 'from collecting bones and harmful plants here when the wandering moon shows her radiant face' (*Sat.* 1.8.21f.). Nominally of course necromancy was simply a means of divination; but the theme of the robbing of graves is evidently much more than this: it evokes a world in which the symbolic means of putting things in their place, of setting things to rights, has gone awry, has lost its efficacy. Hekate, goddess of night-witches, lurked among the tombs and the dried black blood of cemeteries (Theocritus, *Id.* 2. 12f.); hyenas, powerful sorcerers themselves, grub about in grave-yards to find and chivvy human corpses (Pliny, *HN* 28. 104).

Knowledge of ghost-stories, the rituals of the State cult devoted to the dead, reports of disturbed tombs, all contributed to the fear that necromantic rituals did indeed take place. C. Vatinius – of course a Pythagorean, an associate of Nigidius Figulus – was supposed in the 50s BC to have regularly offered perverted sacrifice, boys' noble *exta* (liver and heart), to the Manes, the gods of the Underworld, for the purpose (Cicero, *in Vat.* 14); Varro, who had an elaborate theory of his own about the classification of divinatory techniques, reported matter-of-factly that 'if blood is used (in lecanomancy) one may also consult the dwellers in the Underworld, and that the Greek term for this is necromancy' (*de rerum deorum* 1, frg.IV Cardauns = Augustine, *Civ. Dei* 7.35, tr. Knowles). The blood evidently had to be human. The magician Ostanes was known to have written about necromantic rituals in his book on divination (Pliny, *HN* 30. 14); they certainly appear both in the Demotic Egyptian and in the Graeco-Egyptian receptaries (e.g. PDM xiv 83f.; 259–61; xli 79–94; PGM IV 227; 1928–2005; 2140–4; VII 993–1009; XIII 277–82). A famous inscription from Rome relates how a four-year-old slave belonging to Iulia Livia, the sister of Germanicus and of the future emperor Claudius, was carried off by 'the cruel hands of a witch (*saga*)' and killed by her arts (*CIL* VI 19747 = *ILS* 8522), presumably for necromantic purposes – a neat adaptation of the ancient theme of the child-killing demon.

As we have seen, there are reasons for thinking that it was during the late Republic that the Romans took over the Hellenistic notion of *mageia*, and in particular the Hellenistic history of its development from Zoroaster in Persia, preserved to us by Pliny the Elder, *HN* 30.1–18.[29] I would argue that one reason why necromancy, and more generally the fantastic imagery of the night-witch, became topical in the late Republic and early Principate was their resonance with the ubiquitous theme of moral and religious decline, which was a direct response to the experience of the civil wars (cf. Jal, 1963). It was common ground that the civil wars were an expression of the gods' anger with Rome, that they refused to listen to prayers: in that climate, with access to the symbolic means of re-ordering society blocked, we might expect the spread of a sense that evil was victorious – in a word, a sense of pollution, comparable to that which stimulates the numerous witch-hunting movements of colonial and post-colonial Africa. In effect the night-witch imagery is a reproduction, in a quite different idiom, of Archaic Greek dystopian imagery, in particular of Hesiod's final (sixth) age in his myth of the ages (*Op.* 180–201) – a dystopia generated by the imagined removal of the key social principles of *aidôs* and *nemesis*.

Once imagined, the night-witch was too good to lose: the image survived Augustus' re-establishment of the benign symbolic order, the patching up of the theodicy of good fortune which the experience of civil war had so dented (Zanker, 1988). For she was able to offer the reverse image of the sacrificing princeps, the lynch-pin of the Roman *pax deorum* of the Principate. The night-witch, especially in its female form, became all that the Princeps was not – or should not be, a systematic negation of all four Weberian principles of legitimacy. In that perspective, the Augustan versions – even Ovid's Medea (*Metam.* 7. 149–349) – pale into insignificance by comparison with the vividly-imagined, exhaustive, horrors of Lucan's Erictho (*Bell.civ.* 6.507–88; cf. Gordon, 1987b) and Seneca's Teiresias (*Oedipus* 530–658). Necromancy, one of the key features of the night-witch, becomes a figure for the political other, for emperors who are no emperors: Nero was believed to have attempted to get in touch with the shade of his mother whom he had had murdered (Suet. *Nero* 34.4); one of the losers in the civil war of 193 AD, Didius Iulianus, was supposed to have murdered several boys in order to discover the future (Dio 73.16.5); shortly before his murder in 217 Caracalla was said to have told Flavius Maternianus, the extraordinary commander of the urban troops at the end of his reign, to conduct a necromantic consultation 'by using a dead body' (Herodian 4.12.4).

But there may be a broader consideration yet. In the older representation of the divine order, the gods were conceived as dispensing indifferently good and evil. Hekate in particular could emblematize malign aspects of the divine world, as in a fragment that may be from a fifth-century BC play by Sophron: 'whether you have come hastening from a hanging, or from grinding to death a woman in childbirth, or from ranging among corpses' (Plutarch, *de superst.* 10, 170b = Demiańczuk, frg. dub.2; tr. Parker, 1983/1996: 222f.). The moralization and rationalization of the divine world that slowly took place from the Archaic period had, by the Hellenistic period, made it difficult to accommodate misfortune and evil into the dominant image of the civic pantheon: the notion of Tychê, and the elaboration of a distinct world of *daemones*, were two ways of maintaining belief in a morally univocal heaven. But the development of the image of the night-witch, and particularly of the necromantic witch who threatens the fundamental symbolic distinction between the living and the dead (cf. the wonderful scene of Thelyphron and his wax nose in

Apuleius, *Metam.* 2.21–30), who indeed turns the dead against the living, may perhaps be understood as a further adjustment to a moralized heaven. If the gods will not cause evil, and so make it intelligible, the night-witch can oblige: for she is everywhere and nowhere, a creature precisely of nightmare.

That the night-witch could indeed be seen as a way of responding to the wider issue of the explanation of evil in a rationalized divine world, fulfilling a function analogous to that of the Devil in Christianity, is suggested by a recently-published, though unfortunately incomplete, response (*SEG* 41: 981, cf. Graf, 1992) by the oracle of Apollo at Claros, probably to the city of Sardis, around the middle of the reign of Marcus Aurelius (161–180 AD). The context is evidently the plague which ravaged the Roman Empire in several waves after being brought back by L. Verus' troops from Mesopotamia in 165; recent work has re-emphasized its well-nigh catastrophic social and demographic effects (Duncan-Jones, 1996).[30] The oracle's response, as usual in hexameters, prescribes the performance of a procession in honour of Artemis of Ephesus, evidently for the first time in the city, as a means of protecting the city from threatened danger:

> She will be distressed at the calamity <which has befallen the city>, and by her fiery torches unbind man-destroying magic of plague (*loimoio . . . pharma[k]a*) by melting with her night-flame (the) maumets of wax, the wicked signs of a magician's art (*magou . . . symbola technês*). (ll.6–9)

Although other interpretations have been offered, the most likely scenario is that during an outbreak of the plague some wax maumets were by chance discovered, of the kind discussed elsewhere in this volume by Daniel Ogden, and probably as usual relating to some private feud. But, given the plague, many people assumed that they were its cause – no matter that it was raging all through Asia Minor at the time – thus forcing the city magistrates to take action: the place was polluted, the plague must be the result of malign witchcraft. The oracle finds a solution by authorizing the introduction of the cult of Artemis from Ephesus, a purificatory procession, and a solemn ritual in which the torches of Artemis are to destroy the maumets. If they were destroyed their binding power would be gone: civic cult triumphs over magician's malice. We must be reminded of the medieval and early modern moral panics involving well-poisoners. My argument would be that the availability of the image of the night-witch, who delights solely in the random destruction of human life, whether by murdering children, causing sudden deaths – 'eaten from the inside' like Petronius' hulking great fellow (*Satyr.* 63) – or by blighting the crops in the fields and poisoning the very air (Lucan *Bell. civ.* 6. 521f.), made possible the spontaneous mass re-interpretation of the perfectly familiar, if frightening, objects by which personal enmities might be pursued into the agents of mass-death, the plague. Lucan's detail about polluted air – one of the beliefs about the plague that it was spread, like nineteenth-century cholera, as a miasma – is very much to the point.[31]

Magic as Specious and Vain

All these representations of magic as transgressive derive from its notional illegitimacy as a mode of intercourse with the divine world. It is only an apparent paradox that another important representation of magic conceived it not as powerful for harm but on the contrary as vacant show, as empty nonsense. Although this view is associated generally with the educated élite it was also a view widespread in the population at large: for most of the time, under most circumstances, many people – perhaps more specifically many men – considered the claims of marginal religion absurd. They were disposed to prefer other explanations of any given event, and to consider non-civic rituals mere mumbo-jumbo. This view, once again, was grounded in the belief that valid religion is a collective matter, and that legitimate religious authority belongs in principle to the collectivity.

As we have seen, until Constantine, and indeed after, the ancient city preferred the 'civic compromise' over monopoly of the sacred by a specific class or group. Argument and difference of opinion about the significance of signs of one sort or another could only be resolved by appeal to an outside source, such as an oracle, or by a vote in a responsible instance. But there was no debate about the fundamentals, that civic cult was indispensable to the maintenance of the well-being of the city as a whole, and of its citizens as individuals, and that the rituals handed down by tradition were effective in their contribution to that well-being. Taken all in all, piety consisted

> not in lavish expenditure but in declining to meddle with what their ancestors had bequeathed them; and the consequence was that the blessings of heaven were not bestowed upon them capriciously or harum-scarum but in due season, both for preparing the ground and for gathering in the harvest. (Isocrates, *Areopag.* 30)

Conversely, it was a truism that failure to perform traditional rituals, or collective and individual impiety, both active and passive disregard for proper ritual, led, or might lead, to disaster (cf. Zaidman and Schmitt-Pantel, 1989/1992: 11–15). The Romans' regard for the niceties of ritual observance was by no means peculiar to them.

It is precisely this connection, unquestioned for civic cult, between ritual and efficacy that fails to hold true for illicit religion. There is a vacuum at the centre of illicit cult, a vacancy that is the structural consequence of negating the norm. This prescriptive vacancy, as we might call it, turns magic into failed religion, evoked by a variety of words, particularly those belonging to the *mangan-* and *goêt-* semantic ranges (cf. Burkert, 1962a: 43f.) From the later fifth century BC, these words evoke as often as not the 'smooth hypocrisy' imputed to Hippolytus by his enraged father Theseus: 'Is he not an *epôidos* (one who knows incantations), this man, and a *goês*, so sure that by his easy temper he will master my spirit?' (Euripides *Hippol.* 1038–40 tr. Barrett; cf. *Bacchae* 234). Such language in a tragedy written for public performance implies widespread acknowledgement of this force of the word: Aristophanes actually wrote a comedy entitled *Goêtes*, though its content is wholly unknown. An analogous view is implied by the late fifth-century interest in the Medea who tricked the daughters of Pelias into boiling their father to death (we have seen that both Sophocles and Euripides wrote such tragedies). For one reading of the story might suggest that marginal religion – magic in this case – is merely specious, playing on its customers' foolish and extravagant hopes. That point is certainly made by a joke in Euripides' satyr play, *Cyclops*, in a scene in which Odysseus and the chorus of satyrs are fumblingly attempting to prepare the stake to burn out Polyphemus' eye. Of a sudden, a sideration strikes several satyrs; when Odysseus accuses them of cowardice, the leader of the chorus cries:

> I'm a coward am I? But I can say
> a fine Orphic spell that will make the brand
> fly of its own accord into the skull
> of this one-eyed whelp of Earth and scorch him up.
> Od.: I knew from the first what sort you were,
>   and now I know it better. (*Cyclops* 645–50 [tr. Arrowsmith])

'Orphic' claims are just tall stories. It is to this wider context that the opposition between marginal religion and true piety of the Hippocratic *On the Sacred Disease* belongs:

> Yet I believe that all these professions of piety are really more like impiety and a denial of the existence of the gods, and all their religion and talk of divine visitation is an impious fraud. (3 = 1.28, p. 64.58–61 Grensemann [tr. Chadwick and Mann])

There are other telling examples from the fourth century: a passage of Xenophon, for example, closely associates deception with *goêteia*, sleight-of-hand, making people believe what is not true (*Anab.* 5.7.9); Glaucon in Plato's *Republic* claims 'anything that deceives is wizardry (*goêteia*)' (*Rep.* 413c4; cf. 412e7; 413b1; *Leg.* X, 908d2–4). The link evidently owes a great deal to the rhetorician Gorgias' earlier glorification of *goêteia* as 'soul-gulling' (*Helen* 10 = 82 B11 *DK*). The word *phenakizein*, cheat, cozen, occurs in several of these contexts, notably in relation to the worthless brother of Aristogeiton, who 'performs magic and cheats and professes to cure people who suffer from epilepsy, despite himself suffering from acute blackguardism' ([Demosth.] 25.80). Sosiphanes of Syracuse, a tragic poet of the later fourth century BC, had a character in his lost *Meleager* remark dismissively:

> Every chit of girl in Thessaly can command the moon down from heaven by magic incantations – believe that if you will. (*TGF* 1² 92 F1, cf. Gauly, 1991: 198f)

The motif of changing shape, which evoked in Herodotus' Greeks of Scythia the response *goêteia* – 'I myself do not believe what they say, but they say it nonetheless, indeed swear it' (Hdt. 4.105.2) – reappears in Plato's insistence that the true ontology of god cannot really be as gods are represented in poetry and myth, forever changing shape: 'Do you think that god is a *goês*?' (*Rep.* 380d1–6).

Non-civic religion is thus doomed to be mere show, false appearance. But there were a number of other means of evoking the significance of the contrast between civic and illicit religion. One is the issue of payment. The officials of civic cult acted – by definition – disinterestedly; their perquisites, as it may be the chines, haunches, hides, heads of sacrificial animals, were enshrined in sacred laws, taken for granted (Le Guen-Pollet, 1981). But the representatives of illicit or marginal religion are always understood to be extortioners, to be acting solely for money, merely for self-enrichment, their wares tawdry lies. So Oedipus taunts the seer Teiresias with being a

> scheme-hatching *magos*, treacherous mendicant, who has eyes only for lucre, but as seer was stone-blind. (Soph. *OT* 387–9)

At the end of the fifth century, *On the Sacred Disease* makes the same point:

> If a man were to draw down the moon or cause an eclipse of the sun, or make storms or fine weather by magic and sacrifices (*mageuôn te kai thuôn*), I should not call any of these things a divine visitation but a human one, because the divine power has been overcome and forced into subjection by the human will. But perhaps these claims are not true at all, and it is because these people lack a means of solid livelihood that they have invented all these different arts and play the harlequin so. (4=1.31f., p. 64.69–73 Grensemann [tr. Chadwick and Mann, adapted])

This tradition accompanied the marginal religious practitioner throughout antiquity. A probably fourth-century BC account in the Aesopian corpus describes a woman, a *gynê magos* (itself a most unusual expression, which must date from a much later redaction), who used to sell incantations and 'means of allaying divine anger' – that is, just the kind of person Plato describes in *Rep.* 364b–c, *Laws* 11, 909b – and 'earned pretty well from it'. She was prosecuted for introducing innovation into civic religion (*asebeia*) and condemned to death:

> One of the spectators, seeing her being dragged out of the court said to her: 'How is it, if you claim to be able to avert the gods' anger, that you were not even able to persuade human beings?' (*Fab. Aesop.* 56 Hausrath, 1:77f.= p. 343 Perry)

The point was early taken at Rome, for it appears in one of the very earliest Roman tragedies, Ennius' *Telamo*, based on a Greek original, dating from the first half of the second century BC, where a character denounces diviners:

> Averse to work, or mad, or ruled by want,
> Directing others how to go, and yet
> What road to take they do not know themselves;
> From those to whom they promise wealth they beg
> A coin. From what they promised let them take
> their coin as toll and pass the balance on.
> (Ennius, *Telamo* frg. CXXXIVb Jocelyn [tr. Falconer])

The inefficacy of love-magic is a *topos* of Latin amatory poetry (cf. Tibull. 1.8.24f.; Prop. 2.4; Ovid, *Ars am.* 2.99–106; *Remed am.* 261–90; Nemesianus, *Ecl.* 2.62–73 etc.). Medea is made pointedly to exclaim:

> Dragons and maddened bulls, it seems, I could subdue; a man alone I could not; I, who could beat back fierce fire with wise drugs (*doctis medicatibus*), have not the power to escape the flames of my own passion. My very incantations, herbs and arts abandon me. ([Ovid], *Heroid.* 12.163–7 [tr.Showerman-Goold])

And Deianeira:

> What herbs does Pontus grow, or what does Pindus nourish beneath the rocks of Thessaly, wherein I may find a bane to conquer him? Though Luna should leave the stars and come down to earth, obedient to magic (*carmine mago*); though winter should see ripe grain . . . it will not bend him. ([Seneca], *Herc. Oet.* 465–72 [tr. Miller])

The greed and speciousness of necromancers played their part in the downfall of Q. Marcius Barea Soranus (*cos. suff.* 52 AD). Hated by Nero, he was denounced by Ostorius Sabinus in 66 for plotting in his former province of Asia. His daughter Servilia evidently appealed to some *magi* in an effort to foresee the family fate. When this became public, she had to stand trial before the Senate accused of having given large sums to such persons. The prosecutor asked whether she had indeed done so. She replied:

> My unhappy prayers have had a single aim: that you, Caesar (i.e. Nero), and you, senators, should spare my dear father. I gave my jewels and clothes – what a woman in my position owns – as I would have given my blood and my life if the magicians had wanted them! (Tac. *Ann.* 16.31.1f. [tr. Grant])

She refers of course to the belief that necromancy to be effective requires human sacrifice; and perhaps implies that the magicians' failure was due to her own lack of courage. The Senate required her to commit suicide along with her father, but for Tacitus she is merely a sad, deluded girl. Lovers too are deluded, says Philostratus, so deluded that

> they will accept from [magicians] a box with stones in it which they are to wear, some of the bits of stones having come from the depths of the earth and others from the moon and stars; and then they are given all the spices which the gardens of India yield; and the cheats exact vast sums of money from them for all this, and yet do nothing to help them at all. (*Vit. Apoll.* 7.39, p. 827.13–18 Mumprecht [tr. Conybeare])

The rise of literacy and an education that depended upon it gradually however added to the notion of mere show, predicated on the opposition between civic and marginal religion, a representation founded upon the contrast between city and country, which was at the same time one between urbanity and ignorance. Although the fullest form of this contrast only became possible with the social changes of the Hellenistic period and the disappearance of a sizeable group of city dwellers who went daily out to their farms, it is perceptible already in the jokes of fourth-century comedy, such as the description by Anaxilas in his *Lyremaker*, a lost mid-fourth century comedy, of a country dweller, evidently dressed as disconcertingly as Uncle Benjy for going into town:

> his skin softened with yellow face-cream, dragging his fine robe (in the dust), slopping about in torn house-shoes, chewing bulbs, gobbling cheese, drinking raw eggs, holding ?trumpet-shells, drinking Chian wine, and to cap it all carrying lovely Ephesian letters on pieces of sewn leather (i.e. amulets against various kinds of danger). (*PCG* 2: 285, Anaxilas frg.18)

One common way of eliding the claimed powers of marginal practitioners was to note that only foolish old women, country bumpkins and children believe such stuff: *fabulae aniles* is, as we have seen, Cicero's contemptuous expression (*Nat.D.* 3.12; cf. Horace *Sat.* 2.6.77f.). The inversion civic religion – illicit religion is spatialized, but also temporalized, to correlate with changes in the self-consciousness of the political and social élite:

> Who now credits that the hippocentaur or the Chimaera ever existed? Is there a single old woman to be found who is so unhinged as to be sorely afraid of those monsters in the nether world in which people once believed? Time obliterates falsehoods of common belief. (Cicero, *Nat.D.* 2. 5 [tr. Walsh])

In a similar sense Galen, in the course of his violent attack on Pamphilus' *Descriptions of herbs*, which investigated the use of herbs as amulets and their symbolic associations, denounces his claims as incredible even to small children (*De simpl. med. temp.*, proem. [11: 793f. Kühn], cf. Hopfner, 1921–4/1974–90: 1 §479, p. 266f.).

All these stock attitudes, but above all the notion of speciousness or illusion, are transferred to magic when a strong view of it emerged in the Hellenistic period. Pliny the Elder makes the point in his history of magic (*HN* 30. 1–18), as clearly as can be:

> Let us therefore accept that (the Magian art) is abominable, ineffectual, vain – if there is even a shimmer of truth in it, that shimmer owes more to chemistry than to magic.[32] (*HN* 30.17)

Pliny indeed takes it upon himself in the *Natural History* to perform a service to mankind by exposing *magicas vanitates*, the vanities of the Magi, because of the sway this, the most specious of all the arts (*fraudulentissima artium*), now enjoys all over the Roman Empire, from Persia to Britain, that 'empty void of Nature' (30.1; 13). He finds his most telling evidence in Nero's failure to succeed in his necromantic aims:

> [Nero's] elevation to the greatest height of human fortune aroused desire in the vicious depths of his mind; his greatest wish was to issue commands to the gods, and he could rise to no nobler ambition. (*HN* 30.14 [tr. Jones])

The contrast between public religion, piety, the collective good, on the one hand, and the image of magic as private religion, impiety, personal advantage could hardly be more plain; what is frightful about Nero is that the person who, as *pontifex maximus*, ought to incorporate the civic cult of the Romans, spends his time dabbling in magic, its inverse – when he must have known that it is by definition specious idleness. Apollonius of Tyana makes just the same point to Domitian, speaking of his earlier meeting with Vespasian, his father,[33] at which Apollonius had forecast that he would become emperor:

> For I should not have thought him a fit person for empire if he had either considered me an adept in such art (magic), or resorted to such tricks in pursuit of a crown which it behoved him to win by his virtues alone. More than this, my conversation with him was held publicly in a temple, and wizards (*goêtes*) do not affect temples of the gods as their places of reunion; such places are inimical to those who deal in magic, for they cloak their art under the cover of night. (Philostr. *Vit. Apoll.* 8.7.2, p. 861.17–22 Mumprecht [tr. Conybeare, adapted])

Thereafter, these become the terms within which the contrast between true religion – no longer necessarily understood in terms of civic cult – and magic is expressed. Images of piety, insight, love of god are opposed to false belief, superficial charm, worship of false gods. Lucian's *Demonax* is one of the few of his pieces on an individual that is entirely positive; he describes in it how the Cynic philosopher, who died c.170–80 AD, put down a magician who boasted that he possessed mighty incantations 'by means of which he could 'turn' everyone and provide himself with whatever he wished'. Demonax offered to go with him to the nearest baker and show him how he could get a loaf of bread 'with just one little spell' – meaning a coin 'which had just the same effect as magic' (*Demonax* 23; cf. the joke in Apuleius *Met.* 3.23 ad fin.). One of the key surviving texts in this process is Philostratus' *Life of Apollonius of Tyana*, written in the early third century on the basis of divergent sources, some local, some synthetic, some even documentary, assembled since Apollonius' death about a century earlier (Anderson, 1986: 121–97; Flintermann, 1995: 67–88), which seeks systematically to represent Apollonius as a philosophical sage against earlier views of him, by Moiragenes in particular, as both a magician and a philosopher. One illustration is the account of Apollonius' exposure at Corinth of a *lamia/empousa*, a creature we may characterize as a blend of Count Dracula with the Romantic La Belle Dame sans Merci, familiar from Goethe's ballad *Die Braut von Korinth* (1797) and Keats' *Lamia* (1820).

Menippus was a pupil at Corinth of the Cynic philosopher Demetrius of Alexandria, and had fallen in love with a Phoenician woman. At the splendid wedding feast, however, Apollonius reveals that she is really an *empousa* or *lamia*:

> These beings fall in love, and they are devoted to the delights of Aphrodite, but especially to the flesh of human beings, and they decoy with such delights those whom they mean to devour in their feasts. (4.25, p. 406.12–15 Mumprecht [tr. Conybeare])

All the splendid furnishings and table-settings flutter away out of sight, the slaves and cooks disappear too, and finally she admits what she is, an *empousa*:

> she was fattening up Menippus with pleasures before devouring his body, for it was her habit to to feed on young and beautiful bodies, because their blood is pure and strong. (ibid., p. 406.25–408.3 Mumprecht [tr. Conybeare])

In this story we have a dramatized confrontation between a night-witch figure (cf. Waser, 1905; Herter, 1950/1975: 50–2; Johnston, 1997c: 68 n. 64) and a true lover of God, in which the former is shown to be like the Gardens of Tantalus, that both exist and do not exist, a mere semblance or shadow (cf. 8.7 passim). Apollonius overcame her with the help of Hercules (ibid.); and yet, as he repeatedly insists, he refused to have any truck with civic cult, considering, like Demonax later, blood sacrifice to be an abomination.

In picking up and elaborating the same contrast between the plenitude of true religion and the vanity of paganism, and magic in particular, Christianity thus made itself heir to a venerable classical tradition. Defending Christ against the accusation that he was a mere magician (cf. M. Smith, 1978; Gallaher, 1982), Arnobius has simply to oppose true power to false or specious power:

> Were, then, those things which were done, the freaks of demons, and the tricks of magical arts (*daemonum praestigiae et magicarum artium ludi*)? . . . Who has done (what Christ did) without any power of incantations, without the juice of herbs and grasses, without any anxious watchings of sacrifices, of libations, or of seasons? (*Adv. haer.* 1.43, p. 38.5–12 Marchesi [tr. Bryce and Campbell])

The vanity and speciousness of illicit religion, and so magic, implied not its lack of power – the Christian identification of *daemones* with inherently evil demons foreclosed that option – but its lack of value, itself a consequence of the marginality of the individuals who sought to exercise it (cf. J.Z.Smith, 1978b: 426–9; Segal, 1981). As Tertullian argues:

> If sorcerers call forth ghosts, and even make what seem to be the souls of the dead to appear; if they put boys to death in order to get a response from the oracle; if with their juggling illusions, they make a pretence of doing various miracles . . . how much more likely is this power of evil to be zealous in doing with all its might, of its own inclination, and for its own objects, what it does to serve the ends of others! (*Apol.* 1.23.1 [tr. Thelwall])

The shrillness of Christian apologetics here (cf. Justin, *Apol.* 1, 18.3 and Tertull. *De anim.* 27) is an index of their awareness of the difficulty, once they allowed the issue to be one of miracle-working, of distinguishing between the Christ of the Gospels and the pagan tradition of the marvellous. For if they insisted too much on the theme of juggling, of prestidigitation, they laid themselves open to the same taunt. The only interests which could with equanimity identify magic with illusion in the sense of prestidigitation were the Cynics and Epicureans – and, ironically enough, the magicians themselves. Philostratus makes Apollonius remark on the fact that

> the various devices and artifices by which they work signs from heaven and all sorts of other miracles on a wide scale, have actually been recorded by certain authors, who laugh outright at the art in question. (*Vit. Apoll.* 7. 39, p. 826.24–828.3 Mumprecht [tr. Conybeare])

The sole surviving exposure of this kind is preserved to us in a few chapters of Hippolytus' *Refutation of all the heresies* (4. 28–42 = Totti, 1985 no.78, comm. Ganschinietz, 1913), which explains in detail how magicians achieve their claimed marvels; Philostratus' reference to 'several authors' suggests however a Cynic or Epicurean tradition, analogous to Oenomaus of Gadara's exposure of oracle-mongering, entitled or at any rate often referred to as *The jugglers' deception* (cf. Hammerstaedt, 1988: 11–40).[34] The cast of the work Hippolytus cites from is entirely rationalist, founded on the Cynic contrast between reason and folly (cf. Diog. Laert. *Vit. Phil.* 6.24); the pre-supposition is that magicians were at pains to demonstrate – mostly in darkened rooms – before the eyes of the impressionable a variety of marvels, including bringing down the moon (4.37) and reading sealed letters (28). Many of the details are unknown from elsewhere and also highly specific, such as the account of how to make a skull speak:

> The skull itself is made out of the caul of an ox fashioned into the requisite shape by means of Etruscan wax and prepared gum; when covered in parchment it resembles a skull, which seems to all the spectators to speak . . . (They) obtain the wind-pipe of a crane, or some other long-necked creature, and attach it secretly to the skull, and by this means the accomplice can say what he thinks appropriate. (*Ref. haer.* 4. 41, p. 126.2–7 Marcovitch)

Whether we are here in the realm of the circus mountebank, of the pious fraud so often practised in the context of civic cult, or of sheer imagination, is impossible at this remove to decide. But if marvels existed in the imagination, in 'old women's tales', in traditional mythology, and in the tradition of *mirabilia*, then at some point there was bound to be some physical effort invested in their realisation – the ancient world had no film industry. The magical tradition itself evidently acknowledged as much: there was a genre (Bain, 1998), to which we find occasional reference in the magical papyri, 'the trifles (*paignia*) of Democritus', also known as 'the trifles of Pythagoras' (cf. Σ RVE ad Aristoph. *Nub.* 752, p. 157.14 Holwerda), which listed recipes involving the use of simple chemistry to impress an audience:

> To make an egg become like an apple: Boil the egg and smear it with a mixture of ?egg-yolk (or saffron) and wine. (*PGM* VII 170f. [tr. Kotansky])

But the same list includes recipes hard to distinguish from many of the brief instructions not labelled Trifles, for example that for obtaining an erection: 'Grind pepper with some honey and spread it on your "business"' (185). Who here is having his leg pulled? 'Democritus' trifles' provide the only intentional light relief in the unremitting seriousness of the magical papyri; but they may also half-acknowledge both the tradition of the vanity of magic and the indecipherable status of the serious recipes that otherwise fill these books.

Magic Explained

The tradition of *The jugglers' deception* relied upon an implicit rejection of the conventional understanding of the relation between this world and the Other World – the rejection we associate with the Epicureans and Cynics – in order to arrive at its wholesale denial of the reality of magical action (Hammerstaedt, 1993). If what magicians do is just prestidigitation, merely fraud, a sufficient explanation is to be found in exposing their tricks: the conventional notion of the vanity of magic is pushed here to its very limit (cf. Goulet-Cazé, 1993: 130–2). The Hippocratic author of *On the Sacred Disease* likewise did not feel that he needed a special explanation of how his itinerant healers performed their cures, for they could not cure:

> They also employ other pretexts so that, if the patient be cured, their reputation for cleverness is enhanced, while, if he dies, they can excuse themselves by explaining that the gods are to blame while they themselves did nothing wrong. (2 = 1.20, p. 62.37–40 Grensemann)

But to some, mainly but not exclusively those with an existing investment in the idea of nature as 'implying a universal nexus of cause and effect' (Lloyd, 1979: 49), the claims of marginal religion, and in due course of magic, seemed to raise an interesting challenge to the adequacy of their starting-point. Where do marvels, and in particular marvels induced by qualified persons, fit into the scheme of *physis*, Nature?

Speculation about magic may occur at any level, however, and we begin *exempli gratia* with a couple of what seem to be popular ideas to account for the powers of marginal practitioners, including wise women and root-cutters (leaving aside belief in *daemones*). One is a chance remark of Plato, who alludes elliptically to folklore about 'the Thessalian women', witches, having to sacrifice something very dear to them in order to have the power to draw down the moon (*Gorgias* 513a5–7). An unknown Asclepiades, presumably a Hellenistic commentator on comedy, expands upon this with the information that they would have to kill one of their children or lose the sight of one of their eyes (cited in the apparatus to Zenobius IV.1, ap. *CPG* 1: 83). If the first might be a simple inference from the story of Medea, the second at least may be authentic – we might see here a folk-account that understood partial blindness as a price to be paid for magical power: a hint, that is, of the idea that would be expanded into the diabolical pact. Another possible case is more rationalistic. In a list of a witch's powers, Propertius seems to use the notion of a witch being able to cause floods by means of violent rainstorms as an explanation for the well-known, and evidently by the late first century BC puzzling, reference in the XII Tables to 'spiriting away crops by incantation' (to which we shall return):

> Should she over a trench cast spells with her evil herbs,
> The waters would rise and wash standing crops (*stantia*) away.
>
> (4.5.11f. [tr. Musker])

Transgressive religious power may thus elicit reponses other than fear and rejection: there are many ways of normalizing marvels. In what follows, I select six areas in which we can find evidence of normalizing strategies in the face of magic, six areas in which the marvellous is domesticated, fitted into a wider explanatory frame, sometimes, like atomic theory, wholly personal or individual, sometimes, as in the case of *daemones*, widely shared speculations whose main leverage was upon quite different problems.

The Power of Words (1)   There can be little doubt, judging from the sensitivity to rhythm, assonance, dissonance and other phonetic intensifiers, in early imitations of incantations, such as Circe's spell to turn Odysseus into a pig (*Od.* 10. 320), or Demeter's offer to Metaneira to protect her son Demophoön from illness and malign magic (*Hom. Hymn. Dem.* 228–30) – which contains a remarkable number of non-epic and virtually unexampled words – that many people were interested in the question of how charms worked,[35] and what relation they might have to the capacity of poetry to charm, delight and persuade (de Romilly, 1975). Gorgias' reflections on this matter in the mid-fifth century BC certainly stem from, while also decisively modernising in terms of current medical theory, a tradition of more or less sophisticated interest in the matter, focussing on the word *thelgô* and its derivatives (Furley, 1994: 85–7). His treatment of the theme in the *Helen* (though the force is virtually lost in translation) might almost be part of a commentary upon the Homeric passages describing the song of the Sirens:

> inspired incantations consisting of words bring on pleasure, dissipate pain – for when the influence of the spell meets the opinion-forming part of the mind, it soothes and persuades and finally changes it by magical art (goêteia). Two different arts of incantation and magism have been invented, namely (those producing) delusions of mind, and deceptions of the opinion-forming part of it. (DK 82 B11 §10)

Because for him the point of rhetoric is its brilliant deception, Gorgias can celebrate the words for marginal religious practice used disparagingly by his contemporaries: his psychological model allows him to differentiate between the sense-perception of juggling and of rhetoric (cf. Segal, 1962; Verdenius, 1981). We shall return later to the issue of the effects of magical utterance. Meanwhile it is clear that Gorgias' model works only when the situation envisaged is one in which the practitioner/rhetorician is in the immediate presence of the subject/audience, that is, in the classic magical healing or purificatory context. It was as this model of the addressee changed that theories of the magical word had also to change.

Effluences and Atoms It was however the physical notions of effluences and of atoms which first offered a way of tackling convincingly some reported marvellous phenomena. Empedocles in the first half of the fifth century is reported to have developed a theory of effluences (*aporrhoai*), by means of which he offered an explanation of the working of the magnet, which certainly later, and evidently already, was a *topos* in the register of natural marvels (Alexander of Aphrodisias *Quaest.* 2. 23 = 31 A89 *DK*; cf. 68 A165). But the main theoretical use of effluences was to account for sense perception, including colour, different sense-organs having different sizes of passages for the effluences to enter, which is why we cannot, for example, hear smells (Theophrastus *De sensu* 7 = 31 A86 *DK*). This view was taken over by Leucippus, the originator of the theory of atoms. Democritus of Abdera, contemporary with Socrates, reformulated it in properly atomic terms. In his theory 'images (*eidôla*) of the same shape as the object' continually pour off what one sees and enter the eye after mingling in the air with *eidôla* emanating from the eye itself (*ibid.* 50 = 68 A135 *DK*; Salem, 1996: 129–32). These images are in some way morally differentiated:

> Democritus says that some *eidôla* approach men, some of them beneficent, some maleficent; that is why he desired to 'encounter propitious images'. (Sext. Emp. *adv. math.* 9.19 = 68 B166 *DK*)

This theory of perception was then employed to account not merely for dreams, prophetic and other, but also for the phenomenon of the evil eye:

> Democritus says that these *eidôla* are emanations emitted not altogether unconsciously or unintentionally by the malevolent, and are charged with wickedness and envy. According to him, these *eidôla* with their burden of evil, adhering to their victims and in fact permanently lodged in them, confound and injure both their bodies and their minds. (Plutarch, *Quaest. conv.* 5.7, 682f–683a [tr. Babbit] = 68 A77 D–K)

It has been argued that these malign *eidôla* are in fact to be understood as evil *daemones* (Salem, 1996: 215f.), but it seems more plausible to read Democritus as fitting the evil eye into the larger framework of a theory that explained dreams as caused by individual *eidôla*, charged with movement, will, moral qualities and passions, 'born in the souls of other living creatures' (Plut. ibid. 8.2, 735a = 68 A77 D–K; cf. Dickie, 1990: 272–5). We may also, in passing, remark that much of Plutarch's earlier discussion of the evil eye here revolves around the Empedoclean-Leucippan theory of emanations, though it is more likely in this case that the language is due to Hellenistic (perhaps already even Theophrastan) speculation following up his account of the magnet; the third-century historian Phylarchus called attention to the peculiar power of the Thibeis on the Black Sea coast of causing anyone on whom they breathed, or even looked, to fade away and die (ibid. 680d = *FGrH* 81 F79a) – adding that in one eye they bore the classic mark of the *jettatore*, the double pupil (cf. still McDaniel, 1913), and in the other the image of a horse (F79b = *HN* 7.17). This combination of breath and malign glance recurs as an explanation of Chariclea's mysterious illness, evidently caused by the evil eye, in Helio-dorus' *Ethiopian Romance* (3.7.1–4), most probably to be dated to the first half of the third century AD (Dickie, 1991).

In historical perspective, what is most important about the theory of effluences is that both Empedocles and Democritus assumed that marvels, and indeed specifically magical phenomena, were in principle subject to natural laws, that is, were not 'marvels' at all once rightly understood in terms of a small number of principles, of which the most important was the tendency of like to gravitate to like. That meant that both, but more particularly Democritus, became interesting later to those who wished to defend magic as part of a wider resistance to mechanistic or realistic natural philosophy, and who therefore picked through Nature to find evidence of its marvellous properties. There is a significant sense in which Empedocles and, more still, Democritus are the originators of a theory of natural magic.

Pulling down the Moon Rationalizing explanations of the 'Thessalian trick', the bringing down of the moon, must also have begun in the fifth century BC. One of the two earliest extant references to this form of magical practice occurs in Aristophanes' *Clouds* (423 BC):

> Strepsiades: I've got an idea for dodging interest . . . Suppose I bought a Thessalian slave, a witch (*pharmakis*), and got her to draw down the moon one night, and then put it in a box like they do mirrors and kept a close watch on it.
> Socrates: What good would that do you?
> Strepsiades: Well, if the moon never rises, I never pay any interest. (*Nub.* 747–52 [tr. Sommerstein])

The mention of mirrors, here, although perfect in the context of the joke, may also imply some knowledge of the true practice, which involved reflecting the full moon in a jar or dish filled to the brim with water and using the water as an ingredient in various magical preparations: the folklore of North Africa contains some extremely interesting analogies, in which the literal disappearance of the moon while the water 'boils' is usually insisted upon – another example of the role of narrative in fusing real and ideal (Westermarck, 1926: 2, 553f.; cf. Tupet, 1976: 97–100; Lunais, 1979: 231–3).

Of all extant ancient allusions to this practice (Menander wrote a comedy about it, *The Thessalian Woman*: Pliny *HN* 30. 7; cf. frgs. 192–7 Körte), there are only two passages which seem to show an appreciation of what was involved. In one, a witch speaks of 'the image of the moon descend[ing], brought down by my incantations' (Petronius, *Satyr.* 134.8f. Pellegr.); but only Lucan seems to have understood that the witches valued not so much the disappearance of the moon as the substances produced by its descent:

> Lowered by incantation, [the Moon] suffers greatly, until, almost on the earth, she drops foam (*despumet*) on the ?herbs [or foliage, grass] below. (*BC* 6.505f. [tr. Duff, adapted])

It is this *lunare virus*, 'lunar slime' – *virus* has the sense of an off-putting but striking, pungent, viscous substance, and so becomes a word for a witch-substance, e.g. Ovid *Metam.* 4.501, as well as poison – which Erictho later uses as part of her preparation of the corpse she is about to revive for her necromantic enquiry (669). Valerius Flaccus (*Argon.* 6.447) and Apuleius (*Metam.* 1. 3, *lunam despumari*) allude to this very passage but without elaboration; 'lunar chrism' appears in *PGM* VII 873f. On this account, the descent of the moon inaugurates and validates the claims of natural magic: 'lunar slime' is the ultimate *materia magica*, a substance derived from the very limits of the sub-lunar world, a sort-crosser therefore, which can properly be applied to the transgression of another boundary, between the dead and the living.

One or two passages suggest that the reason for the 'Thessalian trick' was to allow witches to operate under the cover of pitch darkness (Apoll. Rhod. *Argon.* 4. 60f.). But mostly it was explained, as perhaps already at a popular level, as an attempt to cause a lunar eclipse. The earliest relevant passage is Pindar *Paean* 9. 1–3 Snell (463 BC), which describes an eclipse of the sun as a theft; *On the Sacred Disease* mentions bringing down the moon and 'causing the sun to disappear' in the same breath (4 = 1.31, p. 64.68 Grensemann). By the Roman period it is a literary *topos*: Martial, evoking the din of Rome, recalls the clashing of pots and pans 'when the moon is cut (*secta . . . Luna*) and beaten by the magic wheel of Colchis' (12.57.16f. tr. Shackleton–Bailey). The advantage of this account was that it shifted an actual practice into the idiom of popular astronomy, and so confirmed belief in the vacancy of magic. 'Until the time of Democritus,' observes a Scholiast, 'many people called eclipses 'pull-downs' (*kathaireseis*)' (Σ Apoll. Rhod. *Arg.* 3. 533b). But now we know better:

> Long ago was discovered a method of predicting eclipses of the sun and moon, not the day or night but the very hour. Yet there still exists among the common people an established conviction that these phenomena are due to the compelling power of charms and magic herbs, and that knowledge of how to do this is the one area in which women are dominant. (Pliny *HN* 25.10 [tr. Jones, adapted])

As Pliny's remark reveals, the explanation in terms of eclipses also came in handy as a way of representing the otherness of women. This device, which seems to date from the Hellenistic period, is splendidly represented by the story of Aglaonice, a Thessalian woman, who, in the manner of the *prôtos heuretês*, the exemplary inventor,

> through being thoroughly acquainted with the periods of the full moon when it is subject to eclipse, and, knowing beforehand the time when the moon was due to be overtaken by the earth's shadow, imposed upon the (other) women, and made them all believe that she was drawing down the moon.

Plutarch, who several times adverts to this story, gives us the moral: '(a wife) will not swallow any beliefs in magic (*pharmakôn epôdas*) while she is under the spell (*epadomenê*) of Plato's or Xenophon's words' (*Praecept. coniug.* 44, 145c-d [tr. Babbit]).

Daemones   If the identification of the 'Thesssalian trick' as an eclipse may already have been a folk-explanation before being adopted by the educated, we can be more sure of appeal to the daemonic. In the world of dominated practice it was by means of the claim to be able to diagnose and control daemonic intervention that many healers grounded their authority. The claim was also undoubtedly extended to some kinds of divination, for example necromantic oracles, such as those at Ephyra in Thesprotia (Hdt. 5.92η2) or at Phigaleia in Arcadia (Paus. 3.17.8). But this daemonic was unclearly differentiated between gods, unnamed powers, heroes and the restless dead – all belong to the population of the Other World, any of them might be responsible for a given incident or illness (cf. Brenk, 1986: 2073–9). We have also noted briefly that the attempt to distinguish more clearly between morally good gods and morally ambiguous *daemones* is associated with the Pythagoreans, who early attempted to make a distinction that civic religion would later adopt in practice. Part of the value of the civic distinction was precisely to make it easier to distinguish between legitimate and illicit cult, between 'our' religion and 'their' scandal. But we can also find traces in the fourth century and later of the Pythagorean distinction used as a means of accounting for the existence of the wild variety of religious rituals, both of every-day and of the special occasion, in the Greek world, and indeed beyond.

The earliest of these is the well-known account put by Plato into the mouth of the priestess Diotima, which has strongly Pythagorean undertones. Diotima first defines *daemones* topographically – and we have learned from J. Le Goff to pay particular attention to topographic innovation in religious discourse – as 'halfway between god and man' (*Symp.* 202d11–e1). They are then placed in the role of intermediaries between heaven and earth, binding the two together:

> They are the envoys and interpreters that ply between heaven and earth, flying upward with our requests and sacrifices, and descending with commandments, and rewards for the sacrifices. (202e3–5 [tr. Joyce, adapted])

'Pensé verticalement, *daimôn* devient un signe défini' (Detienne, 1963: 139). The effect is to push civic cult and dominated practice together, opening up the crack which Plato is eager to widen, between philosophical religion on the one hand, and the entire gamut of traditional religious practice on the other. But he evidently sees a particular affinity between *daemones* and dominated religious practice:

> [Daemones] form the medium of the prophetic arts, of the priests' rites of sacrifice, rituals for special purposes (*teletai*), and incantation (*epôdai*), indeed of magic (*manteia*) as a whole, that is wizardry (*goêteia*). (ibid. 202e7–203a1 [tr. Joyce, adapted])

The thought of incantation here, as used in rituals of healing, included in *teletai*, leads Diotima/Plato straight on to think of begging-priests and *manteis* as described in *Rep.* 364bc, who offer purification and expiation of sins. On this account, the other traditional notion of the *daemôn* as related to the souls of the dead is elided in favour of a spatial scenario which is evidently also graduated in moral terms; though Diotima says nothing of that here, it is a necessary inference from her account, just as Erôs is midway between deficiency and plenitude (Goldschmidt, 1947: 233f.). Indeed, Xenocrates of Chalcedon, Plato's successor as head of the Academy, explicitly understood *daemones* as ranged along a scale from good to bad (Plutarch, *De Is. et Os.* 25, 360e4f.), and speaks of

> great and strong beings in the atmosphere, malevolent and morose, who rejoice in [unlucky days, religious festivals involving violence against the self, etc.], and after gaining them as their lot, they turn to nothing worse. (ibid. 26, 361b21–3 [tr. Griffiths])

The use of such malign *daemones* by human beings seems not to be even remotely imagined here: Xenocrates' intention was to provide an explanation for the sheer variety of polytheistic religious worship; but it is the potential for moral discrimination offered by the notion of *daemones* which later, certainly by the later second century AD, became one further means of conceptualizing what distinguishes dominated practice from civic religion, and furthering the transformation of that practice into intentional profanation.

Quite when the point was first made remains unanswerable. Much the same thought as Diotima's is to be found in an explicitly Pythagorean context of probably late Hellenistic composition, the *Pythagorean Commentaries*, which evidently draws on older popular representations:

> The whole air is full of souls. We call them *daemones* and heroes, and it is they who send dreams, signs and illnesses to men; and not only to men, but also to sheep and other domestic animals. It is towards these *daemones* that we direct purifications and apotropaic rites, all kinds of divination, the art of reading chance utterances, and so on. (Cited by Alexander Polyhistor ap. Diog. Laert. 8.32 = *FGrH* 273 F93 §32 = Detienne, 1963: 171 no.3)

This account differs from that of the early Academy in reaching back to the other, Archaic, view of *daemones* as souls, and thus anticipates the views of Plutarch and Apuleius in the Principate (Dillon, 1977: 46f.). It clearly implies that *daemones* can cause illness to livestock: this traditional dominated view has now reached the intellectuals. In that context, we may be reminded of the skill of the sieve-diviners (*koskinomanteis*) whose activities are described by Philostratus:

There are certain old women who go about with sieves in their hands to shepherds, also to cow-herds, pretending to heal their flocks, when they are sick, by divination, as they claim, and they say they should be called wise (*sophai*) – indeed wiser than real diviners (*manteis*). (*Vit. Apoll.* 6.11, p. 624.11–16 Mumprecht [tr. Conybeare, adapted]).

If such women could decide through their sieve's answers which *daemôn* was causing the sickness, they could also induce *daemones* to cause illness. But Alexander, having no interest in the point, does not say as much. Nor does the issue occur, so far as I know, in discussions of *daemones* in the early Principate. We must conclude that, despite the attraction to philosophers in the Hellenistic period and the early Principate, and especially the Middle Platonists following up the work of Xenocrates, of a theory of *daemones* to protect God from direct responsibility for human suffering (cf. Plutarch, *De def. orac.* 14, 417d7–e1), but also to avoid the lure of dualism (cf. Brenk, 1986; Donini, 1990), the explanation of malign magic in such terms was of no interest to them – not even to Apuleius. Insofar as they thought of magic in the context of *daemones* at all, they assumed that they had done enough in relating the variety of religious practices to the variety of *daemones*.[36]

The reluctance of the Middle Platonists to discuss the issue is the more remarkable in that from the time of the *Chaldaean Oracles* (early second century AD) it was common to distinguish between an elevated form of magic and a lower (cf. Apuleius *Apol.* 26). As Calasiris the Egyptian priest puts it in Heliodorus' novel *Ethiopian Romance*:

Of our wisdom there is one kind that is common and – as I may term it – creeps on the ground, which is concerned with ghosts and occupied about dead bodies, using herbs and addicted to enchantments (*epôdai*), neither tending itself nor bringing such as use it to any good end. It is often deceived by its own practices and its success is of a vile and terrible sort: that is to say it gives visions of such things as are not, as though they were, and beguileth men of such things as they looked for, a deviser of mischief and a minister of foul and unlawful pleasures. The other, my son, which is the true wisdom, from whence the counterfeit has degenerated, we priests and holy men do practise from our youth. It is conversant with heavenly things, liveth with the gods. (*Aith.* 3. 16 [tr. Underdowne, revised Wright])

This view, which is the premise of theurgy (Iamblichus, *Myst. Aegypt.* 161.10–16=3.26, p. 135 des Places), was made possible by the emergence in the Hellenistic period of a strong view of magic, and necessary by its fusion with private divination in the Principate. Intellectual proponents in Late Antiquity of private contact with the Other World by ritual means were hard put to it to distinguish this aim from magic: they had therefore to stress the moral integrity of their undertaking by distinguishing it as sharply as possible from lower forms (cf. Augustine's comments on Porphyry, *Civ. Dei* 10.9 with Smith, 1974: 81–99). Iamblichus thus insists:

> Let us not, then, disdain to say this also: that we often have occasion to perform rituals, for the sake of genuine bodily needs, to the body's tutelary gods and to good daimones. (*Myst. Aegypt.* 221.1–4 = 5.16, p. 171 des Places [tr. Shaw])

The clearest possible implication is that malign, indeed all 'creeping', magic must be performed by wicked *daemones*; but Iamblichus avoids the issue.

The earliest non-Christian passage familiar to me which seems to adumbrate an account of the daemonic causation of malign magic is Pythagoras of Rhodes' *Psychomanteia*, that is *Necromancy*, probably dating from the late second century AD. This lost book discussed the identity of the spectral phenomena summoned in necromancy:

> first, what the proper term for them (i.e. spectral apparitions) is, whether they are gods or *daemones* or emanations (*aporroai*) of these, and whether (there is but) one *daemôn* who appears now in this form now in that, or whether they are many, all different from each other, some well-disposed, others malign (*agrioi*), some who sometimes speak the truth and others who are utterly fraudulent; he also describes the disagreements of older and more recent writers, and finally reaches the conclusion that spectral appearances are an emanation from (a single) *daemôn*. (ap. Aeneas of Gaza, *Theophrastus* p. 54 Colonna)

Pythagoras of Rhodes here draws on the common Middle and Neo-Platonist distinction (also to be found, at least hesitantly, in the *Chaldaean Oracles*) between good and malicious *daemones*, though he clearly goes beyond it in asking whether the daemonic world, in appearance multiple, may not fundamentally be a unity. But he also evidently appealed to the notion of compulsion to explain how these spectral apparitions appear:

> The gods summoned to appear do not delight in this, but are evidently drawn by some sort of force, some more readily than others. Some, especially if they happen to be good by nature, come as though making an easy habit of it, others, if they appear (at all), are on the look-out to cause harm, especially if the person seems negligent in the (ritual). (Porphyry, *De philosophia ex oraculis haurienda* ap. Eusebius, *Praep. Evang.* 5.7.6 = frg.347 Smith)

As we have seen, although the intellectuals may take note of one or other aspect of dominated or intentional profanation, the explanations they offer are always in terms of their own agenda. Here too, we may suggest, Pythagoras of Rhodes was less concerned to examine the actual practices of necromancy than to distance early theurgic divination from creeping magic, to encourage the apparition of good spectres rather than of wicked and reluctant ones.

The one Platonist text clearly to link wicked *daemones* to the performance of malign magic is to be found in Porphyry's *On not eating meat*, written no doubt c.271 AD. But even this is not quite what we might expect, since Porphyry draws heavily on the traditional conception of magic as mere vanity. Wicked *daemones* are masters of deception, able to fill the mind with fancies:

> On their account misguided people prepare love-philtres and other love-magic. All forms of intemperance, all dreams of wealth and glory are due to them – and deception above all. For theirs is the kingdom of falsehood. (*De abstin.* 2.42.1)

This is in effect the same position as that of Calasiris noted above, contrasting 'creeping magic' with the true Egyptian magic, for whom low magic 'often deceives itself'. For Porphyry seems to be maintaining that it is the wicked *daemones* who suggest impious thoughts and actions to the misguided, rather than that they perform its undoubted effects. It seems clear that a theory of daemonic responsibility for magic could hardly make headway within later Platonism because of its prior commitment to an alternative theory, that of universal sympathy, derived from the pseudo-Democritean tradition.

Magic in History   I have suggested already that the most decisive steps towards the development of a strong view of magic seem to have been taken in the Hellenistic period. We can point to two significant advances at this time, which will be sketched in briefly, since they require fuller discussion than I can here devote to them. Given the dominance of historical narrative as a means of grounding the moral order in antiquity, and especially in the Hellenistic period, it is no surprise to find magic too being represented in such terms (cf. Fox, 1993).

The only reasonably full version that survives is the account summarized by Pliny *HN* 30.1–11 (cf. Gordon, 1987a: 74–8). Unlike the notion of the eclipse, history serves not primarily as a device to explain magic away, but to gather together all the varied manifestations of marginal religious practice, dominated profanation as well as objective, under a single rubric, magic, which has invaded the Greek (and Roman) world from Beyond, namely Persia: its name guarantees its origin in the practice of the magi and in particular the arch-mage Zoroaster, who lived at a specific time in the past, six thousand year's before the death of Plato in 341 BC – or perhaps, though it amounts to much the same date, five thousand years before the Trojan War (30.3f.). Not only can its origin be pin-pointed, but its prescriptive texts can be enumerated – at least from the early fifth century BC, which is the date of the first Ostanes, the author of the oldest surviving manual (30.8). This account in my view probably derives, at least in essence, from Hermippus of Smyrna, in the early third century, who in turn was using the Persian histories which came flooding out following Alexander's conquests (cf. Pliny *HN* 30. 4; *Diog. Laert.* 1.8). Also Hellenistic is the view that Pythagoras, Empedocles, Democritus and Plato all taught magic which they had learned from the wise nations (*HN* 30.9). Pliny's own contribution to this historical framework is solely to extend it to Italy, and the Roman Empire (12f.); these sections are noticeably thinner and lacking in the density of information that characterises the earlier ones.

The achievement of this historical account was to represent as a unified whole a mass of disparate material, some drawn from the religious traditions of complex civilizations in the Fertile Crescent, some from local practices encountered by the Greeks in Asia Minor, and some relating simply to traditional Greek marginal religion. A strong view of magic is constructed by amalgamating the long-familiar practices of Thessalian women (whatever they were exactly – no one of course knew in detail – but admittedly Greek) with the ex-hypothesi marginal religious practices of neighbouring non-Greek peoples such as the Telmessians of Lycia (or perhaps Caria: the sources differ), and putting this amalgam into an entirely new context, the temple traditions of the Egyptians, Medians, Babylonians, Assyrians, Phoenicians and Jews, most of them newly discovered by the Greeks, but at any rate for the first time truly and pressingly topical.

We will not go far wrong in seeing this (pseudo-)historical scheme as the key step in the formation of a strong view of magic in antiquity. It abstracts from the incoherent mass of marginal religious practice, using Homer's *Odyssey* – the story of Proteus, the arch shape-shifter; the song of the Sirens, as an instance of powerful incantation; the episode of Circe, who turned Odysseus' men into swine; the conversation with the dead (skiamancy) of Book 11 – to provide the concrete examples of what magic consists in. These four nodes together provide an image of a practice essentially constrastive – combining cognitive bewilderment, the power of the word over the mind, the unruled female, intercourse with the dead – and fits these instances of the prescriptive Other onto the new model of the geographical Other that emerged with Alexander's conquests. Earlier strategies of the same kind – the established image of the Thessalian woman, the diviners of Telmessus – are effortlessly fitted into the scheme. One advantage is that love-magic and divination other than necromancy now find a place. Another is the creation of a sort of

Huygens' construction: local magical practices, deriving of course ultimately from Persia, could nevertheless be seen as spreading in their own
range – which explains, say, why Greek magicians were not dressed as
Persian magi. But the most important gain is that the frontier between
the proper and the improper use of religious power, which had run
ragged and ill-defined through Greek cult practice, could now be understood as an essentially ethnic frontier: magical practice is objectionable
because it is not Greek. At the same time the historical narrative provided
an account of the sheer attraction or seductiveness of magic, an explanation of how We can simultaneously be They. Magic is implicitly itself
a seduction of the mind, the philtre its perfect synecdoche: it was the
second Ostanes, says Pliny, who aroused the Greeks *ad rabiem, non avidi-
tatem modo*, to a frenzy, not just to eagerness for magic (30.8); and it was
Democritus, who, as everyone agrees, 'more than anyone, instilled into
people's minds its attractive charm (*dulcedo*)' (30.10). The Hellenistic
history would in fact repay analysis in the light of post-Foucauldian
conceptions of ethnicity.

Moreover, it combined its geographical matrix with another, analytical,
one. On this view, magic consists of three aspects, medicine, religion and
divination (*HN* 30.2).[37] Thracian Orpheus, whose powers of healing
legitimated the practice of Thracian healers in the classical period (Plato
Charmides 155e–156e, cf. Furley, 1994: 90f.), was evidently seen as the
emblematic magical healer (Pliny *HN* 30.7). The inclusion of healing
into the Hellenistic notion of magic is exceptionally important, since it is
– naturally enough – normally absent from the stereotype of the malign
witch, whose collection and preparation of herbs is conceived exclusively
in terms of inverted cookery and straightforward poisoning. At the same
time, it allowed a quite different kind of magical medicine, the already
schematized and literate temple-medicine of Babylonia and Egypt, when
it became available in the process of Hellenistic cultural transfer, to be
fitted into an existing, largely negative, category. If 'divination' stands for
all manner of marginal religious practice (Pliny actually takes astrology as
his type of threatening 'magical divination': 30.2), 'religion' gestures
towards the role of the official priesthood, the magi of Persia, the Egyptian temple priests, in developing the practice of magic, and above all in
committing it to writing. It is this written tradition, the books by Ostanes, Zoroaster the 'second', Apollobex the Copt and Dardanus the Phoenician, that both gives magic its authority and underlines its marginality.
The paradox is neatly captured in Pliny's treatment of the famous Greek
magicians Pythagoras, Empedocles, Democritus and Plato: they all went
abroad to learn about magic – for years and years indeed – and, considering it *in arcanis*, one of their special secrets, taught it openly, *praedicavere*
(30.9).

Natural Magic   The second explanatory innovation of the Hellenistic period is the development of the pseudo-Democritean tradition.[38] This tradition set out to collect as much information as possible about marvellous, interesting, useful occurrences both in the natural world and in the world of human (healing and agricultural) practice. Examples of the first might be:

> Even irrational animals protect themselves against the eyes of *jettatori* and wizards (*baskanôn kai goêtôn*) by an uncanny and marvellous instinct. I am told, for example, that as a protection against the evil-eye wood-pigeons strip shoots off the bay-tree and put them in their nests to protect their squabs. (Aelian *Nat. anim.* 1.35 [tr. Scholfield, adapted])

or:

> Pythagoras has recorded that . . . if you throw a holly stick at an animal, it will spontaneously roll nearer the target even if the thrower is not strong enough to hit it and it falls short. (Pliny *HN* 24.116 [tr. Jones, adapted])

Examples of the second:

> Democritus has advised a method of clearing (unwanted) stands of timber by soaking lupin-flower for one day in hemlock-juice and sprinkling it on the tree-roots. (Pliny *HN* 18.47 [tr. Rackham, adapted])

or:

> Democritus . . . devoted an entire book to the chameleon, each body-part receiving separate attention . . . [He] relates that its head and throat, if burnt on logs of oak, cause storms of rain and thunder, as does the liver if burnt on roof-tiles. (ibid. 28.114 [tr. Jones, adapted].

But there was also much information of an apparently straight-forwardly practical kind (Wellmann, 1921), of which the agricultural writer Columella gives us an example, concerning the growing of cucumbers :

> [Bolus of Mendes] advises us to have in our garden, on a site open to the sun and well-manured, fennels and brambles planted in alternate rows, and then, when the equinox is past, to cut them a little below the surface of the ground . . . and then insert the cucumber-seeds, so that, as they grow, they may unite with the brambles and the fennels. (*Rust.* 11.3.53 [tr. Forster and Heffner])

It has recently been urged that the pseudo-Democritean tradition, generally admitted to have been founded by Bolus of Mendes in the Nile Delta in the early second century BC (cf. Fraser, 1972: 1, 440–4), is to be understood as inherited directly from a continuous goetic tradition earlier represented by Empedocles (Kingsley, 1995: 325–8, 335–41). This seems to me a serious distortion (cf. Gordon, 1997a: 134–9). The originality of Bolus lay in his invention of the idea of natural magic. Such a category presumes the prior invention, and assimilation, of the idea of Nature, conceived as possessing its own rules and regularities. In other words, it concedes to the natural scientists and doctors precisely what traditional goetism did not, that natural things have natural causes. But if these writers accepted the idea of Nature, they emphatically did not accept Nature conceived rationalistically: it was the irregularities of Nature that interested them, that aspect of Nature which was most embarrassing to rationalistic natural philosophers (cf. Festugière, 1944/1950: 187–201). Nature is not to be domesticated by being explained: it is to be marvelled at (cf. Wellmann, 1928).

We must accept, as is anyway obvious from the number of pseudepigraphic texts that represent this tradition – the names Zoroaster, Ostanes, Hermes, Pythagoras, Democritus, and several others, crop up repeatedly, quite apart from the writers that used their real names, such as Demetrius, Nigidius Figulus, Anaxilaus of Larissa, Xenocrates of Aphrodisias (Festugière, 1944/1950: 196f.) – that there were many different strands in this movement during the Hellenistic and Roman period. Since the entire tradition has disappeared with hardly a trace, we must also be wary of over-simplification; and the whole topic badly requires a thorough modern treatment. But Pliny often speaks specifically of a group of texts within the pseudo-Democritean corpus as 'the Magi', in keeping with his more general view of the origin of magic; and he cites the Magi in particular for unpleasant, ridiculous or improper remedies. These will be books purporting to be by Zoroaster and Ostanes, which were considered to be simply one group within the pseudo-Democritean texts. Pliny knows when a magical remedy is to be distinguished from a trustworthy one: it is when it appears in one of these books. A magical remedy is a Magian remedy, and vice versa:

> The Magi prescribe sea-urchins to be burnt with vipers' skins and frogs, claiming (*promittentes*) clearer vision as a result. (Pliny *HN* 32.72 [tr. Jones, adapted])

For Pliny, this categorization often means that the remedy is suspect or doubtful, in keeping with the wider view of the vanity of magic. It by no means implies a malign prescription: the context within which Pliny cites these materials makes clear that the books in which they appeared meant by natural magic in principle beneficent magic, although they certainly included amatory magic in this notion:

The blood of a bat, collected on a swab of wool and placed under the head of women, promotes sexual desire; (Pliny *HN* 30.143 [tr. Jones, adapted])

or:

The Magi . . . say that, after piercing a frog with a reed from the sex through the mouth, if the reed is (then) stabbed into (his wife's) menstrual blood by a husband, she will be put off adultery with lovers. (Pliny *HN* 32.49)

It seems likely, however, that amatory recipes were tacitly confined to those which reinforced not merely the asymmetrical relationship between the sexes but also maintained the authority of the marriage-bond (see also the recipe noted below in a similar context). There is much to indicate that Magian remedies included adventurous ones, for intervening into problems with the spirit world:

The Magi tell us that sprinkling with mole's blood restores the delirious to their senses; while those who are haunted by night ghosts and goblins are freed from their terrors if tongue, eyes, gall and intestines of a python are boiled down in wine and oil, cooled by night in the open air, and used as embrocation night and morning; (*HN* 30.84 [tr. Jones, adapted])

or:

'Glossopetra', which resembles the human tongue, does not, we are told, form in the ground [as most stones were thought to do] but falls from the sky during the waning of the moon, and is indispensable to the moon-diviner. (*HN* 37.164 [tr. Eichholz])

Nevertheless there can be no doubt that the pseudo-Democritean books did employ explanatory schemes: many of them at any rate were not bare receptaries, but set out to defend the view that there is in Nature an inherent, marvellous power, which may be used for healing, exorcizing, divining, becoming rich, and many other purposes. The theory is best summarized by the Neo-Pythagorean Plotinus in the mid-third century:

In the arts of the magicians everything is directed towards this linking: this means that magic works by powers which follow on sympathetically. (*Enn.* 4.4.26.3f., 2:109 Henry-Schwyzer [tr. Armstrong])[39]

To that end they ransacked the materials on the natural world already assembled by the Peripatetics to find reports of the extraordinary, the marvellous. That is, they redefined in their own interest examples of natural behaviour already found remarkable by Aristotle, Theophrastus and their followers; many of these in turn had been noted by hunters and farmers, and some, such as the seal and the octopus, were traditional elements of the antique bestiary, noted already in the Archaic period (cf. Detienne and Vernant, 1974; Lloyd, 1983: 7–57). It goes without saying, as we have already noted, that these were not neutrally-reported items of natural history but items already packaged with cultural meaning. But, as far as we can see given the state of the evidence, the pseudo-Democritean writers were not at all interested in the traditional plant lore of wise-folk and root-cutters, nor in their methods of gathering them. They collected mainly from books, not in the field. Like the school doctors, moreover, they completely disregarded the incantatory element of rhizotomic healing practice. They thus sundered an originally unitary practice – precisely the cant phrase for magic 'drugs *and* incantations' – in order to make the claim that the marvellous power inherent in Nature was directly available. Their magic consisted only in 'drugs', not in 'incantation'.

The relation of the pseudo-Democritean tradition to the lore of wise-folk and root-cutters may perhaps be compared to that of, say, Bernardino de Sahagún to the remains of Aztec civilization (Grafton, 1992: 140–7). On the one hand, without a general theory, without an urgent agenda, there would have been no occasion to quarry out and preserve thousands of individual practices often repellent in themselves and at odds both with general conventions of the seemly and with the doctrines of school medicine. These would then, with the passing of the Peripatetic impulse, be lost to us even more completely than they are. Without the Hellenistic encyclopaedic tradition to provide a framing device, no organised sense could have been made of the disjected members of embedded practice. On the other hand, just because the pseudo-Democritean writers were educated outsiders, with their own agenda, the process of selection and combination of elements did violence not merely to the precise manner in which such practices were employed by wise-folk and root-cutters but also to their accounts of them, the sense they made of them. All that was quite irrelevant to the encyclopaedic mind. The coherence of a given practitioner's practice, its inner logic or symbolism, its shifts over time, were likewise of no significance. It is no accident that many of these compilations seem to have been ordered alphabetically: a purely schematic system of ordering, remote from lived experience, neatly emblematizes the divergence between the culture evoked and the thought-world of the pseudo-Democritean tradition.

The main principle these writers appealed to, where possible, as we saw in the example from Columella, was that of sympathy, adapted from Stoic cosmology.[40] In particular, they explained the working of remedies on the principle of antipathy, usually in the verbal form rather than as an abstract noun (Röhr, 1923–4: 34–8):

> The scorpion when pounded up counteracts (*adversatur*) the poison of the spotted lizard – a malign drug [*malum medicamentum*] is made from this lizard: if you drown one in wine, it causes the face of anyone who drinks the wine to come out in blotchy spots. For that reason, wives who want to destroy a concubine's looks kill a lizard in their make-up jar. (Pliny *HN* 29.73 [tr. Jones, adapted])

But the pseudo-Democritean writers were also interested in the exotic marvellous, in the tales of the Orient that they found in the historical and geographical writers on Persia, India and North Africa. These notices powerfully reinforced their claim that Nature abounded in marvels:

> Democritus [tells us of] the *achaemenis* [which is] of amber colour, has no leaves, and occurs among the Taradistili of India; he says that criminals confess all their misdeeds if they drink it in wine: they suffer terribly from apparitions of different demons. It is also called *Horseshy* because mares especially shy away from it. (Pliny *HN* 24.161 [tr. Jones, adapted])

Here too evidence of the working of sympathy (or is it antipathy? – as so often, the choice is arbitrary) might be found:

> Bolus the follower of Democritus, in his book *On Sympathy and Antipathy* [an alternative title for his *Physika dunamera*, *Remedies of (Natural) Potency*], says that in Persia there was a deadly plant, which the Persians introduced to Egypt so that many people should be killed; but the land of Egypt being good, it turned it into its opposite, and caused the plant to produce very sweet fruit. (Σ Nicander *Ther.* 764a, p. 276.4–9 Crugnola = 68 B300 §4 *DK*)

But an Eastern origin may sometimes be merely an indication of authority: 'This remedy [one for preventing drunkenness] was discovered by Orus, king of Assyria' (*HN* 30.145). There is, moreover, good reason to assume that some of the material incorporated into the Magian texts, and into the accounts of marvellous stones in particular, are indeed derived ultimately from Babylonian tradition: the name of Zachalias, who dedicated a book to Mithradates of Pontus (in the first half of the first century BC therefore), is here particularly important (Wellmann, 1935). His book ascribed 'man's destiny to the influence of precious stones'. Pliny reports his account of haematite:

> he is not content with crediting it with curing diseases of the eyes and liver, but places it even in the hands of petitioners to the king, allows it to interfere in law-suits and trials, and proclaims also that to be smeared with an ointment containing it is beneficial in battle. (Pliny *HN* 37.169 [tr. Eichholz])

Reliance upon Babylonian, and Egyptian, traditions supplemented the claim about sympathy by referring awareness of the marvellous power of Nature to the wise nations.

But there was also a specifically Magian argument for the power ascribed to certain animals. This amounted to an adaptation of the traditional strategy of noting animals that were classificatory misfits, what Aristotle calls 'dualizers', and, in effect asking: Why do these animals exist? Why has Nature created them?

A case in point is the tick. This is a quite repellent animal, says Pliny, which is singled out by the Magi for two reasons: it is the only animal without an anus; and the more it eats the quicker it dies (*HN* 30.82). It lives only for an astrological week, but bursts open earlier if it eats to its heart's desire. He expresses that idea more pointedly elsewhere: its own food is the death of it (11.116). Now Aristotle, who was often alerted to dualizers by popular lore, also found animals without vents interesting, for example hermit crabs and sea-squirts, since in his view the vent was one of the three essential parts of animals, the others being the mouth and the intestine (*HA*. 1.2, 488b29ff. etc.; cf. Lloyd, 1983: 38f.). But the Magi known to Pliny had no time for the lower reaches of biology. They found the tick especially interesting because it denies not one but two common-sense facts about animals, that they eat to live, and void excrement.

Pliny stresses that the entire life of the tick consists in burying its head in blood (*HN* 11.116). This suggests that what interested magical prac-titioners in them was that they contain blood. Indeed, most recipes that call for them also specify the kind of animal it must come from — a black dog (PDM lxi.130), a pig-tick (Pliny *HN* 30.84 = Nigidius Figulus, frg.128 Swoboda), for example. Blood, whether as ink or as an indepen-dent agent, is a fundamental ingredient in the Graeco-Egyptian and Demotic formularies (e.g. for activating a drawing or written spell: *PGM* IV 3260; XXXVI. 233–5, etc.; cf. Waszink, 1954b). But the literate Magian tradition was not content with such an explanation, perhaps was not even aware of it: its interest lay in finding reasons for thinking the tick interesting within the frame-work of a Nature already enruled by the philosophers. It proceeded by searching for natural rule-breakers whose oddity could be expressed in terms of uniqueness, taking their cue not from popular lore, evidently, but from the Peripatetic tradition. On the other hand, Aristotle's own awareness of the interest of such unique animals may itself have been in part indebted to an exotic tradition, the sacred animal-lore of Egypt: Herodotus' Egyptian informants had already told him that the crocodile is the 'only animal' which does not move its lower jaw (2.69).

There is a further point about the tick. In the matter of ventlessness, it seems likely that others in the pseudo-Democritean tradition had a different champion of uniqueness. At any rate Pliny elsewhere has an entry about cicadas:

> These creatures are used as food by the peoples of the East, even the Parthians, who have lots of (other) things to eat . . . [The pupae] break out of their cocoons at the solstices and fly out, always at night: at first they are black and hard. This is the only living creature actually without a mouth; they have instead a sort of row of prickles resembling tongues . . . with which they lick the dew . . . When they are disturbed and fly away, they give out moisture, which is the only proof that they live on dew; moreover they are the only creatures that have no opening for their bodily excreta. (*HN* 11.93f. [tr. Rackham])

Now much of this report derives more or less directly from Aristotle, *HA* 5.30, 556a14–b21 (cf. Beavis, 1988: 96–9). The point that it is 'the only animal without exception' lacking a mouth is also derived from him (*HA* 4.7, 532b10–12). Moreover it is clear that even in the fourth century BC there was disagreement about whether cicadas had an excretory vent. Aristotle remarks:

> As they fly up after you have startled them, they discharge a liquid like water: country-folk will tell you this is their urine, – they do excrete, and they feed on dew. (*HA* 5.30, 556b14–16 [tr. Peck, adapted])

But Aristotle's own view was that, because the cicada's sole food was dew, 'it does not have excrement in its abdomen' (*HA* 4.7, 532b14). But what he does not say is that the cicada is 'the only animal without a vent'.

Now Pliny cites Nigidius Figulus (pr. 58 B.C:) – the friend of Cicero 'interested in almost every possible religious and magical tradition' (Rawson, 1985: 94), who wrote a 'Democritean' book *On Animals* – as one of his sources for Book XI. It is tempting to think that Nigidius saw the value of Aristotle's claim for contesting the report of the Magi about the uniqueness of the tick. Although it too has no vent, the cicada is an altogether more elevated animal than the loathsome tick: instead of blood, it lives on dew – 'heavenly dew' remarks Ovid (*Fasti* 1.311) – and, going one better than the tick, has neither mouth nor vent. The 'only animal' formula added by Pliny may therefore derive from Nigidius. Such superiority might suit him, as implying a criticism of 'low' Magian beliefs. But the mere appearance of these two contrasting claims within the pseudo-Democritean tradition based on the same issue suggests that some of these writers at least were eager to justify their claims in scientific terms – precisely because they wanted to be taken seriously by the educated. It also suggests a conscious difference of view within the tradition about the kind of power magic should be aiming at. That is consistent with the point I made earlier about the self-proclaimed differentiation between high and low magic, and indeed suggests that it begins much earlier than the Chaldaean Oracles.

The Power of Words (2)   We may, finally, return to the issue of the force of magical words, and more generally rituals, with which we began this section. The development of a strong view of magic implied that the old view of magical words, that they were just like poetry, came to be felt inadequate. In particular the *Ephesia grammata*, the mysterious letters or symbols used in the making of amulets, presented an inexhaustibly fascinating problem (cf. Hopfner, 1921–4/1974–90: 763–6, §760; Preisendanz, 1962; Le Boulluec, 1981: 2, 174–7). One of several strategies for making sense of them was to claim that they were not names,[41] or pictures, or designs, as others thought, but words, indeed words which tell a sort of story about natural theology. This move is associated with the rather shadowy compiler Androcydes, to whom a book on Pythagorean symbols was later ascribed (Burkert, 1962b: 151f.; Thesleff, 1965: 170):

> Androcydes ... says that the famous [possibly 'notorious'] so-called Ephesian letters are ordered as allegories: *askion* signifies 'darkness', because darkness throws no shadow (*skia*); *kataskion* signifies 'light', since it casts shadow with its light (*kataugazei*); *lix* is an old word meaning 'the earth'; *tetrax* means the 'year', because of the (four) seasons; *damnameneus* means the Sun, which is overpowering (*damazôn*); the *aisia* means 'the true voice'. The allegory intimates that divine things have been arranged in due order, for example, darkness in relation to light, sun to create the year, and the earth to make possible every sort of natural coming-into-being. (Clement Alex. *Strom.* 5.8.45.2–3, p. 356 Stählin)

Androcydes, making use of the Homerists' device of allegory for interpreting inconvenient, or simply unintelligible, passages (Lamberton, 1986), has translated the enigmatic tradition into his own language. The puzzle has been resolved by ingenious evocation from lexical facts (altered if they did not fit) and phonic analogues. For example, the significance 'year' for *tetrax* is tacitly grounded in the double claim that *tetrax* is 'really' *tetras* and that, since a year contains four seasons, the notion 'four' is a code for 'year'. The resolution is completed by the provision of a quasi-narrative link between the decoded elements, which converts the six 'words' into a theological hint. The *grammata* turn out really to be a cryptic form of natural theology: their power is of a wholly intelligible kind. They are the remains of an ancient wisdom, the flotsam of a lost deep knowledge.

The implausibility of this line of argument was apparent as soon as one considered not 'names' in isolation but took incantation for what it obviously was, an illocutionary act. Such acts, on the ordinary model, require addressees. Well, who were the addressees of incantations? One older view, as we have seen earlier, taking the medical incantation as the type case, understood the addressee to be the client or victim. This view remained available well into the Principate. It could be neatly combined with the spatial view of the distribution of belief in magic: Celsus, the Platonist opponent of Christianity in the later second century AD, cites an otherwise unknown Egyptian musician named Dionysius for the view that

> magical arts are effective with uneducated people and with men of depraved moral character, but that with people who have studied philosophy they are not able to have any effect, because they are careful to lead a healthy life. (Origen, *C. Cels.* 6.41 [tr. Chadwick, adapted])

The moral worthlessness of magic has here been turned into an explanation of its possible limits, an explanation highly flattering to the guild of philosophers. This account clearly assumes that magic works primarily against the mind – the model of the love-philtre casting its clear shadow; and Plotinus, seventy-five years later, casually uses the image of 'minds swamped by illness or by magical arts' (*Enn.* 1.4.9.1f., 1:91 H–S., tr. Armstrong). He quite naturally therefore explained the effectiveness of magical incantation at a distance by appealing to a 'super-mind', a mind that links all life together, the World-Soul (4.9.3.4–9, 2:245 H–S.). He evidently thought of it as in some sense a transmission network for magical utterance, and indeed other magical operations: 'a word spoken quietly acts on what is far off and makes something separated by an enormous distance listen' (tr. Armstrong).

It is also in the these terms that Plotinus tried to explain how it was that one of his rivals, Olympius of Alexandria, should have failed to kill him by means of malign magic (cf. Brisson, 1992: 466–8). Evidently Plotinus regularly suffered from painful spasmodic attacks, and came to interpret them as the result of Olympius using star-magic against him. But then Olympius found himself suffering (other) symptoms:

> But when he realised the attack was being turned against himself, he declared to his companions that the power of Plotinus' soul was enormous, in that it was able to beat the attacks on him back onto those who were attempting to harm him. (Porphyry, *Vit. Plotin.* 10.5–9, p. 15f. Henry-Schwyzer, cf. Luck, 1985: 121)[42]

Plotinus' reason for thinking that he had been attacked by magic evidently lay in the character of the symptoms, which he describes in an allusion to Plato's *Symposium* as 'his body being forcibly agitated 'like those bags you pull together with string', his limbs being quite contracted' (10.10–12). The symptoms are on a variety of counts 'strange': one suspects magic at work. At the same time, his account of the fact that he did not die, but merely suffered cramps (or whatever our nosology might offer), was evidently that his soul had been able, through its purity or discipline, to deflect the attacks. We find him saying as much elsewhere:

> How is the good man affected by magic and drugs (*goêteia kai pharmaka*)? He is incapable of being affected in his soul by magic arts, and his rational part would not be affected, nor would he change his mind; but he would be affected in whatever part of the irrational in the All that is in him, or rather this part would be affected . . . Just as the irrational part of him is affected by incantations, so he himself by counter-chants and counter-incantations (*antadai kai antepadai*) will dissolve the powers ranged against him. (*Enn.* 4.4.43.1–6, 7–9 [tr. Armstrong, adapted], cf. Luck, 1985: 120)

The philosopher's essential parts, what makes him a philosopher, his soul and his rational mind, are on this account impregnable to magic, which can only affect that which belongs to the lower man, the irrational. The appetitiveness associated with magic inspires the Neo-platonic solution of the difficulty: the traditional distinction between good religion and bad magic is applied to the inner economy of the soul.

Elsewhere in this same passage however Plotinus shows awareness of a different notion of the addressee of incantation, or magical ritual more generally, namely the gods, or *daemones*. As Apuleius remarks, ordinary people think of the magician as one who

> by verbal communication with the gods, has the power to accomplish everything he dreams of thanks to the extraordinary power of incantations (*incredibili quadam vi cantaminum*). (*Apol.* 26)

If magic is illicit religion, why is it effective? Why do the gods or *daemones* listen to what they ought not to hear? The moralization of the gods naturally gave rise to fresh problems as it solved others. Many different answers must have been canvassed in the ancient world. Virtually our sole indication of this variety is an authorial intervention in the Erictho-scene in Lucan's *Bellum civile*:

> What is this care the gods take to obey their witchcraft, this fear of rejecting it? Have they made an agreement whose stipulations bind them? Are they obliged to obey, or do they do so willingly? Do magicians wield so much power thanks to some secret ritual or does their power come from threats uttered beneath the breath? Do they exercise this sway over the gods as a whole, or do these commanding incantations control one god in particular, who is able to force the world to do what is forced upon him? (*BC* 6. 492–9)

Lucan provides no direct answers to this catalogue of questions: he only introduces it in order to claim the authority to impose his own scheme on the realm of magical action (cf. Gordon, 1987b: 238). But they seem to be ordered in a hierarchy. Assuming that it is correct to interpret the success of magical action in rational terms (so the implied argument runs), it must be by permission of the gods. Their punctiliousness – or is it fear? – might be explained by analogy with legal agreements and obligations. But their relation to magic may be more like their relation with civic cult, in which they take pleasure – but if so, it cannot be a civic piety of an ordinary Graeco-Roman kind. Language is implicitly present in both these options, in the oath or promise associated with legal agreements, in the prayers of civic cult; and it makes its appearance explicitly in the paradoxical notion of 'silent threats', which is evidently taken as the most plausible option, and then briefly elaborated in the question, 'All the gods, or just one grand one?' The authorial voice seems here to suggest that the best – we might say the most economical – explanation of the power of incantation over the natural world is the control it bestows over a single all-powerful divinity (cf. Statius, *Theb.* 4.512–17). This reading seems to be confirmed by Erictho's later successful threat to appeal to the unnamed god at the bottom of Tartarus, in relation to whom the gods of the underworld are 'the gods above' (749). And it is re-echoed in Pythagoras of Rhodes' argument, noted earlier, that all spectral apparitions are emanations from a single *daemôn*. An 'inverted theology' seems to be be in process of tentative formation.

But this was by no means satisfactory to those who maintained the distinction between high and low magic. Compulsion was all very well for reptilian magic, but would not do for them. There must be a better alternative theory. It was found in the notion of divine pleasure (Hopfner, 1921–4/1974–90: 1, 440–51 §717–30; Waszink, 1972). In its classic formulation, Iamblichus picks out as the crux of the matter the *voces magicae*, the apparently unintelligible words that often occur in magical utterance (*Myst. Aegypt.* 257.1–260.2 = 7. 5, p. 193f. des Places; cf. Porphyry, *Epist. ad Anebonem* 2.10, p. 22 Sodano). According to this view, the *a priori* changelessness of the divine world is mimicked in the gods' linguistic conservatism (cf. Origen *C. Cels.* 1.24; 5.45 etc.). Although they do not themselves of course speak Egyptian or any other primeval language, the gods take pleasure in these languages because it was in them that they were first worshipped. Such utterances are thus naturally appropriate to divinity and inherently more effective than artificial prayers which, like those of the Greeks, make sense to those who utter them and whose formulae are therefore subject to constant change. But in practice such languages are preserved in magical contexts only in fragments, consisting of strings of formulae or individual 'words', construed nevertheless as true phrases in these primeval languages. They are to be seen as remnants of a primal order of things (cf. Frankfurter, 1994). In the previous section, Iamblichus insists that none of the assumptions one ordinarily makes about language are valid in the context of the purest forms of such 'words', those known only to the gods and which they have not revealed to us: they do not have a meaning expressible in other terms – that is, there cannot be a lexicon of them. They cannot be grasped by logic – that is, they do not have formal, rational links with the rest of experience. And they cannot spontaneously be uttered – they are ineffable signs lodged in our minds, denoting divinity (ibid. p. 255.17–256.1 = 7.4, p. 192 des Places).

This view of the unintelligible 'words' used at certain points in ritual magical incantation, relying upon the rule that they must be uttered exactly in the correct way, ingeniously claims for them a place in heaven – they are in themselves, as it were, threads attaching down here to up there. Analogously, other accounts of them – for example the *Corpus Hermeticum*, stressing as usual the uniqueness of Egypt – suggest that it is the immanent force (*energeia*) of the words when uttered properly in Egyptian that gives them their effect (*CHerm.* 16.2, 2: 232.5–8 Festugière-Nock, cf. Fowden, 1986: 37f.; also Proclus, *Comm. in Cratyl. 391d-e*, p. 31.28–32.17 Pasquali). Here the motif of the pristine utterance takes on a rather Berlitz tone, for the point is to assert that the only effective magic is Egyptian, as performed by Egyptians. But it is also extremely risky: for the more speculation insisted on the pleasure with which the gods listened to *voces magicae*, the wider the gap yawned between high magic and vulgar magic. But vulgar magic also used these 'words': did the gods take pleasure in them too? Even when they were used for malign purposes? But that amounts to allowing the argument from compulsion in by the back door . . . In the last resort, it was no use in the Principate taking over conventional beliefs from Egypt, where magic had always been the preserve of the higher temple clergy, and where ethical consider-ations in relation to *h3ka* had never had much force. In the world of the Roman Empire, the ethics of magic were all-important.

THE REPRESSION OF MAGIC

We thus come finally to Greek and Roman legal attitudes towards dominated religion, and in particular magic. These naturally were formed within the varied contexts which I have set out in the preceding sections. Although the analogies between them are striking, it will be simplest to take the Classical and Hellenistic Greek world separately from the Roman Republic, and examine the Principate last, for it is in this period that we find the most significant alterations, contingent not merely upon the Hellenistic development of the strong view of magic but, more pro-foundly, upon the new political and ideological situation created by the emergence of an universal autocracy.

The Greek World in the Classical and Hellenistic Periods

So long as 'magic' meant dominated practice, that is, before the emergence of a strong view of magic – and indeed, long after such a view was available in principle to intellectuals – legal sanctions were formulated only against the harm that might be attributed to such practice. The basic principle is tacitly acknowledged in the scene in the *Odyssey* in which Circe turns Odysseus' companions into pigs:

> She brought them inside and seated them on chairs and benches,
> and mixed them a potion, with barley and cheese and pale honey
> added to Pramnian wine, but put into the mixture
> malignant drugs, to make them forgetful of their own country.
>   (Homer, *Od*. 10.233–36 [tr. Lattimore])[43]

The exemplary character of the contrast between harmful and beneficial drugs is made explicit in the same context, when Hermes meets Odysseus as he is on his way up to Circe's palace, and offers him *moly*, a 'good *pharmakon*', to protect him from the effects of a *pharmakon*, therefore 'harmful', which Circe will put into the food she offers him (10.286–92; cf. 326f.). *Moly* (a divine, not a human, name) registers the compulsive polarities of this moral world in its own appearance: for if its root is black, its flower is white as milk (10.304).

But the real world is less gratefully unambiguous. The true properties of natural substances, particularly in combination, were very little under-stood even by professional healers of any stripe. The semantic range of the word *pharmakon*, 'drug', covers equally 'remedy' and 'poison'. While Hippocratic medicine made a determined effort to rationalize and natural-ize conceptions of how drugs might work (Stannard, 1981), the sheer frequency of *pharmakon* in a metaphorical sense in poetry and prose makes it clear that this was the exception: the notion was useful precisely inasmuch as most people could see no value in distinguishing between 'physical' and 'marvellous' effects – and it certainly was not in the interests of traditional healers to attempt to do so (Scarborough, 1991). Indeed, Helen's *nepenthes* neatly captures the inherent ambiguity of the notion: she puts this *pharmakon* into the wine,

> and whoever had drunk it down once it had been mixed in the
>   wine-bowl,
> for the day that he drank it would have no tear roll down his face,

not if his mother died and his father died, not if men
murdered a brother or a beloved son in his presence
with the bronze, and he with his own eyes saw it.

(Od. 4.222–26 [tr. Lattimore])

The authorial voice is at pains here to stress that *nepenthes* belongs to the class of good drugs (227f.); but to whom would it in fact occur to praise unreservedly a drug with such powers that it makes one oblivious of the elementary human feelings of pity and terror? – Ecstasy or crack cocaine have indeed exactly these powers, we might think. Moreover, in its influence upon the mind rather than upon the body, in its ability to influence something as intangible as mood, *nepenthes* is both the model of all psychotropic drugs, beginning with alcohol, and highlights the ideological nature of our own distinction between purely physical ('objective') and purely imaginary ('magical') effects.

At any rate, to practise with drugs was to walk on a knife-edge; and the more marginal the praxis, the more readily the practitioner might be exposed to a charge of manslaughter or even wilful homicide if things went wrong. The danger was apparent to the Hippocratic author of *On the sacred disease*, who accuses magical healers of deliberately

> prescribing no *pharmakon* either to drink or to eat; nor did they make them bathe, so they could not be held responsible (if the patient died). (2 = 1.21, p. 62.40f. Grensemann)

In some states at least, there were explicit injunctions against the use of 'harmful drugs'. Direct evidence for this is known only from the city of Teos on the Ionian coast, but formal rules of this kind must in my view have been relatively common. The text from Teos lists a number of sanctions in the form not of a law but of a public curse, reaffirmed three times a year by the Timouchoi, a board of magistrates specifically charged with this function.[44] The curse relating to the use of harmful drugs comes first in the sequence:

> Whoever employs harmful *pharmaka* against the people of Teos, either against the city as a whole or against a private individual, let him be destroyed, himself and his entire family. (*ML* 30 a1–5)

All the curses are directed against public enemies of Teos. The context is probably the unsettled situation after the return, in the years following the Persian defeat at Mycale (479 BC), of a sizeable group of citizens after more than half a century of voluntary exile. How exactly 'harmful drugs' might be used against the population as a whole is unclear: but the most likely reference is to witchcraft causing unseasonable weather leading to disastrous crop failure, or to an outbreak of disease believed to be caused by drugs.[45] The triannual public reiteration of such execrations is an invitation to take such fears seriously, and by the same token to interpret the death or illness of individuals, their families, and livestock as the result of malign sorcery. The grounds for suspicion, the number and social weight of those who believed themselves affected, the strength of the arguments that could be adduced, the suspect's personal conduct, social figure and reputation, family alliances – all of these were variables in the situation.

Gossip was central, as we can see from a couple of the Hellenistic texts on lead sheet from the sanctuary of Demeter and Persephone at Knidos in Asia Minor. They are examples of a wider class of vindicative texts related to, but distinct from, curse tablets proper, in which individuals, evidently unable to call on more tangibly effective means of redress, seek divine revenge on those who have wronged them, for example by theft or by refusing to return something that had been entrusted to them (Versnel, 1987; 1991). In one of these texts an unnamed woman invokes the goddesses to counteract current gossip that she has 'poisoned' her husband, that is, I take it, that she has tried to control him by means of a philtre:

> I consign to Demeter and Persephone the man who accuses me of giving my husband *pharmaka*.[46] May he burn inside and come with all his family up to (the temple of) Demeter and confess, and may he not find Demeter and Persephone and the gods who dwell with Demeter well disposed to him; but to me may she (show herself) holy and generous, that I may dwell under the same roof (as my husband) or somehow share my life with him [possibly: have sexual intercourse with him in whatever way]; I consign also (to these divinities) the man who has written (a denunciation) against me, or caused one to be written. (*I.Knidos* 150a1–8 = *Syll.*³ 1180 = *DT* 4a)

Presumably the vindicatrix, suspected not merely by the unnamed accusers but also by her husband, cannot appeal to her own family of origin for support in the conflict, or they are too uninfluential to be of much help. Now that the gossip has crystallized into an accusation, having no adequately powerful or effective human friends she can only adopt a weaker strategy, in the hope that a vindicative gesture may to some extent weigh in the balance. Her invocation of the goddesses is based on the acknowledgement that she would run the risk of being punished by them if she were lying. The second curse makes this explicit: a woman named Antigone invokes a curse on herself 'if I have given a *pharmakon* to Asklapiadas or have maliciously schemed against him, or summoned a (wise-) woman to the temple and offered her three half *minae* to curse him to death' (*I.Knidos* 147a6–18 = *DT* 1).

Women such as these had indeed everything to lose if the gossip succeeded seriously in eroding their position and convincing third parties of their guilt. The danger is vividly illustrated by a 'confession text' of the second century AD from Smyrna (Izmir), addressed to Anaitis and the god M(e)is (Men), which – sadly – tells us almost nothing of what we should like to know.[47] The case involved a woman named Tatias, who was believed by her neighbours to have driven her son-in-law Iucundus mad by means of a *pharmakon* – the wider background is not mentioned, but we may suspect that (supposing there is anything in the story at all) she had tried to help her daughter keep her husband's love by giving him, or arranging for the administration of, a philtre; but since her son Socrates was also evidently involved the quarrel may (prior to this) have involved money or property. When gossip hardened to accusation, Tatias tried to defuse the situation by 'raising a sceptre' in the temple, that is taking a solemn oath that she was innocent, calling curses upon herself and offering 'to explain the gossip concerning her' (1.11–13). But evidently she failed: 'the gods ordained a punishment for her, which she did not escape' (14f.) – that is, a court presided over by the priest(s) found her guilty and condemned her to death. Gossip prevailed; and the text burrows down into dead Tatias' mind to find her guilty conscience (1.13). The propriety of this judgement was later miraculously confirmed by an accident: her son Socrates dropped a vine-pruning hook on his foot as he was passing the entrance to the sacred grove and died within twenty-four hours (15–23).[48] Oddly enough, the stele, to the glory of the power of the two gods, is erected not by Iucundus (who was presumably still mad) but by Tatias' four grandchildren, to expiate their grandmother's false oath of innocence and the curses she had called down upon herself, which have been so signally – but not in her sense – vindicated. Their mother, Moschion, who must in fact have been crucial to the entire drama, plays no role in this pious version.

But because the Greek world was in politico-legal terms no unity but a congeries, perhaps even a family, of independent legal codes and traditions, we must assume that the situation in each state was in detail somewhat different. As usual, the only city for which we have a little more information is Athens.

The underlying problem in discussing the issue of the legal treatment of magic at Athens is not merely that before Magic there was only dominated practice but also that Athenian (indeed Greek) conceptions of law, both under the democracy and later, are so alien. Under the democracy the law was concerned only to indicate the forms of action available to plaintiffs, not in any sense to define crimes or torts (delicts) (Todd 1993: 49–73). Most offences or plaints could be prosecuted in several ways, according as the plaintiff saw his advantage (ibid.: 160). Statute law was not easy to discover, since there were no indexes to past decisions of the assembly.

Moreover, just as there were no judges, so there were no experts in the interpretation of laws comparable to the Roman *iuris prudentes*: a law had today whatever meaning a speaker at a trial could successfully convince the jurors that it had — and tomorrow perhaps something different. Indeed none of the words used in Athenian laws had legal definitions: for the most part, law was simply the written form of custom (ibid.: 205).

Apart from the powers of summary execution of robbers, adulterers, and others caught red-handed that could be exercised by the Eleven, which I have already mentioned, offences at Athens could only be prosecuted by individuals, generally those directly affected; though after Solon's introduction of *graphai* in the early sixth century any qualified citizen was permitted to prosecute in many types of case. Nevertheless there was a feeling in the case of crimes against the body that the community as a whole had somehow been injured. A citizen who believed that he had been harmed by magic and wished to take the matter to court had three possibilities open to him.

1. If the complaint was that his health, or that of his family (including slaves), had been harmed by *pharmaka*, or that he had lost livestock or crops by the same means, he could bring a *dikê blabês*, a suit for damages. Although no legal speech survives dealing with such a case, and there is no other direct evidence, the *dikê blabês* certainly was available for a very wide range of harm, intentional and unintentional (Osborne, 1985: 56–8), and we shall see later that Plato simply assumes that damage caused by magic is a form of *blabê*.[49] In other words, the offence lay not in the issue of magic but in the harm to property or health.

2. The same basic point holds good for the more serious offence of killing, or attempting to kill, someone by magic. According to the Aristotelian *Athenian Constitution*, cases involving death by *pharmaka* ('if someone administers a drug and thereby kills another': 57.3) were tried before the Areopagus, the usual court for cases of murder.[50] Since the Areopagus also heard cases of deliberate wounding, we can plausibly argue that charges of attempted murder by malign magic also fell under its authority. But the law evidently mentioned simply *pharmaka*, making no distinction between between what we would term 'purely' physical and magical drugs: once again, it was the death or near-death that was central, not the magic. There could obviously be no clear distinction between using *pharmaka* to harm an enemy's health and attempting to kill him by such means. But in an ordinary *dikê* witnesses did not have to swear an oath, whereas they, and the litigants, were required to do so in trials for (attempted) homicide, the *diômosia*, which might well be more difficult to arrange — witnesses could not be forced to give evidence (there are none in Antiphon's *Stepmother* case for example). Moreover it is clear that, at least in some cases, the accused could hope successfully to argue that the

death had not been intentional, that a *pharmakon* had not been intended to kill but simply, for example, to cause a man to come back to a woman. A Peripatetic text illustrates the notion of 'voluntary (intentional) action' by means of just such a story:

> Thus it is reported that a woman[51] gave a man a philtre to drink, and was subsequently acquitted before the Areopagus. For she had given him the philtre out of love, but had failed of her purpose. So the homicide was clearly not intentional, because she had not given him the philtre with the intention of doing away with him. ([Ar.] *Mag.mor.* 1.16.2, 1188b31–35)

The same ambiguity appears in the story of Aretaphila, who in the early first century BC was forcibly married to Nikokrates, the tyrant of Cyrene, and promptly tried to poison him. When discovered, 'she claimed what she had prepared was not a harmful (*dêlêtêrion*) drug but a philtre, to make her husband love her madly' (Polyaenus *Strat.* 8.38, cf. Plut. *Mul.virt.* 19, 256c).[52]

On the other hand, Antiphon's account of the fate of the concubine of Philoneôs who (genuinely) did exactly the same thing and was executed the same day by the Eleven without trial, shows that everything depended here upon status, upon one's social figure: a female 'citizen' of good character and a wide kin-network might hope to get away with the argument – or rather, since she could not herself appear, her male relatives might use it with some hope of success; a metic hardly (cases involving metics were heard in the Polemarch's court, and the Council had the right summarily to execute any metic); a slave would not be given the chance to argue at all.

3. Our citizen's third choice was rather different: he could try bringing a *graphê asebeias*, an action for impiety, a term which was certainly never defined at Athens but which stood roughly for any behaviour in a religious context which might be construed as out of keeping with Athenian ancestral religion – it was, for example, the charge brought against Socrates (cf. Todd, 1993: 106, 310f.; Parker, 1996: 199–217). The fact that this action was a *graphê*, and the penalty death, points up the collective interest in avoiding possible divine anger through the 'impiety' of an individual (cf. Reverdin, 1945: 208–17).

It seems to me that this tack offered one possible advantage over the first two, in that, the charge being so vague, there was a good chance of victory. For in the context of a city rather than a village it must often have been difficult to show in a private action for damage, or even in a case of supposed murder by *pharmakon*, that the harm had indeed been caused by a particular person (which was the role, for example, of the classic 'encounter, with curse' narrative so common in English witchcraft trials)

— and a failed suit would simply strengthen the enemy's hand.[53] In an action for *asebeia*, perhaps even more than in other types of court-case, general reputation and social figure played a significant role. On the other hand, the charge of *asebeia* could only convincingly be used against someone who was suspected of repeated magical practice — was in fact ideal as a weapon against a marginal practitioner who had acquired a reputation not merely for, say, healing, but also for being capable of doing harm. The *graphê asebeias* came into its own in a context in which malign magic was supposed to be most effective if performed by a professional, a *mantis*, a *teratoskopos*, in Plato's formulation (*Leg.* 11, 933c7): it made it possible to attack not one's suspected enemy but a religious professional who might be shown to have misused his or her powers for ill rather to further the collective weal.[54]

It is evident that *graphai asebeias* were in the fourth century BC a not uncommon means of disciplining what could be represented as undesirable religious innovation (Cohen, 1988; Versnel, 1990: 114–31; Parker, 1996: 163 n. 34) — we have already noted the woman condemned to death for selling 'incantations and means of allaying divine anger'.[55] Of the known cases, the most significant in the present context is that of the Lemnian woman Theôris, who evidently set up as a healer, particularly of people she diagnosed as epileptics. According to Plutarch, she was prosecuted by Demosthenes, 'for being in general detrimental, and in particular for teaching slaves to be deceitful' (*Dem.* 14.6; cf. Philochoros, *FGrH* 328 F60). This must have been a *graphê asebeias*. Another, roughly contemporary, text already cited in a different context, refers scathingly to 'the foul Theôris, that woman from Lemnos, the poisoner — you remember you executed her and her entire family . . .' ([Dem.] 25.79f.). One of the crucial witnesses for the prosecution was one of her slave-women, who was later able to take over her practice.[56]

Several points about this case — granted that once again we know virtually nothing about it — are of interest. The fact that after Theôris' execution her slave was able to carry on her practice clearly implies that at one level what she did was perfectly acceptable — and we have every reason to believe that it included some kind of purificatory healing of the kind denounced by the Hippocratic *On the sacred disease*. Second, Theôris was a metic, and we may suspect that many marginal religious practitioners in ancient cities were of that status — untrammelled by the dense network of social obligation and expectation within which citizens lived their lives, possessing the advantage of a (somewhat) different set of religious themes to work into a personal idiomatic praxis, nudged by their social marginality towards the exploration of charismatic modes rather than fully institutional ones. But as a metic, such a religious specialist was very vulnerable: when the issue of Socrates' uncanny power to attract and influence the young comes up, Meno observes: 'If you did that sort of thing as a metic in another city, you would soon be expelled as a magician (*goês*)' (Plato *Meno* 80b5–7).[57] As a religious specialist of metic status, one might swiftly be considered by the legitimate specialists as aiming at untoward religious or 'salvific' capital. Thirdly, we should note the language that pseudo-Demosthenes – the most nearly contemporary source – uses of Theôris: *pharmakis* he calls her, and goes on to say that the slave who turned Queen's evidence took over her *pharmaka kai epôidas*, her 'drugs and incantations'. So far as I know, this is the earliest example in extant Greek of the word *pharmakis*, which became one of the standard words for 'wise-woman/witch', used as a substantive (cf. Aristotle *HA* 6.22, 577a14, but 7(8).24, 605a5f.; also Ap. Rhod. *Argon.* 4.53).[58] The other expression, 'drugs and incantations', seems also to be a first occurrence in extant Greek, this time of the phrase which came in the Hellenistic period, and more especially in Latin literature, to mean 'magic'.[59] It is a shorthand evocation of a range of words denoting different ways in which marginal practitioners acquired power – Plato tries a list of verbs: 'you are bewitching me, putting a *pharmakon* on me – altogether putting a spell on me' (*Meno* 80a2–3), and Xenophon a little later in the fourth century offers 'with many philtres and incantations and *iunxes*' (*Mem.* 3.11.17). In other words, whatever Theôris was in fact up to – and we cannot exclude that she was believed also to be able to make people mad through *pharmaka* as well as cure them – pseudo-Demosthenes knows how to smear her convincingly: by representing her as nothing more than a female sorcerer, of the sort that anyone would thankfully be rid of.

I would urge, then, that pseudo-Demosthenes' expression 'drugs and incantations' makes a point not explicitly recognised by the law at Athens, that 'poisoning' is sometimes indeed to be distinguished from '(malign) magic'. Plato makes the very same point in his discussion of malign magic in the *Laws*, which is by far the most interesting and suggestive of any account we possess for the Classical and Hellenistic period:

> What gives us pause here is that mankind practice poisoning (*pharmakeia*) in two different ways. [One] is that in which the body is hurt by the action of another body in normal ways (*kata physin*). There is another form which works by conjuring arts – incantations and binding spells, as they are called – and breeds in the mind of the projectors the belief that they possess such powers of doing harm, in those of the victims the conviction that the authors of their sufferings can in truth bewitch (*goêteuein*) them. (*Leg.* 11, 932e6–933a5 [tr.Taylor, adapted])

Plato reproduces here a practical distinction which must have emerged in fourth-century Athens through the trial of cases involving harm caused by magical means, and which was not raised by cases in which death occurred through direct magical action, of which the type was the administration of a *philtron*. The example he gives of the second type of *pharmakeia* is precisely the classic form of binding magic, the maumet:

> It would be labour lost to tell them, if they should perchance see a manikin of wax set up in the doorway, or at the crossroads, or at the grave of a parent, to think nothing of such things. (ibid. 933b1–4 [tr. Taylor])

Such maumets were a sign of a malign magical act that someone had undertaken, a warning that an enemy was out to 'take' one by appealing to the restless dead: they were intended to instil fear, awaken guilt. The very fact that Plato offers maumets as an obvious, unproblematical, instance of *pharmakeia* suggests that by the mid-fourth century, even in courts of law, the concept *pharmakon* was not applied exclusively to drugs that could be ingested or salves that could be applied, but could also be extended to objects which had no physical contact with the intended victim at all, and indeed, evidently, to *epôidai*, incantations, and *katadeseis*, binding curses (for example, what we know archaeologically as curse tablets), which are the terms he uses in the earlier passage I have cited. And in my view, the most likely context for such an extension of the narrower meaning of *pharmakon* were trials for *blabê*, damage, claimed to have been caused by malign magical means.[60]

The second important distinction that Plato makes is that between the effectiveness of professionals, the doctor in relation to natural *pharmaka*, the religious professional, the 'diviner' (*mantis* and *teratoskopos*), in relation to malign magic. Indeed, he goes so far as to claim that just as the layman knows in principle nothing about drugs (poisons), so he knows nothing about malign magic (933c4–7). This difference in competence is reflected in the severity of the proposed penalties: the professional is to be executed for the damage he causes short of death, the layman dealt with at the discretion of the court (933d1–e5). Although such a distinction resonates with Plato's wider interest in professional skill, it surely also reproduces widespread beliefs, in particular that magic is a matter of special, usually secret knowledge, and that malign magic is the most difficult branch of it. Plato's concern with the professional practitioner reflects a real tendency – a more differentiated society could support more full-time specialists of all kinds, and specialism is naturally equated with efficacy; but at the same time we are not far from the claim that knowledge of magic, and not merely the harm it causes, is reprehensible. But it required the conditions of the Roman Principate to bring this issue out into the open.

The Roman Republic and Principate

In some ways, particularly in respect of specific harm caused by magical means, the situation in the Republic is analogous to that in the Greek world; but in others, above all recourse to mass inquisition, quite different. Although it knows no general ban on 'harmful drugs', one of the laws of the earliest Roman law-code, the XII Tables (451–0 BC), formulates an analogous, though more restricted, provision: 'if anyone has cast a spell on the produce of (someone else's) fields . . .', and '[if anyone] has enticed over (to himself) someone else's grain-harvest' (8.8a,b = *RS* 8.4).[61] This title occurs in the context of a series of provisions concerning harm of different kinds, from insult to honour through offensive songs or rhymes to causing significant loss by arson and unauthorized felling of trees. Archaic Roman law thus recognised an action for destroying *fruges* (generally non-grain field-crops) by incantation, and for increasing one's own harvest by 'stealing' neighbours' grain-crops through magical means.[62]

Seneca saw in the first provision a reference to the summons by magic of unseasonable rain or drought (*QNat.* 4.7), which may well be correct; we should add (severe) unseasonable frost, hailstorms, especially with outsize stones, and other freak weather conditions which it might, under certain circumstances, be plausible to blame upon an enemy or a known witch or wise-man. Although the law speaks only of the material harm done to crops, such an allusion would help to explain why the power of magic to command the weather has a much more prominent place in the Roman tradition, starting at latest with Vergil's *Eclogues* (8.99), than in the Greek: by granting such an action against enemies, the Tables also created a paradigmatic form of magical harm.

The significance of the second provision, spiriting away crops – perhaps in particular standing grain – is partly clarified for us by the case of C. Furius C(h)resimus, a freedman, who was accused in the curule aedile's court either in the 190s or 150s BC of using *veneficia*, magical means, to attract away the crops of his neighbours (Pliny *HN* 18.41–3). The prima facie evidence for this accusation was that 'he got much larger returns from a rather small farm than the neighbourhood obtained from very large estates' (41, tr. Rackham). Not only does this incident (the only one of its kind preserved to us) prove that the action granted by the XII Tables was still available perhaps three hundred years after their promulgation – even if the historian Calpurnius Piso's interest in it suggests that actions brought under it, at any rate by the socially significant, were by then a rarity; but it also reveals something of the reasoning of C(h)resimus' neighbours.

They were evidently not small peasant farmers, but were working on the rational expectation, which we know from Cato's roughly contemporary work *On Agriculture*, that relative specialisation of labour, close supervision of the labour force by farm-managers, and progressive refinement of agricultural techniques would together lead to higher yields and so, ultimately, to higher personal income – an expectation fostered by the rapid changes in Italian land-holding that followed upon the Second Punic War in Italy. This 'modern' reasoning was however subverted by the relative success of a much smaller farmer, evidently with only a handful of slaves: it was this confounding of reasonable expectation which here made an accusation of magic plausible; but, as Moses Finley used always to insist, the rationality of estate-owners such as Cato was hardly more than peasant wisdom refurbished. At any rate, we can glimpse here an appeal to the traditional peasant notion of the limited good (Foster, 1965), according to which goods – by contrast with ills – are always in short supply, such that an individual family can only improve its position at the expense of others. With such a fall-back position, it was plausible to argue that C(h)resimus' good fortune must have been obtained at the expense of his neighbours', whose lower-than-hoped-for returns in this perspective appeared as a reduction of the norm, and so indeed as an actual loss. Disappointed 'modernisation' and the persistence of the rationality of the limited good are more important explanations here than the fact that, as a freedman, C(h)resimus was both an outsider and of relatively low status (Graf, 1996: 58–61); in the first part of the second century BC we cannot by any means take it for granted that the larger landowners of the locality were 'insiders' or had held their land over generations.

Although in the end his quick wits won him an acquittal (cf. Gordon, 1987a: 67), C(h)resimus was extremely apprehensive when summoned to the aedile's court for using *veneficia*, malign magical means. And rightly so, for it is precisely at this period, in the years 184, 180–79 and 153 BC, that we hear of a number of cases of Roman magistrates and pro-magistrates ordering mass executions both in the immediate vicinity of Rome and further afield in Italy of persons also accused of using *veneficia* (cf. Polybius 6.13.4 with Walbank ad loc.). In one case, some 2,000 persons were executed (Livy 39.41.5); in another, 3,000 (40.43.2f.). The scale of these investigations and condemnations, which easily outstrips any known from the late mediaeval and early modern periods in Europe, and was made possible by the effectively unlimited police power of Roman magistrates operating under the authority of a *senatus consultum*, is one sharp disconti-nuity with Classical and Hellenistic Greece. Another is the type of offence. Links have been drawn between these inquisitions and the Senate's bloody repression of the Bacchanals in 186 BC; but insofar as they exist they are only of the most general kind. We have rather to do with an example of the fatal conjuncture, familiar from the early modern period, between popular 'pollution' anxieties and state power. Thanks to denunciation and the routine employment of torture and intimidation, the crimes awaiting exposure by the magistrate simply grew like Topsy: after his 3,000 executions, C. Maenius complained in 180 that his 'investigation was assuming ever larger proportions by reason of the evidence received' (40.43.3), and that unless he called an arbitrary halt he would not be able to proceed to his praetorian province of Sardinia. On these occasions (some of) the population both of Rome and of towns and villages in Italy willingly colluded with the authorities to get rid of 'poisoners'.

Livy does not bother to explain what these magistrates included in their notion of *veneficium*. But there is an incident from the early history of Rome which may be enlightening. Although its veridicality must in detail be suspect, the fact of its inclusion in the second-century construction of Rome's early history is telling, for Livy specifically notes that 'this was the first time that there had been trials for *veneficium* at Rome' (8.18.11; cf. Monaco, 1984: 2013f.). The affair, which is assigned to the year 331 BC, developed in the context of an epidemic of illness with high mortality: a number of citizen women, including two patricians, were denounced by a slave woman for 'mixing poison'; they themselves claimed to be making 'healing medicine'. Challenged in court to drink the stuff, they all promptly died; subsequent investigations resulted in the denunciation of many women, of whom 170 were executed (8.18.1–11). We know that during the years 182–180 BC an epidemic of illness had caused so many deaths that it was difficult to recruit sufficient troops for the armies (40.37.14); and that is surely the most plausible context in which to set widespread pollution fears. High mortality triggered a moral panic, whose victims were those who could be fitted into the stereotype of 'poisoner', that is, malign witchcraft, whether because they were directly involved in healing practice or as private enemies. The incident of 331 BC is exemplary in that it literally involved *medicamenta*, potions, which some claimed were beneficial, but which proved to be poison indeed – that is why it is preserved to us; but we do not need to believe that the second-century cases were so clear-cut – both the afflictions and the *veneficia* there were in many cases surely less obligingly palpable.

From 166 BC Livy's *History* is lost: it is uncertain whether there were other similar incidents prior to Sulla's dictatorship 81–79, apart from that of 153, of which we know only that it took place (*Epitome* 48). But we may suggest that it was, among other things, this experience of widespread *veneficium*, dealt with summarily through *ad hoc* commissions (*quaestiones*), which lay behind Sulla's decision in 81 BC to establish a joint *quaestio de sicariis et veneficiis*, a standing commission to try cases of violent homicide and death caused by 'poisoning' (cf. Ferrary, 1991). The fifth chapter of the Lex Cornelia *de sicariis et veneficiis*, clearly based on principles established much earlier in Roman criminal law, authorised the commission to try persons who 'make, sell, purchase, possess a *venenum malum*, a noxious drug, with the intention of killing someone' (Cicero *Clu.* 148 with *Dig.*

48.8.3 pr.). Either at the same time, or more probably later, the law was expressly applied to dealers in medicinal preparations that caused a death (*Dig.* 48.8.3.1). The expression *venenum malum* was intended to exclude medicinal simples and galenicals (cf. *Dig.* 50.16.236); but of course the ignorance and uncertainty of rhizotomic practice meant that the distinction had to be tested afresh in each doubtful case, as we saw in the 'poisoning' of 331 BC. In practice, many cases must have turned upon the question: does *malum* mean 'known beforehand to be poisonous' or 'proved in the event to be poisonous'?

As Mommsen pointed out (1899/1961: 636), the Lex Cornelia did not simply punish murder by poison, but extended the crime to the manufacture and possession of a drug with intent to destroy human life. It left the establishment of intent open to argument; it was also silent on the scope of *venenum malum*. Was this notion intended to apply also to cases in which it was claimed that death had been caused by, say, binding magic? It has recently been urged that the word *dolus* in *Dig.* 48.8.7, 'In the Lex Cornelia *dolus* is taken as the equivalent of the fact' refers to the invisible effects of poison and malign magic (Graf, 1996: 46); but in fact it simply makes the point that, because the crux of the law lay in the phrase 'with the intention of killing someone', which might be hard to prove directly, secrecy and underhandedness were taken as prima facie evidence of intent to kill.[63] The second-century antecedents of the Sullan commission perhaps offer grounds for supposing that the Republican law deliberately intended a narrow definition of 'poison'. The extraordinary commissions of the second century must have revealed the complexity of individual cases in which *venenum* was claimed to have played a part, and the problems this complexity posed for investigating magistrates. I suggest that, in respect of magic, this experience led to a decision that only one term of the hendiadys 'drugs and incantation' should be punishable. This had mainly a pragmatic justification, the virtual impossibility of showing that incantation, and other traditional magical practices such setting out maumets, either had been performed or had had any direct effect in causing death. But it perhaps also suggests a rationalizing attitude towards traditional belief in the power of cursing and binding, as well as a medicalizing view of the nature of *venena*.[64]

However that may be, the Lex Cornelia, which was never superseded by a Lex Iulia, seems to have been limited in the High Empire, with one or two clear exceptions, such as castration and giving false witness in a capital case, to actual homicide. There is nevertheless evidence of pressure to extend it to analogous cases.

One area of uncertainty lay with the *amatorium*, the love-philtre. There evidently was a view that, because such philtres were composed of natural substances, they should count as *venena* (cf. *Dig.* 48.8.3.2), so that their very administration (because of the rule that *dolus* should be taken as the equivalent of the fact) should be punishable under the Lex Cornelia. Quintilian cites the argument that 'not only the person who destroys a life by administering a potion should be guilty of *veneficium* but also the person who destroys a mind <by the same means>' (*Inst.* 9.2.105). The basis of the claimed analogy is the parallel set up between destroying (lit. 'removing') *vita* and *mens*. But he seems implicitly to reject it – he offers the argument as an example of claiming that 'things which seem to be different are the same'. We should perhaps conclude that in the Flavian period it was not yet the ruling of any *senatus consultum*.

On the other hand, one of the pseudo-Quintilianic minor declamations (perhaps first-second cent. AD) both suggests that reflections upon *amatoria*, their working and their classification, were by no means unknown in the courts of the High Principate and seems to accept that the administration of an *amatorium*, as a form of doing harm, might count as *veneficium*. The fictional case concerns a young man who falls in love with a prostitute, and finally gives her a love-philtre to cause her to love him in return. The girl duly falls in love and – this is an inference – refuses to entertain other customers with even the usual simulated enthusiasm. The topic is the pros and cons of the brothel-keeper's suing the young man under the lex Aquilia for his loss: under the terms of the law of damage, he stood to recover the highest value of the thing damaged over the previous twelvemonth (whereas in a criminal trial he would get nothing). It is suggested that the young man's lawyer argue first that a philtre could not have been the cause of the girl's refusal:

Does a philtre have any effect? What if an ugly person administers it, a cripple, a blind man? What if it be administered on behalf of someone not present? Can a chemical substance be given instructions? There is another prior question too: how can a substance alter feelings without harming the body through which it passes? How can it change feelings so as to induce fondness? If there were any such substance, the brothel-keeper would have found a goose to lay golden eggs. ([Quint.] *Decl. min.* 385.5, p. 282 Winterbottom)

These arguments mainly draw upon the Cynic tradition of ridicule of magical beliefs, but one evidently alludes to the lex Cornelia. It is this allusion that prompts the next argument by the defence:

My client was distressed; the old woman came upon him by chance; showed him it. Before he administered the philtre she had shown him, he drank some to make sure it would not harm her. He is guilty of this charge, that he did her harm (but not of damage). (ibid. 6)

The argument is that no action under the lex Aquilia lies, but that one might lie under the lex Cornelia, on the argument that the *amatorium* had 'harmed' the girl (*quod nocuerit*), by having any effect upon her at all.[65] But the young man had tried to anticipate what I take to have been the usual understanding of the law, that 'harm' meant 'fatal harm' – that is why he tested the potion beforehand, to make sure it would not make her physically ill, and so lay him open to the charge that he had tried to kill her: he was acting secretly, and '*dolus* is taken as equivalent of the fact'. Moreover, he had expressly not made an appointment with the old woman, but had come across her by chance: another way of defending himself against the charge of malice aforethought. The clear implication of all this is that in the High Empire administering an *amatorium* without fatal results could give rise to a charge under the lex Cornelia, but that there were accepted ways of arguing that the *dolus* ruling did not apply. And evidently the issue of magic need not arise explicitly at all, even though everyone knew that *amatoria* were made by wise-folk.

The second area applies more directly to magic, indeed malign magic, although as usual in the legal sources of the High Empire, the term is avoided (part of the difficulty with *amatoria* was the question of whether they should count as malign magic). Writing probably under Severus Alexander, Herennius Modestinus (who, quite apart from his legal writing, was also *praefectus vigilum*. i.e. chief of police at Rome), citing a *senatus consultum* of unknown date, ruled 'it is laid down that anyone who performs or possesses *mala sacrificia* is to be condemned under the provisions of this law', i.e. the lex Cornelia (*Dig.* 48.8.13). Though other interpretations have been advanced (e.g. Fögen, 1993: 60f.), the most reasonable position is that the highly unusual term *mala sacrificia* is a calque on the established *mala venena/ medicamenta*, which, as we have seen, meant 'drug within the meaning of the lex Cornelia'. It seems clear from the mention of 'possession' here that *sacrificia* must include objects obtained for the performance of ritual – surely including the ashes and bones of half-burned corpses, the nails used in crucifixions, and criminals' blood (cf. Lucan *BC* 6.534–60). The implication is that just as carrying a weapon with intent to kill was punishable under the law, so was performing a ceremony of malign magic and possession of objects which could be used in such ceremonies: it was legitimate to extend the lex Cornelia in this sense because the natural understanding of such malign magic was that it was intended to kill.[66] It seems to me that it is only to this degree that the lex Cornelia was in the High Empire, through *senatus consulta* but also ultimately through the rulings of *iuris prudentes*, the law that covered magic. As for the date of the *senatus consultum*, it may be instructive that a rescript by Hadrian laid down that 'in cases of *maleficium* we must regard the intention, not the result' (*Dig.* 48.8.4, cited by Callistratus, *On trials*), that is, an act of *maleficium*, malign magic, may fail, but would still fall under the terms of the lex Cornelia. This is simply an explicit application of the *dolus* rule to malign magic, but seems to acknowledge the principle formulated by the *senatus consultum*.

It has been generally supposed, following Mommsen's *Strafrecht*, that there emerged in the late Republic a law or *senatus consultum* against magical practice, which was therefore as such illegal throughout the Principate (Mommsen, 1899/1961: 639–43; Marchesi, 1955: x–xii; MacMullen, 1966/1992: 125; Amarelli, 1988: 131–4). Mommsen conceded that the sources do not allow us to determine precisely 'when and how this concept was introduced into the criminal law' (p. 640) and discussed it separately from the lex Cornelia. This traditional view has recently been challenged from two directions. On the one hand, Marie Theres Fögen (1993), mainly concerned with private divination, has argued that neither such divination nor magic were in themselves legally prohibited until the Tetrarchy and the Christian Empire, when we find a new desire on the part of the emperors to prohibit even the knowledge of how to gain private access to the divine, though she admits that moves were taken in this direction from at least the Severan period, when we find the idea of a normative religious practice as a qualification for true membership in the commonwealth of the Empire (Dio 52.36.2f.). We must distinguish between police action following intermittent *senatus consulta* and legal precepts. In defending this position, she examines critically many of the legal texts which have commonly been held to support Mommsen's position (1993: 55–88). On the other hand, Hans Kippenberg has argued that the proscription of magic emerged gradually in the late Republic and Principate as part of a wider attempt to control and suppress private religion, specifically clandestine rituals (1997). He sees three stages of Roman 'legal discourse' relating to magic: an early one, reflected in the XII Tables, in which harm to property was alone in question;[67] a later one, in which accusations might relate to *amatoria* and *venena* in a wide sense; and finally the persecution of *ars magica* as such, a stage represented by the pseudo-Pauline *Sentences* (5.23.14–19), a compilation of the late third or early fourth century (which he seems however to accept as a genuine statement of the law as understood by the celebrated Severan jurisprudent Iulius Paulus). He reads Apuleius' *De magia*, of the mid-Antonine period, as reflecting a point between the second and third stages, when the prosecution proceeds to list numerous accusations relating to *ars magica* in support of the main charge, above all secret rites, but Apuleius can still defend himself by appealing to a learned conception of *magia* as divine service (1997: 150–2).

It seems to me that both views have some merit, but offer a single insight as though it were the whole truth. Kippenberg, though he is undoubtedly correct about the existence of a rhetoric of public versus private cult, can offer no explanation for the development he discerns – obviously, one might think, because the same preoccupation, with clandestine ritual, is supposed to underlie all Roman official thinking in this context. Fögen rightly stresses the crucial role of Christian debates on Christ's miracles in determining the tone of fourth-century legislation (1993: 210–19) and that we can only place that tone in its proper intellectual context by paying close attention to contemporary arguments – this legislation is not simply a repetition of positions long familiar in Roman law (as Kippenberg, for example, still thinks). But her account is more appropriate to private divination than to magic, and her scepticism of the legal sources sometimes amounts to special pleading.

In my view, the conservative interpretation of the lex Cornelia remained valid for the great majority of individual accusations at least until the last of the Classical lawyers, Herennius Modestinus. The heart of the crime of magic remained the harm it did, not the secrecy of its proceedings. That view is still indeed presupposed in Constantine's law of 321/4 AD, expressly directed against 'those who are discovered to have worked against the well-being (*salus*) of human beings or to have deflected innocent minds to lust, aided by magical arts' (*CTh* 9.16.3), and – the sole law of the Christian Empire to do so – specifically exempts 'medicines intended to heal the human body, or steps taken in country districts, that there may be no apprehension of (heavy) rain when the grapes are ripe, or that they may may not be dashed to pieces by the force of hailstorms . . .'. The major extension to the lex Cornelia in this area admitted only malign magic (*mala sacrificia*), directed in principle against human life. *Amatoria* remained a marginal case, at any rate until Constantine's law, at some point being sanctioned (according to the pseudo-Pauline *Sentences*), together with the administration of contraceptive drugs, as *malum exemplum*, improper professional conduct – another calque on *malum venenum* – so that it was unnecessary to prove *dolus* (5.23.14).

But the underlying issue in accusations of magic, as I have stressed, is not so much the deed as the social figure of the person accused, and beyond that, the multifarious interests and prior assumptions of those who accuse, defend, judge and look on. It is here that the Hellenistic invention of a strong view of magic began to play a determinate role, attacking the basis of the centre-periphery model of the distribution of magical powers and beliefs, according to which only they, out there, foolish as they are, believe such stuff. For this view legitimated a quite new imagery of magic. It confounded indigenous marginal practice with the learned or ritual 'magic' of Babylonia, Egypt and the Jews. It boasted of its divinatory power, its intercourse with *daemones*, its use of the dead as intermediaries.

Its rhetoric claimed to be able to harness not only the powers of Nature but also the powers of the Underworld. In short, the strong view of magic was shot through with intentional profanation.

None of this, so far as we know, mattered in the late Hellenistic kingdoms. But in the crisis of the late Republic and the transition to the Principate it came to matter a great deal. The defining of symbolic boundaries became ever more necessary as the crisis deepened, in an effort to recreate the imagined community of value (we saw that already in the second century BC, in the aftermath of the Bacchanal affair, thousands of persons could be executed for *veneficium*, 'poisoning'). The Senate and magistrates had ample police powers to sanction undesirable behaviour: several kinds of marginal religious practitioners, notably the followers of Isis, were repeatedly expelled from Rome and/or Italy (Mora, 1990: 72–102). Two features of these police measures are here worth stressing. One is the repeated grouping of 'astrologers and magicians', such as those whom Agrippa expelled from Rome as aedile in 33 BC (Dio 49.33.5): what was objectionable about these practitioners was not so much the secrecy of their proceedings – the mere sign of the threat they posed – as their undermining of the status of traditional (not merely public) modes of divination. 'Magic' here really meant new forms of divination, above all astrology (equated with magic by Pliny *HN* 30.2) and necromancy. In 11 AD diviners were forbidden to make predictions to an individual without witnesses being present; and predictions about others' deaths were prohibited absolutely (Suet. *Tib.* 63.1; Dio 56.25.5). This formulation shows beyond any doubt that in the early Principate private divination was not in itself forbidden (Cramer, 1954: 249f.). If divination, and astrology in particular, was not illegal, then neither was magic, with which it was so closely associated.

The expulsion from Rome and Italy of the Greek 'Pythagorean and magician' Anaxilaus of Larissa in 28 BC (Jerome, *Chron.* 28, p. 163.25 Helm; often, though groundlessly, redated to 33) illustrates the second point: that esoteric or occult interests had in the late Republic begun to be shared by some members of the élite and so presented themselves as a new order of threat to conventional religious belief. In the late 40s Nigidius Figulus, another Pythagorean, was believed to have practised 'forbidden arts' in his house (Dio 45.1.4; cf. [Cic.] *Sallust.* 14). These currents were routinely condemned as un-Roman and equated with learned magic: Pythagoras was after all, in the Hellenistic account, a magus (Liebeschuetz, 1979: 126–33).

Jerome says that it was Augustus himself who had Anaxilaus deported. The link between magic and divination made autocracy fearful of it; the link between magic and the non-Roman made it a valuable tool for delators. It is this conjuncture of interests that characterizes the only accusations of magic/divination of which we know any details in the early Principate, the sorry succession of senatorial victims of whose fate Tacitus alone informs us.[68] Typical in a sense is the case of Claudia Pulchra, who, in order to attack her friend Agrippina (Germanicus' widow), was accused in 25 AD of prostitution and adultery, but also of *veneficia in principem et devotiones*, using malign magic against the emperor Tiberius (*Ann.* 4.52.2). 'Magic' is never here more than an item in a list of charges, an index of infamy; its agents and means utterly shadowy. Fögen points out that for Tacitus and Suetonius the repression of divination and magic is above all a political matter (1993: 95–126). It is instructive, for example, that, for all the circumstantiality of the reports that Germanicus met his death in 19 AD through malign sorcery – 'examination of the floor and walls of his bedroom revealed the remains of human bodies, spells, *devotiones* (curses), lead tablets inscribed with the patient's name, charred and bloody ashes . . .' (Tac. *Ann.* 2.69.5; cf. Dio 57.18.9), the recently discovered *senatus consultum de Cn. Pisone patre* shows that the Senate, for all its vindictiveness against Gn. Piso, did not bother with them for a moment: it had sounder charges. Although the Chronicle of 354 claims that it was under Tiberius that *venenarii et malefici* were for the first time arrested and executed, the literary sources for the *senatus consultum* of 16 or 17 AD make clear that this was no more than another routine repression of 'astrologers and magicians' (Dio 57.15.8) – Tacitus indeed mentions only *mathematici*, diviners, especially astrologers (*Ann.* 2.32.5; cf. *Coll. Mos. et Rom.* 15.2.1 [?Ulpian]) – following on the case of the unfortunate Libo Drusus, who, rumoured to have consulted astrologers and indeed a necromancer, was induced to commit suicide in 16 AD (*Ann.* 2.27–32). The self-evident character of the association between magic and divination, and its political import, is clear from the speech Dio puts into the mouth of Maecenas:

> Divination is of course necessary . . . But there ought to be no magicians at all: for such men, by speaking the truth sometimes, but generally falsehood, very often encourage numbers to stir up revolution. (52.36.3)

If the undercutting of the old spatial model and a new awareness of the (ancient) link between divination and magic were two crucial contributions of the Hellenistic account of magic to the early Principate, a third was to supply a new wealth of detail about the practice and performance of magic. For unlike traditional marginal practice, it was not illiterate. Books about it, with authors both named and pseudonymous, abounded – not of course receptaries, which must always have been clandestine, but works belonging to the pseudo–Democritean tradition. The contents of both kinds of books began to filter into shared representations of what magicians might be expected to do, and so became potential stuff for *delatores* and accusers. Apuleius mentions that there was a stir of outrage in the court at his merely mentioning the names of famous magicians – written texts – Carmendas, Damigeron, Moses, Jannes, Dardanus . . . (*Apol.* 91). That is, if the legal interpretation of the lex Cornelia did not change much into the High Empire, the means of justifying an accusation certainly did: the strong view of magic provided a range of new grounds for suspicion of the true character of an accused person, new weapons for attacking his or her social figure.

Here the case of Apuleius is instructive: his accusers brought a charge of *dolus* in relation to the administration of *venenum* under the lex Cornelia; but of course on that count there was hardly anything to say – no one had seen Pudentilla drink an *amatorium*, she had not fallen ill, there was only the ambiguous letter. The only hope was to use circumstantial evidence to suggest that, being a magician, he would have known how to make an *amatorium*. The category 'being a magician' was filled by means of collective representations drawn from many sources, including the strain of intentional profanation in the strong view of magic. This shared knowledge of the category enabled Apuleius' accusers to elicit 'indicative narratives' from informants, which produced the circumstantial evidence that Apuleius attempts to answer in his speech: the mirror, the alleged divination with the boy Thallus, the talismans and strange objects, the claim to heal, the nocturnal rituals, book-learnedness, Platonism. This is in fact just the sort of case that the *delatores* must have made at Rome against Mamercus Scaurus, Lollia, Furius Scribonianus and all the rest of them, though important for us both because the charge was a single and not a multiple one (nor politically motivated), and because through the accident of survival we can glimpse the technique of accusation. In short, there was no *crimen magiae* in a technical sense: there was only circumstantial evidence designed to support a specific charge under the lex Cornelia (or the lex Aquilia, as the case might justify).

Two further points are worth making. First, trials involving magic were surely highly variable in character. Apuleius and the others of whom we hear from Tacitus were granted the right to defend themselves at length only because of their high rank. Citizens of lower social status had no access to a rhetorical education and can rarely have been in a position to gainsay the (circumstantial) evidence against them in the praetors' or governors' court, just as the penalties meted out to them were harsher. Peregrines, the great majority of the provincial population until 212 AD, could hardly expect even so much. The fate of a non-citizen convincingly accused by neighbours of malign magic – normally of course after a long history of such accusations – was probably to be killed out of hand, with at most a cursory trial before the local magistrates, who were not obliged to refer to Roman law (cf. Millar, 1981: 70f.). The nature of the punishments exacted at this popular level are indicative of the strong emotions such cases aroused: Apuleius mentions a plan to stone a witch (*Met.* 1.10); a Greek novel represents a woman accused of being a witch and a poisoner being burned alive (Heliod. *Aith.* 8.9, p. 232f. Bekker) – a punishment also mentioned by a late legal source ([Paul.] *Sent.* 5.23.17). The dissemination of the image of the magician as intentionally profaning religious ritual, and indeed temples (ibid. 5.23.16), largely contributed to the heightening of emotion. Such perversion offended against popular views of the moral order, they were 'enemies of humankind' (*CTh* 9.16.6, 358 AD), and that was enough. Whatever other differences there might be between them, executions of this kind temporarily joined magistrates and people in a moral community of outrage.

This raises the second point. One of Fögen's main claims is that knowledge of magic, as of divination, could not be prohibited until a Christian Empire had undermined the legitimacy of the religious world which sustained belief in magic. This seems unnecessarily categorical. It was a very short step from the circumstantial evidence usually required to obtain conviction to the claim that being a magician, and therefore knowing how to perform magical arts, was itself criminal. 'Magic' – the full Hellenistic story – was easily abbreviated into malign magic, sanctioned both by the lex Cornelia and by popular feeling. It is true that there is virtually no legal evidence prior to Constantine's law of 321/4 that mere knowledge of magic was unlawful. But the issue was familiar in courtroom practice much earlier. A little-known declamatory exercise by the second-century Greek rhetor Hadrian, a pupil of Herodes Atticus, deals with the simulated case of a witch who, when another condemned witch had succeeded in extinguishing the fire that was to consume her (cf. again Heliod. *Aith.* 8.9, where the same thing happens), overcomes her arts and causes the flames to destroy her. The exercise tries to prove that this second witch should herself be condemned to death, claiming that the law itself refutes those who argue 'that it is not women who profess the art (of magic or witchcraft) but those who employ it to wicked ends whom the law punishes' (ap. Polemo, *Decl.* p. 44.8–10 Hinck).

> Some crimes proceed simply from recklessness, from the very fact of being committed, as we say, while others, such as witchcraft, depend upon a learned skill. These are discredited before the act by the very knowledge. Those who have learned to put into practice skills by means of which harm can be done must fall under suspicion from the very desire (to learn them): for those thus facing danger cannot make shift to defend themselves against those who are capable of harming them (after the event), but they must be able to act before they suspect that they have been harmed. (ibid. p. 44.14–23)

Protective magic is here argued to be a form of aggressive or malign magic, on the principle that the most effective form of defence is attack. The inherent ambiguity of magical action, which I have noted earlier, has here been neatly turned into a claim that there can be no passive protection: protection inevitably consists in attacking the suspected enemy (or practitioner) before they have a chance to lay a spell themselves.

> The person who knows about *pharmaka* is a public menace, undertakes to offer (for sale) an art which accomplishes crimes: it is a profession which attacks (others), an art that leads to breaking the law, the right arm of the irreligious. (p. 44.23–45.1)

This text makes clear that, though the dominant view of the lex Cornelia (Hadrian practised rhetoric both at Athens and in Rome, and I take it this exercise was performed in the capital) was that it applied only to malign magic, prosecutors in the late Antonine period might push hard to have mere knowledge condemned. That possibility makes a passage in *Coll. Mos. et Rom.* on divination, which purports to cite Ulpian's commentary on the Duties of the provincial governor (*de officio proconsulis*), all the more interesting:

> The question has been raised whether it is the (mere) knowledge of this class of men (astrologers and diviners) that is punishable, or the exercise and performance (*exercitio et professio*). Among the earlier legal writers it was laid down that it was the performance, not the knowledge, that was prohibited; more recently there have been differing opinions. (15.2.2)

It has been noted that *Coll. Mos. et Rom.* 15.2 is the only section of that work not to be cited elsewhere in the *Digest*, which must make its authenticity doubtful; there can be little doubt that another passage must date from after 294 AD (Fögen, 1993: 63–70). Nevertheless the text tends to support the view that traditional legal views of divination and magic were coming under strain in the Severan period.

The likeliest hypothesis is that it was the third-century crisis which renewed the desire to protect the threatened moral community, and so prepared the way for the legislation of the Tetrarchy and Constantine against divination and magic. The explicit prohibitions on being party to or practising magic and the ownership of 'books dealing with the art of magic' (5.23.17f.) which we find attached to the lex Cornelia in the pseudo-Pauline *Sentences* may well have been added to the law during this period.

At the most general level, then, we can trace the history of magic in the ancient world as a process in which Bourdieu's objective profanation was gradually overlaid, mainly at the level of representation, but also, at least in 'reptilian' magic (learned or ritual malign magic), in some practice, in favour of intentional profanation, in which power was obtained by the inversion or pollution of dominant religious ritual. That process began early, perhaps even in the Archaic period with the specialisation of the *goês* – certainly by the time of the Persian wars; but it was fragmentary and hesitant.

In the Hellenistic world, Alexander's conquests created the conditions whereby learned ritual lore could be transmitted from the high Near Eastern civilizations and turned into a new kind of symbolic resource; the invention of natural magic shifted perspectives upon traditional dominated practice. But it took the crisis of the Republic and the creation of the autocracy to crank the engine of intentional profanation. On the one hand, the night-witch figure constructed a negative inversion of the benign, sacrificant emperor: autocracy required its own Foucauldian other. The disciplining of individuals accused of malign magic, intended to be a theatre of purgation, was at least as much a reminder of the ubiquity of evil. On the other, the inverted imagery undoubtedly had some limited effect upon the practice of malign magic. Essentially, however, intentional profanation was an instrument in the construction of an imagined community, the community of the righteous inhabitants of the Roman Empire. That commmunity did not, and could not, exist except in the mind. But it is in the mind that magic has always been most at home.

BIBLIOGRAPHIC ESSAY

By comparison with historians of late mediaeval and early modern Europe, ancient historians have been reluctant to interest themselves in magic, partly because – despite an important essay on late antiquity by Peter Brown (1970) – in ancient history there has been no Keith Thomas or Alan MacFarlane able to adapt what the social anthropologists had recently been doing, partly because there has seemed so little to get one's teeth into. A devoted band of papyrologists and epigraphers, from Karl Preisendanz to Franco Maltomini and David Jordan, has ensured the (re-) publication of the texts thoughout the century; but they have mainly been used by historians of religion. Insofar as the topic has lately attracted more interest, it is still mainly from that quarter, and in the United States: marginal religious practice, the relation between dominant and dominated discourses, modalities and discontinuities of power, Orientalism – ancient magic seems to open itself to issues of this kind, loosely Foucauldian, which are also topical in other disciplines. A nuanced and attractively-written recent survey (Graf, 1994a, rev. 1996), which has now appeared in English translation (but too late for page refs. to be included here; Graf, 1997a), opens up many fresh topics and surely will succeed, unlike Bernand (1991), in stimulating new graduate work; and a whole range of different, often suggestive, approaches can be found in the rash of recent conference proceedings and analogous publications: Faraone and Obbink, eds. (1991); Johnston, ed. (1994); Meyer and Mirecki, eds. (1995); Schäfer and Kippenberg, eds. (1997); Jordan, Montgomery and Thomassen, eds. (1999).

One key issue is the translatability of the notion magic. Garosi (1976) brilliantly tackled the problem of the construction of the Graeco-Roman term, and her work has been carried further by Graf (1995). As for the Archaic and Classical Greek world, on one view (Burkert, 1984), Greek magical practices developed in the Orientalizing period largely under the stimulus of Near Eastern models, especially Babylonian; a recent book by Sarah Johnston, *Restless Dead* (1999), argues by contrast for the indigenous development of magical practice in close relation to beliefs about the unquiet dead. On the origin of the word 'magic' itself (cf. still Nock, 1933/1972) there is an analogous difference: Kingsley (1994) has argued that the Persian magi were the model of the reference of the term 'magos'; others stress its negative value (Gordon, 1987a; Carastro, 1997: 14–54). Kingsley has also argued for a substantial continuity of magical belief and practice from the Archaic to the Hellenistic periods (1995); others see a decisive caesura in the development of the notion of natural magic (Gordon, 1997a). Some of the characteristic intellectual assumptions of Classical magic have been analysed by Lloyd (1979: 10–32).

Given the massive loss of ancient texts, the study of ancient magic must scrape its evidence where it can find it. Literary sources necessarily play a role which is superfluous for historians of more recent periods (cf. Phillips, 1994). The only recent synthetic account (Parry, 1992), though indispensable for its references, cannot be recommended; but for a better book, more alert to writing strategies, discourses, determinations, we shall doubtless have wearily to wait. Meanwhile, there are good treatments of particular aspects and authors: Moreau (1994) and Clauss and Johnston, eds. (1997) on Medea; Segal (1962) on Gorgias; Johnston (1995) on Pindar *Pyth*. 4; de Romilly (1975) on rhetoric as spell-binding (cf. Seppilli, 1971: 160–229); Goldhill (1991: 261–72) on Theocritus *Idyll* 2; Watson (1991) on Hellenistic curse-poetry. About Latin literature much the same can be said: Tupet (1976), though technically reliable, is utterly pedestrian; and she was sadly never able to complete the volume on the Silver age. Among individual treatments one may single out Viarre (1964), on magical elements in Ovid's *Metamorphoses*, and Fauth (1975) on Lucan's Erictho.

For the historian, there is also oddly little of value on ancient learned or ritual magic. Philological and technical work on the Graeco-Egyptian magical papyri abounds (Brashear, 1995 is an indispensable guide), but there is no good account of the world of the Graeco-Egyptian magician, though Fowden (1986) offers valuable remarks in passing and there are succinct essays by Graf (1991, 1994b) and J. Z. Smith (1978a: 172–207; 1995) on particular themes. Hopfner (1921–24/1974–90) is a magnificent accumulation of material – if one can find what one is after – but the discussions, such as they are, naturally seem now thin and unperceptive. Ritner (1993, 1995) restricts his range to empirical description; more can perhaps be learned from Frankfurter (1994; 1995). Harrauer (1987), Johnston (1990) and Fauth (1995) are valuable accounts of learned strategies of syncretism. Much remains to be done on other aspects of learned magic, notably on the pseudo-Democritan discourse of natural magic: at present there is hardly more than the pages of Festugière (1944/ 1950: 186–216), Fraser (1972: 1, 440–4) and Kingsley, 1995: 325–8, 335–41. Alpers (1984) is an important account of the methods and procedures of one strand of this literature.

The social roles of magic have been very unevenly studied. Pliny the Elder saw healing as a central part of magical practice, and there is an excellent account of what can be disinterred of Archaic and Classical Greek procedures (Lanata, 1967); and likewise of pollution beliefs (Parker, 1983/1996). There is a good study of Pliny's material on magical healing by Martini (1977). On 'love-magic' there is a vivid but very Californian view by Winkler (1991); Faraone directs his attention more to the level of claims, hopes and rights (1990; 1994; forthcoming in Jordan et al, eds, 1999). Faraone is also one of the few classicists to consider the psycho-social role of the Attic curse-tablets (1989; 1991b), though in my view appeal to 'agonism' will not take us very far. Here is an obviously important topic rather neglected by ancient social historians, though Clerc's study of the Principate (1995) is a welcome exception. A good deal of attention has naturally been directed towards the frontier between licit and illicit cult and belief: note especially, for Classical Athens Versnel (1990: 96–205), Garland (1992), Montano (1993), Parker (1996: 199–217); and for the Hellenistic and Roman periods Segal (1973/1981), Poupon (1981), Gallaher (1982) and the fine book by Flintermann (1995). Versnel has also negotiated another frontier, between malign magic and vindicative texts, in an important series of articles (e.g. 1986; 1987; 1991; 1998).

Much has likewise been written on the narrower topic of the sanctioning of magic and more generally impiety. The fragmentary and unsatisfactory evidence for Athens is discussed by Rudhardt (1960), Cohen (1988), and Garland (1996); more particularly on Plato, Reverdin (1945: 169–241), Wyller (1957) and Saunders (1991: 318–23). Despite the incomparably greater amount of evidence, much about the situation at

Rome and in the Roman empire remains controversial. I have found Cramer (1954), Phillips (1986; 1991) and Kippenberg (1997) particularly instructive, without necessarily agreeing with all they have to say; also Coleman (1990) on the theatre of capital punishment. Desanti's insistence (1990) that charges of divination and magic against members of the élite were really charges of *maiestas* seems to me quite out of place. On the intentions and contexts of the legislation of the Tetrarchy and the early Christian Empire against divination and magic, I have found Grodzynski (1974), de Giovanni (1983), Lucrezi (1987), Castello (1990), and Fögen (1993) most useful.

Notes

1. Cf. 'The invention of the barbarian in the early years of the fifth century B.C. was a response to the need for an alliance against Persian expansionism and the imposition of pro-Persian tyrants; but the tenacity of the polarizing ideology after the wars can only be fully understood in the context of the whole conceptual system which underpinned Athenian supremacy' (Hall, 1989: 16f.).
2. Bollack and Wismann (1972: 92–4 frg.14) first realised that 'people of the night'(*nuktipoloi*) must be not an adjective qualifying *magoi* but the term to be defined by the list. Robinson's account is unsatisfactory (1987 frg.43 with p. 85). My interpretation of frg.14b (Heracleitus' objection) is taken from Kahn, 1979: 262f.
3. Burkert, 1962a: 38 n. 12 rightly understood *magoi* here as referring to such people and not to the Persian priesthood.
4. That it is not by Aristotle was shown by Spoerri, 1959: 56, 60, who dated the book to the period 200–170 B.C.
5. This text effectively contradicts the argument of Kingsley (1994) that the word *magos* was adopted into Greek because the Persian magi were indeed magicians. We may note that Miller, in her study of Persian cultural influence on Athens, ignores the entire issue of the magi, a silence we may take as indicative of her position (1997). Eunapius wittily has the rhetor and philosopher Eustathius accused of 'real *goêteia*' by the genuine magi at the court of Shapur I in 358 A.D. (*Vit.Soph.* 6.5.9, p. 27.5f. Giangrande).
6. Cf. the apocryphal tale of a 'Syrian *magos*' foretelling the future to Socrates in Athens, again cited by Diogenes Laertius from the pseudo-Aristotelian *Magikos* (Arist. frg. 32 Rose); in Cicero *De fato* 5.10, cf. *Tusc.* 4.37.80, he is identified with Herodotus' famous Persian exile Zopyros, son of Megabyxus (3.160), on whom see now Miller, 1997: 89–91.
7. Stubble is the traditional Norfolk word for what remains after reeds have been harvested (not in OED), both as a collective and as a term for individual stumps.
8. On the possible sources, cf. Flintermann, 1995: 83; Anderson, 1986: 206–15, defends the partial historicity of Philostratus' Indian material.
9. The word *charactêr* itself, meaning 'incised sign', calls attention to the claim that they are not ordinary letters.

10. Cf. Janko, 1992: 169: '[Hera] perverts her function as protector of married love by performing her conjugal duty'.

11. Closely parallel to the later account of the death of Patroclus, who is killed by Hector but first stunned by Apollo (16.786–868).

12. Cf. Janko, 1992: 101: 'Surely Alkathoos' terrifying paralysis has its equal and opposite reaction, obeying some supernatural law of physics, in the spear's bizarre motion'.

13. Aelian's version modernizes him into kind of renegade Roman soldier exacting illegal payments, a problem typical of the third century A.D.

14. 'In general, for the inhabitants of the Greco-Roman world in the first centuries A.D., the term 'magic' meant the manipulation of supernatural forces by means of spells and rituals which were believed to bring about the desired effect automatically. At the same time, words like *magos* and *goês* were used to stigmatize socially deviant, and therefore undesirable, views and behaviour' (Flintermann, 1995: 67).

15. I very much doubt the view that Agamede is actually to be thought of as the origin of Medea (Will, 1955: 122; Hall, 1989: 35).

16. I am also sceptical of the view (e.g. Hall, 1989: ibid.) that Medea was only turned into a barbarian = outsider in (late) fifth-century tragedy. The argument from vase-painting tells us only about the availability of an inconographical stereotype. Hall herself observes that Medea's paternal grandmother's name is Persê already in the Odyssey (10.138–9), where she is a Sea Nymph 'deckt with long greene haire'. The point is rather that the predominantly negative view of Medea is a fifth-century one: her status as an outsider, from being a source of potency, was turned into an aspect of her culpability.

17. One of the critical signs of bird-divination was 'sittings together' and 'sittings apart' ([Aeschylus], *Prom.* 491f.). A simple form of the theory of sympathy and antipathy is first known to have been used by a mid-fourth century writer on gardening, Androtion (Theophr. *CP* 3.10.3–4, cf. Wellmann, 1903).

18. The line is rejected by most modern editors (West, Solmsen, Mazon), but defended by Sfameni Gasparro, 1997: 71. Whatever the case with l.124f., there can be no doubt that l.252–55 also refer to the same conception of *daemones*.

19. *SEG* 43: 630 = Jameson, Jordan and Kotansky, 1993, accepting the suggestions of North, 1996: 298f. In this case, the shift from spirits of evil to beneficent divinities – reminiscent of Aeschylus' *Eumenides* – is effected through means sanctioned by the community.

20. col. VI.2–4 = Tsantsanoglou, 1997: 95, cf. the translation offered by Laks and Most, p. 11. The souls seem to be those of the newly dead. Tsantsanoglou himself (p. 99) takes the *magoi* as the Persian priesthood, the intention being to claim their authority and prestige for the

writer's claim about the fate of souls. The readings depend heavily upon conjecture, but the mention of the *magoi* seems to me reasonably certain.

21. That is, the texts collected as *PGM* I–XIII, XIXb, XXIIa–b, XXIV, XXXVI, XXXVIII, XLVI, LII, LVII–LXV, LXVII–LXXII, LXXVII–LXXX, and *Suppl.Mag.* nos.70–100. See Ogden, pp. 87 in this volume.

22. That is, the documents collected as *PGM* XV, XVI, XVIIa, XIX, XXXIX, LXVI and *Suppl.Mag.* nos.37–51, 52–8.

23. By 'writing' here I do not mean necessarily to endorse the well-known claims of J. Goody: the word stands for the complex of skills and claims implied by the ideological role of writing in a given culture.

24. The *iunx* is an analogue of the philtre, deceiving the mind by means of its mesmerizing sound (cf. Johnston, 1995: 180–6, 204).

25. The topic of many New Comedies and e.g. so Plautus *Asinaria, Curculio, Pseudolus* etc.; cf. also [Quintilian] *Declam. minores* 385 praef.: 'A young man, being in love with a young slave prostitute, and having given her loads of presents, administered a philtre to her'.

26. Bemarchius, who accused Libanius of magical practice in Constantinople in 343 A.D., also required support: 'He was getting nowhere by setting up this howl all by himself: he required a gang of his own' (1.44, tr. Norman).

27. Although never as rich and prominent as Lepcis Magna, Oea (despite being omitted from *RE*), a municipium already soon after 12 B.C., was granted the status of a colonia within a decade or two of Apuleius' trial. The pitiful quantity of the local epigraphy is due entirely to the poor quality of the local stone (cf. Reynolds and Ward-Perkins, 1952: 65f.).

28. After describing her alarming behaviour, Jerome indeed adds: 'I suppose the intensity of her passion for him was transmuted into madness' (12.4).

29. I do not accept Garosi's view that this account is Pliny's construction and that the notion of *magia* is essentially a Julio-Claudian creation (1976).

30. The use of another oracle, by Alexander of Abonouteichos, as a charm against the plague also in Asia Minor is mentioned by Lucian (*Alexander* 36).

31. The plague – though it must have been an earlier one – is reported to have appeared as a *daemon* at Ephesus in the form of an emaciated old beggar. Apollonius incited the people to stone it to death, after which it was revealed, dead, as a rabid Molossian dog, big as a lion: Philostratus *Vit. Apoll.* 4.10, p. 364.6–10, 364.25–366.3 Mumprecht; cf. Anderson, 1986: 140f.

32. The contrast here is between between *veneficas* and *magicas artes*.

33. This meeting is almost certainly the invention of Philostratus himself: Flintermann, 1995: 144.

34. The dedicatee of Lucian's *Alexander*, Celsus, an ?Epicurean (Caster, 1937: 97f.), had written a book *On magicians*, which Lucian cites in connection with his own account of Alexander's method of reading sealed oracle enquiries (21).

35. Some other examples in Furley, 1994: 100–3; analysis of some actual incantations using historiola, 91–100.

36. A variant is the claim that blood sacrifice *tout court* must be directed to malign *daemones*; but as far as I know this does not occur earlier than Porphyry, *De abstin.* 2.42.3, 2:109 Bouffartigue-Patillon.

37. Pliny uses this division in his introductory critique of magic as a whole, so that it is explicitly his own; but I think there can be little doubt that the Hellenistic writers on magic also used it, at least tacitly.

38. Many of the relevant texts are to be found, assembled apparently by or with the help of M. Wellmann, as 'Sonstiges unechtes' at 68 B300 *DK*.

39. See more extensively *Enneads* 4.4.40–42 = Luck, 1985: 118–20.

40. Kingsley (1995: 298–300), pursuing the theme of a subterranean goetic tradition, suggests that Empedocles' Love and Strife are in fact the origin of the contrast between sympathy and antipathy. One wonders in that case – and Plotinus *Ennead* 4.4.40.5f. provides no kind of counter-argument – why the pseudo-Democritean tradition was not content with this classic formulation.

41. The earliest documentary occurrence of the words *aski kataski aasion endasian, tetrax, trex-, damnameneus* etc., which are evidently closely related to the names that occur in the (late) lists of the *grammata*, is a protective charm from Phalasarna in Crete, dating from the late fourth century B.C. (see now *SEG* 42: 818.6; also Brixhe and Panayotou, 1993; cf. Furley, 1994: 96f., using the old publication of *ICret.* II xix 7). Though much is obscure about this text, it seems clear enough that these words are treated as names, either in the conventional sense, of *daemones*, or as primitive instances of non-lexical 'words' (cf. Kotansky, 1991: 110–12).

42. I take this confession by Olympius as pure decoration, being the necessary 'objective' confirmation of Plotinus' own account.

43. *Pharmaka lugra*, as at 4.230; at 10.394 it is a *pharmakon oulomenon* – *oulomenon* having a semantically vague but highly emotive negative force – that causes their bristles to grow.

44. This board of magistrates was still issuing curses in the second century B.C.: *Syll.* 578.60.

45. When the plague struck Athens in 430 B.C., it was at first thought

that the Peloponnesians had put *pharmaka* into the water-reservoirs which supplied the Piraeus (Thuc. 2.48.2); again, the 'obvious' distinction between physical and marvellous effects is blurred.

46. The text is here unclear: at the end of l.2 the letters *ANA* are written above the line. Newton and Dittenberger implausibly took this to mean *(th)ana(sima)*, 'to kill him'. Bechtel, Audollent, and Blümel read *ana[bai*, 'may he go up', which is the usual formula in this group. My translation differs in several details from Blümel's; the meaning is often obscure.

47. *SEG* 4: 648 = Petzl 1994 no.69, with tr. and comm.; also discussed by Daniel Ogden elsewhere in this volume, p. 000.

48. An exaggeration for effect no doubt – unless there was anaphylactic shock or he bled to death, he most likely died of tetanus, which would normally take two to three weeks.

49. But I confess it is not clear to me whether it might occur to anyone to enter a *dikê blabês* against an opponent in a lawsuit which he had lost, a failure which he blamed on the opponent's judicial curse. I assume that the risks of appearing ridiculous might here outweigh the desire to get even.

50. Dem. 23.65−67 does not mention *pharmaka* however.

51. The use of the word *anthrôpos* of a woman is generally contemptuous; but Aristotle uses it neutrally several times (e.g.*EN* 7.5, 1148b20), and, as will appear shortly, I think that must be so here.

52. Note also the account of the death of Herod's younger brother Pheroras, Joseph. *AJ* 17.4.1 (62). The plea seems to have had a chance of success in Athenian courts, cf. Pl. *Leg.* 9, 865b2−4, b6.

53. Cf. various attempts to use a binding curse to repay a death suspected to have been by sorcery: *Syll.* 1181.3−5 (Rheneia, IIp); Jordan, 1985a: 157f. s.v. no.14, a text of Imperial date from the bank of the Eridanus in Kerameikos (Athens, unpubl.), cursing 'whoever gave a *pharmakon* to Hyakinthos'.

54. Cf. Plato's discussion of *asebeia* in *Leg.* 10, 908d-910b, which is full of reminiscences of the Athenian practice (Wyller, 1957; Saunders, 1991: 318f.).

55. Cf. too Ninos, the priestess of Sabazius: Dem. 19. 281; Joseph. *Ap.* 2.37.

56. It is quite possible that the woman in Aesop's fable 56 was Theôris, though her origin is not further specified.

57. In my view the trope of Socrates' uncanny powers (cf. also Xen. *Mem.* 2.6.10f. – with an allusion to the Sirens; 3.11.16−18, S. as an expert on love magic) was a means of conceding that the *graphê asebeias* against him was not totally groundless.

58. At Aristoph. *Nub.* 749 the word is an adjective qualifying *gynê*, i.e. 'a

herbalist woman' — in this case, a Thessalian, who can haul the moon down. *Pharmakeia*, which in the Principate means 'magic', in the fourth century usually means either 'medical use of drugs' or 'poisoning'. The only exception I know is Ar. *HA* 6.18, 572a22, one of the three parallel passages that mention *hippomanes*, where it is used in a periphrasis to mean 'wise woman/witch'. *Pharmakeus* in Pherecydes *FGrH* 3 F47 (of the Idaean Dactyls) is clearly not part of a genuine quotation, but a summary by the scholiast.

59. As a pair, the terms construct the implicit model of 'magical healing' from earliest times (cf. the sons of Autolykos, Hom. *Od.* 19.456f.), as well as of Circe's magical art (10.236 with 320). But by the fourth century their significance had shifted to become predominantly negative.

60. *Pharmattein*, bewitch, occurs already (in the perf. passive) in Ar. *Thesm.* 534 and [Hippoc.] *Morb. sac.* 4 = 1.40, p. 66.86 Grensemann, meaning 'to have been bewitched'; cf. also metaphorically, Pl. *Symp.* 194a5, *Meno* 80a3 (cited above).

61. It is not quite certain that two different words for crops were used in the two phrases: the earliest evidence for 8.8b = 8.4 *RS*, the historian L. Calpurnius Piso Frugi (cos. 133 B.C.), almost certainly had *fruges* not *segetes* (frg. 33 Peter).

62. In my view the other title which is usually believed, following Pliny *HN* 28.17, to refer to malign magic through incantation (8.1 = 8.1 *RS* with commentary 2: 678f.), does not do so: Pliny misunderstands, or misrepresents for the sake of his argument, the significance of the expression *malum carmen*. Horace *Epist.* 2.1.152–55 is surely decisive.

63. The text is mistranslated by Kippenberg (1997: 153) as 'guilty intention is presumed from the deed'.

64. In the rhetorical schools of the Flavian period, it could still be debated whether incantation should be classed as *veneficium* (Quint. *Inst.* 7.3.7). This suggests that the matter had not yet been decided by any *senatus consultum*.

65. Cf. also the defence's earlier question to the brothel-keeper: 'Are you charging him with *veneficium* when you are suing him for penal damages?' (385.4).

66. The apparent repetition of Modestinus' ruling in [Paul.] *Sent.* 5.23.15 confirms this, since it prohibits 'celebrating or causing to be celebrated perverse or nocturnal rites for the purpose of bewitching, "taking" or binding' (5.23.15f.).

67. Kippenberg also accepts Pliny's interpretation of 8.1 (*HN* 28.18), which I do not: see n. 62 above.

68. Listed by Massoneau, 1934: 172–81; Cramer, 1954: 234 table 4; 237–43; Liebeschuetz, 1979: 133–5; Fögen, 1993: 96 n. 20.

PART 4

The Demonisation of Magic and Sorcery in Late Antiquity: Christian Redefinitions of Pagan Religions

Valerie Flint

INTRODUCTION

The 'demonisation' of 'magic' and 'sorcery' in Late Antiquity came of centuries of thought about demons. It happened on a grand scale only towards the end of the period with which we shall here be concerned, (approximately the first centuries AD until the death of Augustine in 430) but when it happened, it was founded on a real belief in demonic power, a belief made all the more intense by its long gestation.

The characterisation of 'magic' as the work solely of wicked demons, and of 'sorcerers' and 'magicians' as their servants, stemmed from two convergent developments. In the first place, the concept of the 'daimon' changed – a change made in response to extensive alterations in the articulation of religious practices, and in the institutional power attached to them. In the second, 'magia', or 'magic', became the *chief* term whereby the most powerful of the emerging religious systems described, and condemned, the supernatural exercises of their enemies. In brief, as organised and institutionalised religious practice was asked to play an ever more prominent place in the daily life of humans, as an exclusive form of monotheism commanded much of this practice, and as Christianity, in particular, assumed, through some of its officers, a quasi-imperial role, the older, looser, views of the dealings of human beings with the 'daimones' could no longer be tolerated. This 'daimon' was translated, then, into the evil demon of Judaic and Christian literature – a figure who could never help or co-operate with man for his good, but was instead his most bitter foe. Thus, those humans who looked to obtain supernatural help in the older ways and through an older or different 'daimon', came to be viewed by many as terminally deluded, and their exercises seen as magic at its worst. Sorcerers and magicians were then 'demonised' by being declared subject only to the demonic forces of evil, and were described as offering reinforcement to the most wicked of these forces' designs. The process of demonisation was greatly assisted by the extraordinary range of activities which had meanwhile been captured under the name of magic.

One of two actions was required in this situation: the demonically inspired magicians must either be rendered impotent or be converted to Christianity. Simple condemnation, however, came quickly to be recognised as both wasteful and ineffective. Habits had been formed by the older ideas and ways, and these could be tenacious. Some of these supposed supporters of the evil demons had capacities and followings which were precious to the newer religion, and which it could hardly afford to lose. In such circumstances, it became wise to attend carefully to conversion. To this end certain pagan practices might have to be, not destroyed, but redefined. It might become necessary to distinguish between actions described as demonic, to decide that some were less damaging than others, and to look for compromises. This tendency towards compromise was to become a striking feature of the world of Late Antiquity. Efforts were made to preserve some of the older ways, and perhaps some of the older 'daimones', differently conceived; and to restrain the forces of condemnation. Some sorts of magic and sorcery were then tolerated, at the very least for fear of worse, and perhaps because they had some benefits to offer after all. The demonisation of magic was not, therefore, complete even when it came. It brought redefinition in its train.

True religious conversion might require, in addition, the comfort of encouragement; and protection, especially from an over-enthusiastic 'Christian' state. In a further, somewhat unexpected, twist, the process of 'demonisation' allowed the concept of the wicked demon to rescue certain of the 'demonised' magicians from extremes of blame for wrong, wrongful 'magic' included. Christians had strong views about persecution and the right and wrong uses of fear, views eminently relevant to the operation of demonisation. Christianity came to 'cast out fear' (1 *John* 4:18), and particularly the fears through which the wicked demons sought to operate. Christian views on fear, clearly expounded and acted upon, might encourage some of the proscribed magicians to look to the Christian alternative. At times throughout the period, and especially towards its end, encouragement of this kind will be found. Where belief in the wicked demons is intense, attitudes towards fear are of the greatest consequence. This fact needs to be borne very much in mind as we progress.

I shall attempt to follow all these developments here, to their points of collision and compromise. This will be done in the first place by examining the changing concept of the 'daimon' through the centuries, and then through reference to the growing articulation of religious practice. Finally, we shall investigate the many Christian redefinitions of, and compromises with, magic. Throughout the discussion, and especially at its end, I shall maintain that demons were absolutely central to the process of the redefinition of pagan practices by Christianity, and that without this deep belief in them, many of the compromises with, and Christian tolerances of, pagan magic would have been impossible. 'Demonisation', paradoxically, allowed much pagan 'magic' to survive, and some magical practices actively to be condoned. In that it led rather to a widening than to a narrowing of tolerance, then, the Late Antique process of demonisation was very different from some of those we can ascribe to later periods.

I have spoken of 'reference', and advisedly so. This prefatory outline puts the matter far too simply, and there is need of several warning notes. The concept of the 'daimon' changed over the period in reaction to very many differing influences and articulations of practice, and the interrelations of demons with men were viewed at multiple levels of anxiety, only some of which we can recover. Much happened at the interface between the supernatural and the natural, and involved encounters of which only shadows remain. The written evidence for this period is seriously incomplete, and the textual history of much of it is still imperfectly understood. Passionate religious organisers tend to produce records biassed in their favour, and effective proscription will efface the answers of the other side. This happened in the period with which we shall here be concerned to a very high degree. We hear little in the available written record from the condemned magicians themselves and, though creative scholarship continues to make discoveries of the first importance, the point of view of these magicians cannot as yet be thoroughly reconstructed. This warning about the deficiencies of the surviving literature will be repeated frequently during the discussion.

DEMONS OF THE CLASSICAL WORLD

The Greek pagan world teemed with 'daimones'. The word is, of course, difficult precisely to define even at the beginning, as is any word which seeks to portray supernatural power. It is also hard to find exact equivalents for it in other languages, most particularly in English. The Greek 'daimon' might generally be described, however, as a force, or energy, less potent than that of 'theos', or God, but far more so than that of humans. It thus came to occupy an intermediate position in the supernatural hierarchy, a position, on occasion, a little like that of a lesser god, and to be thought capable of interfering in every aspect of human endeavour, should it choose, or be compelled or invited, to do so.

The relations of this 'daimon' with humans were, in Greek literature, ambivalent. Sometimes the 'daimones' were helpfully inclined, sometimes the reverse. In Pindar a 'daimon' might protect and guard a man through life as a form of providence, and give him strength and courage. In this case a man should do his utmost to co-operate with it (Pindar, *Olympian* 9.110, and *Pythian* 3.103–111 and 10.10). However, the 'daimon' might also assist an evil fate to overtake a human, and be then, justifiably, a source of fear (Pindar, *Isthmian Odes* 7.40–45, and *Nemean* 9.27). The 'daimon' of the tragedians is similarly capricious in its intentions (see, for example, Aeschyllus, *The Persians* 158 and 345). The Homeric 'daimon' can be a divinity with which a warrior struggles at his peril (*Iliad* 17.98–99, 103–105). It may well, indeed, override man's sense of his own best interests. In the *Odyssey* we have an early instance of the effects of the 'demon drink', a hazard which caused Elpenor to plunge to an early death (10.64.61–65).

The role of the 'daimones' is a divided one, too, in Greek philosophical tradition. Plato's *Timaeus* (40–2) placed powerful winged forms in the middle air, and the 'daimones' of Plato's *Symposium* (202E) bridge the gap between God and man and thus form the vital connection between the two halves of the universe. Plato describes the 'daimon' here as a great spirits:

> . . . interpreting and transporting human beings to the gods and divine things to men; entreaties and sacrifices from below, and ordinances and requitals from above: being midway between, it makes each to supplement the other, so that the whole is combined in one. Through it [the 'daimon'] are conveyed all divination and priestcraft concerning sacrifice and ritual and incantations, and all soothsaying and sorcery. God with man does not mingle: but the spiritual is the means of all society and converse of men with gods and of gods with men, whether waking or asleep. Whosoever has skill in these affairs is a spiritual man; to have it in other matters, as in common arts or crafts, is for the mechanical. Many and multifarious are those spirits, and one of them is Love. (tr. Lamb, 1967, iii: 178–9)

This passage is of the first importance to the transitions we seek to follow here. In such a guise, 'daimones' appear to be a force primarily on the side of goodness (and, we may add, of a particular social hierarchy). For Plato, divination, priestcraft, incantations and soothsaying did not carry the pejorative overtones a later age would bring to them. These 'daimones' are subject, on the other hand, to passions, just like man. Though they do not seem actually to stoop to evil in Plato's works, some of the 'daimones' of his philosophical heirs might be inclined to do so, through this very susceptibility to passion and emotion. The great Plutarch (d.c. 120 AD) describes potentially wicked 'daimones' of this type. They are:

> stronger than men . . . though they do not possess the divine element in a pure and unadulterated form, but joined in one with the nature of the soul and the perception of the body. This perception is subject to pleasure and pain and to whatever experiences are inherent in changes,

experiences which disturb some people more than others; for daemons, like men, vary in virtue and vice.

Plutarch also speaks of objectionable religious festivals, involving obscenity, self-laceration and foul language — festivals devised, in his view, specifically to placate the passions of the 'malevolent and morose' great 'daimones' of the atmosphere (*On Isis and Osiris* 360E; tr. Griffiths, 1970: 154–7). The exorcism of these malevolent 'daimones' requires, also, a disreputable form of magical incantation.

> The Magi advise those possessed by demons to recite and name over to themselves the Ephesian letters. (Plutarch, *Table Talk* 5 [*Moralia* 706E]; tr. Minar, 1961, ix: 54–5. The *Ephesian Letters* were well known current magical formulae)

Even among these bad 'daimones' however, there are, we should note, already differing degrees of harmfulness.

Apuleius of Madaura, writing perhaps a half-century after Plutarch, gives a full account of demons in his *Apologia* and *De Deo Socratis*. Apuleius's 'daimones' are in many ways like those of Plato:

> I believe Plato when he asserts that there are certain divine powers holding a position and possessing a character mid-way between gods and men, and that all divination and the miracles of magicians are controlled by them. (*Apologia* 43; tr. Butler, 1909: 78)

They inhabit the regions between 'the vault of heaven and our humble abode', and bridge the gap between man and God, taking prayers to the gods and bringing blessings back (including those blessings which support miracles and wonders). The bodies of these demons, though made of the very finest airy substance, prevent them, however, from living in the upper air, or ether, the highest region of the cosmos. Thus, like Plutarch's demons, they cannot themselves be gods and their passions, again, incline them earthwards. The best among them will exercise only a benevolent guardianship over earthly affairs; but some may, again like those of Plutarch, become greedy for an enormous range of honours and sacrificial victims and rites. Good human souls which have left their bodies might join the good 'daimones', and take care of certain parts of that earth they once inhabited. They may even watch over chosen households, as 'lares' or household gods. Less good souls, however, who have made poor use of their time on earth, do not deserve so happy a dwelling place or occupation. They will remain in exile, disconsolately wandering the earth as 'larvae', or malicious ghosts, seeking to do what harm they can (Apuleius, *De Deo Socratis* 6, 8–16; tr. Beaujeu, 1973: 26–37).

This distribution of situation and inclination among the various 'daimones', together with that vulnerability to the passions they shared with man, allowed of a further extension of thought about them – namely, that man was himself subject to an individual good and evil 'daimon' throughout his life. This notion too is traceable in both Greek literature and Greek philosophy. Pindar speaks, as we saw, of a protecting 'daimon' (*Pythian* 5.164ff). Plato and Apuleius believe in guardian demons, a belief which grew, perhaps, out of the idea that man's true soul and his good 'daimon' were the same (Plato, *Phaedo* 107D–108C; Apuleius, *De Deo Socratis* 15–16).

> And as regards the most lordly kind of our soul, we must conceive of it in this wise: we declare that God has given to each of us, as his daemon, that kind of soul which is housed in the top of our body and which raises us – seeing that we are not an earthly but a heavenly plant – up from the earth towards our kindred in heaven. (Plato, *Timaeus* 90c; tr. Bury, 1952 [Loeb], vii: 244–7)

Plutarch speaks clearly of an evil demon attached to humans (*Brutus* 36.3–4).

All such views make it evident how vulnerable mere humans might be to these supernatural powers, powers overwhelmingly superior to humans, yet in some ways oddly like them. The setting for those combats in which 'daimones' and humans are locked together in a struggle for supernatural mastery and salvation, combats so familiar to the history of sorcery and magic and so well dramatised in the figure of Faust, is implicit in such materials. A rise in tension or anxiety about the place of human beings in the universe, about their proper relations with their God, or about the help or harm inherent in the magical arts will easily draw the resources for such struggles from literature of this kind.

One of the most efficient of the purveyors of Greek ideas on demons was Philo Judaeus. As a Jew, educated in Alexandria in the early first century AD, and a prolific author, he was admirably placed to be so. Philo also, (echoing the passage from the *Symposium* of Plato quoted above), describes aery ambassadors or spirit bridge-builders, constantly engaged in going backwards and forwards between God and humans. Their embassies might be either helpful, or maleficent, although, in Philo, the maleficent ones are still under God's control, and act as chastisers – helpful in the end (*On the Giants* 3 and 4). This modification of the demons' extensive powers would help Jews and Christians also to accept, and even encourage, belief in the services of the demons as illuminators of wrong-doing. The neoplatonist Plotinus (c.204–270 AD, and teaching at Rome from 244), together with his pupil, Porphyry, (d.c. 303) and Porphyry's putative antagonist, Iamblichus of Chalcis (d.c. 330) were equally crucial to the transmission of the good and evil 'daimones' to Late Antiquity.

The susceptibility of the 'daimones' to the passions was moreover, for Plotinus, almost a guarantee that these beings might act irrationally, and so (given that, for him, all true good came of reason) wickedly. Plotinus also believed that each man had his own demon (*Ennead* 3.4).

We owe one of the most forceful of all of our expositions of neoplatonic views on 'daimones' to the famous conflict between Porphyry and Iamblichus; and, most importantly for the present discussion, we also owe to it an instructive non-Christian attempt at the demonisation of a form of magic, and a countering insistence on right religion. The expressed antagonism between Porphyry and Iamblichus stemmed from a deep disagreement about the powers and rights of contemporary theurgists. The differences between the two were set out in some detail in the *Letter to Anebo* of the former, and in the *De Mysteriis*, credibly attributed to the latter. The *Letter to Anebo* is lost, and can be reconstructed only by means of the *Praeparatio Evangelica* of Eusebius (3.4, and 5.8–10), the *City of God* of Augustine (10.11) and Iamblichus's *De Mysteriis*. Thus, it is hard to distinguish Porphyry's actual views from those reported by his critics. The *De Mysteriis* survives intact, however, albeit only in manuscripts of the fifteenth century (one of which was corrected and translated by the great Renaissance Platonist Marsilio Ficino), and is a source of deep importance for this subject – one which deserves to be treated more seriously than, in general, it has been. St. Augustine would come to be extremely interested in Porphyry's views upon demonic powers, and the possible influence of the wicked demons upon, to him, 'magical' theurgy and disreputable kinds of wonder-working. Some understanding of the role of the demons in this conflict is essential to all appreciation of the demonisation of magic in Late Antiquity.

The religious system known as 'theurgy' stemmed, it seems, from the activities of one 'Julian the Chaldaean' and his son (also Julian), who practised in the reign of the Emperor Marcus Aurelius (161–180 AD). It had certain features in common with the Greco-Egyptian magic of the papyri, and some of the principles upon which it relied may be disinterred from the extraordinarily difficult, and now fragmentary, *Chaldaean Oracles*. Theurgists declared themselves capable of governing and directing the supernatural powers on earth, though wholly to the end (as they and their supporters averred) of purifying human souls, drawing them up to God and subordinating them to the divine will. Theurgy was supposed 'to intensify the presence on earth of higher beings through the performance of specifically designed rituals' (Shaw, 1985: 1). This was felt, certainly by Iamblichus and his followers, to be the opposite of sorcery, which sought to subordinate the supernatural powers to humans. The conflict between Porphyry and Iamblichus revolved around a distinction between right religion and magic still much in vogue today. According to this distinction, the religious man may be described as one who offers humble submission to the deity in the hope of that deity's assistance. The magician, on the other hand, seeks to compel the higher powers 'to do as he wishes and avert that which he fears' (Barb, 1963: 101).

Theurgists claimed to enjoy particular successes through the arts of divination, but they embraced, in all, an exceptionally broad range of activities. These might involve the calling down of the gods to help man by means of spinning tops (Lewy, 1978: 132), and, according to Book 3 of Iamblichus's *De Mysteriis* (where these exercises are set out in some detail) they included incantations, ecstatic trances and dreams, frenzies and dances (accompanied by flutes, cymbals and tambourines), the consulting of oracles, the interpretation of the entrails of sacrificed animals and of the calls and flights of birds, the calling up of visions on reflecting surfaces such as mirrors or pools of water, conjuring with 'signatures' or mantic signs, or wands, enquiring into the future by means of scattered pebbles or grain, or the movements and dispositions of the stars. The techniques of the theurgists might be divided into two main categories: those which depended primarily upon the use of symbols (vegetable, animal and mineral) and those which employed an entranced medium (Dodds, 1947: 62–8).

There were echoes of contemporary, and discouraged, 'magical' practices within 'theurgic' ones. For instance, that particular and striking rite conveyed through the *Chaldaean Oracles*, whereby the neophyte's body is symbolically buried in order that the soul may be freed was, in certain externals, very like that used by contemporary necromancers (Lewy, 1978: 208–9). The employment of 'symbola', 'characteres' and sympathetic plants and animals as a means of invocation is standard in Greco-Egyptian 'materia magica', such, for instance, as that contained in the famous Paris magical papyrus of c. 300 AD (Paris, B.N: PGM IV). The aims of the theurgists were, however (or so their defenders claimed), altogether different from those of the necromancers and the magicians. Such apparent emulations may well have been part, indeed, of a determined effort to drive real distinctions home, yet still retain a well known and emotionally charged ritual. Such an aim may explain, too, the theurgists' particular fondness for the use of animated statues in the procuring of their oracles. An animated image was a peculiarly powerful way of arresting attention, and the idea of the oracular image had some distinguished devotees. The Emperor Nero, for example, kept one by him to warn him of conspiracies (Dodds, 1947: 63–5). Christians might sneer initially, but they would also come to recognise the ritual power of images, suitably adapted, as we may see even now.

The concept of the Greek 'daimon', complete with its ambivalence, and the problem of the location and nature of those 'daimones' with which the theurgists worked, were and are central to the developments we seek to trace here. They are central both to our general understanding of changing views of 'daimones', and to our particular appreciation of the power struggles which may emerge within evolving religious systems, and which must involve decisions about magic. Were the spirits with which the theurgists conjured good or bad; aids to right religion or wrongful magic? Porphyry doubted the religious value, and indeed the efficacy, of theurgy, and the elements of compromise with magic within theurgy made the movement doubly vulnerable to his criticisms. Theurgic practices could depend, Porphyry argued, upon little more than trickery and falsehood, and so upon the ill-inclined 'daimones', prone to delusion. Augustine gave a clear (and sympathetic) account of Porphyry's argument in the *City of God*:

> He [Porphyry] lets it be understood that this is the work of spirits . . . The spirits are fraudulent . . . As for his view that it is by the use of herbs, stones, animals, certain particular sounds and words, drawings and plastic representations, even by observing certain planetary movements in the revolving vault of heaven, that men create on earth powers capable of accomplishing all sorts of results, all this has to do with those same demons who play tricks on souls that are in subjection to them, and stage as a delicious treat for themselves comedies of human error. (*City of God* 10.11; tr. Wiesen, 1968, iii: 302–5)

Porphyry and Augustine plainly believe in the existence of the 'daimones', but here these have already assumed those devious, and ultimately deeply hostile, forms which Christians would come later to ascribe to them, and which Late Antique Christians would also associate with that magic which must be condemned.

Iamblichus, however, was of another mind entirely. Iamblichus's 'daimones' are divine messengers, like those of Plato; messengers flying through the middle air and translating divine energies into forms humans can understand and use (*De Mysteriis* 1.5). There are good and evil types of demon. The evil demons are evil less because they are in themselves susceptible to the passions, than because they can become contaminated by them when they descend to the material world. They might then do actual physical harm to man, afflicting him with disease and binding him down to the earth and death (*Ibid.* 1.10–15, 18–20 and 2.6). But because their works are good, theurgists must use good demons, thinks Iamblichus. These good 'daimones' will always demonstrate their goodness by responding to the requests of the most purified among humans, and, in doing so, nullify the efforts of the evil demons and their impure human assistants (*Ibid.* 3.13,31). Here, the Greek division between good and evil demons is crucial in forging the distinction between theurgy (acceptable) and 'magic' (not).

For both Porphyry and Iamblichus, the marks of the unacceptable in supernatural exercise, and of 'magic' and evil demons seem to be three: the inflicting of experiences agreed to be unpleasant, such as disease, evidence of false or inappropriate human behaviour, and artifice excessively mired down to the material world (*Ibid.* 2.10 and 3.28–30). They differ only as to whether the works of the theurgists are, or are not, so marked. We might note that the idea of the occult does not loom largely here. The theurgists have secrets, it is true, but they have them because, according to Iamblichus, it is appropriate that they be kept safe from the unworthy. Impurity of life (associated, perhaps, with disease) and offensive crudeness in ritual, rather than secrecy, is that which here chiefly separates condemnable magicians from acceptable ones.

Theurgy was clearly popular, widespread and long-lived. Iamblichus may have had a larger following than Plotinus (Shaw, 1985: 3), and there was a cheering precedent for later Christian compromise in the friendliness theurgy showed towards the milder forms of magic. Thus, to look ahead for a moment, if theurgy 'used the procedures of vulgar magic primarily to a religious end' (Dodds, 1947: 61) as Iamblichus would claim, some Christians would try to do much the same for some of the procedures of theurgy, and so modify attempts to condemn it and all of its works. Proclus, Christian Patriarch of Constantinople (d.446/7), came to approve of many of theurgy's activities and claims, as did other Christians, such as the philosopher Synesius of Cyrene. It may be that Augustine's interest in theurgy was aroused by a similar wish to find a middle way. Some aspects of theurgy were clearly attractive to the newer system, and understandably so. Theurgists were, for instance, concerned for the salvation of the soul of an individual, as were Christian pastors, and the ritual exercises of the theurgists, furthermore, were tailored to each individual's needs. They thus required diagnostic skills of a high order in the officiant, and allowed of a wide range of ability in the neophyte. Purely rational and contemplative capacities were not here quite so important as they were in the pagan philosophical schools; a widening of the way to the divine which held out clear advantages to Christians (Shaw, 1985: 12, 18–19, 26–7). Also, elements close to the sacramental life of the Christian church, such as the elements and 'symbola' in the purification rituals, were already present in theurgy (Lewy, 1978: 184). Some Christians will, therefore, find the aims and activities of theurgists considerably less 'demonic' than those of some of the mystery religions, just as Iamblichus had, and their rites less objectionable than those, for instance, of the cult of Isis. Discoveries of this kind would affect the use of the concept of the Greek 'daimones' in complex ways.

Theurgy, its 'daimones', its exercises and, above all, its attractions to certain types of Christian are central too to another part of this process, and to our understanding of how certain sorts of 'magic' came not merely to be 'demonised' but, in some cases, described in Late Antiquity. Theurgy could, as we have seen, be a source of compromise with the older ways with demons to its more tolerant Christian friends. But, to its enemies, it could also be a repository of much of that which, in condemned magic, they most despised, and it conveniently offered them almost everything they needed to portray it. The activities of the theurgists clearly encompassed, and in some cases may have supplied, much of that technological stock-in-trade which came to be the badge of magic. In a later age, then, and within a different understanding of the works of the 'daimones', it could be used as evidence in the prosecution of many magicians. The fact that Marsilio Ficino preserved and corrected one of the best surviving manuscripts of Iamblichus's *De Mysteriis* is of the greatest interest in this context.

The precise make-up of the Greek 'daimon', and the extent of the belief invested in the concept, are still matters of enormous philosophical and textual complexity, and this is no place to pursue them further. The Greek concept of the evil and good 'daimon' (the latter often firmly renamed as an angel, another element within theurgy which would draw it close to Christianity) (Lewy, 1978: 260–1), was clearly essential by the fourth century AD, however, to the making of distinctions between acceptable and unacceptable supernatural exercises, and so to the demonisation of magic. We are able now to discern, through surviving texts, debatable roles and disputed rituals, certain 'demonic' traits ready for employment in this process, and we have edged towards an understanding of how it was that sorcery and magic came eventually to be demonised in Late Antiquity. Powers which peopled the upper airs were thought surely to exist; and they were superior to man. Some of these aery powers were good, some evil; and, arguably most importantly of all for the present discussion, the distinction between the good and the evil 'daimones', when it came to be made in detail, seemed to depend upon conditioned human values – upon which instances of supernatural exercise a powerful spokesman decided, at a particular time, to defend or deny. When Plutarch or Iamblichus, for instance, spoke, as we saw above, of certain forms of religious festival and exercise they clearly despised, they were able to harness the idea of the evil demons in their support. Iamblichus, in similar fashion, harnessed the good ones to the theurgists, of whose works he as clearly approved. The idea of a supernatural good or evil presence could, in other words, be a most welcome reinforcement to a sense of approval or distaste which might be, at root, one merely of a section of human society, attracted, offended or threatened, at a particular point in time;

and, by allowing such conditioned perceptions to be annexed to it, this idea could help to elevate these senses of approval or distaste into positions far more authoritative than those to which they might, of themselves, lay claim. When that which comes, by some, to be defined anew as 'magic' is again perceived as evil, then the evil demon will be ready once more for condemnation, and the good one for defence. The combination of both ambivalence and power in the concept of the Greek 'daimon' makes it an extraordinarily tempting one to use; and perhaps to abuse.

The end of this first section seems an appropriate place at which to warn again about the evidence, and to advance some general observations about the circumstances which engender and encourage a belief in demons, and the features which appear to be characteristic of this belief. Firstly, the warning. There are clearly aspects of this written evidence of which we should beware. The 'daimones' of Greek literature, for example, may have reached an audience wider than that accessible to the 'daimones' of philosophical and theological controversy, but the latter seem to have commanded the more powerful, and vocal, following in this early period. This will not necessarily be true in later ones. Texts which speak of demons need, then, always to be placed in at least two contexts for their proper understanding; that of their composition, and that of their reception. It will never be possible to give a simple narrative account of the transmission of so essentially dynamic and emotionally charged a concept.

Secondly (and this point is intimately connected with the first), psychological factors were, and are, clearly involved in a belief in demons. Thus, psychological factors will be intimately involved, too, in the fostering of this belief, and, especially, in its association with condemnation. These factors were plainly present in that which I have already described (perhaps a little deceptively) as conditioned human approval and distaste. The concepts of the good and evil demons operated in fact on a far deeper and more powerful level than that of mere taste and distaste, however. They are bound up, indeed, with the chief psychological factor of all, the factor of human insecurity in time and place, together with its associated emotions of hope and fear. Acceptable and unacceptable means of operating upon these emotions were, as I suggested at the beginning with the help of 1 *John* 4:18 on fear, of central importance to Christianity. They would certainly be so to the Church of Late Antiquity when it came to attend to 'magic'.

Human insecurity can find much solace in the concept of the demon. The concept of the good demon assists human beings, of course, in obvious ways. It may help them to hope, and supply them, quite literally, with 'high spirits' in the confidence of friendly supernatural assistance. If, moreover, good demons, not humans, are viewed as the prime opponents of demonic wickedness, then the weight of a person's own responsibility is, or may be, significantly reduced, and the angelic powers will act for him or her instead. Bad demons may also, though such a statement may seem at first surprising, supply a similar solace. One source of solace will lie in the invitation the wicked demon offers to 'demonise', and so to outlaw all which makes humans feel most inadequate or outraged – a tendency it may seem we seek here primarily to examine, and have begun to see in action. This first source of solace is perhaps the most obvious one. These bad demons may also, however, lift burdens of guilt and pain from human shoulders by bearing the responsibility for wrong. The evil demons might, in this way, be ultimately blamed for perceived wicked-ness, in place of a hapless human. If demons are held in truth to be more powerful than human beings, and to control their destinies; if they, not humans, are believed to be the driving forces in human decision-making processes, (to be, in short, man's 'fate'), then the evil 'daimones' might be made ultimately responsible for a great deal of that currently seen as wicked in human behaviour, and penalised in man's place. In this way, belief in the evil demons might obviate a verdict capable of bringing heavy penalties down upon human beings, especially at the hands of a brutal state government; and the exorcising of a demon (provided it is done well and without offence) may seem to some to be a far better way of countering human evil than the possibly harsher means taken by the secular powers. This second view of 'demonisation', the use of demons, that is, as an expedient to release man from both stress and punishment, is less familiar than the first. It is a use, however, which becomes ever more relevant as we approach the world of Late Antiquity. The use of the evil demons as protectors for humans from something far worse than exorcism – from pain, and death, and the loss of the soul – may have played a larger part in the 'demonisation' of magic, and in exciting debate about it in the Late Antique Christian Church, than we have hitherto suspected. These psychological and legal dimensions to the concept of the demon and, above all, that Christian attitude to fear which was mentioned at the beginning of the discussion, need constantly to be thought about as we progress.

Belief in the demons, then, allowed the translation of human problems onto a cosmic plane, and provided 'escapism' of many different sorts. Psychological forces of this order may also, as we have begun to see, readily be translated into moral terms, and be used to reinforce moral dictates. There are, however, prices to be paid for such releases, whenever they occur in the history of human society. The capacity to blame another might sweep away all readiness to accept responsibility for oneself, and the perceived potent presence of 'daimones', of whatever kind, imposes a constant need for their invocation and propitiation, and for affording them their just deserts; a circumstance requiring, perhaps, that attendance upon the higher powers take too great a precedence over other human activities. Psychological forces of this order might be abused by unscrupulous, or deluded, manipulators; by dominant personalities, for instance, who seek unacceptable means of control (a situation still very much with us if we read the twentieth-century press). On occasion, the idea of the demonic may be used to raise the trivial to a status it should not have, and debase the truly important in human affairs. Belief in good and evil demons *can* provide man with ready excuses for a debilitating sense of his own misbehaviour, a rehabilitating means of help and safeguard, and an efficiently directed morality, it is true; but it can also reduce man's sense of stature within the universe, and rob him of the enjoyment of freedoms and capacities truly his own. Elevation and escapism contain both worthy and unworthy elements; 'demonisation' can be an effective, but also a dangerous, source of control.

Demons are not, we should note, the sole claimants to the role of scapegoat or helper in this early period – nor will they be in the later ones. Belief in astrology, and in the overwhelming power of the heavenly bodies, for example, also offered relief from insecurity and anxiety, and from unassisted individual human responsibility. Other creatures could contend with the 'daimones' as providers of this service. To Plotinus the rationality of the stars and planets might be reconcilable with that of man. They might be a better point of reference for man's supernatural progress than the 'daimones'; the stars and planets here, as it were, 'demonise' his demons. Inner contentions of this kind about the roles of cosmic forces superior to man, and about the place of man's reason, will complicate the picture, and will affect both the energy with which the cause of the 'daimones' themselves is urged, and their very configuration.

The 'daimones' of the classical world offered to humans a tremendous range of possible employment and exploitation, as they streamed into the world of Late Antiquity. They could render themselves indispensable to purveyors of a whole range of cosmological, philosophical, psychological and moral directives. This potential ensured their survival into other religions though, of course, many aspects of their pagan features would have to undergo a severe cosmetic change, and their assistance be annexed only with the greatest of care.

THE DEMONS OF JEWISH TRADITION

Hebrew tradition also brought demons to the world of Late Antiquity and, by reason both of the common inheritance of Jews and Christians and, perhaps more importantly, their frequently living as close neighbours, arguably all the more forcefully so. The Hebrew Old Testament has little to say about the Devil as such, although once Christians came to look for him he could conveniently be discovered in such passages as *Isaiah* 14:12–14 and *Ezechiel* 28:12–19. Also, as we shall see below, the Old Testament could conceive of Satan. Neither the Hebrew Old Testament nor the pre-Christian Jewish Apocrypha subscribe with any clarity, however, to the concept of the 'daimones' of the air. Demons such as Azâzêl (*Leviticus* 16:1–28), Lilith, the 'night monster' or 'lamia' of the Vulgate, and Isaiah's goat-demons (*Isaiah* 34:14) are distinctly earthly, and Azâzêl becomes an aery spirit only in the pseudepigraphical *Book of Enoch*. Some elements characteristic of the Greek 'daimones' are to be found in the latter, in other intertestamental literature and in Rabbinic Judaism, but with a striking difference. They are all now, indisputably, forces for evil.

This new clarity of rôle for the 'daimones' sprang in part from the profound changes later Jewish monotheism imposed. Multiple god - 'daimones' for good were no longer acceptable to this monotheism; but we may also turn, once again, to sheer human insecurity for a fuller explanation. A people battling to defend its religion and self-identity, and without hope of victory in military terms, has a special need of a different kind of victory, and to categorise internally all that is most hostile to it. The evil 'daimones' offered themselves readily to Judaism for the task. They were seized upon therefore with enthusiasm. The Jewish 'apocalyptic' books in particular are full of accounts of wicked spirits, all working to undermine God's plans for his people.

The *Book of Enoch* gives us excellent examples of the evil demon of the 'apocalyptic' period of Jewish history (roughly 200 BC to 100 AD) and, especially, of how the concept could be used to reinforce particular moral and behavioural directives. The *Book of Enoch* tells a story about the involvement of demons in the very genesis of mankind. Expanding upon the canonical *Genesis* 6:1–4 it speaks of the fall of certain angels, led by Azâzêl and Semjâzâ, as a result of their lusting after human women:

> And it came to pass when the children of men had multiplied that in those days were born unto them beautiful and comely daughters. And the angels, the children of heaven, saw and lusted after them . . .
>
> And all the others together with them took unto themselves wives, and each chose for himself one, and they began to go in unto them and to defile themselves with them, and they taught them charms and enchantments, and the cutting of roots, and made them acquainted with plants. (*Enoch* 6:1–3, 7:1–2; tr. Charles, 1913, ii: 191–2)

The angels were bound in dark places by God for their deed, but offspring were born of the fallen union, to continue the wrong-doing as evil spirits on earth (*Enoch* 15:9–12)

Here, a wrong which is primarily sexual cast as the source of evil as a whole, as it can be in certain interpretations of the cause of the fall of man in the Old Testament *Genesis*. The evil angels go on, then, to teach *women* forbidden, and magical, arts. A whole host of social dictates is hidden in this short passage, together with a hierarchy of wickedness which is eminently debatable. Demonic forces stand, however, indubitably on the wrong side in the affair, and magic heads the list here of the evils they are purported to have brought to mankind:

> Semjâzâ taught enchantments, and root-cuttings, Armârôs the resolving of enchantments, Barâquîjâl (taught) astrology, Kôkabêl the constellations, Êzêqêêl the knowledge of the clouds (Araquiêl the signs of the earth, Shamsiêl the signs of the sun) and Sariêl the course of the moon. And as men perished, they cried, and their cry went up to heaven. (*Enoch* 8:3–4; tr. Charles, 1913, ii: 192)

The textual transmission of the *Book of Enoch*, and its context, have much to tell about the later demonising of magic and enchantment.

Other books from the apocalyptic period continue the account of the lustful fallen angels, of the subsequent torment of man at the hands of their demonic descendants and of the attempted subversion of the plans of Yahweh. The *Book of Jubilees* and the *Testament of the Twelve Patriarchs* have demonic commanders, Mastêmâ and Belial respectively, urging their legions forward, and adding other temptations to that of lust. The demons' chief rôle here is to throw into relief those precepts of the Law which seemed most important to, and most threatened within, the society which spoke of them; and as the precepts of the Law become defined, so, in return, the idea that demons incite men to break this Law, and sin, adds a further dimension to their wickedness. The evils of sin are now much worse than, for example, those of disease. The arousing of sexual passion, jealousy, drunkenness, murderous rage, greed and pride, together with the encouragement of idolatry and witchcraft, loom largely in these tales of demonic ambition (see, for instance, *Testament of the Twelve Patriarchs* 23:1).

Demons, in that they are here always evil, and help to illustrate a hierarchy of evil so clearly, conjure it forward, in this literature, to the very front of the stage; and humans can, equally clearly, actively co-operate with them. In Greek society, human beings could encourage the baser inclinations of *some* of the 'daimones', as we saw. They could feed their greed with sacrifices and their lust with obscene ritual, and they might engage in trickeries called magic to manipulate the gods. In the literature with which we are concerned here, however, both demons and humans seem able to go far further. There is, in the Jewish demon, a sense of menace hard to equal in the other sources we have so far examined.

The good 'daimones' survive, however, in the form of angels, and so provide a little compensation for this plethora of wickedness. Good, unfallen, angels stand behind the evil ones of the *Book of Enoch*, for instance, and, as protecting spirits, guard the just (*Enoch*, 100:5), much like the Greek protecting 'daimon'. In the *Book of Jubilees* angels are commanded by God to teach the art of medicine to men, in order to protect them from Mastêmâ and his demons of disease; a state of affairs to be found too in the *Chaldaean Oracles* (*Book of Jubilees* 10:12–13; Lewy, 1978: 162). In *Tobit* the angel Raphael gives a prescription against blindness (*Tobit* 6:4–5). In the *Testament of the Twelve Patriarchs* we have those ranks of archangels, angels, thrones and dominions which were to become so familiar to Christians (*Testament* 3:4–9). These angelic spirit messengers of God are found widely too in the canonical Old Testament, helping man. The wicked demons, however, are absolutely everywhere. They can appear in human or animal form (casting shadows) and every sort of colour. They rub up against scholars in such numbers that they wear out the scholars' clothes. They might be conjured up by magic, though this is dangerous. They love the wilderness, ruins, water and every form of uncleanness (such as latrines) and they especially love cemeteries and darkness. They delight in delusion, especially through dreams (Yoma 75a; Berakoth 6a; Berakoth 3a–b).

For 'magic' to be thoroughly 'demonised' two streams of development must, as I suggested at the outset, come together. First of all, demons must be viewed as unambivalently wicked. We have now reached this first point. Judaism, through its own way of rescuing the 'daimones', polarised the good and bad spirits into angels and wicked demons, and illustrated man's place, responsibilities and vulnerabilities in the whole far more clearly than had been the case before. Then, secondly, 'magic' must be given a stature in the hierarchy of religious concern sufficient to command the principal part of the attention of the demons. There are many claims upon the demons' attention in that literature we have just examined, but magic is certainly prominent among them. Magic and the 'teaching of enchantments' seems to have been the first interest of the fallen angelic spirits in the *Book of Enoch*, as we have just seen, and the evils of magic were, in any case, very much present in Jewish tradition. The God of the Old Testament deeply disliked divination (*Numbers* 22:7, 23:23) and every kind of sorcery (*Deuteronomy* 18:10–13). Magic was thus proscribed, and its practitioners allotted dreadful penalties (as, for instance, in *Exodus* 223:18, a favourite of both Anglo-Saxon and later European law-makers, where sorcerers are to be killed). Also, magic was often associated with the bitterest enemies of the Jewish people, and so condemned again. The *Testament of the Twelve Patriarchs* accuses an *Egyptian* woman (who tried to seduce the patriarch Joseph) of summoning magicians and offering love potions (*Testament* 4:9). The Egyptian Pharoah, in a famous passage from

Exodus 7:8–13, confronted Moses and Aaron with magicians. The Babylonian *Talmud* tells clearly of the susceptibility of demons to magical practice (Berakoth 6a). The grounds for a decisive link between wicked demons and magic were, then, very well prepared in Jewish literature and tradition.

THE APOSTOLIC PERIOD OF CHRISTIAN HISTORY

The apostolic period, by which I mean approximately the first two and a half centuries of the history of the Christian Church (ending with the death of Origen in 254), was a period peculiarly rich in demonology. The strains felt within and without the Church as it developed as an institution, and claimed power in the supernatural realm of a widely ranging kind, told at all levels of the written record, and so, of course, upon its record of demons and magic. First of all, many of the wicked demons of Jewish tradition, complete with the hints of them we have found already in the canonical Old Testament, passed into the New. Then, the Devil emerged clearly as the leader of these demons, and as the opponent of all that Christ and his followers sought to do for the Christian God. Lastly, and as a result of these first two developments, opposing religious systems, especially those of the Pagan Roman Empire, invited description as unambiguously the work of the Devil and his evil demons, and were most enthusiastically so described.

Satan was, as I have said, already present in the Hebrew Scriptures. He was shown there intervening at crucial moments of temptation (*Job* 1–2) and judgement (*Zachariah* 3:1–3). Now, however, in the New, the Devil clashes with Christ directly at the beginning of His public ministry (*Matthew* 4:1–11) and with Christ and his apostles continually thereafter (for example *Luke* 22:31–32). Although the older, neutral, sense of the 'daimon' can be found in the New Testament (e.g. *Acts* 17:22, 25:19), demons are regarded here also overwhelmingly as wicked.

The emergence of Satan and his minions as Christ's chief antagonists in the Gospels meant that the role of the evil demons in the Christian Church was assured. There was no question here of the mere accommodation of popular superstition. All the apologists for Christianity believed as surely in the superior powers of the spirit world as their opponents and critics did. Assured too was the idea that humans could be, in some way, possessed by the evil demons, and could either co-operate actively with them, or oppose them. Passages such as those in *Matthew* 10:8 (in which Christ's apostles are urged to cast out demons), *Luke* 8:26–39 (in which Christ himself drives out the evil demons from the man they had occupied, and into the Gadarene swine) and *Luke* 9:1 and 42, (in which Christ gives his apostles total power over such demons), offered enormous scope. So did *Luke* 9:49–50. In this crucial passage the apostle John approaches Christ with a difficulty: 'Master, we saw a man casting out demons in your name, and we forbade him, because he does not follow with us.' Christ's reply is the famous: 'Do not forbid him; for he who is not against you is for you.' The problem of which person is the demons' friend and which his enemy, and so the enemy of Christ, would be rendered capable of enormous discussion and expansion as a result of this little exchange.

Christ's commission to his apostles to cast out demons was echoed in the canonical *Acts of the Apostles* (*Acts* 19:11–20) and, above all, in the Pauline writings. In a famous passage from *Ephesians* (6:11–16) the demons are represented once more as creatures infinitely superior to man:

> Put on the whole armour of God, that you may be able to stand against the wiles of the devil. For we are not contending against flesh and blood, but against the principalities, against the powers, against the world rulers of this present darkness, against the spiritual hosts of wickedness in the heavenly places. Therefore take the whole armour of God, that you may be able to withstand in the evil day.

Paul's demons are not made, like man, of flesh and blood, but of something greatly more elusive, and, though they rule the world, they inhabit the 'heavenly places' of the neoplatonic and theurgic demons. In these writings, the presence of evil demons is sometimes deduced, as it was by Plutarch, from evidence of unacceptable human behaviour (so *I Timothy* 4:1–3). In *I Corinthians* 10:20–1, pagan sacrifices are described as sacrifices made to demons. This is a canonical passage which will be used with great frequency in support of the 'demonisation' of pagan 'magic', and of the idea that magic and pagan sacrifice are much the same. Unacceptable behaviour of this sort is considered here to subordinate man to the wiles of the evil hosts; only the 'armour of God' will protect him. Lists of this kind, both of bad behaviour and of 'wiles', and the question of what exactly is meant by the 'armour of God', are again capable, like the words of *Luke* 9:49–50, of much discussion and extension. Meanwhile, the evil demons are now everywhere, as they are in Rabbinic tradition. They permeate the heavens and the earth, seeking to entrap and seduce by whatever means they can; and 'magic', widely defined, is one of the most important of their snares.

Through the Pauline writings especially, these non-Christian demons enter the Christian world with some of their Greek features still intact, as we have seen, but with a sense of menace and urgency close to that of Jewish apocalyptic. They have now, moreover, an extra dimension to them. Looming behind the amorphous armies of darkness and those of light, each with its infantry of humans, conscript and volunteer, are two named, and supernaturally equipped, arch-enemies; Satan and Christ, present on earth and supplied with both spirit-helpers and human officers. Christ's human officers, led by His apostles, are now especially alerted to the possibility of demonic wickness in all those who try to oppose them by supernatural means. Put in another way, humans who manifest objectionable traits and behaviour may now be *expected* to have demonic helpers, and the practice of 'magic', or supernatural effects by means of these demons, is set to emerge as one of their most abhorrent activities. So charged is the atmosphere now with demonic magic that Christ's Jewish opponents charge Him with being a magician (for instance in *Luke* 11:14–22), just as the apostles charge the Jews. The process of convergence between magic and demons is further assisted by the fact that the apostles seem, in the New Testament, often to be battling with real contemporary magicians, as they are, for example, in *Acts* 16:16–18 when Paul exorcises a divining demon employed by such magicians, or *Acts* 13:6–11, when Elymas the magician is blinded by Paul.

Among the most important of those who took demons and their human helpers seriously in this period were the Gnostics. Gnostic teaching evolved within the schools both of early Christianity and of neoplatonism, and it bears clear traces, too, of Jewish cultural traditions. Some of its extant writings – some of those discovered among the Nag Hammadi codices, for example, – date, it seems, from that same world within which the New Testament canon was formed. Gnostic leaders may have been publicly condemned as early as the start of the second century A.D., perhaps even in *2 Timothy* 2:16–18, and it is at least possible that texts such as the *Gospel of Thomas*, although compiled towards the mid-second century, include traditions which are far more ancient (Robinson, 1977: 117). Eventually both Christians and neoplatonists agreed to exclude the Gnostics from their company. Beginning, perhaps, with their condemnation as heretics by Irenaeus of Lyons in c.180, the hostility of active and orthodox Christian bishops ensured that such proscriptions (most notably those of Epiphanius, Archbishop of Cyprus, 367–403) were effective. This renders our own record of the original form of Gnostic teaching sadly incomplete, and makes it hard, and perhaps unprofitable, to trace the origins and map the evolution of the movement with any precision. The constituent parts and sects of Gnosticism, however, were certainly widely spread, perhaps even as far as Southern India (Conze, 1967: 665), and one preoccupation above all others appears to unite it, namely, its absolute preoccupation with evil.

Gnostic 'dualist' teachings involved the separation of the divine from the created world, and the belief that the latter was subject wholly to the demonic powers of evil. Man was thus helpless against these powers as long as he retained contact with their realm. Demonic trickery could be discerned, some thought, even at Christian baptism, at which moment the demons might receive the seal of baptism with the baptised human being, and stay living inside him or her unless expelled (Kelly, 1985: 63–8). The only way a human had of appreciating his or her plight, and of taking steps to remedy it, was through 'gnosis', or full understanding, both of it and of the nature of God. This understanding required that man face the extent of the wickedness abroad in the created world. It required that human beings know, and counter, the innermost secrets of this wickedness, this as an indispensable preface to their escape from it, and to their salvation in the knowing glorification of the divine. This singular preoccupation with evil meant that Gnostic views upon demons were set out with force – a force made arguably all the more influential (as is so often the case) by proscription. The Nag Hammadi *Apocryphon of John* offers us some sense of Gnostic teaching on demons. This has the wicked demons involved in the very act of creating man and woman, especially the four demons of pleasure, desire, grief and fear, with their attendant evils (Robinson, 1977: 115), and it shows the demonic forces as still very much active in the world. The gnostic *Testament of Truth* presents the God of the Hebrew Bible himself as a demon, and 'orthodox' Christians, therefore, as demon-worshippers.

The Gnostics and their fellow-travellers greatly assisted the process whereby magic and sorcery came to be 'demonised' in Late Antiquity. Through their very obsession with demons, and as a result of a singular irony, they themselves came to be attacked as demonic helpers, calling down 'demonisation' upon their own heads, and, with this, their condemnation as sorcerers and magicians. Thus, the demonisation of the Gnostics provided a near-perfect dress-rehearsal for the later demonisation of magic. In his *De Praescriptione Haereticorum* 43, Tertullian of Carthage (d.c. 225) was happy to add sorcery and magic to his long list of their (to him) absurd activities. The Gnostic insistence on secrecy, and the conviction of certain among them that Gnostic teachers were in possession of mysteries handed down by Christ himself to the few initiate, only compounded their offence (Tertullian, *Adversus Valentinianos* 1), and perhaps hastened the association, in orthodox episcopal eyes, of condemnable 'magic' with the occult. To the most vocal of the Christian bishops on this subject, *public* teaching, confirmed from Rome and issued clearly to the *many*, became the only guarantee of right tradition. The sheer success of the outlawing of the Gnostics encouraged the search for, and proscription of, magicians as demonic helpers even more. Thus, the ghost of Gnosticism shows through many a condemnation of magic, and helps to delineate, and so in some cases to dictate, the characteristic features of demonically asssisted magicians.

We may owe one of the most striking and well told of all the stories of condemned magic and demons which have come down to us, to the problems the orthodox Christian Church had with Gnosticism – a story, or rather set of stories, which will do an enormous amount to stimulate and encourage the wholesale demonisation of magic by the Christian church. This is the story of the battle between St.Peter, Christ's principal apostle, and the 'magus', Simon. Simon Magus first makes his appearance in *Acts* 8:9–24. According to *Acts*, Simon was a magician much revered in Samaria at the time of the apostles, and one who accepted Christian baptism. He was impressed, it seems, by the wonders the apostles performed. Simon aroused Peter's hostility, however, when he attempted to buy these powers from Peter (an exchange specifically condemned by Christ in *Matthew* 10:8). According to *Acts*, Peter took this attempt as a sign of Simon's being subject to 'the gall of bitterness, and in the bond of iniquity', and he outlawed Simon from the apostles' company. Demons are not actually mentioned here, but this condemnation from the mouth of Peter is, in later literature, more than sufficient to bring them in, in alliance with Simon the sorcerer.

The stories about the many subsequent battles between Peter and Simon Magus, stories which take this passage in *Acts* as their starting point, are hard to date exactly. The literary remains of them, however, seem to stem, for the greater part, from the late second and early third centuries AD, and to have a 'popular' flavour, in that they are written in a simple style, and are full of visual images and sensation. Foremost among them are the *Clementine Recognitions* and *Homilies* (so named because they purported to have been written by St. Clement of Rome, held to be Peter's successor) and the apocryphal *Acts of Peter, Acts of Peter and Paul* and *Passion of Peter and Paul*. These stories expand greatly upon the differences between Peter and Simon, in both office and personality, and they concentrate especially upon the victories of the former over the latter. All may, therefore, have been put together in support of certain institutional developments within the Christian Church, especially that of the emerging office of the papacy. The figure here of Simon, Peter's enemy, draws additional strength in this literature from the memory of a Gnostic Simon, also from Samaria. The account of the conflicts between Simon Magus and St. Peter may, then, have been fuelled both by Christian institutional tensions, and by the Gnostic controversy we have just outlined, together with its own organisational divisions and quarrels.

The Peter/Simon Magus literature is pre-occupied with supernatural activity to a very high degree, and one fact is clear from it. The people it addressed expected wonders from their religious leaders. Both Christian orthodoxy and its opposite required the production of these wonders; both, in short, hoped for a kind of magic. Simon Magus is represented as a master of such arts, of the arts both of illusion and real change, and this mastery, it is suggested, was the source of his prestige (although, in the Clementine literature, there is an impressive intellectual dimension to him too). Simon can (like the theurgists) make statues walk, and brazen serpents slither. He can perform shape-shifts, and make himself invisible. He can make bread of stones and compel implements to perform tasks by themselves – rather like the sorcerer's apprentice of the fairy stories. He can heap up riches and walk through fires. He can even call up the dead (*Clementine Recognitions* 2.9,12,15). But Peter too performs great wonders, wonders well outside the common run. He heals the sick and gives sight to the blind, like Christ and the other apostles; but he also offers to correct a shape-shift Simon had made (*Clementine Homilies* 18–23) and gives a dog the power of speech. Finally, and most spectacularly, Peter wins a flying display. Simon, with the help of the demons, succeeds in flying, but Peter (assisted by God's angels) brings him down to his death with a simple command (*Acts of Peter*).

The expectation of wonders from leaders was, in itself, no great thing. Moses had performed, after all, great works of wonder. So, come to that, had the magicians of Moses's great antagonist, Pharaoh, (*Exodus* 7:10–13), and so, above all, had Christ, as we saw. It is not in the fact that it *has* leaders and wonders that the Peter/Simon Magus literature stands out, but in its extraordinary concentration upon these wonders, and in its stark attribution of them. This literature makes, in short, two things plain. Supernatural power is of paramount importance, and the effects it produces are real, but there are clear distinctions between right and wrong in the use of it. Wrong use is ascribed in this literature to 'magic' and 'magicians' and evil demons; rightful to Christ's human officers, Peter above all, and to certain moral imperatives. Peter's wonders are those of God, through Christ His son, and God's angels. Simon's are those of the wicked demons. Simon's wonders were prompted by, and in turn themselves prompted, lust and greed and vain display; Peter's wonders defeated such base desires, and such unjust ambitions.

Magic and demons have, thus, a moral dimension still, but one now plainly conditioned by psychological and institutional needs of the kind mentioned at the end of the first section of this discussion. Peter objects to Simon's magic on the grounds both of his own role as paramount leader, and of Christian morality. Where his leadership is threatened, good demons, in the form of angels, will rescue him. Where his leadership is ignored, and Christian morality defective and uncorrected, evil demons will fly in to exploit the disorder:

But you who shall refuse to receive those things which are spoken by us, shall be subject in the present life to diverse demons and disorders

of sickness . . . when once they have been able, by means of opportunities afforded them, to convey themselves through base and evil
actions into the bodies of men, if they remain in them a long time
through their own negligence, because they do not seek after what is
profitable to their souls, they necessarily compel them for the future to
fulfil the desires of the demons which dwell in them. (*Clementine
Recognitions* 4.14–15; tr. Smith, 1867: 290)

Peter also uses the demons of Simon's magic to explore the problems of
Christian fear and hope, and the involvement in these of the demons:

Were I able to cause earthquakes and do all that I wish, I assure you I
would not destroy Simon and his friends (for not to destroy men am I
sent), but would make him my friend, that he might no longer, by his
slanders against my preaching the truth, hinder the salvation of many.
But if you believe me, he himself is a magician; he is a slanderer; he is
a minister of evil to them who know not the truth. Therefore he has
power to bring diseases on sinners . . . By that evil-working magician,
then, you were stricken with diseases because you revolted from God.
By me, if you believe in Him ye shall be cured; and so having had
experience that He is able, you may turn to good works, and have your
souls saved. (*Clementine Homilies* 7.11; tr. Smith, 1879: 135)

Christian thoughts about that form of fear which is destructive, and so
demonic and 'magical', and that which is salutary, and so God-given, will
become ever more relevant to the definition, and treatment, of magic.

The literature describing the battles for supremacy between Peter and
Simon Magus is a powerful instance of that convergence and collision we
have been seeking. Demons are now viewed as indubitably wicked
creatures, and 'magic' is represented as their principal activity. It would be
wrong to see this convergence as the first. There have been indications of
it before, as we have seen, and much literature is lost. There are, however,
compelling reasons for regarding the Peter/Simon Magus literature as of
fundamental importance; three above all. These are: the singular focus of
this literature upon magic and demons, the scale of its popularity and, in
particular, its presumed object. The growing organisational power of the
emergent Christian Church, and the struggles on behalf of the Roman
papacy, required, at this point, a popularised confrontation. Demons,
magic and magicians, re-configured again, offered themselves for the task.

I have said that the concept of demonic incitement might, on occasion,
rescue individuals from excessive blame and punishment. There is little
immediate sign of this in the writings we have just examined. The early
Peter/Simon Magus literature is confident and triumphalist – even a shade
vindictive. Simon comes to a very painful end. The *Clementine Recognitions*,

in particular, are responsible for an exultant Christianisation, and expansion, of that story of the fallen angels and the teaching of enchantments found in the *Book of Enoch*. In the *Recognitions*, the fallen angels taught *men* these arts:

> that demons could, by certain arts – that is, by magical invocations – be made to obey man; and so, as from a furnace and workshop of wickedness, they filled the whole world with the smoke of impiety, the light of piety being withdrawn.

This teaching was here, as in *Enoch*, one of the causes of the flood; but in the present case, Ham managed to rescue it and hand it on to one of his sons,

> Mesraim, from whom the race of the Egyptians and Babylonians and Persians are descended. Him the nations who then existed called Zoroaster, admiring him as the first author of the magic art; under whose name also many books on this subject exist . . . He attempted these things again and again until he was set on fire, and consumed by the demon himself, whom he accosted with too great importunity. (*Clementine Recognitions* 4.27; tr. Smith, 1867: 297)

The author, or authors, of the *Clementine Recognitions*, from which the above passage comes, clearly thought that this fate was fitting, and thus produced a precedent for the many later burnings of sorcerers and witches. The tale of Ham's degeneracy in matters of magic, moreover, would support a whole series of later condemnations of his supposed descendants. Illicit sexual activity was the main vice to which Ham's 'magic demon' was held to have incited him, but the way was open for many more (Friedman, 1981: 100–2). Such triumphant use of the wicked demons might legitimately call for correction, however, from within the church itself, and this correction is indeed to be found, even in later writings about the Peter-Simon Magus contest. The *Apostolic Constitutions*, for example, (credibly dated to the later fourth century, and possibly influenced by Bishop Epiphanius, hammer of the Gnostics), insist that Peter meant Simon only to be hurt. They are adamant that Peter did not mean to kill him. Thus, according to them, Simon only broke his toes in his fall (*Apostolic Constitutions* 6.9). The version of the *Acts of Peter*, known as the *Vercelli Acts*, agrees that Simon broke only his leg (James, 1924: 331–2). The *Vercelli Acts* are hard to date securely, but they too may be evidence of a later softening; one which would both review ecclesiastical penalties for magic, and, indeed, the definition of condemned magic itself. Such softenings *can*, and I think did, lead to negotiated compromises with magic, and, in Late Antiquity, to a far more sophisticated approach to the problem of magic as a whole than had been common earlier.

A further milestone on the way to the effective demonisation of magic, and perhaps to the correction, too, of some of the ways in which this was to be carried out, is to be found in the works of Justin Martyr (d.c.165 A.D.) Justin was also a believer in the message of I *Enoch*. His second *Apology* (written to the Roman Senate shortly after the accession of the Emperor Marcus Aurelius in 161 A.D.) contains a particularly instructive passage, and one which is clearly dependent, like the *Recognitions*, on I *Enoch* 6:

> God . . . committed the care of men and all things under heaven to angels whom he appointed over them. But the angels transgressed this appointment and were captivated by love of women and begat children who are those that are called demons; and besides, they afterwards subdued the human race to themselves, partly by magical writings, and partly by fears and the punishments they occasioned, and partly by teaching them to offer sacrifices, and incense, and libations, of which things they stood in need after they were enslaved by lustful passions; and among men they sowed murders, wars, adulteries, intemperate deeds and all wickedness. (2 *Apology* 5; tr. Roberts and Donaldson, 1867 ii: 75–6)

There is a connection here between the *wrong* kind of fear, and the employment of magic, a connection which is similar to that we have already found in the passage from the *Clementine Homilies*, and which a thoroughgoing history of fear, should one come be written, will, I am sure, find in much of the literature of this period. The courage of martyrs, including that of Justin Martyr himself, was in part inspired by the need to defy the fear of demonic cruelty, and to manifest the joy and hope of the new dispensation. The demonic, and with it demonic magic, came then also to be defined with reference to the quality of the fear it, and its practitioners, aroused and exploited. In his *Plea*, the second century apologist Athenagoras contributed some vivid passages on the crudity of the fears demons aroused and the need, on these grounds alone, to expose and defeat them. Demons, he says, 'hover about matter, greedy of sacrificial odours and the blood of victims'. They are:

> eager for the blood of the sacrifices and lick them . . . some castrate, as Rhea, others wound and slaughter, as Artemis: the Tauric goddess puts all strangers to death. I pass over those who lacerate with knives and scourges of bones. (Athenagoras, *Plea* chs. 26 and 27; tr. Roberts and Donaldson, 1867: 408–10)

Tertullian wrote in his own *Apology* about the violence and cruelty of the winged demons, and their, perhaps not unconnected, love of the fumes, flesh and blood of freshly sacrificed meat (*Apologeticus* 22). The Christian

Latin author Minucius Felix, writing at the turn of the second and third centuries, is a particularly good example of this type of reference and definition. In his *Octavius* he binds magic, demons, fear and the manipulation of fear, solidly together. Demons, he says, 'range to and fro, the enemies of mankind'. They lurk under the moving statues and images magicians love. They control all the arts of divination, the speaking of oracles, the flights of birds, the casting of lots. They call men away from God and towards the love of material things, and so destroy them. They feed on sacrifices, and, most importantly for our understanding of these attitudes to fear, they creep into human bodies, causing disease and

> strike terror into their minds, distort the limbs, thus driving men to do them worship, in order that, when glutted with the reek of altars or with victim beasts, they may loosen the tightened bonds and claim to have effected a cure. (*Octavius* 26–7; tr. Rendall, 1931: 396–9)

Minucius gives a good list here of those magical exercises which, in his view, supported this manipulation of fear. Such literature helped enormously in the further delineation of the demons and their magic, and in the additional elaboration of possible counters to it. Demons will seek to operate through fear, and so, then, will magicians. The opponents of such magicians will, on the other hand, transform fear into gladness.

It is right, according to this literature, to be a *bit* frightened of these demons, gorged and cruel as they are, involved as they are with magicians and sorcerers, and flitting as they do about graves and tombs and desert places (Clement of Alexandria, *Exhortation* 4; Roberts and Donaldson, 1867, i: 60). But it is very wrong to be so frightened of them as to take to sacrifices or to magical manipulators for their propitiation; to be literally scared almost to death. Those supernatural beings who operate through this sort of fear *must* be defeated by Christians, and Christians must find answers to their powers. The extremes of terror and courage involved in the stark confrontation between Devil and Christian martyr came to form one of the answers, but these confrontations were expensive in every way. They might, then, call legitimately for the comfort of compromise with some of the lesser demons, and they would come to do so. We shall attempt to explore such compromises further in the final section of this investigation. They in fact developed late – or on a public scale at least; but the reasons for them, and something of their style and shape, was being adumbrated already.

Origen (d. 254), the great Alexandrine teacher and Christian apologist, is sometimes viewed as tainted with the 'Gnostic syndrome'. Certainly Origen was extremely interested in the wicked demons, and his writings did a great deal to concentrate attention upon their works, upon the fear they inspired and, once more, upon appropriate ways of obstructing their activities. We may owe first to Origen the idea that Satan enjoyed rights over man quite justly for, at the Fall, thought Origen, man had handed himself over to the powers of evil voluntarily. This idea had a long future (Rivière, 1934). We certainly owe to him a singularly persuasive and alarming image of demonic power, whereby Satan's minions sit at the frontier between life and death and, like a species of infernal customs officer, exact Satan's dues as man tries to pass across this frontier, and into the kingdom of God (Rivière, 1924: 43–64). Origen takes one of his cues from *Luke* 12:58–9:

> And when thou goest with thy adversary to the prince, whilst thou art in the way, endeavour to be delivered from him: lest perhaps he draw thee to the judge, and the judge deliver thee to the exactor, and the exactor cast thee into prison. I say to thee, thou shalt not go out thence, until thou pay the very last mite.

This passage allows him to cast the wicked Greek guardian 'daimon' of every individual in the rôle of the adversary; that is, man's accuser before Satan (*Homilia in Lucam* 12: *PG* 13, 1829).

This last image, which allows the first decision upon man's fate to his wicked 'daimon' and then to Satan (here cast as the judge) seemingly gave the demonic world a tremendous measure of authority, and that at arguably the most frightening moment of man's existence, the point of death. It thus penetrated the very heartland of that region of fear and human insecurity already so well populated by demons. The image drew great support from the description of the ladder Jacob saw in his dream, in *Genesis* 28:12–13. Jacob's ladder in *Genesis* stretched from earth to heaven, and was occupied by angels, climbing up and down it; but it soon came to be loaded both by humans and by demons, in contention for the human souls as they climbed upwards. There are some striking surviving visual illustrations of this concept (one of the best is to be found in the ladder to heaven icon of St Catherine's monastery, Sinai), and it was adopted by many of the most notable of the later Christian apologists, among them the Christian Fathers. John Chrysostom (d. 407) puts the position vividly:

> And if it is difficult to walk by night in a road from land to land, how is it safe in the road that leads from earth to heaven? Know ye not how many demons there are in the intervening space, how many wild beasts, how many spirits of wickedness. (tr. Schaff, 1889, xiii: 371)

Cyril of Alexandria (d. 444) was still making terrifying use of this concept in the early fifth century. These demonic customs officers, he says, are greedy (like those of Plotinus and Plutarch), and they will do battle at the crossing into heaven for every due they think they can exact (Jugie, 1914: 17–21).

When sorcerers occupied themselves with death, then, either by seeking to bring it about, or by calling up, through necromancy, the spirits of the dead (and the evidence of the magical papyri alone tells us that this was one of the favourite arts of the sorcerer), the image of the greedy demons acting beyond the grave was particularly apt for use. It is by no means inconceivable, indeed, that it was formed with such uses in mind. It could certainly be a help to those who wished to outlaw all such activities in the name of true religion, and make further distinctions between helpful and unprofitable sources of fear. Thus, magical necromancy became, with the help of Origen's demons, a point of particular offence, and one with which almost no compromise at all would be possible.

Some of Origen's most trenchant views on demons, on their involve-ment in magic, and, most importantly of all, on the counters to them both, are to be found in his *Contra Celsum*. Dateable perhaps to 248, this treatise has been authoritatively described as 'the culmination of the whole apologetic movement of the second and third centuries' (Chadwick, 1965: ix), and was widely read by the Greek Fathers. In the *Contra Celsum* Origen confronts the pagan philosopher Celsus with, as he hopes, con-vincing proof of the intellectual and social respectability of Christianity. Both Origen and Celsus, apparently (we must note that for the majority of Celsus's writings we have only Origen's word) object to magic, regard secrecy as a sign of it, and view sorcerers as tricksters and illusionists, scruffy racketeers interested primarily in a fee. Both see such activities as a sign of demonic influence. They differ fundamentally, however, in their views of right access to the supernatural and, once again, in their attitudes to fear. For Celsus right access to the divine still lies through the philosophy of the pagan schools, and through stoic 'heroic' morality, including appropriate attendance upon, and sacrifices to, the pagan gods. Thus, Celsus regards Christianity as just one more of those forms of demonically inspired magic he so detests. Origen, in his defence of the Christian way, has therefore to define and distinguish that magic to which he himself objects from those Christian practices he means fiercely to defend. The *Contra Celsum* is thus of especial importance to the present enquiry.

Origen defends the supernatural claims of Christianity, quite simply, on the grounds of the clear divinity of Christ, and by means of its gentler, non-exploitative, manners and moral purposes. Christians, he says,

do not get the power which they seem to possess by means of any incantations but by the name of Jesus with the recital of the histories about Him . . . it is clear that Christians make no use of spells, but only of the name of Jesus with other words which are believed to be effective, taken from the divine scripture. (*Contra Celsum* 1.6; tr. Chadwick, 1965: 10)

Such a statement could embarrass its author, for, in the magical papyri, not to speak of patristic condemnation, there is clear evidence that such spells were used. Also, there were certainly similarities between the wonders of the theurgists and the miracles of Christ and his apostles. This fact was frequently pointed out, and we shall return to it in the final section of this discussion. Rescue came then, for Origen, in the ends for which such 'spells' were employed:

> no sorcerer uses his tricks to call the spectators to moral reformation; nor does he educate by the fear of God people who were astounded by what they saw, nor does he attempt to persuade the onlookers to live as men who will be judged by God. (*Contra Celsum* 1.68, cf. 2.51; tr. Chadwick, 1965: 63, 105–6)

Sorcerers employ them to wrong ends, Christians to rightful ones. Celsus had clearly held to the classical belief in the existence of some good 'daimones' (though not those supporting magicians), but:

> Away with Celsus' advice when he says that we ought to pray to daemons . . . those who have considered the nature of daemons and their purpose and wickedness would never desire to have their goodwill.

The 'fear of God', to Origen, is clearly quite different in quality from the fear aroused by the demons and their power to hurt (*Contra Celsum* 8.26, 35–6; tr. Chadwick, 1965: 471, 478). The former 'fear' is courageous respect, supported by the help and protection of God's angels:

> Let not Celsus scare us, then, by threatening that we shall be hurt by daemons if we slight them. For even if the daemons are slighted, they are able to do nothing to us who are devoted to the Person that is alone able to help all those who deserve it. He does no less than set His own angels over those whose lives are devoted to Him, that the opposing angels and the so-called ruler of this world who governs them may be unable to do anything against those who are dedicated to God. (*Contra Celsum* 8.36; tr. Chadwick, 1965: 479)

Here again, *wrong* magic is chiefly distinguished, for Christians, by the ever present threat of cruelty, and the total lack in it of all promise or hope of permanent protection for man. This way of distinguishing magical practice from Christian would become of prime importance to the Church of Late Antiquity.

Lastly, we may also owe to Origen the somewhat paradoxical notion that the Devil and his demons were not forever damned. This notion is both understandable and illuminating within the present context. Devil and demons alike might, thought Origen, be converted, and return to the kingdom of Christ – albeit at the end, and destruction, of the known world. The notion had its attractions – even, for a while, for certain of the Christian Fathers, such as Jerome (Duval, 1984: 471–94). It rendered the demons, even the demonic customs officers, somewhat less inexorably hostile than they had seemed before, and it made some of their activities perhaps a little less terrifying, and so, again, more amenable to compromise and conversion to Christian ways than many had thought. All of this was cheering, and so was the idea, traceable again to Origen, that the numbers of evil demons were in any case on the wane as a result of the birth of Christ and of the many battles against them Christians had already won (Origen, *Contra Celsum* 1.60, cf. *Homily on Joshua* 15.5; tr. Chadwick, 1965: 54–5), and, in particular, through the capacity of the martyrs to conquer them as their souls flew up to heaven (*Contra Celsum* 8.44; tr. Chadwick, 1965: 483–4).

In the literature of the apostolic period we have surveyed so far, there have been some forthright examples of the Christian demonisation of magic and of sorcerers. Secrecy, love of illusion and unintelligible formulae, depravity and an interest in the unclean, greed for monetary reward, and, above all, cruelty and the attempted arousing and exploitation of terror are now emerging as the signs through which the demon-assisted 'magician' might be detected. Yet there are hints in this literature, too, of a morality which might extend to a little tolerance and selection. The counters to the demons are openness, purity of life, generosity, proper reverence, peace and security, all assisted by the ministering angels (the classical good 'daimones', that is, now transformed into the servants of a single God). These angels, as the Peter/Simon Magus literature shows so clearly, may actively engage in supernatural exercises very like those the demon-magicians enjoyed, and so may certain men. The key lies, it seems, in whether these exercises support the Christian code of morality, and in security from fear.

A further genre of literature will amplify this sense of the evil demons' presence, and, in doing so, will give even more strength to the concept of the wicked demon, to the association of this demon with magic, and to man's need, with the help of the angels, of a species of good counter-magic. This literature will also enliven the discussion about acceptable institutional and moral answers to the wicked demons, and about possible compromises with some of the older ways and their practitioners. We may turn aside now to this rather different genre.

MONASTIC DEMONS

Once it came to be accepted that demons were *especially* attracted to magicians, then it also became possible to use demons as a species of trace-element, as it were, to detect a magician's presence. The tendency to ascribe magic to demons could, in other words, be turned on its head to suggest that, where there were demons, there also must be magic itself, or at least a tendency towards it. Thus, Simon Magus's enemies (and again, we have only the reports of his enemies) were able to identify him as a necromancer, or 'vulgar magician', by means of his 'proven' alliance with the demons. 'Monastic demons' are not, by their calling, primarily connected with magicians; yet they added to the sum and variety of demonic activity and so to the accumulating trace-elements of magic. They gave extra fuel to the magicians' enemies simply by adding further demonic features and demonically inspired activities to those the magicians had already, and in which they might be expected to indulge. Monastic demons were also used to give guidance towards, and perhaps act as special pleading for, specialised safeguards from fear.

The most famous, and perhaps the most engaging (and easy to read) of all Christian accounts of monastic demons is that in the mid-fourth century *Life of Antony*, now credibly attributed to Bishop Athanasius of Alexandria (296–373). The vividness with which the *Life* portrays Antony's besetting demons makes it easy to understand why it had such an enormous impact on artists. The memory of the real St Antony, too, and the admiration he inspired, were prime factors in the ready acceptance of the idea of the demon as a factor useful to monastic progress (though one must beware of assuming that the ways in which demons were portrayed here found favour with everyone).

According to the *Life*, Antony was beset by the Devil and his attendant demons from the moment he decided to renounce his property and family, and go out alone into the desert. The demons of the *Life of Antony* are still creatures of the air, like the Greek 'daimones': 'Great is the number of them in the air around us'. They are now all wicked creatures, however, with a touch of hell-fire about them (tr. Meyer, 1950: 38–9, 41). They put Antony in mind of all he had lost, and incited him to lustful thoughts (*Ibid.*: 22–4). They beat him and tried to frighten him with terrifying sounds and horrifying shapes:

They made such a din that the whole place [the desert tomb, that is, which Antony had made his home] seemed to be shaken by an earthquake. It was as though demons were breaking through the four walls of the little chamber and bursting through them in the forms of beasts and reptiles. All at once the place was filled with the phantoms of lions, bears, leopards, bulls, and of serpents, asps, and scorpions, and of wolves: and each moved according to the shape it had assumed. The lion roared, ready to spring upon him, the bull appeared about to gore him through, the serpent writhed without quite reaching him, the wolf rushed straight at him; and the noises emitted simultaneously by all the apparitions were frightful and the fury shewn was fierce. (*Ibid.*: 27–8)

They tried to tempt Antony with silver and gold, all in the vain hope of deterring him from his purpose. They shewed a marked propensity to adapt themselves to the forms of human failings:

For when they [the demons] come, they conduct themselves as they find us; and in whatever state of mind they find us, so likewise do they represent their phantoms. If they see us panic-stricken with fear, they promptly take possession like robbers who find the place unguarded. (*Ibid.*: 55–6)

Antony's demons are capable of a quite extraordinary range of feats and appearances. They can grow tall and broad. They can sing (including the *Psalms*), and they dance about a lot. They can disappear in puffs of smoke, and reappear, and they can pass through locked doors. They might even, through their superior speed and lightness, appear to foretell the future. Thus, says Antony, they misled the Greeks into believing in their oracles. Loud and irritating noises seem particularly characteristic of the presence of these demons, and often signal their coming,

when we are reading they at once repeat like an echo what we have read. When we go to bed they rouse us to prayers; and this they carry on continuously, scarcely permitting us to sleep at all . . . They talk, they raise clamor . . . They also din loudly, emit silly laughs and hiss. If no one pays any attention to them, they wail and lament as though defeated . . . the attack and appearance of the evil ones is full of confusion, accompanied by crashing, roaring and shouting: it could well be the tumult produced by rude boys and robbers. (*Ibid.*: 41–2, 43, 50)

They will always be vanquished, however, by the sign of the cross (*Ibid.*: 49). Two of Antony's visions contain echoes of Origen's demonic customs officers. In the first, demons bar the way of Antony's soul as it tries to fly to heaven, and call him to account for his acts (they are allowed, indeed, to take account, but they find nothing owing). In the second, Antony sees a vision of souls attempting to fly past a great giant (the Devil). The monster bars some of them as they fly, because they are accountable to him (*Ibid.*: 74–6).

A second important portrayal of monastic demons is that of Cassian (d.c. 432), in his *Institutes* and *Conferences*, drawn up for those sympathetic to the new monastic foundation he had established at Ménherbes, near Marseilles. Cassian pays special attention to demons in Book 7 of his *Conferences*. The soul of the monk is here shewn surrounded by numberless demonic enemies, which are, again like the 'daimones' of the Greeks, aery spirits, far lighter in substance and greater in power than human beings, yet similar to them in certain of their attributes. They are perceptive and intelligent, able to detect a monk's inner weaknesses by means of analysing his external behaviour. Thus, a monk who looks continually and anxiously through his window at the sun shows the demons how greedy he is – avidly reckoning how near is the next meal. Demons will encourage this and other failings by whatever means they can (*Conferences* 7.10–15). Each demon has his own speciality in the matter of temptation; some are good at lust, for instance, others at vain-glory. They vary their onslaughts as time, place or the state and disposition of their chosen subjects demand. Cassian also allows that the aptness of demons to specialise may lead them to be attached to particular places on earth, and that some may be more skilful than others; again, just like humans (*Ibid.* 7.17–20). There are simple demons, such as those who waylay travellers on the roads and in particular haunted places, and who mock and laugh at them, all relatively harmless; or there are truly terrifying demons who inflict real wounds. There are demons on, as it were, night shifts, and some which are particularly devoted to the hour of noon. There is the now familiar, and partly biblically inspired, assemblage of demons in animal shapes – serpents and asps and lions and scorpions (*Ibid.* 7.32–3).

Cassian, then, like Antony, presents us with a wide variety of demonic postures, abilities and possible habitations, all ready for use in the 'demonisation' of a like variety of persons, practices and shrines; and, interestingly, he also offers a form of demonic hierarchy. The feebler among the demons confront the feebler among his monks. As the individual monk progresses in the spiritual life he may, however, suffer assaults of an ever deepening intensity. Cassian, too, adds forcefully to the growing evidence that the most evil of the demons might be *especially* concerned with magic. He argues, like the *Book of Enoch* and the *Clementine Recognitions*, that the wicked Ham allowed magic to survive the flood. Cassian even tells us how. Ham learnt the magic arts from the demonically assisted, and magically adept, 'daughters of Cain'. Then, because he knew that Noah would allow no book containing such arts into the ark, he inscribed their secrets upon water resistant material, metal and stone; all to his own downfall and that of all humans who followed him in this forbidden knowledge (*Ibid.* 8.21).

Monastic demons clearly borrow many of their features from persons, places and practices already 'demonised' by Christianity. The shape-shifting and invisible demons of the *Life of Antony*, for instance, remind us of the figure of Simon Magus, and its hissing demons may well originate in the the unintelligible 'magical' words gnostics and theurgists employed, and which were called 'hissing' by Plotinus (Robinson, 1977: 20). The place-demons of Cassian recall the places of the forbidden pagan shrines. Cassian's elaborations upon the Ham story may also be an attempt to explain surviving magical inscriptions, written on silver or copper sheets, and lead *defixiones*, or cursing tablets, many of which survive now. None of this is surprising. The monastic vocation may sometimes have been precipitated by the survival of such things and their users, and the need for protection against them. Monks and demons are locked here, also, into battles characteristic of the life of the religious; over withdrawal from the family and everyday society, over the strains of incarceration in a monastic community, over the ability to live in solitude, over the deprivation of food and drink and sleep, over the celibate life, and over the need for silence (Valantasis, 1992: 47–79). The turbulence of the noisy demons of the *Life of Antony* is in direct contrast to that imperturbability which is a feature of monastic progress, and, as a characteristic, seems designed to illustrate Antony's capacity of 'being undisturbed' (Williams, 1985: 30–1). Though the descriptions of monastic demons were evidently conditioned by special needs, such demons were still a tremendous reinforcement to the demonisation of magic in Late Antiquity. Many of the characteristics we see here will come to be found both in the demons of later saints' lives and in the demons of the Fathers, especially in Augustine's accounts of demons. Indeed, Augustine was profoundly affected by the *Life of Antony*, as we shall shortly see.

And there is a deeper dimension to the influence of the monastic demons on Late Antiquity even than this. The additional flexibility of this demon, its enlarged capacity to illustrate a moral wrong and, above all, the remarkable range of forms such a demon might assume, was a superb resource for the preacher, as Athanasius doubtless saw in the case of Antony's demons (Brakke, 1995: 255–6). The differing ambitions, and weaknesses, of individual monks produced, in monk-destroying demons, an infinite ability to change and adapt to differing circumstances, allowing such demons to take on different forms, and pose ever stronger challenges as the neophyte strove to mature in the spiritual life. Monastic demons were extraordinarily supernaturally supple; they were behind very many social and moral failings. Should such failings be found by Christian leaders in the larger world, then, this literature could once more justify their ascription to demonic influence, and allow determined critics to see magic, through its trace-elements, the demons, as the root of an exceptionally wide range of social ills. It would, and, as I think, did, then allow of disciplinary action within a very broad compass indeed. Monastic literature added a tremendous potential source of energy to the hunter-down of magicians.

Thus, though the small world of the monastic community, with its exacting virtues and subtle psychological nuances, was not made for imprint upon the world at large, some of the demons described in its literature were too exciting for sections of this larger world to ignore. The variety of, and distinctions between, the multifarious demons who attacked aspiring monks would offer a remarkable array of imprints, clues and justifications, for those who sought to detect, and demonise, magic. Though the concept of the wicked demon was ready in any case for the demonisation of magic and sorcery, as we have seen, and though it had already been widely so employed, this shaping and forging of it in the fires of early monasticism was arguably crucial to its further success in the wider Christian community.

Lastly, the monastic demon also precipitated argument about the appropriate counters to demonic magic. The concept of the monastic demon helped the spiritually adept to make subtle distinctions between the truly demonic and the merely faulty, and so to allow these differences too to apply wherever demons were supposed to be active. Some of the demons of magic might be less evil than others, and so be allowed more scope. Considerations of this kind were of vital importance to the later demonisation of magic. We should note, however, that to appropriate monastic demons in broad condemnation of magic and sorcery is, in a sense, to misappropriate them, almost by sleight of hand. The use of monastic demons as a part of a broader polemic was certainly a double-edged weapon. The more demanding the monastic counters to the demons were made to be, the less inclined might many mere humans be to oppose them. Though the good monk is bound to win, the struggle will be sore (Cassian, *Conferences* 7.21). For the layman, a happy outcome is, in this literature, by no means guaranteed. Monastic demons threatened, I would suggest, to become such a weapon in the hands of certain of the fiercer Christian Fathers. Thus, they could inhibit a truly effective approach to the demonisation of 'magic', and to possibly gentler ways of dealing with the problem. Some solace lay in the counter-magic of the sign of the cross, it is true; but this might, in its turn, obstruct the development of a more nuanced approach to the place of magic as a whole. Monastic demons helped greatly to keep the idea of the wicked demons' ways with humans very much alive, to embellish them and render them capable of a multitude of disciplinary uses; but their transference into the public world of Christianity was fraught with difficulty along the way. The wise 'demoniser' of magic and sorcery would now perhaps lessen the stature of some of the monastic demons, and emphasise rather the certainty of the victory than the severity of the war. Much work remains to be done upon the approaches of the individual Fathers and preachers to the demonisation of magic.

DEMONS, MAGIC AND THE WORLD OF LATE ANTIQUITY

The large world of Late Antiquity may be distinguished from the apostolic period of Christian history in four main ways. Firstly, with the conversion of the Emperor Constantine (commonly dated 312), Christianity became the official religion of the Empire. This event furnished Christianity and its officers with protected status, offered them military power should they have need of it (perhaps for the prosecution of dissidents within the congregation) and so encouraged the state to become interested in Christian affairs. Secondly, bishops became Christianity's principal officers. Their emergence in this role had been long and toilsome, and it was certainly not uncontested now, even under Constantine and his Christian successors. The rise to power of the bishop of Rome was fraught with particular problems, as we saw from the Peter/Simon Magus literature. However, after the impetus given by the conversion of the emperor, the authority of both pope and bishops steadily increased; indeed, if we believe Ammianus Marcellinus, there was hardly a main road free of bishops, galloping to synods by means of the public post-horses (*Res gesta* 21.16,18; Rolfe, 1937–9, ii: 184–5). Thirdly, and largely as a result of these first mentioned events, the Christian Church became more thoroughly structured and organised, especially so through its monastic foundations and liturgy. Fourthly, and perhaps most importantly of all for our present purposes, some fourth century Christian emperors found it increasingly convenient to prosecute their own enemies by means of a charge of 'sorcery' and 'magic'. So, on one startling occasion (the prosecution of Priscillian in 386) did certain bishops. Prosecutions of this kind were of great significance, or so I shall shortly argue, to Late Antique Christian attitudes to demons and to magic.

There is no doubt that the concept of the wickedness of the demons, and the idea that they practised magic above all, came firmly together in this last period. The fusing of the two was in part the result of increased challenges to Christ's style of ministry, to the origins of His power, and so to the origins of that of His imperially supported friends. The association of the wicked demons with magic in this context is especially well expressed by Bishop Eusebius of Caesarea (d.c. 340) in his *Proof of the Gospel*. Eusebius argues here against unnamed, but seemingly increasingly numerous, persons who were accusing Christ Himself of sorcery. In so doing, he describes the character and activities of the contemporary sorcerer, as he saw him, presents him as one of the most loyal of the wicked demons' allies, and, of course, distinguishes all that is orthodox and proper from them both. It is worth quoting Eusebius here at some length because he puts the matter so very lucidly.

Eusebius is well aware of the Greek concept of the good demon – but he will have none of it. All demons are worthless

> from the human sacrifices connected with their rites from ancient days . . . from their deceiving of their questioners through ignorance of the future, through the many falsehoods in which they have been con-victed, sometimes directly, sometimes through the ambiguity of the oracles given, by which they have been proved over and over again to have involved their suppliants in a host of evils. And they have been before shewn to be a vile and unclean crowd from their delight in the low and lustful odes sung about them, the hymns, and recitals of myths, the improper and harmful stories. (*Demonstratio Evangelica* 5; tr. Ferrar, 1920, i: 223)

Sorcerers are the servants of these demons:

> I must again attack my opposer, and enquire if he has ever seen or heard of sorcerers and enchanters doing their sorcery without libations, incense, and the invocation and presence of daemons.

Christians must oppose them to the utmost of their power, as, of course, Christ Himself did:

> It must be clear even to the blind that we who follow Jesus are wholly opposed to such agencies, and would rather sacrifice our soul to death than an offering to the daemons, yea, would sooner depart from life than remain alive under the tyranny of evil demons.

The works of the evil agencies are set out in the course of the argument: 'low' incantations, divination in all of its aspects (prophecy, oracles, birds, entrails, dreams, omens or any sort of sign) and, above all (and much as in the earlier period), the moral standing of the sorcerer:

> A sorcerer, being truly unholy and vile in his nature, dealing with things forbidden and unholy, always acts for the sake of base and sordid gain . . . Once more, sorcerers and real charlatans devote themselves to the forbidden and the unholy in order to pursue vile and unlawful pleasures, with the object of ruining women by magic, and seducing them to their own desires . . . The sorcerer again and the true charlatan courts notoriety and ostentation in all his enterprises and actions, and always makes a boast of knowing more and having more than other people. (*Ibid*. 3.6; tr. Ferrar, 1920: 144, 146)

Here we have that full conflation of wicked demons, magic, and particular kinds of immorality, (the former leading to the latter and, arguably, its prime source), that we saw predicated in such literature as the *Book of Enoch*. We might note, in passing, how well monks are preserved from sharing in the distinguishing marks of the sorcerer, as they are set out here. Monks manifestly do not work for gain, or upon women, or court notoriety, or boast of having more than other people. Research is again badly needed into the relationship between the encouragement of monasticism and the prosecution and suppression of sorcery and magic.

Eusebius had many friends and followers in his description of the associations between magic and the demons. The connection is particularly well made in a popular (perhaps North Italian) late fourth/early fifth century commentary on the *Song of Songs* by one Apponius. Commenting on chapter 4:8, 'from the mountains of the leopards' Apponius points out how wicked demons capture men as leopards capture less wily animals. They do it by leaping out of their mountain dens and eating them up. So do demons devour men's minds through magical incantations, 'maleficia' of all kinds, augury, astrology, 'matheism', predictions from the cries and flights of birds, and from entrails, and the scrutiny of shoulder blades (Vregille and Neyrand, 1986: 159).

Of all the Christian Fathers, St.Augustine of Hippo made the most outspoken use of demons and their connection with magic. Augustine too was concerned to rescue Christ from the charge of being a magician, as in his *Contra Faustum* 29, for instance. This charge does much incidentally to demonstrate how close to magic some Christian churchmen may have drawn in this late period. We shall return to such closenesses in the final section of this discussion. Augustine expresses his views upon demons and magic in very many of his writings (Rivière, 1924: 58–9), but two of them stand out; the slight treatise *On the Divination of Demons* and the immense work *The City of God* (in Book 10 of which, as we saw, Augustine discussed Porphyry's ideas about demonic magic).

The demons of Augustine are still possessed of the now familiar aery bodies of the Greek 'daimones', their capacities and changeability, and their consequent superiority over man:

The nature of demons is such that, through the sense perception belonging to the aerial body, they readily surpass the perception possessed by earthly bodies, and in speed, too, because of the superior mobility of the aerial body, they incomparably excel not only the movements of men and of beasts but even the flights of birds . . . Moreover, how effective is the element of air, in which their bodies surpass, to produce invisibly many visible results, to move, to change, and to overthrow is too long a story to set forth now. (*The Divination of Demons* 3.7 and 4.8; tr. Deferrari, 1955: 426, 429)

Despite this disclaimer, Augustine does eventually set forth a very great deal indeed, and in so doing renders demons capable of seemingly every kind of supernatural activity. He recounts the description Apuleius had given of demons in the *De Deo Socratis* (*City of God* 8, 14–19) but adds his own. They may be lighter than man, and faster, and live in the air, but they are not superior to him, for they are subject to the very passions 'true religion' requires and helps man to renounce (*Ibid.* 8.17). Belief in the fall of Lucifer and his minions, and elaboration of the ways in which man might mount up again to grace, allowed Augustine free rein in his description of these demons as wholly wicked:

> we can by no means accept the theory which Apuleius does his best to prove . . ., namely, that demons are situated midway between gods and men to serve as intermediaries and interpreters, that is to carry our petitions from earth, and to bring back help from the gods. On the contrary we should believe that they are spirits fanatically bent on doing harm, completely at odds with justice, swollen with pride, green with envy and well practised in deceit, who live, it is true, in our air, but do so because they were cast out from the lofty regions of the higher heavens and were condemned in the beginning to dwell in this region, which is, as it were, a prison appropriate to their nature, in just punishment for a transgression from which there is no retreat. (*Ibid.* 8.22; tr. Wiesen, 1968: 100–1)

For man, however, there is a retreat; he might remain within the city of the Christian God.

The *On the Divination of Demons* was concerned primarily to explain how it was that a pagan soothsayer had managed to predict the downfall of the Temple of Serapis in 391. For Augustine, the explanation lay in the fact that the soothsayer was in league with wicked demons, as all such soothsayers are – demons who may, of their aery nature, see further than humans, though always with Divine permission. Such demons might actually possess a human being, inserting their own bodies into his or hers, and permeating his or her thoughts, no matter whether they are waking or sleeping ones (*Divination of Demons* 5.9). In the *City of God* Augustine pursues this theme, again especially with an eye to 'demonic' intervention in the magical arts, and to the arts of divination above all. He moves directly from his castigation of all demons for their lack of 'true religion' to their characterisation as experts in magic. Apuleius's petition-bearing demons in fact now:

cherish 'the thousand arts of injuring' [*Aeneid* 7.338] that the magicians practise in their sorceries and that innocence detests . . . all the miracles performed by magicians, whom he [Apuleius] rightly judges to be worthy of condemnation, are accomplished by the teachings and the actions of the demons. (*City of God* 8.18,19; tr. Wiesen, 1968, iii: 82–3, 88–9)

Again:

demons take pleasure not only in things that good and prudent men loathe and condemn – namely impious, shameful and wicked stories concocted by poets, not about some human being or other but about the gods themselves – but also in the criminal and punishable violation of the law by magic acts. (*Ibid.* 9.1; tr. Wiesen, 1968, iii: 150–1)

Augustine's clear discussion of the demons of the ancient world, his isolation of these demons as evil and his association of their evil powers with magic and sorcery, rendered his works overwhelmingly important in all condemnations of magic as demonic. Sorcery and magic are, in these writings, undoubtedly the *prime* activities of the wicked demons. This triumphant combination had long been prepared for in the literature, as we have seen, and it was certainly in part dependent upon literary tradition. It may be possible now, however, to offer for it explanations which are in advance of those of simple linear descent, or of those of an increased incidence of magical practices. These different explanations are important here, for they are intimately associated with that concept of the demon in his role as scapegoat, and way of escape for man, mentioned at the end of the very first section of the discussion. They also affect, as I think, that anxiety for the redefinition of pagan magic which colours the world of Late Antiquity.

It is possible, in short, that Augustine's pointed descriptions of magicians as the tools of demons betoken a deliberate preference, on the part of the Christian Fathers and Doctors, for 'demonisation' over other sorts of attack on magic. It is possible, too, that this preference brings with it an urgent need to compromise with some of the pagan ways and to preserve some of their practitioners. The demonisation of magic in the world of Late Antiquity may be then, in some of its aspects, less a direct development, conditioned both by the literature and an inherent distaste for different religious practitioners on the part of Christians, than an expedient adopted in response, not directly to the literature or the distaste, but to the particular circumstances of the time.

In a seminal article, written over twenty five years ago now, Peter Brown drew attention to a seemingly greatly increased number of prosecutions for magic in Late Antiquity; a development clearly traceable to the fourth and fifth centuries (Brown, 1970: 17–45). Dissatisfied with the earlier explanations which had been offered for this development (explanations which linked it to a real growth of magical practice), he looked for – and found – another. Emperors, he argued, who could depend upon their servants, and who were suspicious of an aristocracy of a longer lineage and greater confidence than their own, were the true source of these prosecutions, not an increase in magic itself. Certain fourth century emperors came to realise that they might remove their enemies, real or imagined, through a charge of sorcery. The objective of such accusations of magic, then, was less the elimination of magic as such, than the discomfiture of competitors for power, perhaps before they became political conspirators. Fourth-century accusations of sorcery

> mark a stage of conflict on the way to a greater definition of the secular governing class of the Eastern Empire as an aristocracy of service, formed under an emperor by divine right. (*Ibid.*: 23)

Magic had always been a source of fear in the classical pagan world, and had been savagely proscribed by its emperors – by Augustus, for instance (Rolfe, 1951: 170). Apuleius, one of our main transmitters of the Platonic view of 'daimon', was in fact (unsuccessfully) prosecuted for it in the second century A.D. He was supposed to have secured his rich wife by this means, and was charged with magic by a competitor for her fortune (*Apologia* 47).

Interestingly, Augustine himself defends Apuleius hotly from this charge (*Epistulae* 138 to Marcellinus). There may have been far more prosecutions for magic in these early centuries A.D. than those for which we now have evidence, and anxieties about magic and its penalties, legal and supernatural, may have done much to reinforce that obstinate retention of pagan sacrifice so objectionable to Christians, and the cause of so much martyrdom. It does seem to be true, however, that direct, and successful, prosecutions for magic mounted to 'flash-point' in the mid-fourth century (Brown, 1970: 20). The 'divine right' mentioned above was held now to spring, of course, from Christianity, and the Christian emperors' enemies tended now to be the pagan aristocracy.

There are three main sources from which we may gain information about the Late-Imperial prosecutions for magic. The first is the history of the years 96–378 A.D. by Ammianus Marcellinus (d. after 391) The second is the *Autobiography* of the pagan Libanius of Antioch (d. after 393), and the third is the monumental collection of constitutions known as the *Theodosian Code*, a collection ordered to be put together by the Emperor Theodosius II and promulgated in 438. These sources are obviously very different, but in this matter each supports the other. Ammianus observed imperial anxieties at particularly close hand. He produces numerous accounts of fourth century prosecutions for 'magic'. Under Constantius and Gallus,

> if anyone consulted a soothsayer about the squeaking of a field mouse, the meeting of a weasel on the way, or any like portent, or used some old wife's charm to relieve pain (a thing even medical authority allows), he was indicted (from what source he could not guess), was haled into court, and suffered death as the penalty. (*Res Gestae* 16.8.2; tr. Rolfe, 1937–9, iii: 232–3)

Again:

> If anyone wore on his neck an amulet against the quartan ague or any other complaint, or was accused by the testimony of the evil-disposed of passing by a grave in the evening, like a magician who gathers the horrors of tombs and the vain plays of wandering souls, he was condemned to capital punishment. (*Ibid.* 19.12.14; tr. Rolfe, 1937–9, i: 540–1 [emended translation])

Under the Emperor Valens persons were, says Ammianus, framed shamelessly. The imperial officers introduced forbidden substances into their houses – forbidden substances such as 'old-wives incantations or unbecoming love-potions'. The victims were then executed for magic (*Ibid.* 29.2.3; tr. Rolfe, 1937–9, iii: 216–17). The credibility of the persons making such charges seems not to have mattered one bit (*Ibid.* 29.1.42). Even Bishop Athanasius of Alexandria himself, author of the *Life of Antony*, and dweller, as we have seen, upon the prevalence and powers of the evil demons, fell victim for a time to such suspicions and, almost, to such drastic and effective strategies (*Ibid.* 15.7.7–10). Libanius was very nearly prosecuted for consulting a soothsayer about a headache (Norman, 1965: 98–9; see also 30–1 and 38–43). The *Theodosian Code* is full of prescriptions supposedly justifying such prosecutions – yet one should mark immediately how imprecise are the definitions of 'magic' or 'sorcerer', and how much rests upon an assumption that they must all be wicked (see, for instance, 9.16).

Three points should be made about persecution through prosecution of this type, points deeply relevant to our understanding of the association of magic and demons by Late Antique Christian spokesmen. Firstly, it was arbitrary in operation, lacking all but the most token of legal forms. Secondly, it was founded on fear and demanded at least torture, and often death, as penalties. Valentinian, Valens and Gratian denied the Easter release from prison to magicians, ranging them alongside murderers and adulterers (*Ibid.* 9.38.3–4). Constantius added a further incentive to aid in their conviction. He declared the property of magicians forfeit, and thus, presumably, capable of being reassigned to informers (*Ibid.*

9.42.4). Thirdly, 'magic' was an extremely vague term, capable of embracing a great number of distinct activities. From Ammianus and the *Code* together we may distil divination and astrology (when practised outside imperial control), the presenting of petitions at pagan shrines, the owning of 'secret' books, the wearing of amulets, necromancy, incantations, the use of 'occult' (perhaps foreign) words and characters, and the making of love-potions (*Ibid.* 19.12.3–13; Rolfe, 1937–9, i: 534–41). Used for such ends as the emperors appear to have used it, it was, of course, not in the imperial interest closely to define, and so confine, magic.

There is a particular background, then, to that convergence of magic and the evil demons which took place in Late Antiquity, and one which needs fully to be understood, not least because it may differentiate this style of demonisation from many later ones. It is a truism to say that demonisation means discredit, once demons are recognised as invariably wicked; but the demonisation of magic we see in action here was by no means a simple matter of the attacking of magic wholesale by means of the wicked demons. Instead, this style gave some members of the Christian Church a chance to act protectively towards the magician-victim and so, perhaps, to gain friends and converts. Demons could be *exorcised* by Christian exorcists, as we shall see, the magicians they possessed could be re-educated and perhaps converted, and monasticism, in particular, could support and encourage the battle against a whole range of demons, as we have seen already. The 'demonisation' of their practices, then, put magicians in Christian hands, and subjected them to quite different kinds of discipline, many of them (and the monastic one perhaps especially) more humane and more responsive to time and circumstance than the imperial alternatives.

The penalties prescribed by the Christian church for magic certainly stopped short of the imperial ones. The so-called *Canones Apostolorum* 28, thought to record first century practice, forbade even beating as a punishment, even for 'infideles' – this on the interesting ground that it encouraged the wrong sort of fear (*Canones Apostolorum* 28; Mansi, i: 53). We noticed above the different account of the end of Simon Magus given by the later fourth century *Apostolic Constitutions*: Peter would not have him killed. A 513 council of Ancyra (canon 23) urged that confession, followed by a five-year penance, was the proper punishment for

> Augurers and takers of auspices, or those who divined in any way (for example, through dreams), or who taught men to enquire into anything through the magical arts. (Ancyra, 23; Mansi, ii: 534)

Ammianus, himself no Christian, lets slip the fact that the Christians mourned the cruelties of Valentinian, that the Pope, and the priest Liberius, declined to support Constantius's accusations against Athanasius, and that a charioteer, accused of sending his son to be instructed by a magician, tried to take refuge from the death penalty in a Christian church (27.7.5; 15.7.10; 26.3.3; Rolfe, 1937–9, iii, i, ii: 47, 164–5, 580–3). The Spanish bishops who consigned Priscillian to the imperial court, and so to death for sorcery, were condemned both by St. Ambrose and St. Martin, and were exiled for their pains (Chadwick 1976: 78, 129, 148). Ambrose was deeply interested in exorcism, and in Christian penance, complete with the time and disciplines it required (Gryson, 1968: 275–91). St. Augustine himself was evidently concerned to defend the power the Christian bishop had to interevene in, and moderate, secular styles of punishment (Raikas, 1990: 477–8). In his *Oration*, Libanius himself gave evidence of the, to him, somewhat bewildering level of Christian forbearance which could be encountered:

> they might expect more success in doing away with sacrifices if they did away with some individuals who had performed them. But it is not their way, they will say, to hand a man over to execution, even though he be guilty of the most heinous crime. (*Oration* 30.19–20; tr. Norman, 1977, ii: 118–19)

When Christians ascribed magic to demons in this last period, it is undoubtedly true, as we have seen, that they drew upon a very long legacy indeed. It is true too that this legacy was an essential part of all they attempted now. The very richness of the legacy, however, allowed them to draw upon it in many and varied ways, and one of the objects of the demonisation of magic in Late Antiquity seems indeed to have been the offering of a means of escape, for some of the practitioners of magic, from the attacks of quite different agencies, and the proferring of asylum within the Christian Church. Since many of the most articulate of the Late Antique Christian spokesmen on magic, demons, and the association of the two, lived and wrote precisely in this period, this state of affairs is vital to our proper appreciation of their words on the matter, and may indeed, allow us many fresh thoughts about them. The juridical and penitential aspects of 'demonisation' would richly reward further study.

It would be foolish to suppose that protectiveness of this kind was the only motive for the demonisation of magic in Late Antiquity. 'Demonisation' then, as now in some quarters, was an excellent means of condemnation with a touch of salutary fear, and the Scriptures had no liking for sorcery, as we have already seen. The message of Christ, however, added a different dimension to prosecution for wrong, wrongful magic included as may be seen clearly in, for instance, St Augustine's second letter to Januarius (*Epistulae* 55). The age of Christ's grace and mercy was now to replace the literal observance of the Law, and hope was at least supposed to replace fear. Fear, says Augustine squarely, has nothing to do with justice (*City of God* 10.10). Thus, now, in the Age of Grace, wrongful prosecutions for wrongful magic surely deserved the attention of Christian pastors. Peter Brown himself led us almost to this same conclusion. Christianity, he said,

> mobilised a current drift, in the Late Antique world, towards explanations of misfortune through suprahuman agencies in such a way as to bypass the human agent. (Brown, 1970: 28)

Here, I have simply added another level of interpretation, namely, that, through emphasising the invasiveness and power of demons in matters of magic, Christianity may have meant to bypass the punishments for magic recommended by *imperial* human agents, and so save many of the accused, even though a few of them may truly have been magicians.

Motives of this kind cast an important extra light upon that process of convergence between magic and the works of the wicked demons we have tried, here, to follow. Belief in the demons, deftly understood, might achieve unexpected results. The convergence of magic and demons, and even the occasional rescue of some of the practitioners of magic by means of the demons, could be a creative and rewarding one in other ways too, as we shall now see.

CHRISTIAN REDEFINITIONS OF PAGAN RELIGIONS

All of these shapes and kinds of demons bore upon the processes of Christian redefinition. So did the varying attitudes to demons, to magic and to their uses we have tried here to follow. The processes of redefinition were, therefore, exceedingly intricate ones. We may, however, discern three levels of activity within them. One was preoccupied with the now familiar problem of fear. Another laid a particular emphasis upon Christian victory over the demons, a victory whose facets were as multifarious as the demons themselves, and was sometimes brought about with the demons' own weapons. A final one turned aside from victory towards conciliation, compromise and, where possible, conversion. We may take the three in order, although, of course, they act one on another, and none can operate exclusively.

The last discussion has recalled to mind that Christian distinction between proper and improper fear to which we have frequently referred. It was not merely that some persons, and notably the emperors just mentioned, misused the emotion of fear. Demons, and certain kinds of demonic magic themselves, according to the Christian argument, terrified human beings, and robbed them of their true humanity. For Eusebius, for instance, the badge of demonic sorcery was 'cruelty, inhumanity and real viciousness' and its interest in the frightening:

> lifeless matter and dusky caves . . . crows, hawks and other birds . . . the movements of water, the inspection of entrails, the blood of hateful and ugly monsters . . . the bodies of creeping things, like snakes and weasels. (Eusebius of Caesarea, *Proof of the Gospel* 5; tr. Ferrar, 1920: 227, 229)

Even if some such persons escaped secular punishment through the excuse of demonic influence, then, the problems posed by the existence of the demons themselves and, above all, their fearful influence upon humans would still demand urgent attention. Christianity had now to provide this attention, and offer effective counters to the terrors the demons inspired.

This double need for, and double way of, dealing with demonically directed magic, accounts for most of the Christian redefinitions of pagan religions we shall explore in this last section, and for the intricacies of the Christian response. Firstly, the demons and their manipulators must be vanquished in as thorough a way as possible, and the fear they aroused dispelled. Then their victims, now rescued, must be helped as well as they could be helped to conversion and reform. The double need was met in two main ways. In the first place, the evil demons were described as soundly beaten by the superior supernatural powers Christianity offered to all; secondly, and as a result of operations requiring a far greater degree of subtlety than the first form of response, those elements of pagan magic which were perceived to be the most important and most assimilable were drawn into Christian territory, complete with their lesser 'daimones'. These energies were then retranslated and absorbed. Through this last process, the less offensive of the pagan ways came to be preserved; this in the hope that demonic magic, redefined, might both drive the distinction between the old and new religions home with an extra force, and, perhaps, win over some of the adherents of the old.

Should there *exist*, after all, non-Christian magic which was amenable to non-fearful Christian use, and which could therefore be of assistance in controlling from the inside, so to speak, the worst of the wicked demons, then this would offer an enormous resource for conversion to Christianity. To the advantages of custom and familiarity with the older religions might now be added the attractions of the new faith doubly illuminated by the familiarities, yet distinctions, between the old and the new. It will be argued here that amenable magic of this kind did exist, and that many of the redefinitions of pagan magic we shall trace (and there are a great many once we come to look for them) did not, as it were, simply 'trickle down' into Christianity. They were a consequence both of this great weight of belief in, and great need to defeat, the wicked demons, and of the recognition on the part of certain Christian pastors that Christianity needed as many alluring counters to truly evil demonic magic as it could find; including, perhaps, some of the older good 'daimones'. Adaptable forms of pagan magical practice were thus sought out, adopted and even advocated as a result of the clear advantages the linking of 'daimones' and supernatural power offered, through a different understanding of fear, to the purposes of conversion. Christianity made it clear that it could always vanquish the wicked demons in a simple battle of power, but it showed that it might also compel some of them to hand over their best armaments, and even soldiers, to their enemies.

There is much to be said for the idea that, as it progressed in the pagan world, Christianity owed most its first successes to its clear victories over the demons. The tremendous variety of demonic powers we have surveyed, furthermore, gave Christians a correspondingly wide range of opportunity for the manifestation of their might. The most obvious example of the triumphant capture and re-use of demonic armaments is that of the retention of the old good 'daimones', and their redefinition as angels. Angels have already flitted in and out of the picture in the course of the discussion. They were inseparable from the rise, first of the Jewish and then of the Christian religions. The Old Testament mentions them frequently as messengers of God (in the Greek 'angelos', hence the Latin 'angelus'), engaged in the salvation of man. They appear in *Genesis*, (for example, *Genesis* 19:1–17), and continue through the *Exodus* story, and the crossing of the Red Sea (*Exodus* 14:19). Good, unfallen, angels stand behind the fallen ones of such books as the *Book of Enoch*, and guard the way back into paradise (*Genesis* 3:24). The six-winged Seraphim of *Isaiah* 6:2 provide a basis for the idea that angels as a whole are winged and so, like the good 'daimones', are inhabitants of the upper air. Tertullian adopted this idea with some enthusiasm in chapter 22 of his *Apology*. In the New Testament, angels minister to Christ after the Devil has tried, and failed, to tempt Him (*Matthew* 4:11). Angels assist, after His passion, in Christ's ascension into heaven (1 *Timothy* 3:16), and so in the descent of the Holy Spirit upon the apostles (*John* 16:7). Thus, these new good 'daimones' are now clearly set as overwhelmingly forceful counters to the bad.

Athenagoras and Origen would, like Apuleius, allow that these good 'daimones' might have care of particular parts of the world, a little as the old ones did (Athenagoras, *Plea* 24; Origen, *Contra Celsum* 8.31), and there are many Late Antique Christian testimonies to the position, majesty and power of the angels in the new dispensation. Augustine, most notably, accepts the angels as wholly fitting replacements for Plato's good 'daimones' (provided, of course, that they are revered not for themselves, but as messengers of God) (*City of God* 9.21–3 and 10,1–3). He puts the matter with a characteristic bluntness, sweeping aside the worries of Apuleius. Demons, he says,

certainly cannot be friends at all of the good gods whom we call holy angels and rational creatures dwelling in the holy precincts of heaven 'whether they be thrones, or dominions or principalities or powers' [*Colossians* 1:16], from whom they are as far removed in the feelings that rule their heart as is vice from virtue and malice from goodwill . . . So there is no need at all to take a roundabout route through the fancied mediation of demons in order to secure the good offices of the gods, or rather of good angels; the right way is through resembling them in good will, which enables us to be with them, to live with them, and to worship with them the God they worship, even if we cannot see them with the eyes of the flesh.' (*Ibid.* 8.24–5; tr. Wiesen, 1968, xxx: 126–9)

Augustine's trenchant views on angels as, after God, the most effective of the counters to demons human beings had, were vital in establishing confidence in angelic power. Jerome was active in promulgating the idea that each Christian person had a guardian angel, but only a good one; an interesting Christian modification of the Greek concept of each man's own 'daimon', and one surely connnected with the Christian attitude to fear (*PL* 26: 135).

This acceptance of the good 'daimones' as angels, supernatural powers aligned against the wicked demons and helpers in Christ's ascension into heaven and man's salvation there, will allow the angels to play an exceedingly prominent part in further processes. Indeed, the redefined good 'daimones' of the air, and the sense of security they engendered, were essential to the other redifinitions of pagan magic. Good angels, under God, might do anything the demons could do, and far more. They might licence appropriate forms of magic, then, redefined as miracle – a wonder of God, not the devil. They had done this, says Augustine, at spectacular moments in the past. One of the most famous Old Testament stories of opposition to the old magic by the new is the story, in *Exodus* 7:8–13, of the battle between Moses, Aaron, and the magicians of Pharaoh. Aaron, challenged by Pharaoh to 'show signs', changed his rod into a serpent. Pharaoh's magicians did the same in response; but Aaron's serpents ate theirs up. The magicians of Pharaoh were therefore confounded by an activity which was, at root, no more than a superior display of magic. This miraculous form of magic was the work of angels, or so Augustine insists:

For they [Pharaoh's magicians] worked their deeds by the sorceries and magic incantations to which the bad angels, that is demons, have devoted themselves. But Moses, as much more powerful as more righteous, in the name of God who made heaven and earth, with angels as his ministers, overcame them with ease. (*City of God* 10.8; tr. Wiesen, 1968, iii: 282–3)

Angels here employ a species of counter-magic, re-using the older kind of magic to manifest the greater power of the new.

The power of these new angelic 'daimones', the first and most striking of the Christian redefinitions of pagan magic we have, will, together with the concept of the miracle, allow of many future ones, as we shall see. Origen stressed how the demons 'lost their strength and became weak' at Christ's birth. He even suggested that the Magi were prompted to follow the star because, with the birth of Christ, their own magic had ceased to work. The enfeebled demons were now no longer any use to them, being overthrown 'by the angels who visited the earthly region on account of the birth of Jesus'. It was an angel, furthermore, who warned them not to return to Herod (and to their death) but to take a different route to their homeland (*Contra Celsum* 1.60; tr. Chadwick, 1965: 54–5). The Magi thus survived as striking examples of, and precedents for, the possibility of a new magic aided by the angels. Angels could now, therefore, be expected to assist in similar salvations in history. They may illuminate, and so legitimate, acceptable Christian kinds of magi and of magic.

At Christ's death, the defeat of the older magic was, of course, considered absolute and complete. St Athanasius, interested as he clearly was in the wicked demons, puts the position particularly well in his *De Incarnatione Verbi*:

> The Lord came to overthrow the devil, purify the air, and open for us the way up to heaven . . . This had to be effected by death, and by what other death would these things have been accomplished save by that which takes place in the air, I mean the cross? For only he who expires on the cross dies in the air. Thus it was right for the Lord to endure it. For being raised up in this way he purified the air from the wiles of the devil and all the demons. (26; tr. Thomson, 1971: 195–7)

We have seen how their abhorrence of pagan sacrifice allowed Christians to extend the range of the wicked demons into sacrifice, and to describe pagan sacrifice as perhaps the most prominent and objectionable of all of the pagans' magical activities. Yet the Christian counter to this was also a sacrifice, and stressed as such. Christ, by His own sacrifice, redeemed all other sacrifices and, with the help of the angels, drove out the demons and the terrors they induced; but Christ's sacrifice was still, after all, a blood sacrifice, and it was this aspect of it, its capacity, that is, both to outdo and to echo the pagan sacrifices, which the early apologists most liked to emphasise. Among the writings attributed to Justin Martyr, for example, there is an account of the passion of Christ filled with reminiscences of that older magic and those sacrifices we earlier saw so very thoroughly demonised. Justin comments upon a verse in *Leviticus* 14:43:

> And for the purification thereof he shall take two sparrows, and cedar wood, and scarlet, and hyssop.

He does so in these words:

> By that which took place in the running water, in which the wood and the hyssop and the scarlet were dipped, is set forth the bloody passion of Christ on the cross for the salvation of those who are sprinkled with the spirit, and the water, and the blood. (Roberts and Donaldson, 1867, ii: 357)

This is only one of the more vivid of the many passages in the writings of the Apologists and Fathers which echo the forms of the old magical sacrifices in the new. Again, Augustine puts the position particularly clearly in his *City of God*:

> this redeemed city . . . is offered to God as a universal sacrifice through the High Priest who in his passion offered even himself for us in the shape of a slave [*Philippians* 2:7] that we might be the body of so great a head. For it was this shape that he offered, in this that he was offered, because in consequence of this he is mediator, in this he is priest, in this he is sacrifice . . . And this sacrifice the Church continually celebrates in the rite of the altar well known to the faithful, in which it is made clear to her that in her offering she herself is offered to God. (*City of God* 10.6; tr. Wiesen, 1968, iii: 274–7)

This passage is full of pagan echoes redefined. Athanasius indicates how near the two kinds of sacrifice had drawn when he once more defends Christ against the charge of being just another magician:

> if his cross has won the victory over all magic altogether and even over its very name, then it should be clear that the saviour is not a magician, from whom even those demons invoked by other magicians flee as from their master. (*De Incarnatione Verbi* 48; tr. Thomson, 1971: 186–7)

Augustine's mention of the Eucharistic sacrifice – another rich source of charges of magic against Christians (Smith, 1978: 66) – brings to mind the further possibility that even the altar boys, which were so familiar a presence at the Mass, may have been echoes of the boy-mediums of older sacrificial rites (*PGM* V 1–53 and VII 540–78).

The sacrifices of the Christian Martyrs drove the point home even harder, and by means of the same juxtaposition of clear resemblances, yet even clearer differences between pagan and Christian kinds of sacrifice. Many of the accounts of sacrifial martyrdom were in fact composed in the face of the need to counter and compensate for the supernatural effects expected of pagan sacrifice, and some of the deaths themselves may have been, indeed, inspired by this same need. Descriptions of the sufferings of the early martyrs, and later eulogies at their tombs, are filled with the defeat of the demons through the pouring out of sacrificial blood:

> The trophies are exhibited to heaven; the tomb drips with blood; the marks of the bleeding triumph appear . . . Let the triumphant victims take their place where Christ is the victim. Let Him be above the altar who suffered for all; let them be beneath the altar who were redeemed by His suffering . . . Now, you have also heard the demons crying out and admitting to the martyrs that they cannot bear their punishment . . . Yet I do not make use of the demons as a support for the martyrs. Their holy suffering is proved by its benefits . . . The proof which their blood sends forth is stronger, for blood has a piercing voice which reaches from earth to heaven . . . Here blood cries out by disclosing its colour; blood cries out by publishing its work; blood cries out by the triumph of its suffering.

So writes St. Ambrose, in his letter about the discovery of the tombs of Sts. Gervasius and Protasius at Milan (*Ep.* 61; tr. Beyenka, 1954: 380–4). Ambrose here gives spectacular witness to the closeness of the pagan world to the Christians of Late Antiquity, and to the need the church had of its energies, suitably retranslated. His careful separation of demonic, thus terrifying, suffering, from the pain, yet surpassing joy, of Christian martyrdom is worth special note, and so is his mention of martyrdom's trophies. The latter brings to mind the fact that the magic of the pagan world was often used to procure victory; in war, in horse and chariot races in the circus, in athletic contests and the like. The *Theodosian Code* specifically mentions the magical interests of charioteers, anxious to win (9.16.11). Augustine himself was invited to seek victory in a poetry contest through the help of a wizard and pagan sacrifice:

> he [the wizard] was to kill certain living creatures in those his sacrifices, and by these honours to invite the devils to favour me. (*Confessions* 4.2; tr. Watts, 1968, ii: 150–1)

Augustine resisted, but he had felt the pressure and temptation. The idea that a different kind of sacrifice would ensure a far greater victory gains a particular significance when set within this context, and may have been framed specifically to do so. The Christian martyrs Perpetua and Felicity were actually killed during the gladiatorial contests at the games in Carthage, and Perpetua describes herself as being rubbed with oil, like the pagan athletes, in preparation for her contest with, and victory over, the Devil (here portrayed as an Egyptian, in recollection, perhaps, of the magician-enemies of the Jews) (*Passion of Saints Perpetua and Felicity* 10). The *Passion* also draws attention to the rejection of fear implicit in the Christian idea of sacrifice, and the substitution of fear by joy:

> Now dawned the day of their victory, and they went forth from the prison into the amphitheatre cheerful and bright of countenance; if they trembled at all, it was for joy, not for fear. (*Ibid.* 18; tr. Shewring, 1931: 37)

Augustine preached at least three sermons on the sufferings of Felicity and Perpetua, and returned there to the themes of sacrifice for battle victory and, especially, to the contrast between the cruelties of the old religion and the charity of the new.

Augustine's very insistence in his *City of God* on the differences between the pagan sacrifices and those of the martyrs in fact highlights the real and effective resemblances between the two:

> But who of the faithful ever heard a priest standing at an altar, even if it was built over the holy body of a martyr for the honour and worship of God, say, when he prayed: 'I offer sacrifice to thee, Peter, or to thee, Paul, or to thee, Cyprian'? No one, for at their memorials sacrifice is offered to God, who made them both men and martyrs and united them in heavenly honour with his holy angels. This is a ceremony of thanksgiving to the true God for the victories of the martyrs, and at the same time we encourage ourselves to imitiate them in winning like crowns and palms, as we call upon the same God to aid us and as we renew our memory of them. (8.27; tr. Wiesen, 1968, iii: 138–41)

The boundary between Christian and pagan must be carefully preserved and must not, of course, be crossed by Christians. But, provided that the distinctions are clear, some parts of the terrain may be allowed to look similar to that of the enemy, and therefore temptingly familiar to him.

If the martyr is burnt to death, then the smoke of the burning might suffocate the demons in the air, used as they are to feeding upon the smoke of pagan offerings, and thus as unable to digest smoke of this kind as they are to consume martyred flesh (John Chrysostom, *Sermon* 21; Ruinart, 1713: 536–8). The Christian sacrifice will even smell, as the older sacrifices did, but in a wholly different way. St. John Chrysostom stresses this fact especially:

> And other sacrifices also there are, which are indeed whole burnt offerings, the bodies of the martyrs: there both soul and body [are

offered]. These have a great savor of a sweet smell. (*Homily 11 on Hebrews*; tr. Schaff, 1889, xiv: 420)

This contrast between the 'odour of sanctity' and the palpably different odours burnt blood sacrifices released into the nostrils of the votaries was perhaps one of the most striking of the contrasts the new dispensation had to offer, and Christians emphasised it accordingly. Bad smells thus become, in certain of the saints' *Lives*, such as that of Antony, signs of the presence of wicked demons (*Life of St. Antony* 63). Incense helps to distinguish the newly purified air.

Often, too, the deaths of martyrs are reported as bringing about clearly supernatural happenings in their train – happenings manifest perhaps in the changed behaviour of animals or objects, or miracles, often of healing. Predatory birds and animals, such as eagles and wolves, become, instead, protectors of martyred saints. The supernatural forces released by martyrdom alter their natural behaviour, but preserve, at the same time, their places in an older hierarchy (Flint, 1990: 180–1, 198–9). Miracles of healing occurred immediately at the tombs of Ambrose's newly discovered martyrs Gervasius and Protasius for instance (Beyenka, 1954: 381–2; Augustine, *City of God* 22.8), and at the tombs of more martyrs than it is possible to count. These stories all have echoes of an older world, its reverences, its fears, its hopes and its supposed supernatural assistances. The echoes are made necessary by the need both to defeat the demons on their own ground, and to re-occupy that ground through the offering of supernatural help equatable with, yet superior to, that which had been lost. Early Christian proselytisers knew this well.

A further important element in this response to the powers of 'demonic' magic – the response of confounding, yet echoing and re-using, that is – lies in the practice of Christian exorcism. In famous passages from *Luke*, 8:26–39 and 11:14–22, and *Acts* 19:13–16, Christ and His apostles are shown casting out demons – but in ways which were in fact very like those which the non-Christian sorcerers employed; ways which again supported the accusations of enemies that Christians used magic. According to the first account from *Luke*, the demons went into the Gadarene swine, and plunged the swine to their deaths. There is a great deal of popular demonology in this passage. The demons live in desert places and in tombs, like Rabbinic and pagan demons. They make people and creatures behave in extraordinary ways. They have special names and they can be death-dealing. The second passage from *Luke* comes later to be much used by those who wish to condemn Christ Himself as a magician. Christ is accused of casting out demons by another greater demon – Beelzebub. He denies the accusation of course; but in fact by means of the differences *and* similarities between His methods and those of His opponents (*Luke* 11:19). In the passage from *Acts*, the apostles have to deal with Jewish exorcists who operate just as they do. These passages (and I have cited only the three most famous out of very many) are almost a licence for redefinition, provided, once more, that the differences are clear. The differences here reside first in that larger understanding, and awe, of the power of the demonic we have already seen in Christianity, then in a changed attitude to the direction of human action. Exorcism, performed without full realisation of Satan's wickedness, may do more harm than good; as it does in the subsequent passage from *Luke* 11:24–6, when seven worse devils take the places of those evicted by an ordinary sorcerer. The new direction will come from the indwelling of the Holy Spirit, released by Christ (*Luke* 11:13), and be empowered by His ascension and the angels, as we saw. Yet with this realisation of the true extent of demonic wickedness, and with this acceptance of the powers of the angels and the Spirit, the procedures are allowed to be much the same.

Many of the saints' lives of Late Antiquity are filled with stories of exorcism. Jerome's *Life of Saint Hilarion* contains some vivid examples of the ways in which magicians invoked the demons, and of the Christian exorcist's victories over them. A certain young man, for instance, anxious to capture the affections of a Christian virgin, betakes himself to the priests of Aesculapius to learn their arts. As a result,

> Under the threshold of the girl's home, he concealed certain revolting words of magic and hideous figures engraved on thin sheets of Cyprian copper. From that moment the virgin went mad.

Such were the sheets of metal upon which, according to Cassian, Ham the seducer engraved the magical lore he had been given by the fallen angels. There are multiple echoes in this apparently simple passage. St. Hilarion exorcised the demon aroused by the magic and all was well (*Life of Saint Hilarion*; tr. Deferrari et al., 1952: 259–60). One incident in the *Life of Antony* shews that Antony himself was thought to have acted as an exorcist. A young nobleman is possessed by a demon. Antony rebukes the demon and bids it 'be gone to waterless places' (a memory of *Luke* 11:24). The possessed man then attacks the saint, to the annoyance of Antony's companions. Antony, however, says:

> Do not be angry with the young man, for he is not responsible but the demon in him. (*Life of St Antony* 64; tr. Meyer, 1950: 73)

Here we have clear evidence that to 'demonise' could indeed be an act of compassion. In one of his many admiring passages upon the works of St. Martin of Tours, Sulpicius Severus (d.c. 420) speaks in his *Dialogue* of Martin's abilities as an exorcist. He does so in a way which both makes it plain how important it was to contemporaries that the Christian exorcist should outdo (or be thought to outdo) both magician and demons in some striking display of supernatural power, and adduces a Christian moral:

> But if at any time Martin undertook the duty of exorcising the demons, he touched no one with his hands, and reproached no one in words, as a multitude of expressions is generally rolled forth by the clerics; but the possessed, being brought up to him, he ordered all others to depart, and the doors being bolted, clothed in sackcloth and sprinkled with ashes, he stretched himself on the ground in the midst of the church, and turned to prayer. Then truly might one behold the wretched beings tortured with various results – some hanging, as it were, from a cloud, with their feet turned upwards, and yet their garments did not fall over their faces, lest the part of the body which was exposed should give rise to shame. (*Dialogus* 3.6; tr. Roberts, 1894: 48–9)

The exorcism was simply, and not boastfully, performed, and decency was preserved. The mention of Martin's verbal restraint is interesting. There survive many near-contemporary magical spells which are full of mumbo jumbo (*PGM* IV 1227–64), and the gnostics, of course, used complicated formulae. Here, then, one could point out the contrast, whilst keeping the object of attention, the exercise of power over the demons, substantially intact.

Athanasius objects too, in his *De Incarnatione Verbi*, to the use of complex formulae in exorcisms, and advocates, instead, the simple sign of the cross. In doing so he throws an incidental extra light on the continuing concern the fourth century church had with magic and magical operation:

> Formerly everywhere was filled with the deceit of oracles . . . But now, since Christ is preached everywhere, their madness has ceased and there is no longer any augur among them. Previously demons cheated men with their illusions, taking possession of springs or rivers or woods or stones, and thus by their tricks stupifying the simple. But now that the divine manisfestation of the Word has taken place, their illusion has ceased; for a man has only to make the sign of the cross to drive away their deceits. (47; tr. Thomson, 1971: 252–3)

The surviving magical papyri alone show that Athanasius's claim that this world had passed away was itself illusory. Christians, then, must show themselves able to to exorcise the demons in it, yet retain the humans. The sign of the cross was offered here once more both as comparison and contrast. The sign was powerful, yet wholly simple. That simple sign of the cross which would come later, especially in Post-Reformation Europe, to be seen as the merest magical superstition was, in its origins, an important part of a most complex reaction to contemporary magical procedures.

There is a clear precedent laid down here for a whole process of redefinition, provided its end is Christian and the means carefully controlled. Once more, the concept of the wicked demon is used not only to condemn, but to improve the capacity of human beings to appease their anxieties, defend themselves and be saved. And, provided the end is improved Christian understanding, the means may be very closely allied to the non-Christian ways. The great exorcism prayer attributed to St. Ambrose is a fine summary of the style of borrowing exorcism allowed. The apostles have power to tread on snakes and scorpions, to brave dragons and ghosts and desert demons, and to be purified against them by water; to overcome, that is, the lifeless matter and the monsters and creeping things of which Eusebius spoke. The prayer even remembers that man is an image – a sort of statue – made out of mud; though this image has the power of the Christian God behind it (*PL* 17:1109).

Such resemblances, yet clear distinctions, are contained to a particularly high degree in a further extension of Christian power over the demons – the sacrament of baptism. Baptism was easily the most striking of the rituals of the early Christian Church, and one of the most important. It was so because it marked the moment at which Christ's own death on the cross, defeat of the Devil, and resurrection into heaven were imprinted upon, and (it was hoped) repeated in, the life of the individual human being. The rite of baptism was full of echoes of an older world. Catechumens were exorcised several times as they approached the sacrament at which, finally, the Devil, father of the demons, was renounced. Hippolytus (d.c. 236), who wrote the first account of the institutional Christian rite of baptism which has come down to us, insists, moreover, that the first prayer said over the baptismal water be said at cock-crow, the moment when, by tradition, the demons of darkness flee (*The Apostolic Tradition* 21). Cyril of Jerusalem (d. 386) reminds his hearers, in terms reminiscent of a far older demonology, that water could harbour demons. Christ's baptism, however, overthrew these demons, and they would be drowned ever after in the waters of Christian baptism. These passages are full of an old terror confounded (they are echoed too in Ambrose's exorcism prayer, cited above):

According to Job, there was in the waters the dragon that 'draweth up Jordan into his mouth' [*Job* 40:18]. Since therefore it was necessary to 'break the heads of the dragon in pieces' [*Psalm* 73:14] He went down and bound the strong one in the waters, that He might receive power to 'tread upon serpents and scorpions' [*Luke* 10:19]. The beast was great and terrible ... The Life encountered Him, that the mouth of Death might henceforth be stopped, and all we that are saved might say 'Oh death where is thy sting? Oh grave, where is thy victory?' [1 *Cor.* 15:55]. The sting of death is drawn by Baptism. (*Catechetical Lectures* 3.11; tr. Gifford, 1894: 17)

Through its water, the sacrament of Baptism now reshapes an ancient fear of water and its demons into a new hope of salvation. The demons of the waters will

strive to follow you, while you go down into the water, where you are safe, and when you have been purified from all stain of sin, come forth a new man, to sing the new song.

These demons will be drowned, however, says Origen in his *Homilies on Exodus* 5 and 6, just as the Egyptians were drowned in the Red Sea (*Exodus* 14:26–8), and with the help of the countering angels. Though magicians and enchanters must renounce their arts before they can be accepted for baptism (*The Apostolic Tradition* 16, 21–2), elements of these will, then, remain in the new rite.

Tertullian was horrified by the fact that the new rite of baptism could be compared with older, pagan ones; but, through his horror he again illuminates the similarities between the two. He speaks of

other cases . . . in which, without any sacrament, unclean spirits brood on waters . . . Witness all shady founts, and all unfrequented brooks, and the ponds in the baths, and the conduits in [private] houses, or the cisterns and wells which are said to have the property of 'spiriting away', through the power, that is, of a hurtful spirit. Men whom waters have drowned or affected with madness or with fear, they call 'nymph-caught' or 'lymphatic' or 'hydrophobic'.

He describes, with annoyance, how many still believe that water is 'endued with a medicinal virtue by religion' and that 'the devil rivalling the things of God' practises a form of baptism already. All of this draws attention, in fact, to the reconciling advantages of those resemblances he so dislikes. The intervention of an old 'daimon', reclothed as an angel and triumphing over the Devil and his minions, completes the picture. This angel of God grants

his presence to waters to temper them to man's salvation; while the evil angel holds frequent profane commerce with the selfsame element to man's ruin. (*On Baptism* 5; tr. Roberts and Donaldson, 1869–70, i: 237–8)

Angels defeat the demons through baptism, but in a rite which bears resemblances to the older ones of a kind rather to encourage than alarm.

In his *De Anima* Tertullian advocates baptism as the main means by which parents are sanctified and the child protected from the pagan rituals and demons which surround parturition and the new-born. Baptism here becomes an apotropaic ritual similar in intention to the pagan ones (*De anima* 39).

Some aspects of Ambrose's moving descriptions of the baptismal ritual seem, in their efforts to excite the imagination, and in their emphasis on burial in the earth and in the water, to echo certain of the theurgic ones too (Lewy, 1978: 207–8). To Ambrose, again, baptism both replaces and out-performs the older ways, joining the burgeoning rod of Aaron in these triumphs, and substituting ancient terrors with desire (Cramer, 1993: 64–72). Here, baptism once more shows signs of the incorporation of an older magic into the power of the new religion, this with the help of demons redefined; indeed, it is impossible fully to understand the origins and development of this rite without the demons and their magic fully in mind.

The first of those who vanquish, yet re-use and re-define, non-Christian demonic magic for the Christians of Late Antiquity, then, are God's angels, Christ Himself and the martyrs. The ultimate sacrifices of Christ's death and those of the martyrs are pre-conditions for further dealings with the magi, and for the transformation of them and their followers into Christians; yet, as we have seen, they were in one sense concessions themselves. Next come Christ's apostles and their heirs. Through the collective exorcisms and miracles of the latter, and through the concentration of such powers in corporate liturgical activites, such as baptism, the apostles added a further level of conquest and reinterpretation in time. We have touched also upon monastic saints, such as St. Antony and St. Hilarion. The victories of the monks against the demons, and their special successes on the way to the angelic life allowed them perhaps a privileged position as protectors and rehabilitators of the 'demonised' and as authorisers and re-users of Christianised magical powers. Augustine, as so often, summed up this position clearly in his *City of God*:

> a man who is consecrated in the name of God and dedicated to God, in so far as he dies to the world that he may live to God is himself a sacrifice. (10.5; tr. Wiesen, 1968, iii: 272–3)

Such a man might therefore engage more freely with the conquered demons than ordinary mortals, and shew the way to these mortals by apparently magical means. Some will certainly decide to do so.

This over-arching redefinition of pagan magic in terms of victory gave confidence to Christians. The Peter-Simon Magus literature remained popular throughout this period, though with certain changes, as we have seen. It was this confidence, or so I would contend, which encouraged, finally, a further progression. This was the progression from confrontation and absorption to active compromise. The battle was now won, often by means of captured armaments, and the manifest power Christians now had over pagan magic at last permitted a gentler attitude towards the other side. This more tolerant response was not adopted by every Late Antique Christian spokesman by any means. To John Chrysostom, for instance, death was far preferable to the simple wearing of an amulet (*Homily* 8, on *Colossians*). But the successful progress of Christianity under the shelter of the larger redefinitions we have just described, made the idea of compromise perhaps more generally palatable to this late period than to the earlier ones. Also, we might remark, that very range of magical practice the demons had helped to uncover, and which allowed of such a variety of victories, allowed also of a wide choice of tolerances. Ironically, the more vague and sweeping the earlier condemnations had been, the more scope there was now for retractions which might, though belatedly, win some friends.

One very large loophole and means of concession lay in the idea of divination. Much of the demonic magic and witchcraft of the non-Jewish and non-Christian dispensations was, as we have seen, concerned with looking into and, if possible, determining the future. Theurgists were primarily involved in mantic exercises, and so were the 'haruspices' and astrologers of state paganism. No true Christian could doubt that this was wrong. It was an affront both to the idea of Divine foreknowledge and providence, and to the doctrine of the freedom of the will; but there was a way out of the problem. Though the Old Testament hated diviners (*Numbers* 22:7, 23:23), the Jews had been allowed their prophets by their God. Some of these had, moreover, in the eyes of Christians, prophesied the coming of Christ (Iranaeus, *Against Heresies* 4.10). Some form of looking into the future must, therefore, be allowable in its own right.

Origen, even when embattled against Celsus and his pagan demons, had allowed of prophecy. He regarded it, interestingly, as a vital means of preventing the Jewish people from falling into far worse habits than that of consulting their prophets:

> While . . . the heathen were using divination, whether by auguries or by birds or by ventriloquists, or even by those who profess to divine by means of sacrifices or Chaldaean astrologers, all of these things were forbidden to the Jews. But if the Jews had had no knowledge of the future to console them, they would have been led by the insatiable desire of man to know the future . . . and . . . would have turned to heathen divination and oracles, or even attempted something of the kind among themselves. Consequently, there is nothing inappropriate about the fact that the prophets among them uttered predictions even

about everyday matters for the consolation of those who wanted that sort of thing. (*Contra Celsum* 36; tr. Chadwick, 1965: 35)

This recognition of the human need for consolation and encouragement, if the transition from fear to hope in the new religion is properly to be accomplished, is important to our own understanding of Christian compromise.

Augustine came positively to defend the idea of prophecy in the Late Antique Christian Church, and again, it seems, as both a defence against, and a substitute for, the older consolations pagan divination offered:

When Theodosius [II] was pressed by anxious cares, he did not go astray into wicked and forbidden superstitions, but instead sent to John, a hermit established in the desert of Egypt. He had learned from repeated acclaim that this servant of God was endowed with the spirit of prophecy, and from him he received a most reliable assurance of victory. (*City of God* 5.26; tr. Green, 1963/1972, ii: 166–9)

Here, a hermit, made holy by clearly Christian means, is substituted for the pagan diviner and his technology; but the idea that one may look into the future is defended, and the means provided. Adaptations of this kind provide much scope.

The twin ideas of rightful consolation in the face of irreducible human anxiety, and of the appropriate intermediary, in fact allowed of the redefinition of much similar magic in Christian terms, complete with its technology. Thus pagan statues, symbols of so much of that which Christianity most hated in paganism, and among the most notorious haunts of demons, were being admitted to Christian basilicas by at least as early as the pontificate of Damasus (366–84). One notable one was renamed to represent St. Hippolytus himself (Leclercq, 1907: 256). The cure of disease, still often viewed as demonically inflicted, provided many opportunities for transformations of this kind – all in the cause of Christian charity and sometimes, perhaps, in the face of an expensive, or irresponsible, or simply absent medical profession. The first Christian statue known – a town one, in the full pagan tradition of statuary – is carefully described by Eusebius as one of healing. He says it represents Christ and the woman with the issue of blood, though it was most probably a pagan statue, perhaps the empire with a subject province, represented as a woman, kneeling before it (*Ibid.*: 248–9).

Alarms about health and livelihood had often compelled the alarmed to turn to magic in the pagan world and, if we are to believe the evidence of the magical papyri once again, were certainly still doing so in Late Antiquity. Christianity must provide, then, for these alarms too.

Accordingly, Constantine the Great drew a clear line between condemned magic and the protection of harvests or the cure of disease:

> The science of those men who are equipped with magic arts and who are revealed to have worked against the safety of men or to have turned virtuous minds to lust shall be punished and deservedly avenged by the most severe laws. But remedies sought for human bodies shall not be involved in criminal accusation, nor the assistance that is innocently employed in rural districts in order that rains may not be feared for the ripe grape harvests or that the harvests may not be shattered by the stones of ruinous hail, since by such devices no person's safety or reputation is injured, but by their action they bring it about that divine gifts and the labours of men are not destroyed. (*Theodosian Code* 9.16.3; tr. Pharr, 1952: 237)

Some of the Christian Fathers and Doctors of Late Antiquity were adept at supporting such remedies, in both medical and agricultural pursuits. Augustine was once more influential here. In an important passage in his *De Doctrina Christiana* (one in which he discusses herbs and potions and amulets) Augustine seems to allow the use of a wide range of medical remedies, provided they are not *solely* the products of magical exercise:

> where there are no enchantments, invocations, or characters, we can ask these questions. Is the object which is tied or fastened in any way to the body for the restoration of its health efficacious by virtue of its own nature? (If so, we may use this remedy unrestrictedly.) Or, does it succeed because of some signifying bond? The more effectually this seems to do good, all the more cautiously should the Christian beware of it. But, when we do not know the reason for the efficacy of a thing, the intention for which it is used is important in so far as concerns the cure or alleviation of bodies, whether in medicine or in agriculture. (2.29; tr. Gavigan, 1947: 100–1)

This is compromise of a singularly striking sort. The first chapter of St. John's Gospel was used as a healing charm, much as magical incantations were used and possibly because of its inclusion in the Ordinary of the Mass, far into the Middle Ages (Barb, 1963: 122). Augustine himself associates the beginning of the Gospel of St John with sickness and its cure (*City of God* 10.30). Many Christian leaders were allowed to show themselves competent in the protection of harvests. They did so chiefly by means of the contrasting simplicities of the sign of the cross and their own God-given powers of command, but, with this, they were careful to retain an appearance and effect at least equal to those of the magicians. St. Martin, for instance, could protect fields from hailstorms, just as the pagan weather magicians of Cleonae had claimed they could (*Dialogus* 3.7;

Corcoran, 1972, ii: 54–57). The protection of harvests through something very like forbidden pagan incantations was actually allowed, in the very Late Antique Christian Church, to enter the liturgy. The days known as Rogation Days were in origin three days of prayer and litanies for the protection of the harvest, and the Major Rogation directly replaced the pagan feast of the Robigalia, directed to the same end. In c. 470 Bishop Mamertus of Vienne ordered similar prayers (the Minor Rogations) to be linked with the feast of Christ's ascension, contrasting the new ways of exercising power in the heavens with the older ones (Avitus, *Homilia de rogationibus*; *PL* 59: 291).

I have suggested already that it was the confidence of ultimate victory over the demons which, given certain cautions and protections of the kind mentioned by Augustine, allowed of the extension of tolerance in Late Antiquity. Among the over-arching protections mentioned, I included that of the holy men, ascetics and monks. Partly because of the angelic life they sought to follow, but mainly, as I think, because of their multifarious, and well documented, victories over the demons, such men were allowed a special place in the uncovering, re-interpretation and re-incorporation of pagan magic. It may come, then, as no surprise to find one of the most striking of the instances of confident reincorporation in Jerome's *Life of Saint Hilarion*. The incident concerns one of the most treasured of pagan activities, and one for which magical intervention was most fervently sought; the chariot-race. Hilarion does more, in the *Life*, than act as exorcist. He engages in practices even more indisputably magical, and recognised as such by contemporaries. He does so, moreover, to win a chariot-race; not, it should perhaps be made clear, because he has a bet on it, but in response to the pleas of one Italicus (the promoter?), a Christian. Italicus was afraid that his city's rival, Gaza, would win. He explained to Hilarion that

> a Christian could not employ magical arts, but that he could petition help from the servant of God, especially against the people of Gaza, who were enemies of God and were not so much insulting him as they were insulting the Church of Christ.

Convinced, the saint sprinkled the 'horses, charioteers, carriage, and even the bars of the starting stalls' with Holy Water, and the race was won. The losers

> demanded that Hilarion, *the magician of the Christians* [italics my own] be punished, but the victory was incontestable and became the occasion of faith for a great many at this and subsequent contests. (*Life of Saint Hilarion* 20; tr. Deferrari, 1952: 258–9)

Jerome seems to have no objection at all to the description of Hilarion as a magician, nor, remarkably, to the use of supernatural power to this end. The *Life of Saint Hilarion* was read aloud in monasteries and was perhaps written for that purpose. Monks might, then, be allowed to meet popular aspirations in such ways. The line here between pagan and Christian magic seems very slender. Tertullian himself had described the purification rites of Mithras and Isis in terms very similar to those adopted here (*On Baptism* 5).

On Augustine's part the concessions are often reluctant and graded; but they are there. He allows of a semblance of the pagan feast of the parentalia, for instance, under the control of the martyrs:

> Some even bring their food to the [martyrs'] shrines – this is not done by Christians of the better sort, and in most countries the custom is unknown – but in any case those who do so say a prayer when they have laid the food down by the shrine, and then take it away to eat it or to bestow some of it also upon the needy. (*City of God* 8.27; tr. Wiesen, 1968, iii: 140–1)

The Fathers clearly held differing views on the matter, views which would richly reward further study. Augustine's letters to Januarius are full of examples of rather back-handed tolerances of this kind. Though he does not care for it, Augustine allows, in these letters, a famous species of Christian lottery, the *Sortes Biblicae*. This involved the drawing of directions from the random opening of the Bible, or drawing passages from it, in Christianised imitation of pagan lotteries. The *Sortes Biblicae* were often forbidden in church councils, yet, says Augustine, in a concession not unlike that Origen made to the Jews and their prophets,

> It could be wished that they would do this rather than run around consulting demons. (*Epistulae* 55 to Januarius; tr. Parsons, 1951/1953, i: 292)

It may be that Augustine had in mind here the technological competition Christians must wage with the old order if they were truly to win. The magician's tool-chest which Barb describes (Barb, 1963: 112–13), full of paraphernalia suitable for lotteries and surviving from the third century, is a particularly clear example of that which many people must have expected of their religious leaders. It behoved Christians, therefore, to provide something at least comparable themselves.

Augustine also approves of the notion that the Christian Feast of Easter should coincide with the feast of the new corn because the imagery is the same. His reasoning in his second letter to Januarius must have been, and still is, a gift for those looking for ways of reconciliation between the pagan world and the Christian:

If . . . these allegories, taken not only from heaven and the stars, but even from the lower creation, are adapted to the dispensation of the sacraments, they become a sort of eloquence of redemptive doctrine, fit to win the affection of its disciples from visible to invisible, from corporal to spiritual, from temporal to eternal things.

Again:

The church of God, established in the midst of so much chaff and much cockle, tolerates many things. (*Epistulae* 55 to Januarius; tr. Parsons, 1951/1953, i: 272, 291)

In the matter of feasts, we should note that Augustine's concessions were made strictly within the framework of the feasts of Christ's Passion, Resurrection, Ascension and the Coming of the Holy Spirit at Pentecost. No random imitations or simple substitutions were allowed, and certainly no uncontrolled 'trickle down'; this, at least, is the message of his first letter to Januarius (*Ibid.*; 54 to Januarius). Provided the safeguards were there, however, the adaptation of those elements of pagan magic which were relevant to Christian morality seem actively to have been encouraged, from individual and liturgical blessings and 'incantations', to the actual incorporation of pagan imagery into Christian. The moral integrity and right intention of practitioner and practices seem to have justified great numbers of redefinitions. Proof against the demons himself, the tried and trusted apostle of Christ may enjoy *carte blanche* in the practice of Christian magic – or very nearly so.

such miracles as appear to be prophesied or actually accomplished by an act of God, but yet have no connection with the work of the one God . . . are but tricks played by malign demons . . . On the other hand, whatever miracles are so wrought by God either through his angels or *by whatever means they give support to the worship and religion of the one God* [italics my own] . . . these we must truly believe to be the work of those who love us in accord with religious truth, acting either on their own or as instruments, while God himself is active in them . . . Wherefore God, who made the visible heaven and earth, does not disdain to perform visible miracles in heaven or on earth, whereby he may quicken the soul. (*City of God* 10.12; tr. Wiesen, 1968, iii: 306–9)

Quickening the soul is the key. Within such a context, such beliefs as the ancient one in the magical power of barefootedness, much disliked by Augustine himself (*Epistulae* 55), came to be tolerated, and perhaps even actively reflected in the removal, by some monks, of their shoes before the Eucharist (Chadwick, 1976: 17–19).

Demonic magic involves turbulence and aggressive disturbance as we saw, and plays on fear, hatred, anger and ambition. It also likes gifts (*City of God* 8.17):

> Demons . . . resemble foolish and unrighteous men; their bodies are different, but morally they are the same. (*Ibid.* 9.3; tr. Wiesen, 1968, iii: 156–7)

By setting this argument on its head, however, that wonder or 'magic' which brings about peace, calms anger, counters fear, encourages hope and truthfulness, and is, in addition, free, may readily be incorporated into Christian practice:

> It is one thing for magicians to perform miracles, another for good Christians and another for evil Christians. Magicians do so through private contracts, good Christians through a public righteousness and evil Christians through the 'ensigns' or symbols of this public righteousness. (*Eighty Three Different Questions* 79.4; tr. Mosher, 1982: 203)

All that is needed is that these incorporations of non-Christian magical practice be righteous, intelligent, and directed towards the love of Christ. Interestingly, for Augustine the requirement of public righteousness means that astrology can never be made respectable. Astrology, he avers in his *Confessions* 4.3, robs all persons of all sense of sin. Only when astrology too becomes an aid to virtue will the incorporation of astrology be possible to the Christian Church. But for the rest, the saint made great overtures to the pagan world, where he felt he could:

> I cannot approve what is established outside the common custom, and observed almost as if it were a sacrament, but I do not venture to disapprove too freely, even though many things of this sort are to be avoided so as not to scandalize certain holy or troublesome people. (*Epistulae* 55 to Januarius; tr. Parsons, 1951/1953, i: 290)

One reason for these extensions of tolerance may indeed lie in the need to avoid scandal and trouble. It stands therefore at an opposite extreme from that Christian confidence in victory, and that Christian capacity to make moral points through adapted magic and the demons we have explored so far. Instead, it springs from the undoubted fact that, even by the end of the fourth century and the beginning of the fifth, pagan magic was far from dead (Brox, 1974: 179). The very persecutions we examined at the end of the previous section attest to that fact, trumped up though many of them seem to have been. Though magicians and sorcerers were now robbed, for the most part, of public patronage, pagan practices of the kind accommodated by St. Hilarion seem not to have been uncommon. Many of the surviving copies of the magical papyri come from the fourth century, and plentiful lead 'defixiones', or magical cursing tablets, survive from this same period. The Christian Fathers themselves attested to the continuing strength of pagan magical practice by the very vehemence of their denunciations and Augustine clearly recognised some of its abiding power (*City of God* 15.23). Added to these pressures, moreover, were the difficulties and dislocations suffered by whole persecuted communities. No conscientious pastor could fail to feel for such dislocations. Libanius gives us a touching glimpse of them in his *Oration*. He speaks of the fact that in his day

> the temples, great and small alike in which the weary used to find repose, have all been demolished, and those who have suffered this loss are like ship-wrecked mariners, swept from the ships in which they sailed. (30; tr. Norman, 1977: 120–3)

Pastoral concern for displaced persons, and the loss of their places and habits of worship may stand, then, behind at least some of the conciliar rulings against clerical indulgences in magic. Canon 36 of the Council of Laodicea of c.360–365, for instance, forbids outright the practice of 'magia' by the clergy (Mansi, ii: 588–9). The previous canon had forbidden the exaggerated cult of angels – a juxtaposition which at least suggests a connection between the two, and may reveal an over-dependence, on the part of the clergy, on one of those protections we have just discussed, and an excessive enthusiasm for compromise. It is hard to know. There is no suggestion here, however, that clerical self-indulgent superstition alone provoked the rulings. The idea that the unfortunate clergy had transgressed the limits in a laudable effort at tolerance and negotiation is, instead, an interpretation of such evidence which is both permissible, and consistent with the other indications we have examined. It has long been maintained, and plausibly so, that certain identifiably pagan intrusions into Christian iconography may have been encouraged by a tolerant clergy (Leclercq, 1907: 182–4).

Redefinition and compromise, justifiable in theory though they have to be, often come of practical necessity. Figures such as Apollonius of Tyana (d.c.98 AD) may have had some hope to offer. As a magician and wonder-worker Apollonius, after all, was still sometimes compared with Christ (Smith, 1978: 84–6). Augustine admits as much:

> Who could think it a fit matter for laughter that men should try to compare or even prefer Apollonius and Apuleius and other adepts of the magic arts to Christ? Yet, it is more readily bearable for them to compare men to Him rather than their gods, for we have to admit that Apuleius was much better than that originator and perpetrator of so many debaucheries whom they call Jupiter. (*Epistulae* 38; tr. Parsons, 1951/1953, iii: 50)

The magician-successors of Apollonius and Apuleius have now disappeared from our sight; but it may not be pressing speculation too far to suppose that there were some, and that they may have recognised, in the complaisant clergy the councils condemned, persons with whom they could make common cause. Compromise with the less harmful forms of pagan magic, and active absorption of all in it that was acceptable would have helped greatly to convince the more impressive of the opposition, and win them over. It is at least possible to suggest that it was actively meant to do so.

The need to win over the pagan magician, and his following, and to repair the damage caused by the dislocation of religious habit, may, then, have added to those pressures for accommodation we have discussed. Two overall distinctions between the old practices and the new, however, stand out. Few practitioners of the new, Christian, form of supernatural exercise might indulge in relations with the dead, as the pagan necromancers did, and none might charge a fee. Tertullian spells out Christian reservations about tampering with the spirits of the dead in his *De Anima*, and combines them, interestingly, with an account of the types of Christian magic the Old Testament had seemed to him to license. Thus, Moses and Aaron could use magic against Pharaoh's magicians in *Exodus* 7:12, and Paul could blind the magician Elymas in *Acts* 13:8–11. 'God forbid', he says, however, when speaking of the sorceress's claim to conjure up the ghost of the dead Samuel (1 *Samuel* 28:7–16) 'that we should suppose that the soul of any saint, much less of a prophet, can be dragged out of its resting place in Hades by a demon':

> The power of God has, no doubt, sometimes recalled men's souls to their bodies, as a proof of his own transcendent rights; but there must never be, because of this fact, any agreement supposed to be possible between the divine faith and the arrogant pretensions of sorcerers, and the imposture of dreams, and the licence of poets. (*De anima* 57; tr. Roberts and Donaldson, 1869–70, ii: 537–9)

Augustine expressed similar reservations. The sorceress could not possibly have brought back Samuel; the apparition was therefore a demon (*Ad Simplicianum* 2.3.1–2). These firm rulings against bringing back the dead may have owed something to Origen and the demonic customs officers at the frontiers between earth and heaven. Certainly the interest of the demons in death itself prohibited all but the most established of saints from tampering with dead souls.

Revulsion against monetary reward for supernatural service also runs through the literature we have surveyed, from Simon Magus onwards. The Magi of *Matthew* 2:1–12 *brought* material gifts, but received only the immaterial. Tertullian, in his treatise *On Baptism*, contrasted the expense of pagan rituals with the cheapness of Christian baptism, which requires no fee (*On Baptism* 2). Hilarion refused payment for his exorcisms (*Life of Saint Hilarion* 18). This distinction too may have descended in part from the legacy of the demons. The *Book of Enoch* places greed, together with magic, among the vices of the fallen angels. Augustine's demons like gifts and honours, as we have seen. Evidence of greed becomes, then, evidence of demonic presence, and invalidates all claim to righteous supernatural power. This emphasis on greed as a badge of unworthiness may have had the effect of edging out some members of the pagan opposition by robbing them of their livelihood – and perhaps of then encouraging them towards Christianity by promising them, in return for conversion, an organised return. We lack the evidence fully to resolve such problems, although there are indications among the surviving financial mechanisms and concerns of the Church which may perhaps be pursued with profit. At all events, in the matter of the magicians' fees we see once more the idea of the demon active in the encouragement of a particular kind of Christian morality.

The support of Christian charity and hope, and the repelling of fear and avarice, meant that much of the magic of the pagan world was wholly rejected by the Late Antique church. The blood and panoply of pagan sacrifice, the technology and expense of the High priest and magicians, the secrets and mumbo jumbo of the astrologer or wonder-worker must go and be seen to do so. Some of this magic was, however, incorporated, and with considerable adroitness. Within the all-embracing safeguards of the cosmology of the redemptive sacrifice, the living liturgy and the particular moral ends Christianity must now support, a surprising number of demons and pagan exercises were reclothed and put to new service.

CONCLUSION

Demons and magic go together in Late Antiquity, although in ways both more subtle and more surprising than we have always been led to believe. It is clear from the material we have examined that magic was 'demonised' to its discredit, and as a means *towards* (not 'to') its condemnation; but the process of 'demonisation' opened up a whole range of other opportunities. It could support compromises and active concern of quite extensive kinds. Magicians could, as we have seen, be 'demonised' for the purposes of persecution, but also for those of rescue and conversion; and these, in turn, allowed many of the less objectionable exercises to survive and be adopted by the Late Antique Christian Church.

It must be remembered that many of the demons and practices of which we have spoken here were, in one sense, 'popular' ones. The treatises, sermons, saints' lives and letters upon which I have drawn for examples were meant to excite responses from within a theatre larger than that provided by scholarly readers, and perhaps from an audience at an early stage in its spiritual progress (Rousseau, 1985: 134–5). One looks largely in vain for demons and their magic in the learned commentaries on the Bible of the Western Fathers (in, as it might be, Ambrose on *Luke* 8:27–33 or Jerome or Augustine on *Matthew* 10:8) and some of the Christian Fathers, such as St Basil, seem to have been wholly uninterested in demons. Although much more work upon these biblical commentaries, and on those of the later Eastern Fathers too, needs to be done, it seems that the redefinitions we have explored were made largely for the pastor, to assist him in his day by day activities among a particular range of people. The concept of the demon, hovering over, around and even inside the Christian of Late Antiquity, was used primarily psychologically, to sway the emotions of the mass of the people away from the old religions and towards the new.

The demons of this early period in the history of witchcraft and magic are, however, serious players. They are certainly far from the knockabout demons of the late medieval mystery plays; but they are, many of them, also far from those monsters which will be invoked in later prosecutions for witchcraft. The emotions these demons were allowed to sway seem to have been selected very carefully, and they mark a clear contrast with those the demons of early modern Europe often came to arouse. Demons and their magic are conscripted here to drive *out* terror and hatred, and to condemn profit and every form of persecution; and both are expected, in their redefined states, to encourage the very opposite, or so, at least, it was hoped by many of the Christian Fathers. Magic, thoroughly described, and the demons, did come together in the world of Late Antiquity, yet that world too produced some of the most energetic efforts at redefinition we can trace – redefinitions and descriptions of Christian counter-magic which left a permanent mark upon the medieval Christian Church. This church was permeated and sustained by *Christian* forms of magic and indeed of 'witchcraft', with all its wealth; a result wholly unachievable but for this active concern for the right use of demons.

Abbreviations

NOTE

Appended to epigraphical publications is their reference number in Bérard
and Feissel, 1989 (*Guide*).

ABSA	*Annual of the British School at Athens*
AE	*L'année épigraphique*
AION (archeol.)	*Annali dell'Istituto universitario orientale di Napoli. Diparti-* *mento di studi del mondo classico e del Mediterraneo antico,* *sezione di archeologia e storia antica*
AJA	*American Journal of Archaeology*
AJP	*American Journal of Philology*
AM	*Mitteilungen des deutschen archäologischen Instituts. Athenis-* *che Abteilung*
ANET	Pritchard, 1955
ANRW	*Aufstieg und Niedergang der römischen Welt*
ARW	*Archiv für Religionswissenschaft*
BASP	*Bulletin of the American Society of Papyrologists*
BCH	*Bulletin de correspondance hellénique*
BO	*Bibliotheca Orientalis*
CA	*Classical Antiquity*
CIL	*Corpus inscriptionum Latinarum*
CMRDM	Lane, 1971–8
CPG	Leutsch and Schneidewin, 1893–1951
CPh	*Classical Philology*
CT	Gager, 1992
DK	Diels and Kranz, 1951–4
DNP	*Der Neue Pauly* (Stuttgart-Weimar, 1996–)
DT	Audollent, 1904
DTA	Wünsch, 1897
EPRO	Études préliminaires aux religions orientales dans l'Empire romain (Leyden, 1961–86)
FGrH	Jacoby, 1923–58
FHG	Müller, 1853–70

FIRA	*Fontes Iuris Romani Antejustiniani*, 2nd edn., ed. S. Riccobono *et al.* (Florence, 1968)
I.Cret.	M. Guarducci, *Inscriptiones Creticae* (Rome, 1935–50)
I. Délos	Roussel and Launey, 1926–72
IG	*Inscriptiones Graecae*
I.Knidos	W. Blümel, *Die Inschriften von Knidos*, vol 1 = Inschriften der Städte Kleinasiens 41 (Bonn, 1992)
ILS	*Inscriptiones latinae selectae*, ed. H. Dessau, 5 vols (Berlin, 1892)
JHS	*Journal of Hellenic Studies*
JNES	*Journal of Near Eastern Studies*
JOAI	*Jahreshefte des Österreichischen archäologischen Instituts in Wien*
JRA	*Journal of Roman Archaeology*
JRS	*Journal of Roman Studies*
JWCI	*Journal of the Warburg and Courtauld Institutes*
K-A	Kassel and Austin, 1983–
LIMC	*Lexicon Iconographicum Mythologiae Graecae*
LSJ	Liddell *et al.* 1968
Mansi	Mansi, 1757–98
MGH	*Monumenta Germaniae Historica, Auctores Antiquissimi*
ML	Meiggs and Lewis, 1969
OMRL	*Oudheidkundige mededelingen uit het Rijksmuseum van Oudheiden te Leiden*
PDM	= the Demotic papyri trans. by Janet Johnson printed in Betz, 1992
PG	Migne, 1857–66
PGM	Preisendanz and Henrichs, 1973–4/see also Betz, 1992 (numerals between LXXXII and CXXX refer only to Betz)
PL	Migne, 1844–64
RAC	*Reallexikon für Antike und Christentum*
RE	Pauly, 1893–
RHR	*Revue d'histoire des religions*
RIB	Collingwood and Wright, 1965, 1993
RP	*Revue de philologie*
RS	Crawford, 1996
SEG	*Supplementum Epigraphicum Graecum*
SGD	Jordan, 1985a
SHAW	Sitzungsberichte der Heidelberger Akademie der Wissenschaften, phil.-hist. Klasse
SIFC	*Studi Italiani di Filologia Classica*
Suppl. Mag.	Daniel and Maltomini, 1990–2

Syll.[3]	Dittenberger, 1915–24
SVF	H. von Arnim, *Stoicorum veterum fragmenta* (Leipzig, 1903–05)
Tab. Sulis	Tomlin, 1988
Tab. Vindol. ii	Bowman and Thomas, 1994
TAM	*Tituli Asiae Minoris*
TAPA	*Transactions of the American Philological Association*
TGF	Snell, B. *et al.*, eds, 1971–
VD	Faraone, 1991a
ZATW	*Zeitschrift für die alttestamentliche Wissenschaft*
ZPE	*Zeitschrift für Papyrologie und Epigraphik*

Bibliography

Abusch, T. (1974) 'Mesopotamian anti-witchcraft literature: texts and studies, Part I: the nature of *Maqlû*: its character, divisions and calendrical setting', *JNES*, 33: 251–62.

— (1987) *Babylonian Witchcraft: Case Studies* (Atlanta).

Alexander, C. (1991) 'An ideal state', *New Yorker*, 16 Dec.: 53–88.

Alexander, P. S. (1986) 'Incantations and books of magic', in Schürer, E. (1973–87), iii (pt 1): 342–79.

Alpers, K. (1984) 'Untersuchungen zum griechischen Physiologus und den Kyraniden', *Vestigia Bibliae*, 6: 13–87.

Alvar, J., Blánquez, C. and Wagner, C. G. eds (1992) *Héroes, semidioses y daimones*, Proceedings of the first ARYS Colloquium, Jarandilla de la Vera, Dec. 1989 (Madrid).

Amand, D. and Moons, M.-Ch. (1953) 'Une curieuse homélie grecque inédite sur la virginité adressée aux pères de famille', *Revue Bénédictine*, 63: 18–69, 211–38.

Amarelli, F. (1988) 'Il processo di Sabratha', *Studia et Documenta Historiae et Iuris*, 54: 110–46.

Andersen, Ø. and Dickie, M. eds (1995) *Homer's World* (Bergen).

Anderson, G. (1986) *Philostratus: Biography and Belles Lettres in the Third Century AD* (Beckenham).

— (1994) *Sage, Saint and Sophist: Holy Men and their Associates in the Early Roman Empire* (London).

Andres, F. (1918) s.v. Daimôn, *RE Suppl.* 3: 267–322.

Anges et Démons. Actes du Colloque de Liège et de Louvain-la-Neuve 25–6 novembre 1987 (Louvain-La-Neuve 1989).

Archellaschi, A. (1990) *Medée dans le théâtre latin d'Ennius à Sénèque* (Rome).

Armstrong, A. H. (1967) *Plotinus*, iii (London and Cambridge, MA).

Arnold, C. E. (1989) *Ephesians: Power and Magic. The Concept of Power in the Light of its Historical Setting* (Cambridge).

Audollent, A. (1904) *Defixionum tabellae* (Paris), *Guide* no. 746 [*DT*].

Aune, D. E. (1980) 'Magic in early Christianity', *ANRW*, II.23.2: 1507–57.

Aupert, P. and Jordan, D. R. (1981) 'Magical inscriptions on talc tablets from Amathous', *AJA*, 85: 184.

Avitus, *Homilia de Rogationibus*, PL 59: 289–94.

Bagnall, R. S. (1993) *Egypt in Late Antiquity* (Princeton).

Bain, D. (1998) 'Salpe's παίγνια: Athenaeus 322A and Pliny *HN* 28.38', *Classical Quarterly*, 48:262–8.

Barb, A. A. (1957) 'Abrasax-Studien', in *Hommages à W. Deonna*, Collection Latomus, 28: 67–86.

— (1963) 'The survival of magic arts', in A. Momigliano, ed. *The Conflict between Paganism and Christianity in the Fourth Century* (Oxford): 100–25.

— (1966) 'Antaura the mermaid and the Devil's grandmother', *JWCI*, 29: 1–23.

Barnes, J. (1968), 'Legislation against the Christians', *JRS*, 58: 32–50; repr. in idem, *Early Christianity and the Roman Empire* (London, 1984), no 3.

Barnes, T. D. (1985) *Tertullian: A Historical and Literary Study* (Oxford), orig. pub. 1971.

Barrett, W. S., ed. (1964) *Euripides Hippolytos*, with an introduction and commentary (Oxford).

Bathurst, W. H. (1879) *Roman Antiquities at Lydney Park, Gloucestershire* (London).

Bean, G. E. and Mitford, T. B. (1965) *Journeys in Rough Cilicia in 1962 and 1963* (Vienna).

Beaujeu, J. (1973) *Apulée: Opuscules Philosophiques* (Paris).

Beavis, I. C. (1988) *Insects and other Invertebrates in Classical Antiquity* (Exeter).

Bérard, F. and Feissel, D., eds (1989) *Guide de l'épigraphiste*, 2nd edn (Paris).

Bernand, A. (1991) *Sorciers grecs* (Paris).

Berthiaume, G. (1982) *Les rôles du mageiros* (Leiden).

Besnier, M. (1920) 'Récents travaux sur les *defixionum tabellae* latines 1904–1914', *RP*, 44: 5–30.

Betz, H. D. (1983) 'Gottmensch II', in *RAC*, xii: 234–312.

— (1991) 'Magic and mystery in the Greek magical papyri', in Faraone, E. and Obbink, D. eds (1991): 244–59.

— ed. (1992) *The Greek Magical Papyri in Translation, including the Demotic Spells*, 2nd edn (London and Chicago); translation, with additions, of Preisendanz 1973–4; incorporates Greek papyri under *PGM* (with upper-case Roman numerals) and demotic papyri under *PDM* (with lower-case Roman numerals).

Beyenka, M. M. (1954) *Saint Ambrose Letters*, i (New York).

Bilde, P., Engberg-Pedersen, T., *et al.*, eds (1997) *Conventional Values of the Hellenistic Greeks*, Studies in Hellenistic Civilization, 8 (Aarhus).

Boissonade, J. Fr. ed. (1849) *Eunapius, Lives of the Philosophers and Sophists* (Paris).

Bollack, J. and Wismann, H. (1972) *Héraclite ou la séparation* (Paris).

Bonner, C. A. (1932a) 'Witchcraft in the lecture room of Libanius', *TAPA*, 63: 34–44.

— (1932b), 'Demons of the bath', in S. R. K. Glanville, ed. *Studies Presented to F. Ll. Griffith* (London): 10–20.

— (1949) '*Kestos himas* and the saltire of Aphrodite', *AJP*, 70: 1–6.

— (1950) *Studies in Magical Amulets, chiefly Graeco-Egyptian* (Ann Arbor).

Borgeaud, P., ed. (1991) *Orphisme et Orphée, en l'honneur J. Rudhardt* (Geneva).

Bottéro, J. (1987–90) 'Magie A. In Mesopotamien', *Reallexikon der Assyriologie*, 7: 200–34.

Boudon, R. (1995) *Le juste et le vrai: études sur l'objectivité des valeurs et de la connaissance* (Paris).

Bourdieu, P. (1971) 'Genèse et structure du champ religieux', *Revue française de Sociologie*, 12: 295–334.

Bowersock, G. (1990) *Hellenism in Late Antiquity* (Cambridge).

Bowie, E. L. (1972) 'Tradition and reality in the life of Apollonius of Tyana', *ANRW*, II.16.2, 2118–93.

Bowman, A. K. and Thomas, J. D. (1994) *Vindolanda: the Latin Writing Tablets (Tabulae Vindolandenses II)* (London) [*Tab. Vindol.* ii]

Brakke, D. (1995) *Athanasius and the Politics of Asceticism* (Oxford).

Brashear, W. M. (1992) 'Magical papyri : magic in bookform', in P. Ganz, ed., *Das Buch als magisches und als Repräsentationsobjekt*(Wiesbaden): 25–59.

— (1995) 'The Greek magical papyri: an introduction and survey; annotated bibliography (1928–1994)', *ANRW*, II.18.5: 3380–684.

Bravo, B. (1987) 'Une tablette magique d'Olbia pontique, les morts, les héros et les démons', in *Poikilia: études offertes à Jean-Pierre Vernant* (Paris): 185–218.

Bremmer, J., ed. (1987) *Interpretations of Greek Mythology* (London and Sydney).

Brenk, F. E. (1986) 'In the light of the moon: Demonology in the early Imperial period', *ANRW*, II.17.3: 2068–145.

Brisson, L. (1992) 'Plotin et la magie', in idem, Cherlonneix, J-L. *et al.*, eds *Vie de Plotin*, ii Histoire et doctrines de l'Antiquité Classique, 16 (Paris): 465–75.

Brixhe, Cl. and Panayotou, A. (1993), 'Le plombe magique de Phalasarna', in *Hellenika summikta: histoire, linguistique, épigraphie*, Études d'archéologie classique, 7 (Nancy and Paris): 23–38.

Brown, J. P. (1981) 'The Mediterranean seer and shamanism', *ZATW*, 93: 374–400.

Brown, P. (1970) 'Sorcery, demons, and the rise of Christianity from late antiquity into the middle ages', in M. Douglas, ed., *Witchcraft Confessions and Accusations* (London): 17–45; reprinted in P. Brown, *Religion and Society in the Age of St. Augustine* (London and New York, 1972): 119–46.

Brown, P. (1989) *The Body and Society: Men, Women and Sexual Renunciation in Early Christianity* (London and Boston).

Brox, N. (1974) 'Magie und Aberglaube an den Anfangen des Christentums', *Trierer theologische Zeitschrift*, 83: 157–80.

Burkert, W. (1962a) 'ΓΟΗΣ: zum griechischen Schamanismus', *Rheinisches Museum*, 105: 36–55.

— (1962b) *Weisheit und Wissenschaft: Studien zu Pythagoras, Philolaos und Platon* (Nuremberg).

— (1972) *Lore and Science in Ancient Pythagoreanism*, trans. of *Weisheit und Wissenschaft* (Cambridge, MA).

— (1983) 'Itinerant diviners and magicians: a neglected element in cultural contacts', in R. Hägg, ed., *The Greek Renaissance of the Eighth Century BC: Tradition and Innovation* (Stockholm): 115–19.

— (1984) *Die orientalisierende Epoche in der griechischen Religion und Literatur*, SHAW 1984, 1 (Heidelberg); trans. M. E. Pinder as *The Orientalizing Revolution* (Cambridge, MA, 1992).

Burrus, V. (1995) *The Making of a Heretic: Gender, Authority, and the Priscillianist Controversy* (Berkeley and London).

Bury, R. G. (1952) *Plato*, vii (London and Cambridge, MA).

Butler, H. E., trans. (1909) *The Apologia and Florida of Apuleius of Madaura* (Oxford).

Buxton, R. G. A. (1987) 'Wolves and werewolves in Greek thought', in Bremmer, J., ed. 1987: 60–79.

— (1994) *Imaginary Greece: The Contexts of Mythology* (Cambridge).

Cairns, F. and Heath, M. (1990) *Papers of the Leeds International Latin Seminar, 6: Roman Poetry and Drama, Greek Epic, Comedy, Rhetoric*, ARCA 29 (Leeds).

Calder, W. M., III (1963) 'The great defixio from Selinus', *Philologus*, 197: 163–72.

Cameron, A. (1973) *Porphyrius the Charioteer* (Oxford).

— (1976) *Circus Factions: Blues and Greens at Rome and Byzantion* (Oxford).

Caplice, R. (1970) 'Namburbi texts in the British Museum iv', *Orientalia*, 39: 134–41.

Carastro, M. (1997) 'L'apparition de la notion de magie en Grèce ancienne', Mémoire de DEA, École des Hautes Études en Sciences Sociales, Paris.

Castellino, G. (1953) 'Rituals and prayers against "appearing ghosts"', *Orientalia*, 22: 240–74.

Castello, C. (1990) 'Cenni sulla repressione del reato di magia dagli inizi del Principato fino a Costanzo II', *VIII Convegno dell'Accademia Romanistica Costantiniana* (Bologna): 665–92.

Caster, M. (1937) *Lucien et la pensée religieuse de son temps* (Paris).

Chadwick, H. trans. (1965) *Origen: Contra Celsum* (Cambridge); first pub. 1953.

— (1976) *Priscillian of Avila: The Occult and the Charismatic in the Early Church* (Oxford).

Chaniotis, A. (1990) 'Drei kleinasiatische Inschriften zur griechischen Religion', *Epigraphica Anatolica*, 15: 127–34.

Charles, R. H., et al., eds (1913) *The Apocrypha and Pseudepigrapha of the Old Testament in English*, 2 vols (Oxford).

Christophilopoulos, A. P. (1946) *Scheseis goneōn kai teknōn kata to byzantinon dikaion* (Athens).

Clauss, J. J. and Johnston, S. I., eds (1997) *Medea* (Princeton)

Clay, D. (1992) 'Lucian of Samosata, four philosophical lives', *ANRW*, II.36.5, 3406–50.

Clerc, J.-B. (1995) *Homines Magici: étude sur la sorcellerie et la magie dans la société impériale*, Publications Universitaires Européennes, 673 (Bern and New York).

Cohen, D. (1988) 'The prosecution of impiety in Athenian law', *Zeitschrift der Savigny-Stiftung für Rechtsgeschichte, Romanistische Abteilung*, 105: 695–701.

Cohn, N. (1993) *Cosmos, Chaos, and the World to Come: The Ancient Roots of Apocalyptic Faith* (New Haven, CN and London).

Coleman, K. (1990) 'Fatal charades: Roman executions staged as mythological enactments', *JRS*, 80: 44–73.

Collingwood, R. G. and Wright, R. P. (1965) *Roman Inscriptions of Britain*, i (Oxford); *Guide* no. 476 [*RIB*].

Conche, M. (1986) *Héraclite: Fragments* (Paris).

Conze, E. (1967) 'Buddhism and Gnosis', in Ugo Bianchi, ed. *Le Origini dello Gnosticismo: Colloquio di Messina 13–18 Aprile 1966* (Leyden): 651–67.

Corcoran, T., ed. and trans. (1972) *Seneca: Natural Questions*, ii (London and Cambridge, MA).

Corpus inscriptionum Latinarum (Berlin 1863–); *Guide* no. 334 [*CIL*].

Corsini, E. and Costa, E., eds (1990) *L'autunno di diavolo: Diabolos, Dialogos, Daimon*, Convegno di Torino, 17–21 Oct. 1988 (Milan).

Cramer, F. H. (1954) *Astrology in Roman Law and Politics, i: Astrology in Rome until the end of the Principate*, Memoirs of the American Philosophical Society, 37 (Philadelphia).

Cramer, P. (1993) *Baptism and Change in the Early Middle Ages, c.200–c.1150* (Cambridge).

Crawford, M., ed. (1996) *Roman Statutes*, 2 vols (London) [*RS*].

Culianu, I. (1980) 'Iatroi kai manteis: sulle strutture dell'estatismo greco', *Studi Storico-Religiosi*, 4: 287–303.

Cumont, F. (1945) 'Vergile et les morts prématurés', *Publications de l'École normale supérieure, section des lettres*, 2: 123–52.

Daniel, R. W., and Maltomini, F., eds (1990–2) *Supplementum Magicum*, Papyrologica Coloniensia, xvi. 1,2, 2 vols (Opladen); numeration is continuous between volumes [*Suppl. Mag.*].

Daxelmüller, C. (1993) *Zauberpraktiken: eine Ideengeschichte der Magie* (Zurich and Munich).

Deferrari, R. J., *et al.* (1952) *Early Christian Biographies* (New York).

— ed. (1955) *Saint Augustine: Treatises on Marriage and Other Subjects*, trans. C. T. Wilcox (Washington, DC).

Delatte, A. (1938) *Herbarius. Recherches sur le cérémoniel usité chez les anciens pour la cueillette des simples et des plantes magiques*, Académie royale de Belgique: Classe des Lettres . . . Mémoires, sér. 2, 54.4, 2nd edn (Brussels).

— and Derchain, P. (1964) *Les intailles magiques gréco-égyptiennes* (Paris).

Delcourt, M. (1939) 'Le suicide par vengeance dans la Grèce ancienne', *RHR*, 119: 154–71.

— (1957) *Héphaistos, ou la légende du magicien* (Liège).

Derrida, J. (1981) *Dissemination* (Chicago); translation of his (1972) *La dissémination* (Paris).

Desanti, L. (1990) *Sileat omnibus perpetuo divinandi curiositas: indovini e sanzione nel diritto romano* (Milan).

Desborough, V. R., Nicholls, R. V. and Popham, M. (1970) 'A Euboean centaur', *ABSA*, 65: 21–30 with Plates 7–11.

Detienne, M. (1963) *De la pensée religieuse à la pensée philosophique: la notion du* daimôn *dans le pythagorisme ancien*, Collection Latomus 57 (Brussels).

— (1970/1974) 'Les pieds d'Héphaistos', in Detienne, M. and Vernant, J. P. (1974): 242–58 = 'Le phoque, le crabe et le forgeron', *Hommages à M. Delcourt*, Collection Latomus 114 (Brussels): 219–33.

— (1972/1977) *The Gardens of Adonis: Spices in Greek Mythology* (Hassocks); trans. by J. Lloyd of *Les Jardins d'Adonis*.

— and Vernant, J.-P. (1974) *Les Ruses de l'intelligence: la Métis des grecs* (Paris).

— (1978) *Cunning Intelligence in Greek Culture and Society* (Hassocks); trans. by J. Lloyd of *Les Ruses d'intelligence*.

Dickie, M. (1990) 'Talos bewitched: magic, atomic theory and paradoxography in Apollonius *Argonautica* 4.1638–88', in Cairns, F. and Heath, M., eds (1990): 267–96.

— (1991) 'Heliodorus and Plutarch on the evil eye', *CPh*, 86: 17–29.

Diels, H. and Kranz, W. (1951–4) *Die Fragmente der Vorsokratiker*, 7th edn, 3 vols (Berlin) [*DK*].

Dihle, A. (1977) 'Das Satyrspiel 'Sisyphos'', *Hermes*, 105: 28–42.

Dillon, J. (1977) *The Middle Platonists* (London).

Dillon, M. P. J. (1996) 'The importance of oionomanteia in Greek divination', in id. (1996): 99–121.

— (ed.) (1996) *Religion in the Ancient world: New Themes and Approaches* (Amsterdam).

Dittenberger, W. (1915–24) *Sylloge inscriptionum Graecarum*, 3rd edn, 4 vols (Leipzig); *Guide* no. 25 [*Syll.³*].

Dodds, E. R. (1947) 'Theurgy and its relationship to Neoplatonism', *JRS*, 37: 55–69.

— (1951) *The Greeks and the Irrational* (Berkeley).

— ed. and trans. (1963) Proclus, *Theologia Platonica*, second ed. with a commentary (Oxford).

Dohm, H. (1964) *Mageiros. Die Rolle des Kochs in der griechisch-römischen Komödie* (Munich).

Dölger, F. J. (1929–36), *Antike und Christentum: Kultur- und Religionsgeschichtliche Studien*, 5 vols. (Münster).

Domínguez Monedero, A. J. (1992) 'El heroe de Temesa', in Alvar, J. Blánquez, C. and Wagner, C. G., eds (1992): 33–50.

Donini, P. L. (1990) 'Nozioni di *daimôn* e di intermediario nella filosofia tra il I e il II secolo d.C.', in Corsini, E. and Costa, E., 1990: 37–50.

Dover, K. J., ed. (1968) *Aristophanes: Clouds*, with introduction and commentary (Oxford).

Dragona-Monachou, M. (1994) 'Divine providence in the philosophy of the Empire', *ANRW*, II.36.7: 4417–90.

Drew-Bear, T. (1972) 'Imprecations from Kourion', *BASP*, 9: 85–107.

Dubois, L. (1989) *Inscriptions grecques dialectales de Sicile* (Rome).

Dugas, C. (1915) 'Figurines d'envoûtement trouvées à Délos', *BCH*, 39: 413–23.

Dunant, C. (1978) 'Sus aux voleurs!', *Museum Helveticum*, 35: 241–4.

Duncan-Jones, R. P. (1996) 'The impact of the Antonine plague', *JRA*, 9: 108–36.

Duval, Y.-M. (1984) 'Jérome et Origène avant la querelle Origéniste. La cure et la guérison ultime du monde et du diable dans l'*In Nahum*', *Augustinianum*, 24: 471–94.

Dzielska, M. (1986) *Apollonius of Tyana in Legend and History* (Rome).

Eitrem, S. (1924a) *Die Versuchung Christi* (Oslo).

— (1924b) 'Die rituelle *diabolē*', *Symbolae Osloenses*, 2: 33–61.

— (1991) 'Dreams and divination in magic ritual', in Faraone, C. A. and Obbink, D., eds (1991): 175–87.

Elat, M. (1982) 'Mesopotamische Kriegsritualen', *BO*, 39: 5–25.

Elderkin, G. W. (1937) 'Two curse inscriptions', *Hesperia*, 6: 382–95.

Elm, S. (1994) *'Virgins of God': The Making of Asceticism in Late Antiquity* (Oxford).

Elsner, J. (1995) *Art and the Roman Viewer: The Transformation of Art from the Pagan World to Christianity* (Cambridge).

Engelmann, H. (1975) *The Delian Aretology of Sarapis*, EPRO 44 (Leyden).

Evans-Pritchard, E. E. (1937) *Witchcraft, Oracles and Magic among the Azande* (Oxford).

Ewen, C. H. L'E. (1938) *Witchcraft in the Star Chamber* (London).

Fairfax, E. (1621/1882) *Daemonologia: A Discourse on Witchcraft*, ed. W. Grainge (Harrogate).

Faraone, C. A. (1985) 'Aeschylus' *hymnos desmios* (*Eum.* 306) and Attic judicial curses', *JHS*, 105: 150–4.

— (1989) 'An accusation of magic in classical Athens (Ar. *Wasps* 946–8)', *TAPA*, 119: 149–60.

— (1990) 'Aphrodite's *kestos* and apples for Atalanta: aphrodisiacs in early Greek myth and ritual', *Phoenix*, 44: 219–43.

— (1991a) 'Binding and burying the forces of evil: the defensive use of 'voodoo' dolls in ancient Greece', *CA*, 10: 165–205 [*VD*].

— (1991b) 'The agonistic context of early Greek binding spells', in Faraone, C. A. and Obbink, D., eds (1991): 3–32.

— (1992) *Talismans and Trojan Horses: Guardian Statues in Greek Myth and Ritual* (Oxford).

— (1993) 'Molten wax, spilt wine, and mutilated animals: near eastern and early Greek oath ceremonies', *JHS*, 113: 60–80.

— (1994) 'Deianeira's mistake and the demise of Heracles: erotic magic in Sophocles', *Trachiniae*', *Helios*, 21: 115–35 = Johnston, ed. (1994).

— (1995) 'The 'performative future' in three Hellenistic incantations and Theocritus' second *Idyll*', *CPh*, 90: 1–15.

— and Obbink, D. eds (1991) *Magika Hiera: Ancient Greek Magic and Religion* (New York).

Fauth, W. (1975) 'Die Bedeutung der Nekromantieszene in Lucans *Pharsalia*', *Rheinisches Museum*, 118: 325–44.

— (1995) *Helios Megistos: Zur synkretistischen Theologie der Spätantike*, Religions in the Graeco-Roman World, 125 (Leyden).

Felton, D. (forthcoming) *Haunted Greece and Rome. Ghost Stories from Classical Antiquity* (Austin).

Ferguson, E. (1984) *Demonology of the Early Christian Church* (New York and Toronto).

Ferrar, W. J. (1920) *The Proof of the Gospels, Being the Demonstratio Evangelica of Eusebius of Caesarea*, i (London and New York).

Ferrary, J. (1991) 'Lex Cornelia de sicariis et veneficiis', *Athenaeum*, n.s. 69: 417–34.

Festugière, A. J. (1944/1950) *La Révélation d'Hermès Trismégiste i: l'astrologie et les sciences occultes* (Paris).

Fick, N. and Carrière, J.-C., eds (1991) *Mélanges E. Bernard*, Annales litt. Besançon, 444 (Paris).

Flint, V. I. J. (1990) *The Rise of Magic in Early Medieval Europe* (Princeton and Oxford).

Flintermann, J. P. (1995) *Power, Paideia and Pythagoreanism* (Amsterdam).

Fögen, M. T. (1993) *Die Enteignung der Wahrsager: Studien zum kaiserlichen Wissensmonopol in der Spätantike* (Frankfurt am Main).

Fontaine, F. and Kannengiesser, C. eds (1972) *Epektesis: Mélanges patristiques . . . à J. Daniélou* (Paris).

Foster, G. M. (1965), 'Peasant society and the image of the limited good', *American Anthropologist*, 67: 293–315.

Fowden, G. (1986) *The Egyptian Hermes: A Historical Approach to the Late Pagan Mind* (Cambridge).

Fox, M. (1993) 'History and rhetoric in Dionysius of Halicarnassus', *JRS*, 83: 31–47.

Fox, W. S. (1912a) *The Johns Hopkins Tabellae Defixionum* (Baltimore).

— (1912b) 'Submerged tabellae defixionum', *AJP*, 33: 301–10.

— (1913–14) 'Old Testament parallels to *Tabellae Defixionum*', *American Journal of Semitic Languages*, 30: 111–24.

Frankfurter, D. (1994) 'The magic of writing and the writing of magic: the Power of the word in Egyptian and Greek traditions', *Helios*, 21: 189–221 = Johnston, ed. (1994).

Frankfurter, D. (1995) 'Narrating power: the theory and practice of the magical *Historiola* in ritual spells', in Meyer, M. and Mirecki, P., eds (1995): 457–76.

Fraser, P. M. (1972) *Ptolemaic Alexandria*, 3 vols (Oxford).

Friedländer, P. and Hoffleit, H. B. (1948) *Epigrammata: Greek Inscriptions in Verse, from the Beginnings to the Persian Wars* (Berkeley).

Friedman, J. B. (1981) *The Monstrous Races in Medieval Art and Thought* (Cambridge, MA and London).

Furley, W. D. (1994) 'Besprechung und Behandlung. Zur Form und Funktion von ἐπῳδαί in der griechischen Zaubermedizin', in Most, G. W., Petersmann, H. *et al.*, eds (1994): 80–104.

Gager, J. G., ed. (1992) *Curse Tablets and Binding Spells from Antiquity and the Ancient World* (Oxford and New York) [*CT*].

— (1994) 'Moses the magician', *Helios*, 21: 179–88 = Johnston ed. (1994).

Gallaher, E. V. (1982) *Divine Man or Magician? Celsus and Origen on Jesus* (Chicago).

Ganschinietz (Ganszyniec), R. (1913) *Hippolytus' Capitel gegen die Magier, Refut. Haer. IV. 28–42*, Texte und Untersuchungen, ser. 3, ix.2 (Leipzig).

Gantz, T. (1993) *Early Greek Myth: A Guide to Literary and Artistic Sources* (Baltimore).

García Ruiz, E. (1967) 'Estudio linguistico de las defixiones latinas no incluidas en el corpus de Audollent', *Emerita*, 35: 55–89.

Garland, R. (1992) *Introducing New Gods* (London).

— (1996) 'Strategies of religious intimidation and coercion in Classical Athens', in Hellström, P. and Alroth, B., eds (1996): 91–9.

Garosi, R. (1976) 'Indagine sulla formazione del concetto di magia nella cultura romana', in Xella, P., ed. (1976): 13–93.

Gauly, B. *et al.*, eds (1991) *Musa Tragica: Die griechische Tragödie von Thespis bis Ezechiel* (Göttingen).

Gavigan, J. J. (1947) *Saint Augustine: Christian Instruction* (Washington, DC).

Gerson, L. P. (1990) *God and Greek Philosophy: Studies in the Early History of Natural Theology* (London).

Giannini, A. (1964) 'Studi sulla paradossografia greca, 2: da Callimaco all'età imperiale – la letteratura paradossografica', *Acme*, 17: 99–140.

— (1966) *Paradoxographorum graecorum reliquiae*, Classici greci e latini, sez. Testi e Commenti, 3 (Milan).

Gifford, E. H., ed. (1894) *The Catechetical Lectures of S. Cyril, Archbishop of Jerusalem* (New York).

Giovanni, L. de (1983) *Costantino e il mondo pagano: studi di politica e legislazione*, 3rd edn (Naples).

Gnoli, G. and Vernant, J.-P., eds *La Mort, les morts dans les sociétés anciennes* (Cambridge and Paris).

Goetze, A. and Sturtevant, E. H. (1938) *The Hittite Ritual of Tunanawi* (New Haven).

Goldhill, S. (1991) *The Poet's Voice: Essays on Poetics and Greek Literature* (Cambridge).

Goldschmidt, V. (1947) *Les Dialogues de Platon: structure et méthode dialectique* (Paris).

Goodchild, R. G. (1953) 'The ring and the curse', *Antiquity*, 27: 100–2.

Goode, W. J. (1949) 'Magic and religion: a continuum', *Ethnos*, 14: 172–82.

Goodman, M. (1987) *The Ruling Class of Judaea* (Cambridge).

Goodyear, F. R. D., ed. (1981) *The Annals of Tacitus Books 1–6, with a commentary, vol ii, Annals 1.55–81 and Annals 2* (Cambridge).

Gordon, R. L. (1987a) 'Aelian's peony: the location of magic in Graeco-Roman tradition', in E. Shaffer, ed. *Comparative Criticism: A Yearbook* (Cambridge): 59–95.

— (1987b) 'Lucan's Erictho', in Whitby, M., Hardy, P. and Whitby, M., eds (1987): 231–41.

— (1995) 'The healing event in Graeco-Roman folk-medicine', in van der Eijk, P. J. *et al.*, eds (1995): 363–76.

— (1997a) '*Quaedam veritatis umbrae*: Hellenistic magic and astrology', in Bilde, P., Engberg-Pedersen, T. *et al.*, eds (1997): 128–58.

— (1997b) 'Reporting the marvellous: private divination in the Greek magical papyri', in Schäfer, P. and Kippenberg, H. G., eds (1997): 65–92.

— (forthcoming) *Spells of Wisdom: Magical Power in the Graeco-Roman World*.

Goulet-Cazé, M-O. (1993) 'Les premiers cyniques et la religion', in *ead.* and Goulet, eds (1993): 117–58.

— and Goulet, R. eds (1993) *Le cynisme ancien et ses prolongements*, Actes du Colloque CNRS, Paris 22–25 July 1991 (Paris).

Gow, A. S. F., ed. (1952) *Theocritus*, with introduction, translation and commentary, 2 vols (Cambridge).

Graf, F. (1974) *Eleusis und die orphische Dichtung Athens in vorhellenistischer Zeit*, Religionsgeschichtliche Versuche und Vorarbeiten, 33 (Berlin).

— (1991) 'Prayer in magical and religious ritual', in Faraone, C. A. and Obbink, D., eds (1991): 188–213.

— (1992) 'An oracle against pestilence from a western Anatolian town', *ZPE*, 92: 267–79.

— (1994a) *La Magie dans l'antiquité gréco-romaine* (Paris).

— (1994b) 'The magician's initiation', *Helios*, 21: 161–77 = Johnston ed. (1994).

— (1995) 'Excluding the charming: the development of the Greek concept of magic', in Meyer, M. and Mirecki, P., eds (1995): 29–42.

— (1996) *Gottesnähe und Schadenzauber: Die Magie in der griechisch-römischen Antike* (Munich); rev. edn. of Graf (1994a).

— (1997a) *Magic in the Ancient World*, trans. F. Philip (Cambridge, MA and London); English version of Graf, 1996.

— (1997b) 'Medea, the enchantress from afar: remarks on a well-known myth', in Clauss, J. J. and Johnston, S. I., eds (1997): 27–43.

Grafton, A. (1992) *New Worlds, Ancient Texts: The Power of Tradition and the Shock of Discovery* (Cambridge, MA.).

Green, W. M., trans. (1963/1972) *Saint Augustine: The City of God Against the Pagans*, ii and vii (London and Cambridge, MA).

Grégoire, H. (1922) *Recueil des inscriptions grecques chrétiennes d'Asie Mineure* (Paris), *Guide* no. 281.

Griffiths, A. (1995) 'Non-aristocratic elements in archaic poetry', in A. Powell, ed., *The Greek World* (London): 85–103.

Griffiths, J. Gwynn, ed. (1970) *Plutarch's De Iside et Osiride* (Cardiff).

Grodzynski, D. (1974) 'Superstitio', *Revue des Etudes Anciennes*, 76: 36−60.

Gryson, R. (1968) *Le Prêtre selon Saint Ambroise* (Louvain).

Guarducci, M. (1978) *Epigrafia greca*, iv (Rome).

Hall, E. (1989) *Inventing the Barbarian* (Oxford).

Hammerstaedt, J. (1988) *Die Orakelkritik des Kynikers Oenomaus*, Beiträge zur klassischen Philologie, 118 (Frankfurt am Main).

— (1993) 'Le cynisme littéraire à l'époque impériale', in Goulet-Cazé, M-O. and Goulet, R., eds (1993): 403−18.

Hansen, M. H. (1991) *The Athenian Democracy in the Age of Demosthenes* (Oxford).

Hanson, R. P. C. (1980) 'The Christian attitude to pagan religions up to the time of Constantine the Great', *ANRW*, II.23.2, 910−73.

Harrauer, C. (1987) *Meliouchos: Studien zur Entwicklung religiöser Vorstellungen in griechischen synkretistischen Zaubertexten*, Wiener Studien, Beiheft 11 (Vienna).

Harris, W. V. (1989) *Ancient Literacy* (Cambridge, MA).

Hellström, P. and Alroth, B. (1996) *Religion and Power in the Ancient Greek World*, Proceedings of the Uppsala Symposium 1993, Boreas 24 (Uppsala).

Hempel, J. (1912) *Untersuchungen zur Ueberlieferung von Apollonius von Tyana* (Stockholm).

Herter, H. (1934) s.v. 'Telchinen', *RE*, 5A: 197−224.

— (1950/1975) 'Böse Dämonen im frühgriechischen Volksglauben', in *Kleine Schriften*, ed. E. Vogt (Munich): 43−75; repr. from *Rheinisches Jahrbuch für Volkskunde*, 1 (1950): 112−43.

Heubeck, A. and Hoekstra, A. (1989) *A Commentary on Homer's Odyssey*, vol ii, books ix−xvi (Oxford).

Hopfner, T. (1921−4/1974−90) *Griechisch-ägyptischer Offenbarungszauber*, 2 vols in 3, ed. R. Merkelbach (Amsterdam); orig. in Studien zur Palaeographie und Papyruskunde, ed. C. Wessely, 21 and 23 (Leipzig).

Horak, U. (1992) *Illuminierte Papyri, Pergamente und Papiere*, i (Vienna).

Humphrey, J. H. (1986) *Roman Circuses: Arenas for Chariot Racing* (Berkeley).

— Sear, F. B. and Vickers, M. (1972−3) 'Aspects of the circus at Lepcis Magna', *Libya Antiqua*, 9−10: 25−97 and plates 18−37.

Hunink, V. ed. (1997) *Apuleius of Madaura: pro se de magia*, 2 vols (Amsterdam).

Inscriptiones Graecae (1903−) (sundry editors, volumes and editions, Berlin), *Guide* nos. 57−8 [*IG*].

Jacoby, F. (1923–58) *Die Fragmente der griechischen Historiker* (Berlin and Leyden) [*FGrH*].

Jal, P. (1963) *La Guerre civile à Rome: étude littéraire et morale* (Paris).

James, M. R., trans. (1924) *The Apocryphal New Testament* (Oxford).

Jameson, M. H., Jordan, D. R. and Kotansky, R. D. (1993) *A 'Lex Sacra' from Selinus*, Greek, Roman and Byzantine monographs, 11 (Durham, NC).

Janko, R. (1982) *Homer, Hesiod and the Hymns* (Cambridge).

— (1992) *The Iliad: A Commentary* iv: *Books 13–16* (Cambridge).

Jeffery, L. H. (1955) 'Further comments on archaic Greek inscriptions', *ABSA*, 50: 67–84.

Johnston, S. I. (1990) *Hekate Soteira: A Study of Hekate's Roles in the Chaldaean Oracles and Related Literature* (Atlanta).

— (1991) 'Crossroads', *ZPE*, 88: 217–24.

— (1994a) 'Penelope and the Erinyes: *Od.* 20. 61–82', *Helios*, 21: 137–59 = ead. ed. (1994).

— (1994b) 'Defining the dreadful: remarks on the Greek child-killing demon', in Meyer, M. and Mirecki, P., eds (1994): 361–87.

— (1995) 'The song of the *iynx*: magic and rhetoric in *Pythian* 4,' *TAPA*, 125: 177–206.

— (1997a) s.v. Ahoros, *DNP* 1: 303–4.

— (1997b) s.v. Dämonen V, *DNP* 3: 261–4.

— (1997c) 'Medea and the cult of Hera Akraia', in Clauss, J. J. and Johnston, S. I., eds (1997): 44–70.

— (1999a) *Restless Dead. Encounters between the Living and the Dead in Ancient Greece* (Berkeley).

— (1999b) 'Songs for the ghosts: magical solutions to deadly problems', in Jordan, D. R. *et al.*, eds (1999).

— ed. (1994) *Exploring the Shadows: Ancient Literature and the Supernatural*, in *Helios*, 21.2 (whole issue).

Jones, C. P. (1986) *Culture and Society in Lucian* (Cambridge, MA and London).

Jordan, D. R. (1976) '*CIL* viii 19525 (B).2: QPVULVA =Q(UEM) P(EPERIT) VULVA', *Philologus*, 120: 127–32.

— (1980a) 'Two inscribed lead tablets from a well in the Athenian Kerameikos', *AM*, 95: 225–39.

— (1980b) 'Hekatika', *Glotta*, 83: 62–5.

— (1985a) 'A survey of Greek defixiones not included in the special corpora', *Greek, Roman and Byzantine Studies*, 26: 151–97 [*SGD*].

— (1985b) 'Defixiones from a well near the southwest corner of the Athenian agora', *Hesperia*, 54: 205–55.

— (1985c) 'The inscribed gold tablet from the Vigna Codini', *AJA*, 89: 162–7.

— (1988a) 'A love charm with verses', *ZPE*, 72: 245–59.

— (1988b) 'New archaeological evidence for the practice of magic in classical Athens', in *Praktika tou xii diethnous synedriou klasikēs archaiologias 1983–4*, iv (Athens): 273–7.

— (1988c) 'New defixiones from Carthage', in J. H. Humphrey, ed., *The Circus and a Byzantine Cemetery at Carthage*, i (Ann Arbor): 117–40, including, at 134–40, appendix by A. Rosenberg, 'The conservation of lead curse tablets'.

— (1989) 'New evidence for the activity of scribes in Roman Athens', in *Abstracts of the American Philological Association – 120th annual meeting (Baltimore)* (Atlanta), 55.

— (1990) Review of Tomlin 1988, *JRA*, 3: 439–40.

— (1991) 'A new reading of a phylactery from Beirut', *ZPE*, 88: 61–9.

—, Montgomery, H. and Thomassen, E., eds (1999) *Magic in the Ancient World*, Eitrem Seminar, 1 (Bergen).

Jugie, M. (1914) 'La Doctrine des fins dernières dans l'église gréco-russe', *Échos d'Orient*, 17: 5–22, 209–28.

Kagarow, E. G. (1929) *Griechische Fluchtafeln*, Eos Supplements, 4 (Lemberg [Lwów] and Paris).

Kahn, C. (1979) *The Art and Thought of Heraclitus* (Cambridge).

Kahn, L. (1978) *Hermès passé, ou les ambiguités de la communication* (Paris).

Kassel, R. and Austin, C. (1983–) *Poetae Comici Graeci*, 8 vols (Berlin) [K-A.]

Kayser, C. L. ed. (1870) *Philostratus, Life of Apollonius of Tyana* (Leipzig).

Kee, H. C. (1986) *Medicine, Miracle and Magic in New Testament Times* (Cambridge).

Kees, H. (1923) 'Seth', *RE*, 2, Reihe ii.a (Stuttgart) cols. 1896–1922.

Keil, J. and Wilhelm, A. (1915) 'Vorläufiger Bericht über eine Reise in Kilikien', *JOAI*, Beiblatt, 18: 5–60.

Kelly, H. A. (1968) *Towards the Death of Satan: The Growth and Decline of Christian Demonology* (London); published in New York as *The Devil, Demonology and Witchcraft*.

— (1985) *The Devil at Baptism: Ritual, Theology, and Drama* (Ithaca and London).

Kerferd, G. B. ed. (1981) *The Sophists and their Legacy*, Hermes Einzelschriften, 44 (Stuttgart).

Kern, O. (1901) s.v. Daktyloi, *RE*, 4: 2017–20.

Kingsley, P. (1994) 'Greeks, shamans and magi', *Studia Iranica*, 23: 187–97.

— (1995) *Ancient Philosophy, Mystery, and Magic: Empedocles and Pythagorean Tradition* (Oxford).

Kippenberg, H. G. (1997) 'Magic in Roman civil discourse: why rituals could be illegal', in Schäfer, P. and Kippenberg, H. G. eds (1997): 137–63.

Kirk, G. S. (1990) *The Iliad: A Commentary*, ii, books v–viii (Cambridge).

Knigge, U. (1991) *The Athenian Kerameikos* (Athens); translation of *Der athenische Kerameikos* (Athens, 1988).

Kotansky, R. (1991) 'Incantations and prayers for salvation on inscribed Greek amulets', in Faraone, C. A. and Obbink, D., eds (1991): 107–37.

— (1994) *The Greek Magical Amulets. The Inscribed Gold, Silver, Copper and Bronze Lamellae. Part 1: Published Texts of Known Provenance*, Papyrologica Coloniensia, xxii.1 (Opladen).

Laks, A. and Most, G. W., eds (1997) *Studies on the Derveni Papyrus* (Oxford).

Lamb, W. R. M. (1967) *Plato*, III (London and Cambridge, MA).

Lamberton, R. (1986) *Homer the Theologian: Neoplatonist Allegorical Reading and the Growth of the Epic Tradition*, Transformation of the Classical Heritage, 9 (Berkeley).

Lanata, G. (1967) *Medicina magica e religione popolare in Grecia fino all'età di Ippocrate*, Filologia e Critica, 3 (Rome).

Lane, E. N. (1971–8) *Corpus monumentorum religionis dei Menis*, 4 vols (Leyden), *Guide* no. 745 [*CMRDM*].

Lattimore, R. (1962) *Themes in Greek and Latin Epitaphs* (Urbana, Illinois).

Le Boulluec, A. ed., comm. (1981) *Clément d'Alexandrie: Les Stromates*, Sources Chrétiennes, 278–9 (Paris).

Leclercq, H. (1907) *Manuel d'archéologie Chrétienne depuis les origines jusqu'au VIIIe siècle* (Paris).

Le Guen-Pollet, B. (1981) 'La rémunération du prêtre en Grèce ancienne', Thèse de 3e cycle (Paris).

Lesky, A. (1931) s.v. Medeia, *RE*, 15: 29–64.

Leutsch, E. L. and Schneidewin, F. G., eds (1893–1951) *Corpus Paroemiographorum Graecorum* (Göttingen) [*CPG*].

Lewis, O. (1961) *The Children of Sánchez: Autobiography of a Mexican Family* (New York).

Lewy, H. (1978) *Chaldaean Oracles and Theurgy: Mysticism, Magic and Platonism in the Later Roman Empire*, 2nd edn, ed. M. Tardieu (Paris).

Lexicon iconographicum mythologiae graecae (Zurich and Munich 1981–).

Liddell, H. G., Scott, R. and Jones, H. S. (1968) *A Greek-English Lexicon* (ninth ed., Oxford).

Liebeschuetz, J. H. W. G. (1979) *Continuity and Change in Roman Religion* (Oxford).

Lloyd, G. E. R. (1979) *Magic, Reason and Experience: Studies in the Origins and Development of Greek Science* (Cambridge).

— (1983) *Science, Folklore and Ideology: Studies in the Life-Sciences in Ancient Greece* (Cambridge).

— (1987) *The Revolutions of Wisdom: Studies in the Claims and Practice of Ancient Greek Science*, Sather Lectures, 52 (Berkeley).

— (1990) *Demystifying Mentalities* (Cambridge).

— (1991) *Methods and Problems in Greek Science* (Cambridge).

Lowe, J. E. (1929) *Magic in Greek and Latin Literature* (Oxford).

Luck, G. (1962) *Hexen und Zauberei in der römischen Dichtung* (Zurich).

— (1985) *Arcana mundi: Magic and the Occult in the Greek and Roman Worlds* (Baltimore). Portions of this have been used in Part 2 of this volume in a slightly different form; this is with the permission of Johns Hopkins University Press.

— (1986) 'Two predictions of the end of Paganism', *Euphrosyne*, n.s. 14: 153–6.

Lucrezi, F. (1987) 'Constantino e gli aruspici', *Atti della Accademia di Scienze morali e politiche della Società nazionale di Scienze, Lettere e Arte di Napoli*, 97: 171–98.

Luhrmann, T. (1989) *The Persuasions of the Witch's Craft* (Oxford).

Lunais, S. (1979) *Recherches sur la Lune, 1: les auteurs latins . . .* , EPRO, 72 (Leyden).

McCown, Ch. C. ed. (1922) *The Testament of Solomon* (Leipzig).

— (1923) 'The Ephesia grammata in popular belief', *TAPA*, 54: 128–40.

McDaniel, W. B. (1913) 'The 'pupula duplex' and other tokens of the evil eye in the light of ophthalmology', *Classical Philology*, 13: 335–46.

MacDowell, D. M. (1982) *Gorgias: Encomium of Helen* (Bristol).

MacMullen, R. (1966/1992) *Enemies of the Roman Order: Treason, Unrest and Alienation in the Empire* (New York and London).

Maltomini, F. (1979) review of Moke, D. F., *Eroticism in the Greek Magical Papyri: Selected Studies* (Dissertation, Minneapolis 1975), *Aegyptus*, 59: 273–84.

Mansi, J. D. (1757–98) *Sacrorum Conciliorum Nova et Amplissima Collectio*, 31 vols (Florence and Venice) [*Mansi*].

Marchesi, C. (1955) *Apuleio di Madaura: Della magia* (Rome and Bologna).

Margalioth, M. (1966) *Sepher ha-Razim* (Jerusalem).

Mariani, L. (1910) 'Osservazioni intorno alle statuette plumbee sovanesi', *Ausonia*, 4.1: 39–47.

Marinatos, N. (1995) 'Circe and liminality: ritual background and narrative structure', in Andersen, Ø, and Dickie, M., eds (1995): 133–40.

Martinez, D. G. (1991) *A Greek Love Charm from Egypt (P. Mich. 757 P. Michigan xvi* (Atlanta).

Martini, M. C. (1977) *Piante medicamentose e rituali magico-religiosi in Plinio* (Rome).

Massaro, M. (1977) 'Aniles fabellae', *SIFC*, 49: 104–35.

Masson, O. (1972) 'La grande imprécation de Sélinonte (SEG XVI, 573)', *BCH*, 96: 375–88.

Massoneau, E. (1934) *La magie dans l'antiquité romaine* (Paris).

Mauss, M. (1902–3/1972) *A General Theory of Magic* (London); trans. by R. Brain of H. Hubert and M. Mauss, 'Esquisse d'une théorie générale de la magie', *L'Année sociologique*, 7:1–146 = id., *Sociologie et anthropologie* (Paris, 1950), pt i.

Meiggs, R. and Lewis, D. M. (1969) *A Selection of Greek Historical Inscriptions* (Oxford); *Guide* no. 35 [*ML*].

Meillier, C. (1991) 'La logique du rituel magique dans l'Idylle II de Théocrite', in Fick, N. and Carrière, J.-C., eds (1991): 325–36.

Merkelbach, R. (1992) *Abrasax. Ausgewählte Papyri religiösen und magischen Inhalts, Bd. 3: Zwei griechisch-ägyptische Weihezeremonien (Die Leidener Weltschöpfung. Die Pschai-Aion-Liturgie)*, Abhandlungen der Rheinisch-Westfälischen Akademie der Wissenschaften. Sonderreihe Papyrologica Coloniensia, xvii.3 (Opladen).

— and Totti, M. (1990) *Abrasax. Ausgewählte Papyri religiösen und magischen Inhalts, Bd. 1: Gebete*, Abhandlungen der Rheinisch-Westfälischen Akademie der Wissenschaften. Sonderreihe Papyrologica Coloniensia, xvii.1 (Opladen).

Merlan, P. (1954) 'Plotinus and magic', *Isis*, 44: 341–8; reprinted in id., *Kleine Schriften* (Berlin, 1976): 388–95.

Meyer, M. and Mirecki, P., eds (1995) *Ancient Magic and Ritual Power*, Religions in the Graeco-Roman World, 129 (Leyden).

Meyer, M. and Smith, R., eds (1994) *Ancient Christian Magic: Coptic Texts of Ritual Power* (San Francisco).

Meyer, R. T., trans. (1950) *St. Athanasius: The Life of St. Antony* (Westminster, Md. and London).

Migne, J. P. (1844–64) *Patrologia Latina* (Paris) [*PL*].

— (1857–66) *Patrologia Graeca* (Paris) [*PG*].

Millar, F. G. B. (1981) 'The world of the *Golden Ass*', *JRS*, 71: 63–75.

— (1993) *The Roman Near East, 31 BC – AD 337* (Cambridge, MA).

Miller, M. C. (1997) *Athens and Persia in the Fifth Century BC: A Study in Cultural Receptivity* (Cambridge).

Milne, M. J. (1966) 'The poem entitled 'Kiln'', in J. V. Noble, *The Techniques of Attic Painted Pottery* (London): 102–13 (appendix 3).

Minar, E. L. ed. and trans. (1961) *Plutarch's Moralia*, ix (London and Cambridge, MA).

Mitchell, S. (1993) *Anatolia: Land, Men and Gods in Asia Minor*, 2 vols (Oxford).

Mitford, T. D. (1971) *The Inscriptions of Kourion*, Memoirs of the American Philosophical Society, 83 (Philadelphia).

Mommsen, T. (1899/1961) *Römisches Strafrecht* (Darmstadt).

Monaco, L. (1984) '*Veneficia matronarum*: magia, medicina e repressione', in *Sodalitas: scritti in onore A. Guarino* (Naples): 2013–24.

Montano, A. (1993) 'Magia, astrologia, filosofia nel V secolo a.C.: aspetti di una polemica', *Atti dell'Accademia Pontaniana* (Naples), 42: 111–28.

Moore, B. (1997) *The Magician's Wife* (London).

Mora, F. (1990) *Prosopografia Isiaca, 2: il prosopografia storica e statistica del culto isiaco*, EPRO, 113 (Leyden).

Moraux, P. (1960) *Une défixion judiciaire au Musée d'Istanbul*, Académie royale de Belgique, Collection des Lettres, Mémoires, Collection in 8o, 2. LIV, ii (Brussels).

Moreau, A. (1994) *Le mythe de Jason et Medée: le va-nu-pied et la sorcière* (Paris).

Morgan, M. A., ed. (1983) *Sepher ha-Razim: The Book of Mysteries* (Chico, CA).

Mosher, D. L. (1982) *Saint Augustine: Eighty Three Different Questions* (Washington).

Most, G. W., Petersmann, H. and Ritter, A-M., eds (1994) *Philanthropia kai Eusebeia: Festschrift für A. Dihle zum 70. Geburtstag* (Göttingen).

Müller, C. and T. (1853–70) *Fragmenta historicorum Graecorum*, 5 vols (Paris) [*FHG*].

Naveh, J. and Shaked, S. (1985) *Amulets and Magic Bowls: Aramaic Incantations from Late Antiquity* (Jerusalem); 2nd edn, with additions and corrections, 1987.

Nelson, G. W. (1940) 'A Greek votive iynx-wheel in Boston', *AJA*, 44: 443–4.

Nilsson, M. (1967) *Geschichte der griechischen Religion*, i, 3rd edn (Munich).

Nock, A. D. (1929) 'The Greek magical papyri', *Aegyptus*, 15: 219–35; repr. in id. (1972), i: 176–94.

— (1933/1972) 'Paul and the magus', in id. (1972): 308–30; repr. from F. J. Foakes-Jackson and Kirsopp Lake, eds *The Beginnings of Christianity*, i, pt. 5 (London, 1933): 164–88.

— (1950) 'Tertullian and the *Ahori*', *Vigiliae Christianae*, 4: 129–41; repr. in id. (1972), ii: 712–19.

— (1972) *Essays on Religion and the Ancient World*, ed. Z. Stewart, 2 vols (Oxford).

Norman, A. F., ed. (1965) *Libanius' Autobiography, Oration 1* (Oxford).

—, trans. and intro. (1977) *Libanius: Selected Works*, ii (London and Cambridge, MA).

North, J. A. (1996) 'Pollution and purification at Selinous', *Scripta Classica Israelica*, 16: 293–301.

Ober, J. (1989) *Mass and Elite in Democratic Athens* (Princeton).

Ogden, D. (1996) *Greek Bastardy in the Classical and Hellenistic Periods* (Oxford).

Onians, R. B. (1951) *The Origins of European Thought* (Cambridge).

Osborne, R. G. (1985) 'The law in action in classical Athens', *JHS*, 105: 40–58.

Pagels, E. (1980) *The Gnostic Gospels* (London).

— (1995) *The Origin of Satan* (New York).

Palmer, P. M. and More, R. P. (1936) *Two Sources of the Faust Tradition* (Oxford).

Parker, R. (1983/1996) *Miasma: Pollution and Purification in Early Greek Religion* (Oxford).

— (1996) *Athenian Religion: A History* (Oxford).

Parry, H. (1992) *Thelxis: Magic and Imagination in Greek Myth and Poetry* (Lanham, Md.)

Parsons, W. (1951/1953) *St. Augustine's Letters*, i and iii (New York).

Pauly, A. F. von (1893–) *Paulys Realencyclopaedie der classischen Altertumswissenschaft*, ed. G. Wissowa (Stuttgart) [*RE*].

Peterson, E. (1959) *Frühkirche, Judentum und Gnosis* (Herder): 222–45.

Petropoulos, J. C. B. (1988) 'The erotic magical papyri', *Proceedings of the xviii International Congress of Papyrology*, ii (Athens): 215–22.

Petzl, G. (1994) 'Die Beichtinschriften Westkleinasiens', *Epigraphica Anatolica*, 22 [entire volume].

Pfister, K. (1938) s.v. Pflanzenaberglaube, *RE*, 19: 1446–56.

Pharr, C. (1952) *The Theodosian Code* (Princeton).

Phillimore, J. S. trans. (1912) *Philostratus, Life of Apollonius of Tyana* (Oxford).

Phillips, C. R., III (1986) 'The sociology of religious knowledge in the Roman empire to AD 284', *ANRW*, II.16.3: 2677–773.

— (1988) 'In search of the occult: an annotated anthology', *Helios*, 15: 151–70.

— (1991) '*Nullum crimen sine lege*: socio-religious sanctions on magic', in Faraone, C. A. and Obbink, D., eds (1991): 260–76.

— (1994) 'Seek and go hide: literary source problems in Graeco-Roman magic', *Helios*, 21: 107–14 = Johnston, S. I. ed. (1994).

Piccaluga, G. (1976) 'I Marsi e i Hirpi: due diversi modi di sistemare le minoranze etniche', in Xella, ed. (1976): 207–31.

Pinch, G. (1994) *Magic in Ancient Egypt* (London).

Pirenne-Delforge, V. (1993) 'L'iynge dans le discours mythique et les procédures magiques', *Kernos*, 6: 277–89.

Places, E. Des (1966) *Jamblique: Les Mystères d'Egypte* (Paris).

Poupon, G. (1981) 'L'accusation de magie dans les actes apocryphes', in

Les actes apocryphes des apôtres. Christianisme et monde païen, Publ. fac. Théol. Genève, 4 (Geneva): 71–85.

Preisendanz, K. (1926) *Akephalos. Der kopflose Gott* (Leipzig).

— (1962) s.v. Ephesia grammata, *RAC*, 5: 515–20.

— (1972) 'Fluchtafel (Defixion)', *RAC*, 8: 1–29.

— and Henrichs, A. (1973–4) *Papyri Graecae Magicae. Die griechischen Zauberpapyri*, 2nd edn, 2 vols (Stuttgart) [*PGM*]; first edn, 1928–31.

Pritchard, J. B. (1955) *Ancient Near Eastern Texts Relating to the Old Testament*, 2nd edn (Princeton) [*ANET*].

Procopé-Walter, A. (1933) 'Iao und Set (zu den figurae magicae in den Zauberpapyri)', *ARW*, 30: 34–69.

Rabinowitz, J. *The Rotting Goddess: the Origin of the Witch in Classical Antiquity* (New York).

Raikas, K. (1990) 'St. Augustine on juridical duties: some aspects of the episcopal office in Late Antiquity', in J. C. Schnaubelt and F. Van Fleteren, eds *Collectanea Augustiniana* (New York): 467–82.

Ramsey, M. (1988) *Professional and Popular Medicine in France, 1770–1830: The Social World of Medical Practice* (Cambridge).

Raven, M. J. (1983) 'Wax in Egyptian magic and symbolism', *OMRL*, 64: 7–47.

Rawson, E. (1985) *Intellectual Life in the Late Roman Republic* (London).

Rea, J. (1977) 'A new version of *PYale inv.* 299', *ZPE*, 27: 151–6.

Reiner, E. (1988) 'Magic figurines, amulets and talismans', in A. E. Farkas, P. O. Harper and E. B. Harrison, eds *Monsters and Demons in the Ancient and Medieval Worlds: Papers Presented in Honor of E. Porada* (Mainz).

Rendall, G. H., trans. (1931) *Minucius Felix* (London and New York).

Reverdin, O. (1945) *La Religion de la cité platonicienne*, École française d'Athènes, Travaux et mémoires, 6 (Paris).

Reynolds, J. M. and Ward-Perkins, J. B. (1952) *The Inscriptions of Roman Tripolitania* (Rome and London).

Riddle, J. M. (1993) 'High medicine and low medicine in the Roman Empire', *ANRW*, II.37.1: 102–20.

Ritner, R. K. (1993) *The Mechanics of Ancient Egyptian Magical Practice*, Studies in Ancient Oriental Civilization, 54 (Chicago).

— (1995) 'The religious, social, and legal parameters of traditional Egyptian magic', in Meyer, M. and Mirecki, P., eds (1995): 43–60.

Ritter, H. and Plesner, M. trans. (1962) *Picatrix. Das Ziel des Wiesen von Pseudo-Margriti* (London).

Rivière, J. (1924) 'Rôle du Démon au jugement particulier chez les Pères', *Revue des Sciences Religieuses*, 4: 43–64.

— (1934) *Le Dogme de la Rédemption au début du Moyen Age* (Paris).

Robert, L. (1938) *Études épigraphiques et philologiques* (Paris).

Roberts, A., trans. (1894) *The Works of Sulpitius Severus* (Oxford and New York).

— (1867) *Justin Martyr and Athenagoras* (Edinburgh).

— (1869–70) *The Writings of Tertullian*, 3 vols (Edinburgh).

Roberts, A. and Donaldson J. (1867) *Clement of Alexandria*, i (Edinburgh).

— and Rambaut, W. H. (1868) *The Writings of Irenaeus*, i (Edinburgh).

Robinson, J. M., ed. (1977) *The Nag Hammadi Library in English* (New York).

Robinson, T. M. (1987) *Heraclitus: Fragments* (Toronto).

Rohde, E. (1925) *Psyche: The Cult of Souls and Belief in Immortality among the Greeks* (London); trans. from the 8th German edn [9th/10th German edition, Tübingen, 1925].

Röhr, J. (1923–4) 'Der okkulte Kraftbegriff im Altertum', *Philologus Supplementband* 17, 1.

Rolfe, J. C., trans. (1937–9) *Ammianus Marcellinus*, 3 vols (London and Cambridge, MA).

—, trans. (1951) *Suetonius* (London and Cambridge, MA).

Romilly, J. de (1975) *Magic and Rhetoric in Ancient Greece* (Cambridge, MA).

— (1988) *Les grands Sophistes dans l'Athènes de Periclès* (Paris).

Rothschuh, K. E. (1978) *Iatromagie: Begriff, Merkmale, Motive* (Opladen).

Rousseau, P. (1985) *Pachomius: The Making of a Community in Fourth-Century Egypt* (Berkeley and London).

— (1994) *Basil of Caesarea* (Berkeley and Oxford).

Roussel, P. and Launey, M. (1926–72) *Inscriptions de Délos* (Paris); *Guide* no. 134 [*I. Délos*].

Rudhardt, J. (1960) 'La définition du délit d'impiété d'après la législation attique', *Museum Helveticum*, 17: 87–106.

Ruinart, T. (1713) *Acta Primorum Martyrum* (Amsterdam).

Russell, J. B. (1977) *The Devil: Perceptions of Evil from Antiquity to Primitive Christianity* (Ithaca and London).

— (1981) *Satan: The Early Christian Tradition* (Ithaca and London).

Sabbatucci, D. (1991) 'Orfeo secondo Pausania', in Borgeaud, P. ed. (1991): 7–11.

Salem, J. (1996) *Démocrite* (Paris).

Salzman, M. R. (1990) *On Roman Time: The Codex-calendar of 354 and the Rhythms of Urban Life in Late Antiquity* (Berkeley and Los Angeles).

Saunders, T. J. (1991) *Plato's Penal Code: Tradition, Controversy and Reform in Greek Penology* (Oxford).

Scarborough, J. (1991) 'The pharmacology of sacred plants, herbs and roots', in Faraone, C. A. and Obbink, D., eds (1991): 138–74.

Schäfer, P. and Kippenberg, H. G., eds (1997) *Envisioning Magic: A*

Princeton Seminar and Symposium, Studies in the History of Religions, 75 (Leyden).

Schaff, P. (1887) *St. Augustine: The Writings against the Manichaeans and against the Donatists* (New York).

— (1889) *Saint Chrysostom*, xiii and xiv (New York).

Schlörb-Vierneisel, B. (1964) 'Zwei klassische Kindergräber im Kerameikos', *AM*, 79: 85–113.

Schürer, E. (1901–09) *Geschichte des jüdischen Volkes im Zeitalter Jesu Christi*, 4th edn, 3 vols (Leipzig), repr. Hildesheim, 1964 and rev. and trans. as *The History of the Jewish People in the Age of Jesus Christ, 175BC–AD135*, rev. G. Vermes, F. Millar, and M. Goodman, ed. M. Black (Edinburgh, 1973–87).

Scobie, A. (1978) 'Strigiform witches in Roman and other cultures', *Fabula*, 19: 74–101.

Searle, J. R. (1979/1981) 'The logical status of fictional discourse', in id., *Expression and Meaning: Studies in the Theory of Speech Acts* (Cambridge): 58–75.

Segal, A. F. (1981) 'Hellenistic magic: some questions of definition', in R. van den Broek and M. J. Vermaseren, eds *Studies in Gnosticism and Hellenistic Religions [for] Gilles Quispel*, EPRO, 91 (Leyden): 348–75.

Segal, C. (1962) 'Gorgias and the psychology of *logos*', *Harvard Studies in Classical Philosophy*, 66: 99–155.

— (1973/1981) 'Simaetha and the iunx (Theocritus *Idyll* 2)', in id., *Poetry and Myth in Ancient Pastoral* (Princeton): 73–84; repr. from *Quaderni Urbinati di Cultura Classica*, 15 (1973): 32–43.

Seppilli, A. (1971) *Poesia e magia*[2] (Turin).

Seyrig, H. (1935) 'Amulette et sortilèges d'Antioche', *Berytus*, 2: 48–50.

Sfameni Gasparro, G. (1997) 'Daimôn and Tychê in the Hellenistic religious experience', in Bilde, P., Engberg-Pedersen, T. *et al.*, eds (1997): 67–109.

Shaw, G. (1985) 'Theurgy: rituals of unification in the Neoplatonism of Iamblichus', *Traditio*, 14: 1–28.

Sherwin-White, A. N. (1966) *The Letters of Pliny: A Social and Historical Commentary* (Oxford).

Shewring, W. H., ed. and trans. (1931) *The Passion of SS. Perpetua and Felicity MM.* (London).

Singer, C. (1927) 'The herbal in antiquity and its transmission to later ages', *JHS*, 47: 1–52.

Smith, A. (1974) *Porphyry's Place in the Neo-Platonic Tradition* (The Hague).

Smith, J. Z. (1978a) *Map is not Territory: Studies in the History of Religions* (Leyden).

— (1978b) 'Towards interpreting demonic powers in Hellenistic and Roman antiquity', *ANRW*, II.16.1: 425–39.

— (1995) 'Trading places', in Meyer, M. and Mirecki, P., eds (1995): 13–27.

Smith, M. (1978) *Jesus the Magician* (London), 2nd edn 1981.

— (1981) 'The hymn to the Moon, *PGM* IV 2242–2335', in *Proceedings of the 16th Congress of Papyrology* (Chico, CA): 643–54.

Smith, T. (1867) *The Writings of Tatian and Theophilus and the Clementine Recognitions* (Edinburgh).

— *et al.*, trans. (1879) *The Clementine Homilies* (Edinburgh).

Snell, B. *et al.*, eds (1971–) *Tragicorum Graecorum Fragmenta* (Göttingen) [*TGF*].

Snodgrass, A. (1982) 'Les origines du culte des héros dans la Grèce antique', in Gnoli, G. and Vernant, J.-P., eds (1982): 107–19.

Solin, H. (1968) *Eine neue Fluchtafel aus Ostia*, Commentationes humanarum literarum. Societas scientiarum Fenica, 42.3 (Helsinki), see esp. pp. 23–31: 'Eine Übersicht über lateinische Fluchtafeln, die sich nicht bei Audollent und Besnier finden'.

— (1981) 'Analecta epigraphica', *Arctos*, 15: 101–23.

— (1989) 'Analecta epigraphica', *Arctos*, 23: 195–221.

Sourvinou-Inwood, C. (1981) 'To die and enter the house of Hades: Homer, before and after', in Waley, J. ed. (1981): 15–39

— (1988) 'Further aspects of polis religion', *AION* (archeol.), 10: 259–74.

— (1995) *'Reading' Greek Death to the End of the Classical Period* (Oxford).

Spoerri, A. (1959) *Späthellenistische Berichte über Welt, Kultur und Götter* (Basle).

Stannard, J. (1981) 'Hippocratic pharmacology,' *Bulletin of the History of Medicine*, 35: 497–518.

Steier, A. (1933) s.v. Moly, *RE*, 16: 29–33.

Strubbe, J. H. M. (1991) '"Cursed be he that moves my bones"', in Faraone, C. A. and Obbink, D., eds (1991): 33–59.

Suárez de la Torre, E. (1992) 'Les pouvoirs des devins et les récits mythiques', *L'Études Classiques*, 60: 3–21.

Supplementum Epigraphicum Graecum (1923–) (sundry editors, Leyden); *Guide* no. 820 [*SEG*].

Tambiah, S. J. (1973) 'Form and meaning of magical acts: a point of view', in R. Horton and R. Finnegan, eds *Modes of Thought* (London): 199–229.

— (1990) *Magic, Science, Religion, and the Scope of Rationality* (Cambridge).

Ter Vrught-Lentz, J. (1960) *Mors immatura* (Groningen).

Thesleff, H. (1965) *The Pythagorean Texts of the Hellenistic Period*, Acta Academiae Aboensis, ser. A, Humaniora, 30,1 (Åbo).

Thomas, K. (1971) *Religion and the Decline of Magic* (London).

Thomson, R. W. (1971) *Athanasius: Contra Gentes and De Incarnatione* (Oxford).

Tituli Asiae Minoris (Vienna 1901–); *Guide* no. 1801 [*TAM*].

Todd, S. C. (1993) *The Shape of Athenian Law* (Oxford).

Tomlin, R. S. O. (1988) 'The curse tablets', in B. Cunliffe, ed., *The Temple of Sulis Minerva at Bath: ii, The Finds from the Sacred Spring*, Oxford University Committee for Archaeology Monograph no. 16 (Oxford), 59–277; also published separately (but preserving original pagination) as *Tabellae Sulis: Roman Inscribed Tablets of Tin and Lead from the Sacred Spring at Bath*, (fascicule 1 of Monograph no. 16) [*Tab. Sulis*].

Totti, M. (1985) *Ausgewählte Texte der Isis- und Sarapis-Religion* (Hildesheim).

Trumpf, J. (1958) 'Fluchtafel und Rachepuppe', *AM*, 73: 94–102.

Tsantsanoglou, K. (1997) 'The first columns of the Derveni Papyrus and their religious significance', in Laks, A. and Most, G. W., eds (1997): 94–128.

Tupet, A.-M. (1976) *La Magie dans la poésie latine; i: des origines à la fin du règne d'Auguste* (Paris).

—— (1986) 'Rites magiques dans l'antiquité romaine', *ANRW*, II.16.3: 2591–675.

Turner, E. G. (1963) 'A curse tablet from Nottinghamshire', *JRS*, 53: 122–4.

Valantasis, R. (1992) 'Daemons and the perfecting of the monk's body: monastic anthropology, daemonology and asceticism', *Semeia*, 58: 47–79.

van der Eijk, P. J., Horstmanshoff, H. F. J. and Schrijvers, P. H. eds (1995) *Ancient Medicine in its Socio-Cultural Context* (Amsterdam and Atlanta).

Van Rengen, W. (1984) 'Deux défixions contre les bleus à Apamée (VIᵉ siècle apr. J.-C.)', in J. Balty, ed., *Apamée de Syrie: Bilan des recherches archéologiques 1973–79* (Paris): 213–34.

Verdenius, W. J. (1981) 'Gorgias' doctrine of deception', in Kerferd, G. B., ed. (1981): 116–28.

Vermeule, E. (1979) *Aspects of Death in Early Greek Art and Poetry* (Berkeley).

Versnel, H. S. (1985) ''May he not be able to sacrifice . . .': concerning a curious formula in Greek and Latin curses', *ZPE*, 58: 247–69.

—— (1986) 'In het grensgebied van magie en religie, het gebed om recht', *Lampas*, 19: 68–96 (English summary).

—— (1987) 'Les imprécations et le droit,' *Revue Historique de Droit français et étranger*, 65: 5–22.

— (1990) *Ter unus: Isis, Dionysos, Hermes. Three Studies in Henotheism*, Studies in Greek and Roman Religion, 6 (Leyden).

— (1991) 'Beyond cursing: the appeal to justice in judicial prayers', in Faraone, C. A. and Obbink, D., eds (1991): 60–106.

— (1998) '. . . and any other part of the body there may be . . . : an essay on anatomical curses', in F. Graf, ed., *Ansichten griechischer Rituale: Geburtstags Symposium W. Burkert* (Stuttgart and Leipzig): 219–67.

Viarre, S. (1964) *L'image et la poésie dans les Métamorphoses d'Ovide* (Paris).

Voutiras, E. (1998) (Amsterdam).

Vregille, B. De and Neyrand, L., eds (1986) *Apponii In Canticum Canticorum Expositionem* (Turnholt).

Waley, J., ed. (1981) *Mirrors of Mortality: Studies in the Social History of Death* (London).

Waser, O. (1905) s.v. Empusa, *RE*, 5: 2540–43.

Waszink, J. H., ed. (1947) *Quinti Septimi Florentis Tertulliani De Anima* (Amsterdam).

— (1949) 'Mors immatura', *Vigiliae Christianae*, 3: 107–12.

— (1954a) 'Biothanati', *RAC*, 2: 391–4.

— (1954b) s.v. Blut, *RAC*, 2: 459–73.

— (1972) 'La théorie du langage des dieux et des démons chez Chalcidius', in Fontaine, F. and Kannengiesser, C., eds (1972): 237–44.

Watson, A. (1991) *Arae: The Curse Poetry of Antiquity*, ARCA 26 (Leeds).

Watts, W., trans. (1968) *St. Augustine's Confessions*, ii (London and Cambridge, MA).

Wellmann, M. (1903) s.v. Androtion, 2, *RE*, 1: 82.

— (1921) *Die 'Georgika' des Demokritos*, Abhandlungen der Preussischen Akademie der Wissenschaften zu Berlin, 4 (Berlin).

— (1928) *Die Φυσικά des Bolos-Demokritos und der Magier Anaxilaos aus Larissa*, Abhandlungen der Preussischen Akademie der Wissenschaften zu Berlin, 7 (Berlin).

— (1935) 'Die Stein- und Gemmenbücher der Antike', *Quellen und Studien zur Geschichte der Naturwissenschaften und Medizin*, 4.4: 86–149.

Westermarck, E. (1926) *Ritual and Belief in Morocco*, 2 vols (London).

Whitby, M., Hardy, P. and Whitby, M. eds (1987) *Homo Viator: Classical Essays for John Bramble* (Bristol).

Wide, S. (1909) '*aōroi biaiothanatoi*', *ARW*, 12: 224–33.

Wiesen, D. S. (1968) *Saint Augustine: The City of God against the Pagans*, iii (London and Cambridge, MA).

Will, E. (1955) *Korinthiaka* (Paris).

Williams, D. H. (1995) *Ambrose of Milan and the end of the Arian-Nicene Conflicts* (Oxford).

Williams, M. A. (1985) *The Immovable Race: A Gnostic Designation and the Theme of Stability in Late Antiquity* (Leyden).

Winkler, J. J. (1990) *The Constraints of Desire* (New York).

— (1991) 'The constraints of Eros', in Faraone, C. A. and Obbink, D., eds (1991): 214–43 (= Winkler, J. J. 1990: 71–98).

Winston, D. (1979) *The Wisdom of Solomon*, Anchor Bible Series, 43 (New York).

Wolff, G. ed. (1856) *Porphyrii de philosophia ex oraculis haurienda* (Berlin).

Wortmann, D. (1968) 'Neue magische Texte', *Bonner Jahrbücher*, 168: 56–111.

Wright, R. P. (1958) 'Roman Britain in 1957: ii, inscriptions', *JRS*, 48: 150–5.

Wünsch, R., ed. (1897) *Defixionum tabellae [Atticae]*, IG iii.3 Appendix (Berlin); *Guide* no. 63 [*DTA*]; 'Atticae' is not part of the published title of this volume, but is conventionally added to distinguish it from Audollent (1904).

— (1898) *Sethianische Verfluchungstafeln aus Rom* (Leipzig).

— (1902) 'The limestone inscriptions of Tell Sandahannah', in F. J. Bliss and R. A. S. Macalister, eds *Excavations in Palestine during the years 1898–1900* (London): 158–87.

— (1909) 'Deisidaimoniaka', *ARW*, 12: 1–45.

Wyller, E. A. (1957) 'Platons Gesetz gegen die Gottesleugner', *Hermes*, 85: 292–314.

Xella, P., ed. (1976) *Magia: studi di storia delle religioni in memoria di Raffaela Garosi* (Rome).

Youtie, H. C. and Bonner, C. (1937) 'Two curse tablets from Beisan', *TAPA*, 68: 43–77.

Zaidman, L. B. and Schmitt Pantel, P. (1989/1992) *Religion in the Ancient Greek City* (Cambridge); trans. by P. Cartledge of *La Religion grecque* (Paris).

Zanker, P. (1988) *The Power of Images in the Age of Augustus* (Ann Arbor).

Zwierlein-Diehl, E., ed. (1992) *Magische Amulette und andere Gemmen des Instituts für Altertumskunde der Universität zu Köln* (Opladen).

Index

Aaron, 115, 124, 295–6, 327, 337, 346
Abrasax, 49, 76
Academy, Athens, 158
Acanthis (Propertius poem), 123, 194
Achaemenis, 236
Achilles, 131
Acts of Peter, 125–30, 136, 301, 303
Acts of the Apostles, 115, 125, 136
Adonai, 44
Adyton (secret chamber), 107, 153
Aeneas (*Aenead:* Vergil), 75, 111, 121–2, 137
Aeschylus, 282
Aesculapius (deity), 333
Agamede, 179
Agathon, 34
Agesion, 24
Agrippina, 70
Agyrtai (itinerant wizards), 98, 103, 104
Albicerius, 142
Alchemy, 97, 106, 107, 115
Alciphron, 6
Alexander of Abonuteichos (the False
    Prophet), 93–7, 98, 104–6; golden thigh
    131, 146; language of the sorcerer 100;
    Lucian's unmasking 140–1, 142–8, 153–4;
    Manganeumata 99; Simon Magus 127
Alexander the Great, 119–20, 157, 170–1,
    181
Alexandria, 94, 97, 120, 157
Alexikakon (amulet), 100
Alkathoös, 174–5
Allegory, 239
Alphabet, 48
Amaryllis, 62
Amasis (Egyptian king), 131
Amathous, Cyprus, 188
Amatorium, 256–8, 260, 263
Ambrose (Saint), 323, 330, 332, 337; exorcism
    prayer 335
Ammianus Marcellinus, 133, 135, 315, 320–3
Ammon (deity), 119–20

Ammonion, 37
Amorgos, 199
Amulets, 51–4, 99–100, 104–5, 116, 136,
    158, 185, 190, 215, 239, 321, 322; from
    Acrae 115; Petronius' sorceress 138
Anaitis, 247
Anastasi papyri, 109
Anaxagoras, 96, 98, 132
Anaxilaus of Larissa, 121, 233, 261
Ancestors; crimes, 103; worship 117
Anderson, G, 154
Androcydes the Pythagorean, 239
Androsthenes, 27
Angels/angelology, 8, 107, 116, 124, 156,
    290–1, 295, 309, 326–8; Christian baptism
    236–7; Council of Laodicea 345; Jewish
    tradition 293–5; Peter and Simon Magus
    301; ranks of 295
Anguipede 48, 50
Animals, 75–77, 118, 131, 293, 312;
    dissection 139; mythical 142, 144; powers
    of speech 301; protection of saints 332;
    revival of the fish 128; sacrifice 94, 114,
    147, 148–9; speaking dog 127 ; theurgical
    practices 286; *See also:* bats, chameleon,
    dogs, snakes
Animism, 117
Antheira, 12, 21
Anthemion, 34
Antheros (deity), 150
Anthropodaimon (deity in human shape), 101
Anticles, 52
Antigone, *vindicatrix* at Knidos, 246
Antinous, 134
Antiochia, 157
Antoninus, 151–2
Antony (Saint), 310–11, 313, 333, 337;
    odours of sanctity 332
Aphrodite (Venus), 43; girdle of 35, 171–2
Apis (deity), 8, 97

Poisons, 100

Politoria, 67–8

Pollution, 9, 16, 22, 185, 207, 209–10, 254–5

Polymede, 179

Pompey (Sextus), 19

Pompey, Gnaeus Pompeius Magnus, 137

Pontus, 213

Porphyry, 148, 149, 155, 284, 285, 287, 288, 317

Poseidon, 32

Possession, divine, 125, 144, 149

Potio (potion/love potion), 100, 120

Power, 177–80, 181, 183–4, 189, 205, 217, 266

Prayer, 96, 118, 120, 129, 144, 335, 341

Prestidigitation, 162, 217–9, 221

Priapus (deity), 77, 122–3

Priesthood, 95, 103–7, 114–15, 157–8

Princeps, 166

Priscillian (Bishop), 315, 323

Proclus, 149, 288

Profanation, intentional, 179; objective or dominated, 178

Profession, magic as a, 181–2, 250, 252, 260

Prometheus, 206

Propertius, Sextus, 123

Prophecy/predictions, 110–11, 317, 338–9; Apollonius of Tyana 130–5; catastrophies 132–3; Jesus of Nazareth 124; weather 119, *see also* Clairvoyance: Divination; Divination: Oracles

Prosecutions and penalties, 315, 319–23, 348

Proserpina: *see* Persephone

Prostitutes, 34, 68, 194–6, 198, 257

Protasius (Christian martyr), 330, 332

Proteus (deity), 10, 130, 230

Psychagôgoi, 78

Psychology, 290, 292, 348

Ptah (deity), 109–10

Ptolemais, 77

Pudentilla, Aemilia, 199–203,

Pupil, double, 222

Purification, 103, 136–7, 141, 332, 335, 342

Pyrrhias, 24

Pyrrhus, 168–9

Pythagoras, 93–5, 101, 107, 117–19, 164, 166, 181, 219, 230, 231, 232, 233, 261; Alexander the False Prophet 143, 146; Apollonius of Tyana 131–7, 141; golden thigh 118, 131, 146

Pythagoreans, 225, 226, 239, 261

Ra/Rê (deity), 8, 153

Raikas, 323

Ramses II, (Egyptian Pharoah), 109

Ramsey, M., 181

Raphael (angel), 295

Recantations, 145

Reincarnation, 136, 146

Religion, 94–7, 100, 102–3, 126, 139; archaic Greece 117–19; cult of Mother Earth 105; distinctions between philosophy and magic 97–8; magic borrowing from 105; and superstition 101· of everyday, 163; of the special case, 163, 164, 230, 231; *see also* Christianity; Mystery cults/religions

Religious festivals *see* Festivals, Christian: Festivals, pagan

Remora, 169

Renaissance, 285

Rendall, 305

Restless dead, 176–7, 185, 187, 207

Resurrection, 343

Reversal, images of, 205–7

Rhizotomists: see Rootcutters

Rhodes, 179, 188

Ritual magic, 94–6, 98, 100, 151, 152–3, 185–6, 188–91; Alexander the False Prophet 143–7; Apuleius of Madaura 139; Canidia 122–3; Sorcerers' conventional image 103–6, *see also* Initiation rites

Rituals, Christian, 329, 335–7, 343, 346–7; pagan 282, 288–9, 294, 342; and baptism 336–7; expense of 346–7

Rivers, 131

Riviere, 306, 317

Robber Synod of Ephesus, 155

Roberts & Donaldson, 304, 329, 336, 346

Roberts, 334

Robinson, 298, 313

Rogation Days, 341

Rolfe, 315, 320, 321, 322, 323

Roman Law, 136, 139, 153, 157, 255

Rome (Porta S. Sebastiano), 188, (Esquiline), 206–7

Rome/Roman Empire 3–90 *passim;* 93–5, 108, 120–1, 296–309, 347–8; charges against Apollonius 133–6; daemonology and the Roman army 157; Dido's curse 121–2; from conversion of Constantine 315–24; impact of the Empire 157–8; Plotinus and the Egyptian priest 148; repression of magic at, 253–65; Simon